This book is dedicated to
Maruja V. Wahll my wife and best friend who provided support
throughout with her suggestions and drawings; and to our daughter
Ingrid Kirsten and husband Jim Kidd.

BRADDOCK ROAD
CHRONICLES
1755

Gorget of George Washington
Maruja V. Wahll

Compiled and annotated by
Andrew J. Wahll
FROM DIARIES AND RECORDS OF MEMBERS OF THE
BRADDOCK EXPEDITION AND OTHERS ARRANGED IN A
DAY BY DAY CHRONOLOGY

HERITAGE BOOKS, INC.

Published 1999 by

HERITAGE BOOKS, INC.
1540E Pointer Ridge Place
Bowie, Maryland 20716
1-800-398-7709
www.heritagebooks.com

ISBN 0-7884-1205-1

A Complete Catalog Listing Hundreds of Titles
On History, Genealogy, and Americana
Available Free Upon Request

TABLE OF CONTENTS

LIST OF ILLUSTRATIONS

ACKNOWLEDGMENTS

The compiler would like to thank the following people for their help and/or suggestions: Dr. David B. Quinn, Ross Netherton, John T. Phillips, Carney Rigg, Carlisle Wildeman Gentry, J. Martin West, Gregory Johnson, Jim Munson, Paul E. Kopperman, Mike Miller, David B. Wolf, Jane Sween, David Copeland, Steve Pedersen, Ron Vineyard, Leslie Towle, Karen Ackerman, Roxanne Carlson, Roger White, Mr. and Mrs. James Kidd, Sonja Thompson Wahll, and Maruja V. Wahll.

ABOUT THE COMPILER

Andrew J. Wahll a native of Columbus, Ohio currently lives near the march route in Derwood, Maryland. A graduate of Ohio State University, geographer and cartographer by profession is a student of the historical geography of North America and had been interested in the Braddock Expedition for many years.

While living and working in Maine along the banks of the Kennebec River his interest in the colonial New England period was focused on the first English colony in America known as the Popham Colony of 1607, to which he has dedicated more than thirty years of study and research. Mr. Wahll works for the National Geographic Society in Washington, D.C.   Derwood, Maryland, March 1999

INTRODUCTION

BRADDOCK ROAD CHRONICLES 1755 take history students back to the seedtime of the American Republic. It is the pivotal year of 1755 and the English colonies of North America are almost 150 years old. France and England are preparing for yet another war for empire which will be called the French and Indian War, or Seven Years War (1754-1763) that has been aptly termed the "dual for empire".

The causes of the war here in the New World are centered on control of the Ohio Valley and the trade advantage that control of the Ohio Valley would give the victor. Both sides knew this. Since the last colonial war (King George's War) French commerce, in particular the flow of French trade goods to the Indians in the interior of North America, had been limited due mainly to English control of the seas and thereby control of the supply ships to North America. To supply the growing Indian demands for goods, adventuresome hardbitten Scotch-Irish frontiersmen ("white Indians"), rivals from Virginia and Pennsylvania, began overland trading treks to the far off valley of the Ohio and its tributaries. Some of these shadowy men had names: Luke Rown, John Pattin, Robert Smith, Edmund Cartledge, James Le Tort, Charles Poke. Before 1750 as many as fifty traders from Pennsylvania would travel westward to the Ohio country with packtrains trading as far west as the Miami Indian village of Pickawillany (Piqua, Ohio, on the Miami River) whose leader was chief "Old Briton" a friend of the English. There the traders would rendezvous with Indians from further west, trading guns, powder, lead, blankets, rum and other goods for beaver pelts. Twigtwee Town is situated on the NW side of the Big Miamee River and it consists of about 400 families and is accounted one of the strongest Indian towns on the continent. The Twigtwee are the most powerful people to the westward of the English settlements, and much superior to the tribes of the Six Nations. There are other nations or tribes still further to the westward daily coming in to them for trade.

George Croghan and Christopher Gist, at Twigtwee Town and other nearby Indian villages had turned the Indians' trade toward the English. This was a major threat in the very center of New France. It was clear to the French strategists, if the English trading presence were not removed the British might begin to think they could control all trade routes between the Great Lakes and the Gulf of Mexico. On June 22, 1752, France acted and two French traders in league with 240

1

Ottawa Indians attacked Pickawillany destroying the village and killing its defenders both white and Indian. Old Briton was taken, killed and eaten near the fort, in the presence of his tribe. In the attack one white man and fourteen Indians were killed, and five whites were taken prisoner. Governor Duquesne followed up hoping to restore his control of New France by ordering a string of four forts to be built to hem in the English frontier traders from Pennsylvania and Virginia. Fort Presqu'isle on Lake Erie, Fort Le Boeuf on French Creek, Fort Venango, where French Creek empties into the Allegheny River, and Fort Duquesne at the Forks of the Ohio were the frontier forts facing the English in 1754. To the British and their colonials it was equally clear; either destroy the French forts or lose control the Ohio Valley and thereby the interior of North America. George Washington under the orders of Virginia's Governor Dinwiddie began the diplomatic and military counter offensive that resulted in first blood at Jumonville Glen and Fort Necessity in 1754.

A British army led by Major General Edward Braddock, of the Coldstream Guards called to active duty from Gibraltar, who after setting up headquarters at Williamsburg, has gone north, up the Chesapeake Bay and Potomac River and landed at Alexandria in Virginia to launch the conquest of French held North America. He will begin by taking Fort Duquesne at the forks of the Ohio River and then go to Lake Ontario and then to the eastward into the center of New France. Fort Duquesne is a small log and earthen fort which was initially fortified by Virginians under Wm. Trent and Edward Ward but seized by the French under Pierre de Contrecoeur in 1754. At this strategic point the Monongahela and the Allegheny River flowed together forming the fabled "O-heeyo" (in the Seneca, Cayuga & Mohawk languages) or Ohio River.

Governors Robert Dinwiddie (VA) and Horatio Sharpe (MD) are relieved to see Braddock and his army, as both feared the "The Woods" "back country" or Ohio Country would surely be lost to the French *coureurs de bois* forever. A British army in their midst could also be a boon to local economies if handled right.

Braddock's Road is the story of the men, the army and the wagon road they opened to Ohio Country. Passing through the wilderness over the "stoney" ridges of the Allegheny Mountains, this new road crossed over deep ravines of many fast flowing mountain streams, and over upland meadows and swamps in the ancient foreboding forests of

North America. The 2,000 soldiers marched 200 miles in a procession strung out at times for more than three miles. It was made up of 29 pieces of artillery, 407 wagons (150 from Pennsylvania thanks to Benjamin Franklin) pulled by 500 horses. There were 400 carrying (pack) horses, a herd of livestock and even a group of 40 to 50 support women (soldier's wives) of who were officially part of the army and could draw rations (most were sent back to Ft. Cumberland).

Sir John St. Clair, the deputy quartermaster general of the British army arrived early and set the plan. He was the advance man for the army, scouting out roads and the supply situation, making a record of everything. Even General Braddock said "This man is indefatigable, and has done all that man is capable of doing". Nevertheless, the march took three months - progress was unbelievably slow, the column moved no more than two or three miles a day.

The route being improved by British army engineers and pioneers was over paths long used by buffalo, Indian war parties and daring frontier fur traders to cross the Allegheny Mountains. Braddock's Road now being built by the army would enable a wagon link from the Ohio Country lands to tidewater via the Potomac Valley. The colonial geographer, Lewis Evans, concluded the Potomac Valley was the best way to reach strategic Fort Duquesne.

After landing in Alexandria in the Colony of Virginia, the army divided into groups, the larger group (44th Regiment of Foot) headed west through the Piedmont of Virginia was lead by Sir Peter Halkett. The second group (48th Regiment of Foot) lead by Colonel Thomas Dunbar crossed the Potomac River from Virginia in ship's boats to the vicinity of the mouth of Rock Creek in the Colony of Maryland. Colonel Thomas Gage lead the artillery column westward and later the combined army near Fort Duquesne and at first contact with the French and Indian forces.

Both routes crossed the Fall Line just west of Alexandria and at what is now called Georgetown (District of Columbia), where the Falls of the Potomac, beginning with Three Sisters Islands, prevented their transport ships from going further up river. The plan was to trans-ship supplies across the Fall Line barrier and then to use bateaux to ferry supplies to Fort Cumberland. The regiments then passed through newly cleared farm land in Maryland and Virginia by way of wagon roads that became more crude the further west one went, eventually becoming traders' tracks/paths across the Piedmont towards the

Appalachian Mountains. In the distance, further west the route climbed over the Blue Ridge, then outlying ridges toward Winchester, Virginia and Frederick, Maryland. Westward still, deep in the valley of the Potomac and its tributaries, lay frontier plantations and cowpens and the small frontier settlement of the Ohio Company at the confluence of the Potomac River and Wills Creek.

Called Fort Cumberland, it was renamed by General Braddock in honor of the Duke of Cumberland, captain general of the British Army and son of King George II. It was earlier called Fort Mt. Pleasant and known to the Shawnee as Cucucbetuc. Here was the trading post and storage sheds of the Ohio Company built to supply trade needs of settlers heading to their land grants further west on the Ohio River. For defense it was placed well above the Potomac River at the mouth of Wills Creek effectively guarding the trade path and their interests. Westward of Ft. Cumberland civilization ended and the uncharted howling wilderness began.

Braddock's Road has a place in American history as a saga in the continuing struggle for control of North America but more importantly the struggle against the overwhelming forces of nature.

By describing the scenes of building this first road across the Allegheny Mountains through the comments of actual participants, we will understand the nature of the unforgiving wilderness that surrounded and hemmed in the colonies for more than 160 years.

Walter Hough and Ross Netherton, both students of the expedition, provided through their writings ("Braddock's Road Through the Virginia Colony" and "Braddock's Campaign and the Potomac Route to the West") a fuller understanding of the route and the movement of the army through Virginia and Maryland. The route from Will's Creek to vicinity of the Forks of the Ohio is the most difficult part of the traverse, having the greatest physical relief (terrain) differences, and has been the focus of most early treatments of the expedition.

BRADDOCK ROAD CHRONICLES 1755, highlights the road with details written well after by several historians of sites and locales along the way. The compiler points out that retracing the entire road is not his intention; he includes descriptions of the encampments which are fixed sites on the road. A contemporary description of the road would be difficult to do - as Lacock had considerable difficulty doing so in 1914. Today, there is resistance to onsite viewing by local land owners along the route. For detailed descriptions of the road the compiler has relied on site specific comments by earlier students (Sparks - 1847, Atkinson - 1847, Hulbert - 1903, Lacock - 1914, Wallace - 1963, Hough - 1970, and Older - 1995) who as a group are accurate and thorough in their studies. They were not constrained in what they visited and described. Their comments as to the significant sites along the road are included after the appropriate daily record entry in italic type.

Hugh Cleland in *George Washington in the Ohio Valley* aptly writes: "Oddly enough, the only victory his (Braddock's) expedition was to win was not victory over the French but a victory over the forest; not a triumph of arms but a triumph of ax and shovel, of blasting powder and sweating horse. His victory was a road cut over the mountains and down to the rolling Ohio-a road, symbolically enough, built partly with his own bones. The road his men built and died upon became the artery of a people pouring westward to conquer finally with ax and plow the stubborn foes that Braddock could not conquer with the sword and musket".(Material cited is from *George Washington in the Ohio Valley*, by Hugh Cleland, © 1955 by University of Pittsburgh Press. Reprinted by permission of the University of Pittsburgh Press).

Exciting images of early America will be recalled as we follow the army up and down steep grades as it wound its way through the dank, hot and gloomy, breathless forest that isolated and swallowed the expedition muffling the army's sounds: creaking wagons, the tromp of army shoes, clanking of weapons, the incessant chopping of road builders' (pioneers) and bridge builders' (artificers) axes followed by crashing trees as the twelve foot right-of-way was cleared. There were the shrill sounds of whistles and shouts of teamsters, their teams snorting and "streaching" the thick leather harnesses and chain traces. It has been observed that colony horses were smaller than English draft horses and therefore did not fit into English harnesses on the few wagons that were brought over - the men of the army had to make new harnesses. The clamoursome and contentious (even mutinous) "private men" or soldiers moved the train along with shoulders and backs set against wagon boxes. Spiked wrought iron strakes of slowly turning wheels ground over exposed rock surfaces, through the mire of upland swamps or plowed through the ancient humus carpet lying deep on the forest floor. On these early vehicles the iron tires of wheels were put on in sections and spiked in place. Scholars have observed that an ancestral form of the Conestoga wagon was used on the march.

What is interesting is that some men, based on comments in the chronicles, were very much aware of the lands that they were traversing and one can only think that they were comparing America to the lands that they came from (mainly Ireland) with many probably making the decision to stay here at some point in the future.

The culminating event of the march was the Battle of the Monongahela (or the Battle of the Wilderness) where Braddock's army was defeated and routed by a combined force of French and Indians lead by D. Beaujeu and J. Dumas. Alhanase, a Huron war chief from Lorette was there along with other tribal war chiefs including young Pontiac.

While the battle will be addressed, the main emphasis will be on the road, its construction and the recorded events that occurred as the army made its way westward. Fort Cumberland at the mouth of Wills Creek where it flows into the Potomac River was the main staging site of the army on its way to the forks of the Ohio.

Themes inherent in *BRADDOCK ROAD CHRONICLES 1755* include: antecedents to the road (Indian and traders routes); Fort Dusquene; Fort Cumberland; Alexandria; frontier settlements; health conditions; Braddock's Rock; the British Army (regiments, uniforms, wagons, weapons, battlefield tactics - both regular and irregular); the British navy (ships, ordnance, tackle and line); period roads and trails; land grants and surveying; Native Americans; forest warfare tactics; Indian captivity; characteristics of the battle site; the army's retreat and aftermath of defeat on the frontier; and the significance of the road through time.

Two years later with Forbes Road (November 1757) the British opened another route (across Pennsylvania) from the middle colonies to the major tributaries of the Ohio River (Monongahela, Youghiogheny and Allegheny Rivers). Forbes Road was built by the same engineer (Mr. Gordon) who observed the Potomac Route was superior. The army under Brig. General John Forbes succeeded in destroying Fort Duquesne and built on the site, Fort Pitt. With a way now passable on two roads, British control of most of North America east of the Mississippi River was assured.

In retrospect, the events of Braddock's venture, despite the battlefield loss, were of considerable importance to the colonies. The

Allegheny Mountains had been crossed by wheeled vehicles. The colonists found a leader and hero who was George Washington, later to be our Revolutionary War leader and the father of our country. Additionally the colonials witnessed for the first time the vincibility of the soldiers of the British Army. With the defeat, the colonials, no doubt including Washington, thought they might better fend for themselves than depend on the English. Were the ties with the mother country worth keeping? The question was finally asked in 1776. Twenty years earlier the question was raised, according to Benjamin Franklin, "this whole transaction gave the first suspicions that exalted ideas of the prowess of the British regulars has not been well founded". The transaction was the events of Braddock's Expedition.

LIST OF CHRONICLES

* Material from *BRADDOCK AT THE MONONGAHELA*, by Paul E. Kopperman, © 1977 by Univ. of Pittsburgh Press, Reprinted by permission of the Univ. of Pitts. Press.

[+] Material from *BRADDOCK'S DEFEAT*, by Charles Hamilton, © 1959 by Univ. of Oklahoma Press, Reprinted by permission of Univ. of Oklahoma Press.

Material from *MILITARY AFFAIRS IN NORTH AMERICA 1748-1765*, by Stanley Pargellis, © 1936 by American Historical Association.

×Material from *DRS. ALEXANDER AND JOHN HAMILTON COMMENTS ON BRADDOCK'S DEFEAT* by Elaine G. Breslaw, © 1980 by Maryland Historical Magazine, Reprinted by permission of Maryland Historical Magazine.

PEOPLE OF THE CHRONICLES

There is much fascinating material about the road written by fifty-five participants and observers of the expedition including diaries, letters, orderly books, newspaper accounts, and journals of members of the army. These include the diary of Captain Cholmley's batman (or servant), Halkett's Orderly Book kept by Daniel Disney, General Braddock's Orderly Book, the Seamen's Journal, St. Clair's Letter Book, Robert Orme's Journal and Mrs. Browne's Diary.

Just who were these people who were marching through the wilderness of North America. Well lets see:

Charlotte Browne-Mrs. Browne was an English widow and nurse (matron) who left two children back in England and accompanied her brother, a commissary officer in the army. She traveled with the army to Wills Creek taking care of soldiers where she herself became sick of dysentery. Her diary begin back in England which is not included here.

Robert Cholmley's batman –Charles Hamilton speaks of the batman thusly: "picture an energetic youth, shrewd, alert, capable, and adroit scrounger of food in a desolate wilderness. Although only a servant, he carries a firelock and is ready to fight Indians by the side of his master Captain Robert Chomley".

Officer 1 –Again Charles Hamilton gives us an insight as to this person: "The author of the journal could hardly have been more detached if he were a modern historian. Not a single clue does he provide to his identity. That he is a officer is certain, for on June 20 he notes: "...the Huntsmen got us Venison every day but the Soldiers and Bast Men began to find themselves on short allowance".

Officer 2 –A note by Pargellis reads: "There is no endorsement or hint on the authorship of this violent letter, an example of the backbiting that was practiced in the British army before Cumberland became captain general. The handwriting is the same as the scribe's who wrote St. Clair's letter (July 22). It is possible that he may have been Captain Gabriel Christie, who assisted St. Clair on this expedition and had his strong support".

Officer 3 –An officer in one of the regiments with Major General Braddock who wrote to a friend in London describing the march and engagement in the woods with incidents giving a lively idea of the nature of the country, climate, and manner in which the officers and soldiers lived; also the difficulties they went through in that wilderness.

Officer 4 –This regular of the army give a brief account of the battle and the losses of the army mainly equipment. This account first appeared as a letter to the Whitehall Evening Post of October 9-11, 1755.

Duncan Cameron-Private with 44th Regiment of Foot stunned on first volley, awakes to find the action has passed him. He seeks shelter in a tree trunk where he observes much through a knot hole.

Robert Orme-Winthrop Sergeant writes: "Robert Orme, the author of this Journal entered the army as an ensign in the 35th Foot. On the 16th of September 1745, he exchanged into the Coldstreams of which he became a lieutenant on April 24, 1751. He was never raised to a captaincy, though always spoken of as such".

Peter Halkett-Commander of 44th Regiment of Foot who marched through Virginia. Charles Hamilton tells us: "Although wounded in the battle on July 9, young Daniel Disney, quill-pushing adjutant of Halkett's 44th Regiment of Foot, somehow managed to retain both his scalp and the regimental orderly book. The only such document to survive the fight, it is a dramatic record of the orders issued in the weeks just before and after the fateful battle.

Seaman-Leader of a detachment of Seamen ordered by Commodore Kepple to assist on the expedition to the Ohio with boats, ropes, and cannon. This probably was Lieut. Charles Spendelow from HMS Norwich. The detachment had three midshipmen, two boatswains mates, and thirty seamen and was ordered to assist with the tackle and gear needed in handling and transporting the guns and wagons and to construct and navigate floats on the rivers.

Edward Braddock-Leader of British expedition to begin the conquest of French held North America from Fort Duquesene. Served in British Army for forty-three years. Was recalled from Gibraltar to lead the expedition. Wounded in Battle of the Wilderness and subsequently died during retreat and was buried in first wagon road to the west.

Thomas Dunbar-Served in British Army for thirty years. His unit 48th Regiment of Foot marched through Maryland from Rock Creek. Second in command and leader of army after the death of Braddock he carries out Braddock's order to retreat. It was said "He bears the Character of a hearty, Jolly old gentleman". He was superseded in November, 1755, because of the injudicious retreat, and sent into honorable retirement as Lieutenant Governor of Gibraltar; he was never again actively employed. He died 1777.

Charles Lewis-Captain with Virginia volunteers, served under Stephens at Fort Cumberland after the defeat.

Adam Stephen-Captain and leader of First Company, Virginia Rangers. Served in frontier defense at Fort Cumberland after defeat. He is from the area of present-day Martinsburg, West Virginia. He was a skilled forest fighter.

Harry Gordon-Captain with military engineers who built the first road for wheeled vehicles over the Allegheny Mountains.

George Washington-Virginia militia leader who was named aid de camp to the General. Experienced in frontier tactics from Fort Necessity action. Will become first president of the United State of America

Thomas Creasap-Colonel and commissary officer with Maryland Ranger Company. The British officers called him a "Rattle Snake Colonel, and a D_d Rascal" and the Indians called him "Big Spoon", for his generosity to them.

George Croghan-Captain and Chief Indian agent for Pennsylvania. He was on the field of battle with a company of Indians, Andrew Montour and Christopher Gist and his son.

James Smith-Pennsylvania road worker who was captured by Indians and taken to Fort Duquesene where he witnessed the immediate events in the aftermath of battle. He lived in Indian captivity for years.

James Burd-Wrote to Governor Morris describing the kidnapping of James Smith, Pennsylvania road worker.

Pierre de Contrecoeur-French combat commander who lead the Indians and Canadian troops into battle attacking the British regulars. He took command after Beaujeu was killed in the initial exchange of fire. Was one of Celeron's officers traveling the Ohio River placing lead sheets setting forth the claim of the King of France to the lands of the Ohio and Mississippi drainage basin .

Jean-Daniel Dumas-French combat commander who lead with Contrecoeur French and Indians against English.

Pouchot-Canadian military leader to who the Canadian officers reported. He left memoirs that contained Braddock's Defeat material.

Alexander Hamilton-Maryland medical practitioner who treated General Braddock for a cold on his arrival in Virginia.

John Hamilton-Maryland medical practitioner who was privy by correspondence from his brother to battle information.

Benjamin Franklin-Colonial postal official who arranged for the army to get Pennsylvania Quaker provisions and wagons and horses. Published the *Pennsylvania Gazette* in Philadelphia, Pennsylvania.

William Ferguson- Correspondent to Benjamin Franklin from Winchester, Virginia.

John St. Clair-Deputy Quarter Master General who arriving in North America in 1754, was the advance man for the General surveying the region for the army. Sir John St. Clair, remained for a long time in service in America. In 1756, he was made a Lieutenant Colonel of the sixtieth regiment. In 1762, he was made a full Colonel. At the defeat of Braddock he was shot through the body. His Letterbook available on microfilm is selectively included herein - those items that are included have army, historical geography, and or people detail. Transcribing the microfilm was a slow difficult task but rewarding by revealing new unknown details of the Expedition. Words that could not be made out are shown thusly...(with three dots).

Robert Morris-Captain and Aid de Camp of General Braddock who was with 48th Regiment.

Christopher Gist-Came from England when fifteen. He became a Maryland frontiersman who served as pathfinder/scout. Traveled extensively in Ohio Valley for the Ohio Company before 1755.

Thomas Orde-Captain and commanding officer of artillery detachment.

James Furnis-Civilian who was commissary of stores for Ordinance under Capt. Orde.

James Innes-Commander of Fort Cumberland

Philip Huges-Chaplain in Halkett's 44th Regiment of Foot

Thomas Gage-Lieutenant Colonel commanded 2nd company of Halkett's 44th Regiment of Foot.

William Dunbar-Lieutenant with Halkett's 44th Regiment of Foot.

Horatio Gates-Captain and commanding officer of Fourth New York Independent Company.

John Campbell-British soldier and staff member.

Matthew Leslie-Lieutenant with 44th Regiment and Deputy Quarter Master with St. Clair.

Robert Stewart-Captain and commander of Virginia Light Horse.

Pierre Lotbiniere-French Canadian

M. Roucher-French Canadian

Ensign Godefroy-French Army Officer

Officer A-French Army officer
Officer B-French Army officer
Officer C-French Army officer
Thomas Forbes-Author of a journal describing his trip to the French Forts in the Ohio Valley from Quebec ending at Fort Duquesne while a private soldier in the king of France's service.
Scarroyady-Headman of the Aughwick tribe and ally of British. Also known as Monacatootha. He helped George Washington the year before at Fort Necessity after which he moved his tribe to the Upper Susquehanna River.
Gazette newspapers-These three news accounts as one can see by the dates, were delayed by the distance/time needed to get reports from the field to Philadelphia, Annapolis or Williamsburg there to be typeset and then printed. As reflected in the Pennsylvania Gazette the travel time for the express rider to Philadelphia from Fort Cumberland was one week. In most instances it took longer for the news to be accessible to the readers. Gazette entries are placed in the Braddock Road Chronicles 1755 on the date they were published and in all instances they refer to events that happened earlier. Colonial newspapers are an interesting source of information on the expedition. Professor David Copeland, who is knowledgeable about French and Indian War newspaper coverage, suggests that there probably was not a single correspondent, but rather printed news items were culled from many sources (letters, verbal accounts, other newspapers, and diary entries - sometimes being third and fourth hand accounts).

Arthur S. Cunningham in his typescript compilation "MARCH TO DESTINY" lists the names of 527 participants in the Braddock Expedition.

CHRONOLOGY

The following chronology places the movement of the army on the geography of present-day Virginia, Maryland, West Virginia and Pennsylvania and reflects modern place names.

Hampton, Virginia	Feb 20
Williamsburg, Virginia	Feb 20
Chesapeake Bay and mouth of the Potomac River	Mar 13
Alexandria water front	Mar 18
Alexandria Carlyle House	Mar 18
Alexandria Grande Parade (location of the Army encampment is over a large area west of Alexandria)	Mar 18
Mason Island and Braddock's Rock, Camp Hill, Mouth of Rock Creek (Potomac River)	Apr 12
Three Sisters Islands	Apr 12
VA Route 7 Goose Creek	Apr 12
VA Route 7 Leesburg (Nicholas Minors)	Apr 29
VA Loudoun County & Catoctin Creek	Apr 30
VA Route 9 Hillsboro (Edw. Thompson's)	May 1
VA Route 9 Vestal's Gap in Blue Ridge and Vestal's Ferry (Keys Ferry) of Shenandoah River	May 2
MD Route 355 Georgetown	Apr 13
MD Route 355 Rockville (marker)	Apr 14
MD Route 355 Derwood	Apr 14
MD Route 355 Gaithersburg (marker)	Apr 14
MD Route 355 Clarksburg	Apr 15
MD Route 355 Crossing of Monocacy R.	Apr 17
Frederick, MD	Apr 18
Turners Gap or Foxes Gap and Chapmans Ordinary, MD	Apr 29
Crossing of the Antietam River (MD Route 68)	Apr 29
Williamsport, MD (Mouth of Conococheague Creek)	Apr 30
Swearingen's Ferry (Shepherdstown, W.Va.)	
Great Waggon Road, VA (U.S. Route 11)	May 1
Widow Evans	May 1

Widow Billinger (Barringer's)near intersection of Va. 672 & 739 on Apple Pie Ridge	May 3
Charles Town, W.VA.	May 3
Vicinity of Winchester, VA	May 3
Babb's Run, (now Lake St. Clair) Pott's Camp (adjacent to Gainesboro)	May 4
Henry Enoch's Camp (west of Forks of Cacapon)	
Spring Mountain (along Crooked Run)	
Ridges beyond Forks of Cacapon Rivers	May 5
Little Cacapon River, W.VA.	May 6
Ferryfields, W.VA. Cox's Camp(Crossing of Potomac River)	May 7
Oldtown, MD (Col. Thomas Cresap's post)	May 8
Cumberland, MD ("The Narrows" gap in first ridge of Allegheny Mts.)	May 10
Laurel Hill	Jun 4
Allegheny Mountains:	
Big Savage Mountain	Jun 14
Little Savage Mountain	Jun 15
Meadow Mountain	Jun 16
Negro Mountain	Jun 19
The Encampments of the army beyond Fort Cumberland:	
Spendelow Camp (Grove Camp)	Jun 7
Martins Plantation	Jun 14
Savage River Camp	Jun 15
Laurel Swamp	
Little Meadows (east Castleman)	Jun 16
Camp 2 miles west of Little Crossings (Castleman River) (Laurel Spring Camp)	Jun 19
Bear Camp (Maryland)	Jun 20
Squaws Fort Camp (Pennsylvania)	Jun 23
Camp 4 miles east of Gt. Meadows	Jun 24
Orchard Camp (west side of Gt. Meadows)	Jun 25
Rock Fort Camp (Chestnut Ridge)	Jun 26
Dunbar's Camp	
Gist's Plantation	Jun 27
Camp on east side of Youghiogheny (Gt. Crossing or Stewarts)	Jun 29

Camp on west side of Youghiogheny (Main Crossing)	Jun 30
Great Swamp Camp (Terrapin Camp)	Jul 1
Jacob's Cabin	Jul 2
Salt Lick Camp (Salt Lick Cr.)	Jul 3
Thicketty Run Camp (Hillside C.)	Jul 4
Monocatuca Camp (Ridge Camp)	Jul 6
Camp near Stewartsville	Jul 7
Monongahela Camp (Sugar Creek)	Jul 8
Turtle Creek	Jul 9
Monongahela River crossings (2)	Jul 9
Battlefield	Jul 9
Retreat to Fort Cumberland	Jul 20

The compiler points out that the units (44th Regiment, 48th Regiment, artillery and the hospital unit of Charlotte Browne) were at different places on the routes in the daily record entry. In the case of Browne, she followed well behind the other units, leaving Alexandria on June 1st when others had already arrived at Fort Cumberland. She arrived at Fort Cumberland on June 13th.

The Grand Parade probably lies between the intersection of Braddock Road and Russell Road and the Masonic Temple.

Gordon in ABSTRACT OF A JOURNAL lists the following 19 encampments(see daily record entries):

Grove Camp	*Gist's*
Martins	*Steurt's*
Little Meadows	*Main Crossing*
Laurel Swamp	*Terrapin Camp*
Bear Camp	*Jacob's Cabin*
Middle Crossings	*Salt Lick*
Scalping Camp	*Hillside*
Steep Bank	*Ridge Camp*
Spring Camp	*Turtle Creek*
	Sugar Creek

"Styles in farm equipment change slowly and it is probable that the farm-style Conestoga wagon of about 1850 shown above is similar in many respects to the Pennsylvania wagons used by Braddock a century earlier".
From: Bulletin 218: Contributions from the Museum of History and Technology Paper 9: Conestoga Wagons in Braddock's Campaign, 1755. Smithsonian Institution, article and photograph by Don H. Berkebile.

General Edward Braddock

Private, Grenadier Company, 44th Regiment of Foot, 1751

Maruja V. Wahll

Private, Battalion Company, 48th Regiment of Foot, 1742

Maruja V. Wahll

March scene Allegheny Mountains

PLATE 35

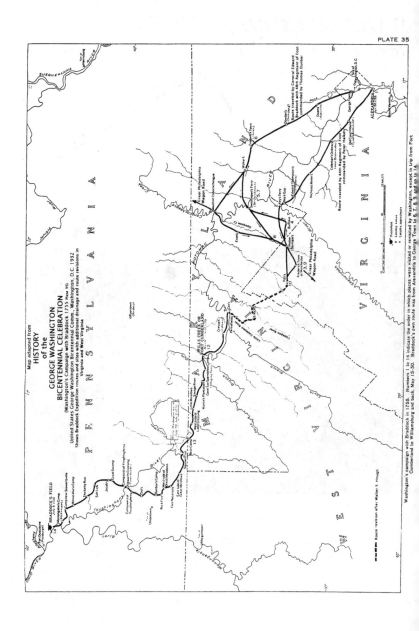

Map of Washington's Campaign with Braddock

DAILY RECORD ENTRIES
January 1755
(Forbes)

About a year and a half ago (1753) I with 120 private Soldiers and our officers embarked in old France for Canada.

Our vessell was a Frigate for forty Guns and another Frigate of 30 Guns sailed at the same time with a company of Soldiers to relieve the Garrison at the Mouth of the Mississippi. After a short Voyage we disembarked at Quebeck, where we were permitted to stay three weeks to refresh ourselves.

The regular Troops in that City did not exceed 300, but I was told that there were many Parties and Detachments quartered up and down the Country all round that place.

Being joined by a Company of 50 Men from that Garrison we went in Batteaus to Montreal under the Command of Lieut. Carqueville and there we spent the last Winter (1753-54).

At our arrival there was a Company of 50 Men in the City where we were quartered, so that in all we made 220 exclusive of Officers. Very early in the Spring we were joined by near 400 more who were drafted out of the several Companies that Garrisoned the Forts and were posted on the Frontiers of Canada. Easter Tuesday (1754) we embarked to the number of six or 700 in about 300 Batteaus or Canoes (not Barken) and took with us a large quantity of Barreled Pork and Meal in Baggs; the Bags weighed sixty or 70 lb each, and I believe there might have been 1500 of them, how many of the Pork there were I never heard nor could I guess, but I believe the Canoes that were not laden with Flour carried five or six Barrels at least, each of them, and the Batteaus received 17 or 20. We were three weeks going from Montreal to Lake Ontario keeping the shore close on board because of the rapidity of the Stream, and at night we went ashore, excepting a few that were left with the canoes, that were fastened to stakes or trees on the shore.

Then we had our Biscuit, which was laid in for the Voyage, delivered to us, with 1 lb of Pork to each, and kindling large fires we cooked our Provisions for next day and slept around the Fires, each of us being provided with a blanket. We kept along the southeast shore of Ontario Lake, and passed so near to the English Fort called Conquen or Oswego that we could talk to the Centinel.

When we came to the Fort at the Falls of Niagara, we landed all our Provisions in which service the Garrison at the Fort assisted and carried them on sleds that were there at the fort, to a little Log House (called le petit Fort de Niagara) three Leagues beyond Niagara Fort, where we put them aboard other Batteaus and Canoes that were there ready to receive them. At our arrival at Niagara there were at the Fort 25 private men, commanded by Lieut. de la Perrie, but Monsieur Contrecoeur was also then in the Fort, and had the Chief command, there was also a Sergeant's Guard at the little fort. The Fort at Niagara is no more than an Emmenence surrounded with Stockadoes or Palisades, which stand about fourteen feet above the ground very close together, and are united or fastened together by three pieces of long scantling that is put transversly on the inside at the distance of three feet or so from each other. These Stockadoes enclosed an Area of near 300 paces square on which is built a House for the Commandant, Barracks for the Men and a Smith's Shop, it is not rendered defensible by any out work or even a Ditch and there are not mounted in it more than four Swivel Guns. As soon as we had put our Provisions on board at the little Fort that I mentioned, we proceeded to Lake Erie with Captain Contracoeur, who had himself now taken the Command of all the Troops in those Canoes. We kept along the Eastern Coast of this Lake to Fort Presqu' isle which I apprehend is about 50 Leagues from Niagara.

This Fort is situated on a little rising Ground at a very small distance from the water of Lake Erie, it is rather larger than that at Niagara but has likewise no Bastions or out Works of any sort. It is a square Area inclose with Logs about 12 feet high, the Logs being square and laid on each other and not more than sixteen or eighteen inches thick. Captain Darpontine Commandant in this Fort and his Garrison was 30 private men. We were eight days employed in unloading our Canoes here, and carrying the Provisions to Fort Boeuff which is built about six Leagues from Fort Presqu' isle at the Head of Buffalo River. This Fort was composed of four Houses built by way of Bastions and the intermediate Space stockaded. Lieut. St. Blein was posted here with 20 Men. Here we found three large Batteaus and between two or 300 Canoes which we freighted with Provisions and proceeded down the

Buffalo river which flows into the Ohio (Allegheny) at about twenty Leagues (as I conceived) distance from Fort au Boeuff, this river was small and at some places very shallow so that we towed the Canoes sometimes wading and sometimes taking ropes to the shore a great part of the way. When we came into the Ohio we had a fine deep water and a stream in our favour so that we rowed down that river from the mouth of the Buffaloe to Du Quesne Fort on Monongehela which I take to be 70 Leagues distant in four days and a half.

At our arrival at Fort Du Quesne we found the Garrison busily employed in compleating that Fort and Stockadoing it round at some distance for the security of the Soldiers Barracks (against any Surprise) which are built between the Stockadoes and Glacis of the Fort.

Fort Du Quesne is built of square Logs transversly placed as is frequent in Mill Dams, and the interstices filled up with Earth; the length of these Logs is about sixteen Feet which is the thickness of the Rampart. There is a Parapat raised on the Rampart of Logs, and the length of the Curtains is about 30 feet, and the Demigorge of the Bastions about eighty. The Fort is surrounded on the two sides that do not front the Water with a Ditch about 12 feet wide and very deep, because there being no covert way the Musqutteers fire from thence having a Glacis before them. When the News of Ensign Jumonville's Defeat reached us our company consisted of about 1400. Seven hundred of whom were ordered out under the command of Captain Mercier to attack Mr. Washington, after our return from the Meadows, a great number of the Soldiers who have been labouring at the Fort all the Spring were sent off in Divisions to the several Forts between that and Canada, and some of those that came down last were sent away to build a Fort some where on the Head of the Ohio, so that in October (1754) the Garrison at Du Quesne was reduced to 400 Men, who had Provisions enough at the Fort to last them two years, notwithstanding a good deal of the Flour be brought down in the Spring proved to be damaged, and some of it spoiled by the rains that fell at the Time. In October last I had an opportunity of relieving myself and retiring, there were not then any Indians with the French but a considerable number were expected and said to be on their March thither. [1]

This initial item in Braddock Road Chronicles comes from Christopher Gist's Journals (William M. Darlington). It is the account of an apparent English speaking/writing soldier who becomes a deserter from the King of France's forces who describes his earlier journey to Fort Duquesne from France.

    Franklin Thayer Nichols in his doctor's degree thesis THE BRADDOCK EXPEDITION mentions three additional deserters who describe the French scene prior to the arrival of the British Army under Braddock. These are Jean Paptiste, Stephen Coffen, and Charles Courteny.

    The English narratives from the Braddock Expedition and others follow as they begin their march from Alexandria, Virginia to the vicinity of the Forks of the Ohio. The Forbes account is a fitting French prelude to this British North American adventure.

January 7 (Tuesday)

MARYLAND-ANNAPOLIS   **(Maryland Gazette)**

    Last Monday Lt. Col Ellington of Col Shirley's Regiment, and Lt. Col. Mercer of Sir William Pepperell's Regiment (who came from England in the <u>Gibraltar</u> Man of War, with some other officers) came to town, and next morning went far out for the Northward. The Gentlemen inform us. that the two Regiments from Ireland, for Virginia may be every day expected in. We hear that his Excellency our Governor is not expected Home from the Camp as Mount Pleasent at Wills's Creek till about the 15th of February.

October 22, 1754

    In a Letter from the Camp at the Great Meadows in Virginia, dated May the 16th (1754) written by an Officer of Distinction, we have the following Particulars: "I have had the Pleasure of a Jaunt down Monongahela within a small distance of the French. The Country is inviting famous for Water, Timber, and Soil. I have obtained a particular description of the River Ohio and the Rivers falling into it, with all the adjacent Lands for the Space of 500 Miles. In my opinion, to possess it would be a greater Acquisition to France than the Conquest of all Flanders. I could demosterate it, but the reasons are too prolix to be inserted in a Letter. It would enable that Kingdom to establish and support a naval strength equal to any in the Universe: and consequently carry the Point they have been aiming at for a Century past. Nature seems to have furnished this Country in the most lavish Manner with all the conveniences and Comforts of Life. I have seen a deal of Limestone, Coal, and rich Iron Oro, all convenient for Water Carriage. [2]

Sir Peeter Halkets Regt and Colonel Dunbars Regt Imbarked
(January 8th) at Cove Near Cork (Ireland) for North America, and
sailed from thence January the 13. From Ireland to Alexandria

Sailing day		miles
Tuesday	Jan 14	124
Wednesday	Jan 15	115
Thursday	Jan 16	118
Fryday	Jan 17	140
Satterday	Jan 18	120
Sunday	Jan 19	77
Munday	Jan 20	120
Tuesday	Jan 21	87
Wednesday	Jan 22	44
Thursday	Jan 23	85
Fryday	Jan 24	96
Satterday	Jan 25	97
Sunday	Jan 26	96
Munday	Jan 27	150
Tuesday	Jan 28	59
Wednesday	Jan 29	60
Thursday	Jan 30	118
Fryday	Jan 31	96
Satterday	Feb 1	66
Sunday	Feb 2	110
Munday	Feb 3	47
Tuesday	Feb 4	28
Wednesday	Feb 5	47
Thursday	Feb 6	111
Fryday	Feb 7	131
Satterday	Feb 8	121
Sunday	Feb 9	178
Munday	Feb 10	154
Tuesday	Feb 11	120
Wednesday	Feb 12	106
Thursday	Feb 13	120
Fryday	Feb 14	104
Satterday	Feb 15	131
Sunday	Feb 16	117

Munday	Feb 17	127
Tuesday	Feb 18	120
Wednesday	Feb 19	85
Thursday	Feb 20	92
Fryday	Feb 21	132
Satterday	Feb 22	118
Sunday	Feb 23	87
Munday	Feb 24	70
Tuesday	Feb 25	116
Wednesday	Feb 26	79
Thursday	Feb 27	51
Friday	Feb 28	49
Satterday	Mar 1	133
Sunday	Mar 2	90
Munday	Mar 3	101
Tuesday	Mar 4	39
Wednesday	Mar 5	00
Thursday	Mar 6	43
Fryday	Mar 7	52
Satterday	Mar 8	106
Sunday	Mar 9	68
Munday	Mar 10	21 (Hampton)
To Alexandria		300
Total miles		5554 [3]

Nichols tells us that in the vicinity Cork, Ireland troops of the 44th were quartered in Kinsale, Charles Fort, and Bandon. Units of the 48th were largely quartered in Cork. Other units included in the army were: 11th Foot (to 44th) at Salisbury - 100 men; the 20th Foot (to 48th) at Bristol - 100 men; 10th and 28th Foot at Limerick - 65 men; and 1st and 26th Foot at Galway - 45 men.

VIRGINIA-WILLIAMSBURG
January 12th 1755
Sir: Gov. Sharpe   **(St. Clair)**

I should have thought myself extremely happy if I had any prospect of finding you at Wills Creek for which place I propose setting out from here by the middle of the week in order to get people to work for building log houses for the greater part of the two regiments for which are daily expected some other ....part of any instructions but by employing a number of the men at the places who are under your

command I not request of you that may expect to our Expedition that
some will...letter to Wills Creek for those commanding officers to give
away any number of...for that Scarce that the troops may rest the
obliged to continue...way of going on and I his place delivering letters
Braddock commands and to...[4]

*As Deputy Quartermaster General, Sir John St. Clair was the advance
man for the army and had been in the colonies since arriving at Hampton Roads
aboard HMS Gibraltar on January 9, 1755. He traveled extensively surveying the
lay of the land and the supply situation for the General in anticipation of the
army's arrival.*

January 14 (Tuesday)
VIRGINIA-WILLIAMSBURG
January 14th 1755
Sir: Mr. Pitcher   (St. Clair)
    I should have thought myself extremely lucky if I had been in
England before you embarked for America... I might have had the
pleasure of your aquaintenance. I take the opportunity of Colonels
Ellison and Morcei who are going northward from hence to levy the
two Regiments of giving them a letter from you to acquaint you of my
arrival and that I have brought with me duplicates of the letters given
to you by Sir Thomas Roberson for the Governor of the respective
provinces in North America.
    Until I got on board, I thought you had proceeded directly to
Virginia, which made me not ask to see your instructions before I left
London so that I am entirely...of your action in this way.
    I now entreat of you to send me the State of the Individual
companies you have mustered that now have it ready to lay before
General Braddock and his...been formerly employed as commisary you
will be better able to judge how necessary it will be that the General
should know their number in case they...be immediately ordered for
Service.
    The Governours of this province desires his compliments to you, I
beg you may likewise accept those of...[5]

January 14th 1755   (St. Clair)
Sir: Provincial Governors

Herewith I transmit to you the letters from the Secretary of State relating to the current Circumstances of Affairs in America.

As his majesty has appointed me Deputy Quarter Master General to the army to be sent forthwith to Virginia and those levies in the different Provinces I have asked those first opportunity of acquainting you of my arrival in Virginia in order to make the major preparations for the Reception of the two Regiments which are to embark at Cork a few days after my Departure from England that we reasonably may expect will arrive in a very short time.

I shall be glad to know the particulars with regard to what may...happended on the travels you command that I may acquaint myself accordingly and have them ready to lay before General Braddock so that on his landing that no time may be lost.

As I am an entire Stranger to the regions in America that be highly necessary to have got the best information of the Situation that I can whether have no other way of doing, but Requesting of you to send any maps or drawings you may have of your province which I shall Return to you after they are copy'd, if you have any of the ground of our back Settlements it will be of use likewise for me to have it where are things that General Braddock will expect I should have that he may be early informed of the distances of places for regulating number of the troops if newly required if this thro the different provinces. Being ordered by his Majesty to correspond with you I am glad of this opportunity of expressing the respect with which I am your most obedient & most humble servant.
PS to the other letter of ye 14th

It would be of the greatest conquences have the proportion of men from your province in readiness for complete the two regiments from 300 men each to 400. [6]

January 21 (Tuesday)

ENGLAND-LONDON   **(Maryland Gazette)**
November 7

We are informed, that the officers of the Train of Artillery, intended for Virginia are to hold themselves in Readiness to embark on Saturday.

Some letter from Dublin say, that orders have been received there for draughting 325 Men out of 5 regiments of Foot on that

Establishment, being 65 out of each Regiment ordered to embark for Virginia.

Two private Grenadiers of the third Regiment of foot Guards have offered themselves Volunteers to go to Virginia; and we hear they are to have Commissions in General Pepperall's Regiment that is to be raised in that Country.

November 9

Sir Peter Halkett arrived at Dublin on Thursday Se-night. The same Day twelve Carriages with chests containing containing 600 Arms, were sent from the Castle of Dublin to Kinsale, for the use of the Draughts who are to embark from thence for America.

The Exedition for Virginia goes on with great Vigor; Numbers of Troops being already embarked, and the Remainder will go on board the beginning of next week so that it is hopped we shall be able in Time to secure our valuable settlements in America, as the Natives there are with great Spirit a specimen of which we experienced in the taking Cape Breton.

November 12

The Embarkation for America are continued, and all the Forces destined for that Part of the World are embarked on Thursday next.

November 13

Yesterday Morning several Officers embarked at the tower, and at the same Time a great Quantity of Ammunition was shipped for Virginia. They are to go first to Cork, in order to join the Regiments there, and then proceed on there Voyage.

Capt. Orme is appointed Aid de Camp to General Braddock.

November 2

Dublin Major General Bligh will shortly set out for Kinsale, to superintend the Embarkation of the Forces destined for Virginia, which are considerably augmented by Draught's from the several Regiments on this Establishment, except those on Dublin Duty.[7]

PENNSYLVANIA-PHILADELPHIA   (Pennsylvania Gazette)

Extracts of two Letters, from an Officer at Wills's Creek to a Gentleman here.

Camp Mount Pleasant, December 19 1754.

"We have No news here, only that about a Week ago, there came to Camp fifteen Indians Allies of the Six Nations, with a white Flag of Truce. We suspected they were French Indians, tho they made their

Speech to us with some belts of Wampum, and told us they came from some nations on or near the Lakes to speak with us as friends; and this day, four of our Friendly Indians came to us from Mr. Crogan's, being sent for on this occasion. Today our Commander in Chief is to return an answer to their belts, the purpose of which shall inform you in my next. Their Indians speak good French, which leaves room to suspect they may be employed as Spies, however, they can observe nothing to our Disadvantage."

Camp Mount Pleasant, January 3, 1755

"The Treaty with the Indians ended the last Day of the year. They insisted strongly, that they came from seven Nations near the Lakes, with seven Belts and strings of Wampum, to make a peace with their Brethren the English, and for that purpose they accordingly made a very long speech, and received our Answer to the same, which a very handsome present, which they accepted with great Joy and Thanks, declaring, that they would represent to their Nations the civility they had received from their Brethren the English. If we can but get the Indians, we shall easily find a method to manage the French, which is the chief thing we want to bring about, and I believe it is what the Indians in general must define."

On Sunday the Cherokee Indians, mentioned in our last, set out from this Place, on their way to Charles Town, in South Carolina.

MARYLAND-ANNAPOLIS
Extract of a Letter from a Gentleman at Wills's Creek, to his Friend here, dated January `17, 1755.

"Yesterday arrived here Sir John St. Clair, Bart: Colonel and Quarter Master General to all his Majestys Troops intended for this Service and sets off Tomorrow Morning with Governor Sharpe. Your worthy Governor has been here about a week, on this his second visit to Camp within two months, and we shall be very sorry, very sorry if he should not cross the Allegheny Mountains with in, in a Station agreeable to himself, and equal to his great Merit.

Three deserters came here Yesterday in 13 days from Fort de Quesne; their mission not public, one of them told me the 15 savages who were here some time ago, arrived 8 or 9 Days at Fort de Quesne before they deserted, and all acknowledged their good usage at Wills's Creek. Two of our Indians were lately sent with a letter from one of the Prisoners at Winchester, when they return we may have some News. We daily expect to hear of the Arrival of General Braddock with the Troops. His Majesty's first Independent Companies here, have built a Fort with several large store Houses, and barracks for all the men, by way of a Fortified camp flanking and flanked by the fort with ten four pounders, besides Swivels, all this since the 12th of September last, without any assistance (either from Virginia or Maryland) of workmen of any kind and even a long while without a sufficient Number of good Tools, beginning only with one spade and two or three axes.

A very good Company from Maryland came here about two months ago, and are in Hutts which they built for themselves near us. We have heard of the Virginia Levies marching almost 4 months ago but none of the appear yet.

We are appraised that in Chester Town, in Kent County, several Men enlisted immediately on the Arrival of the Officer into that Town, before the Drum was beat, and that the Officer wanting 30 men got his Compliment, and marched with them...little while; such is the commendable spirit of that place; they are gone for Wills's Creek , and some young Maryland Gentlemen (true patriots) are gone from thence as Volunteers: The Mother of one of them at parting, took Leave of him with saying, My Dear son, I shall with much greater Pleasure hear of your Death, than your Cowardice, or Ill Conduct.

His Excellency our Governor, and Sir John St.Clair, are returned from Wills's Creek, and gone to Williamsburg; and we hear they came down Potowmack 200 Miles in a Canoe.

Monday Evening last, James Pitcher, Esq. Commissary to the Forces expected in, came to Town, from the Northward, and is now gone to Virginia, expecting to meet them there. [8]

January 26 (Sunday)
MARYLAND-FORT AT WILLS CREEK
My Lord Fairfax: (St. Clair)

As your Lordship was so good as to promise me most everything in your power should be done for the good of the expedition, it is my duty to acquaint you in what I later found...in my way hither.

The float on the shenandoe is now a making by a carpenter sent by your...after promised me to have it finished by the 4th Feb but...I gave him two guineas to employ more hands to rush completion. I imagine it will be finished by the end of the month. The roads now...in construction are vary narrow over the mountains which makes it impossible for waggons to pass one another and present a number of trees along...the land, there are many small rivlets of water which require trees to be laid over them for the commissary of the...

The road from Winchester to the river is very bad, that river has neither canos nor floats only at the fort...and its bottom is very stony, the ford at the Little Cacapon is not near as bad there is neither canoes nor floats over it. I should have been glad to have found the mountain marked out, which was only done at the further end 5 miles from Jos. Pearshall's.

Your Lord's carpenter is to go to the south branch by the first of the month to build a float over the River which are greatly wanted, it will be likewise good to have a float made over Patterson's Creek in the place where the new road that is to be cut is to cross it, I should likewise have been glad to have seen that Road, but no part of it was marked, I could pretty well guess where it comes to the road in the valley.

When I was two miles on this side of the South branch I had a good view of the ground that runs along the Savage River it seems good for a carriage road and might be of great service if you at...would order it to be marked out as I shall soon be obliged to visit all that ground.

I must recommend it to your Lord to give directions that all the new roads which are to be cut may be made at least 30 or 35 feet wide and carried along the ridges of the mountains as much as possible to avoid the valley and should the expense of this be too great for the countys to bear which are only in their infancy. I shall do my duty to recommend to the governor to have a general charge made of it. [9]

January 27 (Monday)
MARYLAND-FORT AT WILLS CREEK   (Sharpe)

To examine the Channel of the River we came down the Potomack by water for a Distance of about 250 miles, the many falls & Shoals in the River which we find render the conveyance of Artillery & other Stores to the Camp by Water impractable, the 5th Day from our leaving the Camp we reached Alexandria or Belhaven a Town on the South Bank of (the) Potomack. [10]

This was a description of the trip down the Potomac as recorded by the Governor in his correspondences. Sir John St. Clair was in the party.

January 31 (Thursday)

VIRGINIA-WILLIAMSBURG   (**Virginia Gazette**)

As I am commanded by His Majesty to raise Recruits to serve in the Regiments of Sir Peter Halket and Col. Dunbar, daily expected into this colony. to drive the French from his Majesty's Lands on the Ohio, the following Encouragement will be given to all Persons inclinable to join for the added Service. viz.

Each man voluntarily offering himself, shall receive a Guinea enlisting money, and Six pence per day, and Provisions, with all arms and Accouterments necessary, and cloathing from Great Briton and when the Expedition and Service is over, they shall be discharged and sent home to their respective Habitations, and if they will repair to Williamsburg, they shall be provided with provisions till the aforementioned Regiments arrive.   Robert Dinwiddie [11]

February 1 (Friday)

VIRGINIA-ALEXANDRIA

Sir: Troop Commanders   (**St. Clair**)

His Majesties Service requiring that twenty Sawyers and sixty others that understand the use of carpenters tools to be commanded by a Captain, two subalterns, three serjents, three corporals and one drummer.

You are hereby ordered to draught from the detachment under your command all men that are carpenters by trade and sawyers, boat or shipbuilders and to appoint a Subaltern, one noncommissioned officer in proportion to the number of the draught with directions to proceed to the nearest Detachment...to their Routes till the numbers required shall be completed or with a number as shall be found amongst the troops and to proceed after passing the several detachments to Alexandria where they are to wait for further orders.

Captain Mercer is appointed to this command, of which you are to give him the earliest intelligence that he may...to his...out at..and must recommend to you in the strongest manner the obedience of the most trusty serjents and corporals in this detachment.

P.S. a copy of this to be sent to the next detachment and so on from one detachment to another.

To: The officer commanding the Troops at Winchester
To: The Officer commanding a detachment of Troops on the march
from Fredericksbg to Winchester (4 copies of this to be...)
To: The Officer commanding the Troops at Fredericksburgh
To: The Officer commanding the Troops at Alexandria [12]

February 2 (Saturday)
VIRGINIA-ALEXANDRIA   (St. Clair)
Memorandum for Mr. Commissary Walker

To buy up in Pensylvania to 4 hundred thousand weight of Flour to
be delivered at Conogoeheog by the 10th day of March the 100
waggons employed for that trip are to proceed to Winchester as
required and are to be paid for by the government.

40 horses are to at the Fort with 200 weight of the...according to
contract they are to present to Mr. Dick at Winchester to be employed
in the Government service you are to appraise Mr. Dick of this and let
him know what he is to lay in at Winchester...For...as much as he can,
the...for a magazine. [13]

Sir: Mr. Dick Commissary   (St. Clair)

As it was impossible for me to be at Fredericksburg by the time I
appointed I take the opportunity of an Officer going to Winchester to
send you this letter, to acquaint you that I have desired Mr. Walker to
send to you at Winchester the 40 horses contracted for which were to
be delivered at the Fort the first week of Feb. with 200 weight of Flour
on each. These horses you are to Employ in carrying of provisions to
the camp it will be necessary to have men enough for each four horses.

It will be necesary that you buy us all kind of provender for horses
and lay it up at Winchester the greater quantity you can get it will be
the better to enable us to transport our Artillery. Should you want
money for purchases, It shall either be sent to you or you may charge
me for it.

I have designated Mr. Walker to go to Pensylvania to contract for
200000 weight of Flour to be delivered at Conogogee the 15th of
March, and that the 100 waggons that should carry it were to be taken
into the Government pay if wanted...will make it necessary that you lay
in what quantity of hay and oats you can at that place.

I shall be glad you will let his Excellency Governor Dinwiddie know from time to time what success you have had, and what provisions you have in view. I am... [14]

February 3 (Monday)
VIRGINIA-ALEXANDRIA
To Major Carlisle: (St. Clair)

As His Majestys service requires it that two months corn and hay be laid in here, for four hundred horses for sixty one days, you are hereby empowered to buy up at the market price 198100 lbs. of hay or corn blades and 1000 bushells of corn or oats, you are to be very clear in making your contracts that what is agreed for may be delivered by the time appointed the sooner the whole is got togeather it will be the better, and on the being brought to this place you are to prepare proper magazines for its reception.

You are from time to time to give me an account of what provender you have got and what you have in view. Given under my hand at Alexandria this 3 day of February 1755. [15]

NEW YORK-NEW YORK
February 3rd 1755
To: Sir John St.Clair   (Delancy)

I had the honour of your letter of the 1st of January by Lieutenant Colonel Ellison and Mercer, whom I have provided with horses in provision of his Majestys Expedition signified to me by letter from Sir Thomas Robenson of the 26th of October. I take this opportunity to congratulate you on your safe arrival at Virginia.

The intelligence I have lately received from Oswego of the 1st of January is that the Indians who Returned from Montreal Report that an officer was arrived there from the Ohio who was to return back this Winter with a reinforcement sufficient to rout all the English from thence; my opinion is that the French will not be able to pass in the winter for the lakes are not hard enough frozen to bear them and they dare not venture by water in this season for one night of hard frost might...'em where they may possible perish.

In August last a party of French Indians of St. Francis and Becanmacourt near Trois Riveries a place on St. Lawrence River between Quebec and Montreal came thro the lake Champlain and St. Sacrement into this province and destroyed a settlement called

37

Hoveck, which is about 18 miles east from that part of Hudson River which is 9 miles above Albany and carry's off the small Remains of an Indian nation which was settled near that place.

As to maps of this country we have none, there is one preparing by Mr. Evans I am told which will soon be published. I use those in Charleviose. As to the knowledge I have of the country, I shall give it (to) you in as few words as I can: the city of New York is seated on Hudsons River, about 21 miles from the Ocean; from New York the city of Albany is about 144 miles the course of the river is north a little easterly, navigable for small sloops. Albany is on the west side of Hudson thence to Schenectdy is...miles, a Town on the Mohawks River which empties itself into Hudson's River from Schenectdy you go up the Mohawks River in canoes or Batteaus to near the head thereof, meeting with only one small carrying place, from the head of the Mohawks River you cross two miles by land into the Wood Creeks which carries you down into the Oneida Lake and go through the lake into the River that leads to Oswego a fort belonging to his Majesty on the side of the Lake Ontario the distance between Albany and Oswego is computed to be 270 miles, It takes 8 days to come up the river St. Lawrence from Montreal to Oswego, from Oswego to the French fort at Niagara its computed to be about 160 miles, I think it is not so much, the great fall of Niagara to the Peninsula on the Lake Erie and thence on to the Ohio and down to Monongehela you will have been better inform'd where you are than I can. I wish you health and success in this service and am Your most O. and most H.S.

James Delancey [16]

While not a member of the Expedition, James Delancy, Governor of the Colony of New York, has been included in Chronicles for the historical geography detail he provides of colonial North America.

February 10 (Monday)
VIRGINIA-WILLIAMSBURG

Williamsbourg Feb[ry] the 10th 1755.   **(St. Clair)**

Sir: Robert Napier

I know no better way of giving you an account of my proceedings in this Country than to transcribe two Letters which I wrote to General Braddock, the one of the 15th of Jan[ry] and the other of the 9th of Feb[ry]; which I hope will be satisfactory. [17]

On the 10th of February St. Clair writes to Napier (above). To explain his activities he includes transcribed letters (Jun. 15th and Feb. 9th) he has written to General Braddock that immediately follow.

Williamsbourg Jany the 15th 1755.

Sir: Robert Napier   **(St. Clair)**

I was very sorry that I had not in my power to receive your Commands before I embarked for America, least you may find any thing neglected on your Arrival. I landed at Hampton the 9th Inst and have ever since been endeavouring to comply with my orders: I shall here send you the Heads of them, and shall inform you what Steps I have taken in the Execution of them.

1st. To provide an Hospital at Hampton or Williamsbourg for 150 Sick.

2dly. To provide provisions against the landing of the Troops and during their stay at Wills's Creek.

3.Bass horses to be provided for the Officers when they arrive.

4. To consult with the Governor the proper Measures for erecting Log Houses or Barns at Will's Creek.

5. Floats or Bathes for the transporting the Artillery and Baggage from the falls of the Potomac to Will's Creek.

6. To settle with the Governor the best and speediest manner to complete the two Battalions with 200 good Men each. The 10th I went to Williamsbourg and delivered my Dispatches to the Govr. The next day I consulted with His Excellency the properest Methods for going to work on this urgent piece of Service. That Day one hundred Horses were contracted for, 40 of which were to be deliver'd the 1st week in Febry and the remaining part the first day of March; each of these Horses are to carry 200 lbs of Flower to Wills's Creek.

The 12th I went with the Governour to Hampton in order to provide an Hospital & lodging for its proper Officers. Next day I went and examined the whole Town of Hampton but cou'd not find any one place Sufficient to contain any Number of Sick; all I cou'd get was two very small Ware Houses; But there are no Houses in Town which will be shut to us on this occasion; So how disagreeable it my be to the Surgeons to have their Sick separate, there is a necessity for it at present. There are Numbers of indigent people who will take the Sick into their Houses, and least Bedsteads may be wanting I have given Directions for 100 Cradles to be built. I have provided extreme good Lodgings at the Town Clerks House for two of the principal Officers of the Hospital, the other may lodge with those people who keep publick Houses until Mr. Graham leaves his dwelling house which will be towards the End of Febry. I shou'd not have hesitated one Moment in running up a large Hospital of Boards if I cou'd have got a Sufficient Quantity of Deal and Artificers, but both are wanting.

I gave Directions to Mr. Hunter (who delivers you this) concerning a Stock of fire wood for the Hospitals, and to get as much fresh Provisions collected togeather for the Sick as possible; as likewise to throw on board of the Transports some Sheep and fresh Pork, and some Beefs if they are to be had.

The Governour has been extremely active and diligent in gathering togeather all kind of Provisions for Wills's Creek, & to make a deposite at Fredericksbourg & Winchester to be near at hand. The Carriage to the Creek is immensely difficult at this Season on account of the Scarcity of Horses, and if we had them, Forage is scarce to (be) had. I am in Hopes we shall be able to collect 200 Horses. If we had more, how are they to be fed? I return'd to Williamsbourg the 13th in the Evening.

Jan: 14th I saw some more Horses brought for the use of the Troops. I wrote Letters to the Governors of all the Provinces & sent my Dispatches to them.

I must, Sir, refer you to the Governour with regard to compleating Sir Peter Halketts & Col: Dunbar's Regiments, all I shall say (is) that Men will not be wanting when you please to call for them.

That part of my Instructions which regards the building of Batteaus or Floats on the Patomack at the Falls of Alexandria, I am obliged to delay executing, as I am informed the doing of it wou'd be in vain, for that in Winter the Stream is so rapide that there is no rowing heavy Boats against the Current, and that in Summer there are many flatts and Shoals which will render the Navigation almost impracticable. On the whole I have acted to the best of my Capacity, and whatever Difficultys may arise I shall do what I can to surmount them.

I propose going to morrow morning from hence to Wills's Creek, I shall go the one Road and return the other; my journey will take me at least twelve Days going and coming back, being 600 Miles with the same Horses; I shall stay there about Six Days which I hope will be Sufficient to see our Barracks in a fair way of being built.

Shou'd you arrive with the Troops before my return I beg of you to send me your Orders by an Express that I may know how to conduct my Self.

I have been talking to the Governour concerning the properest Method of landing the Troops; He is of the opinion they shou'd proceed to Alexandria in their Transports, and march as soon as possible to Wills's Creek; For if they were to land at Hampton & be dispersed about the Country, they wou'd have a long march by land, that all the Horses & Carriages which will be wanted to carry Provisions to the Deposites, wou'd be wanted, to attend the Troops, on their march to Alexandria; and that if they were to march by land, they have Ferrys to cross, which might be attended with a long delay. After examining the situation of the Country, and the quick Dispatch that Affairs require, I am of the above opinion with the Governour, or we shall at least gain three Weeks by going directly by Water.

I am in hopes we shall not want Flower and Salt pork, which is what is easiest to be had in this Country. The Governour had wrote to New England for a Cargoe of Salt Fish, and if you are of opinion that Rice will do for our Men, it may be easily had. We may get some Calavances of the Pea kind which I believe our People will be fond of. That you may be the better Judge of the Difficulty of carriage from Alexandria to Wills's Creek, the Govr pays twenty Shillings for the carriage of each Barrell of Beef for the 400 Men that have been building a Fort at that place & who continue at Work.

I think if no unforseen accident happens to me that I shall return hither the 2^D day of Febry or sooner if I can do my business. I have the Honour of being with the greatest Respect Sir, Your most obedient and most humble Servant.   JOHN ST. CLAIR

pS. If a large quantity of Iron is not brought out with the Artillery, it will be necessary that a Dozen of Quintal should be brought at Hampton to make portable Ovens. [18]

VIRGINIA-WILLIAMSBURG
To: Major General Braddock   (St. Clair)
Williamsbourg
Febry the 9TH 1755.
Sir: General Braddock
I did my self the Honour of writing a Letter to you of the 15th of January, giving you an account of my proceedings till that time, least

you shou'd have arrived during my absence. I shall now let you know in what manner I have been employ'd since the Date of my last Letter, least my Duty shou'd call me from this place or from Hampton, which might deprive me of the pleasure of receiving your Commands until my Return.

The 16th of Jan: I set out for Fredericksbourg, and got to that place the 18th being 104 Miles of very good Road. I saw at that place 190 Men of the Companys raised in this Province, I was from the 19th to the 22d in getting to Winchester which is 93 Miles of very bad Road, I saw a Detachment of 70 men of the same Troops. From the 23d to the 26th I was on the Road to Wills's Creek, this is 85 miles of the worst Road I ever travelled; and greatly lengthen'd by the Roads being in the Channells of the Rivers, when they might be shorten'd by cutting them along the Ridges of the Mountain. Which Lord Fairfax promised me shou'd be done about this time. This will shorten that road about 15 Miles, and avoid the bad Road by Patersons Creek.

When I had got about two Miles on the other Side of the South branch, I had a full view of the Mountains on each side of the Patomack above Wills's Creek, and from what I cou'd see, there is a Road easily to be made across the Country to the Mouth of Savage River which will be gaining 30 Miles: If I am not more deceived than I have been of late with regard to Ground, the Mouth of Savage River is the place where we ought to cross the Alleghany Mountains. I have only been able to find one Woodsman who can give me any distinct Account of that Ground, which gives me great Satisfaction. I have wrote to Lord Fairfax to have the Road marked out to the mouth of Savage River.

I cannot learn what cou'd induce People ever to think of making a fort or a Deposite for Provisions at Wills's Creek; It covers no County, nor has it the Communication open behind it either by Land or Water; the River not navigable and by the least Rains that fall, the Rivers which one has to cross (some of them five times) were without Floats or Canoes, untill within these few Days that they have been set about to be built.

I found the Governour of Maryland at Wills's Creek, who had been at that place but a few Days, not long enough to make any considerable alteration nor to reconoitre the country. He had with him at the Fort (or more properly a small piece of Ground inclosed with a Strong Palisade joined pretty close) three Independent Companys, the one of South Carolina, and the other two of New York: the latter seem to be draughted out of Chelsea. The Excuse they make for having so many old Men do very little Honour to those Companys that are left behind at New York; for they say that they are draughted from them. The Carolina Company is in much better order and Discipline. I likewise saw at Wills's Creek 80 Men of the Troops raised in Maryland, they are a good body of Men, and if the rest of the troops raised in that province be as good (which the Govr has reason to expect) we may get 150 Men from that Province to enable us to complete the two British Regiments.

Least it shou'd be still more advisable to pass the Mountains at Wills's Creek, there are a Number of Trees cut down for erecting Loghouses, and I gave directions for Palisading a House near the Fort for a Powder Magazine.

In my last letter to you, I acquainted you that Governor Dinwiddie told me that the Navigation of the Pattomack is impractical, this I can now affirm from Experience, for Governour Sharp and I found it so for all other vessels but Canoes cut out of a Single Tree; We attempted to go down the River in this sort of Boat, but we were obliged to get on Shore and walk on foot especially at the Shannondeau Falls; So that the getting Batteaus or Floats made for the transport of the Artillery and the Baggage of the Regiments, cou'd serve for no other thing, but to throw away the Governments Money to no purpose, and loose a great deal to time.

As Governour Sharp expected to have found you arrived, he came to this place by Alexandria and Fredericksbourg, at the latter I saw him review 80 Men of the Virginia Troops, which amount by this time to 700 or 800 Men: By what I saw of them, I am afraid the Officers who recruited them, have looked more to their Numbers than to the goodness of the Men. These 80 were the only ones which Govr Sharp has seen. I make no doubt, but that from the Report I made to Govr Dinwiddie of his new Leavies, that their Numbers will be diminished before you arrive.

As the Nature of the Service we are going on, will require a great Number of Carpenters, a Company totally compose of these is now a forming of 100 Men, from whom we may expect great advantage. I wish we may be able to find people to form into two Companys of Rangers.

Whatever Scheme, Sir, you may think proper out of your prudence to pursue; the first thing to be done at all Events is to have our Artillery, Baggage and Provisions carried up to Winchester from Alexandria; for which reason I have ordered all kinds of provender for Horses to be laid in at these two places, in as great quantity as the Country can afford, which is but small. I expect 100 Waggons with Flower from Pensilvania at Winchester by the 15th of March, which Waggons will serve for carrying the Amunition and Stores from Alexandria, least the Horses of this Country employ'd before that time shou'd fall off. On this depends the dispatch we shall be able to make, I hope to get as much Oats, Hay and Indian Corn Blades as will enable us transport the whole to Winchester: But I am afraid we shall not be able to cross the Mountains till the latter End of April when the Grass begins to shoot.

During the Transport of the Artillery to Winchester, there will be sufficient time to cut the Road to Savage River, and to reconoitre the Ground towards the head of the Youghangany, one branch of which seems to lock in with the former.

As I have seen most of this Country, I shall more freely give my opinion with regard to the Disposition of the Troops on their Arrival, both for the Security of our Magazines, Subsistance of the Troops, ease of the Inhabitants and that as few Countermarches may be made as possible.

That the Transports which have on board one Regiment may stop in the River Potomack as near Fredericksbourg as they can, that Regiment may be quartered in the following manner.

3 ½ Companys at Winchester 6 Days march from Fredericksbourg.

½ of a Company at Conogogee 8 Days by Winchester.

6 Companys at Fredericksbourg & Falmouth, one march from their landing.

THE OTHER REGIMENT

5 Companys at Alexandria with the Company of Artillery & Stores of all kind.

1 Company at Dumfries 2 Days march from Alexandria.

1 Compy at Upper Marlbro' 1 Days march.

1 Company at Bladensbourg 1 Days March in Maryland.

2 Companys at Frederick 6 Days march.

By this Disposition the Companys which are quartered at Winchester Conogogee and Frederick form the Chains, to cover our

Magazines, and will be near at Hand to advance either to Wills's Creek or Savage River as you shall Judge most proper.

I have pressed the Governour of Pensilvania to have his Country reconoiter'd toward the head of the Youghangany and to have the Road leading to it marked out, ready to be cut; or if there is any nearer way to the french Forts, to have all these Roads marked out: For that when we cross the Mountains we must depend a great deal on the Supplys of Provisions from that Province. I am with the greatest Respect Sir, Your most obedient and most humble Servant. [19]

To Major General Braddock.   (St. Clair)

I am in Hopes Sir that this will give you some light into our present Situation, if I have not been full enough, great allowance is to be given to one coming into a Country where he is an intire Stranger, and I may say where the Inhabitants are totally ignorant of Military Affairs: Their Sloth & Ignorance is not to be discribed; I wish General Braddock may be able to make them shake it off. I shall undertake to talk to the Germans in the language they have been brought up under in Germany. There is no such thing as to perswade any of them to enlist in the Virginia Companys.

I have not had time to make my self Master of the Indian Affairs, so shall only say in General Terms that I am afraid the French have drawn most of them over to their Interest, especially the Six Nations. We may expect to see a great Number of them, but never to feel them. Since I came from Wills's Creek there are some Letters come to Governours Dinwiddie and Sharp of the 3ᵈ of Febʳʸ which makes them apprehensive of being attacked, as the french are making great quantity of Indian Shoes at their fort, that the first Column of the Indians are arrived, and two more, on their March. The Commanding Officer at the Fort has orders to be on the defensive, but that is not necessary for two of his Company have neither Legs to get upon the Heights nor to run away thro' the Valleys.

I am in great hopes that this advice is true, and that they will make their Attacks in different parts, if so they are already in Pannick; but on the Contrary if they are lying quiet and relieving their out posts often and at irregular Hours, then their attacks will follow and may succeed. I should be pleased they were making Incursion in the Country, for the above reason this is the only thing will awake the sleepy headed Mortals of this and the Neighbouring Provinces.

I shall now acquaint you in what manner I am to be employ'd for some time to come, if General Braddock with the Troops do not arrive.

Governour Sharp goes to morrow for Maryland, being obliged to meet his Assembly the 20th. he takes his Road thro' Fredericksbourg and Alexandria: at the former he is to review the Virginia Detachment, Discharge the bad Men (which are too numberous) and choose out those who are fit to fill up our Regiments; at the latter he is to form the Company of Carpenters to be ready on our Troops landing. I shall carry this letter to Hampton with my others on the 14 (as the 16th is fixed for Capt. Sprys sailing) and shall see the Hospitals and every thing in order for the Sick. I shall return to Williamsbourg the 16th and the 18th set out for Winchester where I shall execute the same thing that Gov[r] Sharp does at Fredericksourg on 600 of the Virginia Troops, and see the Forage is laid in; This may take me up some Days; Then I go to Alexandria either to wait General Braddocks Arrival or go where the Service requires me most. I wish I have not tired your patience with a long Letter, but if you find that I have been too particular, I am sorry for it; I thought it was erring in the safe Side. I with great Sincerity Sir, Your most obedient and most obliged humble Servant.   John St. Clair

pS. In Jeffery'ss Map, Winchester is marked Frederick. Wills's Creek is marked Caicuctuck Creek. The Road to Savage River which I mention runs from a small River which runs from the West into the South Branch. I send you an Account of the Strength of the French which I look upon to be genuine, and an uncorrect Map of the Country on the other Side of the Allegany Mountains. [20]

To Major General Braddock   (St. Clair)

I have had no time to inform myself about the different interests of the Indian Nations but from what I have I am afraid that the french have drawn from the Six Nations their way of fighting I do not apprehend to be formidable...might have been of use to us in supplying us with provisions in the Seasons I have taken the liberty of sending you a proposal which may plague the Indians and not be of any Service to the French, who I am sure deserve all the mischief we can do them.

I am in hopes that the numerous train of small mortars when I mention such to Colo. Napier are sent out with their shells, we shall reap infinate benefits from 'em. I beg Sir that you will take it into your consideration, if Fusees for the officers and Sergents be not proper to be sent out as Spontoons and halberts are of no use on this woods country.

The Reports of the Strength of the French on the Ohio are various, I here with transmit you the most probable amount I have got which I am apt to believe in general.

Nothing will give me greater pleasure than to hear that my proceedings have met with your approbation. I shall act in every respect for the good of the service and with as much frugality as possible. I am with the greatest respect. [21]

February 11 (Tuesday)
VIRGINIA-WILLIAMSBURG   (St. Clair)
Sir: General Braddock

It was not in my power until now to get ready for the sailing of the Gibralter Man of War ever since I landed in Virginia which was on the 9th January I have been employed in endeavouring to execute his Majestys commands the particulars of which I shall inform you after the order that is about them.

I have a better way of acquainting you what I have done, but by transcribing two letters I have prepared for General Braddock on his arrival both as a report of what I have done and in what light things appear to me in the country, this long delay may be too circumstancial but for my own justification I am obliged to work more fully . The first letter is dated March 5th also Jan...and the second the 9th Febry. [22]

The sentence immediately above suggests confused dating but it probably stems from the compilers reading of the faint and small hand writing of St. Clair in his Letterbook. While there is a letter of March 6th from St. Clair to Braddock - it does not fit into the chronology.

PENNSYLVANIA-PHILADELPHIA   (Pennsylvania Gazette)
By a Gentleman, who left Winchester, in Virginia, the third Instant, and from private Letters we have the following Intelligence, viz. that Sir John Sinclair and Governor Sharpe have been to Wills Creek and were returned; and that they had view'd the Great Falls of the Potomack, and were in hopes of blowing them up, so as to make the River navigable for flat bottom'd vessels, which if effected, will be of

the greatest Service in transporting Necessaries for our Forces. That one of our Indians was lately arrived at Wills's Creek from the Ohio, who said, that he could not form a judgment of the particular Number of Troops the French had then in that Country; but that in general they seem'd to be very numerous, Parties daily arriving and marching from Fort to Fort; that they had begun to build another Fort; and that they were not well supplied with Bread, but had enough of other Provisions. That a Party of French and Indians were, not long since, seen a few Miles from our Camp, in order, as it was thought, to get Intelligence of our strength, etc. That Lieutenant Colonel Stephens, with the last Detachment of the Virginia Forces, arrived the first Instant at Winchester, on their way to Wills's Creek, having marched upwards of Ninety Miles in four days, notwithstanding the Deepness of the Roads at this advanced Season. [A good Preface of what may be expected from Troops, animated by the influence and Example of Officers of such Spirit and Activity.] That our Forces, when all join'd at the Camp, will amount to about 1000 Men. That it was reported the Train of Artillery, from England, arrived on the 27th ult. in Virginia, with 150 Matrosses, Cloths, and military Stores, of all sorts, for several Thousand men; that a Camp was mark'd out for them at a Place called Watkin's Ferry; and that they sailed in Company with the Transports bound to Cork, to take on board the two Regiments where for America, which, with General Braddock, may (be) daily expected. And that there were a number of Men at work at Potowmack, building Battoes for transporting the cannon, &c. [23]

February 12 (Wednesday)

VIRGINIA-WILLIAMSBURG

Sir: Governor Sharpe   **(St. Clair)**

As I find that the Company of the Virginia Regiment which I had an order to review at Winchester are now on their march to Wills's Creek; that the service may not Suffer, or any blame laid on me, I beg you may send me a letter to be left at Mr. Gordon at Fredericksburg where I shall be the 19th that I may know if I am to make the same Review at Wills's Creek and if I have any thing to do with the Independent Companies of Carolina and New York and if I am to use what ever of the Maryland detachment will do for our Troops. I am with great respect,

Should I go to Wills's Creek please to let me know if all the Virginia

Troops are to be continued there and the inconvenience of which will certainly occur to you. [24]

February 14 (Friday)
VIRGINIA-WILLIAMSBURG

Sir: Governor of Maryland   (St. Clair)

I did myself the honour of writing a letter to your Excellency of the 1st January in which I beg much of (you) to send me any...or drawings that you may have of Pennsylvania. It has given me a good deal uneasyiness that I have not received your answer which I expected before now in order to have been informed of the situation of your province. I am now alone without any assistance otherwise I should have sent an Engineer to have reconoitered your frontiers, and if I could have been informed from this urgent service I am on here. I should have visited your country myself. I have sent a messenger with this to Philadelphia that your Excellency now is the better informed of our situation and what part expected that you should act for the common good tho 300 troops are daily expected and the service is far advanced, may have no time to leave before they begin their approbation. I have done every thing in my power to facilitate their march from their landing place to the Allegheny Mountains which will be a very great trouble and expense as I make no doubt but that the Troops will unite and then advance togeather to make a stand before we can get on the Ohio which will oblige us to have the assistance of one of the Regiments now raising in the Northern province this stop must pursue the...great deal as they...attack from all quarters. You must be very sensible what a great detail these troops must make by March thro Philadelphia and Frederick in July still crossing the Potomack at the mouth of the Monacasey and joining us at Winchester this would retard our motions. For this Reason I must protest your Excellency in the most earnest manner to open a communication by cutting and repairing the Road toward the head of the Yougheagany or any other way that is nearer to the French Forts by the Map I have of your province there appears to me to be a road from Philadelphia which crosses the Susquehanna a little below the junction of the River Juniata and that there are two paths from your place leading to the blacklog which is a great distance from Youghangany called the Turkey Foot where...the roads not so wanted for this purpose I may mention to...our Excellency that no General will advance with an army

49

without having a communication open to the province in his rear both for the security of his retreat and to facilitate the transport of provisions the supplying of which we must greatly depend on your province. I have sent a commissary to Pensylvania to contract for 100 wagon loads of flour to be delivered at Conogogee by the 20th of March and if wanted are to be taken into the service to carry up our stores I beg of you to give what assistance you can to Mr. Walker who is charged with that commission your Excellency may expect to have the French or other Indians with some Indians making an appearance on your frontiers. You may make what use of these movements you please to your assembly, if you may take my word for it; what if such movements are made, they have no other view in it but to dispatch us in our...and endeavour to...the inhabitants a sure sign that they are in a panic on the contrary if they lie quiet in their new fort they apprehend no danger and me to be dreaded. I hope your people will not look on the road to Ohio as an inlet to our enemies, but lay aside all anamosity and all for the good of the country. Should any small rivers be crossed when the road be a making, I must recommend to have floats made for the crossing of waggon, and that the roads made wide at least 30 feet and carry on along the ridges of the land...to avoid the chance of the runs of water. I have been a good deal employed about this kind of work since I arrived but it is now almost finished.

I am with the greatest Respect, [25]

February 15 (Saturday)
VIRGINIA-HAMPTON
Sir: Colonel Napier   (St. Clair)

After writing you a letter of four or five sheets of paper I thought I should have done at least until another opportunity should offer. In my last letter to you I acquainted you that the troop at Wills Creek were apprehensive of attack from the French, on this remain all the Virginia troops, who are at Winchester have marched thither I suppose to show them...this step has been taken without any orders from Governour Dinwiddie or Sharpe. I am concerned for it as there is no possibility of their staying there for their numbers must consume the provisions and what...that it will give a pleasure to the French to see us weak enough to swallow...is as easy for the fort to contain 10,000 men as the number that is there at present I have sent our expenses to Governour Sharpe to acquaint him with this march as it was agreed that I should put the new levies in some form of order and...him to know if I am to go to Wills Creek the 18th and that I shall wait his answer from Fredericksburg.

I am in the service to both the Governour who were togeather when they received the news of this French intention to attack them, to go and take command at the fort but they did not think that it not necessary, had I gone. I find the need of calling for more troops would have sent two...away of those that were there exclusive of the new levies. Should I go to the fort and by the movements of the french find it necessary to stay I shall make the best disposition I can to save us from...

Let me have your opinion about the New York independent company enlisting a man for a term of years, had they ever any toleration for it?

The Virginia Troops are at a great loss for officers which makes me recommend to be sent out to us Sir James Gabrel on the half in the dutch service he is a good officer as I am told, and I know him to be a brisk young man, he was on the Expedition to Surinam, if he is (in) London you may see him and I dare say you will find him adequate for the character I require of him if he is not in London, Col. York who knows him may soon sent him over from the Hague.

Mr. Pitcher is here who I dare say has made no favorable report of the New York Companies in New York.

If fusees be not sent out for the Sergent and Officers, I beg you may consider if they will not be of more use than the espontoons and Halberds in this woody country.

I have sent you inclosed the Map mentioned in my last and in my former letter is a proposal for getting some Croats to settle on the Ohio. [26]

February 17 (Monday)

VIRGINIA-ALEXANDRIA   **(Carlyle)**
Sir: John St. Clair

Since you left this I have taken every method I could think of to purchase the Hay and Corn fodder you desired, but have not been able to buy above ten thousand weight. I have not yet had any reply from Mr. Diggs of his search in Maryland, I am doubtful he will be able to purchase as much, the people that make quantites not knowing of a certain market have given the most and best of their horses and cattle,

I have purchased and stored about twelve hundred bushels of oats and have agreed for a thousand bushels more, I have secured any quantity of Indian corn, and have...made me of a quantity of hay and corn that will be delivered if wanted at a place on the road to Winchester near halfway, and have mentioned to Col. Sharpe and he seems to think it very proper as by that means the waggons need take the provisions from here as they will be in need of a supply at the middle state.

I have had workmen at work upon the kitchen and the owner of this house is getting up his Ball Room that on the arrival of the Force may depend on every instance in our power. Any commands you have please to lay upon me may depend on my ultimate endeavour to excute and I am your most obedient serv.　　　　　John Carlyle 　[27]

While not a member of the expedition Major John Carlyle was a member of the commissary corps supplying the army. He lived (rented?) in Carlyle House in Alexandria that stands to this day.

Sir: John St. Clair　　　　　　　　　　　　　　**(Dinwiddie)**
I give you the trouble of some letters which I beg you to deliver as directed. When you come to Shanondoe Ferry, order your guide to conduct you to Lord Fairfax who I doubt not will be glad to see you.

I appoint Major Dick Walker commissary of stores and provisions. They have my orders to build boats over the rivers between Winchester & Wills's Creek which I hope over...these are in good fowarding. Col James Innes has the command at Wills's and the direction in building a fort, magazines and barrack, he is a very worthy man. You may freely confide in him for account of what has been done and assistance for what you may think proper to do. I shall be glad if you return by the new road, the north side of Potomack that you may be better judges of the most proper way for carrying up the artillery and other heavy stores.

I wish you health, a pleasent journey, and a happy return. I remain in great truth you most oblig and hum. serv. Robert Dinwiddie [28]

February 18 (Tuesday)
MARYLAND-ANNAPOLIS　　　　　　　　　**(Pennsylvania Gazette)**
Extracts of a letter from a gentleman at Wills Creek, to his Friend here, dated January 27, 1755.

"Yesterday arrived here Sir John St. Clair Bar(onet), Colonel and Quartermaster-General, in all his Majesty's Troops intended for the Service, and forts-off to Morrow morning with Governor Sharpe. Your worthy Governor has been here about a week, on this his second visit to camp within two months, and we be sorry, very sorry, if he should not cross the Allegheny Mountains with us, in a situation agreeable to himself, and equal to his great merit-Three deserters came here yesterday, in 13 days from Fort Du Quesne; their information not publick; one of them told me that 15 savages who were here some time ago, arrived 8 or 9 days, at Fort Du Quesne before they deserted, and all acknowledged the good usage at Wills Creek. Two of our Indians were lately sent with a letter from one of the Prisoners at Winchester, when they returned we may have some news, we daily expect to hear of the arrival of General Braddock, with his troops. His Majesty's Three Independent Companies here, have build a Fort with several large store houses etc. and barracks for all the men, by way of a fortified camp, flanking and flanked by the fort with Ten four pounders, besides swivels; all this since the 12th of September last, with out assistance (either from Virginia or Maryland) of workmen of any kind, and were a long while with out a sufficient Number of good Tools, beginning only with one spade, and two or three axes.

A very good company from Maryland came here about two months ago, but none of them appeared'd yet. We are assured, that at Chester-Town (in Kent County), several men inlisted immediately on the arrival of the Officer into that Town, before the Drum was beat, and that the Officer, wanting but thirty men, got his compliment; and marched with them within a very little while; such is the commendable spirit of the Place they are gone for Wills Creek, and some young Maryland gentlemen (true patriots) are gone from thence as volunteers: The mother of one of them, at parting, took leave of him with saying 'My dear son, I shall with much greater pleasure hear of your death than your cowardice, or ill conduct'.

His excellency-our Governor, and Sir John St. Clair, are returned from Wills Creek and gone to Williamsburg and we hear the two came down Potomack 200 miles in a canoe.

Monday Evening left James Pilcher, Esq. commissary in the forces expected in, came to town, from the northway, and is now gone to Virginia expecting to be met there. [29]

February 20 (Thursday)
VIRGINIA-HAMPTON   (Orme)

The General arrived at Hampton in Virginia, the 20th of February, 1755, and set out immediately for Williamsburg, where Commodore Kepple agreed to meet him, to settle the properest place for the disembarkment of the Troops. Orders were left on board the Centurion to be delivered to each Transport as she arrived, directing the commanding officer to send the sick on shore to the hospitals provided for them by S[r] John S[t] Clair; and orders were given to Mr. Hunter, the Agent at Hampton, to supply the sick and well with fresh provisions at the fullest allowance. [30]

Hampton Roads then as now is one of the largest and most protected anchorages on the Atlantic Coast being very near the mouth of the Chesapeake Bay. The English North American fleets of 1755 contained thirteen transports, two men-of-war and three ordnance ships for a total of 18 vessels.

February 21 (Friday)
VIRGINIA-NORTHERN NECK-FAIRFAX
To Lord Fairfax: (St. Clair)

I did myself the honour of writing to your Lord when I was at Wills's Creek concerning the Roads for the intended Expedition which I am very sorry to hear are not in the forwardness I had reason to expect. I therefore write this to your Lord to know if I am to expect any assistance from this country of which your Lord is proprietor, if not I must attend myself with a large detachment of what troops we have and cutt the proper Road which I am ordered to do by his Majesty, and as I have no proper convenience for want of roads for the subsistence of those men which will be employed for the safety of the country. I have reason to expect that the country will furnish them with provisons.

My reporting, My Lord, at home that the Roads are not finish'd by any frivolus disputes that may happen at your Courts of the Different Countys can be no excuse to me doing my duty. I should with Regret be oblig'd to Report to my Royal Master that it wou'd be much easier to Carry on War from an Enemy's Country than to protect his just Rights to one of his most Loyal provinces in America.

I shall be at Winchester in order to give directions about the Roads at Wednesday the 21st when I shall be glad of receiving your answer that I my take the proper steps for securing our communication which if not done must retard all our operations. I have the honour of being with the greatest regard. [31]

VIRGINIA-FREDERICKSBURG
Sir: Colonel Innes   (St. Clair)
I have received orders to review all the troops at Wills's Creek and Winchester, I have sent Adj. Frazee to both the places in order to prepare things for that service.

I have also enclosed your letter for the command of Officers of the Corps that I am to view that I my not be obliged to stay longer than...with you as I shall see you so soon and have a great deal to say to you I shall add nothing new tha n to assure you that I am always with truth. [32]

VIRGINIA-FREDERICKSBURG
Sir: Commissary Officer at Winchester and Wills's Creek   (St. Clair)
Having received orders to review the troops at Winchester, Wills's Creek, and the Virginia and Maryland detachments I herewith transmit to you a copy of the returns that I beg you will have ruled and filled up for me.

I shall be at your quarters as soon as I can to settle some things of the service that will take me a couple of days in this place.

I have directed Adj. Tranier to proceed to Wills's Creek to prepare the same returns for me. Three duplicates of each will be wanted.

To the Commisary officer at Winchester and Wills's Creek of the Virginia Troops.

To the Independent companies of New York South Carolina and the...detachment. [33]

February 22 (Saturday)
VIRGINIA-FREDERICKSBURG
February 22nd 1755
To: General Braddock   (St. Clair)
I received your Excellencys letter of the 17th instant and was just going to Wills's Creek to execute your commands when I received the enclosed which obliges me to return to Williamsburg. I have taken upon me to move the troops from here to Port Royal in order to make

room here for the British troops I have the honour of being with the greatest respect.

As the Maryland forces will be wanted to complete the English Regiments, I have sent an order to Mr. Pitcher at Wills's Creek that the detachment of Maryland forces now at that place may forthwith march to Frederick to join the rest they will be then at home to be incorporated with the British Regs. [34]

Sir: Gov. Sharp and Maj. Carlyle **(St. Clair)**

As Gen. Braddock with the British forces is arrived, you are hereby ordered to get togeather all the troops provisions you probably can and compleat every thing in earliest manner for their completion as soon as may be. If any carpenter shall be wanting I have directed Captain Mercer to give you what number may be necessary.

Mr. Pitchon the Commissary of muster is going to Wills's Creek and will go from thence to Alexandria you are ordered to provide quarters for himself, servant and two horses. [35]

February 25 (Tuesday) (Pennsylvania, Maryland, Virginia Gazette)
PENNSYLVANIA-PHILADELPHIA

Extract of a letter from an Officer at Will's Creek to his Friend here, dated February 10, 1755.

"Since my last the two Indians, which were sent to Fort Du Quesne with a letter from one of the French Prisoners in Virginia, arrived in this Camp who inform us, that the French Indians, which were some Time since with us, and who pretended in our Council to be Friends with the English, were at the French Fort, and delivered to the Commandant the Speech we made to them, and the Presents they received from us. The Messengers further say, that the French would not admit them into their Council with the French Indians: And that the French Officer told them, he intended, in a very few Days, to march a large Body of French and Indians, and drive us out of our present situation for that we had no Business to build Forts at Wills's Creek. We have put ourselves in a Posture of Defense to receive them, and make no doubt, if they do come that they will meet with a warmer reception than they will imagine. We have cleared all the Land within Cannon Shot of us, both this side of the River, and likewise the other side, beyond the New Store, which is on a higher Ground than our Fort stands upon; but is under the Command of our Guns, about 320 yards distant from the Fort. We expect the first Division of the Virginia Forces to join us this evening when we intend a strong Guard to be mounted at the New Store. [36]

*The multiple source credit used for the first time here (**Pennsylvania, Maryland, Virginia Gazette**) reflects the fact that there is essentially the same material recorded in the sources for the item listed. In the interest of economy only one is included in BRADDOCK ROAD CHRONICLES 1755.*

February 26 (Wednesday)
VIRGINIA-WILLIAMSBURG   **(Braddock)**

His Excellency General Braddock orders that the commanding Officer of each ship upon their arrival in Hampton Road shall immediately send a Return inclosed to Mr. Hunter at Hampton, specifying the number of their sick, the time of their illness, and the nature of them. And that every commanding Officer shall with the utmost dispatch apply to Mr. Hunter for Boats to carry the sick on shore which shall be executed with all imaginable care and expedition, and that a Subaltern Officer of each ship shall see their men safely conveyed to the place appointed at Hampton for their Reception, which Mr. Hunter will shew them; and that the Surgeons or mates of the two regiments and Train shall attend the sick of their own corps. Every commanding Officer is to take particular care that as soon as their sick are sent a Shore all the Hatchways be uncovered, scuttles opened and the Platform thoroughly washed and cleaned, no Officer or soldier, except the sick, to lie on shore upon any acct. The Hospital to continue on board till the General's further Orders. To the companies of Rangers and carpenters:

His Excellency General Braddock orders the commandg officer of each company or Troop to send a weekly Return to the head Quarter's agreeable to the Form annexed; and duplicates of the Returns are to be Remitted weekly to His Excellency, Governor Dinwiddie. The Return for Genl Braddock to be directed to me at the head Quarters. [37]

By His Excellency Edward Braddock   **(Braddock)**

Whereas, an act of Parliament was passed in England, the last Session, to subject all Troops raised in the Colonies to the Regulations and Orders of the article of War, I therefore think it expedient and Order that upon forming the four companies of Rangers, the company of carpenters and Troops of light Horse and whatever Troops are or shall be raised for the service of the present Expedition. That the articles of War be publickly read to the Officers and men, and that every man severaly shall take the Oath of Allegiance and supremacy; and in consequence of these article they are to obey from time to time any orders they shall receive from me or any of their superior Officers. E. Braddock. By His Excel'ys Com'd Feb'y. 26th, 1755 Wil'm Shirley, Secrety. [38]

VIRGINIA-WILLIAMSBURG
February 26th 1755
Sir: John St. Clair   (Braddock)

As the good of his Majestys Service requires that a review should be made of the three independent companies now at Wills's Creek, as well as the forces newly raised in the province of Virginia and Maryland and as the circumstances of affairs puts it out of my power to make that whole review myself.

I therefore order you to make the review of such troops as you shall find at Winchester, Wills Creek, Frederick or else where, and to make a report to me of the state you find them in you are likewise required and directed to order all such men of the independent companies from Carolina and New York of the Virginia and Maryland forces, as you shall find unfit for his Majestys Service giving the reasons why they are so to be forthwith discharged whether formed in to companies detachment or units.

You are likewise to mark down such men as you shall think proper for completing the two British Regiments giving aspects that they maybe in...for them on their finding, and to order them with proper officers forthwith to retain 10...Alexandria and Frederickburg, and to remain there till further orders. All blacks and mulattoes except the young and strong to be discharged the others to be sent to the commissaries with their discharges inclosed. Mr. Dicks or Mr. Walker least they should not chose to employ them, and you are hereby ordered to give such direction with regard to the quartering the Virginia troops as shall be found most convenient for the service, should you think Winchester or Wills's Creek inconvenient. [39]

VIRGINIA-WILLIAMSBURG   (Braddock)
Sir: John St. Clair, Quarter Master General

On the forming the Virginia levies into companies for which you have my order, you are hereby directed and required to administer as commissary to the officers and men of these companies the oath of Allegience for so doing this shall be your sufficient warrant and authority. [40]

VIRGINIA-WILLIAMSBURG
February 26th 1755 **(Braddock)**

Whereas an Act of Parliment was passed in England the last session subjecting all troops raised in the colonies to the regulations and orders of the Articles of War therefore I think it expedient and hereby order that upon forming the four companies of Rangers, company of carpenters, and the troops of light horse, and whatsoever troops are or shall be raised for the service of the present expedition that, the Articles of War be publically read to the officers and men, and that every man severally shall take the oath of Allegience and Supremacy and on consequence of these Article they are to obey from time to time any orders they receive from me or any of their superior Officers. [41]

Nichols writes: "The name Ranger is misleading, for no troops so designated were backwoodsmen or riflemen. Virginia, Maryland, and North Carolina Rangers were largely drawn from tidewater settlements, and they were dubbed Rangers because General Braddock hoped to employ them to cover the Main Body of the Army, and shelter it from all Manner of Surprise. No greater error can be made than to classify these troops with Rogers' Rangers or Morgan's Riflemen of later fame who were especially trained and equipped for Bush fighting and la petite guerre."

February 27 (Thursday)
VIRGINIA-WILLIAMSBURG
Sir: John St. Clair **(Braddock)**

These are to order and direct you when you make the Review of the troops in Virginia and Maryland to make such discharging of the forces as shall appear to you to be most convenient for this Majestys Service at this time by moving the troops from one place to another as well the independent companies of New York and South Carolina as the Virginia and Maryland forces for so doing this shall be your sufficient warrant and authority. [42]

February 28 (Friday)

By His Excellency Edward Braddock, Esq., Gen'l Commander in Chief of His Maj'ty Forces in North America, Quarters of Sir Peter Halkets Regim't:

Orderd, That it proceed to Alexandria in the Transports; five companies to remain in the Town w'th the company of artillery and stores of all kinds.

One company at Dumfries, two days march from Alexandria, thirty miles to Halt the first night after they cross the Ferry of Occoquan; One company at Bladensburg, one days march, they cross the Potomack at Alexandria; One company at upper Marlborough two days march first night at Bladensburg; Two companys at Frederick; These three last cantonments in Maryland; Upon application to Major Carlyl magistrate of Alexandria, the whole will be furnished with Guides Quarters of one Regiment. The Transports which have them on board to stop in the River Potomack as near Fredericksburg as they can; These and an halt company at Winchester, six days march from Fredericksburg, halt a company at Conogogee eight days from Winchester; six companys at Fredericksburg and Falmough on the other side the River Rappahannock.

The five companies of the Regiment that disembark at Alexandria which are to be canton'd to be landed first and to begin their march before the other five debark.

The Engineers and other Officers, not immediatley wanted to be at hand, may be conveniently lodged on the Maryland side of the Potomack leaving a direction where they lodge.

Application is to be made to the several magistrates for carriages to convey the stores. Baggage and Tents of the cantoned companys to be given by the commanding Officers for the numbers employ'd.

The Regiment whose head Quarters are at Fredericksburg, will halt ab't 15 miles from place of disembarking. Waggons will be ordered to attend them. Three companys which are to march to Winchester and Conogogee are to march first to Fredericksburg. The compa Quarterd at Falmouth need not cross the Rappa. Waggon's to each compa to be as asertained, a field Officer to go with each of the five compas and every Officer to go with his compas.

Given under my hand at Williamsburg, this 28th Febry, 1755.

E. BRADDOCK. [43]

VIRGINIA-WILLIAMSBURG
Sir: John St. Clair   **(Braddock)**

I have laid before Governour Dinwiddie a scheme to form a company of carpenters four or more companies of Rangers if men can be found and also one troop of light horse and I have received his honors answer desiring I will establish them as I think most conducive to his Majestys Service.

Therefore order you in the review you are now making to form the companies of above men to be conformable to the establishment you will receive with this and for doing this shall be your authority. [44]

VIRGINIA-WILLIAMSBURG   **(Braddock)**
ESTABLISHMENT OF TWO COMPANIES OF CARPENTERS
First Company
Captain George Mercer
1st Lieutenant William Bromaugh
2nd Lieutenant Thomas Buleek
Sargent 3
Corporals 3
Drum 1
Private man 50
Bat men 3
Second Company
Captain William Colson
1st Lieutenant John Hamilton
2nd Lieutenant Joshua Lucie
Sergents 3
Corporals 3
Drum 1
Private men 50
Bat men 3
Clothing expected daily and will be sent to them as soon as it arrives.
Tools and aprons will be provided by the Quarter Master General.
Every officer will receive a soldiers tent, and a tent will be delivered to every eight men.
No sergeant will be allow'd from the company, each captain will be allowed £20 to purchase two horses for his own and companies tents.

The two subalterns of each company will be allowed twelve pounds between them for the purchase of one horse for their own tents and baggage.

The bat men to have arms to be provided with troops.

ESTABLISHMENT OF FOUR COMPANIES OF RANGERS

First Company

Captain Adam Steven

1st Lieutenant John Savage

2nd Lieutenant Edmond Waggoner

Serjeants 3

Corporals 3

Drum 1

Private 50 Bat men 3

Second Company

Captian Andrew Lewis

1st Lieutenant James McNeal

2nd Lieutenant William Wright

Third Company

Captain Thomas Waggoner

1st Lieutenant Henry Woodward

2nd Lieutenant Walter Stewart

Fourth Company

Captain William Peyronie

1st Lieutenant John Wright

2nd Lieutenant Edward Waggoner

Whatever further companies of Rangers are raised are to be upon the same Establishments.

The staff officer for the two companies of Carptenters and companys of Rangers

Adjutant

Quartermaster

Surgeon

Clothing for the Rangers will be sent as soon as it arrives. Arms and accoutrements are already at Alexandria and Fredericksburg. Every officer, sergeant, corporal and private man to be provided with a Firelock with sling and Bayonet & cartridge box. Every captain to receive £2 and the two subalterns of each company 12£ to supply them with Bat horses. No officer is take more horses than the number above mentioned. Every officer to be furnished with a private mans

Tent and a tent to be delivered to every 8 men. The Bat men company allowed in above compliment to carry no arms.

ESTABLISHMENT FOR THE TROOP OF HORSE RANGERS
Captain Robert Stewart
1st Lieutenant John Mercer
2nd Lieutenant Ca. Gustavies Splitdolph
Serjeants 2
Corporals 2
Privates 30
Bat men 8
The Captain to be allowed £48 for the purchase of Four horses he is to carry all the tents.
The two lieutenants to be allowed £2 each for the purchase of two horses each. The Serjeants Corporals and private men to be allowed one horse each. Four Bat men to be allowed to the companies above the compliment to the Captain and one each of the Subaltern officers. Every officer Sergeant, corporal and private to be armed with a short carbine, case of pistols and a cuttng Sword. The captain to look out for horses and to take care his men are all well mounted, he will receive money for the purchase of them from Governour Dinwiddie.

E. BRADDOCK [45]

(Orme)

The General acquainted Governor Dinwiddie with his Majesty's pleasure, that the several assemblies should raise a sum of money to be employed towards defraying the expenses of the Expedition, And desired he would propose it to his Assembly; And that his Majesty also expected the Provinces to furnish the Troops with provisions and Carraiges. The General desired the Governor would use all imaginable dispatch in raising and convening the Levies to augment the two Battalions to 700 each. He also proposed to the Governor to make an establishment for some provincials, amongst which he recommended a Troop of light horse.

The Governor told the General his Assembly had voted twenty thousand pounds, which sum was to be employed in the purchasing provisions, and the payment of their own troops. That many men were already raised, and that Sr John St Clair had promised him to select the best for the two Regiments, and that the others should be formed into Companies; accordingly two of Hatchet men or carpenters, six of

Rangers, and one troop of light Horse were raised, and their pay fixed at the same, in the currency of that Country, as our Officers of the same rank in sterling. Alexandria was named as the head Quarters, as the most convenient place for forming and cloathing them.

Sr John St Clair came to Williamsburgh and informed the General of his having draughted the best men of the Virginia Levies for the two Battalions; and that about three hundred which were not of proper size remained for the provincial Companies. Sr John St Clair laid before the General a Roll of the Independent Companies, upon which were several men from sixty to seventy years of age, lame and every way disabled; may were inlisted, only for a term of one, two or three years; some were without discipline and very ill-appointed; in short, they were Invalids with the ignorance of militia. were all to be recruited with men who would otherwise have served in the Regiments of Virginia Companies.

Sr John St Clair gave General Braddock a plan for cantoning the two Regiments; one, with part of the Artillery, was to disembark at Alexandria, where five Companies were to remain; two and a half were to canton at Frederick in Maryland, half a one at Conegogee, one at Marlborough and one at Bladensburg. The other Regiment and the rest of the Artillery were to disembark about twenty miles from Fredericksburg upon the Potomack, at which place and Falmouth five Companies were to be cantoned, and the other five at Winchester. As these Cantonments, of only a thousand men, took in a circuit of more than three hundred miles, the General thought it advisable to encamp them; on their arrival; especially as the severity of the weather was then over. He knew that much confusion must arise in disembarking at different places; That it would be impossible to cloath, arm and discipline the Levies when so much dispersed, and that soldiers are sooner and better formed in Camps than in Quarters. He therefore, in conjunction with Mr. Keppel, fixed upon Alexandria to disembark and encamp at; and the Levies for the two regiments were orderd to that place.

The General desired Governor Dinwiddie would inform him of the present disposition of the Indians towards the English; what Nations and number he might expect, and what steps were already taken to obtain them.

The Governor said he had sent a proper person to bring with them the Cherokees and Catawber nations, the latter being about one hundred and twenty fighting-men, and much the bravest of all the Indians; He added a peace was to be concluded at Winchester in April, between the Catawbers and the Six Nations through the mediation of his Government: That he had intended to be present at the Congress; but that he should be prevented by the meeting of his Assembly. However, he would take care, at the Ratification of the Peace, that they should take up the hatchet, and act under the General.

Mr Dinwiddie laid before the General contracts made for eleven hundred head of cattle, eight hundred of which were to be delivered in June and July, and three hundred in August; he said that he had also written to Governor Shirley, for a large quantity of salt fish, that a great deal of flour was already at Fort Cumberland, and that the assembly of Pensylvania had promised to deliver flour, to the amount of five thousand pounds of their currency, at the mouth of Conegogee, in April, in which was to be carried up the Potomack to Fort Cumberland: He had also ordered a great quantity of bacon to be made at the Fort. There were on board the transports one thousand barrels of beef for which the General applied to Mr Keppel and they were landed at Alexandria. Upon making a calculation on these Estimates, there was found to be six months provisions for four thousand men.

General Braddock apprehended the greatest difficulty in procuring waggons and horses, sufficient to attend him upon his march, as the assembly had not passed an Act for the supplying them, but Sr John St Clair assured the General that inconveniency would be easily removed, for, in going for Fort Cumberland, he had been informed of a great number of Dutch settlers, at the foot of a mountain called the Blue Ridge, who would undertake to carry by the hundred the provisions and stores, and that he believed he could provide otherwise two hundred waggons and fifteen hundred carrying horses to be at Fort Cumberland by the first of May. The General desired him to secure the former of these, upon his return to the Fort. At Williamsburgh the General wrote circular letters to all the Governors upon the Continent, informing them of his Commission, and recommending to them the constituting of a common fund, and desiring him to assist and foward as much as possible the general service, that it might answer the end, for which his Majesty had sent troops to their assistance. And, in the letters of Governors Shirley, Delancey, Morris and Sharpe, he desired the would meet him at Annapolis the beginning of April, that he might confer with them on some matters of the greatest importance to the

Colonies, and settle with them a general plan for the approaching Campaign. [46]

VIRGINIA-WILLIAMSBURG   (Maryland, Virginia Gazette)
February 28.

The three Ships of War, of which we mentioned the Arrival in our latest are the Centurion, Commodore Keppel, the Norwich, the Honorable Captain Barrington and the Syren, Captain Poby in the Norwich came passengers, the Honorable Major General Edward Braddock, Commander of all the Forces in North America, Capt. Orme, Aid de Camp, and Mr. Shirley, Secretary, who came to the City last Sunday, where they wait the Arrival of the Forces, who are every day expected.

N.B. The Transports being met with off the Capes, as mentioned in our last, was premature. [47]

The above news item did not appear in the Maryland Gazette until March 20th.

March 1 (Saturday)

VIRGINIA-FREDERICKSBURG
March 1st 1755
Sir: General Braddock   (St. Clair)

I have the honor of acquainting your Excellency that I arrived at this place this day and have taken such steps as will make the carriage of the four 12 pounders very easy, I have given direction for four waggons and two spare wheels to be made with the axel trees and have prepared wood for the bodies of the train so that when the train arrives it will be neccessary that a detachment of a day of them with an officer be sent to this place to give the directions for constructing whose machines, which may be done in two days after the wheels are finished.

I wish your Excellency sent the guns to this place with the train of small mortars and their shells that maybe hauling them up to Winchester. I have appointed Lieut. Woodward for that service to whom they may be...It will be a difficult matter for the commissary to spare 400 shells for each gun if this is the case your excellency has only to...up one twelve pound shott with a letter from Capt. Orme to Lieut. Woodward and he will get the number required made up in their place. If they may not be very expert in casting ball it may be great to have the pattern shott to be of a little less size than usual in these guns while only serve for opening the breach.

When the troops arrive I beg that the inventory of ordnance stores may be laid before the officers of the train to see if they will be powder sufficient, which I am in doubt about if there is not the commander will be able to spare us some if so what we get from the ships will be better in half barrells then whole new. I spoke to Captain Orme to desire that your Excellency would send up Mr. McAllen the Engineer if he cannot to Capt. Somvoy's he will provide him with horses that will carry him to Fredericksburg. Mr. McKeller is an officer who will see the roads finished, which I will set about on going to Winchester. I herewith transmit a letter I received from Lord Fairfax, it is worthy of his Lord the other directed to Gov. Sharpe I likewise transmit as it properly belongs to your Excellency. I have taken a copy of the weekly return the above letters I received since I began to write this letter by the common post which makes it unnecessary for me to send an express. I beg my compliments to the Governor and his Family. [48]

VIRGINIA-FREDERICKSBURG
March 1st 1755
Sir: Capt. Cocke   (St. Clair)
Herewith enclosed your letter to Lieutenant Hamilton which I desire you will immediately send to him by express as the Service requires his being at Alexandria early on Tuesday morning in order to march on Wednesday with the company he belongs to Winchester.

I was pleased to be with you at Port Royal a fortnight hence I should be glad you would continue at Quarters life I see that you maybe in the way of receiving any occasional orders I may have for you. Eng. Frizier likewise is to stay at Quarters.

You will receive some recruits that I have directed Lieut. Woodward who is to stay here to forward to you these man are to be victualed as you can. I am your most hum. serv.
P.S. if Mr Savage is with you with his recruits, they are to remain there till further orders from General Braddock or from me. [49]

March 2 (Sunday)
VIRGINIA-WILLIAMSBURG
Williamsburg, 2 March, 1755   (Orme)
Sir: George Washington

The General having been informed that you expressed some desire to make the campaign, but that you declined it upon some disagreeableness that you thought might arise from the regulations of command, has ordered me to acquaint you that he will be very glad of your company in his family, which all inconveniences of that kind will be obviated.

I shall think myself very happy to form an acquaintence with a person so universally esteemed, and shall use every opportunity of assuring you how much I am, Sir, you most obedient servant. [50]

March 5 (Wednesday)

VIRGINIA-ALEXANDRIA   (St. Clair)
Orders for the Virginia Troops at Alexandria
March 5, 1755

A list of the companys of artificers and the two detachments commanded by Captain Hogg and Lieut. Savage to be made according to the number forming three copies of each to be made.

A return to begun on the arms and accouterments of each company and details to the swords to be given in to Mr. Carlyle who will sign receipts for them.

The officers commanding the companies of artificers are to provide their men, commissioned officers and private men each with a haversack of osnaberg large enough to carry five days provisions the men are to pay for their neglience by a stoppage of their pay which the officer are directed to make.

Each officer commanding a company or detachment is to keep each man...and they are directed to supply their men with all new supplies without taking any profit from the men.

Each man of the artificers to be provided with the following new supplies as soon as possible viz
3 shirts and stocks 3 pr yarn stockings, 2 pair of shoes, shoe and garter buckles Indian spatterdasher and a pair of brown marching spatterdashers.

If any man sell their arms, accouterments, ammunition or clothing he will be severly punished.

The commanding officers at Quarters is to order an officer to visit the hospital every day and to make a report to him.
Orders for Captain Mercer:

You are hereby ordered to remain at this place with the company of artificers under your command, you are to observe good order and disipline in your quarters. You are to receive provisions for your effective men from Major Carlyle for which you are to give him a weekly reciept for his...Given at Alexandria this 5th day of March 1755. [51]

March 6 (Thursday)
VIRGINIA-HAMPTON
March 6th 1755   (Orme)
Sir: John St. Clair

As the transports are...arrived and as the season must necessarily be broke up before the companies can be settled in their several cantonments many inconvienences seeming also to arise from the operation of the troops, it being impossible to dispose, cloth, arm, and disicipline the service in the short time that will be allowed His Excellency therefore orders me to let you know he thinks a camp site in Alexandria will much answer all the purposes and the General therefore intends to order all the ships to proceed to Alexandria and the whole to disembark there and that their own Quartermasters shall work out an encampment...you can arrive when he desires may be as soon as possible and that all the Virginian and Maryland recruits may be ordered to Alexandria with where provisions...may judge necessary and to obviate any inconvenience from...his Excellency will direct all the soldiers bedding to be landed with them. I am your most obd. serv.   Rob. Orme Aid de Camp   [52]

VIRGINIA-ALEXANDRIA
March 6th 1755
Sir: Gov. Dinwiddie   (St. Clair)

I have included this letter to General Braddock who will deliver it to your Excellency. I am under a necessity of sending it by express that I may review your answer on my return to this place. You may easily believe that I must have met with many things on this review and new modelling of the Virginia Forces which I could not foresee, when I received my orders and instruction at Williamsburg. I shall therefore lay before you in what condition I found those I have reviewed and what I have reason to expect from those at Winchester and Wills's Creek.

Capt. Cocke is at Port Royal with a unit of 60 men which have been reviewed he is now joined by number of the recruits raised by Ensign Smith and Mr. Eualache I sent the former from Fredericksburg to take charge of the men after they are reviewed. I have desired Lieut. Woodward to stay at Fredericksburg to see to any artillery or stores landed and fowarded to Winchester.

I have formed the 2 companies of artificers, the first in a very good size and compleat, the (other) wants 11 men which I shall get some way or other and send them to Winchester where they are to march on Saturday. I have formed a detachment of rangers of 7 men and have given the command of them to Lieut. Savage, until your pleasure is known in what manner they are to be disposed of. I have given Capt. Hogg the care of 21 men that I have draughted for the British Battalion and they march to Fredericksburg on Saturday where he will be joined by the other as soon as I review them. I have destined Alexandria for the Maryland draught, you are greatly obliged to Lieut. Savage for the good recruits he has raised that officer has done his duty and preserved your countenance.

I expect to be able to compleat Capt. Lewis's company including the 18 at Jackson's River with the men he marched to Winchester and with those recruited by the man you paid 10 pistols to and to have a half a dozen of men for the British Regiments.

I find by a letter from Col. Innes that he has discharged some of Capt. Waggoners and some of Capt. Peyronie people, that there remain at the fort of the former 65 men and of the latter 58 ones of which I am in hopes to form the two companys for there two captains.

Capt. Stevens and Capt. Stewarts companys are much more numerous at Winchester, you have certainly reason to expect two companys formed from them which if these officers have not put it in my power they are greatly to blame.

This is the state of your forces at present as near as I can judge and from what I have seen I hope to be able to make out 6 companies of rangers if I am not deceived by building too much on Capt. Stewart who I am afraid has not as yet discharged the number of bad men I saw at Fredericksburg.

Lieut. Savage is here with the rangers of his own raising. These men are desirous to serve with him; I did not care to appoint Capt. Stephens to that Company least the men of his company might be worse especially as I saw a great probability of forming six companies which will employ all your captains. If the scheme of forming the six companies of Rangers meets with approbation, Capt. Hogg may be posted to the company here and Capt. Cocke to the other when formed at Port Royal. This will be attended with some little inconveniency with regard to the posting the subaltern officers. Lieut. Savage will be to Capt. Hoggs company. I should wish'd the subaltern officers had not been named 10 companies on account that few of them understand that point of the service, which is that if they had a commission from his Majesty naming them to the a particular company it is in the power of the commanding officer to change them. In case I do not get above 20 men of Capt. Stewarts recruits fit for service and to give him his commission for the troops of light horse before he has his compliment of men compleated.

I beg your Excellency may explain to me what I have requested, should you complete the rangers to six companies I take on me to beg all the commissions may be of the same date, I shall make in every respect for the good of the service and shall lay before you any abuses that has been committed that they may be remedied for the future. I must repeat it to you that if I find any difficulty in forming the 6th company of Rangers the whole blame will be on Capt. Stewart whose company I saw the first time I was at Fredericksburg.

There is a pay master wanting for the troops, I am not able to lay down an establishment for one which Capt. Orme will put you in away of doing a Lieut. is the proper officer for such an employment, and I may venture to say that Mr. Savage has done a great deal for the service, and is deservng of that office for want of such an officer I declare the thing to be almost next to an impossibility of getting the past amounts settled.

No manner of concern has been taken about the arms, I wish I could fix the neglect on any one person, I should lay hold of him I am afraid I shall be under a necessity of concerning some of your young gentlemen how necessary it is to follow military orders.

Be so good as to desire Capt. Orme to see if there is any stuff to make tents of those that have been made hitherto are of no manner of use in the field, the officers small tents when wet are a load for a waggon being made of sail cloth. They will be of great service for magazine tents if we entrench a camp at Savage River. I expect Governor Sharpe here every moment; and shall let you know by postscript what steps we agree on for the Modelling the Maryland forces. On the whole the men of the Virginia forces are much better than I had reason to expect. I am with the greatest respect. [53]

VIRGINIA-ALEXANDRIA
March 6th 1755
Sir: General Braddock   **(St. Clair)**

I find myself under a necessity of sending an express to your Excellency that I may receive further direction on my return hither for the forming the Virginia Forces, I enclose you a letter for the Governor which ought to have been sent to you at least the substance of it but there is not one in this place who I could employ to write for me.

I did my self the honor of writing to your Excellency from Frederickburg and gave you an account of what I have been doing at that place, I could not possibly get thither till Monday noon and am afraid I shall be detained some days longer on account of the great fall of snow and a drift which has filled up the roads, the magistrates are to go with me that I may give them directions concerning the roads as far as Winchester, for that reason I would be glad to have the snow melt so before I leave this I have this for it that the weather changes in this climate every 24 hours.

Since being at this place, I have formed two companies of Carpenters your excellency will by the return I have sent Capt. Orme see that the first is compleat and that the second wants eleven men which shall get them as soon as I can, these latter are under marching orders and will begin their march in Saturday for Winchester. I have picked out twenty-one good men for the British Battalions they march to Fredericksburg on Saturday under the command of Lieut. Hogg, I have formed a detachment of Rangers under the command of Lieut. Savage, they are near compleat, but I am unwilling to form them till my return and that I receive and answer to the enclosed letter.

Your Excellency will easily imagine what a difficult thing I am now about, I shall think myself lucky if I can have my conduct approved of, I have given the soldiers warning of what will happen to them if they come under the lash of the military law, and I dread I shall be obliged to do what will be disagreeable to some of the officers.

I sent an express to Governor Sharpe to know if his affairs would permit him to come to this place, I shall keep this letter open until the express returns. If he cannot come hither, I shall send him an officer concerning the forming the Maryland forces, after I have draughted them at Frederick at which place I shall receive his answer.

The company of Artificers and 47 Rangers that are here in Quarters are very much at a loss for a Sergeant and when the Maryland Forces arrive there may be more...for me; this is the reason I have hurried away the 2nd Company of Carpenters to Winchester and the draughted to Fredericksburg, it would be of great benefit for the Service if you Excellency would get one of the Surgeons or mates of the man of war sent hithter until the troops land, what makes me the more desirous of having a Surgeon is that a very ugly fever is raging in these parts, which I am afraid some our men have got.

I hope this letter will find you employed with the arrival of the Forces from Ireland, if you have no time to write to me, with regard to any article of my letter to the Governor I beg to have directions to enable me to put in execution what the Governor writes me on account of the Forces of the colony I am with the greatest respect. P.S. Since writing the above Governor Sharpe has adjourned his assembly for a couple of days and is come to this place, I should get 150 of his Maryland Forces for the British Battalions and he proposed to me to raise 2 companies of Rangers on the posting of the Virginia ones on condition that I would pay the 150 men or more after I draughted them for the British Battalions which I think is but reasonable...I have agreed to it, it will be 12 days before I can get to Frederick, the roads are I am afraid impassable on the account of the heavy rain that is now falling.

I beg your Excellency will consider if the frame of the vessels is for lake Erie or lake Ontario if for the latter it ought to be sent to New York.

I beg the express may not be sent back soon as I do not think I can return hither in less than 11 days.

Governor Sharpe has promised to give me all the assistance possible in the recruiting Capt. Rutherford for his. I shall order him on the recruiting service, but I can follow expedient for completing Capt. Clarks, Capt. Dumas of the South Carolina Company with command at the Fort. If I can get a spare man for that company they shall have them if the people will enlist voluntarily. [54]

March 7 (Friday)
VIRGINIA-WILLIAMSBURG   (Virginia Gazette)

The Osgood, (Crookshank) and the Fishburn, (Tipple) two of the Transports from Cork, arrived at Hampton last week; the Troops, etc. on Board were extremely healthy, there being not above two or three sick.

Deserted from Petersburg, the 17th Day of January, William Partin, of Virginia, about five feet Inches high, and is thirty five Years old. Whoever secures the said Deserter, and delivers him to Captain Alexander Finnis, shall have a Pistole Reward.   By: Thomas Cocke

Deserted the following Recruits, from King William County, viza Joseph Copeland, about 20 Years of Age, about five feet six inches high, a Shoemaker by Trade, stoops pretty much in his walk, is very remarkable for wearing a small hat, and is supposed to be gone to Prince Edward County. William Holmes a Mullatoe, about about 45 Years of Age, is about six Feet high, Whoever secures the said Deserters, so that they may be again, shall have a Guinea Reward for Copeland, and a Pistole for Holms.

Deserted from Capt. Thomas Waggoner's Company, the following Recruits, viz. Frederick Bougham, born in Essex, is about five feet 7 inches high, darkish color's hair, is 19 Years of Age, had on a blue Duffl Coat, and an old Hat. Jobe Smith, born in Gloucester, about five Feet eight inches high, and of a fair Complexion. William Gardener born in Caroline, about five Feet ten Inches high, and of a fair complexion.

Whoever apprehends and secures the said Deserters, so that they may be conveyed to their Company at Fredericksburg, shall have Two pistoles Reward for each. [55]

March 10 (Monday)
VIRGINIA-HAMPTON   (Orme)

Two Transports being arrived at Hampton, the General and Commodore went thither immediatley, and orders were given to the Commanding Officers of each ship to sail as soon as they received their fresh provisions, and to disembark their men at Alexandria. The soldiers were to take their beds ashore, and Lieutenant Colonel Burton was ordered to Quarter the troops in the town till the arrival of more ships, in case the weather should prove severe. The General waited here three days, but no more ships arriving, he and the Commodore, returned to Williamsburgh.

The General applied to Mr Keppel for some Blocks, Cordage, and other stores, and also for thirty seamen, who he thought would be very serviceable on the march, if it should be found necessary to pass the rivers in floats or in boats. He also desired a carpenter to direct the construction of them; with which the Commodore complied very readily, constantly expressing ardent desire to foward the success of the expedition, and never, I believe, two men placed at the head of different Commands co-operated with more spirit, integrity and harmony for the publick service.

In about ten days, all the transports being arrived, orders were given for all the ships to proceed immediatley to Alexandria; but so little care had been taken at Corke, in the stowage of the cloathing, Arms and camp nesessaries belonging to the Regiments of Shirley and Pepperell, that some was put on board almost very ship; they were removed into one Vessel, and dispatched immediately (March 10) to New York and Boston, which caused a delay of four or five days.

Every thing seemed to promise so far the greatest success. The Transports were all arrived safe, and the men in health. Provisions, Indians, carriages and horses were already provided; at least were to be esteemed so considering the authorities on which they were promised to the General.. [56]

Pargellis includes the following paragraph in his "Military Affairs in North America" which is from:Instructions From the Lords of the Admiralty to Admiral Keppel dated November 1754 (the year before the Braddock Expedion): "Wheoras we have thought it necessary, that Two Lieutenants of His Majesties Fleet should serve under you, in addition to the proper Number of Lieutenants belonging to each ship, to be employed in attending the Land Forces in their Marches, in order to assist in making Floats for their passing the rivers, Drafts (maps) for the Country through which they pass, and on such other Services as you shall find necessary; And we having appointed Lieutenants William Shackerly and Charles Spendelow; he being furnished with Instruments for taking Observation, and making Drafts; and you are to direct him to be very particular therein, and to transmit the same to Us, from time to time, through your Hands."(Material cited is from MILITARY AFFAIRS IN NORTH AMERICA 1748-1765, by Stanley Pargellis © 1936 by American Historical Association).

March the 10   **(Browne)**
At 4 in the Afternoon made Cape Henry, a fair Windy (day). At 7 cast Anchor in Hampton Road. All in great Spirits. 4 Officers came on

Board. Drank out 15 bottles of Port, all in the Cabbin drunk (but Mr. Cherrington) to be free of Hampton. [57]

While the above is the initial entry of Charlotte Browne in BRADDOCK ROAD CHRONICLES, Madame Browne began her diary before departing England aboard the 195 ton hospital transport Neptune. Nichols calls the hospital transport London. The confusion probably stems from the fact Madame Browne was aboard two vessels, the Neptune to Cork and the London to Virginia.

Nichols provides details of her departure from England and the Atlantic Ocean crossing.

(batman)

We Arriv'd at Hampton in Virginia the 10th of March. The Officers went on Shore to get a fresh Supply of Provisions, the town Being very small that one Could not get a Bed for no money, there Being Several Oblig'd to sit by the fire all Night, the Nights Beeing very Cold at that time. [58]

All the transports arrived at Hampton, Virginia between March 10-15 where, after taking aboard provisions and putting ashore the sick they proceeded to Alexandria.

March 11 (Tuesday)

VIRGINIA-HAMPTON

March the 11   **(Browne)**

The Captain went on board the Commodore, (Norwich) and received his Orders to sail up the River Potomack in 28 Hours. My Brother and self went on shore to Hampton in the Pilots Boat. Gave 7s. 6d. for rowing 2 Miles. Went to the Kings Arms and breakfasted. Walk'd till Dinner. A very agreeable place, and all the Houses extreemly neat. Had for Dinner a Ham & Turkey, a Brest of Veal & Oysters, to drink Madeira Wine, Punch and Cyder. Stay'd till 4 in the Afternoon and then went on Board. [59]

VIRGINIA-WILLIAMSBURG   **(Pennsylvania Gazette)**

By an express just arrived from Hampton we are advised that three Men of War are arriv'd there on board of which is General Braddock and several of his Officers of Distinction. The Lightfoot Lane from Dublin and the Charming Anne Baker from London are arrived in York River. February 28, The three Men of War of which we mentioned the arrival of in our last are the Centurion-Commodore

Kepple, the <u>Norwich</u>-the Hon. Capt B..., and the <u>Syren</u>-Capt. Predy.
Of the <u>Norwich</u> are passengers the Hon. Major General Braddock,
Commander of all the Forces in North America, Capt. Orme, Aid de
Camp and Major Shirley, Secretary who came to this city last Sunday,
where they wait the arrival of the forces who are every day expected.
From Hampton we are advised, that two French Men of War have
lately been seen off our coast and it is said the <u>Garland</u>-Capt. Ar..., and
the <u>Gibraltar</u>-Capt. Spry are ordered out in search of them. [60]

March 12 (Wednesday)

VIRGINIA-WINCHESTER
12th day of March 1755   (St. Clair)
By Sir John St. Clair Bar. Quarter Master General to the British
Forces in America

You are hereby Required and directed to March from Port Royal to
Alexandria with the detachment of Virginia Forces under your
command in order that they may be formed into Companys. You are to
begin your march two days after you receive this order, and you are
not to march thro Maryland.

Mr. Commissary Luke will furnish you with provisions for your
march, which your men are to carry, he will likewise furnish you with
Ossnaburg stuff to make Haversacks for the men who have been
Reviewed which the men are to pay for.

During your stay at Alexandria Mr. Carlyle will furnish you with
provisions for your effective men for which you are to give a reciept.

You are to observe on your march and in Quarters good order and
dicipline, and conform yourself in every respect to the Rules and
Articles of War; the officers not to quit their men on their march.

Given under my hand at Winchester this 12th day of March 1755
The recruits which are not received are included in this order.
To Capt. Cocke commanding a Detachment of Virginia Forces at Port
Royal. [61]

VIRGINIA-GREAT CAPACAPON
March 12th 1755
To: General Braddock   (St. Clair)

On my being at Winchester I received a letter from Capt. Orme
acquainting me that your Excellency had come to a resolution that the
troops should proceed to Alexandria and encamp at that place as the

season is so far advanced was to have certainly gained time by keeping our people togeather.

The people of Fairfax County have promised to me that the road passing from Alexandria to the top of the Blue Ridge shall be cut. I carried the overseers with me and pointed out to them that I would have done on my arrival at Winchester I sent expresses for the Overseers of the roads between the Blue Ridge and Winchester from Alexandria and Fredericksburg, they all say they will compleat them immediately, as I am going up I shall take the same steps.

I found the Virginia Troops at Winchester in much the same condition as I suspected, and have discharged 12 of them. I have got 21 men for the British Battalions which was more I had reason to expect, by Capt. Lewis's not coming to Winchester with his company. I shall be obliged to return that way to form his company and give him orders for Augusta County, I may say no officer ever had such a review as their have been what with...I had my hands full but we have got rid of both the one and the other.

I should have wrote this letter from Winchester but I was willing to see Mr. Commissary Duke, who I met at this house, I herewith transmit to your Excellency what he tells me of Mr. Commissary Walker's services at Pensylvania.

I am now making a disposition for my seeing Youghiogany River before I return to Alexandria. This may take me up three days, but it will...doubts with regard to our passing the Potomack.

I shall return to Alexandria as soon as I possibly can, the preparations that I am making are absolutely necessary for our Expedition. I hope to kiss your hand by the 28th of the month and sooner if possible I have got some setts of wheels in this country for our heavy guns, they shall be sent to Fredericksburg.

On the reciept of Capt. Orme's letter, I have ordered Capt. Cocke to march from Port Royal to Alexandria, that the company of Rangers may be formed at that place, and his man draughed and we may have them at Alexandria in three or four days after the troops arrive. I shall take care to have the latter with you, as soon as the Maryland forces.

I am with the greatest respect. [62]

March 13 (Thursday)
VIRGINIA-CHESAPEAKE BAY
March ye 13

We left Hampton and Sailed up the Portwomack (Potomac) River to Alexandria, it Being a pleasent River, having Virginia on the left hand in Sailing up it and Maryland on the Right, it being most of the way up it a Bout two miles Broad and having many gentlemen('s) Houses on Boath Sides which we salluted with our Great Guns and answered again from he Gentlemen Houses with their great Guns and Colours flying. [63]

MARYLAND-ANNAPOLIS   (Maryland Gazette)

Saturday Morning last His Excellency our Governor returned home from Alexandria.

We have now a certain Account of the Arrival in Virginia, of some of the Forces from Ireland. The Ship Fishburn, Capt William Tipple, and the Osgood, Capt. Crookshanks, with 100 Men each beside Officers, arrived at Hampton on the 2d Instant, and last Monday went into Potowmack, to land them at Alexandria. The Men are all well and hearty, and met with no Accident on the Voyage, except the loss of one Man, which fell thro' between the Cross Tree and Gunwale of Capt. Tipple's ship and was drowned.

These two ship left Cork after the middle of January, with the rest of the Fleet, under Convoy of two Men of War but parted from them on the Passage: The whole Fleet consisted of thirteen Transports, and three Ordnance Store Ships viz,

Severn	Capt	Rawlings
Molly		Curling
Anon (?)		Nevin
Halifax		Terry
Terrible		Wright
Prince Frederick		Burton
Fish (?)		Judd
London		-------
Concord		Boynton
Isabel and Mary		Hall
Industry		Miller

And the two which are arrived.

Ordinance Store Ships, the Newall, Capt Montgomorie; the Whiting, Capt Johnson; and the Nelly, Capt.--------.

We every hour expect to hear of the arrival of the other ships. [64]

79

Nichols writes: "The voyage (Hampton to Alexandria) was difficult due to shifting winds and numerous shoals. Weather was biting cold and snow fell as late as March 18th; the London ran aground two days later off Alexandria but her crew broke out her long-boat and yawl and rowed her off the sand bar after an hours heart breaking labor".

March 14 (Friday)   (Virginia Gazette)
VIRGINIA-WILLIAMSBURG

Since our last arrived at Hampton, the Seahorse, and Nightingale, Men of War, the Newall, Montgomery, the Nelly, Ross, the Industry, Miller, the Whiting, Johnson, the _____, Curling, and three or four more of the Transports from Cork, with Troops and stores for the Protection of this Colony. The Troops are all exceeding healthy, and are ordered round to Alexandria immediately, for which Place his Honor the Governor and his Excellency General Braddock propose to set off next Monday. [65]

March 15 (Saturday)
VIRGINIA-WILLIAMSBURG

March 15th 1755   (Braddock)

Sir: John St. Clair

Upon Lieut. Col. Burton's coming to Virginia he having but two companys with him at his request and that of the officer with him I consented that he should go no further than Alexandria and encamp there upon a supposition as every body here agreed that the hard weather was broke up but as I find it is as cold as ever it was and may probably continue, I would desire you to canton them according to the plan we agreed upon but if possible not so far distant, and not less than a company in a place, and that the draughts be sent to there immediately, that they may have time to drill them; the transports all arrived but two and are dispatched away to Alexandria, as Col. Dunbars Regiment is all arrived, you may if you think it necessary send some body to stop them at the landing place on this side and from thence make them marched to their quarters, they tell me the well water at Alexandria is apt to give the flux, if so, the men be cautioned not to drink it as the river is at home; there are not in the whole number of men already come over two sick. I propose to be at Alexandria the twenty second or twenty third instant.

I am with great regard your hum. and Obed serv. [66]

VIRGINIA-CHESAPEAKE BAY
March ye 15   (batman)

We had a vialent (violent) Tack Norwester which Obliged us to lay two all that day. [67]

VIRGINIA-MOUNT VERNON
March 15th   (Washington)
To: Robert Orme

I was not favoured with you polite letter of the 2d inst., until yesterday; acquainting me with the notice his Excellency General Braddock is pleased to honor me with, by kindly inviting (desiring my Company in his family) me to become one of his family in the ensuing Campaign. Its true, Sir, I have ever since I declined a command in this Service express's and Inclination to serve the Ensuing Campaigne as a Volunteer; and this believe me Sir, is not a little encreased, since its likely to be conducted by a Gentleman of the General's great good Character;

But besides this, and the laudable desire I may have to serve, (with my poor abilitys) my King and Country, I must be ingenuous enough to confess, I am not a little bias'd by selfish and private views. To be plain Sir, I wish for nothing more earnestly that to attain a small degree of knowledge in the Military Art...I shall do myself the pleasure of waiting upon his Excellency as soon as I hear of his arrival at Alexandria, (and would sooner, was I certain where) till which I shall decline saying further on this head; begging you'll be kind enough to assure him that I shall always retain a grateful sense of the favor he was kindly pleased to offer me...[68]

MARYLAND-ANNAPOLIS
March 15th 1755   (Sharpe)
Sir: John St. Clair

I had writ to Captain Dagworthy directing in case you chose to draught his company into the British Regiments to preserve and take care of the mens arms, blankets,...canteens apprehending they will be supplied with those articles as soon as they join the Regiments if you approve not of his following those orders. You will be pleased to direct otherwise and you will find Capt. Dagworthy ready to obey you, I have just received a letter from Mr. Carlyle at Alexandria, advising me that three Transports with Col. Burton and some other officer and part of Dunbar's Regiment were just come up to that place where they propose to disembark as yesterday. He also tells me that the General had ordered all the troops to land there and as the season is already far advancing to encamp then appraise in what we pray must be done with the Beeves and flour that have been purchased and ordered to Bladensburg, Rock Creek, Conogogee, Frederick Town and Marlboro. Governor Dinwiddie intimated to me that I might expect the pleasure of seeing the General here soon as he proposes to do me the honour of having an Interview with Gov. Shirley at my house, as soon as I hear of the General's arrival at Alexandria, I shall wait on him. Our assembly is yet sitting but I dispair of persuading them to grant any supplies. The gentleman who present you this is one of the three I mentioned to you were desirous of going volunteer. I have desired that to return again hither before they wait on Col. Halket. If you approve thereof be pleased to order Capt. Dagworthy hither to go recruiting.

I am with the greatest esteem.

P.S. The gun carriage did not answer our expectations but I have sent it to Alexandria. [69]

March 16 (Sunday)

VIRGINIA-CHESAPEAKE BAY   (batman)

The 16 the Storm abated and we sailed again and ariv'd at Alexandria.[70.]

March 17 (Monday)

VIRGINIA-WILLIAMSBURG

Williamsburg March 17. 1755   (Braddock)

Sir: Robert Napier

By the Gibraltar which sail'd about a Fortnight ago I wrote to you to acquaint you with all I then knew; Every thing as I then told you was in the utmost confusion; We have with a good deal of difficulty put our Affairs in some sort of Method. The Transports are all arriv'd, except one, which expected every hour. Without Mr. Keppel I should have been in great distress, the Embarkation having been made in great confusion, Arms, Men, Stores, Officers of different Regiments in one Ship, and as Sir John St. Clair foretold a thousand difficulties rais'd in case I had gone up to Annapolis, as I had propos'd before the

Transports came in, but with the Commodore's assistance, who by the by I think is an Officer of infinite Merit, we have pack'd them all up to Alexandria with very little grumbling, whither I propose to follow them the day after tomorrow, and in all probability be there a day or two before them. There is not one sick Man among them, which is pretty extraordinary considering the length of the passage, in which one Man was wash'd overboard. As to the provisions they made a Rout about there were never known better deliver'd. I at first intended to have canton'd the Troops according to the Account sent you by Sir John St. Clair, but as the Winter seems to be now so far broke up as to admit of their encamping without any ill consquences, I have order'd those that first arriv'd, as I have the other since, to proceed up the River Potomack to Alexandria, there to disembark and encamp immediately, by which means they will have time to discipline their additionals which otherwise would be spent in marching backwards and forwards. The Levies of Virginia and Maryland are likewise to join me at Alexandria; After I have augmented the two English Regiments to 700 Men each with the best of 'em, I purpose to form the others to the following Establishm^t which had been agreed to by Govr Dinwiddie; vizt Two Companies of Carpenters, consisting each of a Captain, two Subalterns, three Serjeants, three Corporals, and fifty Men; Four Companies of Foot Rangers of six, if I can get them, upon the same Establishment; One Troop of Horse Rangers, consisting of one Captain, two Subalterns, two Serjeants and thirty Men: These Companies are to receive from the Province the same nominal pay in the Currency of the Country with the Establishment of his Majesty's Forces, the Difference of Exchange between which and Sterling is about 25 p Cent. I have also settled a Company of Guides, one Captain two Aids and ten Men. I have fix'd posts from the Head Quarters to Philadelphia, Annapolis and Williamsburg, to facilitate the Correspondence necessary for me with those several Governments. There are here Numbers of Mulattoes and free Negros of whom I shall make Bat Men, whom the province are to furnish with pay and Frocks, being resolv'd to allow none our of the Troops.

I hear Governor Shirley's Regiment is near if not quite compleat; I have heard nothing of nor from Sir William Pepperell: Mr. Keppel has sent the Arms Cloathing, Officers and whatever else belongs to those two Regiments to the Northward in two transports under the Convoy of a Man of War.

As soon as I can assemble the Troops provide Forage provisions and other Necessaries for their March I shall proceed to attempt the Reduction of the French Forts upon the Ohio: It is doubtful whether there will be grass on the other side the Alliganey Mountains before the latter End of April, which is indeed as soon as it will probably be in my power to get there.

It is not in my power as yet to give you a certain Account of the Number and Strength of the forces I shall have with me: If I am able to compleat the two English Regiments to 1400, and the provincial Levies to the Establishment above mention'd, I dont find they can amount in the whole with the Independent Companies of New York and Carolina (which two first are good for nothing) to above 2300 or thereabouts. I had propos'd to send for a Detachment from the American Regiments, but as I have thought it necessary to have an Interview with Govr Shirley, and have accordingly sent him Orders to meet me at Annapolis in Maryland I have deferr'd giving Orders on that head till after I have seen him. At this Interview which I expect in about a Fortnight (and at which I have desir'd the Governors of New York and Pensylvania to be present if the Affairs of their Governments will admit of it), I propose to settle the Operations to the Northward; By the first opportunity after it I shall acquaint you with what has been determin'd.

It is likewise impossible for me to give you any certain Account of the French Force upon the River Ohio; If anything can be collected for the various Acco^ts of 'em it is that their Numbers exceed 3000, a considerable part of which are Indians. It is universally agreed that all the Tribes of the Iroquois except the Mohawks are gone over to their Interest; but as the present Attachment of these Nations, and such others of the Southern Indians as are in alliance with them, is attributed to the late Superiority of the French, it may be hop'd that the Appearance of our Army, or at least any Advantage gain'd, may make a great Alteration in their Dispositions.

Sir John St. Clair having inform'd me that we shall be oblig'd to break ground before the Fort upon the Ohio and there having been only four twelve pounders sent out with the Train, I have applied to Commodore Keppel for four more from the Ships with a proper Quantity of Ammunition, and for many other Things that were necessary, all which he has supplied (with) the greatest expedition; and has upon every occasion shewn the utmost Readiness in concurring with me in all measures for promoting the Success of the present Service; He has likewise order'd thirty Sailors with proper Officers to attend the Army, who will be of the greatest use in assisting the Conveyance of the Artillery over the Mountains. I have settled the pay of these Men with Mr. Kepple at 3/6 p day for the Midshipmen, and /6 for the common Sailors which I shall be oblig'd to charge to the Contingencies. I am, Sir, Your most Humble and most Obedient Servant,   E. Braddock [71]

March 18 (Tuesday)

MARYLAND-WILLS'S CREEK

March 18th 1755   (St. Clair)

By Sir John St.Clair Bar. Quarter Master General to the British Forces in North America

You are hereby Required and directed to march from this on Wednesday the 19th Instant and to proceed to Winchester with the men of the Virginia Forces to be discharged on your arrival at that place. You will receive 8 days provisions for your men, and you are to discharge them.

Orders will be left for you at Winchester for your return to the Fort. you are to take Lieut. Speldolf under you command as far as Winchester.

The Officers are not to quit there men on their march and to preserve good order and Discipline conformable to the Articles of War.

Given under my hand at the Fort at Wills's Creek this 18th day of March.

To: Capt. Waggenor of the Virginia Force [72]

MARYLAND-WILLS'S CREEK

March 18th 1755   (St. Clair)

To: Capt. Thomas Clarke Commander of an Indep. Company of N.Y.

Agreeable to the Reviewing instructions given unto me by his Excellency General Braddock commander in chief of his Majestys Forces in North America. It is expected that a Report should be made, that all the troops in his Majesties pay should be compleat and fit for service the 25 of March, and whereas, on making the review of the two independent companies of New York, the company commanded by Capt. Clarke is in great measure found unfit for service on account of a defiency in their numbers and a great number of old men so that the company wants more than half to compleat.

That his Majestys service my suffer as little as possible by this great neglect I hereby order that the independent company commanded by Capt. Clarke do march from this to Frederick in Maryland and there the subaltern officers are to go from thence on the remaining service as that the company maybe compleated with good able bodied men to its establishment by the 25 day of April.

Capt. Clarke is hereby ordered to provide his company with camp equipage and all other necessaries according to the annexed list to be ready to take the field by the 25 of April.

Given under my hand at the fort at Wills's Creek this 18th day of March 1755.[73]

VIRGINIA-ALEXANDRIA   (batman)

Where (Here) we lay in quarter till the Other Ships Ariv'd. As soon as all the Ships Ariv'd, the town Being very small, only Built five years, Obliged us to go to Camp. [74]

A conference was held, at the Grand Parade or encampment (exact location not known for sure) located well back from the tobacco sheds. From SEAPORT IN VIRGINIA - GEORGE WASHINGTON'S ALEXANDRIA we read: "In the mid 1700s Alexandria or Belhaven was a small trading place in one of the finest situations imaginable. The Potomac River above and below the town is not more than a mile broad, but here it opens into a large circular bay of at least twice that diameter. The town is built upon an arc of the bay; at one extremity of which (north) is a wharf; at the other a dock for building ships; with water sufficiently deep to launch a vessel of any rate of magnitude".

In the spring of 1755 the inhabitants of Alexandria crowded the waterfront to watch thirteen British transport ships and three ordnance ships come up river and anchor in the Potomac off the town. The transport ships consisted of the following: Anna, Halifax, Osgood, London, Industry, Isabel and Mary, Terrible, Fame, Concord, Prince Frederick, Fishburn, Molly, and Severn. Additionally there were in the fleet three ordnance ships: Whiting, Newall, and Nelly. These were under escort of two fourth rate war ships: HMS Seahorse and HMS Nightingale. A fourth rate ship has two decks and a net tonnage of 1,100. It has a crew of 350 men and officers and 50 cannon that can deliver a broadside weighing 800 tons.

The village was located on a curving embayment of the Potomac River formed by two points of land. The northern point was the location of the wharf where the Army's provisions, supplies, and baggage were off loaded from the ships and either stored in sheds or carted to the army encampment.

Laying off the town of Alexandria (1748) as surveyed and platted by George Washington against the modern street pattern we see that the colonial village was quite small and on a shoreline long ago filled in. The grand parade where the army encamped was inland - there is a marker at Braddock Road and Russell Avenue. It has been suggested that the encampment was in the vicinity of where the Masonic Temple now stands. The land necessary to canton both the regiments and all the other units, support staff and equipment must have been considerable and probably extended between the Masonic Temple and the Braddock Road - Russell Avenue site. In any event it would appear that the troops used Orinoco Street as their way from the waterfront to the encampment grounds.

March 20 (Thursday)
VIRGINIA-WILLIAMSBURG
Williamsburgh March 20th 1755.   **(Braddock)**
My Lord: Newcastle

In Obedience to your Grace's Commands I take the earliest opportunity that has been in my power to acquaint You with my arrival here, as well as that of all the Transports with the Forces under my Command. My own Voyage was troublesome, but the Transports met with better Weather, and I have the pleasure to acquaint your Grace there has not been one Man sick on board them all.

What Effect His Majesty's Direction to His several Governors upon occasion of the present Expedition may have in the Colonies under their Command, I know not; I cannot say as yet they have shewn the Regard to 'em that might have been expected. I have used, & shall continue to use my Endeavours to excite in 'em a better Spirit, and to prevail upon 'em to bear such a Share of the Expence, which will attend the present undertaking, as their Duty to His Majesty, and the Interest they have in the Event if it requries from 'em. - For this purpose, among others, I have sent Orders to M[r] Shirley to meet me at Annapolis in Maryland, and have desired the Governors of New York & Pensilvania to accompany him thither, if the Affairs of their Governments will admit of it.

I shall not trouble your Grace with the Detail of Business under my Direction in the Service I am engaged in: As I have wrote fully to the Secretary of State by this Opportunity, I beg leave to refer You to my Letter to him for any Particulars you may have an Inclination to be informed of.

As I hear Mr Shirley's Regimt is nearly or quite compleat, and am in hopes Sir William Pepperell may have made some progress in raising his, I shall, immediatley after I have seen Govr Shirley, give Orders for employing those Forces in such manner to be Northward, as may appear most Conducive to the service intended. I shall myself proceed with the Force I shall have with me to attempt the Reduction of the French Forts upon the Ohio, and hope to be on the further side of the Alliganey Mountains by the End of April.

I have receiv'd all possible Assistance from Commodore Keppel, who is an Officer of great Capacity and Merit, I must likewise acquaint Your Grace, that I have met with the readiest Concurrence from the Governor of this Province in every measure I have proposed for the Service of the Expedition, & that the people under his Command seem now dispos'd to contribute largely & chearfully to the support of it, which is more than I can say of the other Governments.

As small coined silver will be greatly wanted for the payment of the Troops, and as no considerable Quantity of it can be got in this Province; I must beg your Grace to direct the Contractors, Mr Hanbury & Mr Thomlinson to send over as soon as possible, if they have not already done it. four or five Thousand pounds, in Piastrines & Half Piastrines: which is the more necessary, as all the Money already brought over by the Regiment Paymasters is in Spanish Gold and Dollars.   I am &ca   E: Braddock
p.s. I have heard nothing yet of the Deputy Paymaster Genl. [75]

MARYLAND-ANNAPOLIS   **(Maryland Gazette)**
We are informed by Mr. Middleton, who came in this Morning from Virginia, that the Fleet from Ireland with the Forces, are all arrived except the <u>Severn</u>, Capt. Rawlings, who had been spoke with and was every Day expected. The had 7 or 8 Weeks Passage from Cork, and are arrived in good Health; the two Regiments will compleat 700 each, when Rawlings arrives. [76]

March 21 (Friday)
VIRGINIA-WINCHESTER
March 21st 1755   **(St. Clair)**
Mr. Perkine
At your request as a civil magistrate, I have delivered over John May to you in order to be prosecuted at civil law concerning a article

which was lost in a scuffle said May had with some of the inhabitants. You cannot be ignorant that the said May was offered up to the civil majestrate on this fray happening, but on their declining the prosecution he was tried by a Regimental court martial and severly punished.

To avoid having any misunderstanding between the civil and the military powers, I have ordered him to be discharged and my duty obliges me to inform you that if this man receives any further punishment or confinement, that I shall lay the thing before his Majestys Attorney General that his Majesty may not be whipped of his soldiers on such frivalous accounts as these.

I am Sir your Hum. Ser. [77]

March 21st 1755
To: Company of Rangers   (St. Clair)
By Sir John St. Clair Bar. Quartermaster
His Majestys Forces in America

You are hereby Required and Directed to March with the first company of Rangers under your command and make the Roads passable for all kind of carriages from Winchester to Enoch's on the Capacapon, when you have cut the Road that far, you are to consult with Henry Enoch the proper place for crossing in a float. You are to cut the Roads down to that place and level the banks of the River for that purpose, should I not be able to join you before you have cut the Roads thus far, you are to pass the river and cut the road blazed out by Henry Enoch to the mouth of the South Branch, he will attend you on this service and has directions from me that all the inhabitants within eight miles of the Road that is to be cut shall attend on this important piece of service for the good of their country. You are to march from hence as soon as you can get tools, and you are to work with 20 men of your company each day who shall be paid six pence British Sterling for their work which the commissary shall have my orders to pay, the commissary has my directions to furnish you with provisions. If this work can be finished before my Return, you are to pass the Potomack to Col Crisipis and march there to the Fort at Wills's Creek. You pass on your march and when encamped to observe good order and disicipline and conform yourself in every respect to the rules and articles of War.

Given under my hand at Winchester, this 21st day of March 1755. [78]

VIRGINIA-MOUNT VERNON
Sir: Robert Orme   **(Washington)**

I find myself much embarrassed with my affairs, having no person to whom I can confide, to entrust the management with. Yet, under these disadvantages and circumstances, I am determined to do myself the honor of accompanying you with this proviso only, the General will be kind enough to permit my return as soon as the...or grand affair is over (if desired). Or, if there should be any space of inaction long enough to admit of a visit (for otherwise I could by no means obtain my own consent, whatever private losses I might sustain) to indulge me wherein and I need not add how much I should be obliged by joining at Wills Creek only, for this the General had kindly promised. These things Sir, however unwarrantable they may appear at first sight, I hope will not be taken amiss when it is considered how unprepared I am at present to quit a family, an estate scarcely settled, and in the utmost confusion....[79]

VIRGINIA-WILLIAMSBURG   **(Virginia Gazette)**

The transports, with the troops, are all now safely arrived; and gone round to Alexandria, where it is hoped, by this time they are all disembarked; tis remarkable that not withstanding a Winter Passage, not one man died since they Left Cork, and only two sick on their arrival.

His Honor the Governor and his Excellency General Braddock are off for the Northward Tomorrow to meet his Excellency Governor Shirley, Esq at Annapolis, in order as it is supposed, to concept the Plan of Operation for the ensuing campaign. [80]

March 22 (Saturday)
VIRGINIA-ALEXANDRIA   **(Orme)**

The 22d of March the General set out for Alexandria, accompanied by the Governor and Mr. Kepple, where they arrived the 26th. [81]

Sir: George Washington   **(Orme)**

The General orders me to give you his compliments, and to assure you his wishes are to make it agreeable to yourself and consistent with your affairs, and, therefore, he desires you will settle your business at home, as to join him at Wills Creek if more convenient to you; and, whenever you find it necessary to return, he begs you will look upon yourself as entirely master, and judge what is proper to be done...[82]

MARCH THE 22 (Browne)

Went on Shore to Bellhaven with Mr. Bass. Extremely hot, but as Agreeable a Place as could be expected, it being inhabited but 4 years. Went with Mr. Lake to every House in the Place to get a Lodging, and at last was Obliged to take a Room but little larger than to hold my Bed, and not so much as a Chair in it. Went on Board at Night. [83]

March 23 (Sunday)
VIRGINIA-ALEXANDRIA (batman)

We Incamped By the town and Recd many Recruits to Both Regiments. From thence we Sent two Recruiting Parties into Maryland. At this place the soldiers Rec'd their Blankets, and all the heavy Baggage that Could not be taken along with (them) was left here in Store. Here we Bought Several Horses but the Baggage was Carried from hence in Wagons. At this place the two Regiments parted. Sir Peeter Halkets Regt marched on the Virginia Side and Colonel Dunbars Regt marched on the Maryland side till they Came to Fort Cumberland and there to join. [84]

MARCH THE 23 (Browne)

Sunday. Was hurried on Shore with all my Baggage to my Lodging. My Brother took one the next Door. I now think myself very happy that I am at Liberty once more, having been a Prisoner in that wooden World call'd the London (ship) 4 Months and 4 Days. I have sail'd since I left England 3 Thousand Leagues. [85]

March 26 (Wednesday)
VIRGINIA-ALEXANDRIA (Orme)

The General arrives in Alexandria. [86]

(Browne)

My Brother went to his Lodgings at a dutchmans. 5 of the Doctors being at a Loss where to go, came to board with us, staid 3 Weeks and then were order'd to Will's Creek. [87]

MARCH 27 (Thursday)
VIRGINIA-CAMP AT ALEXANDRIA

Parole-Williamsburg   (Braddock, Halkett/Disney)
Orders given out in Alexandria
Camp at Alexandria March 27th 1755
The Parole is Williamsburg

Capt Orme of the Colestreem regt. & Capt Morris of Coll. Dunbars
Regt. Are Appointed Aid de Camps to His Excellency Genl Braddock.
His Majesty has pleased to Appoint Capt. Halkett, of Sr Peter Halketts
reg^t Brigade Major.

As the Troops (h)as taken the Field, His Excellence Genl:
Braddock is Desirious the Off^r. & men should be informd of the Duty
he requires of Them, And of some Regulations he thinks benificient to
the Service, And as the two regt^s. now imployd, have served Under
H:R:H: are Acquainted with Military Disciplin, His Excellence
(expects) Their Conduct will be so Conformable to Order, as to sett
the most Soldier like Example to the new lev(i)es of this Country. And
the Genl Orders That the Articles of War be immediately read, & that
every Body may be informed that all Neglects or disobedience of them
or of Any Orders will not be forgiven.

Any soldier who shall Desert tho he Return Again shall be
Hanged without Mercy.

As An Encouragement to the men & to promote their Diligence
And Activity Every man will be allowd every day as much fresh or Salt
provision & bread or Flower, without any stoppage for the same, As
long & in as great propotion (proportions) as it would be possible to
provide Them Unless any man should be found Drunk Negligent or
Disobedient. In such Case this Gratuity shall be stopped. All Orders
relating to the men are Constantly to be read to them by An Offr: of
the Company.

The Oldest Capts Company of each regt. is always to Act as a
Second Grendr: Compny And to be posted upon the left of the
Battallion, leaving the same Intrival as the Grends: upon the right. This
Company to be kept Compleat of Officers & two of Them as well as
of the other Grenr: Company are to be Posted in the Front & the other
in the rear.

The Eight Battallion Companys Are to form eight Firings And to be
Commanded by Their Respective Officers. The Commanding Officers
of each Company is to give the Word. The second is to be Posted in
the Center of the Front Rank & the remaining subaltren Officers of the
Regt: after this Disposision Are to divide The ground in the Rear

92

Equally. These Firings are to begin with the Colo^s. Company, seconded by the Lt. Col^s., and Continued from right to left as fast as posable, but the Two Capt^s of Grend^s: are to take perticuler Care never to give their fire till the Compy^s on the right & left are Loaded. And to Avoid Confusion if the Regt^s. are Order'd to W(h)eel or Fire by Platoons, Every Officer Command^g: a Company is to tell it off in two divisions & to post the second Commissiond Off^r & nonCommissd Off^{rs}. When the Regts: are to decamp or are to form, the Commanding Off^r of the Company is to inspect his Mens Arms, Compleat the files, post the Officers & see (h)is men Are Loaded, that they may wheel up & form the Battalion.

The Officers upon a March to remain in the same Order with their Companys, & those Offr^s: who are placed in the Rear are to March as posted, which will Concequently be upon the flank, As the Reg^t. moves by files. They are therefor required to keep the Soldiers in their files and if many lag behind, one or more of those Officers to be left to bring them up.

Every Off^r leaving his Company upon a march to be Cashered. And every Commanding Off^r will be Answerable for the men of his Company left behind. And the Commanding off^r of each Reg^t are to Order to be punished with the Outmost Severity Any Soldier who shall leave his line without Leave, Sickness or Disability.

Command^g: Officers of Companys are to have Their Arms in Constant good Order & every man to be provided with a Brush & picker & two good spare flints & 24 Cartridges, The Roll of Each Comp^y to be Called by an Off^r morning noon & night, And a return of the Absent or Disorderly men to be given to the Commanding Off^r. of the Reg^t. who is to Order proper punish^t. Each reg^t. to mount a Picquet guard Consisting of 1 Capt 3 Sub(altern)s: and 100 men to be paraded at Retreat Beating, And after report to the Field Offr: of the Day. The two Regm^t are to find (furnish) the Genl^s. Guards, Alternatley Consisting of 1 Lieut & 30 private And to report to the Aid du Camp. The Reg^t who gives the guard to find the Adj^t of the day.

All guards to be Relieved at 8 oClock, all Guards to be told Of(f) in two divison(s) tho ever so small. Guards ordered at Orderly Time are to remain for that Day And a New Detachmt: to be made for any Orderd afterwards.

All Returns are to be signd by the Commanding Offr^s: of Regt^s. Returns of all Commands to be made to the Brigade Major, & every Regt Compny Troop &c Are to make a Dayly Return to him Specifying the Numbers wanting to Compleat them, who is to make one Genl. Return for his Excellence. A daily return of the Sick to be made to the Genl by an Aid du Camp. As the Nature of the Country makes it imposable to provide Magizines of Forage And as it is Apprenhended the Quantity will be very small Uncertain & Difficult to be got, His Excellence Recomends to all the Officers to take no more Bagage then will be Necessary. As the Good of the Service renders the Presence of all the Offr^s absolutely Necessary His Excellence Cannot suffer any Off^r to Act as paymaster. The Genl Therefore desires the Colo^s & Capt^s will fix upon a proper Person as soon as posoble for that purpose.

The Line to find and Field Off^r Daily to be releivd at 9 oClock. This Duty to be done by the Lt Colo^s & two Maj^{rs}. The Field Off^r to Visit the Guards & outposts, Except the Genl^s., And to go the rounds of the Picquet, which as well as the other Guards & posts are to Report to the Field Off^r: And; he is to make his report at 9 oClock of the Whole to the Genl. And in Case of an Allarm the Field Off^r is to repair to the place of Allarm with all Expedition And to send for any Necessary Assistance to the Two Regts who are Immediately to Comply with his Orders. All reports & returns to be made before 9 oClock. Upon any Application made by Sr John St Clear (Clair) Q:M:G: for men the Reg^{ts} are Immediatly to furnish Them. Sr Peter Halkett is to be Applyed to for all Regulations of Provisions And his Orders are strictly to be Complyd with.

All Guards are to Rest & Beat two Ruffs to his Hon^r. Govr Delwiney (Dinwiddie).

The Reg^{ts} to hold Themselves in Readiness for a Muster, Each Compy to be provided with three Rolls, One of them of parchment, & The Officers with new Commissions to have them in their Pockitts. After the Muster the Genl: will Revew the two reg^{ts} by Companys. The Officers to be in Boots & the Men in brown gaters. The Adj^{ts} of the two reg^{ts} & (artillery) Train & also for the Rangers to be at the Major of Brigade's Tent every day (at) 11 oClock to receive Orders, And also a Serjt from the Two Reg^{ts} Artillery & Rangers to Attend the Brigade Major as Orderly And to be releved every Day at guard

Mounting. The Gentlemen of the Hospital And their Serv^{ts} are to morrow to receive Three days provision.

The Adj^t of the Day to send a Serj^t to Sr John St Clear with the Orders.

Field Offr for this Night Lt Col Gage. Field Offr for to morrow Major Chapman.

R(egimental): O(rders): The Serj^{ts} & Corpl^s to be out in the Front of the Camp with Arms & Accouterments.

> For Guard on the Genl: to morrow-Lt Dunbar
> For the Town Guard------------Ensn Kennedy
> For the Quarter Guard-------Ensn Townshend
> For the Picquet this night------Lt Littler
> > Capt Beckwith
> > Ensn William
> > Lt Pottinger [88]

MARYLAND-ANNAPOLIS   (Maryland Gazette)

Since or last we have the Pleasure of hearing of the safe Arrival of Capt. Rawlings at Alexandria; the Forces being now all safe arrived, and landed there. [89]

Nichols writes: "The field officer of the day was the busiest officer in camp, for he had charge of the whole encampment during his tour of duty. He visited all guards, including distant pickets, and received their report. The sentry who did not know the correct parole for the day was sure to be reprimanded by him on his rounds. In case of alarm the field officer of the day took command of all officers and men in the vicinity of the disturbance. All detail of troops destined for drill, work, or guard duty were first drawn up on the "Grand Parade" at the head of the senior regiment before marching off on their particular mission. The two lieutenant colonels and majors of the regulars took turns at this post. The parole was changed daily, and since it was customarily the name of a British city or town, a sentry can hardly be blamed for giving "Winchester" instead of "Chichester," for example."

              (Orme)

The General named his Aid de Camps, and the major of Brigade and Provost Mareschal, and gave out the following Orders, for the better regulation of the camp.

ORDERS GIVEN OUT AT ALEXANDRIA

As the two Regiments now employed have served under his Royal Highness the Duke, they are consequently very well acquainted the Military Discipline. The General therefore expects their behaviour should be so conformable to good Order, as to set the most soldier like example to the new Levies of this country.

As an encouragement to the men, they shall be supplied with a daily allowance of provisions gratis; but if any man be found negligent or disorderly, besides corporal punishment, this gratuity shall be stopped.

The articles of war are to be immediately and frequently read, and all orders relating to the men are to be read to them by an Officer of a Company.

Any soldier that deserts, though he return again shall be hanged without mercy.

The Commanding Officers of companies are to be answerable that their men's Arms are kept in constant good order. Every man to be provided with a brush, picker and two good spare flints, and kept always completed with twenty four rounds.

The Roll of each Company is to be called by an Officer, every morning, Noon and night and a return of the absent and disorderly men is to be given to the Commanding Officer of the Regiment, who is to see them properly punished.

Each Regiment is to have Divine Service performed at the head of their respective Colours every Sunday.

The two Regiments are to find the General's Guard Alternately, which is to consist of a Lieutenant and thirty men, and the Regiment which finds the General's Guard is to find also the Adjutant of the day.

All Guards are to be relieved in the Morning at eight of the Clock. Guards, though ever so small, to be told off into two divisions.

All reports and returns to be made at nine of the clock. Guards, ordered at orderly time, are to remain for that day; and a new detachment is to be made for any ordered afterwards. All returns are to be signed by the Commanding Officers of the Regiments.

Each Regiment, Troop, or Company, is to make a daily return to the Major of Brigade, specifying their Numbers wanting to complete, who is to make a General return for his Excellency.

A daily return of the sick is to be made to the General, through an Aid de Camp. In case of any Alarum, the Virginia troops are to parade before the Church.

The line is to find daily one field-Officer, who is to be relieved at nine of the clock. This duty is to be done by the two Lieutenant Colonels and the two Majors. The field Officer of the day is to visit all Guards and out-parties, except the General's, and to go the rounds of the Picket, which as well as the other Guard and out-parties, are to report to him. He is to make his report of the whole at nine of the clock to the General, and in case of any Alarum, the field Officer is to repair with all expedition to the place where it is, and to send for any necessary Assistance to the two Regiments which are immediately, to comply with his Orders.

The eldest Battalion company is to act as a second Grenadier company, and to be posted upon the left of the Battalion, leaving the same interval as the Grenadiers upon the right.

This company is to be kept complete of Officers, and two of them, as well as of the other Grenadier companies are to be posted in the front, and the other in the rear.

The eight Battalion companies are each of them to be told off into two divisions, that they may either form eight firings, or sixteen platoon, and are alwayes to be commanded by their own Officers, who are to be posted in the same manner as the Grenadier Officers, and that every Company might be complete of Officers, the General made three Ensigns to each Regiment, without pay.

Each Regiment is to mount a Picket guard, consisting of one Captain, two Subalterns and fifty Men which are to report to the field Officer of the day.

Upon any application from Sr John St Clair to either of the Regiments for men, they are immediatley to furnish them.
Sr Peter Halket is to regulate all affairs relative to the provisions.
The Commissary of Provisions is to make two weekly returns; one for the General, the other for Sr Peter Halket. When any man is sent to the General Hospital, he is to carry with him a Certificate, signed by an Officer of his Company, setting forth his name, Regiment, and Company, to what day he is subsisted, and what Arm's and acoutrements he carries with him, which are to be bundled up and marked with the man's name, regiment, and company.

Each regiment is to send to the Artillery for twenty five thousand flints, out of which they are to choose five thousand and send the remainder back; and where any of the troops have occasion for ammunition, or any military stores, the commanding officers are to send to the train for them, giving proper receipts.

The Captains of the two Regiments are to account with their men for their sea pay, giving them credit for their subsistence to the first of

April, and for their Arrears to the 24th of February; and they are to stop for the watchcoats, blankets, and flannel waistcoats.

The men enlisted or incorporated into the 44th and 48th regiments are to have credit for twenty shillings, and are to be charged with the above necessities.

All casualities, or remarkable occurrences in Camp, are to be reported, immediatley, to the General, throught an Aid de Camp. Whenever S[r] John S[t] Clair has occasion for tools, the commissary of the train is to supply them on proper receipts. Those officers of companies, who call the evening roll, are to inspect the ammunition of their respective companies, and report the deficiencies to the commanding officer.

No man, upon a March, is on any account to fasten his tent pole, to his firelock, or by any means encumber it.

The quarter-masters of each regiment are to apply to the assistant quarter master-general, who will show them their store-houses, in which their regimental stores are immediately to be lodged.

The soldiers are to leave in the store, their shoulder-belts, waist-belts and swords, the sergeants their halberts, and those officers that can provide themselves with fusils, their espontons.

The General enquired of S[r] John S[t] Clair the nature and condition of the roads through which the troops and artillery were to march, and also if he had provided the waggons for the Ohio. S[r] John informed the General that a new road was near completed from Winchester to Fort Cumberland, the old one being impassable, and that another was cutting from Conegogee to the same place, and that if the General approved of making two divisions of the troops and train, he might reach Will's Creek with more ease and expedition. He proposed that one regiment with all the powder and ordnance should go by Winchester, and the other regiment with the ammunition, military and hospital stores by Frederick in Maryland. That these should be carried ten miles up the Potomack to Rock Creek, and then up the Potomack to Fort Cumberland.

S[r] John assured the General that boats, batteaux, canoes and waggons were prepared for the service, and also that provisions were laid in at Frederick for the troops. A return was called for of the waggons and teams wanted to remove the train from Alexandria, which S[r] John went up the country to provide.

He told the General two men had undertaken to furnish two hundred waggons and fifteen hundred carrying horses at Fort Cumberland early in May.

Before the General reached Alexandria, the troops were all disembarked, but, very little of the Ordnance stores or provisions were yet on shore, the properest places and methods of unlading them were settled, and they were landed with the utmost dispatch. [90]

The regiments of foot of about 500 men each from Ireland were quartered on the outskirts of town on a flat open area west of Alexandria. The 44th Regiment commanded by Sir Peter Halkett and the 48th Regiment commanded by Colonel Dunbar had already made their way up from the river landing and through the town on Orinoco Street with artillery and munitions train. These regulars were to be augmented to 700 men each by men from New York and South Carolina Independent companies; Virginia and Maryland and North Carolina militia levies. The colonials were called "bobtails" by the regulars because of the short cut of their uniform coats. Regulars were warned not to make loud negative remarks about militia troops during their drills and formations. The regulars had been enlarged in Ireland by drafts from six other regiments still in Ireland and were looked down upon by the officers and non-coms as they were largely taken from jails, slums, gin shops. They were dirty, discontented, insolent and insubordinate with drinking as their pastime.

Mr. Lee McCardell, in his book ILL STARRED GENERAL: BRADDOCK OF THE COLDSTREAM GUARD recreates the scene: "The troops, put ashore by the transport crews, marched up the lane (Orinoco Street) from the river, drums thumping, fifes a-squeal. Frightened hogs and geese, which had the run of the place, scattered. Townsfolk, children, a few farmers, Negro servants watched their first British regulars swing past. Never before had they beheld anything as gorgeous as those yellow face red uniforms with their big shinning buckles and white lace - slightly soiled. Never before had they heard so many drums - twenty to each regiment. The thistle wreathed Roman numerals, were another curiosity.

The soldiers, unkempt by months of cramped living aboard ship, their pigtails smeared with a regulation mixture of flour and tallow, regarded the Alexandrians with much less satisfaction. The blacks were the first Negro slaves some of the soldiers had ever seen. But the long confinement of a transatlantic voyage had aroused more interest in the town. The redcoats marched past a court house, a jail, a whipping post, and a pillory - grouped around the market square. They looked for alehouses - and saw one small tavern. No cook shops. No pastry shops. No coffee houses. No signboards. Along the lane leading to the site of their encampment, the edge of a marsh to the northwest of the town, they passed not more than half a dozen coaches and those with unmatched horses and a plain and dusty as any country carriages they had ever seen in Ireland."(Material cited is from ILL-STARRED GENERAL: BRADDOCK OF THE COLDSTREAM GUARDS, by Lee McCardell, © 1958 by University of Pittsburgh Press. Reprinted by permission of the University of Pittsburgh Press).

March 28 (Friday)
VIRGINIA-CAMP AT ALEXANDRIA

Parole-Albemarle   **(Braddock, Halkett/Disney)**

The Generals Guard to be mounted in Brown Gater's, and the Officers in Boots.

Sir Peter Halkets, Col° Dunbar's and the Royal Regiment of Artillery are to be mustered, on Monday morning at seven o'clock, and afterwards they will be received by General Braddock.

Robert Webster of Sir Peter Halkets Regim[t] is appointed Provoest Marshall and he is to be obeyed accordingly.

One sergeant; one corporal and twelve men to mount as a guard for the Provost Marshal and be relieved every 48 hours.

The Adjutant who does not send in his return to the Major of Brigade, by seven o'clock in the morning will be orderd under an arrest.

The Quarter master of the Corps which is to receive provisions is to give to the Commissary a signed Return of the number he is to draw Provisions for every Saturday at six in the afternoon: The Quarter masters of the different Corps are to be given into Sir Peter Halket a return of the Provisions they delivered out that week, distinguishing the quantitys delivered each Corps; In this return he is to have Colums for the quantitys of each species of Provision's he has receiv[d] that week and a Column for the Quantitys remaining in Store.

To morrow at Orderly time the Adjutants are to deliver in a return of the number of Serv[d] who are not Soldiers and for whom Provisions are to be drawn for; The Commissary are to make two Copy's of this return, one for Gen[l] Braddock, the other for Sir Peter Halkett.

Field Officer to morrow Lieu[t] Col° Burton.

For the Gen[ls] Guard 48th Regiment.

One of the Orderly Sergeants or the Major of Brigade is to carry the Orders to Sir John St. Clair.

A General Court Martial consisting of one Field Officer, Six Captains and Six Subalterns, to sit to morrow morning at 8 o'clock.

L[t] Col° Gage, President. Sir Peter Halkett gives 3 Capt[ns] and 3 Subalterns; Col° Dunbar gives 3 Capt[ns] and 3 Subalterns. Mr. Shirley Judge Advocate; The Picquet to consist of one Capt[n], two Subalterns and fifty men till further Orders. No Officer, Soldier or any other Person to Fire a Gun within a mile round the Camp. [91]

Nichols writes: "The uniform of the private was picturesque. He wore a flat black tricorne hat edged with white, or if he were a grenadier, a tall mitre shaped hat bearing a metal plate marked "GR" for "Georgius Rex". Beneath the hat his hair was clubbed and tied at the nape of the neck with a small black ribbon, and on ceremonial occasions he powdered his hair with flour or rice powder. A white stock and waistcoat set off the striking red coat with its distinctive regimental facings, lapels and wide-turned cuffs of vivid yellow silk for the 44th and of buff for the 48th. Red breeches were tucked into long white spatterdashes, buttoned above the knees and fastened with black garters. On his feet he wore sturdy black shoes. He carried a muzzle-loading, smoothbore, flintlock musket, fitted with an offset socket bayonet, steel ramrod, and white sling strap. A wide waist belt supported a bayonet frog on the left hip and a short sword and scabbard on the right. A shoulder strap held his black leather cartridge pouch in place and another supported his knapsack. The sergeants carried halberds in lieu of muskets, and commissioned officers were armed with espontoons (half-pikes) in addition to their light dress sword. the officer in his powdered wig, scarlet tunic and waistcoat, lace stock and cuffs, gleaming gorget, voluminous red waist sash, and black leather boots was a dashing figure.

All colonial troops wore blue uniforms of the regulation cut, faced with red to set off the blue of their coats and breeches. The arms and equipment of the provincials were similar to those of the regulars although often of inferior quality. Unlike the regulars they carried no short swords. Their smoothbore flintlocks were fitted with bayonets, ramrods, and sling straps. They carried black leather cartridge pouches, for no powder horns were used since only a rifleman or a lazy smoothbore shooter would have employed this clumsy method of loading a piece.

Each regiment carried two flags, or colors: the First or King's Color was the familiar "Great Union"; the Second or Regimental Color was bright yellow in the 44th, buff in the 48th, with the "Union" in the upper right canton and the regimental rank (number) in gold Romans in the center."

VIRGINIA-ALEXANDRIA
March 28th 1755   (St. Clair)
Memorandum for General Braddock

That a proper person of the Artillery should be sent to Rock Creek to receive the stores sent thither by water and lodge them in the storehouses provided by Mr. Beal, that he is to see these stores loaded on waggons for Conogogee, for which he is to take receipts from the waggoners for the quantity loaded and that he is to give a ticket specifying their load where the waggoner is to (go)- the person who is appointed to receive the stores at said place and on that persons signing, a receipt for the load the waggoner will be paid by the commissary of stores at the rate of 16 pence of Maryland money a mile as the law of Maryland directs care is to be taken that they load 2000 weight. Mr. Cresap will provide storehouses at Conogogee.

That a proper person of the artillery should be sent (to) Conogogee to receive the stores sent thither by land from Rock Creek, he is to see that the stores are according to the list sent him from Rock Creek, and give the waggoner a reciept on the back of his tickkett for their payment. He is to see the stores put on boats or canoes and sent to the fort at Wills's Creek, and to consign then to the Officers at the fort, who will receive them, and Mr. Commissary Walker will pay the water carriage.

Then an officer of the artillery should be sent Eight days hence to Wills's Creek to receive all stores sent thither for which there are proper magazines.

That a proper person of the artillery should be sent to Winchester to receive and foward all stores by land in the same manner as the one at Rock Creek.

It is recommended that the commissary of stores for the artillery should consult with Mr. Commissary Duke that he may know what waggonage he is to state to him for the Ordnance of Stores. [92]

March 29 (Saturday)
VIRGINIA-CAMP AT ALEXANDRIA
Parole-Boston   **(Braddock, Halkett/Disney)**
For the General Guard 44th Regiment.

The alarm Post for all the Viginian Troops Quartered in the Town of Alexandria to be before the march.

When any man is sent to the General Hospital he is to bring a certificate signed by an Officer, of his name, Regiment and Company, to what day he is subsisted, and what arms and acoutrements he brings with him. The arms and accoutrements to be bundled up, and marked, with the mans name and Company.

Col[s] Dunbars Regiment to morrow to receive three days provisions.

On Sunday every Regiment in camp is to have divine service at the Head of their Colours.
AFTER ORDERS.

Each Regiment to send to the train for twenty Thousand Flints out of which number, they are to pick five thousand, and to send the remainder back again; The Commanding Officers giving their receipts for what number's they receive.

All the Virginia Troops that are Quartered in Alexandria to be under arms, to morrow morning at half an hour after seven o'clock. The Officers that were formerly appointed Pay masters, to continue so till further Orders and are to issue out in payment to the Troops each a Dollar at 4^e/9^e shil'g.

When either Regiment have occasion for Ammunition, or any Military Stores the Commanding Officers are to send to the Artillery when they will be supplied giving their receipts accordingly.

The General Court Martial where of Lieut Col^o Gage was President is dissolv'd, and James Anderson of Col^o Dunbar's Regiment who was tryed by ye General Court Martial is orderd 1,000 lashes with a Cat and Nine Tails which he is to receive in such manner as the Commanding Officer shall think proper.

Field Officer for to morrow, Lt Col^o Gage.

The Allarm post for all the Virginia Troops Quartered in the Town of Alexandria to be before the Church. When any man is sent to the Genl. Hospital he is to bring a Certificate signd by An Officer of his name Regt: & Company, to what day he is Subsisted. [93]

General Court Martial   (Orme)
Lieutenant Colonel Gage, President

The prisoner ordered one thousand lashes, but part of the punishment remitted. [94]

March 30 (Sunday)
VIRGINIA-CAMP AT ALEXANDRIA
Parole-Chichester   (Braddock)

The two Regiments are to be musterd to morrow morning at seven O'clock but the General will not receive the Troops till further Orders.

The two Regiments from Ireland are to acc^t for their men for their Sea pay giving them credit for their subsistance to the first of March and for their Arms to the 24th of Feb^y; The Captains are to take credit for their Watch Coats, Blankets and Flannell waistcoats brought from Great Britain for their Companys.

The men listed or incorporated into Sir Peter Halketts, and Col^o Dunbar's Regiment are to have credit for twenty Shillings and to be chargd with the above mentiond necessarys His Excellency orders this to be taken from the recruiting Fund, and gives it to those men for their Incouragement that they may do their duty like good Soldiers.

The first company of carpenters are to march to morrow morning to Sir John St Clair for further Order's.

A Return to be sent to morrow morning to Sir Jn° St Clair from Sir Peter Halketts and Col° Dunbars Regiments of the number of Draughts they have received by whom they were enlisted and from what companys draughted. [95]

Alexandria Camp March 30th: 1755   **(Halkett/Disney)**
The Parole Chichester
Morning Orders

James Anderson of Col: Dunbars Regt: who was Try[d] at the Gen[l]: Court Martial is Orderd one Thousand lashes with a Cat of Nine tails which he is to receive in such manner as the Commanding Offr: of the Regt shall think proper.

Field Officer for tomorrow Major Chapman. The two Regts to be mustered to Morrow morning at 7 oClock. But the Gen[l]: will not revew Them till further Orders.

The two Regts from Ireland are to Account with their Men for their sea pay, giving them Creidit for their Subsistance to the first of April and for their Arrears to the 24th of Feb[y]: The Capt[s] are to take Creidit for the Watch Coats Blanketts & Flannel wascoats brough from Brittin for their Companys.

The men listed or Incorporated into S[r] Peter Halketts regt: & Col°. Dunbars are to have Creidit for Twenty Shillings & are to be charged with the above Necessarys. His excellence Orders this to taken from the recruiting fund And given to those men for their Incorigment That they may do their Duty like good Soldiers.

The first Comp[y] of Carpenters are to march to morrow for Winchester, And are to apply to S[r] John S[t] Clear for further Orders.

A Return to be sent to morrow morning to S[r]. John S[t] Clear from S[r] Peter Halket & Col Dunbar's regts: of the number of Draft they have Receiv'd And from whose Company they were Drafted. [96]

March 31 (Monday)

VIRGINIA-CAMP AT ALEXANDRIA   **(Braddock, Halkett/Disney)**
Camp at Alexandria March 31[d]: 1755
The Parole is Darlington
Field Officer for to Morrow Lieut Col Burton
For the Genl[s]: Guard the 44th Regt.

All Casuiltes That happen in Camp to be Reported Immediately to the Gen¹ through an Aid du Camp.

When ever Sʳ John Sᵗ Clear has Occation for Artifficers Tools or impliments he is to Apply to the Commissary of the Train who will supply Him with what he wants taking His or his Assistants Recept for ye same.

The Officers to provide Themselves with Baugt (Bat) Horses as soon as posable.

The Artilery to have their men upon the warfe every morning precisely at 6 oClock to land their stores, And care must be taken that they have their Waggons at the Warfe Exactly at the same time that there may be no Delay. One Serjt or Corpl & 12 men from the two Regts: without Arms to March immediatelly to ye warfe in Order to Assist the Artillery in Landng their stores. This party to be Releivd every morning & to be on the warfe Exactly at 6 oClock. As the Gen¹: has Recommended that the Officers should Carry no more Baggage then what shall be absolutly necessary. They are immediatley to fix upon what they will Carry. And to morrow morning A return to be given from Each Company to the Adjt of what waggons they will want to Carry the Men's An(d) Offrs: Tents as well as the Offrs Baggage to the Next Encampment. As the Officers will be Allowd no baughtmen Or Servts: from the Regts they are to pitch (sic) upon baggage men in the best manner they can from the Country people, which the Government will pay for at the rate of 3s-6d per week each man And the same allowence for provisions as the Soldiers. Store Houses will be provided for the Officers spare baggage at Alexandria, And men that shall be seen Drunk shall be stopd one weeks Provisions.
GENL ORDERS

The Officers not to provide themselves with Baugt men till further Orders. [97]

Nichols writes: "The 44th, 48th, and the artillery were formally mustered at seven on the morning of March 31. The troops were drawn up in review formation, the captain of each company holding his muster roll in his had, and all officers with new commissions were required to carry these in their pockets. Braddock received each company individually as he passed down the brigade line."

April 1 (Tuesday)
VIRGINIA-CAMP AT ALEXANDRIA

Parole-Esse   (Braddock)

Field Officer for to morrow _____

For the Generals Guard 48th Regiment.

Col^o Dunbars Regiment to receive three Days Provisions

The two Regnt are to send to artil^y for 1 Dozⁿ of carts made up
with Ball in order to try if they will fit the men's Firelocks. [98]

VIRGINIA-ALEXANDRIA

1st day of April   (Braddock)

By his Excellency Edward Braddock Esq. General
and Commander in chief of his Majesties forces in North America
To Sir John St. Clair Deputy Quarter Mast. Gen.

In case of your meeting no field officers at Wills's Creek, of
superior Rank to yourself, I do hereby impower and direct you as soon
as you shall get thither, if you shall think it necessary, for his majestys
service to take upon you the command of all the forces there, and all
officers and others whom it may concern, are in such case hereby
required, and directed to obey you accordingly. Given at the Camp at
Alexandria the first day of April 1755.   E. Braddock [99]

Camp at Alexandria April ye 1st: 1755   (Halkett/Disney)

The Parole Essex

Field Officer for to Morrow Lt Col Gage

Genl. Orders

No Soldier is to Cut Wood for the Town people or Suttlers. What
They cut for Themselves to be small wood. No large Trees to be felld
on any acc^t.

The Officers of the Quarter Guard to send a Corpl: & a file of men
every Night at 9 oClock, And to see all lights are Extinguished in the
Soldiers Tents, And is frequinly to send Partoles Round the Regts as
fare as his Centrys are posted, to see that every thing is quiet. And the
Patrol is to take up all soldiers, That are making Any Noise or Any
way disorderly & to releive all Centrys that Suffer Any Disturbence
near their post or otherways (are) negligint.

The Serjt of the Rear Guard is at the same time to take Care that all
Fires, Except the fire for the Guard & the Grand Suttler (are)
Extinguished in the Rear, As likewise to send frequent Patroles And
give Them the same Orders as given to the Qr Guard.

GENERAL: ORDERS
    Each of the two Regts: Are to send to the Artillery for one dozen
of Cartridges made up with ball in order to try if the(y) will fitt the
mens pieces. [100]

April 2 (Wednesday)
VIRGINIA-CAMP AT ALEXANDRIA
Parole-Farnham   **(Braddock)**
Field Officer for to morrow Maj^r Chapman.
For the Generals Guard 44th Regiment.
    The Artillery and Hospital receive three days provision to morrow.
The two Regiments are to apply to the Train for Paper, Powder & Ball
sufficient to compleat every man with 24 rounds which are to be made
up, and distributed as soon as possible.
    The commanding Officers of companys are desird to give particular
directions to their men to be careful of their Ammunition and to inform
them they will be very severly punishd for any abuse or neglect of it,
and the Officer's of company's who calld the Evening Rolls are to
inspect the Ammunition of their several companys and to report the
defficiencys to the commanding Officers of the Regiments who are
desird by his Excellency to keep them compleat with 24 Rounds.
    His Excellency General Braddock Orders that the Soldiers be told
that any man who upon a march by fastning his Tent Pole, or by any
other means incumbers his Fire lock, shall be immediatley and most
severly punished.
    One Corporal and eight men of the Line to attend at 6 Oclock
every morning, to assist the Engineers in Surveying.
    The Artillery, Hospital and Engineers to receive three days
provisions to morrow.
AFTER ORDERS
    One Sergant one Corporal, and twenty men of the Line without
arms to March to the Wharf immediately to assist in disembarking the
artillery.
    The Virginia Troops as appointed to the particular Regiments.
Sir Peter Halkets.
Captn Stephen 1st Company of Rangers
Captn Peyronny A   Company of Rangers
Captn Cock 6th Company of Rangers
Col^o Dunbars Regt.

Captn Waggoner 3rd Company of Rangers
Captn Hogg 5th Company of Rangers
Captn Polson 2^d Comp^a of Artificers

Sir Peter Halketts and Col^o Dunbars Regiments to find three
Corporals one for each Company of Rangers to assist Lieu^t Allayne in
the disciplining the Troops. [101]

Camp at Alexandria April 2^d: 1755   **(Halkett/Disney)**
The Parole is Farnam
Regll: Orders

All Officers to Attend this Night at the Picquet Mounting And to
do all Dutys in boots And never any plain Hatts and Gloves allways.

Genl Orders

Field Officer for to morrow Major Chapman.

The two Regt are to Apply to The Train (for) paper powder & ball
sufficient to Compleat every man to 24 Rounds which are to be made
up & distributed as soon as posable.

Commanding Officers of Compys are disered to give perticular
Directions to their men to be Carefull of their Ammunition And to
inform them They will be severly punished for any abuise or Neglect of
it. The Offrs of Compys who call the Evening rolls Are to inspect the
Ammunition of their severall Compys And are to report the
Difficiencies to the Commanding Offr: of the Regt.

His Excellency Genl: Braddock Orders That every soldier should be
told that every (man) who upon a March by fasning his Tent pool or
by Any other means incumber(s) his Firlock shall be immediatley most
severly punished.

A Corpl: & six men of Line to Attend at six oClock every morning
to Assist the Engineers in survaying. These men to parade at the
Church.

Regimll: Orders

As Soldiers when they are reprimanded or Conversed with by
Officers or Serjts. whilst they are in Liquor often make use of Insolent
Expressions which bring upon them heavy Punishments And sum times
even to indanger their Lives by Words tending to Mutinny, which
words are fare from their sober thoughts And Wholy Occationed by
the Effects of Liquor, All Commissiond & non Commissiond Officers
Are Expresly forbid either to Repprimand or Converse with any

Drunken Soldier but immediatley to Confine Him, And deal with him when sober as they shall think he deserves. [102]

April 3 (Thursday)
VIRGINIA-CAMP AT ALEXANDRIA
Parole-Canterbury   **(Braddock)**
Field Officer to morrow L[t] Col[o] Burton.
For the Generals Guard 48th Regiment.

The Generals Guard is this day reduced to a Corporal and nine men and the Corporal is to report to the Officer of the main Guard.

Sir Peter Halkets Regiment to receive three days Provisions to morrow. [103]

Camp at Alexandria April 3[d]: 1755   **(Halkett/Disney)**
The Parole is Canterbury
Field Officer for to Morrow Lt Col Burton [104]

(Orme)
On the 3rd of April, the General, Governor and Commodore went to Annapolis (arriving in afternoon) to meet the eastern Governors. The General found no waggons were provided for the Maryland side of the Potomack. He applied to Governor Sharpe, who promised above one hundred, which he said should attend at Rock Creek to carry away the stores as fast as they could be landed.

The General was very impatient to remove the troops from Alexandria, as the greatest care and severest punishments could not prevent the immediate (Immoderate) use of spirituous liquors, and as he was likewise informed the water of that place was very unwholsome: Therefore as the Governors were not arrived, the General returned the 7th to Alexandria for the Congress. [105]

April 4 (Friday)
VIRGINIA-CAMP AT ALEXANDRIA
Parole-Dorsett   **(Braddock, Halkett/Disney)**
Field Officer to morrow Major Sparke.
For the Generals Guard 44th Regimt.

Col[o] Dunbars Regiment to have one Corporal and six men ready to march to morrow at 6 o'clock from Alexandria to Frederick with the Hospital stores they are to carry six days Provisions with them and to

take the Arms and accoutrements with which they are to take the field
Each man to have his Blancket (Blankitt) and 29 rounds of Ammun[n].
Col[o] Dunbars Regiment to have three days provisions to morrow. [106]

April 5 (Saturday)
VIRGINIA-CAMP AT ALEXANDRIA
Parole-London   **(Braddock)**
Field Officer to morrow L[t] Col[o] Burton.
For the Generals Guard 48th Regim[t].

The Tents and clothing for the Virginia Company to be brought on
shore as soon as possible; Their tents are to be pitched the first fair day
after they are on shore.
The Artillery Hospital and Engineers to receive three days provisions
to morrow. [107]

Camp at Alexandria Apl: 5th:1755   **(Halkett/Disney)**
The Parole is London
Field Officer for to Morrow Lieut Col Gage [108]

VIRGINIA-WINCHESTER
April 5th 1755   **(St. Clair)**
Proposal for a disposition for advancing the army from Winchester and
Frederick in Maryland

The two brigades being advanced to Winchester and Frederick and
the artillery to Winchester, a detachment of the Winchester Brigade to
march up with it to Wills's Creek to strengthen the convoy and to
cover it but if the road to be cut from the bridge on the Opeckon Bear
Garden proves passable for the artillery then the artillery shall march
along that road, without coming to Winchester which will save them
nine miles and the detachment from Winchester shall march and join
them at Henry Enoch's, and convoy them to Wills's Creek, as that
road is to be constructed soon a report of it shall be made to the
officer commanding the brigade at Winchester.

A detachment to be sent from the brigade at Frederick to
Conogogee, to cover our flour magazine and to adjust in embarking
the stores; this detachment to be made as soon as may be.

As the removal of the Brigade from Winchester and Frederick to
Wills's Creek, must depend upon the quanity of flour that is to be sent
from Pensylvania; The time for their removal from said place can be

fixed, when a proper quantity of that flour is arrived at Conogogee from whence it may also be any time carried by water up to Wills's Creek , and of this timely notice shall be given to the Commander in chief and to the commanding officer of said Brigade, that they may march immediately when the troops are assembled, and the whole got togeather in readiness to march from Wills' Creek to Fort DuQuesne. The march must be tried for one of the two following routes viz

One through the meadows, and crosses the river Yohiogane, being the route taken by Col. Washington last year and the other must be by turning the head of the river if found practicable the latter most elgible since by taking the former, the french may dispute our passages in crossing the river, and give us the trouble of laying bridges, and making work to cover them. The reconoitering of the latter route shall be set about with the utmost expedition and if found practible the troops now at Wills's Creek may be employed in cutting the road open. They may venture to cut the length of 25 miles before the other troops arrive.

The disposition of marching the army from Wills's Creek may be better defered until the above routes round the head of the Yohioganie is reconsidered, then a disposition shall be made and sent with the report of that route.

The commissary have direction to assemble horses and waggons by the 10th day of May, which is the soonest that horses can have grass and if we cannot march by that time the horses and waggons may be employed in bringing such provisions as may be wanting. [109]

April 6 (Sunday)
VIRGINIA-CAMP AT ALEXANDRIA
Parole-Kinsale   **(Braddock)**
Field Officer for to morrow Maj^r Chapman.
For the Generals Guard 44th Regiment.

All Departments for Duty of every nature whatever are to parade at the Grand Parade and to march from thence, Detachments from different corps to draw up by Seniority.

The Grand Parade for this camp is appointed to be at the head of Sir Peter Halketts Regiment.

A report to be made every morning to Sir Peter Halkets, of the Sergeants, Corporals, Drummers and Private men who are Drunk upon Duty, the Sergeants of the Companies they belong to, to keep an exact Roll of their names, Sir Peter Halkett being determined to put a stop to any more prov^{ns} being drawn for such men. Sergeants, Corporals, Drummers, and Private men who appear Drunk in Camp tho they are not upon duty will have their provisions stop'd for one week.

Sir Peter Halketts Regiment to receive three days Provisions to morrow.

The Detachment from the Ordinarys Dutys of camp to change from Right to left every Day.

AFTER ORDERS

One Sergant, one Corporal, and thirty men are to morrow at 6 o'clock in the morning, to go to Alexandria to assist the Officers of the Artillery in loading the Waggons for Winchester and Shipping of Stores for Rock Creek One Officer and thirty men from Col° Dunbar's Regiment to march to morrow for Rock Creek The Officer to call this night upon Sir Peter Halkett who will give him his instructions. [110]

VIRGINIA-WINCHESTER
April 6th 1755
Sir: General Braddock   (St. Clair)

Herewith transmits to your Excellency the disposition for advancing the troops to Wills's Creek which Wm. Mackellar and I hope meets with your approbation. I have taken all the necessary steps with regard to putting it in Execution by giving instructions to the Commisaries for the assembling together 200 waggons and 2000 horses by the 10th of May next.

I have sent to Alexandria a waggon master for the Regt, he is a young man well recommened and was to have gone as a volunteer with the Army, this may give encouragement for the inhabitants to go with you, there will be two wanting, which the commissaries named for me, the one to go to Maryland, and the other to Pensyllvania to asemble the savages, these may serve for Waggon masters to the train if the officers think proper to employ them, if not they maybe paid off when they have done their work. Mr Commisary Walker is gone to Augusta County for those men and to come down waggons...in ten days to Wills Creek.

Mr. Commisary Duke goes from this to morrow for Fredericksburg to hasten up the Guns, the Cohorns with most of the stores are already arrived we have got the powder safely lodged in very proper places and are preparing a place for the ordnance stores which I hope will be finished by to morrow night, and an account taken of the stores.

I hope that Govr. Dinwiddie will excuse me for taking the float of Nowlands ferry on the Potomack, and sending it to Goose Creek for the passage of our waggons.

We found a great many more things to do here than I had reason to expect, which has detained us a day or two longer from going to see the roads cut, I am in hopes to find them in great fowardness: you shall have the report of them sent to Frederick in Maryland. I am a good deal uneasy that there is no Troops at Conogogee, I beg a Detachment may be sent to that place from Frederick to cover our Magazines, in the mean time I shall stop Capt. Dagworth with half his Company who ought to be on their by this time from Frederick the other half will be wanted at Col. Cresaps for Repairing a Road.

Fifteen Waggons go from hence tomorrow for Alexandria which will serve for the march the first Brigade. I missed your Excellency would be Returned from Annapolis, when the Messinger arrives at Alexandria, I have wrote to Sir Peter Halkett about them. What ever steps are taken I shall aquaint you of it from time to time and shall make your stay at Frederick as short as I can, whatever commands you may have for me, I beg they maybe sent to Wills's Creek.

I need not jolt your Excellencys mind, that money is wanting for every thing, if nothing else can be done, paper money or Maryland must be had otherwise ...our carriages will be at a stop. Please to send up as much as is to be had of it to Mr. Commissary Walker at the fort. I have the honor of being with the greatest Respect. Your excel, most obedient and most humble servant. [111]

Camp at Alexandria Apl: 6th: 1755   **(Halkett/Disney)**
The Parole is Kingsale
Field Officer for to Morrow Major Chapman
All Detachments of Duty of every Nature Are to parade on the Genl Parade And to march from thence. Detachments from Different Corps Draw up by seniority. The genl. Parade for This Camp is Appointed at the Head of Sr Peter Halkett regt. Every morning a report to be made to Sr Peter Halket of the Serjts Corpls Drumrs: & Privit men Who are Drunk upon Duty. One Officer & Thirty Men of Col Dunbars regt. is to March to morrow Morning to Rock creek. The

Offr to Call this night on S[r] Peter Halkett who will give him his
Instructions. [112]

April 7 (Monday)
VIRGINIA-CAMP AT ALEXANDRIA
Parole-Dublin   **(Braddock, Halkett/Disney)**
Field Officer for to morrow L[t] Col[o] Burton.
For the Generals Guard 48th Regim[t].

One Officer one Sergeant and 20 men of Sir Peter Halkets
Regiment to hold themselves in readiness to morrow morning to march
to Winchester the Officer at Retreat beating to call upon Sir Peter
Halkett for his Instructions; They are to take six days provisions with
them, subsistance to the 24th of this month and every thing with which
they are to take the Field.

Every Party ordered to march from camp is to have 24 Rounds per
man.

A Greater number of Women having been brought over than those
allowed by the Government sufficient for washing with a view that the
Hospital might be servd; and complaint being made that a concert is
enterd into not to serve with out exorbitant Wages a Return will be
called for of those who shall refuse to serve for six pence per day and
their Provisions that they may be turnd out of camp and other got in
their places.

Col[o] Dunbars Reg[t] is to rec. 3 Days Prov[n] to morrow. Co[lo]
Dunbar's Regiment is to march at 5 Oclock on Saturday Morning for
Rock Creek. [113]

*Nichols writes: "Army life was regulated by drumbeat, just as today the
bugle call is the most familiar sound at military post and camps. Drumming was a
fine art, and the varied patterns of ruffles and taps ordered the soldiers to
assemble, disperse, advance, retreat, and so on. At drill and parades field music of
the fife and drum animated the men. "To Beat the general" did not signify a
drubbing of the commander but meant the assembled drummers were to beat that
particular call designated for a general assembly of all troops."*

*Nichols writes: "Sixty women were permitted to accompany the
expedition, each of the twenty companies being legally allowed three women...In
the main they were honest hard working, lower class women who were carried "on
the strength" (were issued rations) but received no pay. Many of these were the
legal or common law wives of soldiers in the companies to which they were
assigned. Doubtless they were a course lot, but they bravely followed the army
everywhere except into actual battle and did all the washing, cleaning, sewing,*

mending, and probably much of the cooking for the men. Forty-two of these...females boarded the transports at Cork and the remainder of their quota was to be filled in Virginia".

(Orme)

The General returned the 7th to Alexandria for the Congress (with Dinwiddie and Keppel, Orme and W. Shirley). [114]

April 8 (Tuesday)
VIRGINIA-CAMP AT ALEXANDRIA
Parole-Guilford   **(Braddock)**
Field Officer for to morrow Maj[r] Sparke.
For the Generals Guard 44th Regim[t].

The Quarter Masters of Sir Peter Halketts and Col[o] Dunbars Regiment to meet Mr. Leslie assistant Quarter master General this afternoon at 4 Oclock who will show them their Regimental Store Houses.

The Commanding Officer's of each of the Regim[t] as soon as their Regimental Store Houses are fixed are to order their Officers baggage and their mens stores to be immediately lodgd.

The Soldiers are to leave their Shoulder Belts, Waist Belts and hangers behind and only to take with them to the Field one spare Shirt, one spare pair of stockings, one spare pair of Shoes and one pair of Brown Gater's.

For the future the Generals own and all other Guards are to beat a march to him and the Line is always to turn out when the General passes.

As a mistake has happend in regard to the Commissions of the youngest Subaltern of the Rangers; The Commissions of Second Lieu[t] being deliverd to them instead of Ensigns are to be immediately changd to avoid any Inconvenience, which may arise from disrules of Rank.

His Excellency Gen[l] Braddock Orders that all Ensigns bearing Commissions in any of his Majestys Regiments shall take post of the third Officer in any of the Companys of Ranger's.
AFTER ORDERS

Six Companys of Sir Peter Halketts Regiment are to march for Winchester at 6 o'clock on thursday morning; Upon your arrival at Rock Creek you are either to Encamp or lodge your Men as you shall find most convenient and as fast as the Waggons arrive you are to employ them in the Service of ye Regiment and Regulate your Detachment'^s accordingly and to be particularly careful not to use any more Waggons than are absolutely necessary.

You are to leave at Rock Creek an Officer and 30 men who is to remain there till all the Stores of the Train and Hospital are put into the waggons is then to march and form the Rear Guard of the whole.

You are also to leave at Rock Creek a Subaltern and 20 men who are to wait there till the arrival of M^r. Johnston the paymaster and to Escort him to Frederick.

You will be joined at Rock Creek by an Officer and 30 Seamen who you are to take under your command and give them your Orders and Regulations as they will want some conveyance for their baggage you will dispose of it as you find most convenient.

Upon your arrival at Frederick you are to encamp your men the Troops to remain there till further Orders except a Captn, two Subalterns and 50 men who are to be sent immediately on to Conogogee as a covering Party for the magazines and you are to direct the Commanding Officer of this Detach^t to stop all Waggons which shall br^g in Flower, &c, from Pennsylvania and to send a daily...of the numbers which return you are to remit to me unless you should see Sir Jno St. Clair and that he should have secur'd a sufficient number for Transporting the Stores from Frederick to Wills Creek in such case the Waggons are to be dismiss'd.

You will find provisions at Frederick which you are to issue to your men in the same proportions as at Alexandria and to begin upon it as soon as you have expended the Provisions car^d with you.

You are to direct your Officers to provide themselves as soon as possible with Bat horses as no more Waggons will be allow'd after they get to Frederick. [115]

Camp at Alexandria April: 8th. 1755   **(Halkett/Disney)**
The Parole is G(u)ilford
Field Officer for to Morrow Major Sparks

For the future the Genls: Own & all other Guards to receive Him with a March. And The Line is allways to Turn out when the Genl passes. As a Mistake (h)as (h)append in reguard to ye Commissions of the youngest Sub: of the Rangers, Commissions of Second Lieuts being diliverd them in stead of Ensns: wh(ich): are to be Changed Immediatly, But to a Voide any inconvenincess which may happen from Dispuits of rank His Excellence Genl Braddock Orders that all Ensns: bearing Commissions in any of His Majestys Regts: shall take post of the Third Offr of Any of the Compys of Rangers.

Sr Peter Halkett And Co^l Dunbar Regt: to send a Return Immediately to Doc^r Napp(i)er of the Sick they propose leaving in the Genl Hospital. Sr Peter Halketts & Col Dunbars Regts Immediatly to send to the Major of Brigade a Return of their Effective men fitt for Duty. The Qr Masters of Sr Peter Halketts & Col Dunbars regts to meet Mr. Lesslie Assistant Q:M:G: This afternoon at 4 oClock And he will show them their Regimentall Store houses. The Commanding officers of each Regt: As soon as their Store houses are fixt upon They are to Order Their Officers Baggage And mens Stores to be Lodged Immediately. The Soldiers are to leave their Shoulder Belts Wast Belts & Swords in the Stores And take with them to ye field One spare shirt one ditto stockins & one ditto shoes And one pair of Brown spatter dashes (leggings).

AFTER GENL ORDERS

The whole of the Rangers & light Horse Are to March to Morrow for Winchester. Three waggons will be furnished Them by Applying to Mr Lesslies Assistant Q:M:G: Every man is to be furnished with eight days provisions. As soon as They arrive at Winchester the Commandg: Offr of Companys to privide Their Men with Arms as soon as posable, And to make their Applications to Sr Peter Halkett for their direction. Capt Stewart is to Apply Immeddiately to Sr Peter Halkett for 34 Hangers (short swords) for his men which They are to take with Them.

AFTER GENL ORDERS

Six Companys of Sr Peter Halketts regt are to march for Winchester on Thursday at Six oClock (in the morning). Eight waggons will be Orderd to be at the Head of that Regt: on Wednsday Night for the Tents & Baggage &c of Those Compys. Applycations to be made for Mr Lesslie Assistant Q:M:G: for proper Guid(e). Every man to receve eight days provisions to carry Him. The Lieut Co^l (Gage) is to be left with the four remaining Companys till further Orders. All the Sick Are to be left in the Genl Hospital. The Regts: for the Genl Guard as Usual And the proposion (proportion) of Duty is to be made up by Colonel Dunbars Regt: in the Town & other Guards. [116]

The Virginia troops being cloathed were ordered to march **(Orme)** immediately to Winchester, to be armed, and the General appointed ensign Allen of the 44th to make them as like soldiers as it was possible.

Captain Lewis was ordered with his company of Rangers to Green Briar River, there to build two stockade Forts, in one of which he was to remain himself, and to detach to the other a subaltern and fifteen men. These forts were to cover the western settlers of Virginia from any inroads of Indians.

The soldiers were ordered to be furnished with one new spare shirt, one new pair of stockings, and one new pair of shoes; and Osnabrig waistcoats and breeches were provided for them, as the excessive heat would have made the others insupportable, and the commanding officers of companies were desired to provide leather or bladders for the men's hats. [117]

Dear Sir, (Letter I) **(Br. Officer 3)**

You desire me to let you know the Particulars of our Expedition, and an Account at large of the Nature of the Country, and how they live here; also of the Manner of the Service, and which Corps is the most agreeable to serve in, because it has been proposed to you to strive to buy a Commission here, and that you waited my advice to determine. Dear Sir, I love you so well that I shall at once tell you. I reckon the Day I bought my Commission the most unhappy in my Life, excepting that in which I landed in this Country. As for the Climate, it is excessive hot in summer, and as disagreeably cold in Winter, and there is no Comfort in the Spring; none of those Months of Gentle Genial Warmth, which revives all Nature, and fills every Soul with vernal Delight; far from this, the Spring here is of very few Days, for as soon as the severe Frosts go off, the Heat of the neighboring Sun brings on Summer at once, one Day shall be Frost, and the next more scorching for sultry and faint than the hottest Dog-Day in England. What is excessevely disagreeable here is, that the Wealth of the Country consists in Slaves, so that all one eats rises out of driving and whipping these poor Wretches; this Kind of Authority so corrupts the Mind of the Masters, and makes them so overbearing, that they are the most troublesome Company upon Earth, which adds much to the Uncomfortableness of the Place. You cannot conceive how it strikes the Mind on the first Arrival, to have all these black Faces with grim

Looks round you, instead of being served by blooming Maid Servants, or genteel white Livery Men: I was invited to Supper by rich Planter, and the Heat of the Climate, the dim Light of the Myrtle Wax-Candles, and the Number of black half-naked Servants that attended us, made me think of the infernal Regions, and that I was at Supper with Pluto, only there was no beautiful Proserpine, for the Lady of the House was more like one of the Furies; she had passed through the Education of the College of Newgate, as great Numbers from thence arrive here yearly: Most being cunning Jades, some pick up foolish Planters; this Lady's Husband was far from a Fool, but had married, not only for the Charms of her Person, but because her Art and Skill was quite useful to him in carrying on of his Business and Affairs, many of which were worthy of an adept in the College she came from. Among others he made me pay for my supper by selling me a Horse upon Honour, which, as soon as it was cool, shewed itself Dog-lame and Moonblind.

As for eating, they have the Names of almost every Thing that is delicious, or in Fashion in England, but they give them to Things as little like as Ceasar or Pompey were to the Negros whom they call by those Names. For what they call a Hare is a Creature half Cat, half Rabbet, with white strong Flesh, and that burrows in rotten Trees; they call a Bird to much bigger than a Fieldfare, with hard, dry, strong flesh, hardly eatable, a Partridge. The best Thing they have is a wild Turkey, but this is only in Season one Month in the year; the rest it is hard, strong, and dry. As for Beef, the Months of October and November excepted, it is Carrion, that is to say, so lean as it would not be called Meat in England; their Mutton is always as strong as Goat's Flesh; their Veal is red and lean, and indeed the Heat of the Summer and the pinching frost of Winter, makes all like Pharoah's lean Kine. They brag of the Fruits, that they have such plenty of Peaches as to feed Hogs; and indeed that is true, they are fit for nothing else. I do not remember, among the Multitudes that I have tasted, above one or two that were eatable, the rest were either mealy or choaky. Melons grow in Fields, and are plentier than Pumpkins in England, as large and as tasteless; there are such Quanities that the Houses stink of them; the Heat of the Country makes them at once mellow, so that they hardly ever have the fine racy Taste of an English good Melon, for in England you have many bad melons to one good; but here the Heat makes all Fruits like us young Fellows, rotten before they are ripe. With respect to Fish: they have neither Salmon, Carp, Trout, Smelts, nor hardly any one good kind of Fish: they give the Name of Trout to a white Sea-fish, no more like a Trout than a Cat to a Hare; they have one good, nay excellent Kind of Fish, I mean a Turtle; but as scarce as in England. With respect to public Diversions, the worst English Country Town exceeds all they have in the whole Province. As to Drink, Burgundy and Champaign were scarce ever heard of; Claret they have but poor stuff, tawny and prick'd, for it cannot stand the Heat of Summer, which also spoils the Port; the Madeira is the best Wine they have, but that only of the worst Growths, for the best are sent to Jamaica or England; their only tolerable Drink is Rum Punch, which they swill Morning, Noon, and Night. Their Produce is Tobacco; they are so attached to that, and their Avarice to raise it, makes them neglect every Comfort of Life: But the Intemperance of the Climate affects not only all the cattle, Fruits, and Growth of the Country, but the human Race; and it is rare to see a native reach 50 years of Age. I have heard from the best Judges, I mean the kind hearted Ladies most in Vogue, that a Virginian is as old at 30, as an Englishman at 60. The Ladies I speak of are well experienced, and for most of them the Public have for peculiar Merit paid the Passage, and honoured with an Order for Transporation on Record. I would not deceive you so have told you the Truth; I have not exaggerated, but have omitted many disagreeable Circumstances, such as Thunder Storms, Yellow Fevers, Musketoes, other Vermin, & with which I shall not trouble you. The Ship is just going, my Service to Friends, and believe me to be, Dear Sir, Yours, [118]

Nichols writes: "On April 8, after the general's return from Annapolis, a grand review of all troops took place at the Alexandria encampment. Virginia and Maryland society from miles around witnessed this novel and stirring spectacle, after which the great ladies of the vicinity regaled General Braddock and his staff with many delicacies including "delicious Cake, and potted Wood cocks" (this comes from a letter Washington wrote to Mrs. Fairfax, May 14, 1755)."

April 9 (Wednesday)
VIRGINIA-CAMP AT ALEXANDRIA
Parole-Henry   (Braddock, Halkett/Disney)
Field Officer for to morrow Lt Col^o Gage.
For the General Guard 48th Regimt.

Col^o Dunbrs Regiment to send this forenoon two Sergeants and twenty men to Rock Creek to reinforce the Officer there.

A return to be given in this Day of the two Regiments specifying all extraordinary's that have happened since their embarking in Ireland a monthly return of the two Regiments to be given in to General Braddock every first day of the month-The companys of Rangers Artificers and the Troop of light Horse are to be given in a monthly return at the same time: They are to apply to the Major of Brigade, who will shew them the proper form.

The Officers to see that their men are provided as soon as possible with Bladder or thin Leather to put between the Lining and crown of their hats to guard against the Heat of the Sun.

One Subaltorn Officer of Dunbars Regiment to march to morrow morning to Frederick in Maryland who upon his arrival is immediately to take upon him the command of the several Detachments of the Regiment that are now there or may arrive and he is to see yt (that) they are properly provided and Subsisted. [119]

(Orme)

S[r] Peter Halket with six companies of the 44th marched on the 9th to Winchester, and was to remain there till the roads were completed from thence to Fort Cumberland, and Lieutenant Colonel Gage was left with the other four companies to escort the artillery. [120]

April 10 (Thursday)
VIRGINIA-CAMP AT ALEXANDRIA

Parole-Winchester   **(Braddock)**

A Detachment from the two Regiments of a Subaltern, two Sergeants, two Corporals and 20 men is to remain at Alexandria as a Guard for the Hospital and to march with it to Frederick.

The Generals Guard is to be taken off on Friday. A Sergeant and twelve men of Col[o] Dunbar's Regiment to mount as the Generals Baggage Guard and March with it.

The Provost Marshall is to March with Col[o] d Dunbar's Regiment and to have a guard of a Sergeant and ten men who is to make the rear of the whole. Two Officers and forty men of the four remaining companies of Sir Peter Halketts Regem[t] is to mount the Town Guard till further Orders. [121]

Alexandria Camp April 10th 1755   **(Halkett/Disney)**
The Parole is Winchester

121

A Detachment from the two Regts: of 1 Sub 2 Serjts 2 Corpls & Twenty men is to Remain at Alexandria as a Guard for the Hospital And to March with it to Frederick. The Genls: Guard is to be taken of(f) on Friday, a Serjt & 12 men of Co^l Dunbars to mount as the Genls: Baggage Guard & to March with it. The Provoe Marshal is to March with Co^l Dunbars regt: And to have a Guard of 1 Serjt & ten men who is to make the Rear of the Whole. An Officer And 40 men of the four remain(in)g Compys of Sr Peter Halketts regt: is to Mount the Town Guard till further Orders. Col Dunbars Regt: is to March at 5 oClock on Saterday Morning to Rock Creek. Waggons will be Ordered on Friday to Carry the Baggage And what ever Tents may be struck to the boats destained for their Transportation. And at Daybreak on Saterday Morning Waggons will attend at the Head of the Regt: for the Mens Tents &c &c. A subaltren Officer with 3 Serjts 3 Corpls And 30 men are to be sent on Board the Boats And to help to putt Them on Board And to be as a Baggage Guard. All the Boats upon that part of the River Near Rock Creek Are ordered to Attend to Carry the Troops over. The sick men that are not able to march with the Regt to be left in the Genl Hospital. As Col Dunbars regt marches to morrow they are to Receive 9 Days provisions to Carry with Them. The 4 Compys of Sr Peter Halketts Regt And the Royal Artillery Engineers and hospital are to Continue Receving their provision as Usual till further Orders. [122]

VIRGINIA-ENOCH'S CAMP-CAPAPON RIVER

To: General Braddock   (St. Clair)

The road from Frederick to Wills Creek as I have cut it is as near as going all the way thru Maryland, but I shall do all that lies in my power to get the latter Road opened that we may be able to use the Maryland Waggons in case the water carriage shou'd fail us, I must entreat your Excellency to sent up a Detachment of Conogogee for the Embarking any Stores. [123]

Memorandum for the Commissaries   (St. Clair)

As the Army will be able to take the field by the 10th day of May, the commissaries are directed to assemble two hundred waggons and two thousand horses, at the camp of the British Army at Wills's Creek by that day that they are to take all necessary precaution in providing pack saddles and halters for the horses that they shall first hyer (hire) as many waggons with horses as they can and as many as are short of the above number are to be purchased at the best terms possible and to be in readiness at the time mentioned, but the horses not to be delivered until the...of May. [124]

VIRGINIA-ENOCH'S CAMP-CACAPON RIVER
From Enoch' house on Capecapon River
April 10th 1755
To: General Braddock   **(St. Clair)**

I am obliged to send your Excellency an express to acquaint you that Mr. Mackellar and I have reviewed the road leading from the bridge on the Opeckon to this place and we find it passable for all sorts of carriages. I have decided that 34 teams of horses should be at Alexandria on the 18th for transporting the artillery directly to Wills's Creek for if they were to stop at Winchester it might occasion fresh delay, the artillery may stop a day on the road at Mr. Commissary Dicks plantation to refresh their horses, this is on the road 7 miles on this side of Shannondoah Ferry.

I have not heard of any of the proper persons of the artillery other than being sent to Winchester or Conogogee by that neglect of Crp. Find I was delayed two days at Winchester, and was I to go from hence to Conogogee which is 50 miles, the same thing must happen to me. As I make no doubt but what the commissary officer of artillery has very sufficient reasons for neglecting your orders, I do not apprehend it any business of mine to repair his neglects, especially when I am now making this road passable for the carriages and which I expect will be in order for the artillery hopefully by the 14th having only 16 miles more to cut.

I shall execute your Excellencys command in constructing the road to Fort Du Quesne, but to fix on a time for the accomplishing thereof is not in my power, I have given a meeting to one of the commissioners of Pensylvania on Tuesday...the occasion of it you excellency will see by the letters I enclose, there is no flour arrived as yet from Pensylvania, Mr. Cresop advises me that he expects part of it this week.

The road from Frederick to Wills's Creek as I have cut is so near as going all the way thru Maryland, but I shall do all that is in my power to get the latter road opened that we may be able to use Maryland waggons in case the water carriages...fail us. I must entreat your

Excellency to send up a detachment to Conogogee for the embarking our stores and that you will be pleased to order the artillery to be ready by the time mentioned above.

I should be extremely glad to have the return of the messenger by Tuesday at the fort for I hope the next day to be able to go to reconoiter. I have the honour of going with the greatest respect, Your Excellency.

A great number of the levees of eight brought up by Mr. Dick have a very bad look, some them were brought to me in change (chains) that I must not refuse else...would have taken them;

if they are bad as I apprehend it is a most horrid imposition. [125]

April 10th, 1755   (seaman)

Moderate and fair but sultry weather; to-day we received orders to march tomorrow morning, and 6 Companies of Sir Peter Halket's Regiment to march in their way to Wills's Creek. [126]

MARYLAND-ANNAPOLIS   (Maryland Gazette)

Monday Morning last his Excellency General Braddock, the Hon. Governor Dinwiddie, Commodore Keppel, Capt. Orme, and William Shirely, Esq set off from hence for Alexandria. [127]

April 11 (Friday)

VIRGINIA-CAMP AT ALEXANDRIA

Parole-Kendall   (Braddock)

The Officer of the Town Guard to make his report to the General through an Aid de Camp.

AFTER ORDERS

Col⁰ Dunbar Regiment to hold themselves in readiness but not to march till further Orders.

They are to give their proportion of men for the Guard to morrow; one Sergeant, one Corporal and 12 men to parade immediately at the Town Guard of Col⁰ Dunbars Regiment.

They are to take their Knapsacks, Haversacks, and provisions with them, when they come to the Town Guard the Sergeant is to enquire for M[r]. Leslie assistant Quarter master who will give him Order's.

No Person whatever to press or employ any Waggons without an Order from General Braddock the Quarter master Gen[l] or his assistant.

This Order to be read not only to the Soldiers but to the Officers, Servants and followers of the Army as any one who shall be found guilty of disobeying it shall be severely punish'd.

AFTER ORDERS.

As there are Boats provided to carry Col⁰ Dunbars Regiments Baggage to Rock Creek the former orders relative to their march to be obeyed.

Eight Waggons will be orderd to be at the head of that Regiment on Wednesday night for the Tents, Baggage, &c. of those Companys application is to be made to Mʳ Leslie assistant Quarter master for a proper Guide; Every man is to receive 8 Days Provisions to carry with him. The Lᵗ Col⁰ is to be left with the 8 remaining Companys till farther Order's.

All the sick are to be left in the General Hospital.

The Regiments find the Generals Guard as usual and the proportion of Duty is to be made up by Col⁰ Dunbars Regiment in the Town and other Guards. March Rout of Sir Peter Halketts Regiment from the Camp at Alexandria to Winchester.

	MILES
To yᵉ old Court House	18
To Mʳ Colemans on Sugar Land Run were there is Indian Corn, &c	12
To Mʳ Miners	15
To Mʳ Thompson ye Quaker Wʰ yᵉ is 3000 wt corn	12
To Mʳ They's 17 ye Ferry of Shann	17
From Mʳ They's to Winchester	23
Total	97

If the Bridge should not be laid over the Opeckon Canves will be provided for the Troops.

As soon as the Artillery arrives at Winchester a Detachment of their Regiment and what ever part you shall judge proper of the Rangers must be orderd to march with the Artillery to Wills Creek.

But if the road should be cut from the bridge on the Opeckon to Bear Garden and is made passable for yᵉ Artillery, It is then to go along that Road and not by Winchester and your Detachment from Winchester must join them at Henry Enochs_____, A Report will be made to you whether this road is passable or not.

As the Removal of the Troops from Winchester to Wills Creek must depend upon the Quantity of Flower that is to be sent from

Pennsylvania when a proper Quantity is arrivd you shall receive advice of it. [128]

It has been observed that what we know as Braddock's Road (in today's Alexandria city and Fairfax County) was a route created and used by the nearby local farmers to supply the encampment of Braddock's Army with firewood and fodder and other things the army needed. When the army moved they did not use this route but rather went down a roadway that later became Route 7.

Camp at Alexandria Apl:(11) 1755   **(Halkett/Disney)**
The Parole is Hendell (Kendall)
    The Officers of the Town Guard to make (h)is Report Through An Aid du Camp.
    Col Dunbars regt: to hold Them selves in Readiness but not to March till further Orders. They are not to give Their propotion of men for the Guards to morrow. 1 Serjt 1 Corpl & 12 men of Col Dunbars regt. to parade Immedy: at the Town Guard. They are to take their Napsacks Haversack & prov(ision)s: with Them when they Come to the Town Guard. The Serjt is to Enquire for Mr. Leslie Assistant Q:M:G: who will give him Orders. No person to impress or Employ any waggons without an Order from Genl Braddock, The Q:M:G: or his Assi(s)tant. This Order to be Read not only to the Soldiers but to the Officers, Servts: And the followers of the Army, As Any one who shall be found Guilty of Disobaying it will be Severly punished. W(h)ere as Complaint has been made to the Gen[l] that the soldrs: upon their March get Drunk And Abuse the people of the Country & hert their Horses, It is His Excellencys Orders that all Commissioned Officers Commandg. Detachts: to take perticular Care no such Case of Complaint may be given for the Future And All men so offendg: will be most severly punished. [129]

                                                              (seaman)
    April 11th.-Our orders (yesterdays) were countermanded, and to provide ourselves with 8 days provisions, and to proceed to Rock Creek, 8 miles from Alexandria, in the <u>Seahorse</u> and <u>Nightingale</u>'s boats tomorrow. [130]

April 12 (Saturday)
VIRGINIA-CAMP AT ALEXANDRIA
Parole-Leicester   **(Braddock, Halkett/Disney)**

One Company of Sir Peter Halketts Regim[t] to March to morrow Morning, they are to Parade opposite to the town Guard at 6 oclock where they will be joind by five Waggons belonging to the Artillery, which they are to take under their Escort to Winchester. The Town Guard to be reduced to morrow morning to one Subaltern Officer and thirty men.

M[r] Leslie will take care that there shall be at Sir Peter Halketts Quarter Guard this afternoon 3 Waggons, one for the Companys Tents and Baggage and the other two are to carry ye Regiments Spare arms and Stores.

The Men are to take eight days Provisions with them. [131]

(Orme)

As boats were not provided for the conveying of the stores to Rock Creek, the General was obliged to press Vessels, and to apply to the Commodore for seamen to navigate them. At length with the greatest difficulty they were all sent up to Rock Creek, and an Officer with thirty men of the 48th was sent thither with orders to load and dispatch all the waggons as fast as they came in, and to report every morning and evening to the General the number he had fowarded. He was directed to send a party with every division, and to apply for more men as the others marched: and all the boats upon that part of the river were ordered to assist in transporting over the Potomac the 48th Regiment. [132]

Nichols writes: "Small boats from two frigates were used to carry supplies from Alexandria to Rock Creek and to ferry Dunbar's men across the river."

MARYLAND-ROCK CREEK   (seaman)

On the 12th, agreeably to our orders we proceeded and arrived at Rock Creek at 10 o'clock. This place is 5 miles from the lower falls of Potomack, and 4 miles from the eastern branch of it. Here our men got quarters, and we pitched our tents: found here Colonel Dunbar, whose orders we put ourselves under. [133]

(batman)

We Marched from Alexandria to Rock Creek on this side of the Creek. We Crosed the Portwomack River into Maryland, it (being) here about three hundred yards Over. There was flat (boat) to Carry us Over, this days march being 12 miles. In Crosing this River we lost one man. [134]

127

The man lost as per above drowned in the river after they had arrived at Alexandria by a boat overturning on him at Rock Creek. The Maryland Gazette records another death that occurred when a sailor fell over board from the ship *Fishborne* (Capt. William Tipple) on the Atlantic Ocean crossing and drowned (see Maryland Gazette entry March 13). Another account suggests a sailor fell injuring himself and dying aboard ship. Presumably he fell from the rigging and suffered internal injuries for which he was "bled" with out success.

In colonial days the first solid ground on the marshy north shore of the Potomac, now just north of the Lincoln Memorial, was an out crop of Piedmont rocks which jutted into the River. This feature served as the starting point for surveys establishing property lines for early settlers including patents called "Mexico", "Widows Mite", "Port Royal" and "Jamaica" to name a few. On several old maps, it is labeled "Key of all Keys", and for many years it bore a surveyors benchmark. Its more popular name was Braddock's Rock reportedly because General Braddock and his red-coated soldiers, later accompanied by Lt. Col. Washington, crossed over the Potomac River using ships boats after marching from Alexandria on their way to Fort Duquesne.

Above Mason's island lying in the westward trending Potomac River are three islands being the outliers of the fall line that includes the upper and lower falls of the Potomac. These island called Three Sisters mark the limit of navigation on the Potomac River and are part of the fall line - a significant feature of the land in colonial America as well as later. Rivers and streams that run east from the Appalachians flow across the Piedmont, a rocky plateau, then tumble to the Coastal Plain. The fall line - where Piedmont meet plain and where the water falls - was the end of navigation for ships sailing upstream. At the foot of the falls water mills flourished, capitalizing on water power and the break in transportation forms (ships to wagons), this led to settlement that grew to towns and then to cities.

In time the area of Braddock's Rock became a quarry, it is said to have furnished stone for the foundations of both the White House and the Capitol. Later stone from Braddock's Rock was used in the construction of the Chesapeake and Ohio Canal. About 1832, when the canal was extended below Georgetown to connect with the Washington City Canal, most of what remained of the original outcrop of Braddock's Rock was blasted away. The riverside swamps have long since been filled and the land has been raised above the level of the original surface. All that remains of Braddock's Rock can be seen enclosed in a circular granite-lined well south of the grounds of the old Naval Hospital and adjacent to the approach ramps to the Theodore Roosevelt Bridge. An iron grill covers the top of the well, and a ladder 16 feet long leads down to the rock which is usually covered by several inches of water.

The scene of the Army's crossing of the Potomac is between the southern end of Masons Island (Roosevelt Island) and the northern end of Alexander's Island to across the river to the large outcropping of rock in the vicinity of the mouth of Rock Creek. On landing in Maryland the army off loaded provisions and artillery with stores into sheds and awaited wagons from Maryland to move the supplies and baggage to Frederick. They encamped on the slopes of the large rock *outcropping - this physical feature subsequently was called Camp Hill. Early sources call the large rock mass Braddock's Rock on which was located Camp Hill additionally the feature at the water edge is called Braddock's Rock. This is a boulder that has been located at the bottom of the observation well. If the boulder is Braddock's Rock it is indeed a unique touch stone of Colonial America.*

The Potomac has been greatly filled in here and in Braddock's day the shore line extended well back into the land. Some of the well known modern structures built on this fill include the Kennedy Center for the Performing Arts, the Watergate Office Complex, and the Naval Medical Hospital as well as a network of major highways and bridges. In the 1960's John W. Stepp a Star Staff Writer in a story entitled Braddock Rock to be Spared writes: "The boulder (called Braddock's Rock), in fact, is practically consigned to oblivion as it now rests. If General Braddock; after whom it is named, were to land on it with this troops today-as he is believed to have done in Colonial times-he would have to drop down a 12 foot shaft to reach his target".

Two centuries ago the original rock mass jutted like a natural wharf into deep water of the Potomac River. The Potomac shoreline has steadily moved westward toward Roosevelt Island a distance of several city blocks owing to years of landfill operations".

Braddock's at the bottom of the well is a real touch-stone to the colonial period of American history here in the Nation's capital.

Elsewhere in BRADDOCK ROAD CHRONICLES John St. Clair in one of his letters indicates that sheds were constructed at or near the mouth of Rock Creek for the storage of army supplies and munitions.

April 13 (Sunday)
VIRGINIA-CAMP AT ALEXANDRIA
Camp at Alexandria April 13th: 1755   **(Braddock, Halkett/Disney)**
The Parole is Marlbourough [135]

On the 13th of April, the Governors arrived   **(Orme)**
at Alexandria, and with them Colonel Johnston. [136]

VIRGINIA-CAMP ON CAPAPEHON
April 13, 1755   **(St. Clair)**
To: Misters Cocke and Jones

I have this monemt received an express from his Excellency General Braddock complaining that the country people are very dolatory in sending their waggons and teams of horses for our artillery and stores which are lying at Alexandria this is the only thing that...I hope you have sent down the waggons for their 2nd loading but I am sorry to acquaint you that the number which were to have gone down last trip are far short of what I expected.

I am now to acquaint you that 53 waggons are immediatley wanted to be at Alexandria and 24 teams of horses with their harness' besides the 34 teams of horses I ordered Mr. Dick to send down. I would not have the country people plead that they have then ground to plough, this service of the King and country, must be first done, and the people who have their waggones employ'd will soon earn money enough to purchase horses for labor.

You are therefore to warn all the waggoners in the country for his majestys service, the numbers mentioned above to be sent to Alexandria and the others are to load stores at Winchester for the fort taking the road by H. Enoch's and crossing the Potomack at the mouth of the south Branch. Should any one of the inhabitants refuse to go on this service you are to let me know their names that I may apply to Sir Peter Halkett for a Detachment of our soldiers to be Quartered on them, and you may take my word for it that if these people do not go on this service with their Waggons and horses I shall convince them that they had better drawn up our Artillery gratis for Alexandria and been yoaked in place of their horses. [137]

VIRGINIA-CAMP WEST SIDE OF CACAPEHON
April 13th 1755   (St. Clair)
Dear Sir: Richard Orme

I have received yours by an express concerning waggons and horses for transporting the artillery here. I a letter I sent to General Braddock of the 10th I told him what I had done upon that head, but I now find the demands increased and all I can do for this is to persue the steps that I have already taken with diligence and perseverance. I was very well aware of the difficulty we should labour under in regard to the artillery, and therefore look any measures accordingly, but if the commanding officer of that corps and the commissary expect to have their artillery and stores march together, I think they must be disappointed unless they stay until the gear goes up, for I am very well informed that one fourth part of the horses in the country are not ready for the service, I therefore think that the most expeditious method will be to take waggons as they can get them to Wills's Creek. It may indeed be attended with the inconveniency of misplacing a few things or perhaps or perhaps a few, but this I think cannot come in competition, with the dispatch required. I shall however use my endeavours to get as many of them as I can.

I shall order down twenty four teams with harnesses and as many waggons as can be got; when they march they are to proceed by the new road from Opepekon Bridge straight to Wills's Creek and not to go to Winchester.

I told General Braddock between this place and the South Branch would be finished by to morrow night, but I find it will require three or four days more which is the reason of my having stay'd here so long but even that line will be seen enough for their march, the directions in your letter with regard to Sir Peter Halkett and the rangers I shall take caution follow.

I shall be at Wills's Creek on Tuesday next to keep my appointment with the commissioner from Pensylvania which was for that or this day so..., and receive their report with regard to the road to be cut over Laurel Ridge; the report must determine the time of my waiting upon the General at Frederick and if proves favorable, I shall venture to wait upon him, and Mr. Mackellarr and Gordon will undertake to reconitre that road and I shall order them a proper party for their escort on the road to Fort du Quesne which I mean to reconitre before, and...our crossing of the Monongahela and Yoghiogany. If his Excellency does not approve of this, you'll please to let me know by express. I am etc.

P.S. Please to employ all the smiths at Frederick to make the following particulars

Felling axes 100
Horse shoes   10
Whipsaws   12
Miners tools 3 sets breaking and blowing rock [138]

VIRGINIA-CAMP WEST SIDE OF CACAPEPON
April 13th 1755   (St. Clair)
Sir: Peter Halkett

As the road from Opechon Bridge to Wills's Creek with one going to Winchester will be opened in 2 or 3 days, you are to send a detachment of the brigade under our command to Henry Enoch's at that place and to remain here until the artillery arrives from Alexandria and upon their arrival they are to join and escort them to Wills's Creek your detachment may march upon the 22nd instant their first days march to Pottes' and the 2nd to his place. Fifteen days provisions beside the 5 days provisions which they carry will probably be necessary to bring them to Wills's Creek. You shall be acquainted when things are in readiness at that place for marching the remainder of your brigade.

There are some arms belonging to this country in store at Winchester which will probably be taken for the use of your and Col. Dunbars Regiments those that are loose are in very bad repair, and if you will be so good as to employ your armourers while you remain at Winchester to put them in order it will be an acceptable service, and they shall be then fully paid for their trouble I am with the greatest regard. [139]

VIRGINIA-CAMP ON CACAPAPON
April 13th 1755   (St. Clair)
Sir: Officer Commanding the Artillery

As the road from the bridge on the Opechon to Wills's Creek will be open before you come to receive this, You are to take that road with the artillery without touching at Winchester, the waggons with stores are to proceed directly to Wills's Creek in the same manner.

You will find a detachment of Sir Peter Halketts Regiment at that place, who will stregthen your convoys and leave them at Wills's Creek. I am [140]

VIRGINIA-ALEXANDRIA
April 13th 1755   (Orme)
Dear Sir John St. Clair:

The General received your express at 4o'clock to day and has directed me to inform you it gives him much satisfaction some horses are ordered to come to this place tho the number mentioned is insufficient for the conveyance of the train, in a letter I despatched to you dated the 11th, I have laid before you the state of wagons and horses which it is desired you will supplly with all expedition as it retards the service very much not being able to remove the artillery from this town, and care must be taken to provide carriages for the removal of those stores already sent to Winchester from the artillery and one was ordered to Conogogee, who...upon the road but is now proceeding. I beg you will remember to inform Sir Peter Halkett of your resolutions to march the train wide of Winchester, I am Dear sir your most hum.& obed serv. [141]

MARYLAND-ROCK CREEK   (seaman)

On the 13th:-We were employed in getting the Regiment Stores into Waggons, in order to march tomorrow: This is a pleasant situation, but provisions and everything dear. [142]

Sunday April the 13th   **(batman)**
   We halted and had divine service. [143]

April 14 (Monday)
VIRGINIA-CAMP AT ALEXANDRIA
Parole-Oxford   [144]   **(Braddock)**

Camp at Alexandria April 14th: 1755   **(Halkett/Disney)**
The Parole is Oxford   [145]

April 14th   **(St. Clair)**
   I am informed that some of the country people upon Goose Creek and Broad Run have not sent their waggons to Alexandria according to orders, this you can be informed of at Davis's 4 miles beyond Quaker Thompson's and if it is true, I should be glad if you would send orders to your next Division to quarter some soldiers on them at first pass until the whole are past.
                         I am Sir
Sir Peter Halkett or officer commanding the Brigade at Winchester. [146]
                                                                 (Orme)
   On the 14th a Councell was held at which was present General Braddock, Commodore Keppel, Governor Shirley, Lieut. Govr Delancy, Lieut. Govr Dinwiddie, Lieut. Govr Sharpe, Lieut Govr Morris. At this council the General declared to them his Majesty's pleasure that the several assemblies should constitute a common fund for defraying in part the expences of the expedition.
   He showed them the necessity of cultivating a friendship and alliance with the Six Nations of Indians, and asked their opinion if Colonel Johnson was not a proper person to be employed as a negotiator, also what presents they judged proper, and how they should be furnished. (comments on North America military strategy)
   The Governors said, they had severally applied to their respective assemblies to establish a common fund, but could not prevail.
   They were of opinion it was necessary to make a treaty with the Six nations. That Mr Johnson was the properest man to negotiate it, and

They were of opinion it was necessary to make a treaty with the Six nations. That Mr Johnson was the properest man to negotiate it, and that eight hundred pounds should be furnished by the several governments to be laid out in presents for them. (comments on military strategy on Lake Ontario)

The three Governments of Virginia, Maryland, and Pennsylvania were to bear the expense of any additional works at Fort Du Quesne, they were to maintain the Garrison, and also to pay for any vessels that it should be found necessary to construct upon the Lake Erie. (comments on military strategy in New York Mr. Johnson to the Six Nations Speech in the Generals name).

The business of the Congress being now over, the General would have set out for Frederick, but few waggons or teams were yet come to remove the Artillery; He then sent an Express to Sr John St Clair informing him of it, and in a few days set out for Frederick in Maryland leaving Lieutenant Colonel Gage with four Companies of the 44th regiment, who was ordered to dispatch the powder and artillery as fast as any horses or waggons should arrive, taking care to send proper escorts with them. The General at Rock Creek called for a return of the stores, and gave orders for such as were most necessary to be first transported, and for some of the provisions, ordnance, and hospital stores to be left there, the waggons coming in so slow as to render it impossible to convey the whole to Fort Cumberland in proper time. [147]

MARYLAND-BEYOND ROCK CREEK   (seaman)

On the 14th:-We began our march at 6, and were ordered with our detachment to go in front, and about 2 o'clock at one Lawrence Owens, 15 miles from Rock Creek, and 8 miles from the upper falls of Potomack; and encamped upon good ground. [148]

The Owen Ordinary site is located modern-day Rockville, Maryland.

Munday April the 14th   (batman)

We Marched to larance Owings (Lawrence Owens') or Owings Oardianary, a Single House, it being 18 miles and very dirty. [149]

April 15 (Tuesday)
VIRGINIA-CAMP AT ALEXANDRIA
Parole-Petersborough [150]   **(Braddock)**

Alexandria Camp April 15th: 1755   **(Halkett/Disney)**
The Parole is Peterbourough [151]

MARYLAND-BEYOND ROCK CREEK   **(seaman)**
    On the 15th:-Marched at 5 in our way to one Dowden's a Public-
house 15 miles from Owen's, and encamped upon very bad ground on
the side of a hill. We got our tents pitched by dark, when the wind
shifted from the South to the North - from a sultry hot day it became
excessively cold, and rained with thunder and lightning till about 5 in
the morning, when in 10 minutes it changed to snow, which in 2 hours
covered the ground a foot and a half. [152]

Tuesday April the 15th.   **(batman)**
    We Marched to Dowdans (Dowdens's) Oardianary, it Beeing 16
Miles, the Night being very wet and Bad with Thunder and Rain and
the Next Morning a great Quantity of Snow Oblig,d us to halt their.
The day following being Wednesday, April 16, the Snow Being so
Vialent that we where oblig'd to Beat it of(f) the Tents several times
for fear it should Breck the Tent Pools. [153]

April 16 (Wednesday)
VIRGINIA-CAMP AT ALEXANDRIA
Parole-Rochester [154]   **(Braddock)**

Alexandria Camp April 16th: 1755   **(Halkett/Disney)**
The Parole is Queen-Town
    A detachment of S[r] Peter Halketts Regt Consisting of 1 Lieut & 30
men to parade to morrow at 6 oClock in the (morning) at the head of
the Train And to march with all Dispach with Seven Waggons of
powder to Wills's Creek According to The foll(ow)ing March route.
The men Are to take 10 Days provs: One waggon will be sent to ye
head of the Remainying Compys for the mens Tents & Officers
Baggage And what so ever else may be put in to Compleat it to the
Common Load of 2000 is to be done. [155]

VIRGINIA-WINCHESTER   **(Halkett/Disney)**

Sir: John St. Clair, Quarter Mastr. Gen.

Yesterday about eleven, I received your letter one mile on this side of the Bridge they are making, you letter concerning the waggons who have not gone down to Alexandria I sent foward to the Officer commanding the secnd division of my Regiment.

Let me know if one Capt. and two Subalterns with fifty men will be a sufficient escort for the artillery, or if I should order a stronger party, the number of the artillery you expected. I have not heard and canot judge exactly what the escort should be, if the artillery is to be in Brigades, different escorts will be proper, agreeable to the advice I have from you, I shall be directed, all parties shall have fifteen days provisions, besides those that they shall carry.

On Thesday, I shall send off the company of Virginia Rangers who are under orders to march, and they shall have the above provisions with them, upon the 22nd the Escort shall march.

The arms you mention, I shall enquire if there are people among us who can repair them. I shall set them to work after I have some of my own arms repaired.

I have received orders from Britain to augment my regiment with ten Sergents, ten corporals and three hundred men, if I can raise them. I shall have ten additional officers. I wish that you would pick me a few recruits. I have listed five today at one pistole and a dollar and half a dollar to the man who brings a man.

Capt. Stewart hears that you have brought up a considerable number of horses, out of which his troop is to be mounted, he wants to know if it is...if he should or should not buy up horses. Capt. Stewart want to know who he is to apply to for harnesses.

That troop has only got swords, let me know how they are to be provided with other arms and accoutrements fit for a troop, here and at Alexandria there is no leather proper to make bucketts of. Directions must be given for having it from some other place, if he must order the buying of it he wants to know what will be appropriate quanity, by express let me have your answer to the above paricular, and favor me with what besides may ocure to you. Col. Walgrave has got General St. Georges Dragoons, the Seventh and Ninth Regiments of Foot are ordered to Britain and are to be augmented to the British establishment.

I am, sir your most obedient and humble serv. Peter Halkett

Let me know if the officers must have forrage here, or must buy in the country. [156]

VIRGINIA-ALEXANDRIA

Dear Sir John: (Orme)

We have a general want of wagons but particularly on this side. The team demand besides the wagons already sent to Winchester 53 for these plans and 212 horses eighty of which must be furnished with harnesses for the conveyance of their own carriages and ordnance 19 more are wanted for the remainder of Sir Peter Halketts Regiment and baggage and for the clothing of the Rangers, as the whole service is absolutely with this dificiency, the General orders me to inform you of this and desires you will find out some expedient to supply them, and with the greatest expedition.

Sixty wagons are absolutley necessary on the Maryland side. I have applied by the General direction to Governour Sharp who has improved some but any short of the compliment he is expected here tomorrow and his Excellency will again urge him to use every method to procure more, the General has ordered the march of Col. Dunbar's Regiment on Saturday next and a party of a captain and fifty to Conogogee agreeable to your desire, this officer has his Excellency's instruction to retain all those Pensylvania teams to assist us in our march to Wills's Creek, if you have already secured sufficient number for that purpose please to contradict this order.

The rangers foot and horse are gone for Winchester, two wagons start to day with part of their cloths, the General begs of you to give your order for arming and clothing them and to hasten Capt. Stewart in the purchase of his horses that they may be all ready to join you at Wills's Creek and also to provide the serjents of Sir Peter Halketts with firelocks and send a quantity of arms to Wills's Creek for Col. Dunbar's sergents and to furnish whatever recruits which are ordered to be brought to Wills's Creek with an intent to compleat the two regiments to a thousand each in just...of some instructions the General has lately received.

Sir Peter Halkett has received from his Excellency march routes described in your letter and Sir Peter is ordered to remain at Winchester till he receives directions to continue his march, this you will please to relate and also to inform him of the road is cut from the bridge on the Opeckon that he may regulate his detachment accordingly.

For God's sake my dear Sir John prepare everything as fast as possible for our march. I own I fear no thing but the want of horses and carriages, I wish you may be able to provide a sufficient number, I am convinced if there is any deficiency we shall owe it to the impossibility of procuring horses and carriage.

The General proposes leaving this place on Tuesday next, I hope you will let us see you very soon at Frederick many measures of consequence remaining yet to be settled.

His Excellency desires his compliments and I am your most ob. and hum. serv. Robt. Orme [157]

VIRGINIA-WINCHESTER

To: Governor Morris   (Croghan)

He (John St. Clair) stormed like a Lyon Rampant. He said our commission...should have been issued in January last upon his first letter...that the want of a Road and the Provisions promised by Pennsylvania had retarded the expedition...that instead of marching to the Ohio he would in nine days march his Army into Cumberland County to cut the Roads, press Horses, Wagons, etc.; that he would not suffer a Soldier to handle an axe, but by fire and Sword oblige the Inhabitants to do it...that he would kill all kind of Cattle, carry away the Horses, burn the Houses...(He) told us to go to the General if we pleased, who would give us ten bad words for one that he had given. [158]

MARYLAND-BEYOND ROCK CREEK   (seaman)

On the 16th:-On account of the bad wether, we halted to-day, though a terrible place, for we could neither get provisions for ourselves, nor fodder for our horses, and as it was wet in the Camp it was very disagreeable, and no house to go into. [159]

April 17 (Thursday)
VIRGINIA-ALEXANDRIA
Parole-Queen Town [160]   (Braddock)

Camp at Alexandria April 17.1755   (Halkett/Disney)
The Parole is Rochester [161]

MARYLAND-FORT AT WILLS'S CREEK

Sir: Peter Halkett   (St. Clair)

Last night I arrived at this place after having been on the road a week to make them passable on my coming to this place I found every thing in the situation I left it in, that is to say not any one thing done which I had ordered and what is worse, the Pensylvanians have disappointed us in cutting their roads and sending us their flour.

I am under necessity of going to Frederick Maryland to General Braddocks to see if he will march a party of the 2nd Brigade into that province to...wagons loaded with flour, otherwise our expedition must be at a stop. I am able to do but little without some of your regiment at this place. I have now ordered 100 men to cut the road which I expected would have been finished before now and shall want a great many men to work on the two bridges that are to be laid, and must have a strong detachment to go with the Ingeniers to reconoitre the road to Fort Du Quesne. All this I must affect without a strong detachment from you, and if I had men enough of the Independent Company and Virginia forces I have no one officer I could depend on for seeing my orders executed on my absence. You see Dear Sir Peter in what a dismal situation I am, which you can only remedy by coming up here with the corps leaving a detachment at Winchester or by you remaining at Winchester and sending up your Lt. Col. with a large detachment to this place.

The road is to Henry Enoch's 2 days march as before.
From Henry Enoch's to the Spring 9 miles
From the Spring to Col. Cresop's 18 miles, at the mouth of the South Branch you pass the Potomack
From Col. Cresop's to the Camp at Wills's Creek 11miles.

I must remain here until, I receive the return of the express from General Braddock which I expect to morrow, I shall leave my opinion in waiting of what steps I think ought to be taken for carrying on our Expedition. I found this place both destitute of charcol and plank. People seem surprised that I stand in need of the latter. I am

P.S. I beg you would get your amourers to cut a sufficient quantity of Virginia arms for the horse Rangers and give our firelocks and bayonets...in store for your sarjents. [162]

MARYLAND-TOWARD FREDERICK (seaman)

On the 17th:-Marched at 6 on our way to Frederick's Town, 15 miles from Dowden's; the roads this day were very mountainous. After going 11 miles, we came to a river called Mouskiso, which empties itself into the Potomack; it runs very rapid, and after hard rain is 13 feet deep: we ferried the Army over there in a flatt for that purpose, and at 3 o'clock arrived at the town, and put our men and ourselves into quarters, which were very indifferent. This town had not been settled above 7 years, and there are about 200 houses and 2 churches, one English, one Dutch; the inhabitants, chiefly Dutch, are industrious but imposing people: here we got plenty of provisions and forage. [163]

According to records in the Montgomery County Historical Society Library the road being used by Braddock's Army north of the mouth of Rock Creek in 1755 antedates its use by the Army by almost a century. The route being high ground away from the lower wet land was a natural forest route and as settlers took up the land they used this Indian track as a boundary for their land petitions. In 1712 the road was authorized to "run to the upper land of Rock Creek" which means a continuous road from the Potomac to the Monocacy. Patents of land in 1748 then refer to the route as The Rock Creek Main Road.

Thursday April the 17th (batman)

We marched to Frederick. 4 miles this side of Frederick We crossed the River Menurcus (Monocacy), it being a hundred yards Over and only one flat made the Baggage so late before it got Over that we was Oblig'd to lay in Quarters that Night, it being 16 miles in a Pleasant fine Cuntry. [164]

PENNSYLVANIA-PHILADELPHIA (Pennsylvania Gazette)
April 17, 1755
Williamsburg March 13

By an express from Hampton, we are advised that yeasterday morning arrived the Balfey-Capt. Casteton, in whom income passenger Mr. Johnston, Paymaster General of the Forces; who has brought with him sixteen Thousand Pounds Stirling.

Annapolis April 3

This afternoon arrived in Town, from Virginia, his Excellency General Braddock, the Honorable Governor Dinwiddie, Commmodore Keppell, and a good many other gentlemen.

Annapolis April 10

Monday morning left his Excellency General Braddock, the Honorable Governor Dinwiddie, Commodore Keppel, Capt. Orme, and William Shirlely, Esq. set off from hence to Alexandria.[165]

On April 17, 1755, the Maryland Gazette carried a long story on the two Independent Companies from New York and their movement to Wills's Creek. This was addressed: To the Printers of the Pennsylvania Gazette. It is not included here for reason of economy.

April 18 (Friday)
VIRGINIA-ALEXANDRIA
Parole-Salisbury [166]   **(Braddock)**

Alexandria Camp April 18th: 1755   **(Halkett/Disney)**
The Parole is Salsbury [167]

MARYLAND-FREDERICK   **(Orme)**
On the 18th, the 48th Regiment marched to Frederick in Maryland. Colonel Dunbar was ordered to send one company to Conegogee to assist in fowarding the stores from thence to Fort Cumberland, and to remain with the Corps at Frederick till further orders. Thirty more men were ordered to be left with the Officer at Rock Creek.

The sick men of the two regiments, Artillery, and Virginia Companies, were left in the Hospital at Alexandria, and an Officer and twenty men were ordered for its guard and escort. At this place a General Court Martial was held, of which Lieutenant Colonel Gage was president; the prisoner was ordered one thousand lashes, part of which was remitted, and at this place the troops were also mustered.[168]

(seaman)

On the 18th:-At 10 the drums beat to arms, when the Army encamped at the North end of the town, upon good ground: we got our tents pitched and lay in the camp, and the Sutler dieted us here: orders came for us to buy horses to carry our baggage, as there will be no more waggons allowed us. We found here an Independent Vessel belonging to New York under command of Captain Goss. [169]

The last sentence is totally out of context. It refers to FREDERICKSBURG, Virginia a colonial seaport. In September the seamen marched to FREDERICKSBURG to board ship for Hampton, Virginia (see seaman entry for August 11).

Hough writes: "In Frederick the campsite was said to be near the
Washington Street School, and Braddock's headquarters was on West All Saint's
Street in the leading tavern of the town".(Winchester-Frederick County Historical
Society)

Nichols writes: "In Frederick there were 200 houses built by Germans
from the Palatinate".

Fryday April ye 18th   **(batman)**
    We Incamped by the town and one Company of Grannadiers
Marched to Cunnecoejeg (Conococheague/Williamsport) to keep a
pass and there to Remain till we Came. [170]

Conococheague is the place near the mouth of Conococheague Creek
being also a good crossing place of the Potomac River. At this place the Potomac
is wide and without major current. The Great Philadelphia Wagon from Lancaster
southward in the Valley of Virginia uses this crossing and antedates Braddock's
Army by many years. The plan was to move artillery supplies and provisions by
wagon from the mouth of Rock Creek on the Potomac River to Conococheague
Creek and then beyond to use floats all the way to Fort Cumberland. This solved
the problem that the Potomac river was not navigable for a good distance
beginning with Alexandria Falls (the Fall Line from Three Sisters Islands at
Georgetown also known as Little Falls to further up river at Great Falls of the
Potomac River).

April 19 (Saturday)
VIRGINIA-ALEXANDRIA
Parole-Tamworth   **(Braddock)**
    The commanding Officer of the Artillery to apply to M^r. Leslie for
a Store House to lodge their new cloathing in, and the Officers are to
see that their men comply with the Orders of the 8th of Ap^l (viz) to
leave their Shoulder Belts waist Belts and Hangers behind, and are
only to take with them to the field one spare shirt one spare pair of
stockings and one spare pair of shoes and one pair of brown Gaters. [171]

Sir: Robert Napier   **(Braddock)**
    I had the pleasure of writing to you from Williamsburg last March
by a Vessel which was to sail in about a Weeks time, and have since
sent the Duplicate by another. Mr. Shirley with the other Northern
Governors met me at this place last Week, we then settled a plan for
the operations in these parts: Govr Shirley lay'd before me the

Measures concerted between him and Gov' Lawrence for repelling the French from their new Encroachments on the Bay of Fundi, which I approv'd of, and immediately sent orders to Lt. Colonel Monckton to take up on him that Command and carry it into execution. I also settled with the Governors present a plan for the Reduction of Crown Point, which is to be undertaken by provincial Troops alone, rais'd in the Northern Colonies to the Number of about four thousand four hundred to be commanded by Col. Johnson a person particularly qualify'd for it by his knowledge of those parts, his great Influence over the Six Nations and the universal opinion they have of him in the Northern Colonies: I am to supply him with an Engineer. I propos'd of Colonel Shirley to go in person to attack the Fort at Niagara; He express'd the greatest Readiness to engage in it; I therefore order'd him to take his own Regiment which is compleat, and Sir William Pepperell's which will probably be so too by the time he wants them, and to proceed upon it as soon as possible with my Orders to reinforce the Garrison at Oswego with two Companies of Sir William Peperell's and the Effectives of the two Independent Companies at New York, and to put the Works in such Repair as to preserve the Garrison and secure his Retreat and Convoys. Col Shirley apply'd to me to put the two American Regiments upon the same footing as to their provisons with those to the Northward and Southward telling me that from the general Discontent of the Men he was apprehensive of a Mutiny, they being put under Stoppages for their provisions, when the other receive them as a Gratuity. I therefore directed him to give them the same Allowance as the two Regiments, as the Service requir'd their immediate Aid, and might suffer by this Discouragement, and indeed I must say that a Soldier here should have every Advantage as their Fatigue is very great and their pay not near sufficient in the dear and desolate Country. I shall set out to morrow for Frederick in my way to Fort Cumberland at Wills's Creek, where I shall join the two Columns which are now upon ther March at about fifty Miles distance: This Disposition I was oblig'd to make for the Conveniency of Horses and Waggons, by which means I employ those of Maryland which would not be prevail'd upon to cross the Potomack. I have met with infinite Difficulties in providing Carriages &c for the Train nor am I as yet quite relieved from one, a great part still continuing here which has delay'd me for some time; I shall get them dispatch'd tomorrow or next day. I am impatient to begin my March over the Mountains, which in my last I told you were fifteen Miles over, tho' I now know them to be between sixty and seventy, about half way are those Meadows which are not very large, where the French attack's our people that were under Washington. I am to expect Numberless Inconveniences and Obstructions from the total want of dry Forage from the being oblig'd to carry all our provisions with us which will make a vast Line of Baggage and which tho' I reduce as much as possible will nevertheless occasion great Trouble and retard me considerably. I have found it absolutely necessary to appoint eight Ensigns to the two Regiments to act without pay 'till Vacancies shall happen; The Nature of the Country made this Step unavoidable as I am oblig'd to make a Number of small Detachments with every one of which the Service requires an Officer, and without this Expedient the Regiments must have sometimes been left without a sufficient Number of Subalterns. As I have and shall find it often necessary to oblige the Men to take with them seven or eight days provisions, it being frequently impossible to supply them by the great distance from one Magazine to another, in order to enable them to carry; any additional Weight I have lighten'd them as much as possible, and have left in store their Swords and the greatest part of their heavy Accoutrements. I have also made a Regulation which I think will be of great Advantage in posting every Officer in time of Service to his own Company and ordering the oldest Battalion Company to act as Second Grenadier Company upon the left, by which means the eight Companies form so many Firing or sixteen platoons as I shall find necessary commanded by their respective Officers: I was induc'd to make this Regulation on account of the additional Recruits that the Officers and Men might know one another, which by Companies they might easily do, but by Battalion scarcely possible; and in case of Alarm the Men and Officers will know their respective post sooner than by the usual Method. I have receiv'd His Majesty's orders for the Augmentation and immediatley sent an Express to Govr Lawrence who is about seven hundred Miles off to acquaint him of it, and form the spirit and Military Turn of the Northern Colonies I don't doubt of his raising his Numbers, but I fear it will be long before I can compleate these two Regiments as I meet with but few Recruits and those very indifferent. I have not even yet quite compleated them to seven hundred: I have great promises, what the performances will be a little time will shew. The officers and Men of these two Regiments behave well and shew great Spirit and Zeal for the Service, which will be a good Example to the rest. I shall go against the Forts upon the Ohio with a smaller Number of Men that I at first intended because I would not weaken the force destin'd for the Attack of Niagara, but I can't help flattering myself with Success as the plan which I have inclos'd to Mr. Fox, and which I presume you will see, takes in all the considerable Encroachments the French have made upon His Majesty's Dominions in America, in the most important parts in the attacking of which if we succeed it appears to me very evident that the Colonies will be effectually secur'd from all future Encrochments if they chuse it. I have been greatly disappointed by the neglect and supineness of the Assemblies of those provinces, with which I am concern'd; they promis'd great Matters and have done nothing whereby instead of forwarding they have obstructed the Service. When I get to Wills's Creek I will send you an exact account of my numbers and exact Returns of the whole, it being impossible to do it regularly now we are so divided: Also whatever other Information or Intelligence I shall get there, it being impracticable to get any here, the people of this part of the Country laying it down for a Maxim, never to speak Truth upon any account, I beg my humblest Duty to His Royal Highness and believe me to be with the greatest sincerity, Your most Humble and most Obedient Servant,   E. Braddock   Alexandria April 19, 1755

PS. I have appointed Captain Morris of Dunbar's my other Aid de Camp, and have given the Major of Brigade's Commission to Captain Halket, at Sir John St. Clair's Recommendation. [172]

Sir: Duke of Newcastle   **(Braddock)**
...my contingent account will be much greater than I had persuaded myself, or than, I believe, Your Grace imagines; not only as several articles expected from the provinces must be comprehended in it, but from the excessive service of labor, the great number of stores, wagons, boats, etc., and innumerable other circumstances peculiar to the nature of the service in America...[173]

Camp at Alexandria April: 19th: 1755   **(Halkett/Disney)**
The Parole is Tamworth
    The Commanding Officers of Artillery to Apply to Mr. Leslie for a Store house for Their New Cloathing And the Officers Are to see their men compl y with the Orders of the 8th of April (Viz) to leave their shoulder Bellts & Wast Bellts And hangers behind And only are to

take with Them to the field one spair Shirt one spair pair of shoes And one pair of Brown Gaters. [174]

MARYLAND-FREDERICK   **(seaman)**
On the 19th:-The weather here is very hot in the day, but the nights are very unwholesome, occasioned by heavy dews. [175]

Satterday April the 19th.   **(batman)**
We Rested in Camp and Rec'd two days provisions and forige and whiped 4 men, one for Diserting, the Other(s) for getting Drunk - which they rec'd two hundred lashes apiece. [176]

April 20 (Sunday)
VIRGINIA-ALEXANDRIA
Camp at Alexandria April 20th: 1755   **(Halkett/Disney)**
The Parole is London
The men of Col Dunbars regt: left at Alexandria to Guard the Genl Hospital Are to furnish a Centry to it. Any Soldrs that shall be found selling Liquors to any of the Rest of the men will be severly punished. Any Soldiers Wife that shall be detected in the same shall likewise be punished & Drummed out of the Camp. [177]

MARYLAND-FREDERICK   **(seaman)**
On the 20th:-A guard turned out to receive the General. [178]

Sunday April the 20th.   **(batman)**
We Expected the Gen[l] (Braddock) but he did not Come. This town in general is inhabited by the Germans and a fine Cuntry, Plenty of Corn and Milk, here Being two Churches, the English and the Germans. The town have Been in Building only seven years. [179]

There is no entry in the General's Orderly Book this day as he was on the road to Frederick, Maryland.

April 21 (Monday)
MARYLAND-FREDERICK
Parole-Dunbar [180]   **(Braddock)**

ALEXANDRIA-VIRGINIA ^(Halkett/Disney)

(Halkett/Disney)

Camp at Alexandria April 21th: 1755

The Parole is Grantham

A Corpl & six men of Sr Peter Halketts Regt: to parade at the Head of the Train to morrow Morning at 4 oClock. They Are this Night to Recive 10 days provisions & to have 14 Days pay along with Them. They are to take every thing with them They intend for the field. The Corpl to give perticular directions that none of his men snap their firlocks or suffer Them or the Waggoners to smoke & during the Whole March to be perticuler Carefull that no fire is made or brought near the Waggons on Any Acct. what so ever. [181]

MARYLAND-FREDERICK ^(Orme)

(Orme)

Upon the General's arrival at Frederick, he found the troops in great want of provision, no cattle was laid in there; The General applied to Governor Sharpe, who was then present, for provision and waggons, but so little is the Authority of a Governor in that Province, that he afforded the General no Assistance; Upon which the General was obliged to send round the country buy cattle for the subsistence of the troops.

It was above a month before the necessary Ammunition and stores could be transported from Rock Creek to Conegogee, and as the Potomack was not then navigable, even by the smallest canoes, new difficulties arose in providing Waggons to send them to Fort Cumberland; proper persons were sent to the justices of peace of those Counties, and at last by intreaties, threats, and money, the stores were removed.

As the General had met with frequent disappointments, he took the opportunity of Mr Franklin's being at Frederick to desire he would contract in Pensylvania for one hundred and fifty waggons and fifteen hundred carrying horses upon the easiest terms, to join him at Fort Cumberland by the 10th of May, if possible; Mr Franklin procured the number of waggons, and about five hundred horses. As those carriages were to pass through Conegogee in their way to Fort Cumberland, the General sent orders to Cressop the Agent at that place to make use of that opportunity of conveying to Fort-Cumberland the flour which the Government of Pensylvania had delivered there, it being much wanted at the Fort.

As no road had been made to Will's Creek on the Maryland side of the Patomack, the 48th Regiment was obliged to cross that river at Conegogee, and to fall into the Virginia road near Winchester. The General ordered a bridge to be built over the Antietun, which being finished, and provision laid in on the road.[182]

VIRGINIA-WINCHESTER

April 21st 1755   **(St. Clair)**

Of the marching of the troops from Winchester to Wills's Creek the shortest route cut for the artillery

1st From Winchester to Potts's, good camp	12 miles
2d From Potts's to Henry Enoch's	16
3. From Henry Enoch's to Coxes at the Little Cacapehon	12
4 From Coxe's to Col. Cressop's	8
5 From Col Cresopes to the fort	16

Remarks on the above road

1st days march the road is good no run of water to pass of any consequence.

2d days march, should a great body of troops march togeather they may not be able to pass the river of Cacapehon a quarter of a mile from their camp in that case the troops may camp on this side of Cacapehon at Enoch's. Enoch's in this case...only to march 7 miles next day to the head of the mountain where there is a good spring. The floats will be finished by Tuesday next should the troops choose to ford at great Capapehon which will not take them knee deep, they take the road to the right that straight forward I do not answer. If the floats be ready it will be better to use it.

3rd days march it will be best to encamp opposite to Coxe's especially if the water of little Capecahon is high.

4th days march. The officers leading the division of troops may send to Col. Cresaps who can send them down by water what provisions they want from the deposit of provisions at Col. Cresaps. At the mouth of little Caperahon, the troops pass the Potomack in a float four miles from which is Town Creek where our road is building, if road is not ready they may pass in canoes this days march being only 8 miles, the house where the troops encamp belongs to Col Cresap but inhabited by Mr. Jackson who keeps an Inn.

5th days march the commanding officer leading the division is to send to the officer commandng at Wills's Creek to send his wagons to the two creeks to carry them over least the bridges be not ready.

The first creek is three miles from the fort and the second just by.

A Description of the 2nd and longer road to Wills's Creek It being impossible to give a distance by this road.

From Winchester to Jos. Edwards 25 miles at this place the great river of Cacapihon is to be crossed in a float, a good camp at Edward's. From Joseph Edward's to the north river of Capapehon 7 (?) miles, here is a stony foard without float or canoe. 12 miles further is the foard of Little Cacapihon without a float or canoe, but not so deep as the former, the wagon with provisions may unload on he far side of these rivers and return for the soldiers. Ten miles further is Joseph Pearcealls, a tolerable camp.

At Jos. Pearceall's the south Branch of Potomack is to be crossed in a float the best road is along the middle ridge and to pass Patterson's Creek at Mr. Crackon's, here is a canoe, this route had no water on it for 10 miles, but it saves crossing that creek 5 times at bad foards where there is no canoe nor float, from Joseph Pearceall's to John Walker's on the Potomack 25 miles should the Potomack not be passable for wagons and the float not made the officer commanding the Detachment is to send to the Commanding officer at the Fort for a Wagon to carry up his tents and to carry his men over the two rocks near the fort.

From Walkers to the fort, 8 miles in all 88. [183]

VIRGINIA-WINCHESTER
The 21st day of April 1755   (St. Clair)
By Sir John St. Clair Quarter Master General to his Majestys forces in America

You are hereby required and directed to warn or cause to be warned all the wagons on the South Branch and in the neighborhood about to repair immediately to Winchester, to carry up the artillery and stores to the fort, in case the inhabitants refuse to go on this service for the safety of the country, you are to apply to Lieut. Richard Baily of Sir Peter Halketts Regiment, who is sent to encamp at Jos. Pearceall's who will send partys of his troops to be quartered on the inhabitants at free cost for their disobedience to his Majestys orders:delivered to them by me.

Given under my hand at Winchester   John St. Clair [184]

VIRGINIA-WINCHESTER
21st day of April

Instructions for Capt. Polsons Company, the 2d Company of Artificers in consequence of the orders you have received from Sir Peter Halkett to march with what remains of your company at Winchester. You are instructed to join the detachment of your company now building a float on great Cacapehon at Henry Enoch's, which float you are see finished with all possible dispatch, that done you are to march with the assistance of Mr. Byrnce, you are to have oars made for the float at that place and have it tarred for which Mr. Byrnce has my directions. Should you want any provisions for your men you are to apply to Col. Cresop for it, the rope sent for the float on the Potomack is not to be used.

You are to cross the Potomack and go to Town creek where you will find one of the Ingeniers, who will direct you whether you are to stop at that place to build a float or proceed to the fort to build bridges.

Lieut Hamilton with the detachment of your company now at the Opeckon is to remain to escort up the artillery to the fort.
Route:
To Potts 1st day march
To Henry Enoch's 2nd day march'
To Coxes at the mouth of the little Cacapehon
3d day march
To Town Creek 4th day march
Lieut McNeil is to go on the recruiting service.   John St.Clair [185]

VIRGINIA-WINCHESTER
The 21st Day of April 1755   (St. Clair)

Instruction for Lieut. Hamilton of the 2nd Company of artificers. In consequence of the orders given to you by Sir Peter Halkett to take upon you the command of the attachment of the...you belong to who are now making a bridge over the Opeckon. You are to see that bridge finished with our Expedition that done you are to wait for the artillery and march your party to the fort with it in order to repair the carriages on the road, should the artillery not march all togeather you are in that case to divide your people into small squads of which you are to apply to the commanding officer of the artillery to receive his directions concerning the number of men you are to march with each brigade. Given under my had at Winchester. [186]

150

VIRGINIA-WINCHESTER
April 21, 1755
Sir: Lieut. Lewis **(St. Clair)**

I did not receive your letter of the 1st of this month till yesterday, I am sorry that my not getting it in due time, has put it out of my power to grant your request with regard to leave of absence for a few days. Lieut. Hamilton goes to relieve you on your command in order that you may join your company who you will find within a few miles of the fort the service will require your joining it immediately as Captain Steven only waits for you that he may go at recruiting by General Braddocks order. I am with great truth, your most hum. serv. [187]

(seaman)

On the 21st:-At noon the General arrived here attended by Captains Orme and Morris his Aids de Camp, and Secretary Shirley, and went to the Head Quarters, a house provided for him; and Sir John St. Clair arrived here. [188]

Munday April the 21st. **(batman)**

The general ariv'd here (from Alexandria) after being Expected three days. This day we put a Soldier in Stocks for getting drunk to try what it would do, for Whipping would not serve him. [189]

(Franklin)

We found the General...waiting impatiently for the return of those he had sent thro' the back parts of Maryland and Virginia to collect wagons. I stay'd with him several days...and had full opportunity of removing all his prejudices...When I was about to depart, the returns of wagons to be obtained were brought in, by which it appeared that they only amounted to twenty-five, and not all of those were in servicable condition. the General and all his officers were surpris'd, declared the expedition was then at an end, being impossible, and exclaim'd against the ministers for ignorantly landing him in a country destitute of the means of conveying their stores, baggage, etc., not less then one hundred and fifty wagons being necessary.

I happened to say...it was a pity they had not been landed rather in Pennsylania, as in that country almost every farmer had his wagon. The General eagerly laid hold of my words, and said, "Then you, sir, who are a man of interest there, can probaly procure them for us; and I beg you will undertake it". [190]

who are a man of interest there, can probaly procure them for us; and I beg you will undertake it". [190]

April 22 (Tuesday)
MARYLAND-FREDERICK
Parole-Westminster   (Braddock)
One Sergeant one Corporal and 12 men to parade immediately at the Town Guard to March with the Waggons laden with Artillery Stores to Conogogee and to return back with the Waggon's to Frederick as soon as they are unloaded. [191]

Tuesday April ye 22   (batman)
This night the Captain of the Provost patroled Round the town and Brought in Several drunken Soldiers to guard. [192]

VIRGINIA-ALEXANDRIA   (Halkett/Disney)
Camp at Alexandria April 22d: 1755
The Parole is Philadelphia [193]

April the 22   (Browne)
All the Troops march'd to Will's Creek. Left behind 1 Officer and 40 Men, my Brother and self in care of the Sick, having 50 ill. [194]

April 23 (Wednesday)
VIRGINIA-ALEXANDRIA
Alexandria April 23[d]: 1755   (Halkett/Disney)
The Parole is St George [195]

VIRGINIA-MOUNT VERNON   (Washington)
April 23, Wednesday. Mount Vernon
To Hon. Wm. Fairfax
I cannot think of quitting Fairfax (County) without embracing this last opportunity of bidding; you farewell I shall this day set out for Wills Creek where I expect to meet the General and stay - I fear too long as the march must be regulated by the slow movements of the Train, which I am sorry to say will be tedious, very tedious indeed, as I have long predicted, tho' few believed. Alexandria has been honored with five Governours in Consultation, I hope not only of the successes of this Expedition, but of the future greatness of this town. [196]

MARYLAND-FREDERICK   (Braddock)
Frederick, Wednesday, April 23rd, 1755
Parole-Exeter

The commanding Officers of Regiments to order their Officers to provide themselves as soon as possible with Bat men out of such recruits and Levies, as are unfit to do the Duty of sold[er] and such men are to be enlisted as can act as Bat men and are to be taken for any Term and to be allowed as effectives; and according to the number settled in Flanders 3 men to each company and 4 to the staff, you are to go immediately to that part of the Antietum that lies in the road of Connogogee and press such Boats or Canoes as you shall meet with upon the river agreeable to the Orders you shall receive from Governor Sharpe If you shall find any difficulty in execution of this order, you are to send an express to me and you shall be immediately supplied with a party of men to inforce it sending word when they shall join you, and you are to collect all the Boats &c at that pass by the 28th of this month. [197]

Wednesday April the 23d.   (batman)

The govener of Maryland (Horatio Sharpe) Came to town and Was Ordered the Same Compliment to be paid him that governor Dunwiddy (Robert Dinwiddie) had when we were in Virginia. This day and Sunday last after we Came from Church we Beat up (drummed) for Volintears and listed Several Indented Servants. [198]

Frederick April 23. 1755.   (Franklin)

Receiv'd of General Braddock to be laid out in Advance Money to Waggons, &c. Maryland Money and 28 Pistoles £196 06
          720 Ounces Silver
          47 Ounces Gold [199]

TO THE INHABITANTS OF THE COUNTIES   (Franklin)
OF LANCASTER, YORK, AND CUMBERLAND.
Friends and Countrymen:

Being occasionally at the Camp at Frederic a few days since, I found the General and Officers of the Army extreamely exasperated, on Account of their not being supply'd with Horses and Carriages, which had been expected from this Province (Pennsylvania) as most and Assembly, Money had not been provided nor any Steps taken for that Purpose.

It was proposed to send an armed Force immediately into these Counties, to seize as many of the best Carriages and Horses as should be wanted, and compel as many persons into the Service as would be necessary to drive and take care of them.

I apprehended that the Progress of a Body of Soldiers thro' these Counties on such a Occasion, especially considering the Temper they are in, and their Resentment against us, would be attended with many and great Inconveniences to the Inhabitants; and there- fore more willingly undertook the Trouble of trying first what might be done by fair and equitable Means.

The People of these back Counties have lately complained to the Assembly that a sufficient Currency was wanting: you have now an Opportunity of receiving and dividing among you a very considerable Sum; for if the Service of this Expedition should continue (as it's more than probable it will), for 120 Days, the Hire of these Waggons and Horses will amount to upwards of Thirty Thousand Pounds, which will be paid you in Silver and Gold of the King's Money.

The service will be light and easy, for the Army will scarce march above 12 Miles per Day, and the Wagons and Baggage Horses, as they carry those things that are absolutley necessary to the Welfare of the Army, must march with the Army and no faster, and are for the Army's sake, always plac'd where they can be most secure, whether on March or in Camp.

If you are really, as I believe you are, good and loyal Subjects of His Majesty, you may now do a most acceptable Service, and make it easy to yourselves; for three or four such as cannot separately spare from the Business of their Plantations a Waggon and four Horses and a Driver, may do it togeather, one furnishing the Waggon, another one or two Horses, and another the Driver, and divide the Pay proportionably between you. But if you do not this Service to your King and Country voluntarily, when such good Pay and reasonable terms are offered you, your Loyalty will be strongly suspected; the King's Business must be done; so many brave Troops, come so far for your Defence, must not stand idle, thro' your backwardness to do what may reasonably be expected from you; Waggons and Horses must be had; violent Measures will probably be used; and you will be able to seek for a Recompence where you can find it, and your Case perhaps be little pitied or regarded.

I have no particular Interest in this Affair; as (except the Satisfaction of endeavouring to do Good and prevent Mischief) I shall have only my Labor for my Pains. If this method of obtaining the Waggons and Horses is not like to succeed, I am oblig'd to send Word to the General in fourteen Days; and I suppose Sir John St. Clair the Hussar, with a Body of Soldiers, will immediately enter the Province, for the Purpose aforesaid, of which I shall be sorry to hear, because

> I am, very sincerely and truly,
> Your Friend and Well-wisher,
> B. FRANKLIN. [200]

ADVERTISEMENT   **(Franklin)**

Lancaster, April 26, 1755

Whereas 150 Waggons, with 4 Horses to each waggon, and 1500 Saddle or Pack-Horses are wanted for the Service of his Majesty's Forces now about to rendezvous at Wills's Creek; and his Excellency General Braddock hath been pleased to impower me to contract for the Hire of the same; I hereby give Notice, that I shall attend for that Purpose at Lancaster from this Time till next Wednesday Evening; and at York from next Thursday Morning 'till Friday Evening; where I shall be ready to agree for Waggons and Teams, or single Horses, on the following Terms, viz.

1st. That these shall be paid for each Waggon with 4 good Horses and a Driver, Fifteen Shillings per Diem: And for each able Horse with a Pack-Saddle or other Saddle and Furniture, Two Shillings per Diem. And for each able Horse without a Saddle, Eighteen Pence per Diem.

$2d^{ly}$, That the Pay commence from the Time of their joining the Forces at Wills's Creek (which must be on or before the twentieth of May ensuing) and that a reasonable Allowance be made over and above for the Time necessary for their travelling to Wills's Creek and home again after their Discharge.

$3d^{ly}$, Each Waggon and Team, and every Saddle or Pack Horse is to be valued by indifferent Persons, chosen between me and the owner, and in Case of the Loss of any Waggon, Team or other Horse in the Service, the Price according to such Valuation, is to be allowed and paid.

4th[ly], Seven Days Pay is to be advanced and paid in hand by me to the Owners of each Waggon and Team, or Horse, at the Time of contracting, if required; and the Remainder to be paid by General Braddock, or by the Paymaster of the Army, at the Time of their Discharge, or from time to time as it shall be demanded.

5th[ly], No Drivers of Waggons, or Persons taking care of the hired Horses, are on any Account to be called upon to do the Duty of Soldiers, or be otherwise employ'd than in conducting or taking Care of their Carriages and Horses.

6th[ly]. All Oats, Indian Corn or other Forage, the Waggons or Horses bring to the Camp more than is necessary for the Subsistence of the Horses, is to be taken for the Use of the Army, and a reasonable Price paid for it.

Note. My Son William Franklin, is impowered to enter into like contacts with any Person in Cumberland County.   B. Franklin [201]

The two above advertisements for the hire of drivers, wagons and horses that were subsequently printed in Pennsylvania newspapers under the date of April 26, 1755 it would seem were composed at Frederick, Maryland when Franklin visited the army and spoke to the General to arrange terms of supply. As history documents the "Hussar" ruse worked however it is doubtful that St. Clair was a Hussar as none existed in the British army until much later-Napoleonic wars.

Nichols writes: "Franklin gave his personal bond to owners, hence when many of these wagons were destroyed or captured in the campaign to come, the owners sued him for the loss. General Shirley in September gave orders to settle the wagoners accounts for £30,000...The largest claim was for £1,043-17s.-6d to Robert Callendar for the loss of 114 horses".

There were two uses of Pennsylvania farm wagons by the expedition: 1) to carry supplies to Fort Cumberland and 2) to carry baggage and supplies of the expedition to Fort Duquesne. Since the most significant accomplishment of the Expedition was the taking of wheeled vehicles for the first time over the Allegheny Mountains it is worth while to comment on these farm-type conestoga wagons.

Berkebile writes: "The farm wagons used in these operations were often referred to as Conestoga wagons. This term was apparently in general use at least as early as 1750, when the term "Dutch Wagon" was also used in referring to this particular type of vehicle. The Conestoga, deriving its name from the Conestoga valley near Lancaster, was apparently a Pennsylvania adaptation of the English wagon. These (artifacts found in Edmund's Swamp in the route of the Forbes expedition of 1758) indicate a wheel diameter of 64 inches and a tire 2 inches wide. The 2-inch tires are undoubtedly relics of a farmer's wagon. since the various military vehicles had tires no less than 3 inches and often on the heavier types 4 inches wide. The use of strakes also indicates that these early wagons had no brakes such as the large Conestogas of a later period had.

Contemporary letters and newspapers advertisements attest to the fact that farm wagons were the type used by Braddock.

That Braddock's wagons were small is evidenced by the loads carried.

An approximate description of the size of the wagon, taken from the early existing specimens of the same type shows a bed of about 12 feet long on the bottom and 14 feet on the top. Depth of the bed ran about 32 inches and the width was approximately 42 to 46 inches. Through there was little standardization in most features, eight bows usually supported the dull white homespun cover. The diameter of the front wheels varied from 430 to 45 inches, while the rear wheels ran 10 to 20 inches larger.

For a 1759 expedition it was recommended that wagon accessories include drag chains, grass cutting knives, axes, shovels, tar buckets (for lubricating axles), jacks, hobbles, and extra sets of such items as clouts (axle-bearing plates), nails, horseshoes, hames, linch pins and hamestrings. It is doubtful if many teamsters in the 1755 expedition had so complete a selection of equipment.

There is no evidence that the hame bells later to be found on professional teams were used at this early date. The advertisement that was circulated for the 1759 expedition mentions a "slip bell...for each horse" among the items necessary on an expedition, so it is possible that some drivers of the 1755 expedition may have used a single bell on each horse, as was the custom with pack horses. These bells, kept stuffed during the day, were unstuffed at night when the horses were put out to forage in the woods so that they might be more easily found in the morning. Orme mentions no bells, although he writes of other methods used to avoid losing horses at night".

Vineland documents (based on existant examples) all differences between Virginia and Pennsylvania wagons, one of them being that the Pennsylvania wagons could not be disassembled for carrying over mountains. Using a Moravian diary description as a guide, this means that the wagons used on the expedition were emptied and then pushed and pulled up grades by the men and horses, the contents then were carried up to the pass or gap by the men and the horses if the expedition. On the down grades the loaded wagon was controlled by locking the wheels and hanging a tree to the wagon of which all the the brethern took hold as well as drag ropes attached to the wagon.

April 24 (Thursday)

VIRGINIA-ALEXANDRIA

Alexandria Camp April 24th: 1755   **(Halkett/Disney)**
The Parole is Shrewsbury [202]

MARYLAND-FREDERICK   **(Braddock)**

Frederick, Thursday, April 24th, 1755.
Parole-Yarmouth [203]

                  (seaman)
On the 24th:-Very hard showers of rain, and from being very hot became excessively cold and blew hard. [204]

Thursday April the 24th.   **(batman)**

We listed a man for 6 months to take Care of our Horses and several Indented Servants that had been Kidnaped in England and Brought Over hear and Sold to the Planters. Several Prisoners Punished this Evening for being drunk, but one for not learning his Exercise. [205]

April 25 (Friday)
VIRGINIA-ALEXANDRIA

Alexandria Camp April 25th: 1755   **(Halkett/Disney)**
The Parole is Salisbury

One Serjt 1 Corpl & 15 privet men of Sr Peter Halketts regt. to parade to morrow Morning at 6 oClock at the Train of Artillery And there to follow such Directions as Mr. Sowers shall give them. [206]

MARYLAND-FREDERICK   **(Braddock)**
Frederick, Friday, April 25th, 1755
Parole-Appleby

Colo Dunbar's Regiment to hold themselves in readiness to March by the 29th.
AFTER ORDERS.

One Corporal and four men to March to morrow Morning to Rock Creek with four Waggons that came up this Evening; when the party comes t o Rock Creek they are to put themselves under the command of Ensign French. [207]

                                                   (seaman)
On the 25th:-Received orders to be ready to march on Tuesday next. Arrived here 80 recruits and some ordnance stores for the 2 Regiments.[208]

Fryday April the 25th.   **(batman)**
We drew Indien Corn for 6 days and hard that we was to march on Tuesday following. This night we whipped several men for drinking.[209]

April 26 (Saturday)
VIRGINIA-ALEXANDRIA
Alexandria Camp April 26th, 1755   **(Halkett/Disney)**
The Parole Hinsale

The Artillery to have Their Twelve pounders Howitzers 9 pounders Waggons And one Trumbril Loaded with Tools in Readiness to March in a few hours Notice. The Remaining part of S^r. Peter Halketts Regt: to hold Themselves in readiness to march at the same time.

AFTER ORDERS

The Artillery Waggons &c mentioned in this morning's Orders to March to morrow morning under the care of one Lieut & 15 men of the Artillery to be Escorted by one Company of S^r. Peter Halketts Regt: The Genl to Beat at 4 oClock the Troop at 5 & to March immediately. One Sergt & 15 Pioners to go of(f) at Genl Beating with the Bumbril (tumbril) of Tools, And to take their Directions from Mr. Sowers Engineer who will go with Them. The Men who go on this Command to Receive ten Day provision at 5 oClock this Afternoon. Capt Hobsons Company and ye Staff of Sr Peter Halketts regt: to march to Morrow. All the Sick of the Regiment not Able to march to be sent to the Genl Hospital as soon as posable. The Recoverd men of the Americans to march to morrow with Capt Hobsons Compy.

Any man that shall be found Any way in Liquor to morrow when the Company marches will be Severly punished. [210]

MARYLAND-FREDERICK

Frederick, Saturday, April 26th, 1755.   **(Braddock)**

Parole-Bedford

Col^o Dunbars Regiment to furnish 3 Officers for a Court Martial, to try some prisoners of the Independent Company & Captn Gates Presid^t the report to be made to General Braddock. [211]

Satterday April ye 26th.   **(batman)**

One Officer and two drum(er)s and 42 Recruits Joined us, which was Rose (raised) in Maryland in twenty days. Sir Peter Halkets Regt Rec'd the Same Quantity.[212]

Nichols writes: "Much of the difficulty in recruiting for the regulars was also occasioned by the more rigid recruit qualifications:"

"You are to inlist no Irish or any other Country unless you are sure that they are Protestants...All your Recruits must be strait and well made, broad shouldered...you are to Inlist none but shall measure 5 Feet 5 Inches without shoes, from 16 to 20, and 5 feet 6 from 20 to 35 (from Recruiting Instructions, 1755)."

159

April 27 (Sunday)

VIRGINIA-OLD COURTHOUSE

Old Courthouse April 27th: 1755   **(Halkett/Disney)**

The Parole is Lincoln

One Serjt 1 Corpl. & 12 men to mount Guard Immediately upon the Waggons. The Pioners to march off to morrow morning at 4 oClock. The Horses to Harnissed by 6 oClock And the Genl to beat at 7 oClock when the party is to parade & march directly. [213]

MARYLAND-FREDERICK

Frederick, Sunday, April 27th, 1755.   **(Braddock)**

Parole-Chester

Col^o Dunbars Regiment is to march ye 29th and to proceed to Wills Creek agreeable to the following Route:

		MILES
29th From Fred^k on ye road to Conogogee		17
30th From that halting place to Conogogee		18
1st From Conogogee to John Even's		16
2d Rest		
3d To the Widow Baringer		18
4th To George Polls		9
5th To Henry Enock's		15
6th Rest		
7th To Cox's at ye mouth of little Cacapn		12
8th To Col^o Cresaps		8
9th To Wills Creek		16
Total		129

The men are to take from this place three days provisions; at Conogogee they will have more, at the Widow Baringers 5 Days, at Col^o Cresaps one or more Days, and at all these places Oats or Indian Corn must be had for the Horses but no Hay.

At Conogogee the Troops cross the Potomack in a Float When the Troops have marchd 14 miles from Jno Evans they are to take the new road to their Right, which leads from Opeckon Bridge.

When the Troops have marchd 14 miles from George Polle's they come to the great Cacapepon they are to pass that River in a Float, after passing they take the road to the Right.

If the water in the little Cacapepon is high the Troops must encamp opposite to Cox's.

At the mouth of the little Cacapepon the Potomack is to be crossd in a Float Four miles beyond this they cross Town Creek if the Float should not be finished Canvas will be provided.

If the Bridges are finishd over Wills Creek and Evans Creek, Waggons will be orderd to carry the men over. It will be prop^r to get 2 Days Prov^{ns} at Col^o Cresaps ye whole sh^d not arrive till ye 10th.

A Subaltorn and thrity men are to be left behind with a proper number of tents which will be carried for them; these men are to have six days Provisions.

The Generals Guard is not to be relieved to morrow...proper Centrys are to be found from the 30 men orderd to remain. [214]

(seaman)

On the 27th:-We sent 3 of our men to the hospital, vizt., John Philips, Edwd Knowles and James Connor, Employed in getting ready to march. Employ'd in preparing Harness for the Horses. [215]

Sunday April the 27.   **(batman)**

In the afternoon I went forigeing and got two hundred of hay and two days Provisions. [216]

April 28 (Monday)
VIRGINIA-SUGERLAND RUN
The Parole is Nottingham   **(Halkett/Disney)**

1 Corpl & 8 men to mount Guard. The Pioners to march off at 4 oClock to morrow morning. The Waggons to be ready to go by 5. The Genl to beat at that hour & Troop at half An hour after And march Immediately. The Wheels belonging to the Guns to be Greased this night.[217]

MARYLAND-FREDERICK
Frederick, Monday, April 28th, 1755.   **(Braddock)**
Parole-Daventry

The Detachment of Sailors, and the Provost Marshalls Guard consisting of one Sergeant, one Corporal and 10 men to march with Col^o Dunbars Regiment to morrow morning, and to make the Rear Guard.

TO CAPT^N GATES, 28th April, 1755.

You are directed by His Excellency Genl Braddock to proceed with your Company to Conogogee where you are to act as a covering party for the magazines, and you are to remain there till further Orders unless all the Stores, Ammunition, &c, should be come up from Rock Creek and forwarded to Wills Creek, in that case you are to join the General at Wills Creek as soon as possible.

You are to give all possible assistance and use your utmost endeavours in transporting the several Stores, Ammunition, Provision, &c to Wills Creek with the utmost expedition.

Whilst you remain at Conogogee you are to send a Sergant or Corporal with such of your men as are to be trusted with all the Waggon's which arrive at that place from Rock Creek allowing one man to each Waggon and you are to send them immediately back to Rock Creek for more Stores till you shall be informd from the there, that every thing is sent up.

TO ENSIGN FRENCH, AT ROCK CREEK. 28th April, 1755

You are ordered by his Excellency Genl Braddock to forward with all Expedition the ammunition stores &c at Rock Creek or Mr Cresaps Conogogee taking care to send the ammunition Train stores &c first, then the Hospital Stores and Salt Fish.

You are not to wait for the Beeves but as soon as the aforementioned things are gone up you will move with your party and join the Regiment at Wills Creek agreeable to the follow^{g} March Route; as you will find Provisions very scarce on the Road you must take with you as many days of salt Provisions as the Men can carry.

From Rock Creek to Owens Ord^{y}	15
To Dowdens	15
To Frederick	15
On the Road to Conogogee	17
To Conogogee	18
To John Evan's	16
To Widow Baringer's	18
To George Polls's	9
To Henry Enocks	15
To Mr Cox's	12
To Colo Cresap's	8
To Wills Creek	16
Total	174

You must if you should find it necessary, take with you Guides from place to place, and make such halts as you shall find absolutely necessary being carefull not to loose any time.

If the Waggons should come in very slowly make your application to the Civil Officers and if that should not succeed send Parties to fetch in any Waggons you shall hear off (of). Inform Lieu' Breerton of the March Route, and tell him it is the Generals Orders that he make all imaginable dispatch.

As soon as the Paymaster arrives he must also victual his men when the last stores of all kinds which are to be sent and dismissed from Rock Creek, you are to send a Letter to Capt Gates at Conogogee informing him of it.

The hand barrows and wheel barrows of the Train except 6 of each are to be left behind all but the Wheels and Iron Work which are to be fowarded. [218]

(Orme)

Colonel Dunbar marched with his regiment from Frederick on the 28th of April, and about this time the bridge over the Opecon was finished for the passage of the Artillery, and floats were built on all the rivers and creeks. [219]

Munday April the 28. **(batman)**

We Rec'd Orders for Marching on Tuesday and to Carry five days Provisions with us. [220]

April 29 (Tuesday)
VIRGINIA-MR. MINORS

The Parole is Braddock **(Halkett/Disney)**

All the Tents to be piched upon the left of the Artillery Immediatley. 1 Corpl & 8 men to mount Guard & to put two Centrys upon the Forrage & one upon the Rear of the Artillery & Baggage. The Officers Servts to Attend immediatley to get Forrage for Their Masters Horses. The Engineers & Pioners to march to morrow at 8 oClock. [221]

MARYLAND-BEYOND FREDERICK-WALKERS **(seaman)**

On the 29th:-We began our march at 6, but found much difficulty in loading our baggage, so that we left several things behind us, particulary the men's hammocks. We arrived at 3 o'clock at one

163

Walker's, 18 miles from Frederick, and encamped there on good ground; this day we passed the South Ridge of Shannandah Mountains, very easy in the ascent. We saw plenty of Hares, Deer, and Partridges; This place is wanting of all refreshments. [222]

MARYLAND-BEYOND FREDERICK-CHAPMANS ORDINARY

Tuesday April the 29th.   **(batman)**

We marched to Chapmans Oardinary, it being Nigh (near) 18 miles. [223]

Hough writes: "The campsite midway between Frederick and Williamsport was in the wilderness near Boonsboro. In the Seamans Journal the campsite is described as follows: We arrived a 3 o'clock at one, Walkers, 18 miles from Frederick, and encamped there on good ground; this day we passed the South Ridge on Shannandah Mountains, very easy in the ascent...This place is wanting all refreshments. But in the Batman's Diary the same campsite is Chapmans Ordinary, the Batman might have exercised his imagination to honor Major Chapman, a field officer mentioned a number of time in at least three records or Journals covering Braddock's Expedition."(Winchester-Frederick County Historical Society).

Older writes: "Charles Hamilton confirmed to this author (Curtis L. Older) the original journal source stated 'Chapmans Oardinanary.' The author of the Batman's Journal misspelled many words in his journal. The probability a formal name was misspelled in the Batman's Journal is high. Perhaps someone with a last name similar to Chapman lived along the line of march. One name that immediately comes to mind is Chapline. Perhaps the journalist referred to Moses Chapline Sr. when he recorded Chapman. Combining the name and distance records, this author (Older) concludes the stopping place of Dunbar's Regiment the first night out of Frederick Town was the property of Moses Chapline Sr. The names of Chapman and Chapline sound quite similar. The Moses Chapline Sr. property was along the line of march and was in the 17 to 19 mile range from Frederick Town. It was on the west side of South Mountain."

Furthermore, Mr. Older sets forth in his book "The Braddock Expedition and Fox's Gap in Maryland" that Fox's Gap was the route of the Dunbar's Regiment on its way to Conococheague (Williamsport) as well as the route of General Braddock and George Washington on their way to Swearingen's Ferry. Fox's Gap is through South Mountain approximately one mile south of Turner's (Curry's) Gap.

VIRGINIA-ALEXANDRIA

April the 29   **(Browne)**

Words cannot express my Joy; received a Letter from England being the first since I left them, my dear Children and all were well. It was dated the 4 of February. My Mind much more at ease. [224]

April 30 (Wednesday)
VIRGINIA-MR. MINORS

Mr. Minors April 30th: 1755   **(Halkett/Disney)**

The parole is Ohio

The Genl to beat at 5 oClock at which Time the horses are to be put to the waggons, And March Immediately. [225]

Dear Sir, (Letter II)   **(Br. Officer 3)**

I Sent a Letter to you by Captain Johnson, bound for Bristol, with a full Account of the Country, by which you will see the Reasons why it will be highly improper for you to buy into the Troops here; I send this by Ship bound for London.

They make here a Division between the Settlements and the Woods, though the Settlements are what we should call very woody in Europe. The Face of the Country is entirely different from any Thing I ever saw before; the Fields have not the Appearance of what bears that Name in Europe, instead of the ploughed Grounds or Meadows, they are all laid out in Hillocks, each of which bears Tobacco Plants, with Paths hoed between. When the Tobacco is green it looks like a Coppice, when pulled the Ground looks more like Hop-Yards than Fields, which makes a very disagreeable Appearance to the Eye. The Indian Corn also, and all their Culture runs upon hilling with the Hoe, and the Indian Corn grows like Reeds to eight or nine Feet high. Indeed in some parts of the Country Wheat grows, but Tobacco and Indian corn is the chief.

From the Heart of the Settlements we are now got into the Cow-Pens, the Keepers of these are a very extraordinary Kind of Fellows, they drive up their herds on Horseback, and they had need do so, for their Cattle are near as wild as Deer; a Cow-pen generally consists of a very large Cottage or House in the Woods, with about four-score or one hundred Acres, inclosed with high Rails and divided; in a small inclosure they kept for Corn, for the Family, the rest is the Pasture in which they keep their Calves; but the manner is far different from any Thing you ever saw; they may perhaps have a Stock of four or five hundred to a thousand head of Cattle belonging to a Cow-Pen, these run as they please in the great Woods, where there are no inclosures to stop them. In the Month of March the Cows begin to drop their Calves, then the Cow-Pen Master, with all his Men, rides out to see and drive up the Cows with all their new fallen Calves; they being weak cannot run away so as to escape, therefore are easily drove up, and the Bulls and other Cattle follow them; then they put these Caves into the Pasture, and every Morning and Evening suffer the Cows to come and suckle them, which done they let the cows out into the great Woods to shift for their Food as well as they can; whilst the Calf is sucking one Tit of the Cow, the Woman of the Cow-Pen is milking one of the other Tits, so that she steals some Milk from the Cows, who thinks she is giving it to the Calf. as soon as the Cow begins to grow dry, and the Calf grows strong, they mark them, if they are Males they cut them, and let them go into the Wood. Every Year in September and October they drive up the Market Steers, that are Fat and of proper Age, and kill them; they say they are fat in October, but I am sure they are not so in May, June and July; they reckon that out of 100 Head of Cattle they can kill about 10 or 12 Steers, and four or five Cows a year; so they reckon that a Cow-Pen for every 100 Head of Cattle brings about 40 pounds Sterling per Year. The Keepers live chiefly upon Milk, for out of the vast Herds, they do condescend to tame Cows enough to keep their Family in Milk, Whey, Curds, Cheese and Butter; they also have Flesh in Abundance such as it is, for they eat the old Cows and lean Calves that are like to die. The Cow-Pen Men are hardy People, are almost continually on Horseback, being obliged to know the Haunts of their Cattle.

You see, Sir, what a wild set of Creatures our English Men grow into when they lose Society, and it is surprizing to think how many Advantages they throw away, which our industrious County-Men would be glad of: Out of many hundred Cows they will not give themselves the Trouble of milking more than will maintain their Family. - The rest is left out being upon private Affairs. [226]

VIRGINIA-BULLSKIN-FREDERICK COUNTY-WINCHESTER
April 30, Wednesday. Bullskin, FrederickCo.and Winchester.
To: Mrs G.W. Fairfax   **(Washington)**
Dear Madam: In order to engage your correspondence, I think it is expedient just to deserve it; which I shall endeavor to do by embracing the earliest, and every opportunity of writing to you.

It will be needless to expatiate on the pleasures that communication of this kind will afford me, as it shall suffice to say; a correspondence with my friends is the greatest satisfaction I expect to enjoy in the course of this campaign, and that none of my friends are able to convey more real delight than you can to whom I stand indebted for so many obligations.

Out of 4 horses which I brought from home one I have killed outright, and the other 3 are rendered unfit of use; so that I have been detained here three days already and how much longer I may continue to be so time only can discover.

I must beg my compliments to Miss Hannah, Miss Dent, and any others that think me worthy of their enquiries. I am madam your most obedient Servant.   George Washington [227]

MARYLAND-CONOGOGEE   (seaman)

On the 30th:-At 6, marched in our way to Connecochieg, where we arrived at 2 o'clock, 16 miles from Walker's: this is a fine situation, close by the Potomack. We found the Artillery Stores going by water to Will's Creek, and left 2 of our men here. [228]

Wedensday April the 30   (batman)

We marched to Cunnecoejeg where we Incamped By the River Portwomack, it being 18 miles and a pleasent Cuntry. [229]

Hough writes: "Various spellings apply to this campsite such as Connecochieg, Cunnecoejeg, Conogoge, Conegogee, and Connekiege. The 48th Regiment arrived here on the afternoon of April 30 to encamp on the Maryland side near, the spot where the creek empties into the Potomac. Supplies were previously stored here according to a plan to move them up the Potomac to Ft. Cumberland." (Winchester-Frederick County Historical Society)

VIRGINIA-PHILADELPHIA WAGON ROAD   (Orme)

The 31 of April the General set out for Winchester hoping to meet the Indians, but as none were, or had been there, he proceeded to Fort Cumberland, where he arrived the 10th of May, and also the 48th Regiment. Sir Peter Halket with six companies of the 44th, two independent companies and the Virginia troops were already encamped at this place. [230]

Orme misdates this entry - it should read 30 of April.

The route from Conegogee (today's Williamsport, Maryland) to vicinity of Winchester, Virginia (then also called Frederick Town) follows U.S. Route 11. In colonial times this area was in Virginia. In 1864 West Virginia became a state including this area.

May 1 (Thursday)
VIRGINIA-MR. THOMPSONS
Mr. Thompsons May 1st: 1755   **(Halkett/Disney)**
The Parole is Burlington

A Serjt & 12 men to Mount the Bagage Guard And Centrys to be posted on the waggon horses. The Genl to beat at 3 oClock at which Time the Horses are to be put to the waggons. The Waggoners to be Told if Any of their horses were not Ready when the Troop Beats or any that (h)as Horses wanting will be Punished. [231]

VIRGINIA-PHILADELPHIA WAGON ROAD   **(seaman)**
May 1st, 1755. At 5, we went with our people, and began ferrying the Army &c. into Virginia, which we completed by 10 o'clock, and marched in our way to one John Evans, where we arrived at 3 o'clock-17 miles from Connecochieg, and 20 from Winchester. We got some provisions and forage here. The roads now began to be very indifferent. [232]

Thursday May ye 1st.   .   **(batman)**
We marched Cross the River Portwomack Into Virginia to Widow Evens and Carried three days provisions along with us it being 18 miles. [233]

PENNSYLVANIA-PHILADELPHIA   **(Pennsylvania Gazette)**
We hear that Mr. Evan's Map of the British Colonies from Virginia to Rhode Island inclusive; the country of the Six Nations, Ohio, and part of Canada, is nearly done Engraving. [234]

The crossing (ford) of the Potomac River here is very broad with the river having little current. It is a crossing that has been used by Indians and whites for many years. The mouth of Conococheagur Creek is nearby.

Hough writes: "Crossing the Potomac on May 1, the troops marched to John Evan's' place now known as Big Springs on the Valley Pike. The site is about 1 1/2 miles south of the present city limits of Martinsburg" (Winchester-Frederick County Historical Society).

May 2 (Friday)

VIRGINIA-SHARANDO RIVER

The Parole is Halkett   (Halkett/Disney)

The Tents to be piched this Evening Near the Artillery. A Corpl &
6 men to Guard & a Corpl & 6 men as a Guard on the waggons
Horses & Bagage which are not yit Ferried over.

The Gnl to Beat at 10 oClock & the Horses to be put too Immedy
And the party to March. [235]

MARYLAND-FORT CUMBERLAND

May the 2nd 1755

Sir: General Braddock   (St. Clair)

As Governor Dinwiddie made a contract with the bearor of this
Robert Callendar for 100 horses fifty one of which he delivered to Mr.
Commisary Walker as will appear by his reciepts so that there is due
Mr. Callendar £536'12 for various saddles and flour which I am under
the Majesty of applying to you Excellency to direct the Commissary at
Winchester to pay for notwithstanding the contract was made by the
Governor it was at my requests.

Mr. Callendar has likewise at Winchester a number of horses more
to fullfill his contract, which your Excellency may take on the terms
that the persons appointed to examin them shall think proper, as I shall
send on an express the 4th. I have nothing further to add but that I am
with great respect your excellency hum.& obed serv. [236]

*The Sharando River is the Shenandoah River and the crossing was to be
known as Vestal's Ferry. Nearby at the confluence of the Shenandoah River and
Evitt's Run was the earliest iron furnace (bloomery) west of the Blue Ridge built in
1742 for William Vestal by William Mayberry. The area from Cat Tail Run to
Evitt's Run was owned by William Vestal. The elements of Braddock's army who
crossed Vestal's Gap made no mention of this early industrial activity that must
have been noticeable due to extensive burning and smoke as well as clearing of
the land of trees for charcoal. This comes from Historical Archaeology Executive
Summary: U.S. Route 9 Improvement Project by David S. Rotenstein.*

*Hough describes the way of the army down the west side of the Blue Ridge
from Vestal's Gap and shows a photograph of wagon wheel ruts worn into the
shale of the hillside which are approximately half way down to the river. I did see
these ruts and also the river crossing where a ferry operated. At the bottom of the
grade is a broad plain with a dug way down to the waters edge. It is on this bottom
land that Halketts unit encamped prior to being ferried over the river. The dugway
today is filled with wild growing trees and vegetation. Across the river is a quarry*

that is being reclaimed by pumping out water into the river. The army crossed the land of the quarry. All land surfaces have been greatly disturbed and the ruins of the house said to be that of Vestal's (on the west side of the river) has been removed. Hough shows a photo of the walls of the structure taken in 1970. To the east and overlooking the of the river is Vestal's Gap which is crossed by the Appalachian Trail. The gap is not immediately apparent as the road (VA Route 9) curves through the gap on the ridge line of the Blue Ridge Mountain. The road down to the river ferry site is by Route 3 just beyond the gap. Through history beginning well before 1755, the gap and the road down to the river have been used extensively until the construction of the Route 9 bridge over the river at Bloomery.

Also see the entry for Charlotte Browne for June 4 1755 which comments on the route to Vestal's Gap.

Hough writes: "Halkett's 44th Regiment crossed the Blue Ridge at Keys' (Vestal's) Gap on May 2 and marched down the western slope to the Shenandoah River where John Vestal operated a ferry. Vestal owned land on the west side of the river, but on the east side the land was owned by Gershom Keys (Keyes), hence the use of either name in conjunction with the gap and the ferry (established in 1748). The dirt road down the ridge currently designated as W.Va. 32 and 32/1 is, with a few minor deviations, the route traveled by Braddock's troops to reach the ferry. The Braddock Road from Keys's Gap via Keys' Ferry to Charles Town, is with one exception, the route later designated: Alexandria-Warm Spring Road. Ferrying across the Shenandoah River began on the afternoon of May 2 and was completed by midmorning the next day. About 10 o'clock on May 3rd the march was resumed up the road past Vestal's House. The old road past Vestal's house no longer exists due to extension of a large rock-quarry through the area. However, west of the quarry a section remains in use as W.Va. 16 which leads to Route 340 then into Charles Town. The march was over the old wagon road, now Washington St., through Charles Town, turning westward on or near Route 51 to Dicks Plantation." (Winchester-Frederick County Historical Society)

VIRGINIA-PHILADELPHIA WAGON ROAD   (seaman)

On May the 2nd:-As it is customary in the Army to halt a day after 3 days march, we halted to-day to rest the Army, and sent the horses to grass. [237]

We halted. [238]   (batman)

Dunbar's unit used the Great Philadelphia Wagon Road that predated the Expedition by many years. It had been used by European immigrants from the Delaware River port of Philadelphia. This wagon road followed the natural trough right-of-way leading southwest between the ridges of the Allegheny Mountains. With this wagon road the influence of Pennsylvania extended well in to the colonial area of Virginia. This ease of access to Virginia was in part the cause of the bitter rivalry between Pennsylvania and Virginia traders.

Vineland includes an 1753 Single Brethern Moravian Diary that describes travel to the south along the road:" October 18,...At noon we passed Frederickstown (Winchester), which consists of about sixty houses, which are rather poorly built".

From the vicinity of Frederick and due west there were now physical features that lay across the route of the army that would become more and more difficult to pass. These began with the Blue Ridge, Kittochtinny Mountain, South Mountain, and The Devils Backbone.

George Washington and the General met for the first time in the village of Frederick, Maryland when George rode east crossing the Potomac at Swerengen's Ferry (Shepherdstown). It is thought he left Winchester April 30th, or May 1st.

May 3 (Saturday)

VIRGINIA-DICKS PLANTATION

Dicks Plantation May: 3d: 1755   **(Halkett/Disney)**

The Parole is Gage

1 Corpl & 9 men to mount Guard on the Artillery and Bagage. 1 Serjt to take the Number of horses as the(y) Are put into the pasture. 1 Tent to be piched in the Front of the Artillery & another in ye Rear of the Bagage. The Genl to beat to morrow morning (at) 4 oClock & march Immediatley. [239]

VIRGINIA-PHILADELPHIA WAGON ROAD   **(seaman)**

On the 3rd:-We marched at 5 on our way to one Widow Barringer's, 18 miles from Evans: this day was so excessively hot that several officers and many men could not get on till the evening, but the body got to their ground at 3 o'clock. This is 5 miles from Winchester, a fine station if properly cleared. [240]

Hough writes: "The campsite of the 48th Regiment and Mrs. Browne's detachment was thought to be near the spring that gives rise to Hiett's Run. The site is about 200 yards east of the crossroads (Va. 672 & 679) on Apple Pie Ridge, and, as one travels north, about 3.8 miles from Stine's Chapel." (Winchester-Frederick Historical Society)

Satterday May the 3d.   **(batman)**

We marched to Widow Billingers about 19 miles and rec'd two days Provisions and drumed a woman out of the Camp. [241]

On this date the General reaches Winchester and expected an Indian meeting to set up alliances against the French. He waits for the Indians to arrive until the 7th as George Washington barrows money from Lord Fairfax to buy horses.

Hough writes: "On May 3 the 48th marched southward over the valley road to Clearbrook and then turned westward over the same road (now Va. 672) traveled by some of the troops of Halkett's a few days earlier. They passed the site of Hopewell Church, went over Pumpkin Ridge to Widow Barringers. When the troops encamped here (Dicks Plantation) on May 3 the horses were counted and put into the pasture. The site is along Evitts Run, probably near Piedmont - home of Miss Louise Briscoe, about 1 1/2 miles west of Charles Town. Highway 51 is on or near the old wagon road to Middleway over which the troops marched. Included in orders of the day was, 'The Genl to beat tomorrow morning at 4 o'clock & march immediately'. The march continued on or near the present road, W.Va. Highway 51, to Middleway (Smithfield) then turned southward and southwest (W.VA 1 & 1/11) passing the Campbell house then to Opequon Creek which was crossed at Abril's Road. This ford is at the spot where the 4 counties meet. From the ford the march was over a road now designated as Va. 667 to Widdow Littlers Mills now Brucetown."(Winchester-Fredeirck County Historical Society)

VIRGINIA-ALEXANDRIA

May the 3   **(Browne)**

Major Carlile's (Carlyle) Lady came to see me, but I was at a loss to seat her not having a Chair in the House. She sent home for 3. [242]

May 4 (Sunday)

VIRGINIA-THE WIDDOW LITTLERS MILLS   **(Halkett/Disney)**
The Widdow Littlers Mills May: 4th: 1755
The Parole is Winchester

1 Serjt & Twelve as a Guard on the Artillery & Bagage. Centrys to be posted on the Bagage horses two on the Artillery & one on the Bagage. The Corpl in the Waggons to patrole Every two hours. The men of Capt Polsons Company Are to Observe good Order in every perticuler for if They Disobay Milliterry Disiplin They will be severly punished. As to Morrow is a Holting day, all the Carriages to be Greased And every thing done That Lieut McLoud Thinks Necessary. Tents to be piched for the men Immediately. [243]

Hough writes: "The campsite at Brucetown is believed to have been in the vicinity of Littler's Tavern near the road leading westward from the village. The officers of the British army were said to have been entertained at the tavern on the night of the 3rd of May, although the troops did not arrive here until the next day according to Halkett's Orderly Book. The road westward is currently known as the Brucetown Road (Va.672), through Clearbrook, past Hopewell Church and over Pumpkin Ridge. The 44th Regiment passed Barringers and continued westward to encamp at Back Creek. This campsite is the nearest point to Winchester on the line of march, that is about 5 miles by the most direct route. From Barringers the march continued westward over the road currently designated Va. 672 to Cedar Grove then Va. 667 to Babbs Run (Lake St.Clair). The original road us under the artificial lake."(Winchester-Frederick County Historical Society)

VIRGINIA-VICINITY WINCHESTER (seaman)

On the 4th:-Marched at 5 in our way to one Potts-9 miles from the Widow's-where we arrived at 10 o'clock. The road this day very bad: we got some wild turkeys here: in the night it came to blow hard at N.W. [244]

Sunday May the 4th (batman)

We marched to Potses (Potts) Camp, it Being 9 miles. [245]

May 4, Sunday. Winchester. (Washington)

In Company with Braddock arrived at Winchester. [246]

Here GW stays at Williams Cock's Ordinary.

VIRGINIA-ALEXANDRIA

May the 4 (Browne)

This Day was oblig'd to quit our grand Parlour, the Man of the House being at a loss for a Room for the Soldiers to drink Cyder and dance jiggs in. [247]

May 5 (Monday)

VIRGINIA-THE WIDDOW LITTLERS MILLS

The Widdow Littlers Mills May 5th:1755 (Halkett/Disney)

The parole is Cumberland

Four Days provisions to be Dilivered to all the Men Except The Men of Capt Polsons Compy Join(ed) yesterday. At 12 oclock This Day The Serjt of the Guard to be very Carefull That no Fires is made within a Considerable distance of the Artillery on any Acct.

The Genl to be Morrow at ½ an hour after 3 oClock, the Troop at ½ an hour after 4 And March Immediately. [248]

MARYLAND-WILLS CREEK

To William Fairfax: (Washington)

You will naturally conclude that to pass through Maryl'd (when no business required it) was an uncommon and extrordinary route for the

Genl and Colo. Dunbar's Regiment to this place;...the reason, however, was obvious to say that those who promoted it had rather have the communication should be that way than through Virginia, but I now believe the Imposition had to evidently appeared for the Imposers to subject us to the same Inconvenience again. [249]

VIRGINIA-VICINITY WINCHESTER (seaman)

On the 5th:-Marched at 5 in our way to one Henry Enock's at forks of Cape Capon being 16 miles from Potts, where we arrived at 2 o'clock. The road this day over prodigious mountains, and between the same we crossed over a run of water 20 times in a 3 mile distance. After going 15 miles we came to a river called Kahapetin, where our men ferried the Army over and got to our ground, where we found a company of Peter Halket's encamped waiting to escort the Train of Artillery to Wills Creek. [250]

Hough writes: "Enoch's Camp (other designations; Enocks, Enoxes, Kennets) This campsite was probably a short distance west of the river and just below Forks of the Capapon; that is, about a mile from the mouth of Bloomery Run where the Braddock Road struck the Capapon River. To avoid crossing both the Capapon River and North River the road followed down-river along the east bank of the Capapon about a half mile or just below the forks then crossed the river to follow a small run to higher ground. A public road (W.Va. 45/6) enables one to travel by car into Braddock Hollow from the south or by another road (W.Va. 29/3) from the north. It is necessary, however, to abandon your car after going up the ravine about 1 mile and then walk along the stream for another mile crossing it several times before the ancient road leads to higher ground to a dirt road (W.Va. 2/3) that leads to Spring Gap at top of the mountain. The 2-mile stretch up Crooked Run was the roughest part of the road that I encountered." (Winchester-Frederick County Historical Society)

Munday May the 5th. (batman)

We marched to Kennets (Henry Enoch's) Camp after a very Rainy Night and Morning. The tents being very wet made the Baggage very heavy, it being 18 miles. [251]

VIRGINIA-ALEXANDRIA
May the 5 (Browne)

Removed into our first Floor. It consisted of a Bed chamber and Dining Room, not over large. The Furniture was 3 Chairs, a Table, a Case to hold Liquor and a Tea Chest. [252]

May 6 (Tuesday)
VIRGINIA-WINCHESTER

May 6, Tuesday. Winchester.   **(Washington)**

To: John Augustine Washington

   A very Fatiguing ride and long round about, brought me to the
General (the day I parted with you) at Frederick-Town. This is a small
village. 15 miles below the Blue Ridge on the Maryland side of the
Potowmack. From thence we proceeded to this place, where we have
halted since Saturday last, and shall depart for Wills-Creek
tomorrow. [253]

VIRGINIA-BACK CREEK

Back Creek May: 6th: 1755   **(Halkett/Disney)**

The Parole is Wills Creek

   1 Serjt & 12 men as a Guard on the Artillery & Bagage. The Genl
to beat at 6 oClock & the Horses to be put to Immedy. And March at
Troop beating. [254]

   Hough writes: "Potts (Potses) Camp, 48th Regiment
Back Creek Camp, 44th Regiment. The two diaries naming Potts Camp give its
distance from Barringers as 9 miles. Halkett's Orderly Book states that an
encampment was made a Back Creek on May 6, but does not mention distance
from the previous encampment. It is possible that the two regiments used the same
campsite, but if not, the sites are less than a mile apart. The only site designated
Potts that meets reasonable requirements as to distance to the nearest running
water as well as the distance to Barringers and the distance to Enoch's is a site
about midway between Back Creek and Isaacs Creek. This site about midway
between Back Creek and Isaac's Creek. This site is on the hilltop about 350 yards
west of the present Gainsboro School. Traces of the old road are still evident all
the way up the hill from Back Creek, passing between the school and the hilltop.
The site was probably south of the present highway 522 as it curves over the
hilltop, but possibly on the north side of the original road.
   The road westward from Potts campsite is on or near highway U.S. 522,
crossing Isaac's Creek about 200 yards above the present highway bridge, through
Cross Junction to about 3/4 mile beyond Cross Junction where the route continued
directly westward on or near the Whiteacre road (Va. 701) over Timber Ridge
somewhat north of the present road into Hampshire County, then on West Virginia
Road (6/2) to Good, thence on or near W.Va. 45 over Bear Garden Mountain
through Bloomery and down Bloomery Run to the Capapon River. Two
encampments along this route were made by the 44th Regiment that I have not
located accurately. The first of these was on May 7 in, -The wood three miles short
of Mrs. Jennings -; the second was on May 8, - The water of Cape Capon-. The

*latter campsite was probably along Bloomery Run, possibly at or near Bloomery.
According to my measurements, distance via the route just outlined from Potts
campsite to the mouth of Bloomery Run at the Capapon is just slightly in excess of
15 miles. Going down Bloomery Run the road crossed the run twenty times
according to the Seamen's Journal, but when I first traveled that way in the 1920s
crossings were not quite as many and there were at least two plank bridges. Today the modern highway eliminates all fords; the stream and the road have been
straightened so that the modern traveler experiences none of the difficulties of the
past." (Winchester-Frederick County Historical Society)*

VIRGINIA-NORTHWEST OF WINCHESTER (seaman)

May 6th. Halted, as was the Custom to do so every third day. The
Officers, for passing away the time, made Horse Races, and agreed
that no Horse should run over 11 Hands and to carry 14 Stone.

On the 6th:-We halted this day to refresh the Army. [255]

Tuesday May the 6th. (batman)

We halted and Rec'd five days provisions but no forige for our
horses nor any thing to be sold. We should be starved if it was not for
the Kings Allowance. [256]

VIRGINIA-ALEXANDRIA

May the 6 (Browne)

This Unhappy Day 2 Years depriv'd me of my dear Husband, and
ever since to this Day my Life has been one continual Scene of Anxiety
and Care. [257]

PENNSYLVANIA-LANCASTER
ADVERTISEMENT (Franklin)

Lancaster, May 6th. 1755

Notice is hereby given to all who have contracted to send Waggons
and Teams, or single Horses from York County to the Army at Wills's
Creek, that David M'Conaughy and Michael Schwoope of the said
County, Gentlemen, will attend on my Behalf at York Town on Friday
next, and a Philip Forney's on Saturday, to value or appraise all such
wagons, Teams and Horses, as shall appear at those Places on the said
Days for that Purpose; and such as do not them appear must be valued
at Wills's Creek.

The Waggons that are valued at York and Forney's. are to set out
immediately after the Valuation from thence for Wills's Creek, under
the Conduct and Direction of Persons I shall appoint for that Purpose.

The Owner or Owners of each Waggon or set of Horses, should bring with them to the Place of Valuation, and deliver to the Appraisers, a Paper containing a Description of their several Horses in Writing, with their several Marks natural and artificial; which Paper is to be annexed to the Contract.

Each Waggon should be furnished with a Cover, that the Goods laden therein may be kept from Damage by the Rain, and the Health of the Driver preserved, who are to lodge in the Waggons. And each Cover should be marked with the Contractor's Name in large Characters.

Each Waggon, and every Horse Driver should also be furnished with a Hook or Sickle, fit to cut the long Grass that grows in the Country beyond the Mountains.

As all the Waggons are obliged to carry a Load of Oats, or Indian Corn, Persons who have such Grain to dispose of, are desired to be cautious how they hinder the King's Service, by demanding an extravagant Price on this Occasion.   B. Franklin [258]

May 7 (Wednesday)
VIRGINIA-ALEXANDRIA
MARYLAND-CALVERT COUNTY
Maryland May 7th 1755   **(J. Hamilton)**
Dear Brother: (Gavin Hamilton)

I had your letter bearing date Octr 10 at Edinburgh, That by Sir Peter Halket was delivered me in his Tent from his own hands, where we drank your health in particular, with the health of our Brothers and all other Friends in Scotland. Sir Peter's Sea Voyage has agreed well with him, as the air of the Country has hitherto. He told me that he had been Subject to Rheumatick pains, but was then on the first of Aprile quite free from them, and uneasy about nothing but the distance he is at from my Lady Halket, and that the Scene of Action should be so remote from her. As he was sure you would immediately after Recieving it, transmit any account I wrote you of him to his Lady, he requested me not to omit a full relation of that day's visit and of the state he was then in.

You could not without injustice to Sir Peter's character have said less in his praise. I never took so great a Liking to any man, on such short acquaintance. But it is not I only, our whole province, so far as he is known, is full of respect to him, and expressing more concern for his welfare than anything else attendng the affair. Our Brother Alexander went to the same Camp to wait on him, a few days after I was there. I had a ready opportunity by Mr. Jame Dick of London Town of Sending your Letter which came by Sir Peter, with my earnest request that he would not neglect Seeing him. The General was sick while I was at the Camp of a Cold, but did not undergo many days confinement before he went to Anapolis, to meet the Northern Governors, who were not soon enough for the time he staid there. But in a few days they came and waited on him at his Quarters in Alexandria. I saw Coll Dunbar but did not make myself known to him. He bears the Character of a hearty, Jolly old Gentleman. What has been determined by these Gentlemen when they mett and had their Conference I know not, nor are we likely to know For the General has forbid all our Presses the liberty of Mentioning any thing pro or con that related to their affairs, a Caution highly necessary, as we make not the least doubt of the French having many Spies amongst us, where there are great numbers of Papists and Jesuite Priests. Coll. Dunbars Regiment crossed Pottowmack River at Rock Creek and marched to Fredericks Town in this Province. A detachment of Sir Peter's marched with part of the Train a few days after; and last of all Sir Peter followed with the remaining part of the Train, about ten days ago. His Regiment with the Train kept on the Virginia side of the River, only a Small Command left to guard the Hospital, Some Barrels of powder and Carriages which for want of Horses they could not take with them at that time. Their passage here was so Surprisingly good, that the like has scarcely ever been known. When they Arrived at Pottowmack they had lost but one Man, and that by a Fall over board. He was taken into the Ship before he was dead, but a hurt he mett with was fatal. Another drowned in the River 'ere they got to Alexandria by the overturning of a Boat, nor have I heard of loss amongst them by Sickness Since....(rest of letter not relevant to Braddock Expedition)

> Your Affectionate Brother
> Signed Jo. Hamilton
> Maryland Octor 6th 1755 [259]

While not on the Braddock Expedition two brothers: Dr. John Hamilton (Calvert County, Maryland) and Dr. Alexander Hamilton (Annapolis, Maryland) wrote their impressions to a third brother Gavin Hamilton in Edinburgh, Scotland. The two brothers visited Alexandria while the Army was there and "waited on" the

General who was sick with a cold. J. Hamilton gives us our only description of Col. Dunbar.

This letter was written in Calvert County, Maryland. The letter he writes about was received in Alexandria, Virginia and delivered by Sir Peter Halkett.

VIRGINIA-NORTHWEST OF WINCHESTER   **(Halkett/Disney)**
The Woods Three Miles Short of Mrs. Jennings May 7th: 1755
The Parole is Orme
    1 Serjt & 12 men for Guard on the Artillery & Bagage & to patrole from the Front to the Rear. The Genl to beat at 6 oClock & march Immediately after. [260]

VIRGINIA-NORTHWEST OF WINCHESTER   **(seaman)**
    7th:-We marched at 5 in our way to one Cox's, 12 miles from Enock's. This morning was very cold but by 10 o'clock it was prodigiously hot. We crossed another run of water 19 times In 2 miles, and got to our ground at 2 o'clock, and encamped close to the Potomack. [261]

    Atkinson writes: "The Army struck the Little Capapehon about six miles above its mouth, and following the stream encamped on the Virginia side of the Potomac preparatory to crossing into Maryland. The water is supposed to have been high at the time, as the spot is known as the Ferry-fields, from the army having been ferried over. This was about the 4th or 5th of May."

Wedensday May the 7th.   **(batman)**
    We marched to Coxes Camp, Close to the River Portwomack, it being 12 miles. [262]

    On this date the General departs Winchester in his chariot with George Washington as escort with the Virginia Troop of Light Horse.

May 8 (Thursday)
VIRGINIA-CAPE CAPEN RIVER   **(Halkett/Disney)**
The Water of Cape Capen May 8th: 1755
The Parole Cadogan
    1 Serjt & 12 men as a Guard for the Bagage. The Qr Master to go on to Capt Eyres who will give him a party to Assist Him in (im)pressing all the Able Horses he meets with And to Return as Earley as posable to morrow. The Genl to beat at 5 oClock, The Troop half an hour after And march Immediatley. [263]

Dear Sir, (Letter III)   **(Br. Officer 3)**

Since my last, we are got out of the settlements and into the Woods. The Scene is changed, but not for the better. I thought we were then so bad that we had the Consolation of being out of Danger of being worse, but I found myself mistaken. The mutinous Spirit of the men encreases but we will get the better of that, we will see which will be tired first, they of deserving Punishments, or we of inflicting them, I cannot but say the very Face of the Country is enough to strike a Damp in the most resolute Mind; the Fatigues and Wants we suffer, added, are enough to dispirit common Men; nor should I blame them for being low spirited, but they are mutinous, and this came from a higher Spring than the Hardships here, for they were tainted in Ireland by the factious Cry against the L--- L-----, Ld G----, and the Primate; the wicked Spirit instilled there by Pamphlets and Conversation, got amongst the common Soldiers, who, tho' they are Englishmen, yet are not the less stubborn and mutinous for that. They have the Impudence to pretend to judge of and blame every Step, not only on the Officers, but of the Ministry. They, every now and then, in their Defence say they are free Englishmen, and Protestants, and are not obliged to obey Orders if they are not fed with Bread, and paid with Money; now there is often only Bills to pay them with, and no Bread but Indian Corn. In fine, in Europe they were better fed than taught; now they must be better taught than fed. Indeed the Officers are as ill off about Food as they, the General himself, who understands good Eating as well as any Man, cannot find wherewithal to make a tolerable Dinner of, tho' he hath two good Cooks who could make an excellent Ragout out of a Pair of Boots, had they but Material to toss them up with; the Provision in the Settlements was bad, but here we can get nothing but Indian Corn, or mouldy Bisket; the First Bread we must bake in Holes in the Ground having no Ovens, so besides the Mustiness of the Flour, it is half Sand and Dirt. We are happy if we can get some rusty salt Pork, or Beef, which hath been carried without Pickle; for as we cannot carry Barrels on Horses, we are forced to take out the Meat and put it in Packs on Horses Backs; sometimes we get a few live Cattle from the Cow-Pens, but they are so lean that they are Carion and unwholesome. To this is added, the Heat of the Country, which occasions such Faintness, that the Men can hardly carry their Arms, and sometimes when these Heats are a little relaxed, there come such

Storms of Rain, Thunder and Lightening, that all the Elements seems on Fire; Numbers of Pine Trees struck to Shivers, and such Effects of Lightening, that if not seen one could hardly believe; yet we have not as yet had one Man killed by Lightening, but we have had several died by the Bite of Snakes, which are mortal, and abound prodigiously in the Swamps, through which we are often forced to march; there is another Inconveniency, which, tho' it seems small, has been as teasing to me as the greater; that is a Kind of tick, or Forest Bug, that gets into the Legs, and occasions Inflammations and Ulcers, so that the Wound itches and makes one ready to tear off the Flesh; this hath greatly distressed both Men and Officers, and there is no Help nor cure for it but Patience: Indeed they seldom occasion Lameness, tho; sometimes they do; a Soldier of our Company was forced to have his Leg cut off, for the Inflammation caused by the many Bites mortifying. We have nothing round us but Trees, Swamps, and Thickets. I cannot conceive how War can be made is such a Country; there has not been Ground to form a Battalion since we left the Inhabitants. I cannot conceive how we must do if we are attacked, nor how we can get up to attack; but the best is what the General said, to reassure the old Soldiers who are all uneasy for Fear of being attack'd on the long March in Defiles, his Excellency with great Judiciousness says, that where the Woods are too thick so as to hinder our coming at them, they will hinder their coming at us.

Just as I write this we hear the best News I ever heard in my Life, the General hath declared to the Virginians, that if they do not furnish us with Waggons and Provisions in two Days, he will march back he has justly upbraided them for exposing the King's Troops, by their Bragging and false Promises. They undertook to furnish us with Horses, Bread and Beef, and really have given nothing but Carion for Meat, Indian Corn for Bread, Jades of Horses which cannot carry themselves. These Assurances of furnishing every Thing has deceived the General hitherto, and he, out of Zeal for the Service, hath undergone the utmost Difficulties; but now it is impossible to go farther without they comply with the promises they were weak, or wicked enough to make, for certainly they were never able to perform them; it is surprizing how they bragged before we left the Settlements, of what Plenty they would furnish us with at the Cow-Pens, and in the Woods; these assurances has bought the General into the present Difficulties, and he has very justly told them, that if he marched any further without a Supply, he should be justly charged with destroying his Majesty's Troops in the Deserts, and thereby occasion the Destruction of Virgina by encouraging the French, that if he was not supplied in two Days, he would march back, and lay their Breach of Faith before his Majesty.

I now begin to hope that I shall once more have the Pleasure of seeing you, and the rest of my Friends, Pray acquaint my dear Mr. M----, that I desire he would not sell my Farm at ---, since I hope soon to be over. (continued) [264]

VIRGINIA-MARYLAND-POTOMAC RIVER   (seaman)

On the 8th:-We began to ferry the Army over the river into Maryland, which was completed at 10, and then we marched on our way to one Jackson's, 8 miles from Cox's. At noon it rained very hard and continued so till 2 o'clock, when we got to our ground, and encamped on the banks of the Potomack. A fine situation, with a good deal of clear ground around about it. Here lives one Colonel Cressop, a Rattle Snake Colonel, and a vile Rascal; calls himself a Frontier man, as he thinks he is situated nearest the Ohio of any inhabitants of the country, and is one of the Ohio Company. He had a summons some time ago to retire from the Settlement, as they said it belonged to them, but he refused, as he dont want resolution; and for his defence has built a log fort round his house. This place is in the track of the Indians and Warriors when they go to war, either to the Northward or Southward. There we got plenty of provisons, &c.,and at 6, the General arrived here with his Attendants, and a Company of Light Horse for his guard, and lay at Cressop's. As this was a wet day, the General ordered the Army to halt tomorrow. [265]

Thursday May the 8th.   (batman)

We marched to Colonel Crisops (Cresap's) and Crosed the Portwomack River, it being 9 miles. [266]

MARYLAND-ANNAPOLIS   (Maryland Gazette)

Thursday Morning last his Excellency General Braddock left Frederick Town, and is gone to the Army at Wills's Creek. [267]

Hough writes: "Crisops (Cresaps, Cresap, Cressops, Jacksons) the 48th Regiment and Mrs. Browne's detachment encamped here May 8-9 and June 12, respectively. Col. Thomas Cresap and his son, Michael, had a trading post at this place which is now known as Old Town. A log fort built by Col. Creasap stood on the high ground between the river and the C. & O. Canal. The campsite was probably near the fort which is no longer in existence. A log house built by Michael Cresap still stands in the village and is known as A House of History. Col. Creasap was appointed a special agent to obtain and store supplies for the Braddock Expedition. However, both Cresaps failed to live up to expectations, for example, the meat delivered to the troops had to be buried because it was spoiled for lack of pickle, and Michael Cresap allowed the wagon train to pass the storage post at Conegogee without loading provisions when en route from Pennsylvania to Fort Cumberland. As a result, a critical shortage of food supplies developed at the Fort and General Braddock had to act quickly on May 27 when the wagon train arrived. Being thus disappointed in flour and beef the General sent away that night 30 wagons with a Captain's detachment to Winchester for provisions over 60 miles of mountains and rocky country and also 300 carrying horses for flour, with part of the troop of light horse to Conegogee 90 miles distant with orders to bring up Cresop, another commissary being appointed. The march from Cresop's campsite to Fort Cumberland, 15 miles distance, was along the river except for elimination of the river bend opposite the mouth of South Branch, according to Atkinson's report." (Winchester-Frederick County Historical Society)

Atkinson writes: "The Army thence pursued the banks of the river, with a slight deviation of route at the mouth of the South Branch, to the village of Old Town, known at that time as the Shawnee Old Town. The road proceeded thence parallel with the river and at the foot of the hills, till it passes the narrows of Will's Mountain, when it struck out a shorter line coincident with the present county road, and lying between the railroad and the mountain, to Fort Cumberland. From Little Cacapehon to this point the ground was comparatively easy, and the road had been generally judiciously chosen.

May 9 (Friday)

VIRGINIA-GREAT CAPE CAPON RIVER

Great Cape Capon May 9th: 1755   **(Halkett)**

The Parole is Gage

    1 Serjt 7 12 men for the Qr Guard. A Corpl & 6 men to mount as a Guard on the Waggon horses And to patrole every two hours to see their fences Are up And to prevent the Horses geting Away. [268]

MARYLAND-OLD TOWN

Fryday May the 9th.   **(batman)**

    We halted and Rec'd two days provisions. [269]

VIRGINIA-WILLIAMSBURG   (Virginia Gazette)
    Deserted, on the 21st Day of April last from Col. Dunbar's
Regiment, Robert Lynn, of the Colonel's Company, drafted from Capt.
Polson's Company, he is 5 feet, 9 inches and a half high, 26 years of
age, fresh color'd, wore a Wig was born in Londenderry; the Place of
his residence in this Country was at Conicogee in Maryland, a Laborer.
    Deserted also at the same time, Robert Blackburn, from Lieutenant
Colonel Burton's Company, in Colonel Dunbar's Regiment, he is 5
feet 8 inches high, 24 years of age, with brown Hair, Pock marked,
served his Time with William Webb, a Justice of Peace, upon Little
Lan-Tatom, in Maryland, a Laborer.
    Whoever apprehend and conveys the said Deserters to General
Braddock, at the Camp, to the Commissary at Winchester, or to
Williamsburg, shall be intitled to, and receive, Three Pistoles Reward
for each. [270]

May 10 (Saturday)
VIRGINIA-GREAT CAPE CAPON RIVER
Great Cape Capon May:10th:1755   (Halkett/Disney)
The Parole is York
    1 Corpl & men for the Rear Guard And 1 Corpl & 4 to go with
Bagage. The Genl to beat at Day break at wh: time the Horses are to
put to the Guns & waggons And to march Immediately after. [271]

MARYLAND-CAMP AT FORT CUMBERLAND
Saturday, May 10th, 1755   (Braddock)
Parole-Connecticut
Mr. Washington is appointed aid de camp to His Excellency General
Braddock.
Field officer for to morrow Majr Sparke.
    The articles of war to be read to morrow morning, at which time
the servants, women and followers of the army are to attend with the
respective corps and companies that they belong to.
    The two Independent companies and Rangers to receive three Days
provisions to morrow.
    For the Generals Guard 48th Regiment.
    Col Dunbars Regiment to relieve the Fort Guard immediatley, and
the Fort Guard is to march to Fraziers as a Grass Guard, and to be
relieved every 48 hours. Capt Pilson's company of carpenters is to

send one corporal and 6 men with their tools and to make such fences as the officer of the Grass Guard shall think proper.

The Virginia and Maryland Rangers and the company of carpenters to settle their men's accts immediately, giving them credit for what arrears &c are due, and they are for the future to be subisted regularly twice a week as the rest of the troops are.

A return to be given in to morrow morning of the strength of each of the Regiments by companys, the return to be signed by the commanding officers of each corps the Independant Companys, Virginia and Maryland Rangers and the Troops of Light Horse are also to send in a return to morrow morning of their strength, which return is to be signed by the captain of officer commanding each company, and to be given in separately.

The General has fixed the hour for his Levy, from ten till eleven in the forenoon every Day. [272]

(seaman)

On the 10th:-Marched at 5 on our way to Will's Creek, 16 miles from Cressop's; the road this day very pleasant by the water side. At 12 the General passed by, the drums beating the Grenadier March. At 1 we halted and formed a circle, when Colonel Dunbar told the Army that as there were a number of Indians at Will's Creek, our Friends, it was the General's positive orders that they do not molest them, or have anything to say to them, directly or indirectly, for fear of affronting them. We marched again, and heard 17 guns fired at the Fort to salute the General. At 2 we arrived at Will's Creek, and encamped to the Westward of the Fort on a hill, and found here 6 Companies of Sir Peter Halket's Regt., 9 Companies of Virginians, and a Maryland Company. Fort Cumberland is situated within 200 yards of Will's Creek, on a hill and about 400 from the Potomack; its length from east to west is about 200 yards, and breath 46 yards, and is built by logs driven into the ground, and about 12 feet above it, with embrasures for 12 guns, and 10 mounted, 4 pounders, besides stocks for swivels, and loop holes for small arms. We found here Indian men, women and children, to the number of about 100, who were greatly surprised at the regular way of our soldiers marching, and the numbers. I would willingly say something of the customs and manners of the Indians, but they are hardly to be described. The men are tall, well made and active, but not strong, but very dexterous with a rifle barrelled gun, and their tomahawk, which the will throw with great certainty at any mark and at a great distance. The women are not so tall as the men, but well made and have many children, but had many more before spirits were introduced to them. They paint themselves in an odd manner, red, yellow, and black intermixed. And the men have the outer rim of their ears cut, which only hangs by a bit top and bottom, and have a tuft of hair left at the top of their heads, which is dressed with feathers. Their watch coat is their chief clothing, which is a thick blanket thrown all round them, and wear moccasins instead of shoes, which are Deer skin, thrown round the ankle and foot. Their manner of carrying their infants is odd. They are laid on a board, and tied on with a broad bandage, with a place to rest their feet on, and a board over their head to keep the sun off, and are slung to the women's backs. These people have no notion of religion, or any sort of Superior being, as I take them to be the most ignorant people as to the knowledge of the world and other things. In the day they were in our Camp, and in the night they go into their own, where they dance and make a most horrible noise. [273]

Satterday May the 10th.   **(batman)**
   We marched to Willses Creek (Wills Creek). Close by the Creek is the Portwomack River, it Being 15 miles. We pased the fort and Incamped upon the hill above the Fort which is Called Fort Cumberland. When the genll Arived, he was Salluted by the guns in the garrison. Here we Joined the rest of the Army. [274]

   On this day the General in his chariot accompanied by George Washington, Robert Orme and the Virginia Troop of light horse head toward Fort Cumberland along side of the Potomac River passing the 48th Regiment of Foot along the road at mid-day arriving at Fort Cumberland between 1 and 2 p.m.

May 11 (Sunday)
MARYLAND-FORT CUMBERLAND
Camp at Fort Cumberland   **(Braddock)**
Sunday, May 11, 1755
Parole-Albany
Field Officer to morrow [Lt] Col Burton
The Generals Guard 44th Regmt.
   A return to be sent in of the numbers of men who understand the springing of rocks, & those men that are fitt are to be told that they

will receive proper encouragement all the troops are to begin their field Days. Powder may be had from the train by applying for it, and each man is to have 12 rounds for every field Day.

A Return is to be given in to morrow morning at orderly time of the recruits of the whole army, setting forth their age size country and occupation one Sargeant and 6 men from piquet to attend during the time of marketing to prevent Disputes, and if any should happen he is to apply to the capt[n] of the Picquet he belongs to. This duty to be done alternately.

All provisons brought into camp to be settled according to a settled rule, a copy of which well be given to the troops by the Major of Brigade and no person bringing provisions shall presume to ask more nor shall anybody offer less for good and wholesome meat.

The 48th Regiment is to receive their Days provisons to morrow at 10 o'clock.

AFTER ORDERS.

All the out guard to be relieved to morrow morn'g and parade at 5 o'clock.

EVENING ORDERS

It is His Excellencys General Braddocks orders that no officer soldier or others give the Indians men women or children any rum other Liquor or money upon any account whatever. [275]

VIRGINIA-CAMP BETWIXT ENOXES & COVES

Camp   betwixt Enoxes & Coves May 11th 1755   (Halkett/Disney)
The Parole is Ballinroble

1 Serjt & 18 men as a Guard on the Artillery Bagage & Machee's (matches or fuses). The Genl to beat at 3 oClock at which time the Horses to be put to the waggons And the Troop to beat half an hour after and march Directly. The Bagage waggons to be ready to go in the Front. [276]

> *Strong drink was called: "goniga-nongi" by the Indians.*
> *Hough writes: "Spring Mountain (Spring Gap Mt., Spring Gap) Only Mrs. Browne mentions this campsite by name (see Browne narrative June 11). On the other hand, Halkett's Orderly Book has only one entry between May 10 and 18, that is, during the 8 days required to march from Enochs to Wills Creek. During this time the units with artillery and 'Bagage Waggons' was moving through the most difficult part of the march. It is not unlikely that at least one of the nights was spent at Spring Mountain, the only desirable site in the difficult area. Spring Gap gets its name from the fact that a spring is located on the*

187

western slope of the ridge about 25 yards below the crest of a gap in the mountains. The gap is about 250 feet below the crest of the mountain as one looks southward from the gap, and about 450 feet below the highest part of the ridge to the north. In the gap is an area of more than an acre of gentle sloping ground bordering the spring. This was probably the campsite. Braddock's Road was on or near the present dirt road (W.Va. 2/3) that passes close by the spring. The old road leaves the present road about 100 yards below the spring to make a more direct descent of the west slope of the mountain. In several places as one descends the ridge, however, the two roads are still the same, such as at the crossing of the black-top road (W.Va.2) and again going down in a westerly direction for possibly half a mile until the old road that is currently called Dug Hill Road (W.Va. 2/4). The two roads appear to come together again shortly before arriving at the abandoned Dug Hill School. At this place the old road curves slightly southward to follow closely Dug Hill Run to the Little Cacapon River.

After crossing the Little Cacapon near the mouth of Dug Hill Run the march turned north down the Little Cacapon, crossing the river many times before arriving at Cox's Camp where the Little Cacapon empties into the Potomac. The air-line distance is about 3.8 miles but following the stream as it bends among the hills the distance is between 6 and 7 miles. In going the distance to the Potomac there appears to be about 17 crossings on the ripples, the final crossing put the army on he west bank of Little Cacapon slightly more than 1/2 a mile south of Cox's Camp at Ferry Field.

That the Braddock road followed down Little Cacapon to its mouth is attested by T.C. Atkinson. In 1847, Atkinson had his assistant Middleton prepare an excellent map of the route from the mouth of Little Cacapon to the battlefield in western Pennsylvania. The map, known as the Middleton Map, was published in 1848 with explanatory notes by Atkinson that include the following: "The army struck the Little Cacaphon (Cacapon) about 6 miles above its mouth and following the stream encamped on the Virginia side of the Potomac preparetory to crossing into Maryland...the spot is known as Ferry-fields from the army having been ferried over. The Army thence pursued the banks of the river, with slight deviation of route at the mouth of the South Branch, to the village of Old Town. Middleton's Map shows the route a short distance south of Ferry-Fields. It crossed from the east side to the west side of Little Cacapon River a little more than a half-mile south of the mouth of the river."(Winchester-Frederick County Historical Society).

Hough writes: "Friend Cox owned 435 acres of land on the Virginia side at the mouth of Little Cacapon River. The tract of 195 acres along the west bank of Little Cacapon included the flat ground known as "Ferry fields," the campsite from which the army ferried over the Potomac. At that time at least part of the field was sufficiently cleared for cultivation since we find the following note made when the army was returning from its defeat: Sunday Augst ye 3rd. This day we march'd cross the river Portwomack to Coxes Camp, it being 9 miles (from Cresaps). There was some Indien corn growing where we incamped in going up the Cuntry, which Oblig'd us to Encamp Close to the River but on the Virginia side."(Winchester-Frederick County Historical Society).

MARYLAND-CAMP AT FORT CUMBERLAND (Orme)

The General had applied to Governor Morris for some Indians (Aughquick) who lived upon the Susquehannah; about thirty of them met him at this place (Fort Cumberland). The General showed them the greatest Marks of attention and esteem, and the next day called them to his tent, and conferred with them agreeably to their forms and customs.

The General told them of the troops and Artillery his Majesty had sent to their Assistance, and made use of every argument to persuade them to take up the hatchet against the French, and to act with spirit and fidelity under him. After a few days, at another Congress... (see May 19th) [277]

(seaman)

On the 11th:-Orders that the General's Levee be always in his tent from 10 to 11 every day. [278]

(batman)

We had an Assembaly with our Indiens. [279]

May 12 (Monday)

MARYLAND-CAMP AT FORT CUMBERLAND
Parole-Boston (Braddock)
Field Officer to morrow Majr Sparke.
The Generals Guard 48th Regiment.

Whereas Capt. Poulson, one of the Virgina company of carpenters desired a court martial to enquire into his character, having been accused of being in arms in the late Rebellion in Scotland His Excellency has been informed that the accusations is scandalous and groundless; if therefore any person whatever can prove Captn Polson to have been in the late Rebellion they are desired immediately to send their accusation to the General; if not His Excellency entirely frees him from any imputation of that kind, and desires that no reflection of the future may be thrown on Captn Polson on that acct.

AFTER ORDERS.

A General Court Martial to sit immediately at the President's Tent, it is to consist of one field officer, 6 Captns and 6 Subalterns.

    Majr Sparke President.
    Mr Shirley Judge Advocate.

His Excellency has thought proper to Brigade the Army in the following manner and they are for the future to encamp accordingly:

The 1st Brigade, Commanded by Sir Peter Halket:

	Compliment-Effective
44 Regiment of Foot	700-700
Captn Rutherford's Indep Co NY & Captn Gates	100 95
Capt. Polson Carpenters	50 48
Capt. Peronnee's Virg.Rangers	50 47
Capt Wagner's Virginia Rangers	50 45
Capt.Dagworthy's Maryl.Rangers	50 49
The Second Brigade, Commanded by Colonel Dunbar:	
48th Regiment of Foot	700 700
Capt. Demerie's S.C. Detacht	100 97
Capt. Dobb's N.C. Rangers	100 80
Capt. Mercer's Co. Carpenters	35
Capt. Stevens Virginia Rangers	50 48
Capt. Hogg's Virginia Rangers	50 40
Capt. Cox's Virginia Rangers	50 43

Any soldier or follower of the army who shall stop any one bringing in provisions or forage to the camp shall immediately suffer death.

No out post to march from or to camp with beat of drum, nor is any beat of drum to beat before the Troop unless when any of the Troops are out at exercise, and of which they are to acquaint the General the night before thro' one of His aid de camps.[280]

(Orme)

We had been promised the greatest plenty of all kinds of provisions at this place, but none fresh could be procured. The General was greatly concerned to see the want of all refreshments begin so early, fearing it would disable the men from undertaking the fatigues and hardships they were to meet with on the March to the Ohio. They had already marched two hundred miles through an uninhabited wilderness without any other but the salt provision that they had carried with them, or that had been laid in for them upon the road. The General offered large rewards, and lent several people his own money to enable them to provide the camp, and give all manner of encouragement to such as would bring provision. Everything brought to camp was to be sold at a particular place, and any person was to suffer death who should dare to interupt or molest anybody bringing provision, or should offer to buy of them before it was carried to the public market, which was put under the care and inspection of the Captains of the

Picket, and a Sergeant with a small Guard of the Picket to attended the market to prevent all quarrels or confusion.

As a further encouragement, the price of provisions was raised a penny in the pound, and no good meat was to be sold at less than the fixed price, lest the Peasants should be distress'd when they had brought it many miles. These regulations and encouragements produced some supplies, tho' by the nature of the country inadequate to the wants of the camp. [281]

(seaman)

On the 12th.:-Orders this morning that there will be a congress at the General's tent at 11 o'clock, at which time all the officers attended the General, and the Indians were brought; the Guard received them with their Firelocks rested. The Interpreter was ordered to tell them that their Brothers, the English, who were their old friends, were come to assure them that every misunderstanding that had been in former times should now be buried under that great mountain (a mountain close by). Then a string of wampum was given them; then a belt of wampum was held forth with the following speech, vizt.: that this wampum was to assure them of our friendship; that everybody who were their enemies were ours; and that it was not the small force only that we had here, but numbers to the northward under our great War Captains, Shirley, Pepperrell, Johnston, and others that were going to war, and that we would settle them happy in their country, and make the French both ashamed and hungary: But that whatever Indians after this declaration did not come in, would be deemed by us as our enemies, and treated as such. The General then told them he should have presents for them in a few days, when he should have another speech to make to them, so took their leaves after the ceremony of Drams round. In the afternoon Mr. Spendlowe and self surveyed 20 casks of beef by order of the General and condemmed it, which we reported to the General. This evening we had a gust of wind, with lightening, thunder and rain, which drove several tents down, and make the camp very uncomfortable. [282]

Munday May the 12th.   (batman)
    I went into the Cuntry to buy us a Cow to give Milk for here it is very scarce or none, for we have pased the Inhabited Cuntry a Bove 20 miles. [283]

May 13 (Tuesday)
MARYLAND-CAMP AT FORT CUMBERLAND

Parole-Charleston   **(Braddock)**

Field Officer for to morrow Lt Col Burton.

For the Generals Guard 44th Regiment.

The quartermasters, Camp colour men, and Pioneers of the two Regiments with two men of the Independent Companies with proper Tools for clearing the ground in the Front to parade at five o'clock in the Evening at the head of the 48th Regiment, and to remain there for the Field Officer of the Day's orders.

The Picquetts are to lay advanced and to remain at their parade till they receive the Field Officers orders. Each of the two Regiments to send 6 tents to the companies in each Brigade, and also to send 6 tents each for the men of their advanced Picquets. The centrys on the advanced Picquetts not to suffer any body to pass unquestioned after sun set.

The Picquet returns at 6 o'clock in the morning.

The quarter Guard of Sir Peter Halketts Regiment for the future to be posted on the right flank. [284]

                                                                       (seaman)

On the 13th:-The weather is now extremely hot. This day as the Corporal came to exercise our men in the evening, I went to see the Indian camp, ¼ mile from ours, in the woods. Their houses are 2 stakes driven into the ground, with a Ridge pole, and bark of trees laid up and down the sides, but they generally have a fire in them. This is all the shelter they have from the weather when they are from home. As soon as it was dark they began to dance, which they do round a fire in a ring. Their music is a tub with a sheep skin over it (Tay wa'egun), and a hollow thing with peas to rattle (Sheshegwon). It is a custom with them, once or twice a year, for the women to dance and all the men sit by. Each woman takes our her man that she likes, dances with him and lies with him for a week, and then return to their former husbands, and live as they did before. [285]

Tuesday May the 13th.   **(batman)**

We Rec'd two days provisions and at Night the Picqet (sentry) advanced in the front of the line. The Reason was in the day they heard that there was a Body of the French Indiens within a mile of our Camp to the number of five hundred but it was all false. [286]

May 14 (Wednesday)
MARYLAND-CAMP AT FORT CUMBERLAND
Parole-Dimfries   (Braddock)
Field Officer to morrow Lt Col Burton.
The Generals Guard 48th Regiment.

The General Court Martial is dissolved. Luke Woodward soldier in the 48th Regiment, commanded by Col Dunbar, having been tryed for Desertion by a General Court Martial whereof Maj^r Wm Sparke was president, is by sentence of that Genl Court Martial adjudged to suffer death. His Excellency Genl Braddock has approved of the sentence, but has been pleased to pardon him.

Thomas Conelly, James Fitzgerald and James Hughes, soldiers in the 48th Regiment, and tryed for theft by the said Court Martial whereof Major Sparke was President, are by the sentence of the s'd Court Martial adjudged to suffer the following punishments:

Thomas Conelly one thous^d Lashes att the Head of the line.

Jas Fitzgerald, eight hund^d Lashes att the Head of the line.

Jas Hughes eight hund^d Lashes att the Head of the line.

Also that they be obliged to make satisfaction for the Kegg of Beer stolen by them to the value of thirty three shilgs Maryland Cur^y, and that proper stopages be made out of their pay by their officers for that purpose; His Excellency has approved the sentence, but has been pleased to remit one hundred lashes from the punishment of Conelly and two hundred from each of the other two. Conelly is to receive 900 lashes at 3 different times 300 lashes each time. Jas Fitzgerald and Jas Huges are to receive 600 lashes each at two different times, 300 lashes each time. The 48th Regiment to send the Drummers to the head of ye line, to put the sentence in execution, the first time of punishment to be to morrow morning at troop beating. The two Picquetts formed from the Independent Companies Virginia and Maryland Rangers, to consist of one Captn 2 Subalterns, 2 Sargeants, 2 Corporals and 38 Centinals.[287]

May 14, Wednesday. Fort Cumberland.   (Washington)
Dear Brother:(John Augustine Washington)

I overtook the General at Frederick-Town, in Maryland, and proceeded with him, by way of Winchester, to this place which gave him a good opportunity to see the absurdity of the route, and of damning it very heartily [288]

May 14, Wednesday. Fort Cumberland   **(Washington)**
To John Carlyle:

Colo. Dunbar's Regiment was oblig'd to cross over at Connogogee and come down within 6 miles of Winchester to take the new road up, which gave me infinite satisfaction. [289]

Fort Cumberland, 14 May,1755   **(Washington)**
Dear Brother:(John Augustine Washington)

As wearing boots is quite the mode, I must beg the favor of you to procure me a pair that are good and neat, and seen them to Major Carlyle, who I hope will contrive to forward them as quickly as my necessity requries.

I seen no prospect of moving from this place; as we have neither Horses nor waggons enough, and no forage for them to subsist upon but what is expected from Philadelphia; therefore I am well convinced that the trouble and difficulty we must encounter in passing the Mountain for want of proper conveniences, will equal all the other Interruptions of the Campaigne; for I conceive the March of such a Train of Artillery in these Roads to be a tremendous undertaking: As to any danger from the Enemy I look upon it as trifling, for I believe they will be oblig'd to exert their utmost Force to repel the attacks to the Northward....

The Gen'l. has appointed me one of his Aids de Camps, in which Character I shall serve this Campaigne, agreeably enough, as I am thereby freed from all commands but his, and give Order's to all, which must be implicitly obey'd.

I have now a good oppertunity, and shall not neglect it, of forming an acquaintence, which may be serviceable hereafter, if I can find it worth while pushing my fortune in the Military way.

I have wrote to my two female corrispondents by this oppertunity, one of which Letters I have inclos'd to you, and beg y'r. deliverance off. I shall expect a Succienct acc't of all that has happended since my departure. [290]

On the 14th:-This day 2 of our men arrived from Frederick hospital, and our men from Connecockieg that were left to assist the Artillery. Orders to send the returns of our people to the Brigade major every morning. ²⁹¹

Wedensday May the 14th. **(batman)**

We had a Genll Coart Marshall. One Soldier was tried for disartion and sentenced to Suffer death. Three more was tried for Stealing a Barrel of Beer in the Cuntry and Was Odered three hundred lashes a man with the Cat of Nine tails. ²⁹²

May 15 (Thursday)

MARYLAND-CAMP AT FORT CUMBERLAND

Parole-Portsmouth **(Braddock)**

Field Officer to morrow is Majr Sparke.

For the Generals Guard 44th Regiment.

The Officers who were ordered to get themselves in readiness to go with the paymaster are cont^d

On subaltern, one sergt 1 corpl and 30 cent'l to march this evening to Mr Martin's where the troop of Light Horse graze, the men to take tents with them and provisions for three days, the officer to receive his orders from Capt Stuart of the Light Horse; this guard to be relievd every 3d Day.

One Serg^t, one Corpl and 12 men to parade att the Fort Guard this Day at 12 o'clock.

The Surgeant will receive his orders from Capt Orme.

AFTER ORDERS.

The Subalterns Guard that was ordered to march to Martin's is countermanded. ²⁹³

On the 15th:-Mr. Spendlowe and self surveyed 22 casks of beef, and condemmed it, which we reported to the General. ²⁹⁴

Thursday May the 15th. **(batman)**

We had a field day. The Regt was out at Exercise at five in the morning and after Exercise we Rec'd provisions. ²⁹⁵

May 15, Thursday. Fort Cumberland **(Washington)**

I was sent to Col.(John) Hunter for a supply of money and arrived as far as Winchester on the day following. [296]

May 15 Fort Cumberland   **(Scarroyady)**
To: Colonel Johnson
I hope you will send what warriors you can spare to join us.[297]

PENNSYLVANIA-PHILADELPHIA   **(Pennsylvania Gazette)**
We hear from the counties of Lancaster, York and Cumberland, that notice being given there that waggon and carriages were wanting for the use of the Army, great numbers were immediately offered and 250 waggons, laden with oats, Indian corn and other forage were dispatched to the camp in a few days and many more might have been had if wanted the people offering with great readiness and cheerfulness from a zeal for his Majesties Service. [298]

Nichols writes: "Mohawks did not go on the expedition as they believed southern Indians (Catawbas) were part of Braddock's force-their enemys".

Scarroyady (Scaroodaya) was also known as Monacatootha who after helping George Washington on the campaign the year before (1754 - Fort Necessity) removed his people from the Ohio Country to the upper Susquehanna River area.

May 16 (Friday)
MARYLAND-CAMP AT FORT CUMBERLAND
Parole-Winchester   **(Braddock)**
Field Officer to morrow Lt Col Gage.
For the Generals Guard 44th Regiment.

Any Indian Trader, Soldier or follower of the army who shall dare to give liquor to any of the Indians or shall receive or purchase from them any of their presents made to them by His Majesty thro' His Excellency Genl Braddock, shall suffer the severest punishment a court martial can inflict.

There will be a public congress of the Indians to morrow at 12 o'clock at the Genls tent. [299]

VIRGINIA-WINCHESTER
May 16, Friday. Winchester.   **(Washington)**

To John Hunter

I have Letters from the General and Paymaster with Bills and proper Instructions, all of which I shall deliver when I have the pleasure of meeting you, and this I expect will be in Williamsburg on Wednesday next as I am now on my way down and shall delay no time on the journey. [300]

(seaman)

On the 16th:-Arrived here Lieut. Col. Gage, with 2 companies of Sir Peter Halket's, and the last division of the train, consisting of 3 field pieces, 4 howitzers, a number of cohorns, and 42 waggons with stores. Departed this life Captain Bromley of Sir Peter Halket's. [301]

Fryday May the 16th.   **(batman)**

The first division of the train of Artilary Ariv'd here with two Companies of Sir Peeter Halkets Regt from Alexandria. [302]

May 17 (Saturday)

MARYLAND-CAMP AT FORT CUMBERLAND

Parole-Eskaw   **(Braddock)**

The congress of Indians mentioned in yesterdays orders is put off.
Field officer to morrow Lt Col Burton.
For the Generals Guard 48th Regiment.

The Two Regiments, the Independent compys, the companys of carpenters, the Virginia and Maryland company of Rangers and the Troop of Light Horse are to send immediately to Mr Lake, commissary of Provisions a separate return of the number of persons they each of them draw provisions for, this return to be signed by the commander of the two regt and by the captains or officers commanding each of the Independent companys &c. The form of this return is sent to the Brigade Major and is to be given in regularly every eight Days.

His Excellency expects that this order will be punctually obeyed, as the commissary will not be able to provide a proper quanity of Provisions for the army unless he has the above return sent to him regularly.

One Subaltern, one Sergt 1 corporal, & 30 men to mount as a guard on the artillery, They are to parade this afternoon at 5 o'clock and to be relieved every 48 hours. [303]

On the 17th:-Had a survey of our men's arms, and found several of them unserviceable. All the officers are desired to attend Captain Bromley's funeral tomorrow morning, and at the General's tent at 12.[304]

Satterday May the 17th.
This day a Capt[n] (Bromley) belonging to Sir Peeter Halkets Regt dyed of a vilant Feaver which this Cuntry is very Subject to. [305]

May 18 (Sunday)
MARYLAND-CAMP AT FORT CUMBERLAND
Camp at Wills's Creek May:18th:1755   **(Braddock, Halkett/Disney)**
The Parole is Farnham

Genl: Orders There will be a publick Congress of The Indians heald This Day at 12 oClock at the Genls: Tent. Field Offr for to Morrow Major Sparks.

1 Corpl & 8 men of the Line to Attend The Engineers in Survaying. They Are to parade at 9 oClock. His Excellency Genl: Braddock Has been pleasd to Appoint Capt Lt Richard Gethins to be Capt to The Late Capt Bromleys Company & Lieut Terence Molloy to be Capt Lieut in his room & Ensn Williams to Lieut in his room & Mr. Geo: Pennington to be Ensn in the Room of Ensn: Williams & They are all to be Obayed as such.

Each regt Indipendent Compys &c in the making up of their Cartridges Are to Allow 36 rounds with ball to a pound of powder And for field Days & Excercise Are to allow 46 (with or with out Ball) to a pound of powder. Six Women per Company Are Allowed each of the two regts: & the Indipendent Companys, 4 Women to each of the Company of Carpenters Virginian & Maryland Rangers, 5 Women to the Artillery, 2 Women to the Detachment of Seamen & 2 Women to the Troop of Light Horse. His Excellency Expects that this Order is puntualy Complyd with As no more provisions will be Allowd to be Drawn for Then the Above Number of Women. The Surgons of the Two regts Indipendt: Artillery Are to meet (Capt Morris) Aid du Camp to Genl Braddock At his Tent to Morrow Morning at 11 oClock. 1 Sub: 1 Serjt 1 corp & 30 men to parade to Morrow morning at 6 oClock. They are to have Three days provisions and the officers (sic) is this night to receive his Orders from S[r] John S[t] Clear. [306]

On the 18th:-Excessively hot. At 10 o'clock we all attended the funeral, and the ceremony was a Captain's guard marched before the corpse, with the Captain of it in the rear, and the fire locks reversed, the drums beating the dead march. When we came near the grave, the guard formed 2 lines facing each other; rested on their arms, muzzles downward; and leaned their faces on the butts: the Corpse was carried between them, the sword and sash on the coffin, and the officers following two by two. After the Clergyman (Mr. Philip Hughes) had read the service, the guard fired 3 vollies over him and returned. At 12 we attended the General's tent when all the Indians came, and the General made a speech to them for this purpose. He desired they would immediatelly send their wives and children into Pensylvania, and take up the Hatchet against the French: that the great King of England, their Father, had sent them the presents now before them for their families, and that he had ordered arms &c. to be given to their Warriors; and expressed concern for the loss of the Half-King killed last year. The presents consisted of strouds, rings, beads, linen, knives, wire, and paint. They received their presents with 3 belts and a string of wampum, and promised their answer next day. And to show they were pleased, they made a most horrible noise, dancing all night.[307]

The Captn was Buried. This day was held a Congrace (congress) with the Indiens.[308]

May 19 (Monday)

MARYLAND
CAMP AT FORT CUMBERLAND
Parole-Guilford   (Braddock)
Field officer to morrow Lt Col Gage.
For the Generals Guard 44th Regiment.

Each Brigade to send a man to the Gen'l Hospital as Orderly who are to receive and obey the directions of Doct[r] Napper Director of the 2d Hospital.

All the troops are to acct with the Director of the Hospital once in three months or as soon after as can be, for stoppages at the rate of 5 pence stirl'g per Day, for every Man that is admitted in the Gen'l Hospital; this stoppage to commence for the 24th of May ensuing.

As soon as the Retreat has been beat this night the Drum Maj[r]. of each of the two Regimets are to march with the Drummers and Drumers to the Head of the artillery where they will receive orders.

AFTER ORDERS

A return to be given into the Brigade Major to morrow at orderly time of the number of smiths and carpenters that are in the two Regiments, Independent Companies &c. [309]

Camp at Wills's Creek May 19th: 1755   **(Halkett/Disney)**

The Parole is G(u)ilford

Field Officer for to Morrow Lieut Col.Gage

A Congress to Morrow will be held with the Indians at the Genls Tent at One oClock. Each Brigade to send a man to the Genl: Hospital as Orderly who are to receive And Obay the Directions of Docter Nap(i)er. All the Troops to Acct with the Directer of the Hospital once in Three Months or as soon after as can be for stopages at the rate of five pence Sterg: per Day for every Man that is Admitted into the Genl Hospital.

As soon as the retreat is beat this Night The Drum Major of each of the two regts Are to march with Their drummers & Drums to ye Head of the Artillery where they will receive their Orders. [310]

(Orme)

(cont.)A few days after, at another Congress, they (the Indians) informed him (the General) of their resolutions to serve with him, and declared war against the French according to their own ceremonies. They desired leave to return to the Susque hannah with their wives and children (to whom the General made considerable presents) and promised to rejoin him in a few days, only eight of them remaining with him (the General), who were immediatley employed in getting intelligence (see list of names of the Indians). The others never returned to the General, but about sixteen of them advanced as far as Colonel Dunbar's Camp. The General sent messengers to the Delawar and Shawnee Indians to invite them to join him. [311]

(seaman)

On the 19th:-Captain Gate's New York Company arrived here. This evening the Indians met at the General's tent to give their answer, which was, that they were greatly obliged to the Great King their Father, who had been so good as to send us all here to fight for them, and that they would all give their attendance, and do what was in their power of reconnoitring the country and bringing intelligence. That they were obliged to the General for his expressing concern for the loss of the Half-King our Brother, and for the presents he had given them. Their chief men's names are as follows: Monicotoha, their wise man who always speaks for them (Monicatoha their Mentor);--Belt of Wampum or White Thunder, who has a daughter called Bright Lightning - he keeps the wampum: the next is the great Tree and Silver Heels (Jerry Smith and Charles), with many others belonging to the Six Nations. The General told them he was their Friend, and never would deceive them, after which they sung the war song, which is shouting and making a terrible noise, declaring the French their perpetual enemies, which they never did before. After this the General carried them to the Artillery, and ordered 3 Howitzers, 3 ½-Pounders, and 3 Cohorns to be fired, all the drums and fifes playing, and beating the point of war, which astonished and pleased the Indians greatly. They then retired to their own Camp, where they ate a bullock, and danced their war dance, which is droll and odd, shewing how they scalp and fight, expressing in their dance the exploits of their ancestors, and warlike actions of themselves. [312]

Munday May the 19th.   **(batman)**
     We had a Congrace with the Indiens and after Retreat Beating the Train fired three piece of Cannon and threw several Shels in the Air to let the Indiens see the way that we proposed to proceed with the French. They seemed greatly divarted. [313]

May 20 (Tuesday)
MARYLAND-CAMP AT FORT CUMBERLAND
Parole-Hendon   **(Braddock, Halkett/Disney)**
Field officer to morrow Lt Col Burton;
For the Generals Guard 48th Regmt.
     One Subaltern, 1 Sergt, 1 corp & 24 men to parade to morrow morning at 5 o'clock they are to have three Days Provisions with them and the officer is this night to receive his orders from Sir John S[t]. Clair. [314]

                                                          (Orme)
     About the 20th of May, the Artillery, which marched in two divisions, arrived. They had remained at Alexandria a fortnight after the General had left it, through the want of waggons and horses, nor

could they at last have marched without press parties, which Lieutenant Colonel Gage sent for many miles round, and he was obliged to continue this method the whole march, having neither pasture nor forage on the road, not even at those places where it had been said to have been provided. This march was over a prodigious chain of mountains, and through deep and rocky roads. The troops were now joined, except a North Carolina company, commanded by Captn. Dobbs, which was daily expected.

The General had now frequent opportunities of seeing and hearing of the appearance and disposition of the Virginia Recruits and companies. Mr Allen had take the greatest pains with them, and they performed their evolutions and firings as well as could be expected, but their languid, spiritless, and unsoldierlike appearance considered with the lowness and ignorance of most of their Officers, gave little hopes of their future good behavior.

Guards were posted upon the Patomack and Will's Creek, and two other guards were ordered for the security of the horses that were grazing in the woods; and Detachments of the Picket lay advanced from retreat beating till daylight, having been informed some Indians had been seen near the Camp. [315]

Dear Sir, (Letter IV)   (Br. Officer 3)
In my last I acquainted you with the joyful News that our General resolved not to be any longer put upon by the Virginians, Orders were given for our March back, but the Day before that was appointed there arrived five Quakers decently dressed, they were pure plump Men, on brave fat Horses which, by the way, were the first plump Creatures I had seen in this Country. Then, as I told you before, I believe Virginia was peopled by Pharaoh's lean Kine(kin), but these Quakers seem to come from the Land of Goshen, they looked like Christian People, they went directly to his Excellence, and Curiosity carried us all to the general Quarters. They came with Thanks to the General from the People of Pensilvania, for the great Labour he had gone through in advancing so far into the Wilderness for the Protection of his Majesty's dutiful Subjects. They acquainted him further, that they had been cutting Roads to meet him with a Number of Waggons loaded with Flour, Cheese, Bacon, and other provision; tho' this was good News I did but half like it, I fear's it would occasion our Stay, and prevent our marching back; besides it was ominous, your Cheese and

your Bacon being the Baits that draw Rats to Destruction; and it proved but too true; this Bait drew us into a trap where happy was he that came off with the loss of his Tail only. This Evening we saw the Road and Waggons, and the Men eat, this was a Duty so long disused, that it was a Tour of Fatigue to the Teeth. The Fellows who drove the Waggons, tho' they would have made but a shabby Figure among our Hampshire Carters, yet here they looked like Angels compared with the long, lank, yellow-faced Virginians, who at best are a half-starved, ragged, dirty Set; if by Accident they can clear enough by their Tobacco to buy a Coat, they rather chuse a half-wore gaudy Rag, than a substantial coarse Cloth, or Kersey; they are the very Opposites to the Pensilvanians, who buy Coats of Cloth so strong as to last as long as the Garments of the Israelites in their March through the Desert; a Coat serves a Man for his Life and yet looks fresh, but this comes from their never wearing them at Home; when out of Sight they work half naked. They are a very frugal People, and if they were not so would be as beggarly as their Neighbours the Viginians. The Ground does not bear half the Crops as in England; they have no Market but by Sea, and that very dull, if you consider they are forced to put their Flour in Barrels after grinding and sifting, all at their own Charge, and no Consideration thereof in the Price which the English Farmer only thrashes his Wheat, and sends it to Market. Tho' Pensilvania is a Paradise to Virginia, it is a very poor Country compared to England, and no Man in his Senses that can live with Comfort in England stays here; as soon as they get Estates they come over to England. The Proprietor, a most worthy Gentleman, and universally admired, went over, and out of Compliance staid a little Time with them, but soon returned back to England, where he resides. If Pensilvania could be agreeable to any one it would be so to him, who is one of the most amiable Men living, and the whole People used their utmost Endeavours to make the Place agreeable; but alas, the Intemperature of the Climate, the Nearness and Frugality in their Manner of Living, necessary to carry on the Cultivation; the Labour that most are forced to undergo to live, prevent their giving Way to Pleasure, and the rest, as soon as they by Labour and Frugality get enough to come to England, leave that Country, there are not People enough at ease to n... an agreeable Society; nor to occation the Improvement in Gardens, Buildings, and Parks, as would make Life agreeable, much less is their Numbers enough of Rich to afford Encouragement to support publick

Diversions; so that America is a very disagreeable Place, the least Shire-Town in England has more Pleasures than the best Town in North America.

But to return to our Quakers, the Chief of them told the General that he fear'd greatly for the Safety of the Army; that the Woods, the further we went, would be the more dangerous, and the French were a subtle and daring Enemy, and would not neglect any Opportunity of surprising us; that the further we went the more difficult it would be to supply us with Provisions, and that the Country was not worth keeping much less conquering. The French not yet knowing our Force were in Terror, and if he sent would perhaps come into a Treaty; that Peace was a heavenly Thing; and as for the Country in Dispute it was misrepresented by those Projectors, who had some private Advantage; for it was fit for none but Indians, the Soil bad, far from the Sea, and Navigation; therefore he thought if the French would abandon and destroy their Forts, and we do the same, and leave the lands to their rightful Owners the Indians, on Condition that that Nation should pay some Furrs and Deer Skins, by Way of Tribute, to our most gracious King George, a Pacification might be established til the matter was made up before his Majesty. That General Oglethorp had in that Manner settled all Differences with the Spaniards on the Southern Frontiers, towards Florida, and the Accord lasted to this Day; on the other Hand, he said, that if the French refused, then the Indians, who are a free and warlike Nation, and much too powerful to be despised, would probably take our Side; if we would pull down the French Forts, and our own also, they would be the Guard of our Colonies with very small Expense to England.

The General not only heard this Proposal with Pleasure, and communicated it to most of the Officers, but doubted if he had Power to execute it. Some of the Braggadocio Virginians, who last Year ran away so stoutly, began to clamor against the Quakers and the General; so we marched....(continued) [316]

May 20, 1755

To Governor Morris: **(Croghan)**

Tomorrow what Indian women and children came to Fort Cumberland with me will be sent back to Aucquick by order of the General, the Men entirely go with the General, and the General insists on my going with him, so that it is out of my power to provide for those Women and Children. The messenger I sent to the Shawnese, Twightwees and Owendots, are not yet returned but I hear they are coming, so that I hope they will join the General before the Army gets to the Ohio. [317]

(seaman)

On the 20th:-Arrived here 80 waggons from Pennsylvania, to assist in the expedition, and eleven waggons from Philadelphia, with presents for the officers of the Army.

Arrived 80 waggons from Penslyvania with stores; and 11 likewise from Philadelphia, with Liquors, Tea, Sugar, Coffee, &c., to the Amount of £400, with 20 Horses, as presents to the Officers of the 2 Regiments.

An Indian arrived from the French fort in 6 days, and said; they have only 50 men in the fort, but expect 900 more; that when our Army appears they will blow it up. I believe this fellow is a villain, as he is a Delaware, who never were our friends. [318]

Tuesday May the 20th. (batman)

It being genll Orders that six Wimen a Company should march up the Cuntry with the men, therefore he Ordared the Doctors to search and see who was clean and proper to. This day I Crosed the River Portwomack in a little cannow and Returning Back there was an Indien Came Over with me who was for making her go with his hands and I not understanding him Made us Boath in dainger. [319]

> Berkebile writes: "Early in May detachments of the Army began to arrive at Wills Creek. During the advance to Wills Creek, the lack of transportation had been keenly felt. Wagons had been forced to shuttle back and forth between camps in order to keep all stores and provisions moving forward. By the latter part of May the Pennsylvania wagons were coming in; about 90 arrived on May 20. That same night 30 wagons had to be sent on to Winchester to bring up to Wills Creek the provisions which could not be brought earlier for lack of wagons".

May 21 (Wednesday)
MARYLAND-CAMP AT FORD CUMBERLAND
Parole-Ilchester (Braddock, Halkett/Disney)
Field officer to morrow Maj Chapman.
The Generals Guard 44th Regmt.

No soldier that is employed as a Baker by Mr Lake, commissary of Provisions, is to be put upon any duty whatever till further orders.

It is His Excellency's orders that no Sutler give any liquor to the Indians on any account; if any one does he will be severly punished.

The provost is to go his round every Day through all the Roads leading to the camp, Every soldier or woman that he shall meet with on the other side of the River, or beyond the advanced Picquets without a pass from the Regiment or from the officer commanding the company to which they belong, he is to order his excutioner to tye them up and give them fifty lashes and to march them prisoners thro' the camp to expose them.

One gill of spirits mixed with three gills of water may be allowed each man per Day, which the officers of the picquet are to see delivered out every day at Eleven o'clock, any settler that shall sell any spirits to the soldiers without an officer being present shall be sent to the Provosts.[320]

(seaman)

On the 21st:-There are 100 Carpenters employed, under the Carpenter of the <u>Seahorse</u>, in building a Magazine, completing a Flatt, and squaring timber to make a bridge over Will's Creek; the Smiths in making tools; the Bakers baking biscuits; and Commissaries getting the provisions ready for marching. Arrived here a troop of light Horse, and 2 companies of Sir Peter Halket's (A Troop of Light-Horse and 2 companies of Sir P. Halket's Regiment, under the command of Major Chapman, came in from Winchester.).[321]

Wedensday May the 21th.   **(batman)**

This day two Companies of Sir Peeter Halkets Regt Joined us. This day all the Bakers in the Army were Called to bake Biskake for the march. We Rec'd three days Provisions.[322]

VIRGINIA-ALEXANDRIA

May the 21   **(Browne)**

Extremely hot. Discharged my servant Betty, having found of mine in her box, a pair of ruffles, a pair of stockings and an Apron.[323]

May 22 (Thursday)

MARYLAND-CAMP AT FORT CUMBERLAND

Parole-Kensington   **(Braddock, Halkett/Disney)**

Field Officer to morrow Maj[r] Sparke.

The Generals Guard 48th Regiment.[324]

On the 22nd. the Indians had arms   (seaman)
and clothes given to them. [325]

Thursday May the 22d.   (batman)
    This day we Rec'd ten Horses to the Regt for the Subletans
(subalterns) from Pensilvenia and many Other Presents, Rum shugar
tea Cheese Coffee Biskake. This day was tryed an Indien for Joining
with an Irish man and going twenty miles from the Camp and Stoping
our Wagons telling them they had Better stay there along with them
for the French would Soon Be with them. [326]

VIRGINIA-CLAIBORNE'S FERRY   (Washington)
    Proceeded myself thro Fairfax where I was detained a day getting
horses. At Clayburne's Ferry the 22d I met the express I had sent (to
Williamsburg) as he was returning...proceeded on to Williamsburg
where I arrived the same day. [327]

VIRGINIA-ALEXANDRIA
May the 21 (read May the 22)   (Browne)
    Mr. Wood gave my Brother and self an Invitation to go to see his
Daughter. It was 4 Miles up the River. Set of at 4 and came to her
House at 6 but to great Disappointment she was out; but her Mother
receiv'd us with a friendly wellcome. We stay'd till 8 and then with
great difficulty got into our Boat, it being a Shore; and when we had
got half way home our Cockswain run us a ground, and we were some
Hours before we could get clear. At 11 we got home, but I was much
fatigued with my journey. [328]

PENNSYLVANIA-PHILADELPHIA   (Pennsylvania Gazette)
    We hear from the camp at Wills's Creek that his Excellency General
Braddock, and all his forces were arrived there. That Captain Dobbs,
son of Governor Dobbs was also arrived from North Carolina, with a
fine company of 100 men, and that Scarroyday had himself got in the
camp, with a number of Indians. Since our last a Gentleman came in
town from the camp who informed us, that on the 26th ult. Sir John
Sinclair, with the first division of the Forces, marched from the Great
Meadows for Fort Du Quesne; and that the General, with the whole
army proposed to be there as on this day. He likewise says, that since

the murder of Williams, etc. mentioned in our last, a number of the inhabitants going to Fort Cumberland from the North Branch of Potowmack, for fear of being attacked by the French Indians were fired at by a party of them from the woods, by which six were killed and afterwards scalped and that a boy was likewise knocked down & scalped, but recovering ran into the river, where he was some time after found almost dead and carried to Wills's Creek; and proper care being taken of him it was thought he would recover.

The report we had of some of our waggoners being intercepted by the enemy, is entirely groundless.

Forty-one waggons are immediately needed, to carry each a Load of Oats and Indian Corn from Philadelphia to Will's Creek, for which they are to be paid at their Return Twelve Pounds each Waggon. Protection and Passes will be given the Waggoners by Authority of the General, to prevent their being impressed or detained after Delivery of their Loads. They are to set out together on Thursday the 29th Instant. Apply to Benjamin Franklin, in Philadelphia. Note - Several Neighbors may conveniently join in fitting out a Waggon, as was lately done in the Back Counties. If the Waggons cannot thus be obtained, there must be an impress.   B. Franklin   [329]

May 23 (Friday)

MARYLAND-CAMP AT FORT CUMBERLAND

Parole-Lincoln   **(Braddock, Halkett/Disney)**

Field officer to morrow Maj^r Chapman.

For the Genls Guard 44th Regemt.

A General Court Martial to sitt to morrow morning, at 8 o'clock at the Genl's Tent to consist of one Field officer, 6 capt^{ns} 6 Subalterns.

Lt. Col Gage President.

Mr Shirley Judge Advocate.

If any officer, soldier or follower of the army shall dare to give any strong liquor, or money to the Indian Men or Women, if an officer he shall be brought to a General Court for disobedience of orders; if a non commissioned officer soldier or follower of the army he shall receive 250 lashes without a C't Mart'l. [330]

Dear Sir, (Letter V, cont.)   **(Br. Officer 3)**

As the Intention of marching back continues, another Courier is to be sent which Opportunity I take, not only to let you know I am well,

but to desire my Cousin_____ would not send any Money to
Mr._____ to be remitted to me in Virginia. As the Pen is in my hand,
I will give you an Account of a Diversion we had some Nights ago, it
was an Indian Dancing, which I cannot call a Ball, though it was a
Kind of Masquerade, the Habits being very antick; but this as every
Thing in this Country is, was in the Stile (Style) of the Horrible; the
Sal de Ball was covered with the Canopy of Heaven, and adorned with
the twinkling Stars, a large Space of Grass was mark'd out for the
Dancing-Place, round which we the Spectators stood, as at a Cricket-
match in England, in the Centre of it was two Fires, at a small Distance
from each other, which were designed as an Illumination to make the
Dancers visible; near the Fires was seated the Musick, which were a
Number of Men and Women, with a Kind of Timbrels or small Kettle-
Drums, made of real brass Kettles, covered with Deer Skins made like
Parchment by the Indians, and these they beat, and keep good Time,
although their Tunes are terrible and savage; they also sing much in the
same stile, creating Terror, Fear, and all dreadful Passion, but no
pleasing ones. After this noise had gone on for some Time, at once we
heard a most dreadful Shout, and a Band of horrid Figures rushed into
the Ring, with a Nimbleness-hardly conceivable; they struck the
Ground in exact Measure, answering the rough Musick; at once all the
Descriptions of the Fawns and Satyrs of the Latin Poets came into my
Mind. and indeed the Indians seemed to be the same Kind of brown
dancing People, as lived under King Faunus, some 3000 Years ago in
Italy; they are most chearful and loving to their Friends, but implacable
and cruel to their Enemies. They drink and act when drunk much like
Silenus and his Satyrs their whole Life is spent in Hunting, War, and
Dancing, what they now perform'd was a War Dance; as soon as this
Surprize ceased the Dancers followed one another, treading a large
Ring, round the two Fires and Music, and ceased singing; the Timbrels
and Voices in the Centre set up a Tune to which they continued
dancing, and follow'd one another in the Ring with a very true
Measure, antick Postures, and high Bounds, that would puzzle our
best Harlequins to imitate; soon after, to every five Dancers came out
a Boy, carrying in their Hands flaming Splinters of light Wood instead
of Torches, which cast a glim Light that made Things as
distinguishable as at Noon-Day; and indeed the Suprisingness and
Newness of the Spectacle made it not unpleasing; the Indians being
dressed some in Furs, some with their Hair Ornamented with Feathers,

others with the Heads of Beasts; their Bodies naked, appearing in many places, painted with various Colours, and their Skins so rubbed with Oyl as to glitter against the Light, their Waists were girded round with Bear or Deer Skins with their Hair on, and artificial Tails fixed to many of them that hung down near unto the Ground. After they had danced some Time in a Ring, the Music ceased, the Dancers divided into two Parties, and set up the most horrid Song or Cry; that ever I heard, the Sound would strike Terror into the stoutest Heart. They then formed themselves into two Bodies, four deep. all which they did still dancing to the Tune and Measure; they ceased singing, and the Music began, on which the two Bodies run in at each other acting all the Parts the Indians use in their Manner of Fight, avoiding Shot, and striving to surround their Enemies, Some Time past in this Manner, and then at the Signal of a dismal Cry the Dancers all at once rushed out agin, leaving one only behind them, who was supposed to have mastered his Enemy; he struck the Ground with his Tomohawk or Club, as if he was killing one lying there, then acting the motions of scalping, and when holding up a real dried Scalp, which before hung upon him amongst his Ornaments; he then sung our the great Achievements which some of the Nation had performed against the French, told the Names of the Indian Warriors, and how many of French each had scalped, and then the Dance ended, etc. (continued)[331]

(seaman)

On the 23rd:-Both the Regiments exercised and went through their firings (formings). Sent 3 of our men to the Provost for neglect of Duty and disobedience of orders. [332]

Fryday May the 23d.   **(batman)**

There Being a field day today and the men fired (at) our Indiens thinking it was the French that had Ingaged us. They Ran immediately where they heard the fireing with all their Articals of War along with them. This day all the Wimen that goes up the Cuntry was taken to the Doctors to see if they was Clean and Ready to march. [333]

VIRGINIA-WILLIAMSBURG

May 23, Friday Williamsburg.   **(Washington)**

To Robert Orme

In pursuance of His Excellency's commands I proceeded with all convenient dispatch to this place...As I am much fatigued and a good deal disordered by constant riding...I shall proceed more slowly back.[334]

VIRGINIA-WILLIAMSBURG   (Maryland, Virginia Gazette)
   On Friday the 11th of this Instant arrived at Fort Cumberland upwards of a Hundred Indians for different Nations, amongst them three or four French Indians and they were all kindly entertained by His Excellency General Braddock, who arrived there the Day after, with the last Division of the Troops. On Sunday the 12th they were all drawn up under arms, the Officers in a line by themselves when the General made a speech to the Indians and gave a belt of Wampum to which they answered and returned another belt. [335]

   The above story appears in the Maryland Gazette on June 12, 1755 and has a date line of Williamsburg, May 23. This shows how news was shared and the time lag caused by distance that affected when stories appeared in the other colonial newspapers.

May 24 (Saturday)
MARYLAND-CAMP AT FORT CUMBERLAND
Parole-Monmouth   (Braddock)
Field officer to morrow Lt Col Burton.
For the Genls Guard 48th Regmt. [336]

May 24, 1755   (Braddock)
Governor Morris:
   You will...be informed of the situation I am in by the folly of Mr. Dinwiddie and the roguery of the Assembly, and unless the road of communication from your province is opened and some contracts made in consequence of the power I have given I must ineviably be starved...Cresap...has behaved in such a manner that if he had been a French Commis(ary) he could not have acted more for their interest. In short, in every instance but in my contract for the Pennsyulvania wagons, I have been deceived and met with nothing but lies and villainy.   General Braddock [337]

Camp at Wills's Creek May 24th: 1755   (Halkett/Disney)
The Parole is Munmouth
Field Officer for to Morrow Lieut Col: Burton

Six men of the line to be at the Head of the Train without Arms to Morrow Morning at 5 oClock And to Attend Capt Hinds Orders. [338]

General Court Martial   (Orme)
Lieutenant Colonel Gage, President
    The punishments put in execution, all corporeal ones. [339]

                                                                      (seaman)
    On the 24th:- Our Force here now consists of 2 Regiments of 700 men each; 9 companies (Virginia) of 50 men each: 3 Independent Companies of 100 men each: one Maryland Company of 50 men; 60 of the train (2 New York, 1 Independent Carolina Companies of 100 men, 1 Company of Artillery of 60) and 30 seamen. This day 2 men were drummed out of Sir Peter Halket's Regiment for theft, after receiving 1000 lashes, and preparations making for marching. [340]

Satterday May the 24th.   (batman)
    This day an Accident hapn'd. Two Soldiers Exerciseing Opwards (of) Each Other, and another man had loaded one of their pieces to shout a Dear. The men not knowing the piece to be loaded, when they Came to the firings they fired and the piece went of(f) and Shot the Other man dead. Their hapn'd to be a genll Coart Martial Sitting when the Prisoner Came to Camp. He Immediately was tried and Acquitted. [341]

VIRGINIA-ALEXANDRIA
May the 24   (Browne)
    5 Waggons came in, we wait for 4 more. Mr. Napper sent us 2 Markeys. Very busy in getting ready to march. [342]

May 25 (Sunday)
MARYLAND-CAMP AT FORT CUMBERLAND
Parole-Norwich   (Braddock)
Field Officer to morrow Majr Sparke
For the Generals Guard 44th Regmt.
    If any non commissioned officer or soldier belonging to the army is found gaming he shall immediately receive three hundred lashes without being brought to court martial, and all standers by or lookers on shall be deemed principals and punished as such.

One Capt[n], 1 Leut, 1 Ensign and 70 men of the 2 Brigades to parade immediatley att the Fort. They are to take Tents and 10 days prov[ns] with them. The Capt is to receive his orders from Sir John St Clair.

A Genl Court Martial of the Line, to sitt to morrow to try Lt McLead of the Royal Regt of Artillery confined by Genl Braddock to consist of one Col. 2 Field Officers. and 10 Captns.

    Sir Peter Halkett President.

    Mr Shirley Judge Advocate.

To sit at the Presidents tent and to meet at 12 o'clock. [343]

Camp at Wills's Creek May 25th: 1755   **(Halkett/Disney)**

The Parole is Norwich

Field Officer for to Morrow Major Spark

The Genl Court Martial where of Lieut Col: Gage is President is Adjurnd till to morrow morning at 9 oClock and to Sitt at The President's Tent. If any non Commissiond Officer or Soldier belonging to the Army is found Gaming he shall Immediately Receive 300 lashes without being brought to a Court martial And all Standers by or lookers on shall be Deemed Principles And punished as such.

An Exact Return to be given into the Genl: as soon as posable of the Two Regts. Signed by the Commanding Officer of each Corps as also of the Artillery Indipendent Compys & by their respective Captains or Officers Commanding Their companys. 1 Capt 1 lieut 1 Ensn & seventy men from the Two Brigades to parade Immediately at the Fort. The men Are to take Ten days provisions with Them. The Commanding Officer is to Call on S[r] John S[t] Clear or Capt Orme for Orders.

A return to be given in to the Genl. to morrow morning at 11 oClock from the Two regts: Indipendent Compys, The Companys of Carpenters, Virginian & Maryland Rangers, The light horse & Detachment of Seamen of the no of Persons each Draws provisions for Daily. Mr. Lake Commissary is also to give in at the same time A Return of the Numbers of Guides, Indians, Workmen That draw provisions Daily And John Scott Waggon Master Gen'l is to Send in A return at the same time of the Numbers of Waggoners And Horse men That draw provisions daily. His Excellency Expects That Commanding Officers of corps & Companys &c will be very Exact & particuler in this Return.

A Genl Court Martial of the Line to sitt to morrow upon Mr. McLoad of the Artillery confined by the Genl. It is to Consist of 1 Col Two Field Officers And Ten capts: And to sitt at the Presidents Tent at 12 oClock, Sr Peter Halkett President Field Officers Major Chapman & Lieut Col Burton. [344]

(Orme)

About the latter end of May, the Pensylvania waggons came up to us, but brought very little flour from Conegogee, occasioned by the infamous neglect of Cressop the agent at that place, who suffered almost all the waggons to pass without giving them the Order before mentioned. Much about the same time this man's father was employed by Governor Sharpe to salt a quantity of beef for the use of the Maryland troops; which beef had been reckoned in the estimate of those provisions designed for the March; it was no sooner brought to Camp but it was condemned to be buried by a survey. The Surveyors reported that it had no pickle, and that it was put into dry casks, which could never have contained any.

Being they was disappointed in flour and beef, the General sent away that night thirty waggons with a Captain's detachment to Winchester for provisions over sixty miles of Mountainous and rocky country; and also three hundred carrying horses for flour, with part of the troop of light horse, to Conegogee, ninety miles distance, with orders to bring up Cressop, another commissary being appointed.

Most of the horses which brought up the train were either lost, or carried home by their owners, the nature of the country making it impossible to avoid this fatal inconvenience, the whole being a continued forrest for several hundred miles without inclosures or bounds by which horses can be secured: they must be turned into the woods for their subsistance, and feed upon leaves and young shoots of trees. Many projects, such as belts, hobles, &c., were tried, but none of these were a security against the wildness of the country and the knavery of the people we were obliged to employ: by these means we lost our horses almost as fast as we could collect them, and those which remained grew very weak, so we found ourselves every day less able to undertake the extraordinary march we were to perform.

The General, to obviate as much as possible these difficulties, appointed a waggon Master General, and under him waggon masters over every forty waggons; and horse Masters over every hundred horses, and also a drover to every seven horses; the waggon and horse master with the drovers were to go into the woods with their respective divisions, to muster their horses every night and morning, and to make a daily report to the waggon master General, who was to report to the General.

These regulations remedied in a great measure that evil. Some Indians arrived from the Delawars, with whom the General conferred, and to whom he made presents. They promised to join him with their Nation upon the march, which they never performed.

Of all the Indians promised by Governor Dinwiddie, none had joined the General; and a few days before we marched the person sent to the Catawbers and Cherokees returned; He informed the General that three hundred of their warriors had marched three or four days with him in their way to the Camp; but one Pearus (Paris?) an Indian Trader had by means of a quantity of liquor diverted them form their undertaking; advising them to call upon Gist (who was the person employed) to shew some written and sealed authority by which he acted; who not being provided with any instrument of this nature from the Government of Virginia, they judged him an imposter, and returned to their towns.

The General wond'red that the Governments of Carolina had not been applied to for obtaining these Indians, as being their natural allies.

While these disappointments were still fresh, one Hile a Virginian, with whom the commissaries appointed by Governor Dinwiddie had made a contract for five hundred Beeves to be delivered at Fort Cumberland, came to the Camp and informed the General, the Committee of the Virginia Assembly would not confirm the contract, and that it was consequently void. He had already received a part of the money, and the General offered to pay him the balance, but he said he had recalled his Factors from Carolina, and would not make another contract without an advanced price; and even then would not engage to preform 'till September. The General therefore resolved to supply himself elsewhere.

General Braddock had applied to the Governor of Pensyslvania, soon after his arrival in America, to open a road from that country towards the Ohio, to fall into his road to that place from Fort Cumberland, either at the great meadows, or at the Yoxhio Geni, that he might keep open a communication with Pensylvania either for reinforcements, or convoys. The Governor had laid this before his Assembly, and had represented to them in the strongest terms the use, and indeed necessity, of such a measure; but they would pay no regard to it. Upon a farther acquaintance with the nature and state of Virginia, and the frequent disappointments the General experienced from that Province, he thought it would be imprudent to depend entirely upon contracts made with, or promises received from them; he therefore wrote again to Governor Morris to desire he would once more apply to his Assembly to open a road and as he was every day the more convinced of the necessity of such a communication, he desired that it might immediately be begun and carried on with all possible expedition, and that he would undertake to defray the expense of it, in case they should again refuse it. The Governor through his Zeal for his Majesty's service, had it carried into great forwardness in a very short time.

Mr Peter the Secretary of Pensylvania, who had been to inspect the road, waited upon the General at Fort Cumberland to inform him of its progress; The General desired Mr Peters would in conjunction with Governor Morris make a contract in his name for a magazine of provisions to be formed at Shippensburgh, sufficient to subsist three thousand men for three months, and to be completed by the begining of July; he desired they would appoint some proper person to forward the whole or part with all expedition when demanded. This contract was concluded, and the deposit made agreeable to the time mentioned. The General also fixed with Mr Peters that the junction of the two roads should be at the Crow foot of the Yoxhio Geni.

The General called a Council of War Consisting of:

      Colonel Sr Peter Halket
      Lieu^t. Colonel Gage
      Major Chapman (Russel)
      Colonel Dunbar
      Lieu^t Col^o Burton (Ralph)
      Major Sparks (William)
      Major Sr John St Clair, D.Q.G.

The General acquainted the Council he had formed a plan of March and encampment upon the Nature of the service, Country, and Enemy he was engaged in and expected to be opposed by; That he offered it to them for their opinions, in which he desired they would be very explicit, and make such objections, and offer such amendments, as they should judge proper, by which some general plan might be formed which would effectually answer the end proposed, of marching and encamping with the greater security. He said he should be very much encumbered with a vast number of carriages and horses, which it was absolutely necessary to secure from the insults of the Indians from whom he apprehended frequent annoyance. It would be therefore necessary to divide the troops into small parties to cover as much as possible the baggage, which would be obliged to march in one line through a road about twelve foot wide, and that it appeared to him also necessary to extend small parties very well upon the flanks, in the front, and in the rear, to prevent any surprise which the nature of the country made them very liable to; and he proposed, as it would be impractiable to have a regular parade, that every commanding officer of a company should regulate that company's duty by detaching always upon his flanks a third of the effectives with a Sergent, which Sergent was to detach a third of his men upon his flanks with a Corporal; these out parties were to be relieved every night at retreat beating, and to form the advanced pickets.

Each regiment was to find one Captain and three subalterns for the picket of each flank; and the independent companies, Virginia, Maryland, and Carolina rangers, One Captain and two Subalterns for each of the flanks of their division; and the field Officer of the day was to command the whole. The officers of the pickets were to march upon their respective flanks. The waggons, Artillery, and carrying horses were formed into three divisons, and the provisions disposed of in such manner as that each division was to be victualled from that part of the line it covered, and a commissary was appointed to each. The waggon master were to attend their respective divisions to proportion the goodness of teams, and to assist at every steep ascent by adding any number of horses from other waggons, till their respective divisions had passed.

The waggons were subdivided again into smaller divisions, every company having a certain number which they were to endeavor to keep togeather, however the line might be broke: The Companies were to march two deep that they might extend the more, be more at liberty to act, and less liable to confusion.

A field officer was to march with a van, and another with a rear guard. Sr Peter Halket was to lead the column, and Colonel Dunbar to bring up the Rear. The field officer of the Picket had no fixed posts. There was also an advanced party of three hundred men to precede the line to cut and make the roads, commanded by a field officer or the quarter master general. This detachment was to be either a day's march before the line or to move earlier every morning, according to the country we were to pass through, or the intelligence we could get of the enemy.

The form of the encampment differed very little from that of the march. Upon coming to the ground, the waggons were to draw up in close order in one line, the road not admitting more, care being taken to leave an interval in the front of every company. When this was done the whole was to halt and face outward. The serjeants' flank parties were to divide, facing to the right and left, and to open a free communication by cutting down saplings and underwood, till they met the divisions of the other serjeants' parties: they were then to open a communication with the corporal in front, who was to keep his men under arms. The serjeant was then to advance half of his party, which was to remain under arms whilst the corporal opened his communications to the right and left. All this was carried on under the inspection of the Picket Officers of the respective flanks. Whilst this was executing, half of each company remained under arms, whilst the other half opened the communication to the right and left, and to the serjeants in front, and also cleared ground for the tents, which were pitched by them, and placed in a single row along the line of baggage, facing outwards. These parties were then to be relieved, and the corporal's party was all posted in centinels, which made a chain of centinels round the camp. The grenadiers were to encamp across the road, and each company to advance a serjeant's party.

Upon beating the General, the men were to turn out, but not to strike their tents till they received orders; upon the Assembly the horses were to be loaded; and upon beating the March the Corporal were to join their parties, and the whole was to face upon the right and left.

When the waggons were all closed up, the waggon and horse-master were to assemble in some particular place their respective divisions, and to give their orders to the waggoners and drovers. The horses were then to be turned out within centinels, very sentinel having orders not to suffer any horse to pass him.

It was the opinion of the Council this line of march and plan of encampment would answer extemely well for the service we were engaged in; every field officer was to have a copy of it, and they were desired to assemble the Captains and explain to them fully the duty they were to perform.

Some Indians returned from a reconnoitring party, and informed the General about a hundred soldiers were then in Garrison at Fort Du Quesne, but that they soon expected greater reinforcements from Montreal and Quebec.

Two days after, the General called another Council of War. He informed them of the present state of the Garrison, and read to them some letters of intelligence, that he had received from the Governors of New York and Pennsylvania.

The General told the Council, that he found by his returns, That he had not above forty waggons over and above the hundred and fifty he had got from Pensylvania, and that the number of carrying horses did not exceed six hundred, which were insufficient to carry seventy days flour and fifty days meat, which he was of opinion was the least he could march without running great risques of being reduced to the utmost distress before the Convoy could be brought to him if he should meet with any opposition at the Fort. And he desired to know their opinions of a measure he had formed for carrying eight days more provision and for saving some days in the march.

The General reminded the Council of the Waggons sent to Winchester for provisions, which could not return in less than seven days, and this time would absolutely be lost if the march of the whole was delayed for their return. The General therefore proposed the sending forwards of a party of six hundred men, workers and coverers, with a field officer, and the Quarter-master-Generall; that they should take with them two six-pounders, with a full proportion of ammunition; that they should also take with them eight days provisions for three thousand two hundred men; that they should make the road as good as possible, and march five days towards the first crossing of the Yoxhio Geni, which was about thirty miles from the camp, at which place they were to make a deposit of the provisions, building proper sheds for its security, and also a place for arms for its defence and the security of the men. If they could not in five days advanced so far, they were at the expiration of that time to choose an advantageous spot and to secure the provisions and men as before. When the waggons were unloaded, the field officer with three hundred men was to return to camp, and Sr John St Clair with the first engineer was to remain and carry on the works with the other three hundred. The

General proposed marching from Fort Cumberland to the first camp in three divisions, as it would be impossible for the whole line with the baggage to move off the ground in one day.

Sr Peter Halket with the 44th Regiment was to march with the first division, taking with him about a hundred waggons of provisions, stores and powder.

Lieutenant Colonel Burton with the independent Companies, Virginia, Maryland, and Carolina rangers, was to march with the artillery, ammunition, some stores and provision, and to form the second division.

Colonel Dunbar, with the 48th, was to make the third division, and to take with him the provision waggons from Winchester, the returned waggons from the advanced party, and all the carrying horses.

The whole of the General's plan was universally approved of, and agreed to; and the Resolutions of the first, and of this Council of War were signed by the members. [345]

Sunday May the 25. (batman)

This day they Began to load their Wagons with Ammunition and Provisions. This day an Officers Command went out after 9 at Night to Winchester. This day we had no prayers, the Minister Being Sick [346]

On August 18th, 1757 George Croghan delivered the following letter to Mr. Peters, Secretary to Governor Morris. It is included here as it is appropriate to the material in Braddock's Orderly Book for the above date.

(Croghan)

The Government continued to maintain the Indians that lived at my house till the Spring, when General Braddock arrived. They then desired Governor Morris to let me know that they would not maintain them any longer, at which time Governor Morris desired me to take them at Fort Cumberland to meet General Braddock, which I did. On my arrival at Fort Cumberland, General Braddock asked me where the rest of ye Indians were? I told him I did not know: I had brought with me about 50 men which was all which was at the time under my care and which I had brought there under direction of Gov. Morris. He replied "Governor Dinwiddie told me at Alexandria that he had sent for 400 which would be here before me." I answered I know nothing of that, but that Capt. Montour the Virginia Interpreter was in camp and could inform his Excellency; on which Montour was sent for, who informed the General that Mr. Gist's son was sent off some time ago for some Cheroquces Indians, but whether they would come he couldn't tell: on which the General asked me whether I could not send for some of ye Delawares and Shawnese to Ohio. I told him I could; on which I sent a messenger to Ohio who returned in eight days and brought with hime three chiefs of the Delawares. The General had a conference with these chiefs in company with those 50 I had brought with me, and made them a hansome present, and behaved as kindly to them as he possible could during their stay, ordering me to let them want for nothing. The Delawares promised In council to meet ye General on the road, as he marched out, with a number of their warriors, but whether the former breaches of faith on the side of the English prevented them, or that they had before engaged to assist the French, I cannot tell; but they disappointed the General and did not meet him.

Two days after the Delaware Chiefs had left the camp at Fort Cumberland, Mr. Gist's son returned from the Southern Indians where he had been sent by Governor Dinwiddie, but brought no Indians with him. Soon after the General was preparing for ye march with no more Indians than those I had with me, when Col. Innis told the General that the women and children of the Indians which was to remain at Fort Cumberland would be very troublesome, and that the General need not take above ten men out with him, for if he took more, he would find them very troublesome on the march, and of no service; on which the General ordered me to send all the men, women, and childern back to my house in Pennsylvania, except eight or ten which I should keep as scouts: which I accordingly did.

But I am yet of opinion that had we had fifty Indians instead of eight, that we might in a great measure have prevented the surprise, that day of our unhappy defeat. [347]

VIRGINIA-ALEXANDRIA
May 25   (Browne)
Most of this Day spent in making a Tilt for my Waggon which is to be my Bed Chamber on my March to Wills's Creek. [348]

May 26 (Monday)
MARYLAND-CAMP AT FORT CUMBERLAND
Parole-Oxford   (Braddock)
Field Officer to morrow Lt Col Gage.

For the Generals Guard 48th Regiment.

The General Court Martial whereof Lt Col Gage was President is dissolved His Excellency having approved of the several sentences allotted them.

John Nugent of the 44th Regiment having been tryed for theft and found guilty of the crime laid to his charge as an accomplice in receiving a share of the money that was stole, is adjudged to receive one thousand lashes, and to be drum'd out of the Reg't through the line with a halter about his neck.

Samuel Draumer, of the 44th Regim't and George Darty of Capt Derere's Independent Company having been tryed for desertion are adjudged each of them to receive two hund'^d lashes.

Henry Dalton, of the 48th Regt't having been tryed for shooting Henry Pelkington, sold'r in the said Regiment the Court Marshal is of opinion that the said Dalton did not shoot the said Pelkington with design but that it was done by accident, therefore His Excellency Gen'l Braddock has ordered him to be released and to be sent back to his duty.

If any soldier is seen Drunk in Camp he is to be sent immediately to the quarter guard of the Regmt he belongs to, and the next morning he is to receive two hundred lashes without a Court Martial. [349]

May 26th 1755 Camp at Wills's Creek   **(Halkett/Halket)**
The Parole is Oxford
Field Officer for to Morrow Lieut Col:Gage

A Return to be given in to Sr John St Clear by the Qr Master of each Brigade And Artillery of the Quantity of provisions drawn from the Commissary And a Return to be given in to Sr John St Clear every Monday of the Quantity of provisions Drawn the proceeding Week.

The Genl Court Martial where of Lt Col: Gage was President is disolved, His Excellencey having approved of the Sentence of the Said Court Martial. The Prisoners Are to receive the Several punishments Allotted Them. John Nugent of the 44th Regt having been tryd for Theft And found Guilty of the Crime laid to his Charge As An Accomplice in receiving share of the money that was Stole is Adjudged to receive One Thousand Lashes And be drumd out of The Regt. with a halter about his Neck. Samuel Dranan of the 44 Regtr. & Geo. Desby of Capt. Demmeres Compy having been tryd for Desertion Are Adjudg'd to Receive Each of Them Two Hundred lashes. Henry

222

Dalton of the 48 Regt. having been tryd by the Court Martial where of Lieut Col Gage was President for shooting Henry Pilkington Soldier of the Said regt. The Court Martial is of Opinion That the Said Dalton did not shoot the Said Henry Pilkinton with a design but that it was done by Accident And Therefore His Excellency Genl Braddock has Ordered him to be Released And Sent back to his regt: If any Soldier is found Drunk in Camp he is to be sent to the Qr Guard or his Own Regt. And the Next day he is to Receive Two Hundred Lashes without a Court Martial. [350]

General Court Martial   (Orme)
Sr Peter Halket, President
    To try Lieutenant McLeod, of the Artillery. Part of the sentance remitted. [351]

Munday May the 26th.   (batman)
    This day we had a genll Coart Martial to try a Lieutenant of the Train and some Diserters. All the Carpenters Smiths and Bakers and Taylors are Imployed at their Seperate trade. [352]

VIRGINIA-ALEXANDRIA
May the 26   (Browne)
    My new Servant came. Sent a Letter to England by the Man of War, Capt. Deggs, bound for Hampton. [353]

May 27 (Tuesday)
MARYLAND-CAMP AT FORT CUMBERLAND
Parole-Petersfield   (Braddock)
Field Officer to morrow Lt Col Burton.
For the Generals Guard 44th Regiment.
    The party of the Picquets that lay advanced to load with raming ball, the rest of the picquets to load with powder and to have their ball in their pockets.
    The following detachments to march on Tuesday morning to parade at Revelle beating. The men to be provided with two days provisions ready dress'd. The 44th, 48th Regts are to furnish 1 field officer, 4 capts 12 subalterns and 250 rank and file.
    Capt Rutherford's Capt Demere's Independent Companys, Capt Waginer's Capt Peyrouneys Companies of Virginia Rangers and Capt

Polson's Company of Carpenters are also to march with this detachment, who are to take them their camp equippage and baggage.

Major Chapman Field Officer for the detachment. The Independent Company and companys of Virginia Rangers ordered for this Detachment to furnish no men for the guards to morrow and any men that they may have upon the out Guards are to be relieved immediately. Particular care is to be taken that the men's arms are in good order and that each man is provided with ten flints and compleated to 24 rounds of ammunition.

The Tools and Tomahawks of the 2d Brigade are to be given at Gun firings this evng to the quarter master General at his tent and a dem'd to be made to morrow nig(ht) at 6 o'clock of ye number of Tools each Brigade will want, the quarter master to attend. [354]

Camp at Wills's Creek May 27th: 1755   **(Halkett/Disney)**
The Parole is Petersfield
Field Officer for to Morrow Lt Col: Burton

The Genl Court Martial where of Sr Peter Halkett (was President) is disolved. The following Detachts: of the Line to parade on Thursday morning at Revalley Beating in Order to March. The Men to be provided with Two Days provisions Dressed. The 44th & 48 Regts Are to furnish 250 privit 12 subaltrens 12 Serjts 4 Capts: & one field Officer. Capt Rutherfords Company Intire Capt Demmers Capt Wagoners Capt Peroneys Capt Polsons the whole of the Detachment to March with their full Equipage. The Tools & Tomioks (tomahawks) of the Two Brigades to be given in at Gun firing This Evening to the Qr Master Genl at His Tent And a demand to be made to morrow morning at six oClock of the No of Tools each Brigade will want. The Quarter Masters Are to Attend the Several Compys Ordered for service. They Are to do no (sic) further Duty And Any men upon out Guards are to be Releieved Immediately. Perticular Care must be taken to have the Arms in good order And every man to have Ten flints And to be provided with 24 Rounds of Amunition. The Detachts: of the Picquet that March is to be Loaded with a Running (ramming) ball And Those that remain in Camp to be loaded with powder, And to have Their balls in their pouches. Field Offr for the Above Detach: Major Chapman. [355]

On the 27th:-We have now here 100 waggons, which the Commissaries are loading with provisions. In the evenings a Captain's Guard marched for Winchester, to escort the provisions to the Camp. Some Indians came in here belonging to the Delawares. [356]

Tuesday May the 27th.   **(batman)**

This day there was two men of Sir Peeter Halkets Regt that Rece'd a thousand lashes a piece for Stealing some Money and Diserting. They were drum'd through the line with halters about their knecks. [357]

VIRGINIA-WINCHESTER   **(Washington)**

The 27th I arrived at Winchester-set out on the 29th and arrived at Camp the 30th. [358]

VIRGINIA-ALEXANDRIA

May the 27   **(Browne)**

Went with Capt. Johnson's Lady to Mr.Roshar's in Maryland. We were receiv'd with great Politeness. The neatest House I have seen since I left England, and furnish'd in Taste. We stay'd till night. [359]

Berkebile writes: "According to the accounts of the commission later appointed to settle wagoner's claims, 146 wagons with teams, and about 510 pack horses were provided by Pennsylvania to accompany the army.

In many communications, there appears a certain looseness in reporting numbers in round figures, and also in using the words "wagons" or "carriages" in an all inclusive sense. It is obvious that such figures must often have included any wheeled vehicle, and some times even the gun carriages. Thus the figure 200 undoubtedly includes 145 Pennsylvania wagons, plus a number of British Army wagons, tumbrils, and perhaps gun carriages.

From the beginning of the march, the roads were a challenge, for both Braddock's and Burd's roads presented what appeared to be insurmountable obstacles. An examination of the terrain over which they had to pass causes far greater respect for these road builders and drivers than is usually accorded them".

May 28 (Wednesday)

MARYLAND-CAMP AT FORT CUMBERLAND

Parole-Quarendon   **(Braddock)**

Field officer to morrow Maj Sparke.

Generals Guard 48th Regt.

The Regulation of stoppages with the Director of the Genl Hospital to commence from the 24th of this month.

As it is necessary to employ the soldiers in making and amending the roads His Excellency has been pleased to appt the followg allowances:

	s	d (Sterling per Day)
To every sub: officer	3	0
To every sergeant	1	
To every corporal		9
To every drumer and private centinal		6

But as at present there is no public market and of course the men will have no opportuinty of making use of the ready money His Excellency is so kind as to promise that he will see that they are punctually paid whatever is due to them when they arrive in winter quarters therefore whatever Subaltern officer or sergeant has the command of any working party as soon as they are relieved or come back they are to make an exact return of the number of men of their party and give it in to the quarter master Genl.

But if hereafter there should be any public market or that the money will be found to be of use to the men upon a proper application His Excellency will give orders for their being paid.

The companies of Rangers are for the future to furnish their proportion of men for duty with the rest of the line.

As there will be an express going in a few days, any officers that have any letters to send to Great Britain are desired to give them to either the Genl's aid de camps or to Mr. Shirley.

AFTER ORDERS.

The men of the Detachment that march to morrow to be commanded by the officers of their own corps or company.

Sixteen men from line to be appointed to the Guns to morrow that march and to be under the dirction of the officer of artillery.

The Independent company and Rangers of the two Brigades to mount but one picquet. [360]

MARYLAND-CAMP AT FORT CUMBERLAND
May 18, 1755   **(Braddock)**

Instruction to Sir John St. Clair Deputy Quarter Master General
1. You will proceed with a detachment of six hundred men, ordered for that purpose, under the command of Major Russell Chapman, to

open and repair a road over the Allegany Mountains, toward the great meadows to a distance not exceeding forty miles.

2. You will acquaint Major Chapman whom I have directed to consult you in the execution of his orders, what part of the detachment you shall think necessary to be employed in opening and repairing the road, and you will also give him your opinion with regard to the disposition of the remainder for the defence of the working party and the convoy under his escort.

3. You will cease opening and repairing the road at the end of seven days or...if it shall be thought advisable and shall pass upon such a spot as shall appear proper to yourslef and the engineers ordered upon this service for construction a place of defence for the party and the provisons ordered the provisions to be lodged there.

4. Upon major Chapman's leaving you, you will employ the remaining part of the detachment, which will be left under your command, is complete the place of the defence and you will make such dispositions and preserve such discipline as the service requires. [361]

Camp at Wills's Creek May: 28th: 1755   **(Halkett/Disney)**
The Parole is Quarandon
Field Officer for to Morrow Major Sparks

As it will be Necessary to Imploy the Soldiers in making and mending of Roads, His Excellency has been pleas'd to appoint The following Allowences. To Every Subaltern Officer 3s: to every Serjt 1 S to Corppl. 9d: or to every Drumr: or privet Centinal Six pence Sterg per Day. The Companys of Rangers for the future to do Their propotion of all Dutys with The rest of The Line.

The Detachments of men from the Different Corps that marches to morrow Are to be Commanded by their Own Officers. Sixteen men of The Line to be appointed to the Guns That goes with the Detachment to morrow. They are to be Under the Direction of The Officer of Artillery. [362]

(seaman)

On the 28th:-At 11, the Delawares met at the General's tent, and told him that they were come to know his intentions, that they might assist the Army. The General thanked them, and said he should march in a few days toward Fort De Quesne. The Indians told him they would return home and collect their warriors togeather, and meet him on his march. These people are villians, and always side with the strongest.[363]

Wedensday May the 28th.   **(batman)**

At noon it blowed and rained hard.

We Recd Orders that a Detachment of 6 hundred men was to march on thursday. My Master was Ordered for that Command and to take one days provisions and two piece of Cannon and two Cow Horns (cohorns). [364]

The advance mentioned here was to open the road to Little Meadows and to build there a small fort to serve as an advance supply base. The army and supplies could not move due to lack of wagons and horses that were then on their way from Winchester.

VIRGINIA-WINCHESTER

May 28, Wednesday. Winchester.   **(Washington)**

I should have received greater relief from the fatigues of my journey, and my time would have been spent much more agreeably, had I halted below, rather than at this vile post; but I little imagined I should have to wait for a guard who should have waited for me, if either must have waited at all. I came to this place last night, and was greatly disappointed in not finding the Cavalry, according to promise. I am obliged to wait 'till it does arrive, or 'till I can procure a guard from the Militia; either of which, I suppose will detain me two days; as you may with (almost) equal success, attempt to raise the dead, as the force in the Country. [365]

Washington was concerned as he had with him several thousand pounds sterling he obtained in Williamsburg from Mr. Balfour assistant to John Hunt (paymaster) to be delivered to the General.

VIRGINIA-ALEXANDRIA

May the 28   **(Browne)**

Capt. West's Lady came to see me, and found me very busy packing up. Spent the Evening at Capt. Johnson's, much intreated to stay all Night, but did not. [366]

May 29 (Thursday)
MARYLAND-CAMP AT FORT CUMBERLAND

Parole-Queensbury **(Braddock)**
Field officer to morrow Lt Col Gage.
The Genls Guard 44th Regiment.[367]

Camp at Wills's Creek May 29th: 1755 **(Halkett/Disney)**
The parole is Queensbourough
Field Officer for to Morrow Lieut Col Gage [368]

(seaman)

On the 29th:-A detachment of 600 men marched towards Fort de Quesne, under the command of Major Chapman, with 2 field pieces, and 50 waggons with provisions. Sir John St. Clair, 2 Engineers, Mr. Spendlowe, & 6 of our people to cut the road, and some Indians went away likewise (and 6 seamen with some Indians were ordered to clear the Roads for them). [369]

MARYLAND-NORTHWEST OF FORT CUMBERLAND
Thursday May the 29th. **(batman)**

This day we marched about seven miles and was 8 hours of marching it, it being very Bad Roads that we Where Oblig'd to halt Every hundred yards and mend them. As soon as we Came to our (encampment) ground their was a working party sent out to Cut the Roads, and a Covering party to guide them, the Working party Being 200 men, and the Covering party 100. [370]

VIRGINIA-ALEXANDRIA
May the 29 **(Browne)**

Received a Card from Mrs Salkeldat, with her Comp'ts and desired my Company to her Husband Funeral at 2. He had been dead a Month. It is the Custom of this Place to bury their Relations in their Gardens. [371]

PENNSYLVANIA-PHILADELPHIA **(Pennsylvania Gazette)**

We hear from the camp, at Wills's Creek, that his Excellency General Braddock was to march in a few days for the Ohio; That Mr. Croghan had arrived there with a Number of Indians; and that more were daily expected to come in. [372]

May 30 (Friday)

MARYLAND-CAMP AT FORT CUMBERLAND

Parole-Rochester   (Braddock)
Field officer to morrow Lt Col Burton.
General Guard 48th Regmt.

The troops to hold themselves in readiness to march in 24 hours warning.

Whatever Barrells the Regiments; and companys have got belonging to the artillery are to be sent back immediatley   with their troops to the foreman of the train. [373]

Camp at Wills's Creek May 30th: 1755   (Halkett/Disney)
The parole is Rochester
Field Officer for to Morrow Lt Col Burton

The Troops to hold Themselves in Readiness to March at 24 Hours Notice. Whatever Barrels the Troops may have got with powder from the Train, They Are to Return them with Their Hoops to Mr Furnis of the Train. [374]

                                                              (Orme)
This (the) detachment of six hundred men commanded by Major Chapman marched the 30th of May at daybreak, and it was night before the whole baggage had got over a mountain about two miles from the camp. The ascent and decent were almost a perpendicular rock; three waggons were entirely destroyed, which were replaced from the camp; and many more were extremely shattered. Three hundred men, with the miners (of whom the General had formed a company), had already been employed several days upon that hill.

The General reconnoitred this mountain, and determined to set the engineers and three hundred more men at work upon it, as he thought it impassable by Howitzers. He did not imagine any other road could be made, as a reconnoitring party had already been to explore the country; nevertheless, Mr. Spendelow, Lieutenant of the Seamen, a young man of great discernment and abilities, acquainted the General, that in passing that mountain, he had discovered a Valley which led quite round the foot of it. A party of a hundred men, with an engineer, was ordered to cut a road there, and an extreme good one was make in two days, which fell into the other road about a mile the other side of the mountain.

From this place the General wrote to Colonel Shirley and Colonel Johnson, desiring them to use all possible dispatch in the carrying their expeditions into excution, and he wrote also to the Governor of New

York, to desire he would afford them all possible assistance in his Government, as they must necessarily depend entirely upon it for their subsistance.

Mr. Shirley represented to the General the weakness of Sir William Pepperell's regiment, and applied for the five hundred men under the command of Colonel Schyler, who were raised in New Jersy for the Crown Point expedition; which men the Governor, Assembly, and Colonel Schyler, were willing should join Mr. Shirley. The General therefore acquiesced, and wrote to that purpose to Governor Belchier.

The Governor of South Caroline sent the General bills for four thousand pounds, being part of six thousand which was voted by that assembly towards a common fund. These bills were remitted to Governor Morris to pay in part for the magazine at Shippensburgh. This was the only money raised by the Provinces which were passed through the General's hands.

The General wrote to the Governors of Virginia, Maryland, and Pensylvania, desiring the two former to have their Militia ready to escort his convoys, if he should not be able to detach a sufficient number of men from his own body; and also desired the three Governments to provide Artillery for the Fort, in case he should make himself master of it, as he could not leave any of his Ordnance in that place. He also informed them that the French had threatened to fall with their Indians upon the back Inhabitants as soon as the Army should march, and the General desired they would make the best use of that information.

A proper Commissary was appointed at Conegogee, with orders to send up all the flour to Fort Cumberland. and directions were given for gathering to that place all the provision which had been left for want of carriages at Alexandria, Rock Creek, Frederick, and Winchester. Thus two Magazines were formed in different parts of the country, from either of which the General might supply himself as he should find most convenient.

It appearing to the General absolutely necessary to leave some proper person to superintend the commissaries, and to dispatch the convoys, and also to command at the Fort, Colonel Innys was appointed Governor of it. Instructions were given to him, and money was left with him for contingent expenses, lest the service should for want of it to meet with any checks. The General fixed with the several Governors of Virginia, Maryland, and Pensylvania proper places for laying horses for the more ready conveyance of their expresses: men were also employed with proper badges; and orders were given in the several Governments to supply them with horses upon a proper application.

A company of guides were established under two Chiefs; each regiment had three guides. The General had one, and the Quartermaster General three.

An Hospital was left at the place, and the most infirm Officers and men remained in Garrison.

Every thing being now settled, Sr Peter Halket with the 44th regiment would march on [marched] the 7th of June.

Lieutenant Colonel Burton with the independent Companies and Rangers on the 8th, and Colonel Dunbar with the 48th regiment on the 10th, with the proportions of baggage, as was settled by the Council of War.

The same day the General left Fort Cumberland, and joined the whole at Spendelow camp, about five miles from the Fort.

ORDERS GIVEN AT FORT CUMBERLAND

None of the men that came with the Regiments from Ireland to be suffered to act as Bat-men.

All the troops to be under arms, and to have the Articles of War read to them, at which time the servants and followers are to attend.

A return to be made of such men as understand mining, to whom proper encouragement shall be given.

The troops to begin immediatley their field days, each man to have twelve rounds of powder.The troops are to be immediately brigaded in the following manner:(Note: this appears in Braddock's log on May 12)

FIRST BRIGADE, COMMANDED BY SR PETER HALKET.

	Compliment	Effective
44th Regiment of Foot	700	700
Captn Rutherfordsand Ind. Co. NY	100	95
Captn Gates		
Captn Polson's Carpenters	50	48
Capt. Peronnee's Virginia Ra	.50	47
Capt Wagner's	50	45
Capt Dagworthy's Maryland Ra.	50	49

SECOND BRIGADE, COMMANDED BY COLONEL DUNBAR

48th Regiment of Foot	700	700

Capt. Demeries's S.C.Detach	100	650
Capt Dobb's S.C. Rangers	100	80
Capt. Mercer's Carpenters	50	35
Capt Steven's	50	48
Capt Hogg's Virginia Ra.	50	40
Capt Cox's	50	43

The Detachment of Seamen to encamp with the Second Brigade and the Troop of light horse separately.

The General is to be acquainted through an aid de Camp the night before the regiments are to excercise.

Prohibitory Orders were given against spirituous liquors (goniga-nongi) being sold to the Indians, or any soldiers going into their camp.

Proper Victualling returns were ordered to be given in to the Commissary General of the stores, signed by the commanding officers of the Regiments and artillery, the several Companies, Detachment of Seamen and Troop of light horse, the Director of the Hospital, Waggon-Master General, and Indian manager, specifying the names and qualifications of those persons, who drew provisions under their command of directions.

All the troops were to account to the director of the hospital once in three months for stoppages at the rate of four pence sterling per day for every man that was admitted into the General Hospital.

It was also ordered, that no suttler should dare to sell any more spirits to the men than one gill a day to each, which an Officer of the Picket was to see delivered out at eleven of the clock and mixed with three gills of water; any suttler offending against this order was to be sent to the Provost.

If any non-commissioned Officer or soldier shall be found gaming, he shall immediately receive three hundred lashes, and the standers by shall be deemed principals and punished as such.

If any soldier is seen drunk in Camp, he is to be sent immediately to the Quarter Guard, and to receive two hundred lashes the next morning.

Agreeably to a resolution of a Council of War, it was ordered that every subaltern superintending the work upon the road should receive three shilling per day; each serjeant one shilling, each corporal one pence; and every drum or private man six pence. But as it was thought this would weaken too much the Military Chest, and there being no publik markets, the General promised to settle with them in their winter quarters.

Any soldier or followers of the Army that shall be detected in stealing or purloyning any of the provisions, shall suffer death.[375]

May 30, Friday. Fort Cumberland.   **(Washington)**
I arrived with my charge safe into the Camp the 30th of last month, after waiting a day and piece at Winchester.[376]

(seaman)
On the 30th:-Arrived here a Company from North Carolina under the Command of Capt Dobbs.[377]

MARYLAND-NORTHWEST OF FORT CUMBERLAND
Fryday May the 30th.   **(batman)**
We marched at 6 oClock. The party that Cut the Roads marched at four. We marched till Eight at Night and only marched three miles. The great Quantity of Wagons delayed us and the Roads Being all to Cut and make passable.[378]

Lacock writes: "From Fort Cumberland westward Braddock had to make a road for his troops across mountains divided by ravines and torrents, over a rugged, desolate, unknown, and uninhabited country. In any discussion of this subject three things should be borne clearly in mind: (1) the irregular topography and mountainous nature of the country through which the road had to be built, for there were as many as six ranges of the Alleghenies to be crossed, besides other mountain elevations and passes that presented as great and serious difficulties; (2) the wooded character of the country; (3) the fact that the road had to be constructed by the soldiers of the army. It is noteworthy that the road which Braddock made followed every closely the course of the so-called Nemacolin Indian trail, and that it was used as a pioneer road as far west as Jumonville until late in the first quarter of the nineteenth century.

On May 30 a detachment of six hundred men commanded by Major Russell Chapman set out to clear a road twelve feet wide from Fort Cumberland to Little Meadows, twenty miles away; but in spite of some work previously done on Wills Mountain, just west of the fort, they had some great difficulty in passing the elevation that on the first day they got but two miles from the starting-place. In the process, moreover, three of their wagons were entirely destroyed and many more shattered.

So great was the difficulty experienced by the advance party in passing this mountain (Wills) that General Braddock himself reconnoitered it, and had determined to put 300 more men at work upon it when he was informed by Mr. Spendelow, lieutenant of the seamen that he had discovered a pass by way of the Narrows through a valley which led round the foot of the mountain. There upon

Braddock ordered a survey of this route to be made, with the result that a good road was built in less than three days, over which all troops and supplies for (from) Fort Cumberland were subsequently transported."

VIRGINIA-ALEXANDRIA
May the 30   **(Browne)**
    Extreem hot. Very busy making Bread and Ginger Bread and boiling Hams for our March. Had Company to dine with us in our Anti Chamber which is as hot as a Bagnio. We are to march on Sunday for Will's Creek if Mr. Falkner our commanding Officer does not get lit in his upper Rooms and forget it. [379]

      George Washington arrives at Fort Cumberland on this day with the money, 15 days after leaving for Williamsburg.

May 31 (Saturday)
MARYLAND-CAMP AT FORT CUMBERLAND
Parole--------   **(Braddock)**
Field Officer to morrow Maj^r Sparke.
Generals Guard 44th Regiment. [380]

Sir: John St. Clair   **(St. Clair)**
    It was very far form my intention that our detachment should be seven day march from me, I proposed that the road you should make in seven days I might be able to march it on three or four are...but according to the amount I hear of it I must be much longer marching it that you and my carriages are heavier and more numerous which is by no means what I proposed I must therefore desire you to make no more haste than good I...let me have your answer by bearer, and believe me to be your most obed.& hum. serv. [381]

Camp at Wills's Creek May 31st: 1755   **(Halkett/Disney)**
The Parole is Stafford
Field Officer for to Morrow Major Sparks
    1 Corpl & Eight men of the Line to parade every Morning at Eight oClock. They Are to be directed by Mr. Lake Commissary in Unloading of Waggons &c &c. [382]

MARYLAND-NORTHWEST OF FORT CUMBERLAND
Satterday May the 31st.   **(batman)**

We marched about three Miles and when we Came to our ground after Receiving Provisions and Cooking it, the Working party was Ordered to Cut the Roads up a large mountain and a Covering party along with them to guide em. [383]

VIRGINIA-ALEXANDRIA

May the 31 (Browne)

Spent this Day in packing up and loading my Waggon and fixing my Tilt. Sup'd at Capt. Johnsons and lay'd at Mr. Moxly's (ordinary) but had no sleep not having lay'd on a Bed since I left England. [384]

June 1 (Sunday)
MARYLAND-CAMP AT FORT CUMBERLAND
Parole-Tamworth (Braddock)
Field officer to morrow Lt Col Gage.
Generals Guard 48th Regmt. [385]

Camp at Will's Creek June: 1st: 1755 (Halkett/Disney)
The Parole is Tamworth
Field Officer for to Morrow Lieut Col Gage [386]

MARYLAND-CAMP AT GEORGES CREEK

June 1st 1755 (St. Clair)

Sir: General Braddock

I received your Excellency's letter by Capt. Orme and would have answered it, had he not returned to your head Quarters, as he could acquaint you more fully of our situation having seen it on the spot.

It never was my intention to go on and leave any road to be cut by the body of the army, unless it is the five miles next to the fort, which may be easily repaired by the troops before they march. I carried out with me this morning 15 men to Savage River which road will be completed this evening so that we may move our camp tomorrow to that place. I have sent back a working party of 200 men five miles toward the camp to repair the damages done by our carriages, which I dare say they will complete this afternoon, I shall report its situation in a postscript to this letter.

Your Excellency need not be apprehensive of us gettng too far ahead, I wish with all my heart that the ground would permit it. I believe with much difficulty we shall be able to get to the little

Meadows the 7th day but should be sorry to stop at that place for fear
of destroying your forage more than one night. Could we get on ten
miles farther to Bear Camp and think its advisable, and leave the Little
Meadows for the Rendevouz of the Army for should your Excellency
ever attempt to march your whole convoy in one body, you will be
under an absolute necessity of falling into divisions, so that it appears
to me that it will be the best manner to march in three divisions and
join the whole at the Little Meadows the van guard excepted.

I shall be glad to know your Excellency's sentiments on this head
that I amy guide my self according. I shall undertake nothing which
will put it out of our power to send back the empty waggons by the
time appointed for their arrival at the fort. Should the whole number of
Guides not have joined the Brigade, the bearer of this Grymess (?) is
recommended to me as a person who knows the country very well. I
have the honour of being with the greatest respect,

Your Excellency's most obed. & hum. serv. [387]

(seaman)

June 1st:-We hear the Detachment is got 15 miles: Mr. Spendlowe
and our people returned. [388]

MARYLAND-NORTHWEST OF FORT CUMBERLAND
Sunday June the 1st.   (batman)

We halted and sent a party of men to Cut the Road Over Halligany
(Allegheny) Mountains, which they finished Near 6 Miles. [389]

VIRGINIA-WEST OF ALEXANDRIA-OLD COURTHOUSE
June the 1   (Browne)

At 4 in the Morning I was call'd upon by Mrs. Johnson who came
to take her leave of me, and at 8 we March'd for Wills's Creek with
one Officer, my Brother, self and Servant, 2 Nurses, 2 Cooks and 40
Men to guard us, 12 waggons with the sick, Lame, and Blind, my
waggon in the Rear. My Equipage, 3 Horses and a Mare, good in
Spirit but poor in Flesh; which I mention'd to Mr. Gore (my
Coachman), who told me that if they were right fat they would faint by
the Way. My Brother came padding on his horse in the Rear, but as
my Friend Gore observ'd there was no fear of his fainting by the Way
being very poor in Flesh. We had march'd 3 Miles when my Coachman
was for taking a better Road, but the Sentrys forbid it; but he said it
was very hard if the other Waggons drove to the Old Boy he must

follow them. We halted at 3 and din'd on a Piece of salt Port and Water to Drink. At 6 we came to the old Court House 17 Miles from Bellhaven. Laid in a Room with but 3 Beds in it. [390]

Nichols writes: "Although each regiment in the Army had its surgeon, surgeons mate, and chest filled with medicine, bandages, and surgical instruments, a general hospital with full medical equipment was added to the expedition. The hospital staff included "Director" James Napier, two master surgeons, two master apothecaries, three surgeons mates, three apothecary mates and a matron, one Charlotte Browne...Browne left Alexandria June 1st and arrived at Fort Cumberland on June 13th. She was escorted by one Company of Halkett's command under Lt. Thomas Faulkner with 50 sick soldiers in 13 wagons with both sick and blind".

Hough writes: "This campsite is about 0.4 miles southwest of Tysons Corner, at the intersection of Old Court House Road and Chain Bridge Road. An appropriate marker at this intersection states: From this spot stood the first Court house of Fairfax County. Built in 1742. Abandoned because of Indian hostilities about 1752. Erected by the Fairfax Chapter D.A.R. The 44th Regiment camped here April 27, 1755 and Mrs. Browne's hospital unit on June 1.

Fry & Jefferson Map (printed in 1754, roads added 1755) shows but one road westward out of Alexandria. This road forked at Cameron's Ordinary: the right (north) fork led to the Shenandoah Valley via Miners (Leesburg) and Vestals Gap in the Blue Ridge: the left (south) fork also led to the Valley but via West's Ord (near Aldie) and Williams (Snickers) Gap in the Blue Ridge. Evidently sentries posted at the fork (exact location not known, but possibly near the corner of Episcopal High School grounds where the street named Braddock Road crosses King Street or within a mile westward of this corner were to direct all marching units onto the right fork which was the older route.

Furthermore, all of the diaries now available confirm the fact that only one Virginia road was used from Alexandria to the Valley, the other route being through Maryland. The street named Braddock Road from downtown Alexandria to the vicinity of Episcopal High School Grounds is probably the road traveled by the 44th Regiment and Mrs. Browne's unit when enroute to Old Court House.

From the campsite at Old Court House the route westward was over Old Court House Road (Va. 677) until its identity is lost in modern developments. In general, however, the route went toward Leesburg and modernization of the Leesburg Pike eliminated many of its curves and changes of direction. Sometimes sections of the ancient road are currently part of the secondary road system; for example, in the Dranesville area it curves north of U.S. 7 as much as half a mile (now designated Va.743), and in the Sugarland Run area it is almost half a mile south of the same highway where its current designation is Va. 604." (Winchester-Frederick County Historical Society).

June 2 (Monday)
MARYLAND-CAMP AT FORT CUMBERLAND

Parole-Weybridge   **(Braddock)**

Field Officer to morrow Lt Col Burton.

Generals Guard 44th Regiment.

The Hatchet men of the two Regements and one man per company from the rest of the line to Parade this afternoon att 3 o'clock at Mr Gordon's (Engineer) Tent.

Four Sergeants 2 corporals & 100 men with arms 1 subaltern, 1 sergeant 1 coporal and 30 men with arms to parade to morrow morning at Revelle beating at the head of the Line and to receive their orders from Mr Gordon Engineer.

His Excellency has been pleased to appoint Col Innes Governor of Fort Cumberland.

MONDAY EVENING

Three subaltern officers to march with the detachment of 100 men without arms, which is to parade to morrow morning at Reville beating. [391]

Camp at Wills's Creek June: 2nd: 1755

The Parole is Waybridge   **(Halkett/Disney)**

Field Officer for to Morrow Lt Col Burton

The Hatchett men of the Two Regts: & 1 man per Company of the rest of the Line to parade This Afternoon at 3 oClock at Mr Gordons Engineers Tent. 4 Serjts 2 Corpls & 100 men without Arms 1 Sub: 1 Serjt 1 corpl & 30 men with Arms to parade to morrow Morning at Revalley beating Att the Head of the Line & to receive Their Orders form Mr. Gordon Engineer. His Excellency Genl Braddock has been pleased to Appoint Col (James) Innes to be Governeur of Fort Cumberland. [392]

MARYLAND-CAMP AT SAVAGE RIVER

June 2nd 1755   **(St. Clair)**

Sir: General Braddock

I am this moment favored with your Excellencys command by Capt. Orme and beg leave to inform you that I by no means intended to march beyond the 7th day march at any rate and such time I hope will carry us to the Little Meadows or very near them and as we shall I think have no reason to fortify ourselves there, the convoy of waggons shall be return. The next day after our arrival which will shorten the time of your Excellency stay at Cumberland Fort.

Our present convoy has this day got over the hill on this side Georges Creek and with a...trouble as we could hope for. We have taken a great deal of paine upon the road over it, but some part of it cannot be made very good in so short a time, we shall likewise continue to make it from thence to the Little Meadow, as well as the nature of the ground and the time will...determine all, I hope we shall get on Wednesday night for there is no nearer place to encamp all.

I beg leave to inform your Excellency that if you Rendevouz the whole at Georges Creek you will find it difficult to pass the rear of your convoy from thence like late the 2d day or perhaps the 3rd.

If your Excellency disapprove of our marching forward to the little Meadows you'll please to inform me tomorrow and we shall stop at Laurel Run and only cut the road forward.

Monocahuka is arriv'd with the Indians but wants to go to the fort unless Montour comes to them to morrow therefore beg your excellency may please to send him. I am [393]

Sir: John St. Clair   **(Orme)**

The General received your letter and has ordered me to inform you that he does not choose to have you advance more than the seven days and he is very desirous of getting from this place as soon as possible and that his Excellency intends a junction of the whole convoy at Georges Creek instead of the Little Meadows and he would have the road repaired as much as it will admit of.

Your most hum. & obed serv. [394]

                                                           (seaman)

On the 2nd:-Col. Burton, Capt. Orme, Mr. Spendlowe and self went out to reconnoitre the road. Mr. Spendlowe left us, and returned to Camp at 2 o'clock, and reported he had found a road to avoid a great mountain. In the afternoon we went out to look at it, and found it would be much better than the old road, and not above 2 miles about.[395]

MARYLAND-NORTHWEST OF FORT CUMBERLAND
Munday June the 2d.   **(batman)**

We marched about 6 Miles, the Rocks being so large that we where obliged to Blast them several times before we Came to our (camp) ground. [396]

VIRGINIA-WEST OF ALEXANDRIA-COLEMANS
June the 2   (Browne)

At Break of Day the Drum beat. I was extremely sleepy but got up, and as soon as our Officer had eat 6 Eggs and drank a dram or two and some Punch we march'd; but my Waggon being in the Rear the Day before, my Coachman insisted that it was not right that Madam Browne should be behind, and if they did not give way they should feel the soft end of his Whip. He gain'd his point and got in Front. The Roads are so Bad that I am almost disjointed. At 12 we halted at Mr. Colemans, pitch'd our Markeys and dined on Salt Gammon, nothing better to be had. [397]

NEW YORK-NEW YORK   (Pennsylvania Gazette)

Last Sunday Sen'night a French trader, with a woman (said to be his wife) arrived here from Montreal, in Canada, which place he left about a month since: we hear he reports, that two Detachments of men amounting to 700, were sometime before his departure from thence, sent to the Ohio; that another party of 250 were soon to follow; and that their whole force on the Ohio this summer, would not (if we have faith enough to believe a Frenchman) exceed 1200 men, exclusive of Indians; that at Quebeck they were very busy in building not less than 500 batteaus; and t'was tho't some new expedition was on foot, as the Gazette of April 16 may appear. [398]

Hough writes: "Richard Coleman's house stood on a knoll on the east bank of Sugarland Run slightly more than 0.4 mile upstream (south) from the present U.S. 7 bridge over that stream. The original house is no longer standing but its foundation is plainly visible. The 44th Regiment encamped here April 28, 1755, and Mrs. Browne's unit stopped here on June 2."(Winchester-Frederick County Historical Society).

June 3 (Tuesday)
MARYLAND-CAMP AT FORT CUMBERLAND
Parole-Yarmouth   (Braddock)

A General Court Martial of the Line consisting of 6 captains & 6 subalterns to sit to morrow morning at 8 o'clock at the Presidents Tent.

Major Sparke President.
Mr Shirley Judge Advocate.
Field Officer to morrow Lt Col Burton.

Generals Guard 48th Regiment.

Four Subalterns, 5 Sergts, 5 Corpls, and 150 men without arms to parade to morrow morning at y[e] head of the line at Revelle beating.

One Subaltern, 1 Sergt, 1 Corpl, and 30 men with arms to parade at the same time and act as a covering party; they are to receive their Order from Mr. Gordon, Engineer. [399]

Camp at Wills's Creek June: 3d: 1755   **(Halkett/Disney)**
The Parole is Yarmouth
Field Offr: for to Morrow Lieut Col Gage
For the Genls Guard 48regt

A Genl Court Martial of the line Consisting of One Field Offr & Six Capts Six Subaltrons to sitt to morrow Morning at 8 oClock at the Presidents Tent Major Sparks President Mr Sherly Judge Avocate.

4 Subs: 5 Serjts 5 Corpls And 150 Men Without Arms to parade to morrow morning at Reveillie beating att the head of the Line. 1 Sub 1 Serjt 1 Corpl & 30 men with Arms to parade at the same time As a Covering party. They are to receive their Orders from Mr. Gordon Engineer. Lieut Howard of y[e] 48 regt to be one of the Subs. for the Working Party. [400]

General Court Martial   **(Orme)**
Major Sparks, President

The punishments put in execution, all corporal ones. [401]

                                                         (seaman)
On the 3rd:-This morning an Engineer (Mr. Engineer Gordon) and 100 men began working on the new road from Camp, and Mr. Spendlowe and self with 20 of our men went to the place where the new road comes into the old one, and began to clear away, and completed a mile to-day. [402]

NAME OF ENCAMPMENT   **(Gordon)**
From Ft. Cumberland to Grove Camp-Dist. 5 Miles
WORK DONE TO THE ROAD

A great deal of cuting and digging and some blowing
N.B. the road by Will's Creek is impassable in wet weather, all through a Defile, but pretty level
QUALITY OF THE ROAD

The hill rough, its rise quick, its fall quick and narrow, the rest

tolerable
QUALITY OF THE CAMP
Open, moist, good feeding, plenty of tolerable Water
Days halted 2 [403]

Temple comments that colonial records suggest that there already was a road from Ft. Cumberland to Turkey Foot in 1751 that was 30 feet wide and 80 miles long - probably an exaggeration to impress the King. Temple further comments that Washington reported to Dinwiddie in 1754 the work needed to "amend and alter" the first 20 miles of the road form Wills Creek to Little Meadows took 60 men from April 25 to May 1 when 160 men continued the work until May 9. An analysis of the figures means that on an average 87 men could "amend and alter" one mile of road a day. Furthermore one year later John Armstrong reported to Gov. Morris that 60 men could make one mile of entirely new road in one day through mountain wilderness (this was on the Pa. Road to the Turkeyfoot).

MARYLAND-NORTHWEST OF FORT CUMBERLAND
Tuesday June the 3d.   **(batman)**

Last Night about ten at Night we was Alarmed by several Shots fireing at a distance which made us stand to Arms Immediately which we did till two in the morning and after that we lay upon our Arms all Night and in the morning we marched 6 miles and sent a working party to Cut the Roads as usal. [404]

VIRGINIA-WEST OF ALEXANDRIA-MINORS
June the 3   **(Browne)**

At 3 in the Morning was Awak'd by the Drum beat, but was so so stiff that I was at a loss to tell whether I had any Limbs. I breakfasted in my Waggon and then set off in front; at which all the rest were very much inrag'd, but to no Purpose for my Coachman told them that he had but one Officer to Obey and she was in his Waggon, and it was not right that she should be blinded with Dust. My Brother the Day before left his Cloak behind, so sent his Man back for it on his Horse, and march'd on Foot. On the Road met with Mr. Adams a Parson, who left his Horse & padded with them on foot. We halted at Mr. Minors. We order'd some Fowls for Dinner but not one to be had, so was obliged to set down to our old Dish Gammon & Greens. The Officer and the Parson replenish'd their Bowl so often that they began to be very Joyous, untill their Servant told them that their Horses were lost at which the Parson was much inrag'd and pop'd out an Oath, but Mr. Falkner said "Never mind your Horse, Doctor, but have you a Sermon ready for next Sunday?" I being the Doctors country woman he made me many Compts. and told me he should be very happy if he could be better acquainted with me, but hop'd when I came that way again I would do him the Honour to spend some Time at his House. I chatted till 11 and then took my leave and left them a full Bowl before them. [405]

Hough writes: "The 44th Regiment encamped at Nicholas Minor's place on April 29 & 30. Mrs. Browne slept in Minor's House on June 3 according to her diary. Although the house is no longer standing, its site at Leesburg is 0.7 miles southeast of the junction of E. Main and E. Loudoun Streets. The site is on a small knoll on the south side of U.S. 7 and just within the current city (1970) limits. Braddock's Road westward from Minors went along the north side of Tuscarora Creek then up Dry Mill Branch through Clarke's Gap, thus bypassing the 60 acre tract that became the site of Leesburg. In Clark's Gap the old road crossed the present U.S. 7 highway and continued westward through Hillsboro to Keys (Vestals) Gap in the Blue Ridge."(Winchester-Frederick County Historical Society)

June 4 (Wednesday)
MARYLAND-CAMP AT FORT CUMBERLAND
Parole-Doncaster   **(Braddock)**
Field officer to morrow Lt Col Burton.
For the Generals Guard 44th Regiment.

    The 44th Regiment and Capt Mercer's Company of Virginia Carpenters to hold themselves in readiness to march in an hour's warning. The working Party to be relieved to morrow morning, and by the same number. [406]

Camp at Wills's Creek June 4th: 1755   **(Halkett/Disney)**
The Parole is Duncaster
Field Offr for to morrow Lt Col: Burton
For the Genl Guard 44th Regt.

    Sir Peter Halketts Regt: & Capt Merors (Mercer's) Company of Carpenters to hold Themselves in readiness to March at An hours warning. [407]

                                                  (seaman)

    On the 4th:-Went out today, and cleared another mile (1 Midshipman and 20 men cleared ¾ of a Mile). [408]

MARYLAND-NORTHWEST OF FORT CUMBERLAND
Wedensday June the 4th.   **(batman)**

We halted by the River Lorel (Laurel Hill Creek) and after Receiving Provisions and Couking (cooking) a party went to work and a Covering party Along with them to guarde them. This day our Hunter went a shouting (shooting) and Brought home a Bear and killed a Wolf and followed a panter Better than 6 miles but did not get him.[409]

VIRGINIA-WEST OF ALEXANDRIA-QUAKER'S
June the 4   **(Browne)**

At break of Day my Coachman came and tap'd at my Chamber Door and said Madam all is ready and it is right early. I went to my waggon and we moved on. Left Mr. Falkner behind in Pursuit of his Horse. March'd 14 Miles and halted at an old sage Quaker's with silver Locks. His Wife on my coming in accosted me in the following manner: "Welcome Friend set Down, thou seem's full Bulky to travel, but thou art young and that will enable thee. We were once so ourselves but we have been married 44 years & may say we have lived to see the Days that we have no Pleasure therein". We had recourse to our old Dish Gammon, nothing else to be had; but they said they had some Liquor they call'd Whisky which was made of Peaches. My Friend Thompson being a Preacher, when the soldiers came in as the Spirit mov'd him, held forth to them and told them the great Virtue of Temperance. They all stared at him like Pigs but had not a Word to say in their justification. [410]

   Hough writes: "In other words, the present highway (U.S. 9) follows, in general, Braddock's Road from Clark's Gap through Hillsboro and Keys Gap. Of course, there is evidence that the modern highway eliminated many bends in the original road." (Winchester-Frederick County Historical Society).
   He does include a map drawn by him that shows the road from Minor's (Leesburg vicinity) to Thompson's house using routes 699 to Clarks Gap and then route 9 to Thompson's (Hillsboro).

June 5 (Thursday)
MARYLAND-CAMP AT FORT CUMBERLAND
Parole-Boston   **(Braddock)**
Field Officer to torrow Major Sparke.
For the Generals Guard 48th Regiment.

   The working party to be relieved to morrow morning and by the same number of men.[411]

Will's Creek, June 5, 1755   **(Braddock)**
Sir: Secretary of State of Pennsylvania

    Before I left Williamsburg the Quarter Master General told me that I might depend upon twenty five hundred horses and two hundred wagons from Virginia and Maryland; but I had great reason to doubt it, having experienced the false dealing of all in this country with whom I had been concerned. Hence, before my departure from Frederick, I agreed (desired) with Mr. Benjamin Franklin, Postmaster in Pennsylvania, who has great credit in that Province, to send here (hire me) one hundred and fifty wagons and the necessary number of horses. This he accomplished with promptitude and fidelity, and it is almost the only instance of address and integrity which I have seen in all these provinces.[412]

Wills's Creek June 5th 1755   **(Halkett/Disney)**
The Parole is Bolton
Field Officer for to Morrow Lieut Col:Gage
For the Genl Guard 48 Regt.[413]

                                          (seaman)
    On the 5th:-We went out as before, and at noon, Mr. Spendlowe and I went to the other party to mark the road for them, but at 1, it came to blow, rain, thunder, and lighten so much, that it split several tents, & continued so till night, when we returned to the camp.[414]

MARYLAND-NORTHWEST OF FORT CUMBERLAND
Thursday June the 5th.   **(batman)**

    We marched to the little Meadows, it being 4 miles, very Bad Roads Over Rocks and Mountains almost unpassable. We was ten hours in marching it. This day our hunter Shot us two Elks and one Bear and a Dear and Wounded two more. Today we dined on Bear and Rattle Snake. [415]

VIRGINIA-WEST OF ALEXANDRIA
June the 5   **(Browne)**

    My Lodgings not being very clean, I had so many close Companions call'd Ticks what deprived me of my Nights Rest, but I indulg'd till 7. We halted this day, all the Nurses Baking Bread and boiling Beef for the March to Morrow. A fine Regale 2 Chicken with

Milk and Water to Drink, which my friend Thompson said was fine temperate Liquor. Several things lost out of my Waggon, amongst the rest they took 2 of my Hams, which my Coachman said was an abomination to him, and if he could find out who took them he would make them remember taking the next. [416]

PENNSYLVANIA-PHILADELPHIA   (Pennsylvania Gazette)
We hear from Wills Creek that the waggons and horses lately contracted for in the counties of Lancaster, York and Cumberland were safely arrived at the camp, and gave great satisfaction to the General, and the other officers being for the most part by far the best of any that have been engag'd in the service of the Army since their arrival.

We likewise hear that there are fine Bottoms for several miles round the Camp in which there is a great deal of good grass and other food for the Horses and that the Army in general were very healthy, impatient to enter on action, and wait chiefly for the arrival of the forage purchased in this province.

In a letter from Susquehanna, dated the 31st ult. it is mentioned that a person was just returned from the Camp and brought Advice that before he left it, two men came there, who appeared to be spies, one of them being known to have been among the Virginia forces on the same business before Washington's defeat last summer. They own'd they came from the French Fort, and pretended they were very numerous there, One of them attempted to make his escape, and being a good runner, was overtaken by one man, who brought him back, when he was immediately put in irons, and it was thought soon to be hang'd. [417]

June 6 (Friday)
MARYLAND-WILLS'S CREEK
Wills's Creek June 6th: 1755   (Braddock, Halkett/Disney)
The Parole Carlile
Field Offr for This Day in the room of Col Gage Major Sparks
Field Officer for to Morrow Lt Col: Burton

Sr Peter Halketts regr: to march to morrow morning. The Sick of the Regt: unable to march to be sent This afternoon to the Genl Hospital And One Subaltern Offr to be left behind with Them. The men of that regt now upon Guard, when They Are Releived or Order'd to Come off Are to be Assembled to Gather And to be Marchd Regulary to the regts by an Officer. Capt Gates's Independent Company And the Remaining Companys of provincel Troops to March on Sunday Morning with the Whole Park of Artillery.

No more women to March with each regt: or Compy Then His Excellency Allowd in ye Orders of the 18th: of May: Any Soldier Suttler or Woman or Any person what ever belonging to the Army who shall be Detected in Stealing plundering or Wasting any of the Provisions shall suffer Death. Sir Peter Halketts regt. to Receive Two Day('s) provisions. As ye women are to receive Eight Day('s) provisions, The men Are to receive Theirs at 3 oClock this afternoon & the women at Six. The Genl Court Martial where of Major Sparks was President is disolved. Richd: Shelton & Calbib Curry Soldiers in Capt Edward Brise Dobs Compy of Americans Tryd for Desertion Are by the Sentance of the Court Martial found Guilty And is Adjudged to receive one Thousand Lashes Each. John Igo a convict Servt: being Accused of Theft is found Guilty of receiving and concealing of Goods The property of soldiers in His Majestys Service And is Adjudged to receive five Hundred Lashes with a Cat of Nine Tails. John McDonell Soldier on Sir Peter Halketts regt. Accused of being Concernd with John Igo in Concealing of Goodes The property of Soldiers in His Majestys (service) with An intent to Desert, The Court Martial being of An Opinion That sufficient Evidence is not produced in support of the Charge Against him Therefore do Acquit Him. The Guards Advanced up Wills's Creek The Pottomack And the flatts to be taken of(f) to morrow morning And Join their Severall Corps. The other Guards to Remain And be relieved As Usual. No soldiers Wife to be suffered to march from the Camp with a Horse (As Their Own). [418]

(seaman)

On the 6th:-We went out as usual, and at 2 o'clock completed the road, & returned to Camp. This Evening I was taken ill. [419]

MARYLAND-NORTHWEST OF FORT CUMBERLAND
Fryday June the 6th. **(batman)**

We halted and unloaded all the Wagons and sent them to Fort Cumberland where we came from. The Rest of the Army they went for more provisions and three hundred men along with em to guarde them.

This day a working party went a Clearing the Ground Round the Meadows. This day we dined on Snake and Bear and dear. [420]

VIRGINIA-TOWARD FORT CUMBERLAND-THOMPSONS
June the 6   (Browne)

Took my leave of My Friend Thompson who bid me farewell. A great gust of Thunder and Lightning and Rain, so that we were almost drown'd. Extreem bad Roads. We pass'd over the Blue Ridge which was one continual mountain for 3 Miles. Forg'd through 2 Rivers (Catoctin Creek & Shenandoah River). At 7 we halted at Mr. Keys. The Soldiers desired my Brother to advance them some Whisky for they told him he had better kill them at once than to let them dye by Inches, for without they could not live. He compiled with their Request and it soon began to operate; They all went to dancing and bid defiance to the French. My Friend Gore began to shake a leg. I ask'd him if it was consistent as a Member of his Society to dance; he told me that he was not at all united with them, and that there were some of his People who call'd themselves Quakers and stood up for their Church but had no more Religion in them than his Mare. I then told him I should set him down as a Ranter. [421]

> Hough writes: "Edward Thompson, a Quaker, owned the land at Hillsboro where the 44th Regiment encamped on May 1. Mrs. Browne's detachment camped at the same place on June 4 & 5."(Winchester-Frederick County Historical Society).
>
> Thompson a Quaker has been described in all the literature as a resident of the early settlement what would become Hillsboro, Virginia. Fairfax Harrison in The Virginia Magazine of History and Biography ("With Braddock's Army", Oct. 1924) describes these two crossings as Catoctin Creek and Shenandoah River. Harrison (page 310) and The Atlas of Early American History (page 4-5) suggest an alignment that passes through Waterford, Virginia, an 1732 Quaker village located on the South Fork of the Catoctin..
>
> John T. Phillips, knowledgeable about Loudoun County colonial history, observed to the compiler that elements of Braddock's Army did not pass through Waterford, Virginia. His observation is based on his study of roads and county land records.
>
> See entry for May 2 for additional detail on Mr. Keys Plantation. From land ownership records the name Keys is used in 1852 when Humphrey Key's is shown as the owner of the saw mill (Brown 1852).

June 7 (Saturday)
MARYLAND-CAMP AT FORT CUMBERLAND

Parole-Doncaster

Capt Yates's Independant companies & the remaining companies of Provinicial Troops & ye whole Park of Artillery to march to morrow morning and to be under the command of Lieut Col Burton.

The artillery & companies that march to morrow to receive this afternoon Provisions to compleat them to the 11th inclusive & y[e] women to the 17th.

The 48th Regiment to take all the Guards to morrow; the men of the 48th Regiment now upon ye train Guard are to join their corps to morrow morning when the artillery marches off & that Guard to be mounted by the companys that march to morrow. The 48th Regiment to hold themselves in readiness to march on Monday next.

AFTER ORDERS.

The Generals Guard is to be reduced to morrow to 1 Sergt 1 corpl and 12 men who are not to be relieved but to remain with the Genl's Baggage. [422]

(seaman)

On the 7th:-A rainy day, with thunder and lightning. Sir Peter Halket and his Brigade marched with 2 field pieces, and some waggons with provisions. A midshipman & 12 of our people went to assist the train. [423]

MARYLAND-NORTHWEST OF FORT CUMBERLAND
Camp at About six Miles from Will's Creek June 7th   (Halkett/Disney)
The Parole is Doncaster

Two Serjts Two corpls: & 48 Men to Mount Guard Directly & to place 16 Centrys & every Centry is to be placed within Sight of one another & is to open Comunication to one Another by Cutting down the Brush. One Serjt 1 Corpl with the one third of the Effective men of Each Company to Mount Guard to Morrow Mornig at 8 oClock And to divide Their Ground Equaly on the right Side of the Waggons. An Officer of a compy to go to the Suttlers with Two men of a Tent And to see delivered to every Three men yt desires it One pint of spirits or Any Quantity less that they shall desire. They Are to Mix it with a propotionable quantity of Water. Mr Disney is to see That The centinals Are Advanced to Such a distance that there shall be a Sufficient quantity of Grass betwixt Them And the line of Waggons, And That there is An opening cut betwixt the Centrys Cross which They Are to allow no Horses to pass. If They should They Are

250

immediatley to bring Them back. The brush which They cut down to be thrown to the out Side of the Oppening. [424]

Satterday June the 7th.   (batman)

The working party went a Clearing the Camp, and some to Build a house Over the Provisions. This day we Recd five days provisions. Five men of the Carralina Companies Intended to depart after Receiving provisions but was Apprehended by one of them who Informed on the rest. Today we dined on Bear. [425]

VIRGINIA-TOWARD FORT CUMBERLAND
June the 7   (Browne)

Having no room to lodge in I lay'd in the chimney, so wanted no calling in the Morning having no sleep all Night. At 4 we began to march. Left Mr. Falkner behind, who did not choose to March with an empty Stomach. Great Gusts of Rain, My Waggon and everything in it wet, and all the sick allmost drown'd. At 4 we halted at my Friend Laidlers who bid me wellcome, but had no Whiskey which was the Soldiers first Enquiry; for the were still in the opinion that they could not live without it. We now live high, had for Dinner a Qr. of Lamb and a Pye, to drink my Friend Thompson's temperate Liquor Spring Water. I spent the evening very agreeable; Mr. Falkner favour'd me with several Tune on his Flute. Chatted til 10 and then retired. [426]

Atkinson writes: "The first brigade under Sir Peter Halket, lead the way on the 8th, and on the 9th the main body followed. Some idea of the difficulties they encountered, may be had when we perceive they spent the third night only five miles from the first. The place of encampment which is about one third of a mile from the toll-gate on the National Road, is marked by a copious spring bearing Braddock's name. From the western foot (of Wills Mountain), the route continued up Braddock's Run to the forks of the stream, where Clary's tavern now stands, nine miles from Cumberland, when it turned to the left, in order to reach a point on the ridge favorable to an easy descent into the valley of George's Creek. It is surprising that having reached this high ground, the favorable spur by which the National Road accomplishes the ascent of the Great Savage Mountain, did not strike the attention of the engineers, as the labor requisite to surmount the barrier from the deep valley of George's Creek...passing then a mile to the south of Frostburg, the road approaches the east foot of Savage Mountain, which it crosses about one mile south of the National Road, and thence by very favorable ground through the dense forests of white pine peculiar to the region, it got to the North of the National Road, near the gloomy tract called the Shades of Death".

On this the first day of movement of the army from Fort Cumberland it was apparent that the march was to be made in several parts. These have been described in a work entitled George Washington (volume 2 page 46) as follows:

1. From Fort Cumberland westward to the Great Crossing of the Youghiogheny, a distance of about thirty miles through Maryland and Southern Pennsylvania, across Wills Mountain and the main barrier of the Allegheny Range at an elevation of approximately 3000 feet.

2. From the Great Crossings northwestward to Great Meadows and the site of Fort Necessity, a stretch of not more than fifteen miles, but over the forbidding grades of Laurel Hill, at a maximum elevation of about 2400 feet.

3. From Fort Necessity northwestward and northward to the crest and along the higher sweeps of Chestnut Ridge, at 1800 to 2200 feet, until the vicinity of the Jumonville Camp was reached, a distance of about eight miles.

4. From Jumonville Camp North along Chestnut Ridge and thence downgrade to Stewart's crossing of the Youghiogheny; a total of twelve miles.

5. From Stewart's Crossing to the Monongahela in the vicinity of the Narrows of Turtle Creek - thirty-four miles of rolling country, 1200 to 1300 feet above sea level.

6. From the Monongahela and the narrows to Fort Duquesne itself, eleven to thirteen miles according to the choice of routes, at an elevation of 800 to 1200 feet.

The total distance to be covered in these six stages thus was about 110 miles, the greater part of it through rough, heavily wooded country. Dependence, to repeat, was to be upon the main base at Fort Cumberland; the column had to be self-sustaining because the country itself would supply nothing.

June 8 (Sunday)

MARYLAND-CAMP AT FORT CUMBERLAND
Parole-Essex   (Braddock)

Capt[n] Gates's Independant Company and the remaining companys of the Provinicial Troops and artillery are to march to morrow.

The 48th Regt to march on Tuesday as Col Dunbars Regiment is not to march to morrow the Genl's Guard to be relieved to morrow morning.

The Companies that march to morrow to send immediately 1 Sergeant corporal & 12 men to assist Mr Lake commissary of Provisions at the Fort.

A Return to be sent immediately from Col Dunbar's Reg't Capt Gates's company & the American Troops of the number of men they have fitt for Waggoners or Horse Drivers.

In the return of Col Dunbar's Regt they are only to include those men that have joined the Regiment since they have been landed in America. [427]

Sir, (Robert Napier)   (Braddock)

I had the pleasure of writing to you from Frederick the latter End of April, when I gave you an Account of all I then knew. On the 10th of May I arriv'd here; the Train who have been very near a Month on their March, arriv'd the 17th; and the whole of the Forces are now assembled, making about two thousand Effectives, the greatest part Virginians, very indifferent Men, this Country affording no better; it has cost infinite pains and labour to bring them to any sort of Regularity and Discipline: Their Officers very little better, and all complaining of the ill Usage of the Country, who employe'd them last Year without pay or provisions. I am told they have made a pretty good hand of this year's recruiting Affair, tho' I can get no proof of it. This part of the Country is absolutely unknown to the Inhabitants of the lower parts of Virginia and Maryland, their Account of the Roads and provisions utterly false. From Winchester to this place which is Seventy Miles is almost uninhabited, but by a parcel of Banditti who call them selves Indian Traders, and no Road passable but what we were oblig'd to make ourselves with infinate Labour. It would take up too much of your Time were I to tell you particularly the Difficulties and Disappointments I have met with from the want of Honesty and Inclination to forward the Service in all Orders of people in these Colonies, which have occasion'd the great Delays in getting hither, as well as my being detain'd here a Month longer than I intended. I was assur'd at Williamsburg that two hundred Waggons and two thousand five hundred Horses would be here by the 10th of May, as also great Quantities of Forage at proper distances upon the Road, where the Artillery and Waggons were to pass, and that proper persons and such as could be depended upon were employ'd for that purpose; but I soon found that there was hardly any Forage in the Country and that the promises of the people of Virginia and Maryland were not to be depended upon: If we press'd Waggons, as we were oblig'd to let the Horses go into the Woods to feed, they went off directly, the pack Horses the same, for which reason I determin'd before I left Frederick to desire Mr. Franklin of Pensilvania (a province whose people tho' they will contribute very little to the Expedition are exact in their Dealings, and much more industrious than the others) to contract in my name for an hundred and fifty Waggons and a number of pack Horses to be sent to this place with all expedition. It was well I took this precaution, for the Number of Horses and Waggons procur'd in these Colonies do not amount to the tenth part of what I was promis'd: Mr. Franklin undertook and perform'd his Engagements with the greatest readiness and punctuality. By this means I hope to leave this place to morrow with a less Quantity of provisions than I propos'd from the Disappointment of the Waggons and Weakness of the horses. To remedy as much as possible this Inconvenience I have sent forward a strong Detachment with a large Convoy of provisions to be lodge'd upon the most advantagious spot of the Alliganey Mountains with directions for the Waggons to return with a proper Escort. My being oblig'd to draw my supplies from distant provinces lays me under a Necessity of employing a Number of Assistant Commissiaries, none of which will serve without exorbitant pay and am forc'd to make more Contracts than I otherwise should, to guard against the failure of some of them, in which Contracts the people take what Advantage they can of our Necessity. Nothing can well be worse than the Road I have already pass'd and I have an hundred and ten Miles to march thro' an uninhabited Wilderness over steep rocky Mountains and almost impassable Morasses. From this Description, which is not exaggerated you conceive the difficulty of getting good Intelligence, all I have is from Indians, whose veracity is no more to be depended upon (than) that of the Borderers here; their Accounts are that the Number of French at the Fort at present is but small, but pretend to expect a great Reinforcement; this I do not entirely credit, as I am very well persuaded they will want their Forces to the Northward. As soon as I have join'd the Detachment, who have been seven days making a Road of twenty four Miles, I shall send people for Intelligence, who I have reason to believe I can confide in. I have order'd a Road of Communication to be cut from Philadelphia to the Crossing of the Yanghyanghain, which is the Road we ought to have taken, being nearer, and thro' an inhabited and well cultivated Country, and a Road as good as from Harwich to London, to some Miles beyond where they are now opening the new Road. I am inform'd the long expected Arms for the New England Forces bound to Nova Scotia are Arriv'd and that they are sail'd. Boats and Floats are preparing for the Troops destin'd to Niagara and Crown point, the province of New York have been dilatory in regard to that Service of which I presume you will have a particular Account from Governor Shirley, who is upon the Spot and which he may convey to you as soon as to myself untill the Communication can be open'd. Inclos'd I send you the Return of the Forces I propose to proceed with, had I more it would be out of my power to subsist them, With these I flatter myself to be able to drive the French from the Ohio, and to open a Communication with the rest of His majesty's Forces in the other provinces. Captain Bromley of Sir Peter Halket's is dead, I have dispos'd of the Commissions in the Regiment according to Seniority. Mr. Hervey has the Ensigney. I receiv'd a Letter from Sir William Peppperel complaining of his ill State of Health from his sufferings at Louisbourg, and to let me know his Regiment is near compleat; as it is some time since, I presume they are so by this time. Shirley's has been so long since. I have wrote to them both to send their Returns to England by the first opportunity.

I am, dear Sir, Your Most Humble and Most Obedient Servant

E. Braddock [428]

Fort Cumberland Wills's Creek   **(Braddock)**
June 8th 1755.

I receiv'd this Morning a Letter from Sr Wm Pepperel who tells me his Regim^t is not half compleat, occasion'd by the great Numbers that have enlisted for Nova Scotia and Crown point. [429]

MARYLAND-NORTHWEST OF FT CUMBERLAND
Camp About Six Miles from Wills's Creek June 8th   1755
The Parole is Essex   **(Halkett/Disney)**

A Return of the Number of men fitt for Waggoners or Horse drivers that is in each Company of Those that (h)as Joind since the Regt Landed in America to be given in immediatley. [430]

Sunday June the 8th.   **(batman)**

The men went to work at Clearing the Camp. Some of our Indiens Advanced about five miles in the front of the Camp till they Came up with many of the French Indiens Roasting dear. As soon as they saw our Indians they Ran away and left their victals behind em. Our Indiens not being very Strong Returned to Camp to get a fresh Supply of men, which was one Captain one Lieut one Ens(ign) and two drums and 50 private (who) Immediately Advansed with Indiens but did not take them. The 4 men that was for Departing last Night was Punished to day. One Recd a thousand lashes, one Nine Hundred and the Other

255

two, five hundred a piece. Its thought if they had got away they would have gone to the French, which might have Been of great service to them, for they would Inform them our Numbers and where they lay, which they might have brought a greater force against us, which might have cut us of(f) Before we Could get Any Relief from the Grand Army. [431]

VIRGINIA-TOWARD FORT CUMBERLAND-BELLINGERS
June 8   (Browne)

I slept but poorly, laying on a deal Feather Bed. Having had no sleep for 2 Nights did not hear the Drum. We march'd at 4. At 9 we halted at my Friend Bellingers who bid me wellcome. My Brother set off for Winchester, 8 m. off, but Mr. Flakner said he would do himself the Pleasure of staying with me. We spent the day very agreeably: had for Dinner some Veal and greens, to drink french Wine, and for Supper Milk Punch. [432]

June 9 (Monday)
MARYLAND-CAMP IN FORT CUMBERLAND
Parole-Fallmouth   (Braddock)

Col Dunbars regiment to send their sick unable to march to the General Hospital and to leave a subaltern officer behind with them.

One sergeant, 1 corpl and 24 men without arms to parade to morrow morning at Day break to assist Mr. Lake, commissary of Provisions in loading of ye waggons. [433]

Ft Cumberland, June 9th, 1755   (Braddock)
Sir: (W. Shirley)

I have found it necessary to discharge a number of women who are wives to soldiers belonging to the forces under my command, and must beg of you to give orders that they be subsisted in your government; their names are contained in the Passes I have given 'em for their Protection, and I have taken care to order stoppages to be made of one-third Part of thier Husbands' Pay to defray the expence of their maintenance;

I am, sir, your most obedient and most humble servant,

E. Braddock

By his Excellency Edward Braddock, Esq. General and commander in chief of all His Majesty's Forces in North America.

256

I do hereby certify that the Bearers, Mary Welch, Elizabeth
Webster, Mary Walker, Mary Crab, Dorkey Moreton, Margaret Wray,
Margaret Gates, Catherine McFarland, Jane Campbell, Catharine
Watson, Annie Manning, Susanna Duncan, Annie McDonald, Mary
Ryo, Margaret Doggett, Elizabeth Rickerby, Annie Anderson, Jean
Anderson, Mary Scott, Annie Totle, Christiana Fergason, Mary
Dimond, Eieanor Lemmon & Sara Lord, are wives to soldiers
belonging to forces under my command; And all persons whatsoever
are hereby required to suffer 'em to pass without hindrance or
molestation.

Given at the Camp at Fort Cumberland, the 9th day of June, 1755
By His Excellency's Command   E. Braddock [434]
W. Shirley

The person to whom this is addressed is not clear - it could be Colonel
Innes, Governor of Fort Cumberland or the Governor of the Colony of
Pennsylvania (Philadelphia) where the women were being sent.

On the 9th:-Orders for Col. Dunbar'sBrigade   **(seaman)**
to march tomorrow morning. [435]

MARYLAND-NORTHWEST OF FORT CUMBERLAND
Camp six Miles from Wills's Creek June 9: 1755   **(Halkett/Disney)**
The Parole is Falmouth

No fires to be Allowed to be made less then sixty yards from the
Waggons And those that Are made Are to be on the right & left of the
Waggons.

The Out Centrys Are to rest (arms) to no One not even the Genl,
And the Serjts Guard is only to Turn out with Shouldered Arms
Facing the Front. Six little houses to be made immediately for the Use
of the (men). They Are to be upon the right Side & four to be made
for the Offrs on the Left Side at a proper distance one from Another.
This to be a Standng Order Tho the Troops stay but one night in
Camp. Any Centry who shall be found Sitting on his post will be
immediately relieved And Tryd by a Genl Court Martial. All Trees that
lays betwixt Advance Centrys to be immediately Removed And
Thrown in the Front of Them. [436]

Munday June the 9th. **(batman)**

The men went to work a Clearing the wood out of the place from where they fel'd it and to lay it Round the Camp for a Brest work Against the Enemy. This day a Soldier was tryed for Sleeping when Sentry, a great Crime here. But he haveing a good Carractor was forgiven. This day all the Volintears and the Indiens Advanced to the Great Meadows to see it the French was there as was Reported. They propose Returning in 4 days. [437]

VIRGINIA-TOWARDS FORT CUMBERLAND

June 9 **(Browne)**

Lay'd on some Planks. Halted all this Day, the Nurses busy baking Bread and boiling Beef and Washing. Mr. Falkner went a shooting, return's and brought me some Squirrills. Dressed them for Dinner. My Brother return'd from Winchester, there came with him Mr. Savage an officer and thirteen Recruits, and a Waggon with a nurse and Four sick men, one at the Point of Death. [438]

June 10 (Tuesday)

MARYLAND-CAMP AT FORT CUMBERLAND

Parole------ **(Braddock)**

The Fort Guard to join their Regiments as soon as Governor Innes has taken possession of it and placed his centrys. [439]

MARYLAND-CAMP AT THE GROVE (First Camp from Fort Cumberland) **(Braddock)**

Parole-Gainsborough

All the officers of the Line to be at the Gen's tent to morrow morning at 11 o'clock.

No Fires to be made upon any acct whatever within 150 yards of the Road on either side, any person acting contrary to this order shall be very severely punished.

All the waggons to be drawn up to-morrow morning as close as possible and as soon as the waggons belong to the detachment under the command of Majr Chapmen have closed up to the rear of the Artiller y that Detachment then to join the respective Corps.

Col Dunbars Regiment to encamp to morrow morning upon the left of the whole, according to the line of Encampment. [440]

Lacock writes: "After leaving the gap (Narrows) the road turned into the valley of Braddock Run. The methods employed by Braddock's engineers in laying out the road indicate the its course was probably that afterward followed by the National turnpike to a point near the northwest corner of the Alleghany Grove Camp Ground just beyond which and south of the turnpike is a distinct hollow or trench. The neighborhood of the Alleghany Grove was unquestionably the place of the first encampment, Spendelow Camp.

The three engineers who accompanied Braddock's expedition made striking use of a series of absolutely straight lines in laying out the road except where the fording of a river required a tortuous route, or where the topography of the country was such as to render their plan utterly impracticable. This device, which impressed itself upon the writer and his party as they were crossing Wills Mountain, afterwards proved of great value to them in their efforts to pick up the road where traces of it were completely obliterated for rods at a time in cultivated fields."

MARYLAND-CAMP AT LITTLE MEADOWS

June 10th 1755   **(St. Clair)**

Sir: General Braddock

Monocatua's son is this moment arrived from Fort Du Quesne, he left it on Sunday afternoon and brings accounts that he saw at that place in all 70 Indians and 100 French who were preparing set out as yesterday morning to harass on our march. That they were daily in expectation of a reinforcement of 200 more but were delayed by the water being low.

I would have sent this young Indian to your Excellency this evening but he is inclined to go early in the morning to appease his father at the great meadow least he should be in any danger from the Enemy.

He further says that the Delawares have sent to the Shawnees and the Mohawks in the French interest to withdraw from the French and hold council with them, and that the French are now mounting six 4 pounders which they have lately received. The French had an account of our being ready to march by a Desciter (deserter) of the Independent Company who deserted from our van guard, I am . [441]

(seaman)

On the 10th:-The Director of the Hospital came to see me in Camp, and found me so ill of a fever and flux, that he desired me to stay behind, so I went into the Hospital, & the Army marched with the Train &c., and as I was in hopes of being able to follow them in a few days, I sent all my baggage with the Army, and in the afternoon the

General, his Aids de Camp &c., with a company of Light Horse, marched.

The last division of His Majesty's Forces marched from Will's Creek or Fort Cumberland, with General Braddock and his Aides de Camp, &c [442]

(Halkett/Disney)

Camp About Six Miles from Wills's Creek
June: 10th: 1755
The Parole is Gansbourough

No firing to be within Two Miles of the Camp. Any one found to disobay this Order will be Try(ed) by a Court Martial for the same. Those of Indipindent Company of Rangers And the Detachment under the Command of Major Chapman to give 1 Capt & 2 Subs: for the Picquet. S[r] Peter Halketts regt gives 1 Capt & 2 subs: for their Picquet. The Officers of the Different Picquets Are to Visit Their Own Guards & Centrys in the same way they were Orderd to do it at Wills's Creek.

   Field Officer for This Night Lt Col Gage
   Field Officer for to Morrow Lt Co Burton

Those Troops who have not yet Detached Their Guards to do it Immediatley, post Their Centrys And Conform in every respect to the late plan of march given by his Excellency Genl Braddock. All The Officers of the Line to be att the Genls Tent to morrow morning at 11 oClock. No fires to be made on any Acct. what ever within 150 yards on either Side of the road. Any person Acting Contrary to the Order will be severly punished. All the Waggons to be Drawn up to Morrow morning as close as possible And Major Chapmans Detachment As soon as the Waggons Are Closed up to ye Rear of the Artillery To Join their Respective Corps. Col Dunbars Regt to Incamp to Morrow Morning upon the Left of the Whole According to the line of Incampment. [443]

Tuesday June the 10th.   **(batman)**

This day the men worked at the Brest Work and one Indien a Spy is Ariv'd from the French and Brings us word that the French is making from the Great Meadows to Ingage us.[444]

Tuesday June 10th.   (Br. Officer 1)

All ye remaining troops marched from Fort Cumberland (at Wills
Creek) to ye Amount of 1500 Men; a Detachment of 600 & two
Engineers having marched some days before to clear the roads: the
March was attended with many difficulties owing to ye road and
cariages being bad, & through ye line of March was intended to be only
two Mile & an half in Extent, Yet they were frequently twice that
distance. This was a circumstance impossible to be helped, accidents
occasioning many halts in different parts of the line. At first all our
provisions and Amunition were caried in Waggons, & loaded as farr as
18 or 20 hundred weight each, but after the first days March they
found it Absolutely necessary to lighten ye cariages to 12 or 14
hundred & carry all they could on horses backs. The better to ease the
Train which whey looked upon to be too much, they sent back the
next Morning two Six pounders with their allotted ammunition: So
that the train now consisted of 4 twelve pounders; 4 six pounders; 4
Howitzers & 15 Coehorns with 300 rounds for each; & 3 Months
provisions for 2000 Men.

It was recomended to ye Officers & to every one else to lighten
their baggage as much as possible which they did & every thing was
sent away to the Fort (Cumberland): this Fort is a Square, the sides
about 120 feet built of large Logs fixed upright in the ground as close
as can be; fastened within side with a rail: at the joyning of these Logs
they have fixed plank to make it nearly of an equal thickness, & cut
loop-holes for small Arms; there are 9 or 10 four Pounders in the faces
& flanks of this fort. The Situation is high & pleasant, on a neck of
Land formed by the Potomack on one side & Wills Creek on the other.
The first Days March was about 5 Miles & we were obliged to halt till
ye 13th. [445]

(Cameron)
We march'd from Wills-Creek under the command of General
Braddock, a brace old experienced Officer, in whom we had a great
deal of Confidence, and his Dependence was chiefly upon us Regulars
that he brought from Ireland, being 1000 Men compleat, which with
above 1200 New-rais'd, and Three Independent Companies, made in
the whole upwards of 2500 Men, besides Officers; we had 200
Baggage Waggons, about 1500 Pack Horses, and a fine Train of
Artillery. The Way was very rugged till we got over the Alleghany
Hills, when gradually it grew better as we proceeded.[446]

June 10   **(Browne)**

Up before the Sun and march'd till 12. Extreem hot and very bad road. I was obliged to walk. We halted at My Friend Rogers (probably at or near Bloomery, W.Va.) who had nothing for us to eat. Mr. Falkner and Mr. Savage went a shooting and brought me some Pidgeons; had them for Supper which made us a fine Regale, to drink Milk and Water. At 10 I went to bed in my Waggon, but lay'd exteemly cold. Mr Falkner order's a Centinal to be at my waggon all night so that no one should molest me. [447]

June 11 (Wednesday)
MARYLAND-CAMP AT THE GROVE
Parole-Hartford   **(Braddock, Halkett/Disney)**

Capt[n] Rutherford and Cap[n] Gates Indep companys and all the American's Troops to be under arms immediately at the head of their respective encampments.

Any person whatsoever that is detected in stealing shall be immediately hanged with[t] being brought to a Court Martial.

One Subaltern Officer 1 Sergt 1 corporal & 40 men with[t] arms from each of ye two Regimen[t] to parade immediately at ye head of the artillery.

One Sub: 1 Sergt 1 D[r] & 30 Men of the line to Parade in the Rear of Col[o] Dunbars Reg[t] as soon as they have come to their proper ground The Officer is to receive his Orders from Maj[r] Sparkes.

Whatever number of Horses are furnisd by the Officers are to be paraded as soon as possible in the Rear of Col[o] Dunbars Regim[t] and to be reviewed by Maj[r] Sparkes.

The Officers are desird to acquaint Maj[r] Sparkes which of their Horses for carrying Horses and which are for Draught and to be so good as to send with the carrying Horses, Bat-Saddles & etc. if they have them.

The Command[g] officers of the two Regt[ts] & the captn[s] of the Independ[t] and Provinicial Troops to send in a Return to the Genl of the number of Horses furnished by their respective Officers, and opposite to the Officier's names, The number of Horses furnished by each officer; that the Genl may be able to inform His Majesty of the

Inclination and readiness of the particular Officers in carrying on the service.

AFTER ORDERS.

No more than two Women per company to be allowd to march from the Camp, a List of the names of those that are to be sent back to be given into Captn Morris that there may be an Order sent to Col^o Innes at Fort Cumberland to Victual them-A List of the names of the women that are allowed to stay with the troops to be given into the Maj^r of Brigade and any woman that is found in camp and whose name is not in that List will for the first time be severely punished and for the second suffer Death.

AFTER ORDERS

Col^o Dunbar's Reg^t is immediately to furnish a Serg^t & 12 Men as a Guard for the Provisions on their Left and the Serg^t is to receive his orders from Mr Lake Com^y of Pro^{ns}.

The Line is to furnish two Sergt^s & 30 Men with^t arms who are to attend Mr Lake Com^y of Pro^{ns} to morrow mon^g at Day break & assist in loading the Horses.

It is the Genl Orders y^t Mr Lake Com^y of Pro^{ns} with his People & ye party y^t Party is allowed him begin weigh^g out ye Flour & oth^r Pro^{ns} for back 2ds to morrow m^g by day b^k & his Excellency y^t every th^g will be in readiness by 1 Oclock in ye afternoon. [448]

MARYLAND-VICINITY OF FORT CUMBERLAND
June the 11th 1755
Sir: John St.Clair   (Orme)

The General ordered me to deliver you his thanks for the intelligence you have sent him he is now encamped at the foot of the First Hill and proposes marching forward tomorrow. The General desires you will use all methods to procure further information and immediately advise him of it. I am your obed. & hum. serv. [449]

MARYLAND-SPENDELOW CAMP   (Orme)
Lieutenant Colonel Burton represented to the General that he and been two days in marching about five miles on a better road than we were to expect afterwards, occasioned by the extreme faintness and deficiency of the horses.

The General thereupon called togeather all the Officers, and told them, that through this inconvenience it would be impossible to continue the March without some alterations, which he was convinced they would readily assist in, as they had hitherto expressed the greatest spirit and inclination for the service. He recommended to them to send to Fort Cumberland all such baggage as was not absolutely necessary, and told them, if any of them had able horses, which they could spare to the publick cause, he would take care that such testimonies of their regard to the service should not be forgotten, and excited them to it by his example; he and his family contributed twenty horses, This had such an effect, that most of the Officers sent back their own, and made use of Soldiers tents the rest of the Campaign, and near a hundred able horses were given to the publick service.

June 11th. The General called a council of war, consisting of
    Colonel Sr Peter Halket,
    Lieut. Col^o. Gage,
    Major Chapman,
    Colonel Dunbar,
    Lieut. Col^o. Burton, Major Sparks.

In which it was agreed to send back two six-pounders, four cohorns, some powder and stores, which cleared near twenty waggons. All the King's waggons were also sent back to the Fort, they being too heavy, and requiring large horses for the shafts, which could not be procured; and country waggons were fitted for the powder in their stead.

This day was employed in shifting the powder, fitting the waggons, and making a proper asortment of the stores.

The loads of all the waggons were to be reduced to fourteen hundred weight; seven of the most able horses were chose for the Howitzers, and five to each twelve-pounder, and four to each waggon. The other horses were all to carry flour and bacon. Every horse was by the contract to have carried two hundred weight, but the contractors were so well acquainted with our situation (which did not permit us to reject anything), that most of the horses furnished by them were the offcasts of Indian traders, and scarce able to stand under one hundred weight.

A detachment of a Captain, two subalterns, and fifty men, were sent as a covering party to the workers upon the Pensylvania road; and fifty of the worst men from the Independents and Rangers were ordered to reinforce the Garrison at Fort Cumberland; and only two women per company were allowed to be victualled upon the March, but proper provision was made for them at the Fort, to which place they were sent back.

Some orders were found necessary for the farther regulation and security of the Camp.

We were now encamped accordng to the plan approved of by the Council of War. When the carriages were closed up, leaving proper intervals of communications, the extent of the Camp, from the front to the rear guard, was less than half a mile.

ORDERS GIVEN AT SPENDELOW CAMP

The captains of the picket are to be at the field officer of the day's tent to receive the countersign, which they are to give to the subaltern, the subaltern to the serjeants, the serjeants, to the centinels, who are not to suffer any person to come within ten paces without receiving the countersign; and all advanced corporals and centinels are to have their baynets fixed.

The field officer of the picket is to be received as grand rounds, whenever he goes his round either night or day.

No person whatever to fire a piece within a mile of the Camp.

No hutts or bowers to be built by the advanced pickets or centinels.

One tumbril with tools is to march in the front and another in the center of the carriages, and one engineer with part of the pioneers in the center.

It required two days to new load the waggons, and put everything in order, which being settled we marched on the 13th to Martin's plantation, being about five miles from Spendelow Camp. [450]

MARYLAND-NORTHWEST OF FORT CUMBERLAND

Wedensday June the 11th. **(batman)**

This day the men went to work as Usual. The Indiens and the volintears Returned to Camp and Brings us Word that they did not see Any thing of the French, Neather on this side of the Meadows nor at them. The duty is Excesive hard here, haveing only One Night in Bed. The day that they are of(f) guard, they go to work so that they Either mount guard or go to work Every day, and only salt meat and water to live on and not having sufficient of that. [451]

VIRGINIA-TOWARD FORT CUMBERLAND

June 11 **(Browne)**

The Drum beat and awakened me but I was at a loss for some time to tell where I was. My coachman put the Horses to the Waggon and march'd on and desir'd me not to disturb myself. The Roads were so bad that the poor Horses were not able to keep on their Legs, which I observ'd to my Coachman who said they were right tough and good, and that everyone was not to be taken by their Looks, and as to Black & Brown they were as good as ever stretched a Chain. We left one of the Nurses and a sick man behind, he not being able to march any further. 2 of the Waggons broke down, halted till they were mended. I walked till my feet were blister'd. We came to a Place call'd Spring Mountain (see Hough comments May 11) and there we encamped. We drank Tea and supt on the Stump on an old tree. We had nothing to eat but salt pork, to drink humble Grog. We chatted till 11 and were very merry and then retired to our respective Waggons. [452]

June 12 (Thursday)
MARYLAND-NORTHWEST OF FORT CUMBERLAND
Mr. Spendloes Camp   **(Braddock, Halkett/Disney)**
June 12: 1755 (Grove Camp)
The Parole is Ilford
Field Officer for to Morrow Lieut Col:Gage

The picquets Are to Load with Cartridges & not with running (ramming) balls to Challange & demand the Counter-sign Till Troop beating, And The Field Officer of the picquet to be received As Grand rounds when ever he goes his Rounds eigher (either) by Night or Day.

The Advance Corpls: & Centrys to have Their baynotts fixt. The Detached party from the Serjts Guards to have Corpls with Them. The Advance Centrys not to Suffer Any person to Come within Ten paces of their Arms Without receiving the Counter Sign. The Advance partys not to Build Any Bowers (shelters) upon pain of Sever punishment. Those Allready Built to be destroyed. These Orders to be read to the men by the Officers of the Picquet befor the Guards Are posted.

Where ever the Communuications Are not Oppend betwixt Serjts Guard & Serjts-Corpls Guard & Corpls Guard, They are to be done Immediatley. This to be a Standing Order in All Camps. No person to fire his peice within a Mile of the Camp but in Case of An Alarm of being Atact. This Order to be Read to the men by the Commanding Officer of a Compy And The Orders Relative to the picquet to be read to the Men by the Officers of the Picquets before they Advance there

Guards. The Capts: of the Picquets to be at the Field Officers Tent of the picquet An hour before the Beating of the retreat, To Receive the Countersign from him. As There Are some Waggons going to Fort Cumberland lighly loaded The Officers of the Line Are desird to send Their Baggage there And Govenour Innis will Take Care of it. The Troops Are this Afternoon to receive provisions to the Sixteenth Inclusive And the Waggoners & horse Drivers to the 26th Inclusive. What ever Women Are to be sent back to the Fort Are to March with Capt Hogs Detachment. Sir Peter Halketts Grends: And four Battallion Companys of that Regt to March Immedy: to the Crossing of the Old & new Road, And a little beyond where the Detachment of Seamen are now Encamped. They Are to Encamp theire, The Grendr: Compy Crossing the road And the Battallion Companys According to the Present line of Encampment Covering the Advance Waggons.

The Commanding Officers to take Care to Advance his picquets in the same Manner and proportion of Numbers As Orderd in the Dispotion of March And to take Care yt his Advance picquets Comply with the Orders of this Day. The Detachment of Seamen Commanded by Mr.Spendeloo to be disposed of in Such part of ye Line as he shall think proper And Their Arms & Accoutrements Are to be carried in What ever Waggons he shall Appoint. Three Hatchett men of the line with their Tools to remain Constantly with the Detachment of Seamen And to receive their Orders from Mr. Spendeloo. One Tumbril with Tools to March in the Front, immediately after Capt Polsons Compy of Carpentors And another Tumbril with Tools to March in the Center of the Carriages. One Engineer to March with Capt. Polsons Company And An other Engineer to March in the Center of the Carriages. The Pioners of the Line with Their Tools (Except those that Are Orderd to the Detacht: of Seamen) to march Constantly in the Center of the Carriages & to be Under the Direction of the Engineer that Marches in the Center. The Troops to March to Morrow morning. The Genl to beat at 4 oClock in the morning. [453]

MARYLAND-CAMP AT THE GROVE
June 12, 1755   (Orme)
Sir: John St. Clair

The General has received your letter by Lieut. Woodward and orders me to inform you he proposes to march from this camp to morrow and will be at the little Meadows on Sunday, his Excellency desires you will not proceed upon any further work upon the road and only employ them in the business of securing the camp till he can deliver your party and would not have you fatigue your men by too much labour. The General has retrenched very much the number of waggons and increased by many means the back lodes. I am your most hum. & obed serv. [454]

Thursday June the 12th.   (batman)

The men went to work at the Brest Work and I went to the grand Army (then en route to the Little Meadows) to see if I Could buy some fresh Provisions which I Bought, 6 loafs of Bread and some Mutton. [455]

MARYLAND-TOWARD FORT CUMBERLAND
June 12   (Browne)

At 2 in the Morning the Drum beat, but I could have wish'd it to have stay'd a few Hours longer, being very sleepy. We marched but there is no describing the badness of the Roads. I walked as far as I was able. The poor horses no longer regard the smack of the Whip or beat of the Drum, and as to Black she could go no further. 2 of the Waggons broke down. At 10 we came to the River (Potomac) and waited 6 hours before we could ferry over. At 8 at night we halted at a Rattlesnake Colonels nam'd Crisop. Had for supper some Lamb, to drink some very bad Wine, which was but 5s. a Quart! I could get no bed so went to my Waggon. [456]

PENNSYLVANIA-PHILADELPHIA   (Pennsylvania Gazette)

Governor Morris sends from Philadelphia fifty two waggons each carrying 50 bushels of grain, one half oats & the other Indian corn.

We hear that near 60 waggon laden with forage for the Army, have been dispatched from this city within a few days to Wills's Creek; the Inhabitants of most of the townships in this county having cheerfully given considerable bounties to the waggoners, to encourage them to undertake the Journey. We hear also that a number of waggons laden with forage are likewise gone from the counties of Lancaster and Berks. Since our last, an officer and a number of Matrosses, arrived here from New York, on their way to the camp at Will's Creek. [457]

MARYLAND-ANNAPOLIS   (Maryland Gazette)
May 15.

Tuesday last about Noon, his Excellency our Governor returned in good health from his interview with General Braddock at Virginia, to the great satisfaction of People of all Ranks among us. [458]

Nichols writes: "Postal service express riders-Pennsylvania supplied relays of horses on roads into Fort Cumberland. A regular post between Philadelphia & Fort Cumberland left the Quaker City every Thursday."

June 13 (Friday)
MARYLAND-CAMP AT_____
Parole-Hertford   (Braddock)
Field officer to morrow Major Chapman.
The line is not to march to morrow. [459]

2nd Camp from Ft Cumberland June 13th: 1755
The Parole is Kingston   (Halkett/Disney)
Field Officer for to Morrow Major Chapman

The plan now Drawn is the line of March for the Security of the Convoy And differs in the Method of their Encampment only in this respect, that when the Halt for the Day is Orderd, the line of provisions Amunition Artillery Stores &c Are to Close up as much as posable. As soon as this is done the whole to Face outwards And The Qr Master Genl is to go round the Flanks, And to Advance the Serjts & Corpls Partys As far as the Ground will Admit of in Order to have greater room to Forrage the Horses. And where it will not Admit a Sefficient Quantity on one Flank, to advance them the more on the other. When these Detachments are moved to their proper Distance, all the Corpls Guards Are to remain under Arms facing outwards till the Serjts have Opend Communications with each other which is to be done by Dividing their partys And cuting Away the under Wood And small trees till they meet their partys upon the right & Left. When the Genl: Beats the men to form at the Head of the Encampment but not to Strick their Tents till Orderd. The Advance Guards to to the same. The outposts after a march to be Immediatley relievd upon comming to the Ground. At other times at Retreat beating all the Corpls: Guards upon Comming to their Ground Are to remain Under Arms facing outwards till the Serjts Guards have Oppend Communications one with another, both on the right & Left, As likewise with their respective Compys. When that is finished the Serjt is to Dispach half his remaining Men to the Corpls: Guard who are to be under Arms till the corpls. have Also Oppend Communications one with Another laying any trees that shall be cut down in their Front. Dewering this time the Companys to remain by their Arms, And when this is finished, the Advance Men to Join their Serjts Again, both Guards to remain Under Arms, And the Compys to pich Their Tents. The advance Serjts will then pitch Their Tents, And when that is finished, The Corpls: will post Their Centrys. The Troops not to March to Morrow. [460]

Camp of the Van Guard of the Army   **(St. Clair)**
at the little Meadows, June 13th 1755.
Sir: Robert Napier

    Since General Braddocks arrival about the 20th of Feb[ry] I have not wrote to you, I delayed it from time to time expecting to be able to give you a full account of our Situation: I certainly shou'd have wrote to you on the arrival of all our Troops at Wills's Creek, but I was employed about cutting the Roads, that I had not one Moment to spare.

    In my last letter to you I acquainted you that I was to review the Independent Companys and to form the Provincial Troops of Virginia and Mayland in which Service I was employd till the 24th of March, they being scattered all about the Country. On my coming that day to Alexandria I found the British Troops disembarked and beginning to land their Stores. The 26th General Braddock and Governor Dinwiddie arrived. I left Alexandria the 2d of April, in order to foward the Transport of our Artillery & Stores to Wills's Creek, but did not get to the fort till the 16th being obliged to repair old Roads and cut new ones, in which I made very great progress considering that we had Snow in the Mountains till the 15th of April. The Roads leading to the Fort were not cleared till the 1st of May; the next Day the first Divisin of our Troops arrived and the 10th the last Division; the first Division of the Artillery the 16th of May & the last the day following: from that Day till the End of the Month, things were preparing for the march of the whole.

    The Situation I am in at present put it out of my power to give you a full description of this Country; I shall content myself with telling you that from Winchester to this place is one continued track of

Mountains, and like to continue so for fifty Miles further. Tho our Motions may appear to you to have been slow, yet I may venture to assure you that not an Hour had been lost; considering that no Magistrate in Virginia or I believe in Maryland gave themselves the least trouble to assist in collecting the Country Peope to work upon the Roads, and to provide us with Carriages: But on the Contrary every body laid themselves out to put what money they cou'd in their Pocketts, without forwarding our Expedition. In this situation we never could have subsisted our little Army at Wills's Creek, far less carried on our Expedition had not General Braddock contracted with the People in Pensylvania for a Number of Waggons, which they have fullfilled; by their Assistance we are in motion, but must move slowly untill we get over the Mountains. I cou'd very easily forsee the difficultys we were to labour under from having the Communication open only to Virginia, which made me Anxious of having a Road cut from Pennsylvania to the Yaugheaugany; I wrote to Govr Morris the 14th of Feb^{ry} on this Head, notwithstanding of which, that Road has not been set about till very lately. The last report that I had of it, was that it woul'd be finished in three Weeks hence; the two Communications will join about forty Miles from hence, but it is not fixed on which side of the Yaugheogany.

The little knowledge that our people at home have of carrying on War in Mountaneous Country will make the expence of our Carrigaes appear very great to them.., that one Article will amount near to £40,000 Stir.

Thus far I do affirm that no time had been lost in pursuing the Scheme laid down in England for our Expedition; had it been undertaken at the beginning from Penslvania it might have been carried on with greater dispatch and less expence: I am not at all surprized that we are ignorant of the Situation of this Country in England, when no one except a few Hunters knows it on the Spot; and their Knowledge extends no further than in following their Game. It is certain that the ground is not easy to be reconoitered for one may go twenty Miles without seeing before him ten yards.

The Commanding General pursues his Schemes with a great deal of vigour and Vivacity; the Dispositions he makes will be subject to be changed in this vast tract of Mountains, I mean instead of marching the whole togeather (the Van Guard excepted) in one Body, he will be obliged to march in three Divisions over the Mountains and join about the great Meadows, fifty two Miles from the fort. The General is bent on marching directly to Fort du Quesne, he is certainly in the right in making his Dispositions for it: But it is my opinion he will be obliged to make a halt on the Monagahela or Yaughangany until he gets up a Second Convoy, and until the Road is open from Pensylvania, which the Inhabitants will not finish unless they are covered by our Troops.

I have not as yet talked to the General of this, nor shall I until we get over the Mountains, for then things may appear in another light, and I am unwilling to propose any thing which might look like starting Difficultys. The marching to the french fort is certainly practicable with this present Convoy; but in what light must we appear if we are obliged to abandon our Conquests for want of Sustenance. What was looked on at home as easy is our most difficult point to surmount, I mean the passage of this vast tract of Mountains; Had we a Country we could subsist in after we get over them, the thing wou'd be easy.

I am at this place with 400 Men as a Van Guard, and to cut the Roads, I was not able to reach this Ground till the 8th Day, 'tho only 20 Miles from Wills's Creek it is certain I might have made more dispatch but I was charged with a Convoy of 50 waggons. The Roads are either Rocky or full of Boggs, we are obliged to blow the Rocks and lay Bridges every Day; What an happiness it is to have wood at hand for the latter!

One of our Indians who left the french Fort the 8th Inst, tells me that there are only 100 french & 70 Indians at that place; that they were preparing to set out the Day after to dispute the passage of the Mountains. I have seen nothing of them as yet, nor do I expect that they will come so far from home. They have lately received Six 4 pounders which they were busy mounting when the Indian came away. I should be glad to have a Visit from them at this Camp, it is a very good one Surrounded with an Abattis.

I expect the General with the Army will be at this Camp the 15th and that I shall receive his Orders to move on the same Day. I shall take care to let you know every thing that happens amongst us which I dare say will be to your Satisfaction. I am with the greatest Regard, Sir, Your most obedient and most humble Servant, John St. Clair [461]

(Orme)

It required two days to new load the waggons, and put everyting in order, which being settled we marched on the 13th to Martin's plantation, being about five miles from Spendelow Camp. The first brigade got to their ground that night, but the second could not get up before the next day at eleven of the clock, the road being excessively mountainous and rocky. This obliged the General to halt one day for the refreshment of the men and horses.

ORDERS GIVEN AT THE CAMP AT MARTIN'S PLANTATION

Upon the beating of the General, which is to be taken from the 44th Regiment, all the troops are to turn out, accoutre and form two deep at the head of their encampments upon all halts, tho' ever so small; the pickets and companies are to face outwards. The officers of the pickets are to take care that their pickets keep at a proper distance upon their flanks. Upon the firing of a cannon, either in front, centre or rear, the whole line is to form, to face outwards, and to wait for orders.

The field officers, excepting him that commands the Van Guard, are to take no particular post, but to see that the men assist in getting up the waggons at any steep ascent, or difficult pass.

In case any waggon should break down, it is immediately to be drawn out on one side of the road, and a report of it with its lading to be sent to the Waggon Master-General, who is to order it to be repaired and fall in the rear, or the load to be divided among the other waggons, as he shall think proper.

The carrying horses having suffered very much by bearing their loads so long the day before, they were ordered with an escort of two campanies upon the right of the 44th to proceed to the little meadows, at which place Sr John St Clair was encamped with the three hundred men, not having been able to proceed further in the five days. [462]

Lacock writes: "A short distance beyond the Hoffman coal mines, on the north side of the road, is a very deep scar, which is probably a part of Braddock's roadbed. At the top of the hill the road turns northward at almost a right angle in order to avoid what was formerly a very wide swamp, and then passes over the ridge and down through Layman's orchard, where there is a deep scar. Near the end of this ridge, overlooking Frostburg and about five miles from Spendelow Camp, is the site of the second encampment, Martin's Plantation."

MARYLAND-NORTHWEST OF FORT CUMBERLAND
Fryday June the 13th.   **(batman)**

The men went to work at the Roads and a Covering party along with to guarde them. We Expect the French Indiens to attack us Every day. We dined this day on Snake and Bear. [463]

Friday ye 13th. (Br. Officer 1)

The General beat at 4 a clock & we were soon on our March; this days March was closer than the former, but still was tedious and with some accidents; we marched 6 Miles to George's Creek, there we halted ye next day, & marched Sunday ye 15th within 4 Mile of the little Meadows. [464]

MARYLAND-TOWARD FORT CUMBERLAND
June 13 (Browne)

At 3 we march'd but I was so ill I could not hold up my Head. 3 of the Waggons broke down at 4 in the After Noon. Mr. Bass came to meet us and gave me some Letters from England. At 6 we came to Fort Cumberland the most desolate Place I ever saw. Went to Mr. Cherrington who receive'd me kindly, drank Tea and then went to the Governor to apply for Quarters. I was put into A Hole that I could see daylight through every Log, and a port Hole for a window; which was as good a Room as any in the Fort. [465]

June 14 (Saturday)
MARYLAND-CAMP AT MARTIN'S
Parole-Leicester (Braddock)
Field Officer to morrow Lt Col Burton.

Upon the beating of the General which is to be taken from Sir Peter Halketts regiment, all ^{ye} troops are to accoutre turn out and form two deep at ye head of their respective encampments, and there wait for further orders and no soldiers tent to be suffered to be struck till ordered by the General.

As soon as the tents are struck they are to be immediately loaded as also the officers baggage and then the troops are to lay upon their arms till they receive an order to march and upon the beating of ye march the whole to face to the right and left.

The Field officers are not to be particularly posted excepting the one who marches at ye head of ye vanguard.

The number of carriages to be equally divided and Sir Peter Halkett and his Field officers with the troops of his brigade are to take under

274

their care half of carriages and see that their officers order their men to assist the waggoners upon any point or difficulty that may happen. Col Dunbar and his Field officers with ye troops of the second brigade to act in the same manner with the remaining number of carriages.

In case any wagon should break down in such a manner as to be unable to keep with the Line it is immediately to be drawn out on one side of the road and a report of it with what it is loaded to be sent to Mr. Scott Wagon master general who is to order it to be repaired, or see that the load is divided among the rest of the wagons as he shall think proper.

Upon any halt, tho' ever so small the Companys are to form two deep and face outward.

Upon a march the captians and officers of ye picquet to visit frequently their out detachments, and see that they keep at a proper distance from their companies.

Upon ye firing of a cannon either in ye front, centre or rear the whole line to form face outwards and then wait for further orders.

When the troops came to Savage River the servants, bat men Waggoners and horse drivers must take particular care to prevent their horses from eating of laurel, as it is certain death to them. The General to beat to morrow morning at 4 o'clock.

AFTER ORDERS.

Upon the beating of the General to morrow morning two companys from the right of Sir Peter Halkett's regiment to strike their tents and march as an escort to the carrying horses of ye army The Commanding officer to apply to Capt. Morris to morrow morning for his orders. [466]

Here is an omission of two days orders, which cannot be supplied, but a blank is left in the records to show gap.

PENNSYLVANIA-GEORGES CREEK   (Washington)
June 14, Saturday. Georges Creek, Pennsylvania. Dear Brother: (John Augustine Washington)

As I wrote to you twice since the 1st Instant, I shall only add, that the difficulties arising in our March (from having a number of Waggons) will, I fear, prove an unsurmountable obstacle....of transporting our provisions and Stores. [467]

RIGHT-OF-WAY   (Gordon)
    From Grove Camp to Martins Plantation-Dist.5 Miles
WORK DONE TO THE ROAD
    a great deal of cuting, digging and Bridging
QUALITY OF THE ROAD
    one mile level but swampy, 2 1/2 very rough and steep, the rest
tolerable but here and there swampy
QUALITY OF THE CAMP
    open, dry, very good feeding, fine water Days halted 1 [468]

                                              (Halkett/Disney)
Martins Plantation-2d Camp from Fort Cumberland June 14th: 1755
The Parole is Lester
    All prisoners to be Confind on the picquets Guards of the Compys
They shall belong to. Any Serjt who shall Neglect Reporting (h)is
prisoners to the Adjt by Troop beating will be reduced. All Guards to
receive the Parole from the round or Any Number of people
Approaching Them, before they suffer them to Advance. The Countersign is for the Centrys Only. The Guards And Centrys when ever
the(y) gett under Arms or Challenge are to Face the Way yt they Are
approched, except in the Day time betwixt beat (of) the Troop & the
Retreat. If the Guards have then Occation to Turn out to the Genl or
for any other Reason They Are to face the Front & the Centrys likwise
And both to Stand Shoulder'd. The Guards & Centrys to Receive all
rounds with Rested Arms with their Thumbs upon the cocks of their
Firelocks which is more intended for their Own Security then Any
Compliment. The Advance Centrys after Retreat beating to have their
Bayonets fixt & when the(y) Receive the Countersign to plant it at the
Brest of the person that gives it them. The Serjts to Act in the same
manner when the(y) Receive the Parole. A Centry allways to be posted
on each Serjts Guard to give the Alarm. These Orders to be Read to
the men going on the Advanced Guards every Evening before they
mount by the Offr who Call's the Roll for a Fortnight.
Field Officer for to Morrow Lieut Col: Burton
    Upon beating the Genl which is to be taken from Sir Peter Halketts
regt all the Troops are to Accouter, turn out two deep And from at the
head of their respective Encampments And there wate for further
Orders. And no soldiers Tent to be sufferd to be Struck till orderd by
the Genl. As soon as the Tents Are Struck they are to be immediately

loaded as also the Officers Bagage. Then the Troops Are to lye upon their Arms & wate for Orders for to March. And upon the beating of the March the Whole to face to the right & left. The Field Officers Are not to be perticulery posted Except the One who leads the Van Guard. The Number of Carriages to be Equaly Divided. Sr Peter Halkett & his Field Off^{rs}: with The Troops of the first Brigade to take under their Care half the Carriages And to their Officers Order their Men to Assist the Waggons When Any pinch of a hill or Diffuculty That may Append. Col: Dunbar And his field Officers with ye Troops of the Second Brigade is to Act in the same manner with the Remaining Carriages. In Case any Waggon should break down in such a manner As to be Unable to keep up with the Line it is Immediatley to be drawn out on one side of ye Road And a report of it with what it is loaded with to made to Mr. Scott Waggon Master Genl. who is to Order it to be Repaird or to seen the Load be divided amongst the rest of the Waggons, As he shall think proper. Upon all Halts tho ever so small the Companys Are to form two deep And face out Wards. Upon a March the Capts & Officers of the picquet Are frequently to Visit the out Detachments And to see the(y) keep at a proper distance from their Companys. Upon the Firings of a Cannon either in front Center or Rear the Whole line immediately to form face outwards And wate for Orders. The Genl to beat to Morrow morning at 4 o'Clock When the Troops Comes to Savage River, the Servts Battmen Waggoners And horse drivers must take perticuler care to prevent their horses eating of Lawrell As it is Certain Death to them. His Excellency Genl Braddock has been pleas'd to Appoint Ensigns Daniel Disney Quintin Kennedy Robert Drumond to be Lieutenants in Sir Peter Halketts Regt of foot as Also Mess(r)s: Thos Gamble James Allen Ely Dagworthy to be Ensigns in the Said regt. And are to be Obayd as such.

Upon the Beating of the Genl to Morrow Morning Two Compys from the right of Sr Peter Halketts regt. to Strike Their Tents And March as An escort to the Carrying Horses of the Army. The Commanding Officer to Apply to Capt Morris for his Orders. [469]

Lacock writes: "At this point, one-fourth mile west from Braddock Park, the ascent of Big Savage Mountain begins. Although there are some level spots on the western slope of the mountains, the ascent of more than two miles is very steep and rocky, and the cut is several feet deep in places. On the summit of the mountain, a few hundred years to the north of the road, is St. John Rock, 2930 feet above sea level, from which is a magnificent view of the surrounding country is to be had. The descent for a half mile or more is also very rugged and in places extraordinarily steep.

At the foot of the mountain the road unites with a highway and follows it for a half mile then fords Savage River. Near a school house on the north bank of Savage River and a short distance west of the mouth of Carey Run the road begins a very steep ascent of Little Savage Mountain. A little over a mile westward, the road comes to the farm of Henry Blocher which mark the location of Braddock's third encampment, Savage River Camp.

It is an interesting fact that throughout the route, the fording of a stream was in every case at or slightly below the mouth of a tributary. At such a place there is usually a riffle caused by the formation of a bar of sand, gravel, and mud, the crest of which offers a very practical opportunity for fording. Some of the apparent deviations of the road from what would seem to have been the natural course may have been made for the sake of avoiding a depth of water which might have rendered the streams impassable except be bridging. in other instances a circuitous route may have been the most practicable way of passing a swamp or a bog.

From this point to some woods less than a quarter of a mile westward there is no trace of the road, but through these woods there is a well-marked scar for over half a mile to Two Mile Run. Near this stream are the renowned "Shades of Death", once a deep forest the tops of whose towering trees intertwined. Dense forests of white pine formerly covered this region, which from the deep gloom of the summer woods and the favorable shelter that the pines gave to the Indian enemy, came to be spoken of as the "Shades of Death". The writer's party was told that the old wagoners who used to drive from Baltimore to Zanesville dreaded this locality as the darkest and gloomiest place along the entire route. Of the former gloomy forest, however, nothing now remains except the stumps, The trees were cut down years ago, sawed up, and shipped to market."

Atkinson writes: "This was the 15th of June, when the dense gloom of the summer woods and the favorable shelter which those enormous pines would give an Indian enemy, must have made a most sensible impression on all minds of the insecurity of their mode of advance".

MARYLAND-NORTHWEST OF FORT CUMBERLAND
Satterday June the 14.   **(batman)**

This day the men went to work at the Brest Work and Clearing the Camp. [470]

Halted for day [471]   **(Br. Officer 1)**

MARYLAND-FORT CUMBERLAND
June the 14   **(Browne)**

I was taken very ill with a Fever and other Disorders which continued 10 Days and was not able to get out of my Bed. [472]

June 15 (Sunday)
MARYLAND-NORTHWEST OF FORT CUMBERLAND

Camp at Savage River June 15th: 1755

The Parole is Malbourough **(Halkett/Disney)**

Field Officer for to Morrow Lt Col: Gage

The Troops to March to Morrow. The Genl to beat at 4 oClock. [473]

NAME OF ENCAMPMENT **(Gordon)**

From Martins Plantation to Little Meadows Camp-Dist. 10 Miles

WORK DONE TO THE ROAD

a great deal of cuting, digging and Bridging and a great deal of blowing

QUALITY OF THE ROAD

4 miles up and down the ridge very rough and steep, the rest for about 3 miles tolerable, 1 mile very rough, a hard pinch

QUALITY OF THE CAMP

inclosed with an Abbatis, dry, fine feeding, good water source

Days halted 3 [474]

(Orme)

June 15th. The line began to move from this place at five of the clock; it was twelve before all the carriages had got upon a hill which is about a quarter of a mile from the front of the Camp, and it was found necessary to make one-half of the men ground their arms and assist the carriages while the others remained advantageously posted for their security.

We this day passed the Aligany Mountain, which is a rocky ascent of more than two miles, in many places extremely steep; its descent is very rugged and almost perpendicular; in passing which we intirely demolished three waggons and shattered several. At the bottom of the mountain runs Savage river, which when we passed was an insignificant stream; but the Indians assured us that in the winter it is very deep, broad and rapid. This is the last water that empties itself into the Potomack.

The first Brigade encamped about three miles to the westward of the river. Near this place was another steep ascent, which the waggons were six hours in passing.

In this day's march, though all possible care was taken, the line was sometimes extended to a length of four or five miles. [475]

Lacock writes: "From "Shades of Death" the road passes up Red Ridge, crossing another road a few rods to the north of a house; thence it runs to Wolf Swamp and Red Run, and on to the foot of Meadow Mountain. On the western slope is the location of the fourth encampment".

Nichols writes: "On the fifteenth (June) the difficult passage over Savage Mountain exhausted both men and beast...one of the few surveying errors of the Braddock Road caused this trouble for the engineers overlooked an excellent spur, affording a much easier crossing (Olden Times, 11, 542).

Temple writes: "Just beyond Frostburg the steep ascent of Big Savage mountain begins. Here as elsewhere the road climbs squarely up the grade. Though there is an ascent of 1,000 feet in about two miles, some portions of which are remarkably steep, there is no movement along the mountainside to make the slope more gradual. Fronting the ascent squarely the wagons would be higher, of course, in front than at the rear, but one side of the wagon would be no higher that the other and the danger of overturning would be reduced to a minimum. The army had no time to make a "side hill cut" over every steep mountain it must cross."

Marched to within 4 Mile of the little Meadow. [476]   **(Br. Officer 1)**

NAME OF THE ENCAMPMENT   **(Gordon)**
Little Meadows to Laurel Swamp (aka Camp 2 miles west of Little Crossings)-Dist. 4 miles
WORK DONE TO THE ROAD
a little blowing digging and bridging, a great deal of cuting
QUALITY OF THE ROAD
3 ½ very good, ½ mile very stoney and rough
QUALITY OF THE CAMP
bad in all respects [477]

(seaman)

The 15th.-The General and all the Army arrived at the little Meadows, which is 22 miles from the Fort. He found here that the number of carriages, &c., that he had with him occasioned his marches to be very short, and that in all probability if they continued to do so the French fort would be reinforced before he got before it. He therefore thought proper to take 1200 of the choicest men, besides Artillery and Sailors, with the most necessary stores that would be wanted to attack the Fort, making up all 51 carriages, and left all the heavy baggage, &c. with Col Dunbar, and the rest of the forces to follow him as fast as possible, and marched accordingly, and continue so to do without being molested (except now and then losing a scalp, which in the whole amounted to 8 or 9, a number far less than expected). [478]

> Lacock writes: *"On June 15th, 1755, the entire force had reached Little Meadows, where at a council of war it was determined that General Braddock and Colonel Halkett, with a detachment of the best men of the two regiments (in all about 1400, lightly encumbered), should move forward. Colonel Dunbar with the residue (about 900), and the heavy baggage, stores, and artillery, was to advance by slow and easy marches."*

> Atkinson writes: *"This doubtless had a share in causing the council of war held at the Little meadows the next day. To this place, distant only about twenty miles from Cumberland, Sir John Sinclair and Mayor Chapman had been dispatched on the 27th of May, to build a fort; the army having been seven days in reaching it...This interesting locality (Little Meadows) lies at the west foot of the Meadow Mountain, which is one of the most important of the Alleghany Ridges where it constitutes the dividing ridge between the eastern and western waters. A rude entrenchment, about half a mile north of the Inn on the National Road kept by Mr. Hudson, marks the site of this fort. Here it may be well enough to clear up an obscurity which enters into many narratives of these early events, from confusing the names of the Little Meadows and Great Meadows, Little Crossing, and Great Crossings which are all distinct localities. The little Meadows have been described as at the foot of Meadow Mountain; it is well to note that the Great Meadows are about thirty-one miles further west, and near the east foot of Laurel Hill. By the Little Crossing is meant the Ford of Casselman's River, a tributary of the Youghiogheny; and by the Great Crossings, the passage of the Youghiogheny itself. The Little Crossing is two miles west of the Little Meadows, and the Great Crossing seventeen miles further west."*

Sunday June the 15th.   **(batman)**
    The men worked at the Brest Work. This day Came in two Companies of Sir Peeter Halkets Regt with two hundred Horses loaden with Flower and Bread from the grand Army. [479]

June 16 (Monday)
MARYLAND-CAMP AT LITTLE MEADOWS   **(Halkett/Disney)**
Camp at the Little Meddows June 16th: 1755
The Parole is Norwich
Field Officer for to Morrow Major Chapman
    One Capt 4 Subs: & Eighty men of the Line to parade to Morrow at daybreak to take up the Guards now posted by the Command under Sir John S[t] Clear. To Morrow at daybreak three Guards to parade,

Each Consisting of 1 Serjt 1 Corpl. & 12 men who are to Releive the Genls. Guard & the other two Serjts guards in the Front. [480]

Monday ye 16th.   **(Br. Officer 1)**

The General (beat) at 3. & altho' ye distance was short, two very long steep Hills hindered the last Brigade from reaching ye Meadows that day which they did tuesday morning it being halting day. The weather being very hot, & water bad, it caused many fluxes & feavers among the Men.

The General finding that such a number of cariages delayed our March very much, & not thinking ye Enemy to be so powerfull as we unfortunately found afterwards, he was resolved to march forwards with a thousand Men. Accordingly a disposition was made immediately; 700 Men of ye Old Standers were picked out of the two Regiments; one Company of Carpentars & two of Rangers; four twelve pounders; two Six; four Howitzers & three Coehorns with 70 rounds for each; & between 30 & 40 days provisions for the Men; so that the cariages in all did not exceed fifty. [481]

Letter V   (continued)   **(Br. Officer 3)**

On the (16th of June) the General got as far as the Meadows, where, to hasten our March, he fortified and intrenched a Camp, and left the heavy Baggage, sick Men, and spare Provision, &c and to cover our Communication, he left Colonel Dunbar with 800 Men. This Place was the only one where regular Troops could make Use of their Discipline and Arms, and it is all open Ground, therefore the General made this Camp as a Place of Arms, where a Fortification being erected would supply the Army as they should want, and might receive, and lay up the Provisions in Safety, as they arrived from Pensilvania; the General also said, that as this place was on the West Side of the Allegane Mountains, it preserved his Majesty's Rights against the French, who pretended that those Mountains bounded his Majesty's Dominions. Here we halted and refreshed ourselves bravely, by the Help of the Pensilvania Provisions, and of Deer, wild Turkeys, and Game of several other Kinds brought in by the Indians, which though we should deem it bad enough in England, for there is not above one Deer in ten that is fat, yet here our former Wants made these delicious. [482]

June 16th. We marched from the Camp near Savage river to the little meadows, which is about ten miles from Martin's Plantations, where the first brigade arrived that evening, but the second did not all arrive till the 18th. A great part of this day's march was over a bogg which had been very well repaired by Sr John St Clair's advanced party with infinate labour. (Note: this was the famous shades of death)

By these four days' marches it was found impossible to proceed with such a number of carriages. The horses grew every day fainter, and many died: and the men would not have been able to have undergone the constant and necessary fatigue, by remaining so many hours under arms; and by the great extent of the baggage the line was extremelly weak'ned.

The General was therefore determined to move foward with a detachment of the best men, and as little incumbrance as possible. [483]

(Cameron)

At the Place call's the Little Meadows, our General ordered about 1200 Men to be pick'd out for a hasty March to the French Fort Du Quesne on the Fork of the Ohio; I happe'd to be one of 800 old Regulars pick'd out for that Purpose; we march'd forward with hasty Marches, having about 80 Waggons, the chief Part of the Artillery, with necessary Ammunition with us; leaving Col Dunbar to bring up the Remains of the Army, &c. [484]

Monday June the 16th.   **(batman)**

The men went to work at the Brest work. This day most of the grand Army Joined us here at the little Meadows. To day as one of our Raingers was a Shouting (shooting) he Comes up with some of our Own Indiens a Shouting dear. He taking them to be a party of the French Indiens fireing at him, he Immediately Returns to Camp, acquaints the genll. There was Immediately a party sent out against them. When they Came up with them, it was our Indiens that had shot three dear. [485]

PENNSYLVANIA-PHILADELPHIA   **(Pennsylvania Gazette)**

From Fort Cumberland there is advice that on the 14th instant 250 men marched from thence, to protect the workmen that are cutting a road from the back parts of this province towards the Ohio, from the French or their Indians: That an Indian man and woman had lately come there from Fort Du Quesne and positively say, that there are not above 200 men, French and Indian, in that Fort; and that a party of the Indians, with some French, were to set out soon, in order to harass any stragglers from our Army on the march. [486]

Berkebile writes: "By June 16, when the first brigade reached Little Meadows, Braddock realized that the advance of his column was being retarded and his troops weakened by the number of wagons in his train. Washington who had profited from his 1754 experience in Pennsylvania, previously had recommended that Braddock use more pack horses and fewer wagons. It became obvious that wagons, while ordinarily superior to pack animals, lost this advantage if the roads were not sufficiently opened to admit their easy passage. In view of this, Braddock decided to advance from Little Meadows with a picked detachment of 1,300 men and a minimum of wagons, about 30 in number, and to leave the heavier baggage with 84 wagons in charge of Colonel Dunbar and his 850 men. Prior to this reorganization at Little Meadows, four horse teams had been used in accordance with the terms of Franklin's advertisements. Now, however, the advance unit of the army marched with six horses to a wagon, a change necessitated equally by the rugged terrain and the hastily constructed roads with which they were forced to contend, and by the poor condition of the horses. While this lightened column moved forward more rapidly, the mountainous and rocky roads continued to impede the progress of the army".

June 17 (Tuesday)
MARYLAND-CAMP AT LITTLE MEADOWS
June the 17th Morning Orders   **(Braddock, Halkett/Disney)**
    The Troops to draw provisions this afternoon for 5 Days to the 21st Incle: if the Commissary is not to be got Lieut Wright of Capt Peronees Compy; to deliver the provisions. The men at work on the Bridge to be taken of(f) Immediatly. At half An hour after 12 oClock the Twenty (women) to be at Docr. McKinleys Tent And Any Woman that shall be Absent will be sent back.
The Parole is Oxford (Orford)
Field Officer for to Morrow Lt Col: Burton
    A Detach: to march to morrow morning at 4 Clock Consisting of 1 Field Officer 2 Capts. 6 Subaltrens 12 Serjts & 200 Rank & File of the Two Regts. Capt Gates & his Two Subs: 2 Serjts 2 Corpls & fifty privets of his Indipendent Compy Capt Waggoners & Capt Peronees two Compys of Rangers. Lieut Col. Gage to Command this party. A Detachment to March on Thursday Morning at 4 oClock Consisting of One Col. one Lieut Col & one Major And the Two oldest Compys of

Grends: 5 Capts 12 Subs: 22 Serjts And five hundred Rank & File of the Two Regts. Sir Peter Halkett Lieut Col. Burton & Major Sparks Field Officers for this Detachment. The Kings Colours of the 44 Regt & the Second Coulour of the 48 Regt for this Detachment.

The Men of the two Regts that Are to March with the Detachment of to Morrow & Thursday to be taken out of those Landed from Ireland. The Commandg. Officer of each of the Regts to be Answerable to His Excellency that this Order is puntualy Comply'd with. A Return to be Sent in to morrow morning to either of the Aid du Camps Signd by the Commanding Officers of Companys of the Two Regts: of the Names & Countrys of the men That Are for the Above two Detachments their time of Service & Regts they have Served in.

His Excellency has been pleased to appoint the following Capts: & Subaltrans Officers for the Above two Detachments, And desires they will take as little Bagage with them as posable. For the Detachment Under Col. Gage, Capt Beckwith Lts: Littler Treby Cleark of the 44th Regt, Capt Lt Morris Lts Hanserd Barbutt Ensn Dunbar of the 48th Regt: For the Detachment on Thursday Capts: Saml: Hobson Gethins Lts Halkett Bayly Pottinger Simpson Lock Kennedy Townshend Enss: Nartlo(w) Pennington Preston of the 44th: Regt: Capts Dobson Chumley Boyer Lieuts Walsham Hawthorn Hedmanston (Edmestone) Coop (Cope) Bralton (Brereton) Hart Ensns: Corvert (or Cowart) Harrison Crow Mr Mulling (McMullen) The Surgeons Mate of the 48th Regt: to March with this Detachments. Capt Rutherfords Indpendent Compy And Capt Stevens (Stephens) Company of Rangers to March to Morrow morning with the Detracht: Under the Command of Lieut Col Gage And to Return to Camp at Night. 1 Corpl & 4 light Horse to march to morrow And Remain with Col Gage. The Detachment of Seamen and Capt Stewart with one Sub: & Eighteen light horse to March on Thursday. His Excllency has been pleas'd to appoint Lieut. Buccannon (Buchanan) of the Artillery to March with the Two Guns to Morrow. Capt Lt Smith & Lt McLoad of the Artillery to March with the Detacht on Thursday. The man (men) that Marches to Morrow & Thursday to be Compleated with Twenty four Rounds per man. [487]

MARYLAND-CAMP AT LITTLE MEADOWS
Tuesday June the 17th.   **(batman)**

285

This day all the Army Join'd us here. This day 6 hundred men went to work at the Roads and a Covering party along with them to guarde them. Tomorrow we Expect to March towards the great Meadows. [488]

June 18 (Wednesday)

MARYLAND-CAMP AT LITTLE MEADOWS   (Halkett/Disney)

Camp at the little Medows June: 18th: 1755

The Parole is Petworth

The Detachment Orderd Yesterday to parade tomorrow Morning at 4 oClock without (outside) the Abbots: (abatis) Adjoining the Medows. The Detacht that Marches to Morrow to receive Two days provisions Beef or Pork but no flower. [489]

(Orme)

Therefore a detachment of one field-officer with four hundred men and the deputy quarter master general marched on the 18th to cut and make the road to the little crossing of the Yoxhio Geni - taking with them two sixpounders with their ammunition, three waggons of tools, and thirty five days provision - all on carrying horses. [490]

Wedensday June the 18th.   (batman)

This day five hundred men marched towards the great Meadows and a Command of a thousand men is to follow them to Morrow Morning. This last Command is all Chosen men out of all the Army, Except the two youngest grenadiers Companies and they Remain behind with Colonel Dunbar. All the Wimen Except two a Company is Ordered to stay behind or to go to Fort Cumberland where they may Stay and Receive Provisions. [491]

June 19 (Thursday)

MARYLAND-LITTLE MEADOWS   (Halkett/Disney)

Camp at The little Medows June: 19th: 1755

The Parole Readford

Field Officer for this day Major Sparks for to Morrow Lieut Col: Burton

The Qr Masters immediatly to see Communications cut betwixt the Guards & Centrys & betwixt the Guards & the Divisions they Are detached from. 1 Sub 1 Serjt & 25 R & File to mount the Genls: Guard. The 44th regt gives the Genls. Guard this day. The picquets of the Detacht: to Consist of Two Capts: 6 subs; 6 Serjts & 200 R & F.

The Eldest Capt of the Picquet to Visit the Guards upon the Left Flank Genl to beat at six oClock to Morrow And front Guard of the Grends. The youngest Capt to Visit the right Flank & Rear Guard of the Grends:

For the Genls: Guard to Morrow the 48 regt:

The Retreat to beat An hour befor Sunsett. The Genl to beat at six oClock to Morrow morning the Assembly at 7 oClock and to March immediately. A Detacht to parade to morrow morning at Genl Beating Consisting of 1 Capt: 3 Subs: 3 Serjts And 100 Rank & File. [492]

Lacock writes: "A short distance from Little Meadows the road crosses Chestnut Ridge. Thence proceeding westwardly, it intersects the National turnpike about one mile east of the Little Crossings bridge over the Castleman River. A quarter of a mile farther westward it intersects the National turnpike near Stanton's old mill; but, after it veers off to the south, crossing the Castleman River about three hundred yards above the Little Crossings bridge near a point locally known as Hickory Hole.

At the foot of the western slope of Shade Hill, the road crosses Big Shade Run, this was the place of the fifth encampment. At this point, in plain view of the National turnpike, the road begins the ascent of Negro Mountain."

Atkinson writes; "The line of march, now more compact was resumed on the 19th. Passing over ground to the south of the Little Crossings, and of the village of Grantsville, which it skirted."

MARYLAND-NORTHWEST OF FORT CUMBERLAND   (Orme)

And on the 19th the General Marched with a detachment of one Colonel, one Lieutenant Colonel, one Major, the two eldest Grenadier Companies, and five hundred rank and file. The party of Seamen and eighteen light horse, and four howitzers with fifty round each, and four twelve pounders with eighty rounds each, and one hundred rounds of ammunition for each man, and one waggon of Indian presents; the whole number of carriages being about thirty. The Howitzers had each nine horses, the twelve pounders seven, and the waggons six. There was also thirty five days provisions carried on horses.

This detachment marched and encamped according to the annexed plan.

The Indians were ordered to march with the advanced party; this day Monocatuca the Indian Chief being at a small distance from the party was surrounded and taken by some French and Indians. The former were desirous of killing him, but the Indians refused, declaring they would abandon them and join with us if they persisted in their design; They agreed at last to tye him to a tree, and leave him: But his son who was with him escaped, and informed our Indians, who went soon after and brought him off.

We this day crossed the first branch of the Yoxio Geni, (Note: Castleman's River at Little Crossings ford) which is about four score yards over and knee deep. After having marched four miles from the little meadows we came up with the rear of the advance party, and were obliged to encamp, as they were then at work in cutting a travers-road over an immense mountain, which could not be finished till the next day. Immediately upon coming to our ground, some guides ran into us, extremely frightened, and told us a great body of the enemy were marching to attack our advance guard. The General sent forward an aid de camp to know the truth of this report, who found Lieutenant Colonel Gage in possession of the top of the mountain, and his men very advantageously posted. Our Indians had discovered the tracks of several men very near the advanced party, which had given rise to this alarm. Lieutenant Colonel Gage remained about two hours under arms, but no enemy appearing he sent parties to scour the neighboring woods, and upon their return proceeded with the work, leaving proper parties to secure the heights, and encamped there that night.

As the advanced party was to move forward early in the morning, the General ordered a detachm^t. of a Captain and one hundred men to march at daybreak, and to occupy that eminence till he should pass it with the Artillery and baggage.

Every field-officer had an orderly light horseman by whom they were to inform the general of all accidents, stops or delays in their respective parts of the line; by which means, the extent of the carriages, upon the march, was very seldom above half a mile; and the encampments was but three hundred yards from the front to the rear.

ORDERS AT THE CAMP ON THE WEST SIDE THE LITTLE CROSSING OF THE YOXHI GENI

June 19. The quarter masters are constantly to see the communications opened.

The pickets of the detachment to consist of two captains and the subaltern officers parties that are advanced upon the flanks in the front and in the rear.

The eldest captain of the picket is to command and visit the pickets of the front Grenadiers and the left flank, and the youngest captian the picket and the rear Grenadiers and the right flank. The retreat is to beat an hour before sunset, at which time the picket is to be relieved, that the officers may have light to reconnoitre the ground and to post their centinels.

From thence we marched about nine miles to Bear Camp over a chain of very rocky mountains and difficult passes. [493]

Nichols writes: "The superiority of the flying columns over the former marching order was becoming apparent. Instead of a column three or four miles long and an encampment one half mile along the road, the line of march was now seldom over one half mile and the encampment was but 300 yards from front to rear. Captain Orme gives us detailed descriptions of the new march order and encampment in two of the six maps drawn to illustrate his journal.

The line of march consisted of a point, vanguard, main body, and rear guard and included adequate flank parties along the entire column. The main body marched on both sides of the road, along which the artillery and wagons were moving, and packhorses, spare horses, and beef on the hoof moved along both flanks between the marching columns of men and vehicles and flank parties.

The encampment of the whole force represented a closing-up and telescoping of the entire flying column.

On June 20, the flying column made an excellent nine mile jump to Bear Camp, the route covering "a chain of very rocky mountains and difficult passes"."

Thursday yᵉ 19th.   (Br. Officer 1)

Every thing being in readyness we marched foward, & reached about 8 Mile, leaving yᵉ comand at yᵉ meadows to Coll: Dunbar. Imediately on our coming to our ground we were alarmed by some Indians who were sent to Spy into our Motions; the reason of this alarm was, Monacatothe the half King or cheif of our Indians being out on yᵉ advance the day before, was met by 70 Indians & some French at their head, who bound him & were going to kill him; but an Indian of his own Nation being among them, entreated that he might have his liberty, which after some difficulty was granted. They asked him many questions about our numbers & what Artillery, & were excessively surprised at his account. However yᵉ French they had with them endeavoured to perswade yᵉ Indians it was impossible to march Artillery through such a country, & that what Monacatothe said was entirely false. Nevertheless the French not knowing how to credit what he said, sent 5 Indians to reconnoitre who met some of ours & asked them if what they heard yᵉ day before was true; they said it was & if they would stop a little they would be convinced, which they did, & were no sooner so, than they ran away saying the French should come themselves next time; this alarm was made general, but every thing was soon quiet. [494]

Thursday June the 19th. (batman)
This day their was a Command of a thousand Men Marched of(f). My Master was one for this Command. As soon as we Came to our ground we was Alarm'd by the Indiens and lay upon our Arms for two after. When we found they would not Ingage us we pitched our Tents as Usal, it being 6 miles. [495]

Dear Washington: (Morris)
I am desired by the General to let you know that he marches tomorrow and the next day but that he shall halt at the Meadows two or three days. It is the desire of every particular in this family and the General's positive commands to you not to stir but by the advice of the person under whose care you are till you are better which we all hope will be very soon...   Roger Morris [496]

MARYLAND-ANNAPOLIS (Maryland Gazette)
June 5.
We hear from Wills's Creek, that the Waggons and Horses lately contracted for in the Counties of Lancaster, York, and Cumberland, were safely arrived at the Camp, and gave great satisfaction to the General, and the other Officers, being, for the most Part, by far the best of any that have been engag'd in the Service of the Army since their Arrival. We likewise hear that there are fine Bottoms for several Miles round the Camp, in which there is a great Deal of good Grass and other Food for the Horses: And that the Army in general are very healthy, impatient to enter on Action, and wait chiefly for the Arrival of the Forage purchased in this Province.
In a Letter from Susquehanna, dated the 31st ult. it is mentioned, that a Person was just return'd from the Camp, and brought Advice, that before he left, two men came there, who were supposed to be spies, one of them being known to have been among the Virginia Forces on the same business before Washington's defeat last Summer. They own'd they came from the French Fort;, and pretended they were very numerous there. One of them attempted to make his Escape, and

being a good runner, was overtaken only by one Man, who brought him back, when he was immediately put in Irons, and it was thought would soon be hang'd.

We are told that his Excellency Mayor General Braddock, and all the Forces under his Command, are gone from Will's Creek towards the Ohio. May the Great GOD OF HOSTS Crown their Enterprize with Success. [497]

This was the day when George Washington was taken ill with the bloody flux which left him prostrate. This was at Bear Camp, he managed to travel further in a wagon to Squaw's Fort camp where he stayed until July 2nd when he was well enough to travel.

Lacock writes: "At this camp, Washington, prostrated by a violent attack of fever, was left under a guard to await the arrival of Dunbar with the rest of the army. The road proceeds over Keyser Ridge, where although there is a very luxuriant growth of underbrush, the trace of the road for a little over two miles is so distinct as to leave no doubt in regard to its course over this rocky and very difficult pass. From the woods it emerges into the bottom of the north fork of Mill Run, less than half a mile from the Pennsylvania and Maryland boundary line at Oakton, Maryland. Here, in one of the most picturesque places for an encampment along the entire route, was Bear Camp".

June 20 (Friday)
MARYLAND-BEAR CAMP
Bear Camp June: 20th: 1755   **(Halkett/Disney)**
The Parole is Sumersett
Field Officer for to Morrow Lt Col:Gage
For the Genls Guard to Morrow 44th Regt.
The morning Assembly at 7 oClock And to March immediatly. A Detacht to parade to morrow morning at Genl Beating Consisting of 1 Capt: 3 Subs: 3 Serjts And 100 Rank & File. [498]

(Orme)
We could not reach our ground 'till about seven of the clock, which was three hours later than common, as there was no water, nor even earth enough to fix a tent, between the great Mountain and this place.
We halted here two days, having a road to cut in the side of a mountain, and some swamps to make passable.
ORDERS AT BEAR CAMP; June 20th.

The men of the pickets are always to load afresh when they go on duty, and to take particular care to save the ball, which the commanding officers of companies are to see returned to the train.

The troops that are encamped here are to be formed into Companies according to the number of Captains present.

The Articles of War are to be read to the men, and that article relating to the alarming of camps to be particularly explained to them.

The general having observed upon the March some neglects upon the out detachments, orders that for the future the subalterns' parties, when the ground will possibly admit of it, keep at least one hundred yards distance from the line, and that the serjeants keep their parties within sight of the subaltern's from which they are detached; and upon every halt, through ever so small, the men are to form two deep, face outward, and stand shouldered.

The Officers and serjeants are to be very attentive to the beat of the drum, taking care always to halt when they hear the long roll beat at that part of the line from which they are detached, and to march upon beating the long march.

The field officers and all officers commanding any part of the line are to be particularly careful to beat the long roll and long march upon their halting and marching.

Exact victualling returns are to be given in to the commissaries, signed by the commanding officer.

The quarter masters of the two regiments are always to attend at the delivery of provisions, and to receive from the commissary the full quantity for their respective corps, which they are to distribute to the serjeants of the companies, who are to issue it to the men. The Artillery, seamen, and light horse, and waggon masters, are to do the same. [499]

NAME OF ENCAMPMENT   (Gordon)
Laurel Swamp (from west of Little Crossings) to Bear Camp-Dist. 7 miles (Abstract of a Journal give distance from Little Meadows to Bear camp as 10 miles)
WORK DONE TO THE ROAD
a great deal of cuting and digging, and a few bridges
QUALITY OF THE ROAD
½ mile in steep turnings, ½ mile good, 2 miles very rough and stoney, 4 miles tolerable

QUALITY OF THE CAMP
open, good in all other respects Days halted 2 [500]

Friday the 20th. (Br. Officer 1)

The General beat at 3, & we marched at 5. The road was Stony & some hills, but we marched about 8 Miles; the Huntsmen got us (the officers) venison almost every day; but the Soldiers & Bast (Bat) Men begun to find themselves on short allowances; the road not being cleared we were obliged to halt there till ye 23d. [501]

Letter V (continued) (Br. Officer 3)

On the 4th of July (this should read June 20th as per other accounts) our Indians were defeated in the Woods by the French Parties; a few only was killed, but their chief Man was taken; the French have treated them very kindly, and declare they intend no War against the Indians. The General is apprehensive this will make an ill Impression on them, therefore does not care to trust them any further; he has publickly said he will advance himself with 1200 Men, drive the Enemy of the Woods, and invest Fort Du Quesne; he is resolved to be prepared for all Accidents, therefore leaves Colonel Dunbar with a strong party to make good this Camp. The Ground round the Camp is open, and Situation so advantageous, that this Camp is defensible against all the Efforts the French can make, if any Accident, should happen to the General; and he had declared, he has put it in this Condition, that his Majesty's Affairs may not suffer if he should miscarry. [502]

Fryday June the 20th. (batman)

This day we Marched to a place they call Bears Camp, it being 8 miles, very Hilly, but the Camp leavel. [503]

PENNSYLVANIA-PHILADELPHIA (Pennsylvania Gazette)

Sunday last an Express arriv'd here from Wills's Creek, who brought advice, that General Braddock, with the last Division of the forces, marched on Tuesday, the Tenth Instant, for the Little Meadows, whence they will be join'd by the rest of the Army, and then proceed to the Ohio: and that he has left Colonel Innes Governor of Fort Cumberland, with a sufficient Garrison for the defense of it, and a magazine of provisions, Forage and Stores, that are left there.

We hear that several bodies of French troops have lately been seen passing in Batteaus on Lake Ontario, in their way, as is supposed to the Ohio. [504]

June 21 (Saturday)

MARYLAND-BEAR CAMP

Bear Camp June 21th: 1755   **(Halkett)**

The Parole is Forester

Field Officer for to Morrow is Maj.Sparks

The Men upon the Advance picquets to be Loaded & non(e) but them.[505]

Satterday June the 21st.   **(batman)**

We halted and sent out a working party to Cut the Road up a large hill and the Covering party along with them to guarde them, and at Night we sent the advance Piquet out in the Front of the line. In the Night a Sentry Fired at two Men as he thought which alarm'd the Camp but nothing Extraordinary hapn'd all the Night. [506]

Atkinson writes: "The army spent the night of the 21st at the Bear Camp, a locality I have not been able to identify, but suppose it to be about midway to the Great Crossings, which it reached on the 23d."

June 22 (Sunday)

MARYLAND-BEAR CAMP

Bear Camp June 22d: 1755   **(Halkett)**

The Parole is Winchester

Field Officer for to morrow Lt Col Burton

For the Genl Guard to Morrow the 48th Regt

The Genl: to beat to Morrow Morning at 4 oClock & the Assembly at half An hour after And to March Immediately. [507]

Sunday June the 22d.   **(batman)**

This day we halted here and the Advance party Marched to the great Crosins (the Great Crossing of the Youghiogheny). This day we Rec'd two days Provisions. [508]

Lacock writes: "Leaving Bear Camp, the road, after crossing Mill Run, intercepts the Pennsylvania boundary line, and a few rods farther on crosses the National turnpike less than one-forth of a mile west of Oakton."

June 23 (Monday)
PENNSYLVANIA-SQUAWS FORT CAMP
Camp June 23d: 1755   **(Halkett/Disney)**
The Parole is Alsford
Field Officer for to Morrow Maj Sparks
For the Genl Guard to Morrow the 48th Regt
    The Genl: to beat to Morrow Morning at 6 oClock, the Assembly half An hour after & march Immediatly. Its Genl Braddocks Orders that no fires Are lighted with in 150 yards of the Carriages. [509]

(Orme)
On the 23rd of June we marched from this Camp to the Squaw's fort, making about six miles of very bad road.
    Three Mohawk Indians pretending friendship came to the General and told him they were just come from the French fort. They said that some reinforcemen[ts] were arrived from Montreal, and that they were in expectation of many more: that they had very little provision at the fort, and that they had been disappointed of their supplies by the dryness of the season having stopped the navigation of Buffler river.
    The General caressed them, and gave them presents, but they nevertheless went off that night, and with them one of our Indians, whom we had very long suspected, This fellow had frequently endeavored to conceal himself upon the flanks on the March, but was always discovered by the flank parties. Nothwithstanding this, we could not punish him, as the Indians are so extermely jealous that we feared it would produce a general disaffection. [510]

Nichols writes: "One of Braddock's Indians, Jerry by name, deserted the army in their company and fought for the French thereafter. Jerry later scalped several British soldiers, was captured, and for some reason, pardoned by Col. Dunbar. In 1756 Jerry was murdered at Schenectady by soldiers of the 44th Foot who remembered him from the previous year - his head found next morning on a post at the head of the 44th Regiment".

NAME OF ENCAMPMENT   **(Gordon)**
    Bear Camp to Middle Crossings camp-Dist. 8 Miles (aka Squaws Fort camp, Great Crossings)

WORK DONE TO THE ROAD

a great deal of cuting and digging, and a few bridges

QUALITY OF THE ROAD

3 miles tolerable with a few hard pinches, the ridge ½ up in zigzags, 2 miles stoney, 2 ½ miles in a Defile

QUALITY OF THE CAMP

Open, dry, tolerable feeding, water bad [511]

Monday y[e] 23d.   **(Br. Officer 1)**

The General beat at 5, & we marched to within a Mile of ye Yaughyaughgany (Youghiogheny). [512]

(batman)

This day we marched Eight Miles and drove many French Indiens before us. [513]

Lacock writes: "The road strikes north of the north branch of Braddock Run, and about half a mile beyond comes to the forks of the run. Between these forks, and possibly a short distance westward, is the ground which formed the seventh encampment, called Squaw's Fort. From this point the road follows Braddock Run to its mouth, fording (without bridging) the Big Crossing of the Youghiogheny at or near the mouth of Braddock Run, about half a mile above where the National road now crosses the river. Keeping on down the west bank of the stream, it begins a sharp ascent of Wolf, or Turkey Garden Hill, at a point opposite Somerfield, and follows the northern side of this hill, for some distance before entering Jockey Hollow."

Atkinson writes: "The route (from Great Crossings) thence to the Great Meadows or Fort Necessity was well chosen, though over a mountainous tract, conforming very nearly to the groud now occupied by the National Road, and keeping on the dividing ridge Between the waters flowing into the Youghiogheny on the one hand and the Cheat River on the other."

June 24 (Tuesday)

PENNSYLVANIA-CAMP 4 MILES EAST OF GREAT MEADOWS

1st Camp from the Gt Crossing June 24:1755

The Parole is Buckingham   **(Halkett/Disney)**

Field Officer for to Morrow Lieut Col:Gage

The Troops to receive as soon as they come to their Ground One days bread & One Days flower And half a pint of Beans.

For the Genl Guard to Morrow the 44th Regt

It is His Excellency Genl Braddocks Orders that no fires Are lighted within one hundred yards of the Carriages And this to be a Standing Order. Before the men of the Advance picquets turns out in the morning they Are to Examine their pans And Supply Any diffiiencey with fresh powder. The Genl to beat to morrow morning at 7 oClock, the Assembly at 8 And to March immediatly. [514]

The 24th of June **(Orme)**

We marched at five in the morning, and passed the second branch of the Yoxhio Geni, which is about one hundred yards wide, about three feet deep, with a very strong current. In the day's march, we discovered an Indian Camp, which they had just abandoned: our Indians informed us that, by their hutts, their number was about one hundred and seventy. They had stripped and painted some trees, upon which they and the French had written many threats and bravados with all kinds of scurrilous language. We marched this day about six miles, and at night joined the two detachments.

ORDERS AT THE CAMP ON THE EAST SIDE THE GREAT MEADOWS

At daybreak the men of the advanced pickets are to examine their panns and to put in fresh priming.

The subalterns upon the advanced parties are to keep one of their men within sight of the line, whom they are to have always in view; and the serjeants are to do the same by the subalterns.

The General is determined to put the first officer under arrest whom he shall find any ways negligent in any of these duties. [515]

Tuesday ye 24th. **(Br. Officer 1)**

We crossed very early in the Morning. The crossing of this river was extreamly beautifull & aforded us a plesant prospect; it undoubtedly appeared to us much more so having had nothing but a continued thickett to march through since our first setting out. Close to ye crossing of this River is a small Log Fort built by the Indian Women last year to secure themselves & childern in when Mr. Washington was engaged with ye French; we marched this day 5 Miles the other side of the River. On our March ye Guides imagined they saw some Indians frequently lurking round our line which we had reason afterwards to think true. A Wagoner going out next morning to bring in his horses was surprised by a party of Indians who shot him in 4 places in the belley & His horse in the Neck, he made shift to return to Camp, but after lingering some days he died; ye same morning 4 people more going out to look after their Horses were killed and scalped. One of the Guides shot an Indian or French Man as was Judged by the quantity of blood on the ground for at least an 100 Yards where they found a french Gun & ye place where somebody had been newly buried. [516]

(seaman)

On the 24th:-A man came into the Fort, and reported that a party of Indians of about 20 had surprised, killed & scalped two families to the number of about 14 or 15 people, and not above 3 miles from this place.[517]

NAME OF ENCAMPMENT   (Gordon)
   Middle Crossings Camp to Scalping Camp-Dist.7 Miles (aka Camp 4 miles east of Great Meadows)
WORK DONE TO THE ROAD
   digging, blowing, bridging, a great deal of cuting, chiefly old timber
QUALITY OF THE ROAD
   swampy for a mile, ¾ up hill, rough and steep, ½ mile good, a steep Hill, 1½ mile rough, the rest tolerable
QUALITY OF THE CAMP
   open, dry, indifferent feeding, Water bad [518]

Tuesday June the 24th.   (batman)
   This day we marched 10 miles and drove great many of the French Indiens before us, and one of our Indiens diserted to them. We lay two hours after upon our Arms. [519]

June 25 (Wednesday)
PENNSYLVANIA-CAMP ON WEST SIDE OF THE GREAT MEADOWS   (Halkett/Disney)
Camp beyond Great Medows June 25th: 1755
The Parole is Cumberland
Field Officer for to Morrow Lt Col Burton
   1 Capts 2 Subs: 2 Serjts & 50 Rank & File of the Line with 1 Serjt & 8 of the light horse to parade immediatly at the Front Gun. 1 Sub & 20 of this detacht. to be detached to the rear & some on each side of the roads And to bring to Camp all stray horses. The Subaltrens

Officers who marches with the Out detachments upon the Flanks Are to keep one of their Men within Sight of the Line And the Officers And the rest of these partys where the Ground will posably Admit of it Are never to be nearer to the Line then 100 yards. And the Serjts & Corpls. Detachts: Are never to be nearer to there Officers then 50 yards. His Excellcy Expects this Order will be striclty Complyed with As he is determind to put the first Officer under An Arrest that he finds Negligent. [520]

Lacock writes: "No other part of the old Braddock Road presents such difficulties as this section of it over Division Ridge, for the underbrush is so thick in places that one is compelled to crawl on hands and knees in order to keep the road. The slopes are very rocky and the passes are exceedingly difficult, but with plainly marked scars. At the western foot of this ridge was situated the camp of the Twelve Springs, which Orme designated as "the camp on the east side of the Great Meadows".

Berkebile writes: "On the morning of June 25 so steep a grade was encountered that the men were obliged to ease the carriages down with tackles. Throughout the remainder of June and the early part of July the column was so retarded by the road conditions that only a few miles could be covered each day".

PENNSYLVANIA-GREAT MEADOWS (Orme)
ORDERS AT THE CAMP ON THE EAST SIDE THE GREAT MEADOWS

At daybreak the men of the advance pickets are to examine their panns and to put I fresh priming.

The subalterns upon the advanced parties are to keep one of their men within sight of the line, whom they are to have always in view; and the serjeants are to do the same by the subalterns.

The General is determined to put the first officer under arrest whom he shall find any ways negligent in any of these duties.

On the 25th, at daybreak, three men who went without the centinels, were shot dead and scalped. Parties were immediatley sent out to scour the woods on all sides, and to drive in the stray horses.

This day we passed the Great Meadows, and encamped about two miles on the other side. We this day saw several Indians in the woods; the General sent the light horse, our Indians, and some volunteers, to endeavor to surround them, but they returned without seeing them.

About a quarter of a mile from this camp, we were obliged to let our carriages down a hill with tackles, which made it later than usual before we got to our ground.

The soldiers were now so accustomed to open the communications, and understood so well the reason and method of our encampment, that they performed this work with great alacrity and dispatch; and the marching through the woods, which they at first looked upon as unnecessary fatigue, they were are convinced to be their only security, and went through it with the greatest cheerfulness.

Some French and Indians endeavored to reconnoitre the camp, but wherever they advanced, they were discovered and fired upon by the advanced Centinels.

Two Captain's Detachments of 50 men each, were ordered to march at 10 o'clock in the morning with guides. One party was to march out at the front and the other in the rear. They were to divide the detachments into small parties, and to lie upon their arms about half a mile wide upon each flank of the encampment. At break of day the pickets were to advance, and at the same time these small parties were to move forward towards the camp.

By this measure, any Indians who had concealed themselves near the camp must have been taken; but these parties returned without having seen any of the enemy.

ORDERS AT THE CAMP ON THE WEST SIDE OF THE GREAT MEADOWS, June the 25th.

The Advanced pickets are to take no more blankets than will be sufficient to cover their centinels.

The line is never to turn out upon any account but by order from the General, or the field officer of the picket.

Every soldier or Indian shall receive five pounds for each Indian scalp. [521]

Lacock writes: "The road runs down Hager Hill south of James Bishop's, a quarter of a mile south of Fort Necessity. For a mile and a half from the James Bishop house the road can be very accurately followed to the point at which it intersects the National turnpike, - a point, it may be noted, about a stone's throw south of the spot where lies the mortal remains of General Braddock. At this intersection the road leaves the turnpike never again to rejoin it, and turns somewhat to the northwest in order to gain a favorable pass over Chestnut Ridge, the last mountain ridge to be crossed. About a quarter of a mile northward from Braddock's grave was "the camp on the west side of the Great Meadows." the Orchard Camp."

Atkinson writes: *"About one mile west of the Great Meadows and near the spot now marked as Braddock's Grave, the road struck off more to the north-west, on order to reach a pass through Laurel Hill what would enable them to strike the Youghiogheny, at a point afterwards known as Stewart"s Crossing and about half a below the present town of Connellsville. This part of the route is marked by the farm known as Mount Braddock".*

Wednesday ye 25th. **(Br. Officer 1)**

We marched about two Mile the other side ye great Meadows. It was strongly imagined if we met with any opposition, ye Meadows would be ye place; but we marched through without any Molestation or alarm. There are about 150 Acres of Meadow-land entirely clear. In ye middle of this spot is Fort Necessity; built by Mr. Washin(g)ton last Year when he retreated from the French; it was a small fourside figure, with a trench dug round it; they had some very good Swivells wch: when they retreated from thence, the french entirely disabled, but left them in the ditch. There are many human bones all round ye spott; but at present every thing is entirely pulled down. [522]

Wedensday June the 25th. **(batman)**

We being Alarmd at four in the Morning by some Indiens fireing at our Wagonars fetching in their horses and wounded two in three places, and Scalped one man, a Servt to Major Halket. Our Indiens Immediately upon hearing them fire went out against them and gave them one fire, but seeing they was two many of them, they Returned into the Camp and a Strong party Advanced to bring in all the Wagoners horses that was a stray. This day we marched Eight miles and Marched a Cross the large Meadows, it being a Mile long and two hundred yards Broad. This day we killed a French Indien. [523]

June 26 (Thursday)
PENNSYLVANIA-ORCHARD CAMP-ROCKFORT
June 26th: 1755 **(Halkett/Disney)**
The Parole is Chester
Field Officer for to Morrow Major Sparks

1 Capt 2 Subs: 2 Serjts & 50 Men of the Line to parade to morrow Morning at 1 oClock at the Head of the Front Gun. 1 Capt 2 Subs 2 Serjts & 50 men of the line to parade at the same time at the head of the rear gun. The Capts to receive their Instructions from Lieut Col

Gage. The Genl to beat to morrow morning at 4 oClock the Assemble at 5 And the Troops to March immediatley After. The out picquets Are to have no more Blankets then will cover their out Centrys. The Line never to turnd out on Any Acct whatever but by an Order from the Genl. Or the Field Offr of the Day or the Commandg; Offr of each regt: Any person whatsoever who presume to turn out the line by any other metthod Shall be Immediatly Confind. If An Offir he shall be Casherd. If An non Commissioned Offr or Soldr: he shall Receive 1000 lashes. If Any Soldr or follower of the Army bring into head Quarters An Indian Scalp (he) shall Receive five pounds from the Genl for every Scalp.

For the Genls Guard to Morrow the 44th: Regt.

The Troops Are immediately to Receive four days flower and two days fish & one days Pork which compleats them to the 30th Inclusive And they are to manage it Accordingly. The Officers And Soldrs: of the Two Regts upon Detacht with Sr John St Clair to be releived to Morrow uppon the Troops Comming to their Ground. The Genl to beat to morrow Morning at 5 oClock the Assembly at six And March half An hour after. If upon a March Any Soldier shall fall Sick his Arms & Accoutrements Are to be put into one of the Waggons that is Coverd (by the division the Soldier belongs to). The provisions to be dilivird to the men As soon As posable After they come to their Ground. [524]

Lacock writes: "A short distance from this camp (Orchard Camp) the road runs south of Nemacolins Wigwam, and a few rods northward near a schoolhouse enters the wooded part of Chestnut Ridge, on the eastern slope of which it passes the spot called Peddler's Rocks. On the western slope a sort of transverse road, the traces of which are easily followed except for about a quarter of a mile, was cut to join a township road near the house of John Henry Rankin, three miles and a half from Braddock's grave. A few rods distant on the west side of the township road are the Half King's Rocks, better known as the Great Rock, where the old camp of the Half King was located; and close by these rocks and south of the road is "Washington Springs," the place of Braddock's tenth encampment, called Rock Fort, two miles south of Dunbar's camp. This Indian camp was in a strong position, being upon a high rock with a very narrow and steep ascent to the top. It had a spring in the middle, and stood at the termination of the Indian path to the Monongahela, at the confluence of Red Stone Creek."

NAME OF ENCAMPMENT   (Gordon)
   Scalping Camp to Steep Bank Camp Dist. 7 Miles (aka Orchard
Camp)
WORK DONE TO THE ROAD
   cuting old and standing timber, a little bridging and digging
QUALITY OF THE ROAD
   all along pretty good, excepting a steep bank in the rear of the
camp
QUALITY OF THE CAMP
   pretty secure, feeding distant, water bad [525]

June the 26th.   (Orme)
   We marched at five o'clock, but by the extreme badness of the road
could make but four miles. At our halting place we found another
Indian camp, which they had abandoned at our approach, their fires
being yet burning. They had marked in triumph upon trees, the scalps
they had taken two days before, and a great many French had also
written on them their names and many insolent expressions. We picked
up a commission on the march, which mentioned the party being under
the command of Sieur Normanville. This Indian camp was in a strong
situation, being upon a high rock with a very narrow and steep ascent
to the top; it had a spring in the middle, and stood at the termination of
the Indian path to the Monongehela, at the confluence of Red-stone
creek. By this pass the party came which attacked Mr. Washington the
year before, and also this which attended us. By their tracks, they
seemed to have divided here, the one part going straight forward to
fort du Quesne, and the other returning by Red-stone Creek to the
Monongohela.
   A Captian, four subalterns, and ninety volunteers, marched from
this camp with proper guides to fall in the night upon that party which
we imagined had returned by the Monongohela. They found a small
quantity of provisions, and a very large Batteau, which they destroyed,
and the Captain according to orders joined the General at Gist's
plantation, but saw no men. [526]

NAME OF CAMP   (Gordon)
   Steep Bank Camp to Spring Camp-Dist. 3 1/2 Miles (aka Rock
Fort Camp, Half King Rock)
WORK DONE TO THE ROAD

cuting old and standing Timber, a little bridging and digging
QUALITY OF THE ROAD
   2 miles tolerable but stoney, descent of the hill steep,
the rest good.
QUALITY OF THE CAMP
   pretty secure, dry, indiferent feeding, fine water [527]

(seaman)
   On the 26th.:-An account came in of 2 more families being scalped
within 2 miles of us. The Governor sent out a party to bury the dead,
as well as to scour the woods for the Indians. They found a child of
about 7 years old, standing in the water scalped & crying; they brought
it into the Fort and the Doctors dressed it: it had 2 holes in its skull,
besides being scalped, but was in spirits, and had its skull not been
wounded might have lived, (they brought it to the Doctor, who
dressed it) but as it was it died in a week. It would be too tedious to
recount every little incident here in the Fort, therefore will return to
the Army, and give an account of their proceeding from the time they
left us. [528]

The 26th.   (Br. Officer 1)
   We marched about 4 Mile & crossed a very high & steep
Mountain. Our encampment was under a rocky hill where 150 or 200
french & Indians had encamped y[e] Night before. They had drawn many
odd figures on y[e] trees expressing with red paint, y[e] scalps and
Prisoners they had taken with them; there were three french Names
wrote there, Rochefort, Chauraudray, & Picauday; from this place
Capt. Dobson with 70 Volunteers set out for Redstone creek, where a
party of french & Indians had been all Winter. They found nothing but
a Batteau & some Canoes, with some pieces of pork & beef which
they burned; at going out they took a biscuit & a gill of rum each Man,
on which they were obliged to live 48 hours. [529]

   This high steep mountain is what we know today as Chestnut Ridge.

Thursday June the 26th.   (batman)
   We marched Eight miles and at twelve at Night we was Alarmed by
the Indiens fireing at our Sentrys. Immediately after their was two
Captns and a hundred men Ordered to march out of the Camp a Mile,
one to face one Side of the Camp and the Other the Other side and

there to lay till the genll Beating in the morning, and then to march down all in a Brest to see if they Could Surround them, but to no purpose at all. My Master was on this Command. [530]

Lacock writes: "From Washington Springs the line follows the course of the present road for about a mile, with distinct marks at intervals along the sides; it them continues in a northerly direction eastward of the present road to a point east of Jumonville and of Jumonville's grave. Jumonville marks the northernmost point reached by Dunbar's regiment. Near the grave is the ledge of rock on which Washington and the Half King took position in their attack on Jumonville, May 28, 1754. From here it keeps its northerly course along a very narrow crest of the mountain, past the Honey Comb Rock, and thereafter in the main follows the dividing line between North Union and Dunbar townships to a point about one mile south of the old Meason house on the Gist Plantation, when by a slight deflection northwestward it crosses Cove Run and the Pennsylvania Railroad to Gist's Plantation, the place of the eleventh encampment. Between the tenth and eleventh encampment the traces of the road so plain that one does not have to rely on inference."

June 27 (Friday)
PENNSYLVANIA-GISTS PLANTATION   (Halkett/Disney)
Camp at Guests house June 27th: 1755
The Parole is London
Field Officer for to Morrow Lieut Col Gage
For the Genls Guard to morrow the 48th Regt
The Commanding Officers of each Compys of the Two Regts: of the Artillery the detracht of Seamen And Troop of light horse to Send into Mr Leslie Immedy: a Return of the No of Serjts Corpls Drummers & privet men bearing Arms Exclucive of Battman & Servts: in Each Compy. And the Serjts to Attend Mr Leslie to Morrow Morning At 5 oClock to receive a quantity of Rum for each man which his Excellency is pleasd to give the men in Consideration of their good Behavour. Capt Gates with a Detachment of his Company And a Detach of 2 Serjts & 50 R & File of the Two Regts: now Incamped hear with Capt Polsons Company of Carpenters Capt Waggoners & Capt Perrnes Compy of Rangers to parade to Morrow Morning at day break At the head of the Front Gun to March of(f to) Sr John St Clairs Camp & put themselves Under his Command. The Whole detacht of the Two Regts now Under the Command of Sr John St Clair to Join their Respective Corps to Morrow morning At 5 oClock Except Lieut Littler of the 44th & Lieut Hanserd of the 48th Regt: The Waggons &

horses which Sr John St Clair leaves behind him to fall into Our Line
And to be disposd of in the same Order of March. The Troops to hold
Themselves in Readiness to March at half An hours warning. [531]

> *Lacock writes: "The last mountain barrier had been passed. Along this*
> *narrow road, cut but twelve feet wide and with the line of march often extending*
> *four miles at a time, the army had toiled on day after day, crossing ridge after*
> *ridge of the Alleghany Mountains, now plunging down into a deep and often*
> *narrow ravine, now climbing a difficult and rocky ascent, but always in the deep*
> *shadow of the forest".*

NAME OF THE ENCAMPMENT   **(Gordon)**
   Spring Camp to Gists-Dist. Miles 8 (aka Gist's Plantation/Camp,
Gists House or Plantation)
WORK DONE TO THE ROAD
   A great deal of cuting and digging, a few bridges
QUALITY OF THE ROAD
   2 miles pretty good, 1/2 mile steep, 3 miles rough and stoney, the
rest somewhat soft
QUALITY OF THE CAMP
   open, moist, good feeding, good water but muddy [532]

June 27th.   **(Orme)**
   We marched from the camp of Rock fort to Gist's plantation,
which was about six miles; the road still mountainous and rocky. Here
the advanced party was relieved, and all the waggons and carrying
horses with provision belonging to that detachment joined us, and the
men were to be victualled from us. [533]

The 27th.   **(Br. Officer 1)**
   We Marched to Guest's plantation over a long & steep mountain
our course to ye Eastward of the North; here ye mountains begin to
diminish & a fine pleasant rich Soil is seen. [534]

Fryday June the 27th.   **(batman)**
   We Marched 7 miles, to guests Plantation and Rec'd Provisions. [535]

June 28 (Saturday)
PENNSYLVANIA-CAMP ON THE WEST SIDE OF
YOCHOGHIOGHENY   **(Halkett/Disney)**

Camp on the Yochoganney June 28th: 1755

The Parole is Waterford

Field Officer for to Morrow Lt Col: Burton

    The Genl to beat Immediately. One Field Officer 2 Capts 4 Subs. & 150 men of the Two Regts: to parade Immediately And Remain upon the Ground. 1 sub & 40 men of the two Regts: to parade at the same time for a Rear Guard. [536]

(Washington)

June 28, Saturday. Great Crossing of the Youghiogheny, Pennsylvania.

Dear Brother: (John Augustine Washington)

    Immediately upon our leaving the camp at George's Creek, on the 14th instant, (from whence I wrote you) I was seized with violent fevers and pains in my head, which continued without intermission 'till the 23d following, when I was relieved, by the General's absolutely ordering the Physicians to give me Doctr. James's Powder w'ch is one of the most excellent medicines in the world for it gave me immed. ease, and removed my Fev'rs and other complaints in 4 Days time. My illness was too violent to suffer me to ride; therefore I was indebted to a cover'd wagon for some part of my transp'n; but even in this I could not continue for the jolt'g was so great that I was left upon the road with a guard, and necess'rts, to wait the Arr'l of Colo. Dunbar's Detach., which was two days march behind. The Genl. giving me his word of hon'r, that I should be brought up, before he reach'd the French fort; this promise, and the Doct'rs threats that, if I persever'd it wou'd endanger my Life, determin'd my halting for the above Detach't.

    As I expect the Communication between this and Wills Cr. will soon be too dangerous for single persons to pass, it will possibly stop the interchange of Letters in any measure; therefore I shall attempt (and will go through if I have strength) to give you an acct. of my proceeding, of our situation, and of our prospectss at present; which I desire you may communicate to Colo. Fairfax, and my Corrse'ds, for I am too weak to write more than this letter. In the Letter wh'ch I wrote fr'm Georges Creek, I acquainted you that unless the numb'r of Wag'ns were retrenched and the carr'g Horses increased that we never should be able to see Duquisne: this, in 2 Days afterwards which was about the time they got to the little Meadows with some of thier First Waggons and strongest Teams, they themselves were convinced off, for they found that besides the almost impossibility of gett'g the wag'ns along at all; that they had often a rear of 3 or 4 miles of Waggons; and that the Sold'rs Guarding them were so dispersed that if we had been attack'd either in Front, Center, or Rear the part so attack'd must have been cut off and totally dispersed before they cou'd be properly sustained by any other Corps.

At the little Meadws there was a 2d. Council call'd, for there had been one before therein it was represented to all the Off'rs of the diff't Corps the great necessity there was for Horses and how laudable it wd. be to retrench their Baggage and offer the spare Horses for the Publick Service. In order to encourage this I gave up my best Horse, (w'ch I have nev'r heard of since) and took no more baggage than half my Portmanteau would easily contain....

The General before they met in Council ask'd my private Opinions concern'g the Expedition. I urg'd it in the warmest terms I was Master off, to push on; if we even did it with a chos'n Detacht. for that purpose, with the Artillery and such other things as were absolutely necessary; leav'g the baggage and other Convoys with the Remainder of the Army, to follow by slow and regular Marches, which they might do safely, while we were advanced in Front. As one Reason to support this Opinion, I inform'd the Genl. if we could credit our Intelligence, the French were weak at the Forks but hourly expect'd reinforcements, which to my certain knowledge cou'd not arrive with Provisions or any supplies during the continuance of the Drought as the Buffalo River (The River aux Boeufs, or French Creek) down w'ch is their only communication to Venango, must be as Dry as we now find the great xing of the Youghe., which may be pass'd dry shod. This was a Scheme that took, and it was det'd that the Genl. with 1200 chosen Men and Officers of all the differ't Corps, with the following Field Officer's (viz,; S^r. Peter Halkett who acts as Brigadier), Lt. Colo. Gage, Lt. Colo. Burton, and Major Sparke, with a certain number of Waggons as the Train would absolutley require, shou'd March as soon as things cou'd be got in readiness for them, which was compleated, and we on our march by the 19th, leav'g Colo. Dunbar and Maj. Chapman, with the residue of the two Reg's, Companys most of the women and in short every thing behind except such Provision's and other necessary's as we took and carried upon Horses.

We set out with less than 30 Carriages (Incl'g all those that transported the Howetzers, 12 pounders and 6 pounders, etc.), and all of those strongly Horsed; which was a prospect that convey'd the most infinate delight to me tho' I was excessively ill at the time. But this prospect was soon over turn'd and all my sanguine hopes brought very low when I found, that instead of pushing on with vigour, without regarding a little rough Road, they were halting to level every Mold Hill, and to erect Bridges over every Brook; by which means we were 4 days gett'ng 12 miles; where I was left by the Doct'r's Advice and the Genl's absolute Orders, otherwise I wou'd not have been prevailed upon to remain behind my own Detach't as I then imagn'd, and believ'd I shall now find it not very easy to join my own Corps again, which is 25 Miles advanced before us; tho' I had the Generals word of Hon'r pledg'd in the most solemn manner, that I sh'd be brought up before he arrived at Duquisne. They have had frequent Alarms, and several Men scalp'd; but this is only done to retard the March, and to harass the Men if they are to be turn'd out every time a small party of them attack the Guards at Night; (for I am certain, they have not sufficient strength to make head against the whole).

I have been now 6 Days with Colo. Dunbar's Corps, who are in a miserable Condition for want of Horses, not hav'g more one half enough for their Wag'ns; so that the only method he has of proceeding, is to March on himself with as many Waggons as those will draw, and then Halt till the Remainder are brought up which requires two Days more; and I believe shortly he will not be able to stir at all; but there has been vile management in regard to Horses and while I am mention'g this I must not forget to desire that you'll acq't Colo. G. Fairfax that I have been made the most strick enquiry after his Man and Horses, but can hear nothing of either; at least nothing that can be credited. I was told that the Fellow was taken ill upon the Road while he was with Sir John St. Clair's Detacht. the certainty of this I can't answer for, but I believe there is nothing more Cert'n than that he is not with any part of the Army. And unless the Horses stray and make home themselves, I believe there is 1000 to 1 against his every seeing them again: for I gave up a horse only one Day, and never cou'd see or hear of him afterwards: My strength wont admit me to say more, tho' I have not said half what I intended concerning our Affairs here. Business, I shall not think of, but dep'd solely upon your management of all my aff'rs, and doubt not but that they will be well conducted. You may thank my friends for the Lett'rs I have rec'd which has not been one from any Mortal since I left Fairfax, except yourself and Mr. Dalton. It is a piece of regard and kindness which I should endeavor to acknowledge was I able and suffer'd to write....Make my Complim'ts to all who think me worthy of their Enquirys.

P.S. July 2d. A great Misfortune has attended me in my sickness was, the looseing the use of my Servant, for poor John was taken about the same time that I was, with near the same disorder; and was confin'd as long; so that we did not see each other for several Days. he is also tolerably well recover'd. We are sure advan'd almost as far as the g't Meadows; and I shall set out to morrow morning for my own Corps, with an Escort of 100 Men which is to guard some Provision's up; so that my Fears and doubts on that head are quite remov'd. I had a Letter yesterday from Orme, who writes me word that they have pass'd the Youghyangane for the last time, that they have sent our Partys to scour the Country thereabouts and have Reason to believe that the French are greatly alarm'd at their approach. [537]

NAME OF THE ENCAMPMENT **(Gordon)**
From Gist's Plantation to Steuart's-Dist. 5 Miles (aka Camp on West side of   Youghiogheny)
WORK DONE TO THE ROAD
a great deal of cuting chiefly old timber, several bridges
QUALITY OF THE ROAD
in general good, the soil rich and in many places soft and deep
QUALITY OF THE CAMP
secure, dry, indiferent feeding, water tolerable [538]

June the 28th. **(Orme)**
The troops marched about five miles to a camp on the east side of the Yoxhio Geni. [539]

The 28th. **(Br. Officer 1)**
We marched within half a Mile of ye great crossing of the Yaughyaughgany, over exceeding fine ground; our course Northerly.[540]

Satterday June the 28th. **(batman)**
We marched 7 miles, the terable Rain that Ever hapnd. It was 7 in the Evening before we Came to our ground. This day a Captn (Dobson) and Eighty soldiers went to hunt the Indiens. They traveled

Eighty miles and saw neather man, woman, Nor Child but a Bear sitting in a Mulbery Tree and a fine Boat in the River, the prittyist that Ever was seen. It would hold twenty People and one man might Carry it on their Backs. [541]

Lacock writes: "Leaving Gist's Plantation the line runs abruptly to the northward, eventually keeping the higher ground to a point about a quarter of a mile east of Leisenring, where it turns into the valley of Opossum Run and follows the stream to its mouth in the Youhiogheny. On the west side of the Youghiogheny, near Robinson's Falls, was the place of the twelfth encampment. Although no trustworthy scars of the road from Gist's Plantation to this point are discernible, there can be little doubt that this was the line of march."

June 29 (Sunday)
PENNSYLVANIA-YOUGHIOGHENY RIVER   **(Halkett/Disney)**
Camp at the Crossing of the Yochoganney
June 29th: 1755
The Parole is Tunbridge
Field Officer for to Morrow Major Sparke
For the Genl Guard the 48th Regt:
    One Sub: Two serjts And forty men to parade Immediatly At the head of the Rear Gun & to March As a Grass Guard to the Batt Horses &c. The Officer to receive his Ordrs from Capt Morris.
    The Commanding Officers of each Regt: & Capts. of the severall Companys Detacht: of Seamen Light horse to send in to the Train their damaged Cartridges, And to apply to ye Commandg: Officer of the Artillery who is Ordered to deliver them fresh ones. As soon as the Troops have Received from the Train As many Cartridges has will compleat each man to 24 Rounds, They Are then to send in to Capt Ord All their spair ball and what ever powder they have from the Cartridges they have been oblidge to break up. Where as by the Connivence of some of the Officers several of the men fired their pieces this morning in a very Ireguler manner It is His Excellencys Orders that for the future if Any Offr of whatsoever Rank shall suffer the men to fire their pieces in that Ireguler manner They shall be put Under An Arrest. And When ever it shall be found Necessary to fire an(y) of the mens peices that cannot be drawn (unloaded) the Several Commandg: Officers of all the Troops are to Apply to the Genl through An Aid du Camp for his leave. A Detacht: of One Capt 3 Subs: 4 Serjts & 100 men to parade to morrow Morning at half an

hour after three oClock At the Front Gun to March to Sr John St Clairs Camp and there Receive Orders. The Troops to receive Immediately two days flower & Two (sic) days Bacon which Compleats them with provisions to the Second of July Inclusive. It is recomended to the men as they halt this day to Bake their flower into bread. One sub. One Serjt and Twenty Rank & File to parade this day at Twelve oClock as a Grass Guard. [542]

Lacock writes: "Braddock forded the Youghiogheny at Stewart's Crossing, below the mouth of Opossum Creek, to a point on the opposite side of the river above the mouth of Mounts Creek, half a mile below Connellsville. His next encampment, which was on the east side of the fording, a mile north of the mouth of Mounts Creek, cannot be definitely fixed; but most probably it was on Davidson's land, southeast of the Narrows. Between this point and the battleground there were still some highlands to be crossed, which, though trivial in comparison with the mountains already traversed, were yet rugged enough to present serious difficulties to the troops, already worn out with previous labors and exertions."

Atkinson writes: "This second crossing of the Youghiogheny was effected on the 30th of June. The high grounds intervening between the river and its next tributary, Jacob's Creek, though trivial in comparison with what they had already passed. it may be supposed, presented serious obstacles to the troops, warn out with previous exertions."

NAME OF THE ENCAMPMENT   **(Gordon)**
   From Steuarts to Main Crossing (of Youghiogheny River)-Dist. 2 Miles
WORK DONE ON THE ROAD
   digging, some cuting, one bridge
QUALITY OF THE ROAD
   a steep Bank in the front of the Camp, uneven to the ford, the ford rough, the rest good
QUALITY OF THE CAMP
   open, dry, tolerable feeding, water good, very fine coal here Days halted 1 [543]

                                                          (Orme)
ORDERS AT THE CAMP ON THE EAST SIDE OF THE YOXHIO GENI, June the 29th.
   Whereas by the connivance of some officers several of the men have fired their pieces in a very iregualr and unmilitary manner; The

General declares that, for the future, if any officer, of whatever rank, shall suffer the men to fire their pieces, he shall be put under arrest. And it is ordered, that whenever it is found necessary to fire any of the men's pieces, that cannot be drawn, the commanding officers of the several troops are to apply to the General for leave, through an Aid de Camp.

The commanding officers of regiments, troops, and companies, are to send to the train all their damaged cartridges, and to apply to the commanding officer of the Artillery for fresh ones in the lieu of them. [544]

The 29th. **(Br. Officer 1)**

We crossed the river without any opposition, which was not expected; we encamped on the other side; our course to ye northward. [545]

Sunday June the 29th. **(batman)**

We marched 4 miles, it being a Pleasent Cuntry, the land being so good that the weeds hide me when on horse from seeing the men march at twenty yards distance. [546]

June 30 (Monday)

PENNSYLVANIA-YOUGHIOGHENY RIVER **(Halkett/Disney)**
Camp After the Crossing the Yochoganney
June 30th: 1755
The Parole is Wells
Field Officer for to Morrow Lieut Col Gage
For the Genls: Guard for 44th Regt:

For the future the Soldiers ten(t)s Are allways to be piched in a Single line facing out wards And no Officer is to pitch his Tent or have his picquet of horses in the front of the soldiers Tents but Always in the rear And that there may be sufficent room for that purpose It is His Excellencys Orders that as soon as the Troops are come to their Ground And the Carriages Closed up that the Commandg: Officers of each Regt. Order their Several Detachts: to Advance 25 paces from that part of the Line of Carriages which they Seperatly Cover And there pitch their Tents. The Officers upon the Advance picquets And the Serjts & Corpls that are Detached from them Are upon no Acct. whatever to Suffer any fires to be lighted in their Front. The Genl to beat to morrow Morning at 5 oClock & the Assembly at 6 And the Troops to March Immediatley After. [547]

June the 30th.   (Orme)

We crossed the main body of the Yoxhio Geni, which was about two hundred yards broad and about three feet deep. The advanced guard passed, and took post on the other side, till our artillery and baggage got over; which was followed by four hundred men who remained on the east side 'till all the baggage had passed.

We were obliged to encamp about a mile on the west side, where we halted a day to cut a passage over a mountain. This day's march did not exceed two miles.

Part of the flour having been unavoidably damaged by severe rains, the General sent an order to Colonel Dunbar to forward to him with the utmost diligence one hundred carrying horses with flour, and some beeves, with an escort of a Captain and one hundred men.

Upon this day's halt the men's arms were all drawn and cleaned, and four days provision served to the men that they might prepare a quantity of bread, and dress victuals to carry with them.

ORDERS ON THE WEST SIDE OF THE YOXHIO GENI

The men's tents are to be pitched in a single line facing outwards, and no officer is to pitch his tent or have his picket of horses in fronts of the soldiers tents. And that there may be sufficient room for this, it is the General's order that as soon as the troops come to their ground and the carriages close up, that the commanding officers of each regiment order their several detachments to advance twenty five paces from that part of the line of carriages which they covered, and there to pitch their tents. No fire upon any account to be lighted in front of the pickets. [548]

(Washington)
June 30, Monday. Camp between the Great Crossing and the Great Meadows.

To James Innes:

I have been excessively ill but am now recovering from violent Fevers and Pains of wch my disorder consisted. [549]

The 30th.   (Br. Officer 1)

Remained in Camp, the working party only advancing to clear ye road for ye next days march. [550]

Munday June the 30th.   **(batman)**
    We halted and rec'd Provisions. [551]

*This is the place that has seen much change in the intervening years. In
1755 the road descended down by a valley to the broad bottom land of the river
where the river is easily forded. From the ford the road headed west via a broad
valley to the higher elevations. A three arch stone bride with an inclined roadway
was built at the crossing to carry the National Road. In the 1930's a flood control
program of the U.S. Army Corps of Engineers called for a dam on the river just
down stream from the crossing. This resulted in a large impoundment called
Yough. River Lake and the route west known as U.S. Route 40 was put on a new
high bridge over the reservoir. When the reservoir filled the stone bridge and
several valley settlements disappeared beneath the waters.*

*Records indicate that just before the army passed the crossing there was
an Indian village nearby that was recently abandoned. Archaeology indicates the
site had been an Indian village site well back into history.*

*Due to the orientation of the road in a northeast direction the army came
first to the camp on the west side of the Youghiogheny and then continuing in a
northeasterly direction crossed the river at Stewart's Crossing and then soon came
to the camp on the east side of the Youghiogheny.*

*Sparks writes: "On the 30th of June the army forded the Youghiogany at
Stewart's Crossings and then passed a rough road over a mountain. A few days
onward they came to a great swamp which detained them part of a day in clearing
a road."*

July 1 (Tuesday)

PENNSYLVANIA-NEAR JACOBS CABIN   **(Halkett/Disney)**
Camp Near Jacobs Cabbin July the 1d: 1755
The Parole is Barkway
Field Officer for to morrow Major Sparks.
For the Genls Guard to Morow 48th Regt.

It is His Excellencys Orders that no Tents are pitchd nor any
Blanketts carried for the partys that lyes on the Advance picquet upon
Any Acct whatever. When the Troops comes to their Ground to
Morrow One Field Officer one Capt: 3 Subs: and 100 Rank & File
from the Two Regts to Join the Advance party And one of the
Companys of Rangers now with the Advance party to Join our Line
and Encamp in the rear. For the future all Returns for the Demand of
provisions to be Signd by the Commanding Officer of the Troops that
the person belongs too for whom the provisions are Drawn for And
the Names of the persons for whom provisions Are Demanded is to be

mentioned in the Return Specifying the different Cappasites they serve in Such as Officers Serjts Corpls Drummers Soldiers Carrying Arms in this Detacht., Battmen, Servts. The Officers & Soldiers upon Advance partys to be Included in this Return. The Staff are likewise to send in a Return of the same nature. This Return to be given to the Major of Brigade at 7 oClock to morrow Morning. His Excellency Expects that the Officers who Sign the Above Return will be very puntual has he is ditermind to punish with the Outmost Severity Any Neglect in the above Returns.

Field Officer for the Detacht Major Sparks. [552]

Lacock writes: "Here, at a place called Jacob's Cabin, still on the east side of Jacob's Creek, the army encamped. On the night of July 1 the army seems to have bivouacked in order that a swamp which extended for a considerable distance on either side of Jacob's Creek might be made passable. The army, which was close at the heels of the advance or working party, had to halt there till a corduroy road could be thrown across the swamp, a process that required time."

Wallace writes: "No. 14, July 1: Terrapin Creek (Great Swamp Creek). Lacock was correct in placing "the great swamp" at Green Lick Run. Captain Orme noted that, after having traveled "about 5 miles" from the last camp (which was one mile north of the crossing of the Youghiogheny at Connellsville), they "could advance no further by reason of a great swamp which required much work to make it passable."

NAME OF THE ENCAMPMENT   **(Gordon)**

From Main Crossing to Terrapin Camp-Dist. 7 Miles

WORK DONE TO THE ROAD

chiefly cuting, some bridges

QUALITY OF THE ROAD

4 miles somewhat stoney, the rest tolerable but in some places stoney

QUALITY OF THE CAMP

open, dry, indiferent feeding, water distant [553]

        (Orme)

On the first of July, we marched about five miles, but could advance no further by reason of a great swamp which required much work to make it passable. [554]

July the first.   **(Br. Officer 1)**

   We marched early over a very long & high ridge, the
Yaughyaughgany running on each side of us. There was frequently
found peices of coal which when tried burned like pitch; this days
march we went 8 or 9 Mile, ye soil good & tollerably level; our course
Northerly. [555]

Tuesday July the 1st.   **(batman)**

   We marched 9 miles in a pleasent Cuntry. The gentlemen begins to
be afraid that we are passing the Fort (Duquesne). [556]

MARYLAND-FORT CUMBERLAND
July the 1   **(Browne)**

   My Brother was taken ill with a Fever and Flux and Fits. My Maid
taken ill with a Fever. [557]

July 2 (Wednesday)

PENNSYLVANIA-JACOBS CABIN   **(Halkett/Disney)**
Camp at Jacobs Cabbins July the 2d: 1755
The Parole is Bugdon
Field Officer for to Morrow Lieut Col Gage

   The Genl to beat directly, Capt Waggoners Compy is allways to
take the Guard over the Waggons of provisions And to detach One
Serjt & Six as Rear Guard. [558]

                                                                   (Orme)

On the 2nd of July, we marched to Jacob's cabin, about 6 miles
from the camp. A field officer was sent from the line to take the
command of the advanced guard, and the disposition thereof was
settled according to the annexed plan.
ORDERS AT JACOBS CABIN.

   No more bell tents are to be fixed: the men are to take their arms
into their tents with them; and an officer of a company is to see at
retreat beating that the men fix on their thumb stalls. [559]

   *Lacock writes: "Notice the words "from the camp." The preceding stop
was then a bivouac, not a camp. The camp referred to was the encampment one
mile on the east side of the Youghiogheny, at Stewart's Crossing. This day's march
would be about one mile, and the place of encampment Jacob's Cabin. The two
halting places were evidently both on the east side of Jacob's Creek. What is*

commonly known as the Great Swamp Camp was only the bivouac to which reference has been made."

Wallace writes: No. 15, July 2: Jacobs Cabbins (Jacob Cabin). Lacock was wrong in supposing that from the camp at the swamp the army marched only one mile to Jacobs Cabin, which he took to be on the south side of Jacobs Creek. Captain Orme, Cholmley's batman, and the anonymous British officer agree the Jacobs Cabin was about six miles from the preceding camp (Green Lick Run). Gist puts the distance at five miles. It (the cabin) was on a gentle ridge just east of what was once Jacobs Swamp (since drained) and on or near a still passable road about two and a quarter miles north of the head of Eagle Street in Mount Pleasant. In other words, Jacobs Cabin was five and a half miles, by the Braddock Road, from the crossing of Green Lick Run."

Sparks writes: "They next advanced to Salt Lick Creek, now called Jacob's Creek, where a council of war was held on the 3d of July to consider a suggestion of Sir John St. Clair that Colonel Dunbar's detachment should be ordered to join the main body. This proposal was rejected on the ground that Dunbar could not join them in less than thirteen days; that this would cause such a consumption of provisions as to render it necessary to bring forward another convoy from Fort Cumberland".

The 2d.   **(Br. Officer 1)**
     We marched early about 3 & reached 6 Miles to a place called Jacobs Cabin; our course still to ye Northward. [560]

NAME OF THE ENCAMPMENT   **(Gordon)**
     From Terrapin Camp to Jacob's Cabin-Dist.5 Miles
WORK DONE TO THE ROAD
     bridging a swamp, digging a bank,cuting a great deal of old Timber
QUALITY OF THE ROAD
     in general good
QUALTY OF THE CAMP
     open, dry, good feeding, fine water [561]

PENNSYLVANIA-BETWEEN GT CROSSINGS & GT MEADOWS
July 2, Wednesday.   **(Washington)**
Dear Brother: (John Augustine Washington)
     We are advanced almost as far as the Great Meadows and I shall set out tomorrow for my own Corps. [562]

Wedensday July the 2d. **(batman)**

We marched about 6 Miles in a pleasent Cuntry and Came to our ground in time. We Begin to be scarce in Provisions that we only Received three Quarters of a Pound of Flower and half a pd of Bacon Each day pr man, the Other Provisions being So far behind and the wagons so loaded and wanting Horses. They (the horses) dye so fast that when they march they Cannot draw a Bove half of the wagons so when they Come to their ground they are oblig'd to send the Horses Back for the Remainder of the Wagons which delays them so that they Cannot Over take us.[563]

July 3 (Thursday)

PENNSYLVANIA-SALT LICK CAMP **(Halkett/Disney)**

Camp at the Deers lick July the 3rd: 1755
The Parole is Cambridge
Field Officer for to Morrow Major Sparks
For the Genls: Guard to morrow the 48th Regt.

The Commanding Officers of Companys to Revew their Mens Arms this Evening at retreat beating And to see they Are Clean & put in the best Order posable to Morrow Morning. At Assembly Beating all the Troops are to Load their peices. The Centrys from the Advance picquets Are to be doubled Not by An Additional number of Centrys but by planting two Centrys at each post. The Officers upon the Advance picquets during the Night time to have half their picquets Constanly Under Arms with fixt Bayonets And Releive Them every two hours. The half that is releivd may lay down by their Arms, but Are not to be sufferd to quit their picquets. The Capts of the Picquets to lye out At Nights, And when they Are not going their Visiting Rounds, they are to be found At the head of the Center Picquet of that Flank which: they Are Appointd: to Visit. [564]

July 3rd. **(Orme)**

The swamp being repaired, we marched about six miles to the Salt Lick Creek (Jacob's Creek). Sr John St Clair proposed to the General to halt at this Camp, and to send back all our horses to bring up Colonel Dunbar's detachment.

The General upon this called a council of war consisting of
Colonel Sr Peter Halket,
Lieut. Colonel Gage,

Major Sparks,

Lieu^t. Colonel Burton,

Major Sr John St Clair, D.Q.G.,

And informed them of the proposition made to him by Sr John, and desired their opinions thereof. Then the following circumstances were considered:

That the most advanced part of Colonel Dunbar's detachment was then at Squawse fort, and the other part a day's march in the rear, from which place with our light detachment we had been eleven days. And tho' we had met with some delays while the roads were making, yet, when the badness of them was considered, and the number of carriages Colonel Dunbar had with him, it was judged he could not perform the march in less time:

That the horses could not join him in less than two days:

That no advantage seemed to accrue from this junction, as the whole, afterwards, could not move togeather:

That Colonel Dunbar was unable to spare many men:

That, besides, he would be more liable to be attacked than at his present distance;

That the horses through their weak situation were not judged capable of performing it:

That by the loss of so many days the provision brought with us from Fort Cumberland would have been so near expended, as to have laid us under the necessity of bringing up a convoy, had we met with any opposition at the fort:

That by these delays the French would have time to receive their reinforcements and provisions, and to entrench themselves, or strengthen the fort, or to avail themselves of the strongest passes to interrupt our march: That it was conjectured they had not many Indians or great strength at the fort, as they had already permitted us to make many passes which might have been defended by a very few men:

Upon these considerations, the council were unamimously of opinion not to halt there for Colonel Dunbar, but to proceed the morning.

The General sent for the Indian manager, and ordered him to endeavor to prevail with the Indians to go towards the fort for intelligence, which the General had often assayed, but could never prevail upon them since the camp at the great Meadows. They now

320

likewise refused, notwithstanding the presents and promises which he constantly made them.

ORDERS AT SALT LICK CAMP.

The commanding officers of companies are to view their men's arms this evening before retreat beating, and to see them put in the best order.

At the beating of the assembly to-morrow, all the troops are to load with fresh cartridges. The centinels upon the advanced pickets for the future to be doubled at night, by placing two sentinels at every post.

The officers upon the advanced pickets during the night time are to have half their men constantly under arms with fixed bayonets and to relieve them every two hours; and the half that is relieved may lye down by their arms, but are not to be suffered to quit their pickets.

When the captains of the pickets are not going their rounds, they are to remain at the head of the center picket of that flank which they are appointed to visit.

Whenever any advanced centinel fires his piece in the night, the captain of the picket of that flank from which the shot is fired is immediately to go a visiting round to that part of the picket, and to send word to the field officer of the occasion of the shot being fired. [565]

Lacock writes: "Extending a mile westward from the intersection of the Mount Pleasant, Hempfield and East Hempfield township lines is a great swamp of several hundred acres, which the road skirts to the eastward to the Edwin S. Stoner farm near Belson's Run (a tributary of Sewickley Creek). According to local tradition, this farm is the site of the Salt Lick Camp, a view in support of which there is much to be said.

Wallace writes: "No. 16, July 3: Lick Camp (Salt Lick Camp). Where was this salt lick? Christopher Gist said it was four miles from "Jacobs Cabbins". What used to be called "Goudy's Fording" of Sewickley Creek (at Hunkers, about a mile southwest of New Stanton) is exactly four miles from the cabin by way of the Braddock Road. On Sewickley Creek, about half a mile beyond that crossing, there was formerly a salt mine. No doubt, Lick Camp was a little west of Goudy's Fording and on the edge of the salt swamp of which these vestiges remain."

Atkinson writes: "On the 3d of July a council of war was held at Jacob's Creek, to consider the propriety of bringing foward Col. Dunbar with the reserve...the measure was rejected on sufficient grounds.

NAME OF THE ENCAMPMENT   (Gordon)
From Jacob's Cabbin to Salt Lick-Dist. 4 Miles

WORK DONE TO THE ROAD
   several Banks dugg, cuting and bridging
QUALITY OF THE ROAD
   in general good
QUALITY OF THE CAMP
   secure, dry, very good feeding, tolerable water [566]

The 3d.   **(Br. Officer 1)**

We marched at 4, & got to Lick Creek, the ground in some parts a little uneven, but mostly very good. This Creek takes its Name from a lick being there, where Deer, Buffaloes & Bears come to lick ye salt out of ye Swamp; this days march was about 5 mile & to ye Westward of the North. [567]

Thursday July the 3d.   **(batman)**

We marched about five miles, very good Roads But hilly. [568]

PENNSYLVANIA-PHILADELPHIA   **(Pennsylvania Gazette)**

General Braddock, with the Army under his command, was at a place called Bear Camp, near Great Meadows on the Twenty First ult.

Extract of a letter from Winchester, dated June 26. "This morning arrived here from Pattison's Creek, on his way to the Honorable Thomas Lord Fairfax, Abraham Johnson, who informed that the Indians had killed and wounded several people on said creek, and that many were missing. It is said Eleven are murder'd and that a number of the inhabitants are now coming down here. The number of Indians is not known, but they are still about the creek.

Another letter from Carlisle, dated June 29, mentions the murder of one Williams, his wife, and grandson, a few days before, on the North Branch of Potowmack, about 12 miles above the mouth of Wills's Creek, by a parcel of Indians; one of which being killed, proved to be an Indian who had lately been at our camp as a Friend, and was well treated there.

We hear that reinforcement of 150 men are come back to the Garrison at Fort Cumberland from the Army.

Since our last, several of the waggoners, who went with Forage etc, to the camp at Wills's Creek, have return'd to this city, all well. [569]

MASSACHUSETTS-BOSTON (Maryland Gazette)
June 12.

AND WHEREAS the General Court of this Province have voted, That a Bounty or Encouragement be granted and allowed to be paid out of the Public-Treasury to the marching Army that shall be employed for the Defense of the Eastern and Western Frontiers from the Twenty-fifth of this Month of June until the Twenty-fifth of November next;

I have though fit to publish the same; and I do hereby promise, that there shall be paid out of the Province-Treasury to all and any of the said Forces, over and above their Bounty upon Enlistment, their Wages and Subsistence, the Premiums of Bounties following, viz.

For every Male Indian Prisoner above the Age of Twelve Years, that shall be taken and brought to Boston, Fifty Pounds.

For every Male Indian Scalp, brought in as Evidence of their being killed, Forth Pounds.

For every Female Indian Prisoner, taken and brought in as aforesaid, and for every Male Indian Prisoner under the Age of Twelve Years, taken and brought in as aforesaid, Twenty-five Pounds.

For every Scalp of such Female Indian or Male Indian under Twelve Years of Age, brought as Evidence of their being killed, as aforesaid, Twenty Pounds,

Given under my hand at Boston, in the Province aforesaid, this Twelfth Day of June, 1755, and in the Twenty-eighth year of the Reign of our Sovereign Lord GEORGE the Second, by the Grace of God, of Great-Britain, France, and Ireland, KING, Defender of the Faith, &c. By his Excellency's Command,

J. Willard, Secr'y   W. Shirley

GOD save the KING [570]

MARYLAND-ANNAPOLIS (Maryland Gazette)

On Saturday last, his Excellency our Governor sent down the following message, viz.

Gentlemen of the Lower House of Assembly,

I have just received Letters from Colonel Innes at Fort Cumberland, and from the Back inhabitants of Frederick County, advising me, the a party of French Indians, last Monday Morning, fell on the Inhabitants of this Province, and killed two Men and one Woman (who have been since found dead); eight other Persons they have taken Prisoners and carried off. The names of the persons who were murdered and left, are John Williams, his Wide and Grandson;; and with their Bodies was also found that of a French Indian. "The Persons carried off, are Richard Williams (a Son of John who was murdered), with two Children, one Dawson's Wife, and four Children. Richard Williams's wife, and two Brothers of the young Man that is killed, have made their Escape. This Accident, I find, has so terrified the distant Inhabitants, that many of them are retiring and forsaking their Plantations. Another Letter from Winchester in Virginia informs me, that a Party of Indians have also attacked the Back Inhabitants of the Province, of whom they have killed eleven, and carried away many captives.

Apprehending the French would proceed in this Manner, as soon as General Braddock and the Troops under his Command, should have passed the Mountains, and being confirmed in my opinion by an intimation in the General's Letter, I issued a Proclamation near a Month since, cautioning the distant and outer Inhabitants of this Province, to be on their Guard, and unite for their common Defense and safety at the same Time, I sent peremptory Orders and Instructions to the Officers of the Militia of Frederick County, frequently to muster and discipline their several Troops and companies once a Fortnight at least; and in case of an Alarm, that the Enemy was approaching, or had fallen on the Inhabitants, to march out and act either offensively or defensively, and use all Means to protect and defend the Inhabitants from the Devastations of the French, or their Indians. [571]

New England as Nichols suggests had been fighting Indians long before the southern colonies had to consider it - this news item reflects Massachusetts realistic response to a life or death matter. Nichols further suggests that Braddock was sent to Virginia as the New Englanders would fight the French and Indians on their own.

PENNSYLVANIA-PHILADELPHIA   (Maryland Gazette)
June 20.

Sunday last an Express arrive here from Wills's Creek, who brought Advice, that General Braddock, with the last Division of the Forces, march'd on Tuesday, the Tenth Instant, for the Little Meadows, where he will be join'd by the rest of the Army, and then proceed to the Ohio: and that he had left Colonel Innes Governor of

Forth Cumberland, with a sufficient Garrison for the Defense of it, and the Magazine of Provisions, Forage and Stores, that are left there.

We hear that several Bodies of French Troops have lately been seen passing in Battoes on Lake Ontario, in their Way, as is supposed , to the Ohio.
June 26.

From Fort Cumberland there is advice, that on the 15th instant 150 Men march's from thence, to protect the Workmen, that are cutting a Road from the back Parts of this Province towards the Ohio, from the French or their Indians: That an Indian Man and Woman had lately come there from Fort Du Quesne, and positively say, that there are not above 200 Men, French and Indians, in that Fort; and that a Party of the Indians, some French, were to set out soon, in order to harass any Stragglers from our Army on their March. [572]

July 4 (Friday)

PENNSYLVANIA-THICKETTY RUN CAMP   (Halkett/Disney)
Camp at The Thickett Run July ye 4th: 1755
The Parole is Darlington
Field Officer for to Morrow Lt Col Burton
For the Genls: Guard to Morrow the 44th

When Any Advance Centrys fires his piece in the Night time the Capt of the picquet for that flank from which the Shot is fired is immediatley to go a Visiting Round to that part of the picquet And to send word to the field Officer the Reason of the Shots being fired. The Drumrs: of the Advance party to beat the Pionners March instead of the Genl. The Detacht of 100 men from the Two Regts: that Joind the Advanced party to be Releived this Evening. Field Officer for this Detacht: Lieut Col Gage. The Troops to Halt to Morrow. [573]

Lacock writes: "After crossing Sewickley Creek the road veers away northwest to join the Sewickley and Hampfield township lines to the farm of D.F. Knappenberger, which offers all the requirements favorable for a camp, and is probably the place of the sixteenth encampment, Thicketty Run."

Wallace writes: "No 17, July 4 and 5: Camp three miles from Lick (Thicketty Run Camp). Gist and Lacock agree that this camp was beside a small run a mile southeast of Madison. The modern road crosses it at the approximate site of the camp."

Sparks writes: "On the 4th the army again marched and advanced to Turtle Creek, about twelve miles from its mouth, where they arrived on the 7th inst."

Atkinson writes: "From the crossing of Jacob's Creek , which was at the point where Welchhanse's Mill now stands, about 1 1/2 miles below Mount Pleasant, the route stretched off to the north, crossing the Mount pleasant turnpike near the village of the same name, and thence by a more westerly course, passing the Great Sewickley near Painter's Salt Works, thence south and west of the Post Office of Madison and Jacksonville, it reached the Brush Fork of Turtle Creek."

NAME OF THE ENCAMPMENT   **(Gordon)**
  From Salt Lick to Hillside (Thicketty)-Dist. 3 Miles
WORK DONE TO THE ROAD
  some bridging and cuting, a little digging
QUALITY OF THE ROAD
  in general good with a few hard pinches
QUALITY OF THE CAMP
  open, dry, bad feeding, water indiferent
Days halted 1 [574]

July 4th.   **(Orme)**
  We marched about six miles to Thicketty-run; the country was now less mountainous and rocky, and the woods rather more open, consisting chiefly of white oak.
  From this place two of our Indians were prevailed upon to go for intelligence towards the French fort; and also (unknown to them), Gist, the General's guide. [575]

The 4th.   **(Br. Officer 1)**
  We marched at three & got about 6 Mile. This day two of our Indians went to reconnoitre the french Fort. [576]

Fryday July the 4th.   **(batman)**
  We Marched a Bout 6 miles and Came within 16 miles of Fort De Cain.

MARYLAND-FORT CUMBERLAND
July the 4   **(Browne)**
  All greatly alarm'd with the Indians scalping several Families within 10 Miles of us; one poor boy brought in with his Scalp off, he liv'd 4

Days. Several Familys left thier Homes and came to the Fort for Protection.[577]

July 5 (Saturday)

PENNSYLVANIA-MONACATUCA CAMP   **(Halkett/Disney)**

Camp Near Thickett Run July ye:5th: 1755

The Parole is Rumford

Field Officer for to Morrow Major Sparke

For the Genls: Guard the 48th Regt:

    The Genl to beat to Morrow as six oClock. Monacatuthaws son will be interred this Evening.[578]

PENNSYLVANIA-ALLEGHENY MOUNTAINS

5th July, 1755

Honored Sir: Governor Morris   **(Burd)**

    We have now got this far with the road, but at present are under a very great dilemma, the cause of which is as follows: We had thought it necessary to make use of an empty house, 47 miles from Anthony Thompson's, for a store-house for our provisions, and we sent a guard of seven men, armed, to said store house. They immediatley fortified the house, and had received some of our provisions. We were like to be short of meat. etc., and hearing that there were wagones, and supposing cattle, upon the road, one Mr. Robert McCay, who had the command of the store and the people there, sent a boy called James Smith, about sixteen years of age, down the road to hurry up the cattle and wagons. Said Smith meeting a man sent up by Mr. Adam Hoops, at Ray's Town, received information that the wagons were just at hand, upon which the boy returned with Mr. Hoops' man hither, the wagons at this time being behind. The wagons arrived at the store the 3d curr't, at noon. Inquiry was made of the wagoners where Mr. Hoop's man and the boy were, and they replied that they had not seen them; upon which they went out to search for them. They first found the boy's hat, and then Mr. Hoop's man's (named Arnold Vigouous) gun, and about ten perches from thence, Arnold lying dead, being shot through with two bullets and scalped. Mr. McCay immediately dispatched an express to me to the camp, about twelve miles from the store. I went down with a party of twelve men of Captain Hogg's company, and saw the corpse and got it buried, but could find nothing of the boy, only his horse we have got. That night, being the evening of the 3d curr't, we mounted guard at the store. About 9 o'clock we were attacked by Indians; their number we could not know. Two of our sentinels fired at two to the Indians which they saw, and I myself pursued singly the said two Indians, it being dark amonst the trees, could not see them nor overtake them, but heard them plainly about fifteen yards before me. The next day, being the 4th curr't, I returned to our camp, and was under a necessity to call the people togeather, and make use of all the arguements I could to unduce them to continue in the service until we had finished. But, unfortunately, we had an alarm last night. One of the sentinels on the picket guard challenged three times and fire his musket, which has struck a great terror into the laborers; thirty of them are gone home this morning, and the remainder are very much dissatisfied, as they have no arms to keep them much longer. However, the Governor may depend upon my utmost endavours to carry out the work, and that I won't leave my duty while I have ten men to work, or am recalled by your Honor.

We are obliged to send off this morning a guard of twelve men and a serjeant of Captain Hogg's Company for a covering party for our returning wagons, and to bring up out horses but with a guard. Our roads are all way laid in order to cut off our provisins and any straggling men they can. Mr. William Smith is likewise under a necessity to go home this morning, as the boy that is taken prisoner (as we suppose) is his brother-in-law. We have now about three days' provisions.

Please to excuse unconnections.

I am, respectfull, your honor's most obed't, h'ble. servant. [579]

The 5th.   **(Br. Officer 1)**
We remained in Camp except a reconnoitering party with Sir John St. Clair & an Engineer who returned ye same Evening. This day a Party came in from Coll: Dunbar with 100 Oxen & a large quantity of flour, a very seasonable supply, (we) having lived on salt provisions the whole time. [580]

Satterday July the 5th.   **(batman)**
We halted and Recd provision and a Fresh Supply of Bullocks from Colonel Dunbar. [581]

July 6 (Sunday)

PENNSYLVANIA-MONACATUCA CAMP

July the 6th: 1755 (Halkett/Disney)

The Parole is Colchester

Filed Officer for to Morrow Lt Col: Gage

    The Field Officer and the Detacht: of 100 Men that Joind the Advance party at the Camp Near the Thickett Run to be Relieved This Evening. Field Offr Lt Col: Burton. The Officers & men of the two Regts: that came up with Capt: Stephens to Join their respective Corps to Morrow Morning. At Genl Beating Capt Stephens Lieut Brenns & Lieut Gray with two Serjts & fifty Rank & file of the Detacht that Came from Col Dunbars to Join Lieut Col Burton to Morrow at 4 oClock. The Genl to beat to Morrow Morning at 5 oClock. A Detacht of 1 Sub: & Rear Guard Consisting of Capt 1 Subs: 2 Serjts & 50 R & File. [582]

(Orme)

    The Indians returned on the 6th, and brought in a French officer's scalp, who was shooting within half a mile of the fort. They informed the General that they saw very few men there, or tracks; nor any additional works. That no pass was possest by them between us and the fort, and that they believed very few men were out upon observation. They saw some boats under the fort, and one with a white flag coming down the Ohio.

    Gist returned a little after the same day, whose account corresponded with their's, except he saw smoke in a valley between our camp and Du Quesne. He had concealed himself with an intent of getting close under the fort in the night, but was discovered and pursued by two Indians, who had very near taken him.

    At this camp the provisions from Colonel Dunbar with a detachment of a Captain and one hundred men joined us, and we halted here one day.

    On the 6th July we marched about six miles to Monakatuca Camp, which was called so from an unhappy accident that happened upon the march.

    Three or four people loitering in the rear of the Grenadiers were killed by a party of Indians and scalped. Upon hearing the firing, the General sent back the Grenadier company, on whose arrival the Indans fled. They were discovered again a little after by our Indians in the front, who were going to fire upon them, but were prevented by some fired upon them and killed Monakatuca's son, notwithstanding they made the agreed countersign, which was holding up a bough and grounding their arms. When we came to our ground, the General sent for the father and the other Indians, condoled with and made them the usual presents, and desired the officers to attend the funeral; and a gave an order to fire over the body.

This behavoir of the General was so agreeable to the Indians, that they afterwards were more attached to us, quite contrary to our expectations.

The line of carrying horses extending very often a prodigious length, it was almost impossible to secure them from insults, tho' they had yet marched without any interruption, every Bat-man having been ordered to carry his firelock, and small parties having kept constantly upon the flanks. The disposition of march for these horses had varied almost every day, according to the nature of the country; but the most common was to let them remain upon the ground an hour after the march of the line, under the guard of a Captain and one hundred men: by which means there was no confusion in leaving the ground, and the horses were much eased. They were now order'd, when the woods would permit, to march upon the flanks between the subalterns' picket and the line; but whenever the country was close or rocky, they were then to fall in the rear, and a strong guard marched thither for their security, which was directed to advance or fall back in proportion to the length of the line of carrying horses, taking particular care always to have parties on the flanks.

ORDERS AT MONAKATUCA CAMP

If it should be ordered to advance the van or send back the rear guard, the advanced parties detached from them are to remain at their posts, facing outward.

Whenever there is a general halt, half of each of the subalterns' advanced parties are to remain under arms with fixed bayonets, facing outwards, and the other half may sit down by their arms. [583]

Nichols writes: "The Frenchman killed by Braddock's Indians was Pierre Simard, age 23".

Wallace writes: "No. 18, July 6: Monacatootha Camp (Monacatuca Camp). This camp, named for the unhappy accident by which Monadatooths's (Scaroyady's) son lost his life, was, according to local tradition, beside a stream in a wide, comfortable valley where the late William B. Howell's house fronts a road that undoubtedly Braddock's. But, if Gist correctly measured the distance from the *preceding camp, Monacatootha Camp was a mile and a half beyond the Howell house. Orme, the British officer, and the batman agree with Gist that the distance between the two camps was "about 6 miles". A march of six miles over these pleasant hills from Thicketty Run by the almost straight north-northwest course of the Braddock Road would bring the army to a spot two miles Southwest of Irwin, and two miles north of Rillton. The site here proposed for Monacatootha Camp not only fits the recorded mileage's up to that point, but also agrees with (as the Howell house site does not) the new evidence for the recorded distance - two miles - between Monacatootha Camp and the one following it."*

(Letter of Attorney, Harrisburg, PA.)

This is to certify that Mr. Christopher Gist executed the Office of head Guide with the great Sobriety Prudence & Fidelity to which Office he was appointed by Genl Braddock the 27th of May 1755. And I do farther certify that he was sent to bring intelligence from the French Fort which Service he performed with great Risk being for a long time pursued. Upon his return the Genl being very well satisfied with his behavior ordered Mr. Shirley the Secretary to pay him his 50 thirty six Shilling Pieces.[584]

NAME OF THE ENCAMPMENT   **(Gordon)**
From Hillside (Thicketty) to Ridge Camp-Dist. 6 Miles 6(aka Monakatuca Camp)
WORK DONE TO THE ROAD
cuting through four thickets,and digging three banks
QUALITY OF THE ROAD
in general good, turned off the Indian path to avoid a long run
QUALITY OF THE CAMP
open, dry, bad feeding, water at a distance [585]

The 6th.   **(Br. Officer 1)**
We marched very early. About ten a clock ye two Indians who went to reconnoitre returned with a french scalp. They told us they saw some Canoes coming down the Monongahela with Men & provisions to ye Fort which we had reason afterwards to be sorry for; they said the french had made no alterations in their Fort, except their changing their flag from one Bastion to another, & yt: (that) they had no advanced post whatever. After we had marched about 6 miles we were allarmed by some Indians who fired on our right flank. This put ye Men in a good deal of confusion. However we returned ye fire very briskly & obliged them to retire; there was no damage done in either side

except at ye begining of ye fire, our own Indians interfering; unluckily one of them was Shott by our own people, it was Monacatothe's Son who had brought in ye scalp ye same Morning. When we halted we had him buried with all ye decency in our power, which ye rest of ye Indians seem much pleased with; Old Manacatothe his Father, who undoubtedly is a very good Man was hardly able to support his loss; he said had he been killed by the french it would have been trifling, but what he regretted most was his being killed by our own people. We sent a party imediately to pursue the Indians & traced blood a considerable way; they found two Spears, & some other little things belonging to ye Tawwaws (Ottawas); we went on ye rest of ye Day without opposition & halted after a March of ten Miles. [586]

Sunday July the 6th.   (batman)

We marched in the morning. Our Indiens Came up with a French man in a Cannow. They waited till he came on Shore and then shot him and Scalped him, but they was in great hast, being far from our Army and they not knowing but their might be a large body of the Enimy Nigh (at) hand made them in hast in taking of(f) his Scalp so that they skined it the second when they Came to our Army before they shewed it to the genll. A Bout Eleven in the Morning the French Indiens Attacked our Baggage on the March in the Rear and Scalped a Soldier and a woman. The woman Belonged to the genll('s) Cows. They wounded one man in the Shouldear and Began Scalp a Nother Soldier but had not got it of(f) before our Rear guard Came to his Relief. About one in the After Known (afternoon) we Start(l)ed a Parcel of the French Indiens. Our Soldiers Immediately Began to fire after them. Our Indiens Comming to our Asistance, our men taking them to be a Nother party of the French Indiens began to fire upon (them) Immediately. Altho they grounded their Arms and Ran up to them According to Orders, they (the soldiers) killed One of our Own Indiens and wounded two. The Indien that was Shot was our Kings Son. He was put in the Wagons and Carried to the Other ground and there he was Buried and the Soldiers fired Over him, the same as tho he was a Cristian. This day we marched about 6 miles. [587]

PENNSYLVANIA-FORT DUQUESNE   (Roucher)
July 6th 1755

The Hurons who had been out on the discovery, brought Advice that the English were within 8 leagues marching brisklly with their Artillery.

The Chevalier de la Parade an officer; was sent with some french and Indians to be certain of the discovery the Hurons had made; but his Guide (who was an Iroquois of the five Nations settled on the River Ohio) [not wishing] to conduct him above 3 or 4 leagues, he as obliged to return

The [Ottawas]and Missillimakinaks, from the falls, who should have gone in a party that day against the English; were detained by [the] other Nations to hold a Conference with Monr; Contrecoeur; at which it was [held] that all the Indians Nations should march togeather; and the Expeddition was defered till next day.

Messr: de Contrecoeur & Beaujeu sent Monsr: De la Parade & Mr: Bailleul with a party of french and Indians on the discovery by two different Routes.

We understood at the Return of these Gentlemen, and that of Mr. Regoville (out ever since the 28th; of last month with 120 Indians; Hurons and of the Nations from the falls (Detroit), & 10 french men. in a party against the english) that they were but 8 Leagues distant that they marched in (a) body of 3000 Men with a strong train of Artillery.

Mr. Roctoyade, who had been out with a party of Indians & french on the same design, informed us that his party had fixed on the Enemy and had kill'd some of them; but the Indians (according to their cruel Custom) had not been able to scalp them; the English always keeping in good order.

After all these discoveries which confirm'd one another, together with the Certainty Mr. Contrecoeur had of the Approach of the English with a train of Artillery which seemed considerable, it was resolv'd we should the next day march out to meet them with all the Indians, only reserving some french for the Defense of the Fort. [588]

(Godefroy)

The 6th (of July), we learned from an Indian of the Five Nations that the English were on the bank of the Monongahela River. The chevalier de La Perade was detached to reconnoiter. [589]

Charles Hamilton writes in <u>Braddock's Defeat:</u> *"The king, or chief, was a noted Oneida, known in Virginia as Monacatootha and in Pennsylvania as Skirooniatta. He remained friendly with the English during his life, claiming to have participated in thirty-one combats. Tattooed on his chest was a tomahawk and on each cheek a bow and arrow. In May, 1755, he made an eloquent speech to the Indians at Fort Cumberland, urging them to join Braddock's expedition."*

July 7 (Monday)
PENNSYLVANIA-CAMP NR STEWARTSVILLE **(Halkett/Disney)**
Camp on The East side of Turtle Creek
July y^e: 7th: 1755
The Parole is Dublin
Field Officer for to Morrow Major Sparke
For the Genls: Guard the 48th: Regt.

1 Serjt 1 corpl & 10 men to be Added to the rear Guard Immediately. The Batt Horses to March betwixt the line of March & picquets of the Left Flank And when the wood is so thick that they Cannot proceed they Are to fall into the rear and As soon As the wood oppens the(y) Are Again to March forwards. If upon a march it should be found proper to Advance the line the Advance partys Are to remain at their proper Posts facing Outwards. Upon the march when the Troops halt half of each advance party remain Under Arms with fixt Bayonets facing outwards And the other half may Sitt down. The Genl to beat to Morrow Morning at 5 oClock. A Detacht of 1 Sub; & 20 Grands: from each Regt (and) one Capt One Sub: & 20 Rank & File from the Line to parade at 1 oClock in the Morning at the RearGun.[590]

Lacock writes: "In Circleville the road seems to pass east of Long Run Church, and a few rods northwest of it crosses the Pittsburgh and Philadelphia turnpike. Here, in the neighborhood of Circleville and Stewartville, the army encamped again.

At this point General Braddock, after causing an examination of the country between the camp and Fort Duquesne to be made, abandoned his design of approaching the fort by the ridge route, being deterred by the deep and rugged ravines of the streams and by the steep and almost perpendicular precipices to the eastward of Circleville and Stewartsville."

Wallace writes: "No. 19, July 7: Blunder Camp (Camp near Stewartsville). Of all the camps, this one raises the most questions. Where was it? What was Braddock trying to do here? What was the blunder? How did he retrieve it? Lacock avoided committing himself to any precise location; he said only that it was "in the neighborhood of Circleville and Stewartsville". It is now possible with the new evidence to place the site more confidently, and in doing so to explain the blunder that caused Christopher Gist to give the camp its intriguing name.

Having decided to give up the ridge route (to Fort Duquesne) and to avoid the dangerous narrows of Turtle Creek as well as those on the Monongahela, Braddock and his army retraced their steps a little and camped that night, July 7, at a spot which the British officer said was within six hundred yards of where the had first halted. Because of the time lost, they advanced, according to Gist, only two miles that day. Gist's figure is corroborated by the batman, who wrote, we marched about two Miles and Incamped Near Turtels Creek.

Next morning they went down the west side of the ridge (taking elaborate precautions to avoid ambush in the valley of Long Run) and camped with "a Small Mile" of the Monongahela at what it now McKeesport."

Sparks writes: " I suppose this to have been the eastern branch or what is now called Rush Creek, and that the place at which they encamped was a short distance northerly from the present village of Stewartsville. It was General Braddocks intention to cross Turtle Creek, and approach Fort Duquesne on the other side; but the banks were to precipitous, and presented such obstacles to crossing with his artillery and heavy baggage that he hesitated and Sir John St.Clair went out with a party to reconnoiter. On his return, before night, he reported that he had found the ridge which led to Fort Duquesne but that considerable work would be necessary to prepare a road for crossing Turtle Creek.

Atkinson writes: "It must strike those who examine the map that the route, for some distance, in the rear and ahead of Mount Pleasant, is out of the proper direction for Fort Duquesne, and according we find on the 7th of July, Gen. Braddock in doubt as to his proper way of proceeding. The crossing of Brush Creek, which he had now reached, appeared to be attended with so much hazard that parties were sent to reconnoitre, some of whom advanced so far as to kill a French officer within half a mile of Fort Duquesne. Their examination induced a great divergence to the left, and availing himself to valley of Long Run, which he turned into, as is supposed, at Stewartsville, passing by the place now known as Samson's Mill, the army made one of the best marches of the campaign and halted for the night at a favorable depression between and stream and Crooked Run and about two miles from the Monongahela. At this spot, about four miles from the battle ground, which is yet well known as Braddock's Spring, he was joined by Washington on the morning of the 9th of July."

(Orme)

On the 7th July we marched from hence, and quitting the Indian path, endeavored to pass the Turtle Creek about 12 miles from the mouth, to avoid the dangerous pass of the narrows. We were led to a precipice which it was impossible to descend. The General ordered Sr John St Clair to take a captain and one hundred men, with the Indian, guides, and some light horse, to reconnoitre very well the country. In about two hours he returned and informed the General that he had found the ridge which led the whole way to fort Du Quesne, and avoided the narrows and Frazier's, but that some work which was to be done would make it impossible to move further that day. We therefore encamped here, and marched the next morning about eight miles to camp near the Monongahela. [591]

The 7th.   **(Br. Officer 1)**
Advanced both parties. After we had marched 5 Miles along a very fine ridge, we were obliged to halt at least four hours, the Guides having lost their Way; we kept to ye right of ye Old Indian path to avoid some bad Swamps which put the Guides entirely out, however after some reconnoitering we found a tollerable good road but were obliged to halt within 600 yards of ye first halting for want of Water. Through our accounts before we came into ye country were favourable for us in regard to having it good, we found our selves much streightened for it, being obliged to go generally half a Mile or more & even then very bad. [592]

Letter V (continued)   **(Br.Officer 3)**
The General seems very anxious about marching through the Woods, and gave very particular Orders; Powder and Bullet were given out, and every Thing fit for action; two Lieutenant-Colonels were ordered to command the advanced Party. The General followed with the Gross of the two Regiments from Europe, the Americans followed, and the Rear was brought up by Captain Dumary's and another independent Company. We marched on in this Manner without being disturbed, and thought we had got over our greatest Difficulties, for we look'd upon our March through the Woods to be such: We were sure we should be much above a Match for the French, if once we got into the open Ground near the Forts, where we could use our Arms. We had a Train, and a gallant Party of Sailors for working our Guns, full sufficient to master better Works than those of the French Forts, according to the Intelligence we had of them. [593]

NAME OF THE ENCAMPMENT   **(Gordon)**
From Ridge Camp to Turtles Creek-Dist. 3 Miles
WORK DONE TO THE ROAD
cuting chiefly old timber
QUALITY OF THE ROAD
All very good

QUALITY OF THE CAMP
Strong, dry, bad feeding, bad water and scarce[594]

Munday July the 7th.   (batman)
We marched about two Miles and Incamped Near Turtals (Turtle) Creek. This day our light horse Came up with two of the French Indiens. They fired after them and they Ran away and Rose thirty more of them. They all made their Escape. [595]

MARYLAND-FORT CUMBERLAND
July the 7   (Browne)
My Brother extreemly ill, he was Blister'd. Several who call'd themselves friendly Indians came to the Fort but the Gates were ordered to be shut. They stay'd 4 Hours and then went to the Camp, and we had not a drop of Water there being no well in the Fort. [596]

(Godefroy)
The 7th, he reported that the enemy was near. That same day, a detachment was prepared to engage. [597]

(Fr. Officer A)
M. de Contrecoeur, captain of infantry, commandant of Fort Duquesne of the Belle Riviere, having been informed that the English were arming in Virginia in order to come and attack him, was told soon afterwards that they were on the march. He dispatched scouts into the countryside, who advised him faithfully of their route. The 7th of this month he was told that their army was composed of three thousand English troops and was six leagues from the fort. He used the next day to make arrangements...[598]

Nicholas writes: "The French commander at Fort Duquesne did the only possible thing under the circumstances (relentless advance of the British Army), but we have noted how Braddock's vigilance foiled the small parties sent out by Contrecoeur and reduced them in their impotence to the inscription of pornographic insults on trees and the taking of an occasional stragglers scalp...Ensign Godedroy, a member of the Duquesne garrison, noted in his journal the departure of some of these raiding parties: Cadet Normanville and a large party of French and Indians set out for Braddock's army on June 8; another group compsed of seven Frenchmen and 130 Indians went out on the eighteenth under Cadet Niversville. On June 26 and 30 two small parties left Fort Duquesne to scout the British and to pick off stragglers. Their combined efforts produced one scalp. A detachment of 33 Indians tried its luck on July 5 but returned empty handed. That same day a young Canadian militiaman was killed and scalped by Braddock's Indians within one half mile of Fort Duquesne (the victim was Pierre

337

Simard aged 23-doubtless this lad was the "officer" whose scalp was brought to Braddock on July 6 by two Aughwick Indians) The French Indians agreed to march against the enemy on the seventh. That day Peyrode reported that the British were near, and on the eighth, Cadet Normanville located their camp on the Monongahela. Ensign Bailleul also conducted a reconnaissance that day".

July 8 (Tuesday)

PENNSYLVANIA-MONONGAHELA CAMP   **(Halkett/Disney)**
Camp Near Monagahelia July the 8th; 1755
The parole is Burntwood
Field Officer for to Morrow Lt Col: Burton
For the Genls Guard to Morrow the 44th

  The field Officer and Detacht. of 100 men that Joind the Advance party at Monacutha's Camp to be Releivd this Evening And to parade at the Front Gun. Field Officer for the Detacht Lieut Coll Gage; The Troops to receive Immedy; Two days Meat & Two days flower which compleats them with provisions to the Tenth Inclucive. All the men but those who mount the picquet this Night to draw their peices and to Load with frish Cartridges to morrow at Genl Beating And the Commandg: Officers will be Answerable to the Genl for any firing without Applycation. The Company of Grends; of the 44th & 48th Regts: to parade to Morrow Morning At Two Oclock at the head of their Respective collours And to March from thence to the Advance party And there put themselves under the Command of Lt Col Gage. The Men Are to be Compleated with 24 Rounds of powder & ball And Are to take their napsacks & Haversacks but Are to leave their Tents behind. The Grends: to March Compleat with Offrs & 70 Rank & File. The Officers not to take their Bagage but to leave it in Charge with the Qr Master of their respective Regts. The Genl to beat to Morrow Morning at 4 oClock the Assembly at 5 And the Troops to March Immediatley after. [599]

  Lacock writes: "From half a mile east of the boundary line between Allegheny and Westmoreland counties the road follows naturally down the valley of Long Run at or near the present bridge to a point about two and a half miles westward, where the army encamped at a very favorable depression now known as McKeesport, two miles north of the Monongahela River and about four miles from the battlefield. A magnificent spring of water marks the site of this encampment, which was called Monongahela Camp."

Wallace writes: "Camp No. 20, July 8: Head Sugar Creek (Monongahela Camp). At two o'clock on the morning of the July 9, Lieutenant Colonel Gage advanced with between three and four hundred men to secure the fords of the Monongahela. There was no opposition. By early afternoon the whole army had made the double crossing and the men, as one them wrote, "hugg'd themselves with joy..."

Nichols writes: "Daniel Dulany, not an eyewitness, was told that when Gage's party arrived at the second ford, "They suspected the enemy had just passed it from the muddiness of the water, and of this they saw evident signs when they had passed the river in the moisture of the earth and the impression of many feet".

Sparks writes: "This (ridge) route was finally abandoned, and on the 8th the army marched eight miles and encamped not far from the Monongahela, west of the Youghiogheny and near what is called in an old map 'Sugar Run'. When Braddock reached this place it was his design to pass through the narrows, but he was informed by the guides who had been out to explore that the passage was very difficult, about two miles in length, with a river on the left and a high mountain on the right, and that much work must be done to make it passable for carriages. At the same time he was told that there two good fords across the Monongahela where the water was shallow and the banks not steep."

(Orme)

We marched the next morning about eight miles to the camp near the Monongahela.

When we arrived here, Sr John St Clair mentioned (but not to the General), the sending a detachment that night to invest the fort; but being asked whether the distance was too great to reinforce that detachment in case of an attack, and whether it would not be more advisable to make the pass of the Monongahela or the narrows, whichever was resolved upon, with our whole force, and then to send the detachment from the next camp, which would be six or seven miles from the fort, Sr John immediately acquiesced, and was of opinion that would be a much more prudent measure.

The guides were sent for, who described the Narrows to be a narrow pass of about two miles, with a river on the left and a very high mountain on the right, and that it would require much repair to make it passable by carriages. They said the Monongehela had two extreme good fords. which were very shallow, and the banks not steep. It was therefore resolved to pass this river the next morning, and Lieutenent Colonel Gage was ordered to march before break of day with the two companies of Grenadiers, one hundred and sixty rank and file of the

44th and 48th, Captain Gates's independent company, and two six-pounders, with proper guides; and he was instructed to pass the fords of the Monongehela and to take post after the second crossing, to secure the passage of that river.

S[r] John S[t] Clair was ordered to march at 4 of the clock with a detachment of two hundred and fifty men to make the roads for the artillery and baggage, which was to march with the remainder of the troops at five.

ORDERS AT THE CAMP NEAR THE MONONGAHELA

All the men are to draw and clean their pieces, and the whole are to load to-morrow on the beating of the General with fresh cartridges.

No chests or baggage are to be taken with Lieutenant Colonel Gages's party. [600]

PENNSYLVANIA-NEAR FORT DUQUESNE   (Washington)
July 8, Tuesday. Near Fort Duquesne.

The 8th of July I rejoined (in a covered wagon) the advanced Division of the Army, under the immediate command of the General [601]

NAME OF THE ENCAMPMENT   (Gordon)
From Turtles Creek to Sugar Creek-Dist. 8 Miles (aka Monongahela Camp)
WORK DONE TO THE ROAD
cuting chiefly old timber and some digging
QUALITY OF THE ROAD
4 miles very good, 2 miles through a bad defile, the rest good
QUALITY OF THE CAMP
open, dry, bad feeding, bad water and scarce [602]

PENNSYLVANIA-SUGAR CREEK or MONONGAHELA CAMP
July 8th
To: Not stated   (Gordon)

We crossed the long run which was a small rivulet that runs into the Monongahela about 12 miles from the French Fort. We were oblig'd to cross it many times, in the span of two miles, in which distance we came along a narrow valley at the widest a quarter of a mile, very much commanded on both sides sides by steep hills. In this march every proper precaution was taken to secure us, by detaching all

340

the men that could be spared from the advanced party, that day commanded by C. Burton. On our flank the General likewise ordered 350 men to take prossession of the heights on each side; and the grenadier company of Sir P. Halket Regt., the advance of the advance party, to gain the rising ground, which shut up the valley in our front. No enemy appeared and we encamped on the last mentioned rising ground which brought us within a small mile of the River Monongahela. [603]

The 8th.   **(Br. Officer 1)**

Marched very early. In this days march was a hollow Way through which we were obliged to pass, the greatest breadth for at least 3 miles was about 50 Yards, two very steep hills surrounding us; there we were obliged to reinforce our flanks, but ye fatal stroke was reserved till next day; which our Superiors thought would never happen. It may be satisfactory to be particluar in the next days account, wch. is as follows (continued). [604]

                                         (seaman)

....till the 8th of July, when he encamped within 8 miles of the French Fort, and there held a Council of War, which agreed that as they were to pass over the Mongohela river twice (this river is a ¼ mile broad, and 6 miles from the French Fort), that the Advanced party should parade at 2 o'clock to secure that pass, as on the contrary if the Enemy should have possession of it, they would not be able to get over without a great loss. They likewise agreed that the Army should march over the river in the greatest order, with their baynonets fixed, Colors flying, and Drums and Fifes beating and playing, as they supposed the Enemy would take a view of them in the crossing. [605]

Tuesday July the 8th.   **(batman)**

We marched 7 miles and as soon as we Came to our ground my Master went upon the Advance party to Cover the working party, it being Eight O Clock before we came to our Ground. [606]

MARYLAND-FORT CUMBERLAND
July the 8   **(Browne)**

My Brother still the same and maid very ill. I can get no Nurse, so that I am very much fatigued. [607]

PENNSYLVANIA-FORT DUQUESNE (Smith)

In May, 1755, the province of Pennsylvania agreed to send out three hundred men, in order to cut a wagon road from fort Loudon, to join Braddock's road, near the Turkey Foot, or three forks of Yohogania. My brother-in-law, William Smith, Esq. of Conococheague, was appointed commissioner, to have the oversight of these road-cutters...We went on with the road, without interruption, until near the Alleghany mountain; when I was sent back, in order to hurry up some provision-wagons that were on the way after us. I proceeded down the road as far as the crossings of Juniata, where, finding the wagons were coming on as fast as possible, I returned up the road again towards the Alleghany mountain in company with one Arnold Vigoras. About four or five miles above Bedford, three Indians had made a blind of bushes, stuck in the ground, as though they grew naturally, where they concealed themselves, about fifteen yards from the road. When we came opposite to them, they fired upon us at this short distance, and killed my fellow-traveller, yet their bullets did not touch me; but my horse making a violent start thew me, and the Indians immediately ran up and took me prisoner. The one that laid hold on me was a Canasatauge, the other two were Delawares...When we came to this camp, we found they had plenty of turkeys and other meat there; and though I never before eat venison without bread or salt, yet as I was hungary I ate it, relished very well. There we lay that night, and the next morning the whole of us marched on our way for fort Du Quesne. The night after we joined another camp of Indians, with nearly the same ceremony, attended with great noise, and apparent joy, among all except one. The next morning we cantoned our march, and in the afternoon we came in full view of the fort, which stood on the point (near where for Pitt now stands). We then made a halt on the bank of the Alleghany, and repeated the scalp hallo, which was answered by the firing of all the firelocks in the hands of both Indians and French who were in and about the fort, in the aforesaid manner, and also the great guns, which were followed by the continued shouts and yells of the different savage tribes who were then collected there.

As I was at this time unacquainted with this mode of firing and yelling of the savages, I concluded that there were thousands of

Indians there ready to receive General Braddock; but what added to my surprise, I saw numbers running towards me, stripped naked, excepting breech-clouts, and painted in the most hideous manner, of various colors, though the principal color was vermillion, or a bright red; yet there was annexed to this black, brown, blue, &. As they approached, they formed themselves into two long ranks, about two or three rods apart. I was told by an Indian that could speak English, that I must run betwixt these ranks, and that they would flog me all the way as I ran; and if I ran quick, it would be so much the better, as they would quit when I got to the end of the ranks. There appeared to be a general rejoicing around me, yet I could find nothing like joy in my breast; but I stared to the race with all the resolution and vigor I was capable of exerting, and found that it was as I had been told, for I was flogged the whole way. When I had got near the end of the lines, I was struck with some thing that appeared to me to be a stick, or the handle of a tomahawk, which caused me to fall to the ground. On my recovering my senses, I endeavoured to renew my race; but as I arose; some one cast sand in my eyes, which blinded me so that I could not see where to run. They continued beating me most intolerably, until I was at length insensible; but before I lost my senses, I remember my wishing them to strike the fatal blow, for I thought they intended killing me, but apprehended they were too long about it.

The first thing I remember was my being in the fort amidst the French and Indians, and a French doctor standing by me, who had opened a vein in my left arm: after which the interpreter asked me how I did; I told him I felt much pain. The doctor when washed my wounds, and the bruised places of my body, with French brandy. As I felt faint, and the brandy smelt well, I asked for some inwardly, but the doctor told me, by the interpreter, that it did not suit my case.

When they found I could speak, a number of Indians came around me, and examined me, with threats of cruel death if I did not tell the truth. The first question they asked me was how many men were there in the party that were coming from Pennsylvania to join Braddock? I told them the truth, that there were three hundred. The next question was, were they well armed? I told them they were all well armed, (meaning the arm of flesh.) for they had only about thirty guns among the whole of them; which if the Indians had known, they would certainly have hove and cut them all off; therefore, I could not in conscience let them know the defenceless situation of these road-cutters. I was then sent to the hospital, and carefully attended by the doctors, and recovered quicker than what I expected.

Some time after I was there, I was visited by the Delaware Indian already mentioned, who was at the taking of me, and could speak some English. Though he spoke but bad English, yet I found him to be a man of considerable understanding. I asked him if I had done any thing that had offended the Indians which caused them to treat me so unmercifully. He said no; it was only an old custom the Indians had, and it was like how do you do; after that, he said, I would be well used. I asked him if I should be admitted to remain with the French. He said no; and told me that, as soon as I recovered, I must not only go with the Indians, but must be made an Indian myself. I asked him what news from Braddock's army. He said the Indians spied them every day, and he showed me, by making marks on the ground with a stick, that Braddock's army was advancing in very close order, and that the Indians would surround them, take trees, and (as he expresed it) shoot um down all one pigeon. [608]

July 8th 1755   (Roucher)

All the Indian Nations were called togeather, & invited to joyne & assist the french to repulse the English who came to drive them out of that land they were then in possession of.

Mr. Beaujeu began to Warsong & all the Indian Nations Immediately joined him except the Poutiawatamis of the Narrows (Detroit), who were silent. Which occasioned all the other Nations to desire not to march till next day.

The Chawanons & Iroquois of the five Nations, who (are) all near Fort Duquesne came to wait on Mr: Contrecoeur & told him that being informed he was determined to oppose the English who was very near, they came to joyne him and assist to repulse them.

They were genteelly entertained in order to engage the other Nations, and not to spin out time, all there demands were granted; & in consequence thereof were arm'd & equipt the same day. [609]

The 8th, the Indians wished to delay. But the   (Godefroy)
prudent Normanville brothers persuaded them to
reconnoiter, and they found the enemy at six leagues distance. [610]

July 9 (Wednesday)

PENNSYLVANIA-FIELD OF BATTLE

July 9th. **(Orme)**

The whole marched agreeably to the Orders before mentioned, and about 8 in the morning the General made the first crossing of the Monongahela by passing over about one hundred and fifty men in the front, to whom followed half the carriages. Another party of one hundred and fifty men headed the second division; the horses and cattle then passed, and after all the baggage was over, the remaining troops, which till then possessed the heights, marched over in good order.

The General ordered a halt, and the whole formed in their proper line of march.

When we had moved about a mile, the General received a note from Lieutenant Colonel Gage acquainting him with his having passed the river without any interruption, and having posted himself agreeably to this orders.

When we got to the other crossing, the bank on the opposite side not being yet made passable, the artillery and baggage drew up along the beach, and halted 'till one, when the General passed the detachment of the 44th, with the picket of the right. The artillery waggons and carrying horses followed; and then the detachment of the 48th, with the left pickets, which had been posted during the halt upon the heights.

When the whole had passed, the General again halted, till they formed according the (annexed) plan.

It was now two o'clock, and the advanced party under Lieutenant Colonal Gage and the working party under Sr John St Clair were ordered to march on 'till three. No sooner were the pickets upon their respective flanks, and the word given to march, but we heard an excessive quick and heavy firing in the front. The General imagining the advanced parties were very warmly attacked, and being willing to free himself from the incumbrance of the baggage, order'd Lieutenant Colonel Burton to reinforce them with the vanguard, and the line to halt. According to this disposition, eight hundred men were detached from the line, free from all embarrassments, and four hundred were left for the defence of the Artillery and baggage, posted in such manner as to secure them from any attack or insults.

The General sent forward an Aid de Camp to bring him an account of the nature of attack, but the firing continuing, he moved forward himself, leaving Sr Peter Halket with the command of the baggage. The advanced detachments soon gave way and fell back upon Lieutenant Colonel Burton's detachment, who was forming his men to face a rising ground upon the right. The whole were now got togeather in great confusion. The colours were advanced in different places, to separate the men of the two regiments. The General ordered the officers to endeavor to form the men, and to tell them off into small divisions and to advance with them; but neither entreaties nor threats could prevail.

The advanced flank parties, which were left for the security of the baggage, all but one ran in. The baggage was then warmly attacked; a great many horses, and some drivers were killed; the rest escaped by flight. Two of the cannon flanked the baggage, and for some time kept the Indians off: the other cannon, which were disposed of in the best manner and fired away most of their ammunition, were of some service, but the spot being so woody, they could do little or no execution.

The enemy had spread themselves in such a manner, that they extended from front to rear, and fired upon every part.

The place of action was covered with large trees, and much underwood upon the left, without any opening but the road, which was about twelve foot wide. At the distance of about two hundred yards in front and upon the right were two rising grounds covered with trees.

When the General found it impossible to persuade them to advance, and no enemy appeared in view; and nevertheless a vast number of officers were killed, by exposing themselves before the men; he endeavored to retreat them in good order; but the panick was so great that he could not succeed. During this time they were loading as fast as possible and firing in the air. At last Lieutenant Colonel Burton got togeather about one hundred of the 48th regiment, and prevailed upon them, by the General's order, to follow him toward the rising ground on the right, but he being disabled by his wounds, they faced about to the right, and returned.

When the men had fired away all their ammunition and the General and most of the officers were wounded, they by one common consent left the field, running off with the greatest precipitation. About fifty Indians pursued us to the river, and killed several men in the passage.

The officers used all possible endeavours to stop the men, and to prevail upon them to rally; but a great number of them threw away their arms and ammuntion, and even their cloaths, to escape the faster.

About a quarter of a mile on the other side the river, we prevailed upon near one hundred of them to take post upon a very advantageous spot, about two hundred yards from the road. Lieutenant Colonel Burton posted some small parties and centinels. We intended to have kept possession of that ground, 'till we could have been reinforced. The General and some wounded officers remained there about an hour, till most of the men run off. From that place, the General sent Mr Washington to Colonel Dundar with orders to send waggons for the wounded, some provision, and hospital stores; to be escored by two youngest Grenadier companies, to meet him at Gist's plantation, or nearer, if possible. It was found impractiable to remain here, as the General and officers were left almost alone. we therefore retreated in the best manner we were able. After we had passed the Monongahela the second time, we were joined be Lieutenant Colonel Gage, who had rallied near 80 men. We marched all that night, and the next day, and about ten o'clock that night we got to Gist's plantation. [611]

Lacock writes: "On the morning of July 9 the army turned into the valley of Crooked Run down what is now known as Riverton Avenue, fording the Monongahela to the north of the mouth of the run in order to avoid the narrow pass on the east side of the river. The route follows down the western bank of the Monongahela through what is now Duquesne, fording the river a second time a short distance west of Turtle Creek. Here, on the eastern bank of the Monongahela, the battle took place."

Nichols writes: "When the main body arrived at the second ford at about 11 o'clock, St. Clair's work party was employed on the further (east) side of the Monongahela cutting away the perpendicular 12 foot river bank in order to make a passable slope (dugway) for the heavy 12 pounders and 8 inch howitzers. The artillery wagons and pack train drew up on the near side of the ford. By noon the work was completed and the main body began to cross".

PENNSYLVANIA-MONONGAHELA-NEAR FORT DUQUESNE
July 9, Wednesday.   (Washington)

On the 9th I attended him (Braddock) on horse-back, tho' very weak and low. On this day he was attacked, and defeated by a party of French and Indians, adjudged not to exceed 300. When all hope of rallying the dismayed Troops and recovering the ground, was expired (our Provisions and Stores being given up) I was ordered to Dunbar's Camp. [612]

(Washington)

In the early part of the Action some of the Irregulars (as they were called) without direcns. advanced to the right, in loose order, to attack but this, unhappily from the unusual appearance of the movement being mistaken for cowardice and a running away was discountenanced, and before it was too late, and the confusion became general an offer was made by G.W. to head the Provincial and engage the enemy in their own way; but the propriety of it was not seen into until it was too late for execution. After this, many attempts were made to dislodge the enemy from an eminence on the Right but they all proved ineffectual: and fatal to the Officers; who by great exertions and good examples endeavoured to accomplish it. In one of these the Genl. recd. the Wd. of which he died; but previous to it, had several horses killed and disabled under him. Captns. Orme and Morris his two Aids de Camp. having received wounds which rendered them unable to attd. G.W. remained the sole Aid through the day, to the Genl...No person knowing in the disordered State things were, who the surviving Senr. Officer was. and the Troops by degrees going off in confusion; without a ray of hope left of further opposition from those that remained; G.W. placed the Genl. in a small covered Cart, which carried some of his most essential equipage, and in the best order he could, with the best troops (who only contind. to be fired at) brought him over the first ford of the Monongahela; where they were formed in the best order circumstances would admit on a piece of rising ground. [613]

NAME OF THE ENCAMPMENT   (Gordon)
     From Sugar Creek to Field of Battle-Dist.6 Miles
WORK DONE ON THE ROAD
     a little cuting, some digging
QUALITY OF THE ROAD
     a bad defile for near a mile
QUALITY OF THE CAMP
     retreated to Gist's before we encamped
Total Halting days 10
Total Marching days 14 [614]

On Wenesday the 9th Inst. We were advanced within 9 miles of Fort du Quesne, & in order to reach it were to pass the Monongahela in 2 different places. by 2 in the Morning Col: Gage with the 2 Companies of Grenadiers, to wch I belonged, with 150 Men besides was ordered with 2 six pounders, to cross the River, & cover the March of the General wth the Rest of the Army. This We executed without any disturbance from the Enemy, and when we had yet possession of the Bank of the sd crossing, we were remained drawn up, till the general came with the rest of the Army, & passed the River in a Column. The Ground from thence to the French Fort, we were told was pretty good, & the woods open, but all upon the ascent Col: Gage was then ordered with his advance party to march on, and was soon followed by the general. We had not marched above 800 yards from the River, when we were allarmed by the Indian Hollow, & in an instant, found ourselves attacked on all sides. their methods, they immediately seise a Tree, & are certain of the Aim, so that before the Genl came to our assistance, most of our advanced Party were laid sprawling on the ground. our Men unaccustomed to that way of fighting, were quite confounded, & behaved like Poltrons, nor could the examples, nor the Intreaties of their officers prevail with them, to do any one (what was ordered.)

This they denied them, when we begged of them not to throw away thier fire, but to follow us with fixed Bayonets, to drive them from the hill & trees, they never minded us, but threw their fire away in the most confused manner, some in the air, others in the ground, & a great many destroyed their own Men & officers. When the General came up to our assistance, men were seized with the same pannic, & went into as much disorder, some Part of them being 20 deep. The officers in order to remedy this, advanced into the front, soon became the mark of the Enemy, who scarce left one, that was not killed or wounded: when we were first attacked, It was near one o'Clock, & in this confusion did we remain till near 5 in the Evening, our Men having then thrown away their 24 Rounds in the manner above mentioned, & scarce an officer left the head them, They then turned their backs, & left the Enemy in possession of every Thing. What officers were left, endeavoured to rally them at the first crossing of the River, but all to no purpose, terrified at the notion of having no Quarter & being scalped, they ran witht knowing where & most of them threw their

Arms from them(.) The French & Indians not imagining our Pain & Consternation were so great, as they really were, pursued us no further than the first crossing otherwise 100 of them, might have cut the Remainder of us to Pieces. We marched all night in the utmost horrour & distress, most of us wounded, without a bit of any thing to eat & nothing to cover us. On Friday the 11th We arrived at Col: Dunbars Camp 56 Miles from the Place of action. Our Strength before the Engagement amounted to 1100 Men.

Killed & wounded 823. [615]

Wednesday July the 9th. **(Br. Officer 1)**

As we were to cross ye Mona(n)gahela that day & so near the Fort as we were drawing, it was found absolutely necessary to detach a party to secure the crossing. Accordingly Lieut: Coll: Gage with 300 Men & the Grenadier Companys with two peices of Cannon marched before day break and before the road was cleared. At day break the whole detachment marched, tho slowly, having a great deal of trouble with ye road; after 5 Miles march we came to ye first crossing of the river which was extreamly fine having a view of at least 4 Miles up the river & ye breadth about 600 Yards; near this first crossing our advanced party scared some Indians from their holes, finding many spears & their fires newly burning. From this crossing to the other was near two miles & much the finest of the two; on the other side ye second crossing ye advanced party had halted at Fraziers house close to ye bank which was very steep & took us two hours to make it passable for ye cariages. The General now thinking ye dangerous passes were over did not suffer ye advanced party to proceed any farther than ye distance of a few Yards from the main body. It was proposed to strengthen ye flanks but this was unhappily rejected. Between 12 & 1 after we had marched 800 yards from ye river our first flank upon the left was fired on & every Man of them killed or wounded; the alarm quickly became general & ye fire was brisk from right to left, ye Indians were all planted behind trees & fired with the utmost security; the ground where the Enemy was posted was rising & advantagious. Upon our right were a couple of immense large trees fallen on each other which the Indians were in possession of & annoyed us from very much; but an Officer & a party of men soon dislodged ym, & by a pretty brisk fire kept our right tollerably easy; ye Guns which were all rather to ye left fired both round & grape shott doing great execution. The Indians whether ordered or not I cannot say kept an incessant fire on the Guns & killed ye Men very fast. These Indians from their irregular method of fighting by runing from one place to another obliged us to wheel from right to left, to desert ye Guns and then hastily to return & cover them. At ye first of ye firing the Genl; who was at ye head of ye detachment came to ye front, & ye American Troops through without any orders run up immediately some behind trees & others into ye ranks & put ye whole in confusion. The men from what storys they had heard of the Indians in regard to their scalping and Mawhawking, were so pannick struck that their Officers had little or no command over them, & if any got a shot at one the fire imediately ran through ye whole line though they saw nothing but trees; the whole Body was frequently divided into several parties, & then they were sure to fire on one another. The greatest part of the men who were behind trees were either killed or wounded by our own people, even one or two Officers were killed by their own Plattoon. Such was ye confusion, that ye men were sometimes 20 or 30 deep, & he thought himself securest who was in the center; during all this time the Enemy kept a continual fire & every shot took place. The General had given orders that they should fire in Platoons (which was impossible to be effectd) which would not have answered at all as the Enemy were situated. Within about two hours & an half the Men were obliged (or at least did) retreat three or four times & were as often rallied. We found that we should never gain ye day unless we dislodged them from the rising ground, upon which Lt: Coll: Burton with the Grenadiers pushed & attempted ye Hill; for sometime we were in hopes of their sucess, but some Shot killing 2 or 3 of them, the rest retreated very fast, leaving their Officers (entreating & comanding but) without any regard to what they said. The Indians were scalping at the begining of the affair which we heard was a sign they were dubious of Success, but (it) is certain they never gave ground. General Braddock who was in the heat of ye Action the whole time, was greatly exposed: he had 4 horses shot under him & shot through several parts of his cloaths; at the latter end of ye affair an unlucky Shot hit him in the Body which occasioned his death in 3 or 4 days afterwards. Sir Peter Hackett (sic) was killed at y^e: begining & many more Officers.

After the Men retreated from the hill, they made some stand & ye Cannon kept a tollerable good fire, but very soon for want of a sufficient Guard to it, the men were obliged to leave them. During this time ye Wagoners who imagined things would turn out badly, had taken the gears from their Horses & galloped quite away so that if Fortune had turned in our favor we had not one horse left to draw the Train forwards. However after about 4 hours of incessant firing & two thirds of y^e: Men killed or wounded, they as if by beat of Drumm turned to y^e: right about & made a most precipitate retreat every one trying who should be the first. The Enemy pursued us butchering as they came as farr as the other side of ye River; during our crossing, they Shot many in ye Water both Men & Women, & dyed ye stream with their blood, scalping & cutting them in a most barbarous manner. On the other side of the river we most of us halted to resolve on what to do; but ye Men being so terrified desired to go on, nay indeed they would; melancholy situation! expecting every moment to have our retreat cut off (which half a dozen men would easily have done) & a certainty of meeting no Provisions for 60 Miles. I must observe that our retreat was so hasty that we were obliged to leave the whole Train; Amunition, Provision & bagage to ye plundering of the Indians. The Mens wounds being fresh, many of them retreated with us though in ye utmost agonies. In making y^e: road we (had) marked y^e: trees on each side of it, which we found of very great use to us in our retreat, for being obliged to keep marching y^e: whole night through a continued Wood, ye people frequently lost their way, & had nothing to put them right except feeling for the Marks; nevertheless many of the Rear lost their Way, & of ye wounded entirley lost. The General in the Night found himself extreamly bad, so they contrived a kind of Litter to be caried on Mens Shoulders; it was with y^e: utmost difficulty they could get Men to carry him on though large promises were made; the Men indeed had not eaten any thing since very early on the day of ye Action nor (had) one Moments rest, which was some (tho small) excuse. [616]

Letter V (continued)   (Br. Officer 3)

Then we marched on, and when within about ten Miles of Fort DuQuesne, we were, on a sudden, charged by Shot from the Woods. Every Man was alert, did all we could, but the Men dropped like Leaves in Autumn, all was Confusion, and in Spight of what the Officers and bravest of the Men could do, Numbers run away, nay fired on us, that would have forced them to rally. I was wounded in one Leg, and in the other heel, so could not go, but sat down at the

Foot of a Tree, praying of every one that run by, that they would help me off; an American Virginian turned to me, Yes, Countryman, says he, I will put you out of your Misery, these Dogs shall not burn you; he then levelled his Piece at my Head, I cried out an dodged him behind the Tree, the Piece went off and missed me, and he run on; soon after Lieutenant Grey, with a Party of Dumary's Company came by, who brought up the Rear; the Firing was not quite ceased, he told me the General was wounded, and got him carried off. [617]

> *Nichols writes: "Another rescue story concerning Lt. Treby of the 9th Company of the 44th is probably authentic although it first appeared in Thomas Mente' History of the Late War (London 1772)p.28. Mente had been an engineer during the war and doubtless had met Treby. The Lieutenant, wounded in both legs, lay helpless until Mr. Farrel, a volunteer, caught him on this back and carried him from the field. Farrel was not an officer in 1755 but Mente stated he was a captain in the 62nd Foot in 1772."*

(Br. Officer 4)

In advancing toward the Enemy the Fire in Front was thick and heavy; and two of our Parties, one of three hundred, the other of two hundred Men, falling back, caused such Confusion and Pannick that no military Expedient thought of had any effect upon our Men; who, after firing away, in the most irregular Manner, all their Ammunition, ran quite off, leaving to the Enemy the Artillery and Baggage. The main Body was with Col. D---, or the whole Army would have been destroyed: Loss of Horses and Want of Carriages for the Wounded, made us destroy Ammunition and superfluous Provision. The whole Artillery is lost. The Troops are so weakened by Deaths, Wounds, and Sickness, that it is judged impossible to make any farther Attempt for the present. It is affirmed, that the military Chest, with £25,000. to pay the Army, and all the General's Papers are lost. Capt Waggoner, with 170 Virginians, went up to where the Enemy was hid and routed them: but O unhappy! our Infatuateds seeing a Smoke, fired and killed him with several of his Men.

Capt. Polson, another brave Virginian, with his Company, attacked the Enemy a little before the Retreat was beat, which they hearing, surrounded theses brave Fellows, and cut the Captain and most of them to Pieces. It is with Regret I send this sad Account.

P.S. D---'s hasty Retreat seems still a great Mystery. [618]

On the 9th of July we cross'd the Mononghale (a Branch of Ohio) in two Places, and soon after the second Crossing, when our advanc'd Guard had got about one Mile from the River, a Firing began in the Front: The Enemy were advantagiously posted on two Hills, one on each Side of our Way, which Hills joined in our Front: The Firing as a Signal began in the Front, and immediately was follow'd from behind the Hills and Trees all-along each Flank: Our Troops keeping in regular close Order, not a Shot of theirs, posted to such Advantage, could be well shot amiss; and yet they shot too high: Our Officers as well as Men generally behaved well; and all the Blame that can be properly laid, is in not having proper Scouts out to have prevented our falling into such an Ambush; however, our Army was defeated by a Number equal if not superior, posted as well as their Hearts could wish. Near 400 of our Men were left dead on the Spot, between 2 and 300 wounded got off, about 100 were left wounded not able to get off. Among the Kill'd to our very great Grief, was our brave Colonel Sir Peter Halket, and his Son. As soon as the Remains of our Army had recross'd the River, and got out of Gun-shot, the Indians, a merciless Crew that compos'd Part of the French Army, began immediately to scalp the Dead and Wounded; this I heard and saw, though escap'd being seen by them; for I being one of the first that was wounded, and was for a while pretty much stunn'd, was left among the Dead of the advanc'd Guard of our Army; when our Army retreated, the Enemy follow'd close, by which Means the Ground where the Battle began in the Front was deserted for a Time both by Friends and Enemies, and in that Time I made shift to get away and hide myself at some small Distance in a hollow Tree; and I had not been long there before these ravenous Hellhounds came yelping and screaming like so many Devils, and fell to work as before-mentioned: About a Foot above the Entrance into the Tree I was in there was good Foot-hold for me to stand on, upon which I stood, and against my Face where was a small Knot-hole facing the Field of Battle, by Means of which I had a fair Prospect of their Cruelty: But Oh! what a Pannic was I in, when I saw one of those Savages look directly at the Knot-hole, as I aprehended, give a Scream, and came directly up to the Tree? But what Inducement he had for doing it I canot tell, for he went off again without shewing any signs of his discovering me. The whole Army of

354

the Enemy fell to plundering, &c. Through I must do the French Commandant this Justice, that as soon as possible he could, he put a stop to the Indians scalping those that were not yet quite dead, and ordered those Wounded to be taken Care of. Among the Plunder they found near Two Hogsheads of Rum, and the Indians, as likewise the French Soldiers, fell to drinking, and soon got themselve pretty drunk, and went off, as I aprehended, at Night to the French Fort, without carrying off, much of their Plunder, neither could they do it by reason of the Intoxication: They did not leave so much as a Guard on the Field of Battle; neither did they pursue our Army farther that the River; so that if our People had halted but Half a Mile from the Field of Battle, they might have returned that Night, and destroyed most of the Baggage. At Night when the Coast was clear, I got me out of my Hiding-place. [619]

On the 9th July, 1755.-The advanced party consisted of 400 men and upward, under the command of Lieut. Col. Gage, and marched according; and about 7 o'clock started a party of about 300 Indians, but they got off. About 7 o'clock, some Indians Rushed out of the Bushes, but did no Execution, The party went on and secured both Passes of the River; and at 11 the Main Body began to cross, with Colours flying, Drums beating, and Fifes playing the Grenadiers' March, and soon formed: when they thought that the French would not Attack them, as they might have done it with such Advantage in crossing the Monongohela. They marched on and secured both crossings of the river without interruption. The main body marched about 6 o'clock and about 11 began to cross over as proposed in the Council of War, and got over both passes, when they began to think the French would not attack them, as they might have done with so many advantages a little time before.

The Advance Party was now about ¼ of a mile before the Main Body, the rear of which was just over the river when the front was attacked. The 2 Grenadier Companies formed the 2 flank advance Picquets, 2 Companies of Carpenters cutting the Roads, and the rest covering them. The first fire our men received was in front, and on the flank of the flank Picquets, which in a few minutes nearly cut off the most part of the Grenadiers and a Company of Carpenters. The first fire the Enemy gave was in front, and they likewide galled the Picquets in flank, so that in a few minutes the Grenadiers were nearly cut in

355

pieces, and drove into the greatest confusion, as was Captain Polson's company of Carpenters. As soon as the General with the Main Body heard the Front was attacked, they hastened to succour them, but found the Remains retreating. Immediately the General ordered the cannon to draw up and the Batallion to form. By this time the Enemy began to fire on the Main Body, who faced to the right and left and returned it, and the Cannon began to play, but could not see at what, for our men were formed in the open road they had just cut, and the Enemy kept the Trees in front and on the flanks. On the right they had possession of a hill, which we could never get possession of, though our Officers made many attempts to do it: but as the Officers dropped, which was generally the case, or that the Enemy gave a platoon of ours advancing up the hill a smart fire, they immediatley retreated down again. As numbers of our Officers declared they never saw above 4 of the enemy at a time the whole day, it struck a panic through our men to see numbers daily falling by them, and even their comrades scalped in their sight. As soon as the General saw this was the case, he ordered that our men should divide into small parties and endeavour to surround the Enemy, but by this time the greatest part of the Officers were either killed or wounded, and in short the Soldiers deaf to the commands of those few that were left alive. It was in an open Road that the Main Body were drawn up, but the Trees were excessive thick around them, and the Enemy had possession of the Hill to the Right, which consequently was a great advantages to them so many officers declared that they never was above 5 of the Enemy at one time during the whole affair. Our soldiers were encouraged to make many attempts by the Officers (who behaved Gloriously), to take the Hill, but they had been so imtimidated before by seeing their comrades scalped in their sight, and such numbers falling, that as they advance up towards the Hill, and their Officers being pict off, which was generally the case; they turned to the Right About, and retired down the Hill. Then the General perceived and was convinced that the soldiers would not fight in a regular manner without Officers, he divided them into small parties and endeavour to surround the Enemy, but by this time the major part of the Officers were either killed or wounded, and in short the soldiers were deaf to the commands and persuasions of the few Officers that were left unhurt. The General had 4 horses shot under him before he was wounded, which was towards the latter part of the Action, when he was put into a Waggon with great difficulty, as he was very solicitous for being left in the Field. By this time, too, the greatest part of the Train were cut off, having fired between 20 and 30 rounds each cannon, for the Enemy made a mark of them and the officers.

The General had 4 horses shot under him before he was wounded, which was towards the latter end of the Action, for when the General was put in a Waggon the men soon dropped out of the field, and in a little time became too general after standing three hours, and with much difficuly got the General out of the Field (for he had desired to be left). It was the opinion of most of the Officers there, that had greater numbers there, it would have been the same, as our people had never any hopes of getting the field, for they never got possession of the ground the front was attacked on. But very luckily for us they pursed us no further than the Water, and there killed and scalped many. One of our Engineers, who was in the front of the Carpenters marking the road. saw the Enemy first, who were then on the run which plainly shows they were just come from the Fort, and their intention certainly was to secure the pass of the Monongahela, but as soon as they discovered our Army, an Officer at the head of them dressed as an Indian, with his gorget on, waved his hat, and they immediatley dispersed to the right and left, forming a half-moon. It was impossible to judge of their numbers, but it believed they had at least man for man. [620]

(Stephen)

July the 9th: about two o'clock in the Afternoon. The first of our forces consisting of about 1300 Men & Officers under the Command of General Braddock was attacked by a Party of French and Indians near to the River Monongahela about 8 Miles from Fort Du Quesne.

The Private Men of the two Regiments were entirely at a loss in the Woods. The Savages and Canadians kept on their Bellies in the bushes and behind the Trees, and took particular Aim at Our Men, and Officers especially, most of whom are killed or wounded: The British Troops were thunderstruck to feel the Effect of a heavy Fire, & see no enemy; they threw away their Fire in a most indescreet Manner, and shamefully turned their Backs on a few Savages and Canadeans. General Braddock strove most incessantly to rally them, and make the proper Disposition, but all was in vain They kept in a mere huddle in spite of the most ardent Endeavours of many brave officers, and tho' our Numbers were sufficient to have surrounded them, fought them in their own way, and pursued our March. Shame unto the infamous Dogs! Their Numbers only served to increase the Number of the Killed. They were infatuated to such a pitch, that they would obey no Orders, killed one another & deserted the Colours; and after about 3 1/2 hours-(Shame! That it should be ever heard of) run from a small number of French and Savages, leaving them an easy Prey of a most valuable Train, a Stock of Ammunition, Provision and Baggage. In short the Enemy obtained an easy and compleat Victory. The few independents and Virginians that were engaged behaved better and suffered much. There were but few of them engaged, as General Braddock had unhappily placed his confidence and whole Dependence on the Regiments. But his Excellency found to his woeful Experience, what had been frequently told him, that formal attacks & Platoon firing never would answer against the Savages and Canadeans. It ought to be laid down as a Maxim to attack them first, to fight them in their own way, and go against them light & naked, as they come against Us, creeping near and hunting Us as they would do a Herd of Buffaloes or Deer; whereas you might as well send a Cow in purssuit of a Hare as an English Soldier loaded in their way with a Coat, Jacket, &c. &c, &c., after Canadeans in their Shirts, who can shoot and run well, or Naked Indians accustomed to the Woods. I escorted a Convoy of 100 Bullocks, and 100 Horse Load of Flour from Col. Dunbar's Camp to the General's which was 50 Miles. I had only 100 Men, and was dogged night and day by the Indians; but by Vigilance, which is the only thing can secure one against such an Enemy, joined the General four Days before the Engagement without the loss of a Man or Bullock. We beat them out of ther Ambushes, & always had the first Fire on them. The British Gentlemen were confident they never would be attacked, and would have laid any Odds, that they never should, until they come before the Fort, yea, some went further, and were of opinion, that We should hear the Explosion of the French Fort blown up and deserted, before We approached it. These Notions which were very ill-grounded, served to lull them into a fatal Security which contributed not a little to the fatal Event which has lately happened.

I always declared openly & at the time was not the better thought of for it, that they would be attacked before they arrived at the fort, My Reasons were, that the French must lose the Use of their Indians, if they did not. They had collected a Body of them, and they would not be cooped up in the Fort; and the character of the People We had to deal with would not permit Us to think but the French would take all Advantages. I had the Honour to receive the General's Thanks for my Service in the Field; and if he had lived a Week, I should have been provided for. Twelve Virginia Officers were engaged, six of whom were killed. I have two Bullet Holes in my Body at this instant. Lieut. (Walter) Stewart is wounded. Sr. Peter Halket fell in the begining of the Day. Secretary Shirley & thirteen Officers of the Regiment are killed. Almost all wounded.[621]

Wedensday July the 9th.   **(batman)**

The Advanced Party Marched at two in the Morning, Consisting of two grannadier Companies and a hundred Pattallion. My Master Commanded the Pattallion. We marched to take Possession of a Pass Over the River which is Called Muningahele (Monongahela) River, we having all the morning two pieces of Cannon which was very troublesome to get forward before any Road was cut which there was not at that time for the working party being b'hind at that time.

A Bout Eight in the Morning we Came to the River after Marching Near Seven Miles. When we Came Close to the River some of our men saide they saw (a) great many of the French Indiens on the Other side of the River. Some saide their was not Any but to be Shure Colonel Gage who Commanded the Party Ordered the Cannon to be taken of(f) the Carriges and to be drawn Over by the men, Ready to Ingage if accation (action). The men all marched Over in line of Battle with the Cannon till they Came to the Other side of the River where we had a Bank to Rise Eight yards parpendiquler that we was oblig'd to Sloape before we Could Rise the hill. The River is betwixt two and three hundred yards Over and not much more than knee deep. After we had Rose the Bank we had not a Bove two hundred yards to Frayzors Plantation where we marched and our Command went no further at that time.

So as soon as we arived their, the Sentryes was posted and Everything made secure. The men that had anything to Eate they eate it for their Breckfast, it being then about half an hour after Nine, but I believe where there was one that had any thing to Eat their was twenty that had Nothing. Some men had Nothing most of the day Before. My Master Eat a little Ham that I had and a Bit of gloster Shire cheese and I milked the Cow and made him a little milk Punch (of) which he drank a little. About half an hour after ten the working party Came Over the

River and a Bout a(t) Eleven the grand Army begins to Come Over. As soon as they Came to the River we Rec'd Orders to march on again. Sir John Sincklare (St. Clair) asked Colonel Gage if he would take the two piece of cannon with us again. Colonel Gage Answered, no Sir I think not, for I do not think we Shall have much Occasion for them and they being troubolsome to get forwards before the Roads are Cut. So we began our March again, Beating the grannadiers March all the way, Never Seasing. There Never was an Army in the World in more spirits than we where, thinking of Reaching Fort de Cain the day following as we was then only five miles from it. But we had not got above a mile and a half before three of our guides in the front of me above ten yards spyed the Indiens lay'd down Before us. He Immediately discharged his piece, turned Round his horse (and) Cried, the Indiens was upon us.

My Master Called me to give me his horse which I tooke from him and the Ingagement began. Immediately they began to Ingage us in a half Moon and still Continued Surrounding us more and more. Before the whole of the Army got up we had about two thirds of our men Cut of(f) that Ingaged at the First. My Master died before we was ten Minuits Ingaged. They continualy made us Retreat, they haveing always a large marke to shoute (shoot) at and we having only to shoute at them behind trees or laid on their Bellies. We was drawn up on large Bodies together, a ready mark. They need not have taken sight at us for they Always had a large Mark, but if we was of them five or six at one time (it) was a great sight and they Either on their Bellies or Behind trees or Runing from one tree to another almost by the ground. The genll had five horses Shot under him. He always strove to keep the men together but I believe their might be two hundred of the American Soldiers that fought behind Trees and I belive they did the most Execution of Any. Our Indiens behaved very well for the Small Quantity of them. Their was a man his Son thought to have killed a Bout sixteen men (of the enemy). The father, after (having) Spent all his Ammunition, lay down his gun till he went to get a fresh Supply. In the mean time one of our men found her (the gun) and to hinder the Enemy for having Any service from her he knocks her Round a tree and bent her like a Bow. Soon after the man Comes and finds his piece all Bent. He was seemingly very Angry. He afterward said he should do the same. He spyes a French Indien that had shot several Shots from behind a tree. He Immediately Called his

Son to Shout (shoot) at him, which he did and shot him dead. They begin to Inclose us more and more till they had Nigh Inclosed us in. If it was not for their Barbaras Usage which we knew they would treat us, we should Never have fought them as long as we did, but having only death before us made the men fight Almost longer then they was able. Their was about three Quarters of an hour (after being nearly encircled) before we Retreated. I Expected nothing but death for Every one of us, for they had us surround(ed) all but a little in the Rear, which they strove for with all their Force. But our men knowing the conciquances of it preserved the pass till we Retreated. The generall was wounded and a great many Officers was killed with about five hundred private men, and about four hundred wounded out of Better than twelve hundred. The Ingagement began before one and Ended half and hour after four, when we Retreated. They prosued us Better than a mile and Cut many of(f) in going through the River. All the wounded that Could not walk fell in the Enemys hands but was given no Quarters. My Masters horse Rec'd a Ball in the Shoulder and after that the genll('s) horse was Shot and I mounted him of(f) my Masters. Near half an hour after their was Other horses Ready, I advised him to mount another As he (the horse) was wounded. I was a fear'd he (the horse) should fail with him (Braddock); but I did not leade him (the horse) above half an hour Before a Ball Struck him in the Rib and he died Immediately. I had seven horses in the field and one Cow and they was all lost but two horses. When we Retreated we marched all Night and the Next day without any thing to Eat or drink Except water untill we Came to guests Plantation before we halted, it being Better than Sixty Miles, and then we had Eight miles to Colonel Dunbar('s) Party but it being so late, then Eight O Clock and the men so forteagud (fatigued) (there) not being a hundred Ariv'd at that time made us halt there that Night. And we sent a party to Colonel Dunbar('s) party to fetch us some provisions to be with us Early in the morning, which they did, and after couking, we marched on the Other party (Colonel Dunbar's). The few that was up that Night was oblig'd to stand Sentrys Over the Wounded. The genll, we was oblig'd to Carry him on two long poals (poles) and a Bed upon it for him to lay on, in way of a horse litter. We was six of us Carrying him at once. I had of my Master('s) Baggage that was saved a Bout two quarts of Rum and Nigh the same quantity of wine which the genll hereing of desired that I would save it for him, which I did, their being not so much saved in all the Army besides.

In going Over the River there was an Indien Shot one of our Wimen and began to Scalp her. Her Husband being a little before her Shot the Indien dead. There was another Indien Immediately Shot him through the Arm, but he made his Escape from them. Just after we had passed the River a Captn that was wounded in the foot Bege'd that I would lend him my Horse which I did, although I had about two hundred miles to march on foot before he could get a horse. [622]

PENNSYLVANIA-FORT DUQUESNE (Smith)

Shortly after this, on the 9th day of July, 1755 in the morning, I heard a great stir in the fort. As I could then walk with a staff in my hand, I went out of the door, which was just by the wall of the fort, and stood upon the wall, and viewed the Indians in a huddle before the gate, where were barrels of powder, bullets, flints, &c., and every one taking what suited. I saw the Indians also march off in rank entire; likewise the French Canadians, and some regulars. After viewing the Indians and French in different positions, I computed them to be about four hundred, and wondered that they attemped to go out against Braddock with so small a party. I was then in high hopes that I would soon see them fly before the British troops, and that General Braddock would take the fort and rescue me.

I remained anxious to know the event of this day; and, in the afternoon, I again observed a great noise and commotion in the fort, and though at that time I could not understand French, yet I found that it was the voice of joy and triumph, and feared that they had received what I called bad news.

I had observed some of the old country soldiers speak Dutch: as I spoke Dutch, I went to one of them, and asked him what was the news. He told me that a runner had just arrived, who said that Braddock would certainly be defeated; that the Indians and French had surrounded him, and were concealed behind trees and in gullies, and kept a constant fire upon the English, and that they saw the English falling in heaps, and if they did not take the river, which was the only gap, and make their escape, there would not be one man left alive before sundown. Some time after this I heard a number of scalp halloos, and saw a company of Indians and French coming in. I observed that they had a great many bloody scalps, grenadiers' caps,

British canteens, bayonets, &c. with them. They brought the news that Braddock was defeated. After that another company came in, which appeared to be about one hundred, and chiefly Indians, and it seemed to me that almost every one of this company was carrying scalps; after this came another company with a number of wagone horses, and also a great number of scalps. Those that were coming in, and those that had arrived, kept a constant firing of small arms, and also the great guns in the fort, which were accompanied with the most hideous shouts and yells from all quarters; so that it appeared to me as if the infernal regions had broke loose.

About sundown (on July 9) I beheld a small party coming in with about a dozen prisoners, stripped naked, with their hands tied behind their backs, and their faces and part of the bodies blackened; these prisoners they burned to death on the bank of the Alleghany river, opposite to the fort. I stood on the fort wall until I beheld them begin to burn one of these men; they had him tied to a stake and kept touching him with firebrands, red-hot irons, &c., and he screamed in a most doleful manner; the Indians, in the mean time, yelling like infernal spirits.

As this scene appeared too shocking for me to behold, I retired to my lodging both sore and sorry.

When I came into my lodgings I saw Russel's Seven Sermons, which they had brought from the field of battle, which a Frenchman made a present to me. From the best information I could receive, there were only seven Indians and four French killed in this battle, and five hundred British lay dead in the field, besides what were killed in the river on their retreat.

The morning after the battle I saw Braddock's artillery brought into the fort; the same day I also saw several Indians in British officers' dress, with sash, half moon, laced hats, &c., which the British then wore.

A few days after this the Indians demanded me, and I was obliged to go with them (up the Alleghany river by canoe). [623]

Nichols writes: "The total number of prisoners taken to Fort Duquesne was 20, seven of whom were army women from the handful who had accompanied the flying column. The remaining eight women were those Gordon saw tomahawked earlier near the Monongahela while he was fording it. The seven women prisoners either died at the stake or entered the huts of their captors for there is no further record of them. One or two atrocity stories dealing with women captured in July 9 have been recorded. One, which sounds authentic, concerns Pontiac's cannibal Ottowas (Mississippi Valley Historical Review, XIII, 74), and another more fanciful, describes the harrowing experiences and cruel death of a woman alleged to have been Braddock's mistress".

July 9th. 1755   **(Roucher)**

Mr. Beaujeu proposed to march at daybreak, but the Indians not being quite ready retarded him. He was oblig'd in order to hurry them to advance with the detachment of french two Musket shot from the fort; from whence he could not march till 8 o'clock, the Indians not having joyned him sooner. The Poutiawatamis march'd with the rest.

Detachment of French & Indians that marched against the English

3 Captains Vist. Messrs; Beaujeu, Dumas & Deligney

4 Lieutenants, Messrs. Courtmanch, La Bourque, Mommidy & Carqueville

6 Ensigns. Messrs. Longueville, La Parade, Bailleul, Corbreare, Bleury; & the Chevr. de (Celeron)

23 Cadets. Messrs. Pecudy, Courtmanch, Beaulac, St. Cherre, Hartell, Cabanac, (Demuy,) Rocheblas, Saqueppec, Soanna, St. Simon, Labourque, Linctot, the Elder, (and the younger), Daillebout, La Framboise, Normanville, Roctorade, Calaron, Blanville, Monsr. St. Ours & Monandiere

112 (72) Regular Troops

146 Militia

637 Indians

891 Men in all

At one in the Afternoon we heard from Fort Duquesne (the) blast of great guns & Musquetry which made us apprehend our detachment had joined in with the English Army nearer than the imagined, & that they were ingaged.

Our Scouts had indeed about that time discovered the English Army (had called) the Halt (who probably had receiv'd intelligence of us) & immediately acquinted Monsr. Beaujeu who was at No very great distance. That Commander directly advanced with his detachment & was soon engaged with the English Army; The Indians instantly set up the War Cry as is their Custom, our detachment was posted in the woods, it was very clear. The English Army which form'd a Coloum of about 15 men in front made a brisk fire from both Artillery and Musquetry with all the order imaginable, & was answer'd with the same Vivacity by our detachment who having advanced under cover of the Woods and the Indians being posted behind the Trees, attack'd the column of English in front, of whom they made a great Slaughter.

The English seeing that the fire of the Musquetry made no impression on our Detachment, their Artillery was of no more service, & that our fire did not Slacken; broke their Ranks, which gave fresh Courage to our detachment, they retreated in good order, but we did not fail to pursue them for 4 or 5 hours; The Indians seeing us Master of the Field of Battle & Artillery stoped to Scalp, we french then halted by parts return'd to carry off the wounded, the remainder with some Indians pursued the English as far as the River Monongahela 3/4 of a League from the Field of Battle, which they had forded that Morning, but now repast in disorder.

Messrs. Dumas & Lignery when they marchs home left Messrs. Courtmanch, Montigny & Bleury to take care of the Artillery and sent to demand an hand to strengthen the guard whom Mr. Contrecoeur sent under the command of Monsr. Godfiore; and Indian frighten'd at the first discharge took flight and alarmed us in the fort about 4 of the Clock in the afternoon with an account that french and Indians were defeated.

But two hours after we learn'd the Victory which our detachment had gain'd over the English; however our joy was mingled with grief as we understood that Mr. De Beaujeu was kill'd the third discharge; Mr. Dumas having taken on him the Command, appeared at the head of the detachment with a real bravery and encouraged the troops all he could by his Countenance.

Monsr: Deligney was nothing behind him, several Officers & Cadets wounded likewise some soldiers & Militia; but could one gain so compleat a Victory without some loss; the Indians also have lost men and some wounded.

The Officers, Cadets, Soldiers, a great part of the Militia & almost all the Indians fought with an invincible Courage; we may judge it by the loss of the English which is very Considerable, in spite of their strength and Artillery whose number or Quantity we are as yet ignorant of. We reckon they were from 1500 to 2000 men, all regular troops.

Mr. De la Bourque, Lieutt. Mr. Bailleul Ensign, Messsrs. Normanville, Hartell & St. Cerre, Cadets, all wounded march'd on foot to the fort, Messrs. Carqueville & Laparade were carried, but Monsr. Carqueville died on his Arrival.

Mr. Rocheblas Cadet brought in the same evening on horseback two (iron) Cohorn morters. [624]

We will give here an account, as received from some Canadian Officers who were present, of the order of battle in which the English were found.

M. de Contre-coeur being appraised by the Indians, of the march of a large body of English from Fort Cumberland, who were opening the road from day to day as they advanced;-sent a detachment of two hundred men Canadians and colonial troops, under Captains Beaujeu and Dumas, with several other officers, having under them Indians of the upper country, and our domiciliated Indians, to the number of five hundred. This detachment expected to meet the English at some distance, and hoped by some surprise or check, to retard their march, rather then to prevent them from reaching Fort Du Quesne, as the officers were told that the enemy was in greatly superior force.

But the latter, confident in their numbers, proposed to come and form an establishment, feeling assured that it would cost them little beyond the trouble of showing themselves, and convinced that they could take the fort in a day, They, however, marched with great caution, and upon arriving within three leagues of Fort Du Quesne, they halted after crossing a little stream near the house of a blacksmith named Frazer, a German who had settled there to begin his trade with the Indians, but had left when the French began to occupy upon the Ohio.

About eleven o'clock in the morning, the English began to defile over a hill forming a little mountain, with twenty cavalrymen at the head, ten carpenters, two companies of Halke(t)'s grenadiers, the seven companies of that regiment, six recent companies of Virginia troops, three on the right and three on the left, while the regiment of Dunbar, and its grenadiers formed the rear guard. Then followed the laborers and twenty horsemen, forming the column under the orders of General Braddock. The artillery was in the center, and the regimental baggage munitions and provisions were in the rear. All these equipages were well protected by troops who were ranged by companies in alternate order.

The cavalry upon reaching the hill top, having discovered the French who were marching down a hill, fell back upon the advance guard, who were distant from them a full musket shot.

The French, on their part, upon seeing the English, threw themselves behind trees and began to fire, while the Indians passed to the right and left of the hill. They were thus exposed to a fire of musquetry and artillery from the column, and were not accustomed to hear such loud discharges, but seeing the French remain firm, and noticing that the fire was not very destructive, they with their accustomed cries, resumed each a place behind every tree.

The English were not expecting this attack, yet they held a firm aspect, facing to the front and flanks, but seeing that they covered too much ground, they made a movement to advance, and returned a very sharp fire, their officers on horseback, sword in hand, animating their men. After the death of M. de Beaujeu, who was killed on the first fire, M. Dumas took command of the French, or rather, they continued each one to do his best in the place they were in.

Soon afterward, the English abandoned two pieces of artillery, and fell back toward the rear of their columns, which still pressed towards the front, to attack, but they lost their canon one by one, and were thinned out by the musketry during a space of five hours. The Indians taking this movement of the column from the front towards the rear, as a tendency to retreat, rushed upon them with their tomahawks, as did the French also, when they disbanded, and a great massacre followed.

They pursued the English, who threw themselves into the stream to swim, and many were killed in crossing. They did not, however, pursue far, because the Indians could not wait to plunder and drink...The total loss was estimated at 1,270. They abandoned their wounded, who mostly perished in for forest. Of one hundred and sixty officers, only six escaped...

This action, the most important and glorious that the Indians had ever witnessed, and which was partly won by the accuracy of their own fire, only cost them eleven killed, and twenty-nine wounded.

If on a battle field, with no natural advantages, this event should happen to brave and well disciplined troops, from not knowing how to fire steadily, and not being acquainted with the kind of enemy they had to deal with it is an impressive lesson upon these two points. This victory, which was received on the 9th of July, put the whole country in good spirits. [625]

The 9th, the day of the action, M. de Beaujeu left with about 150 Frenchmen, as many officers as cadets, and in addition regulars, militiamen, and five hundred Indians. He marched at 8:00 A.M. Three hundred of the Indians took a route different from that of their commander. They crossed the Monongahela River, so that as it approached the enemy and the detachment was very weak, but as it prepared to strike the the three hundred Indians rejoined the party at a point about three and one-half leagues from Fort Duquesne, where the enemy had stopped to eat. The enemy troops cried out and struck back from high ground, which was very disadvantageous to us, but although on three occasions we retreated slightly, it was not more than ten paces. They had their cannon charged with grapeshot. M. de Beaujeu was killed on the third volley, and M. Dumas took command. The Canadians held firm to the front of the enemy troops, facing their cannon, while the Indians fired on the opposing army from both flanks. They both did their duty so well that although the battle lasted until 4:00 P.M. they did not fall back, and they forced the enemy to abandon their principal pieces of cannon, which fired more than eighty rounds. The English numbered two thousand men. They were always in column, unfortunately for them, for that made them easy to kill. But when they left the field, they did so in such good order that they did not seem to retreat, that instead by half-ranks they wheeled right and left, and regrouped to charge from the rear. [626]

Nichols writes: "Captain Dumas, the French field commander, now lost control over his 600 howling savages, and for a time even his regulars joined in the mad pillage. Apparently some of the French cadets participated in this ghoulish pickpocket game. Cadet Rochablaue squabbled with La Choisle over a well filled purse filched from 'the body of an English officer, richly dressed'. La Choisle won the arguement, but the following morning he was found murdered and his purse of gold missing. Rochablaue was strongly suspected, but there was no evidence of the cadet's guilt (Grignon's Recollection, Wisc. Hist. Soc. Colls. III, 214-215).

Note: La Choisle is not identified in any of the standard sources - he probably was a "private man" in the Canadian militia."

Nichols writes: "One French account asserted that the French and Indians, almost out of ammunition when the British retreated 'were ab't to retreat, but seeing the English begining to leave the field stayed till they got some of the ammunition the English left behind them, and then pursued them as far as the river killing all they could' (Examination of William Johnson, Oct. 26 1756, Pa. Arch., III, 17)."

Nichols writes: "Wounded French officers lay helpless and neither red nor white man could be induced to succor them. Dumas ordered cadets Normanville and St. Simon to round up the regulars. When a number had assembled, they picked up the wounded officers and carried them back to Fort Duquesne. Dumas unable to find anyone to carry Capt. Beaujeu's body from the field, was forced to hide the corpse in a ravine 'a little removed from the road'. He did this to prevent his own Indians from scalping their dead commander. The wounded officers were: Lt. Le Borgue, Lt. Carqueville, Lt. Mommidy, Ensign Bailleul, Ensign Peyrode, Cadet Hertel, Cadet Normanville, Cadet St. Cherre".

(Fr. Officer A)

...On the 9th he (M. de Contrecoeur) detailed M. de Beaujeu, seconded by MM. Dumas and de Lignery, all three captains, with four lieutenants, six ensigns, twenty cadets, one hundred soldiers, one hundred Canadians, and six hundred Indians, with orders to lie in ambush in a favorable spot which had been reconnoitered the night before. Before it had reached this station, the detachment came into contact with the enemy, some three miles from the fort. M. de Beaujeu, seeing that his ambush had failed, decided to attack. This he did with so much vigor that, although the enemy awaited us in the best possible order, it was stunned. But when their artillery fired a round, our company was shaken in its turn. The Indians also, terrified by the noise of the cannon rather than by the harm it had done, began to give ground. When M. de Beaujeu was killed, M. Dumas at once applied himself to reanimating his detachment. He ordered the officers in command of the Indians to lead them in attacking the enemy's flanks, while he, M. de Lignery, and the other officers who led the French, attacked the front. This order was executed so promptly that the enemy, which had been shouting "Long live the King," now were occupied with defending themselves. The battle was unyielding on both sides, and success was long in doubt, but at last the enemy collapsed. Vainly were commands given in an attempt to make the retreat an orderly one. The war cries of the Indians, echoing throught the forest, struck terror in the heart of the enemy. The rout was complete....Such a success, which no one had expected, is the fruit of M. Dumas's experience, and of the activity and valor of those officers under his command. [627]

The army that had been assembled for action by the Belle Riviere was composed of regiments of regular troops, which had been sent from England to Virginia, and of regiments of militia, which had been formed in that and adjoining colonies. It totaled three thousand men, at the time when General Braddock took command, and marched against Fort du Quesne. The sieur de Contrecoeur, captain in the Canadian troops and commandant of the fort, had been informed of the preparation being made in Virginia, but he did not expect to be attacked by such a large force. Having sent different detachments to points along the English route, he learned on July 8 that (they were only six leagues from the fort and that) they marched in three columns. He immediately formed a detachment of all he could spare from the fort, in order to engage them. This detachment was composed of 250 Frenchmen and 650 Indians. Sieur de Beaujeu. who commanded it, had with him the sieurs Dumas and Ligneris, and in addition several subaltern. He marched at 8:00 A.M., and by 12:30 he found himself in the presence of the English, about three leagues from the fort. He attacked them immediately, with great spirit. The first two volleys from the enemy artillery caused his small force to fall back a little. On the third volley, he had the misfortune to be killed, but the sieur Dumas, who took command, as well as the sieur de Ligneris and the other officers-followed by the French and Indians-fell on the English with such vigor that they forced them to fall back in their turn. The latter continued to fight boldly for some time, but finally after four hours of fierce firing they collapsed, and the rout was general. Our forces pursued them for some time, but sieur Dumas, having learned that General Braddock had left some leagues to the rear a corps of seven hundred men under the orders of Colonel Dunbar, ordered a halt. The English have lost nearly 1,700 men. Almost all of their officers are dead, including General Braddock, who died a few days after, from his wounds. [628]

Nichols writes: "In all Canada there were slightly over 2000 regular troops, of whom perhaps 500 were in the Ohio Country.

These troops were colony regulars and had no regimental organization. Although they were not marines, they were often called "troops de la Marine" since they were subject to the Minister of the Marine and Colonies. Most of them had formerly belonged to regular French regiments which had been sent to New France to be disbanded there.

The Canadian militia was composed of all the able-bodied men in New France. The Governor had absolute control over it and could order the habitants to take up arms at any time. The militia in Ohio therefore, was made up of men pressed into that service.

Captain Stone and Captain Floyer were present as volunteers at the battle. They were members of the 47th Regiment stationed at Nova Scotia who had come to the American colonies on recruitment efforts".

July 10 (Thursday)

PENNSYLVANIA-TOWARDS FORT CUMBERLAND   **(Orme)**

We marched all that night, and the next day, and about ten o'clock that night we got to Gist's plantation. [629]

(Br. Officer 1)

On leaving Coll: Dunbar's party at ye meadows, the General had given him orders to remove to Guests, about 50 Miles from ye place of Action, but having a great number of carriages & vary bad Horses he could not reach within 12 miles of the place; however by means of an express, we met with provisions a few miles from his Camp where we halted the next night & joyned next Morning. Provisions & rest were very seasonable for the Men not having of either for 48 hours. The Men of Coll: Dunbars party hearing of our defeat, were extreamly frightened, nay so much so, that upon seeing 2 or 3 of our own Indians returning, the greatest part began to run away; but were stopp'd when they were convinced of their mistake.

Coll: Dunbar having had charge of y^e: amunition & provision except wt: we had taken with us, & not having Horses to carry them back to y^e: Fort, he was obliged to destroy the whole, except a little they preserved to support the Men to y^e: Fort: they brake all ye Shells, buried the shott, burned all y^e: composition, provision & wagons.

Our remains retreated all night, and got to Col. Dunbars Camp the next day, which was near 50 miles from the field of action, and then the General ordered Col. Dunbar to prepare for a retreat, in order to which they were obliged to destroy all the Ammunition and provisions they could not possibly carry, and the reason of so much was the absolute necessity there was for a number of waggons to carry the wounded officers and men: the General's pains increased in such a manner-for he was shot through the arm into the body-togeather with the great uneasiness he was under. [630]

PENNSYLVANIA-FORT DUQUESNE (Contrecoeur)

Monsieur de Contrecoeur, captain of infantry commanding at Fort
Duquesne, having been informed that the English would march out
from Virginia to come to attack him, was warned a little time
afterward that they were on the road. He put spies through the country
who would inform him faithfully of their route. The 7th of this month
(July) he was warned that the army, composed of 3,000 men of the
regular English forces were only six leagues from his fort. the
commander employed the next day in making his arrangements, and on
the 9th of the month he sent Monsieur de Beaujeu against the enemy
and gave him for second in command Monsieurs Dumas and de
Lignery, all three of them being captains, with four lieutenants, six
ensigns, 20 cadets, 100 soldiers, 100 Canadians, and 600 savages, with
orders to hide themselves in a favorable place that had previously been
reconnoitred. The detachment found itself in the presence of the enemy
at three leagues from the fort before being able to gain its appointed
post. Monsieur de Beaujeu seeing that his ambuscade had failed, began
a direct attack. He did this with so much energy that the enemy, who
waited us in the best order in the world, seemed astounded at the
assult. Their artillery, however, promptly commenced to fire and our
forces were confused in their turn. The savages also, frightened by the
noise of the cannon rather than their execution, commenced to lose
ground. Monsieur de Beaujeu was killed, and Monsieur Dumas rallied
our forces. He ordered this officers to lead the savages and spread out
on both wings, so as to take the enemy in flank. at the same time he,
Monsieur de Lignery, and the other officers who were at the head of
the French attacked in front. This order was executed so promtly that
the enemy, who were already raising cries of victory, were no longer
able even to defend themselves. The combat wavered from one side to
the other and success was long doubtful, at length the enemy fled.

They struggled unavailingly to keep some order in their retreat. The
cries of the savages with which the woods echoed, carried fear into the
hearts of the foe. The rout was complete. The field of battle remained
in our possession, with six large cannons and a dozen smaller ones,
four bombs, eleven mortars, all their munitions of war and almost all
their baggage. Some deserters who have since come to us tell us that
we fought against two thousand men, the rest of the army being four

leagues farther back. These same deserters tell us that our enemies have retired to Virginia. The spies that we have sent out report that the thousand men who had no part in the battle, also took fright and abandoned their arms and provisions along the road. On this news we sent out a detachment which destroyed or burned all that remained by the roadside. The enemies have lost more than a thousand men on the field of battle; they have lost a great part of their artillery and provisions, also their general, named Monsieur Braddock, and almost all their officers. We had three officers killed and two wounded, two cadets wounded. This remarkable success, which scarcely seemed possible in view of the inequality of the forces, is the fruit of the experience of Monsieur Dumas and the activity and valor of the officers that he had under his orders. [631]

PENNSYLVANIA-PHILADELPHIA   (Maryland Gazette)
July 3.
Extract of a Letter from Oswego, on Lake Ontario, dated June 9
    "Within these three Weeks have passed by about 36 Battoes, with eight or ten French and Indians in each of them.
We are busy getting a fine Row Galley ready, in order to stop their Passage for the future. They are obliged to pass in Sight of our Fort, which lies on the edge of the Lake, on the South Side, and cannot keep far from the Shore, because of the frequent Squalls of Wind that happen, and would certainly overset them, if they could not quickly reach the Shore. Our People work on Sundays as well as other Days. Several larger vessels are going to be built. Some Carpenters arriv'd here Yesterday from Boston.
    Since our last several of the waggoners, who went with Forage, &c. to the Camp at Wills's Creek, have returned the city, all well. [632]

PENNSYLVANIA-PHILADELPHIA (Maryland, Pennsylvania Gazette)
    Mr. Evan's map of the middle British colonies, and the Country of the Six Nations, comprehending Ohio, etc is just finished engraving; and next Saturday Proposals for publishing the same by subscription will be given gratis at the Printers hereof.
    We hear from Tulpehocken, the John Shickealani, an Indian chief, arrived there last week, and informed, that the French Fort on the Ohio had been strongly reinforced lately with both Frenchmen and Indians: That General Braddock would not allow his Indians to scalp any

Frenchmen that might fall into their Hands, which had occasioned a good many of them to leave him, and would not engage till they should hear from the English Governors and that they wanted much to know whether it was war or peace. [633]

Nichols writes: "Little is known of the detailed composition of Beaujeu's force of 637 Indians. They fall into three main divisions: first the praying Indians principally the Caughawagas from Sault St. Louis, the Abenakis of St. Francis, and the Huron of Lorette; secondly, the Ohio Indians formerly in alliance with the British, mainly Shaweness, Delawares, and Mingos (English name for Iroquois who had migrated to Ohio); and finally, the fierce western tribes, the most important of which were the Ottawas, Ojibways, Pottawattamies, and Michillimackinacs."

July 10th. 1755   **(Roucher)**

Monsr. de Courtmanche, who had remain'd all Night to guard the Artillery sent to desire Canoes in order to carry them off having heard nothing of Mr. Godfiore who having wandered in the woods during the Night had not then joyn'd him.

Monsr. Contrecoeur immediately dispatched 12 Canoes with six men each Commanded by Mr.de Coleron the elder. Mr. Laparade died and was buried with Monsr. Carqueville deceased the Night before.

The greatest part of the Indians who had remained behind to scalp and plunder arrived with may horses loaded with spoils of the English consisting of furniture Cloaths, Utensils, Gold, Silver &c. they brought in but 20 prisoners whereof Seven Women or Girls were on the Number, but they brought an infinite Number of Scalps.

Some Indians afraid that the French would wrong them of their plunder Spread the Report that the English had rallied & were on the March to recover their Cannon, Orders were immediatelly sent to Mr. De Celeron to halt and send out parties on the Discovery.

After a long deliberation, it was determined, that as the Artillery was the principal subject to hinder the English from attempting a second Attack this Year, it was absoutely necessary to be Masters of it.

Captain Dumas offered to conduct that Expedition Mr. de Lerie (whom Mr. Contrecoeur had prevented going to the Engagement the day before, by command (that he oversee) the Artillery and Works.) was given him for a Second with a detachment of 100 french & some Indians to go on the look out.

Mr. Dumas having rejoyn'd Mr. De Celeron sent some french & Indians in the Discovery, who reported that the English were retired having seen nothing but dead bodies for more than six Leagues from the field of battle; this news made our detachment pass the night a great deal more at their ease.

The Utoweawas, Misillimakinaks & Poutiawatamis at the Narrows demanded leave of Mr. Contrecoeur to return home to their Wives and Children, having drove the English back a great way.

Mr. Contrecoeur, replyed, that they were not so far off, perhaps, as they Imagined, & that they ought to defer their departure: but notwithstanding all the Arguments he made use of, they departed the next day with their horses & a great booty. [634]

Nichols writes: "Early the next morning, July 10, a runner sent from the battlefield by Lt. Courtmanche arrived at the fort with an urgent request that pirogues be sent up the Monongahela to transport Braddock's ordnance to Fort Duquesne. Captain Contrecoeur immediately sent Ensign Celoron the elder and 12 canoes with 6 men each up the river to bring off the artillery. Soon after Celoron's departure the greatest part of the Indians who had remained behind (on the battlefield) to scalp and plunder arrived with many horses loaded with spoils of the English consisting of furniture, cloths, utensils, gold, silver, etc...they brought an infinite number of scalps (Roucher Journal, GD. 8/98).

Nichols writes: "Dunbar's earliest knowledge of the disaster was gleaned from terrified wagoners who galloped into his camp early on the morning after the battle" These were: Michael Houber, Jacob Novre, and Matthew Laird".

July 11 (Friday)
PENNSYLVANIA-GIST'S PLANTATION
July 11th.   (Orme)

Some waggons, provisions, and hospital stores arrived. As soon as the wounded were dressed, and the men had refreshed themselves, we retreated to Colonel Dunbar's Camp, which was near Rock Fort. The General sent a serjeant's party back with provision to be left on the road on the other side of the Yoxhio Geni for the refreshment of any men who might have lost their way in the woods. Upon our arrival at Colonel Dunbar's camp, we found it in the greatest confusion some of his men had gone off upon hearing of our defeat, and the rest seemed to have forgot all discipline. Several of our detachment had not stopped 'till they had reached this camp.

It was found necessary to clear some waggons for the wounded, many of whom were in a desperate situation; and as it was impossible to remove the stores, the Howitzer shells, some twelve pound shot, powder, and provisions, were destroyed or buried. [635]

(Washington)

...by the Genls. order, he (G.W.) rode forward to halt those which had been earlier in the retreat: Accordingly, after crossing the Monongahela the second time and ascending the heights, he (G.W.) found Lieutt. Colo. Gage engaged in this business to whom he delivered the Genls order and then returned to report the situation he found them in. When he (G.W.) was again requested by the Genl. whom he met coming on, in his litter with the first halted troops, to proceed (it then being after sundown) to the second division under the command of Colo. Dunbar, to make arrangement for covering the retreat, and forwarding on provisions and refreshments to the retreating and wounded Soldiery. To accomplish this, for the 2d. division was 40 odd miles in the rear it took up the whole night and part of the next Morning, which from the weak state in which he (G.W.) was, and the fatigues, and anxiety of the last 24 hours, rendered him a manner wholly unfit for the execution of the duty he was sent upon when he arrived at the Dunbars Camp. To the best of his power however he (G.W.) discharged it, and remained with the secd. division till the other joined it. The shocking Scenes which presented themselves in this Nights March are not to be described. The dead, the dying, the groans, lamentation, and crys along the Road of the wounded for help (for those under the latter descriptions endeavoured from the first commencement of the action, or rather confusion to escape to the 2d divn.) were enough to pierce a heart of adamant. the gloom and horror of which was not a little encreased by the impervious darkenss occasioned by the close shade of thick woods which in places rendered it impossible for the two guides which attended to know when they were in, or out of the track but by groping on the ground with their hands.

Happy was it for him, and the remains of the first division that they left such a quantity of valuable and enticing baggage on the field as to occasion a scramble and contention in the seizure and distribution of it among the enemy for had a pursuit taken place, by passing the defile which we had avoided; and they had got into our rear, the whole, except a few woodsmen, would have fallen victims to the merciless

376

Savages. Of about 12 or 13 hundred which were in this action eight or 9 hundd. were either killed or wounded; among whom a large proportion of brave and valuable Officers were included. The folly and consequence of opposing compact bodies to the sparse manner of Indian fighting, in woods, which had in a manner been predicted, was not so clearly verified that from hence forward another mode obtained in all future operations.

As soon as the two divisions united, the whole retreated towards Fort Cumberland; and at an Incampment near the Great Meadows the brave, but unfortunate Genl. Braddock breathed his last. He was interred with the honors of war, and as it was left to G.W. to see this performed, and to mark out the spot for the reception of his remains, to guard aganst a savage triumph, if the place should be discovered, they were deposited in the Road over which the Army, Waggons &ca. passed to hide every trace by which the entombment could be discovered. thus died a man, whose good and bad qualities were intimately blended. He was brave even to a fault and in regular Service would have done honor to his profession. His attachments were warm, his enmities were strong, and having no disguise about him, both appeared in full force. He was generous and disinterested, but plain and blunt in his manner even to rudeness. [635]

The above passage was composed by George Washington for use in a biography and reflect his thoughts of the events but were written down at a later date. When he uses "he" the reference is to himself - George Washington.

Sir: (addressee not named)   **(Innes)**
   I have this minute received the melancholy account of the Defeat of our Troops, the General killed and Numbers of our Officers, our whole Artillery taken; in short the Account I have Received is so very bad, that, as pleased God I intend to make a stand here, it's highly necessary to raise the Militia everwhere to defend the Frontiers.
       Your humble servant, James Innes
  Fort Cumberland July 11th 1755
  To all to whom this may Concern [636]

MARYLAND-FORT CUMBERLAND
July the 11   **(Browne)**
  My Brother much better. All of us greatly alarm'd; a Boy came from the Camp and said the General was kill'd 4 Miles from the

French Fort, and that allmost all Sr. Peter Hackets Regiment is cut of by a Party of French and Indians who were behind Trees. Dunbar's Regiment was in the rear so that they lost but few Men. It is not possible to describe the Distraction of the poor Women for their Husbands. I pack'd up my Things to send, for we expect the Indians every Hour. My Brother desired me to leave the Fort, but I am resolv'd not to go but share my Fate with him. [637]

Nichols tells us that the boy was a runaway wagoner with the expedition who brought the first news.

July 11th 1755   (Roucher)
    At 4 of the Clock this morning a Piece of brass Cannon of 12 lb. bore was brought here which Messrs. De Lerie & Dumas had put on board a canoe the preceding Evening. At 3 in the afternoon those Gentlemen return'd, & brought with them
    3 Peices of Brass Cannon of the same bore.
    2 Peices of Brass Cannon 6 lb. bore
    4 Mortars brass of 7 1/2 Inches diameter
the same evening this artillery was brought into the Fort, there was likewise brought in about 80 head of horned Cattle with which the Indians made as great Slaughter as they had done with the English.
    They return'd without the Body of Mr: Beaujeu which they could not find altho strongly recommended to them.
    Messrs: de Montisembert was also sent with some french & Indians (to) observe the Retreat of the English.
    A Party of the Mississaque Indians came in this Evening (with a) Scalp, which they told us was of an Officer belonging to the English army, (whom) they had found in the morning six leagues or thereabout from the field of (battle) And told us that the Enemy no longer march'd in Order.
    Messrs. de Montigny & Corbrere returned from the field of Battle & brought in their Canoes the Body of Monsr. de Beaujeu in a coffin sent on purpose: He was buried with all the marks of Honour due to his Bravery.
    These Gentlemen brought with them in their Canoes 19740 Musquet Cartridges fill'd
    17 Barrels of Powder, each 100 lbs:
    192 Bombshells of 43 lb. Weight

55 Grenadoes of 6 1/2 lb.

175 Twelve pound Balls

57 Six pound Balls. Shovels &c.

The French & Indians at the time of Battle have kill'd a Quantity of Horses, they have kill'd a great many more since, broke all the Carts & destroyed every thing they possibly could. Powder & Flower are scatter'd over the Field of Battle the Indians have brought off a great deal of the last.

The bodies of a great number of men kill'd & those of eight Women or Girls entirely strip'd, lie promiscuously with dead horses for more than half a League.

It is assured that the General of the English Army, whom they called Mr: Braddock is kill'd with the Officers of Artillery and Engineers; there is all the just appearance that, the army will not rally again, as the Principal Officers are left on the field of Battle.

That Army march'd not to attack a wooden Fort, but the Strongest fortified in Canada. Without saying too much of it, one cannot say enough. [638]

July 12 (Saturday) (Halkett/Disney)

PENNSYLVANIA-CAMP ON WEST SIDE YOUGHIOGHENY

Camp 6 Miles of this Side Guests

July ye 12th 1755

The Troops to parade this Evening At Retreat beating At the head of their Respective Regts. & Companys with their Arms & Accoutriments. The Surgons of the Line to get their several Sick & wounded men put into Waggons this afternoon. They Are to Apply to Mr Scott waggon Master Genl. for waggons that the men Are to go in, And to Conform to the Orders of this Morning Relative to ye men going in them. The Genl to beat to Morrow Morning at 4 oClock, the Assemble at 5 when the troops Are to March. The Officers fitt for Duty to parade this evening with their men. [639]

(Croghan)

Mr. Croghan came over on Saturday (July 12) to Shippensberg, he had a free sight of the Enemy as they approached, says they were about three hundred, the French in shirts, & the Indians naked, that they were lead by three French officers with hats in their hands and with which they gave a signal for the firing. He was informed 400 Onandago Indians came to the Fort the day before, that there were 100 Delawares, 60 Wiandots, 40 Puywas, 500 Pawwaws, the Shawnees who lived about Logtown, and some of all other tribes, that some of the Wyandots now going down to Philadelphia were in the action against us, but says the attack was not made by above three hundred, but is was intended to dispute every inch of Ground between the river and the Fort, that the Indians had all the plunder and next day went off-all the prisoners and wounded who could not get off the Field were killed in cold blood and only one man and three Women got into the Fort. The firing was over excepting a few shots now and then a Quarter of an hour before our people retreated, & the enemy had fired for some time at such distance that the Bullets came in quite dead-that the Indians never expected a (British) defeat, by reason they began to scalp immediately but when the Grenadiers, (who gave the fire at 200 yards distance, instead of receiving it) began to retreat, that the Indians hollowed and began act vigorously-many of our people fired twenty-four rounds and never saw the enemy, not above two hundred and Fifty were left dead on the Ground, and it is supposed one hundred and Fifty were killed by our own people & it appears to me, that had there been any officers to have rallied the men on retreating even at last the Enemy would not have got the six cannon and mortars, & perhaps they might have Advanced toward the Fort, for when the men were going off, many of the officers called out Halt, Halt, which the men mostly did, but the Officers continued on and got the heels of them. The unfortunate General Braddock was intirely deserted in the waggons with only his servants and a person or two more, & it was some time before they got a party of men to Guard him. There is an anecdote which possibly you have heard as to the greatness of his despair & his wanting to die as an old Roman, & endeavouring to lay hold of Croghan's pistoles, this you may credit, as I privately inquired of Crogghan as to the truth of it. [640]

(seaman)

On the 12th, at 8 at night, he (the General) departed this life, much lamented by the whole Army, and was decently, through privately, buried next morning. The number killed, wounded and left on the Field, as appeared by the returns form the different companies, was 896, besides Officers, but cannot say any particular Company suffered more than another, except the Grenadier Companies and Carpenters; from out of Colonel Dunbar's Grenadiers, who were 79 complete that day, only 9 returned untouched, and out of 70 of Halket's, only 13.

Amongst the rest, I believe I may say the Seamen did their duty, for out of 33, only 15 escaped untouched: and every Grenadier Officer either killed or wounded. Our loss that day consisted of 4 field pieces, 3 howitzers, and 2 wagons, with Cohorns, togeather with the 51 carriages of provisions and Ammunition, &c., and Hospital stores, and the General's private chest with £1000 in it, and about 200 horses with officers baggage. [641]

Satterday July ye 12th. **(batman)**

We halted and broak and distroyed all the Ammunition and provisions and Buried them in the ground. The Reason for distroying them was because we wanted the wagons to Carry the Wounded. The Horses dying so fast oblig'd us to fire about a hundred for want of horses to draw them.

Provisions that was so Scarce about two days before became so plenty that the men would have hardly any thing but hams. I my self got six or Eight it beeing as many as I Could well Carry on my Horse. The men had the Choice of all the Wagons which Could not be less then (than) a hundred. All the provisions and Wagons that Could not be taken with us was all set on fire to hinder them falling in the Enemees (enemies) hands. All this day we lay Ready to march [642]

MARYLAND-FORT CUMBERLAND
July the 12 **(Browne)**

My Brother better. No news from the Camp so we hope that it is not true what the Boy said... [643]

Nichols writes: "On the morning of July 12, the Huron set out for their distant home despite the French commandant's pleading that they remain. Two days earlier the Sachems of the other western tribes, the Michillmackinac, Ottawa, and Pottawatami, had demanded permission to return home to their wives and children."

July 13 (Sunday)
PENNSYLVANIA-ROCK FORT CAMP **(Halkett/Disney)**
Camp at Lawrel Hill July the 13th: 1755
The parole Whitehall
Field Officer for this Night Major Sparks
One Capt 2 Subs; 2 serjts 2 Corpls & 60 men of the Line to parade Immediatelly & Receive their Orders from Col Dunbar. They Are to

go to the Meddows as a Grass Gd. The commanding Officers of each Company to give in Immediatley A Return of the Effective Serjts Corpls & privet Men fitt for Duty Now in Camp & likewise of the Officers. This Return to be given in to the Brigade Major. The Retreat beating, all the Picquets to Stand to their Arms. They Are to Advance one third from each (other) As Out Centrys And see they Are posted properly. The Officer of each Picquet is by turns to go their Rounds from 9 oClock till Genl Beating Every two hours. On the Drums Call for beating the Genl all picquets Are to Stand to their Arms And the Out Centrys Are to look out sharp and Are to Remain untill a long roll beats And then they Are to Join their respective Picquets. When the Long Roll beats all the Tents Are to be Struck And Immediatly Loaded & Repair to the Front of the Line where they Are to March Constantly And all the Women are to march Constantly in the rear with the provost. Any Battman or Woman Disobaying this Order will be severly punished. Capt Cristy of Col Dunbars Regt. is appointed to Act as Qr Master Genl to this Army the Quarter master Genl being indisposed. The Genl to beat tomorrow morning at 5 oClock. The Line is to March 4 deep. The Officers & Serjts Are to see they March Regulery. The Officers Are desired to keep Constantly to their posts And at all times to march on the Flanks. One Capt 2 Subs & 60 men to make the Advanced Guard, And One Sub with one Serjt & 20 men to make the Rear Guard. The Advanced guard to Advance 1 Serjt & 12 men to help 60 guards Advanced of him. 2 Serjents with 12 men for each Flank. [644]

Although Sir Peter Halkett was killed in the battle, his adjutant Daniel Disney although wounded in the battle continues to keep Halketts Orderly Book.

We marched from hence to the Camp, near   **(Orme)**
the great Meadows, where the General died. [645]

Letter V (continued)   **(Br. Officer 3)**
    When we arrived at the Meadows, we found Colonel Dunbar did not think it expedient to wait for the French there, but retired, and carried us, the wounded, with him to Wills's Creek. I have writ till I am faint. [646]

Sunday July ye 13th.   **(batman)**

We marched and in the Evening the Genll died of his Wounds and severall Other Soldiers, this beeing the first place that the men was dressed since the Ingagement. The wether being very hot Ca(u)sed a great many magets in the men's wounds when they were drest. This day('s) march beeing 10 miles. [647]

MARYLAND-FORT CUMBERLAND
July the 13   **(Browne)**

An Officer is come from the Camp and confirms all what the Boy said. [648]

July 14 (Monday)
PENNSYLVANIA-ORCHARD CAMP   **(Halkett/Disney)**
1st Camp from the great meddows July ye 14th: 1755
The Parole is St James's
Field Officer for this Night Lt Col Gage

46 men to parade Immediatley in Order to go with the Sick waggons. The Two Regts & American Troops finds Each a Capt for the Picquets this Night upon the Retreat beating. The Whole Troops to stand to their Arms And each Corps & company to turn out one third to form a Chain of Centrys Round the Incampment As the Field Officer shall think proper, And if he finds the Number Turnd out more then Necessary to form the chain He is desired to lett them Join their respective Corps. Those Centrys Are to be Releieved every two hours And rounds to go As Usual. The Americans Troops to Appoint An Officer to Act as Adjt. for the whole who is to Attend the Major of Brigade for Orders. They Are also to Appoint a man per Company as Batt men. All the batt of the Line to Assemble near Col. Dunbars Tent whenever the Oderly Drum beats their Call. The Genl to beat to Morrow morning At 5 oclock. The picquet & out Centuries to Observe the Orders given last Night in the Reguard of their Marching. An Orderly Serjt from each Corps to Attend Col: Dunbar. The Qr Masters to Call on Mr Lake Commissary of provisions for fresh meat for the Sick Officers and Soldiers [649]

Munday July ye 14.   **(batman)**

Early in the Morning we marched and after we had got a little distance from our old ground we halted till their was a grave dugg'd for the genll, where we Buried him in two Blankits in the high Road that was cut for the Wagons, (so) that all the Wagons might March Over him and the Army (as well) to hinder any Suspision of the French Indiens. For if they thought he was Buried their, they would take him up and Scalp him. To day we march'd 10 miles.[650]

PENNSYLVANIA-FORT DUQUESNE   (Contrecoeur)
French Account of the Action Near the Ohio River on July 9, 1755.

In relation to the action which occurred on the Ohio River three leagues from Fort Duquesne on July 9, 1755 between a detachment of 250 Canadians and 650 Indians, commanded by Captain De Beaujeu and a body of 2000 English men commanded by General Braddock.

Extract from the letter written by Mr. De Contrecoeur, commandant at Fort Duquesne to the Marquis De Vaudreuil, Governor General, dated from the aforesaid fort on July 14, 1755.
Dear Sir: (Governor General)

Since the beginning of this month, I haven't stopped sending (I continue to send) French and Indian detachments to harass the English that I know number around 3000 from 30 to 40 leagues from the fort who are preparing to lay siege to it in the future. These troops maintain their guard so well, marching always in battle formation so that all the efforts that the detachment made against them became useless.

Finally, learning that the troops were still approaching, I sent officer La Peyrade with several Frenchmen and Indians in order to know precisely where it (the army) was, he told me the next day, the eighth, that the English were about eight leagues from the fort.

I sent another detachment to the field which told me the same day that they were no more than six leagues away and that they were marching in three columns.

The same day I formed a party of everyone I could put (I could spare) outside the fort to go meet them. It was composed of 250 Frenchmen and 650 Indians, which made up a group of 900 men commanded by Captain De Beaujeu. There were two captains who were named Dumas and Lignerie and many other subordinate officers.

This party started to march on the ninth at 8:00 in the morning and found themselves at 12:30 in the presence of the English about 3 leagues from the fort. They began to fire on each other, with enemy artillery fire making our party fall back a little two times. De Beaujeu was killed and the third officer in charge, Dumas, took command. He did his best with our courageous French soldiers supported by the Indians, even though they had no artillery to fire, they, in turn, made the English, who were fighting in battle order in good countenance, give way; and the latter, seeing the ardor of our people who were rushing (attacking) with infinite vigor, were finally obliged to yield completely after four hours of firing. Dumas and Lignerie, who only had twenty Frenchmen with them did not engage them at all in the pursuit; they returned to the fort because a large party of Canadians, who unfortunatley were only children, had pulled back at the first salvo, the best had stayed at the Aux Boeuf River in order to portage the provisions. Besides, a party of Indians were occupied only in taking scalps and pillaging. If the enemy had returned with the 1000 fresh troops which they held in reserve a little distance from them, and of which we didn't know the distance (whose location we didn't know), we would have been at a loss.

Lieutenant Courtemanche bedded down on the battlefield while officers who were returning from pursuing the runaways, at whom they shot until night, with the Indians which had followed them.

Dumas and Lignerie replaced De Beaujeu well in the battle. All the officers in general distinguished themselves in battle, the cadets did wonders as well as our soldiers.

All the Detroit Indians and the Michili-Mackinac left on the day after the action, without my being able to stop them. These Indians, like the residents and those from the Belle River, did very well. It was necessary to recompense them.

I am sending today a small detachment in order to discover what became of the English; and to know if they have the intention of returning to attack us or to go back.

If you want to kept that river, it is necessary to establish a larger force there.

ATTACHMENTS

The state of artillery, war munitions and other effects belonging to the english which were found on the battlefield after the action.

4 cast iron cannon of English manufacture,
11 lb caliber (11 pounders)
4 of the same of 5 ½ lb
4 mortars of cast iron howitzers of 7 ½ inch diameter
3 other grenade mortars of 4 ½ inch diameter

17511 lb bullets
57 6 ¾ shells
17 barrels of powder of 100 each
19740 live cartridges for muskets shell for artillery
other tools necessary for siege
large quantity of rifles, serviceable and out of service
quantity of broken wagons
400 to 500 horses, some of which were dead
about 100 horned beasts (steers)
a large number of broken barrels of powder and flour
about 600 dead men, of which a large number were officers,
and a proportionate number of wounded
20 men or women made prisoner by the Indians
a large quantity of loot, furniture, clothing and tools a quantity
of paper which one did not have time to have translated one
recognized among others the plan of Fort Dusquesne with the
exact proportions Note: The Indians pillaged a lot of
gold and silver money. List of officers, soldiers, militiamen and
Canadian Indians where killed in action.
Dead:
Commandant De Beaujeu
Lieutenant De Carqueville
Ensign De La Peyrade
3 officers
3 Canadians
2 soldiers
15 Indians of different nations
Wounded:
Lieutenant Le Borgues, broken arm
Ensign Bailleul, (lightly wounded)
Cadet Hertel Sainte Teresa (lightly wounded)
Cadet Montmidy (lightly wounded)
12 Indians (lightly wounded)
For extraction to Quebec August 8, 1755
French narrative of the action of July 9 at Monongahela,
near Ohio River, 1755. [651]

July 15 (Tuesday) (Halkett/Disney)
PENNSYLVANIA-CAMP ON EAST SIDE OF YOUGHIOGHENY

Camp after Crossing of the Yaughagany July ye 15th: 1755
The Parole is Cumberland

The Picquets & out Centrys to be posted as mentioned in last Nights Orders. The Orderly men upon the Waggons to Attend & pitch the Hospital Tents when Necessary. A Return to be given in to the Major of Brigade at 8 oClock this Evening from each Regt indipendent Company & provincial Compy of the Number of Officers or Commissiond Offrs And Soldiers That was with Genl Braddock in the late Ingagement Near Frassers Plantation specifying the Officers Names And Ranks And in the Margin Mark the Killd Wounded And Returnd not wounded. Such as Are not known to be Killd or Wounded And have not yet Joined us to be returned in the Column missing. The Several Surgons Are to take the greatest Care to see the Number of Wounded Allotted to their Care by the Director of the Hospital Are Carefully dressed every day. They are also to make the Strictest inquery this Night of the Wounded that Are Able to March that they may be sent forward to the Hospital. The Surgons Are desired to make a Return at the same time of the Number that Are necessary to be sent in waggons And it is Required & Expected they see them put into waggons when they Are to march And if the(y) see lumber (stored Articles) of Any kind in the Waggons but what they Are Convinced belongs to the Sick they Are to Order it out. The Troops Halts to Morrow. The Advance & Rear Guards Consisting of 1 Capts 3 Subs; 120 Privet to be Releived to morrow morning at 8 oClock. The Officers who goes the Morning Rounds Are to send a Sergt of each picquet after Revalle beating to Order every other Centry to Join their Respective picquets. On the long Roll beating the Serjts Are to Acquaint those who Are to Come in on the Signal being given And An Offr of each picquet is to Visit their Out Centry at 6 oClock to see these Orders Are Comply'd with And the Remaining Centrys Are to be Relieved every two hours. Each corps to send a Carry Kettle to the Hospital for the Sick immediatly. The Eldest Capt of the picquet to go to the Grand rounds. [652]

PENNSYLVANIA-LITTLE MEADOWS
July 15, Tuesday. Little Meadows.
To James Innes: **(Washington)**

I doubt not but you have had an acct. of the poor Genls. death by some of the affrighted waggners who ran off without taking leave. James Innes. [653]

Tuesday July ye 15th.   **(batman)**

We marched and after we had Marched about six Miles there was a Captn('s) Command (led by Dobson and Washington) of seventy men Marched with the Wounded Officers Towards Fort Cumberland. I thought it would be best for me to march with the first Command (of seventy men) as I had no Victuls but what I Carried on my Own horse until I Come to Fort Cumberland. We lay this night upon a large Rock Close by a large Spring, it being so stony that we hardly Could get our Tents Pitched, here beeing on this ground great Quantities of Rattle Snakes, this days march being 12 miles. [654]

VIRGINIA-WINCHESTER
Winchester, Va. July 15, 1755
To: Benjamin Franklin   **(Ferguson)**

By good Authority from the Forces we learn, the Generall is not killed, as reported at first. He is wounded in the body, but its thought not mortal. He had three horses killed under him: Capt. Orme AD Camp is wounded in the thigh and Secretary Shirley killd. Sir Peter Halkett killd dead, with a great many more officers of Account. All the Artillery taken and the whole put to the rout by a few Indians.
William Ferguson [655]

July 16 (Wednesday)
PENNSYLVANIA-SQUAWS FORT CAMP
Camp After the Great Crossing July ye 16th 1755
The parole is Hampton Court   **(Halkett/Disney)**

All the Wounded returnd Able to March with a little Assistance Are to parade at the Genl Beating at the Front Gun When Surgon's Campble & Lee Are to attend with Their Medicins And to March with them to Fort Cumberland. One Sub & twenty men of the Line are (to) Escort Them And to give them all the assistance that lays in their power. [656]

Wedensday July ye 16th.   **(batman)**

We marched toward the little Meadows, it beeing 16 miles. Very Rainy here. We Incamped upon our old ground. [657]

July 17 (Thursday)
MARYLAND-BEAR CAMP

Bear Camp July ye 17th: 1755

The Parole is Winsor   **(Halkett/Disney)**

        The Genl to beat to morrow morning at 5 oClock And march half An hour after.[658]

(Br. Officer 1)

    Being now very light as to cariages, we returned to the Fort (Cumberland) by ye 17th, where y^e: Men were dressed & most of them are in a good way. The balls that were cut out of Ye: Wounds were all of them chewed & many Sluggs & other ragged peices of lead were found in them.

    On our coming to ye Fort ye number of killed & wounded were cast up, & are as follows.

    An Account of the Detachment commanded by General Braddock at the late engagement within 6 miles of Fort Duquesne on Fraziers Plantation near the Monongahela river July the 9th 1755.

Name	Status	Not Wounded	Status
Genl: Braddock died of his	w	Capt: Robt: Dobson	
Capt: Orme	w	Capt: Llt: Wm: Morris	
Mr. Sherley	k	Lieut: John Walsham	
Sir Peter Hackett	k	do: Jno: Hawthorn	
Capt: Charles Tatton	k	do: Jno: Cope	
do: Richd: Gethin	k	do: Joseph Cowart	
Lieut: James Halket	k	do: Hen. Harison	
do: Robt: Townshend	k	Ensign Jno: Dunbar	
Ensign Wm: Nartlow	k	Surgeon's Mate Jno: Lee of Hospital	
Lieut: Jas: Allen died of his	w	Doctor Napier	
Lieut: Coll Ths: Gage	w	Doctor Adair	
Lieut: Wm: Littler	w	Doctor Swinton killed	
do: Wm: Dunbar	w	Mate Williams	
do: John Treby	w	Mate Campbell	
do: Andrew Simson	w	Engineer Mackellar wounded	
do: Robert Lock	w	do: Henry Gordon wounded	
do: Danl: Disney Adjt:	w	do: Adams Williamson wounded	
do: Quintan Kennedy	w	Artillery	
Capt: Sam: Hobson	not wounded	Capt: Thos: Ord not wounded	
do: John Beckwith	do:	Capt: Lt: Robt: Smith died of his wounds	
do: Francis Halket	do:	Lieut: Wm: Mcleod wounded	
Lieuts: Thos: Falconer	do:	do: James Buchanan do:	
do: Richard Baily	do:	do: Jno: McCulloch do:	
do: Jas: Pottinger	do:	Americans	
Ensign Geo: Clerk	do:	Capt: Wm.Polson	killed
do: Wm: Preston	do:	do: Chevr: Peronie	died of w
do: Geo: Pennington	do:	do: Horation Gates	w
do: Thos: Eyre	do:	do: Adam Stephens	w
Chaplain Phill: Hughs	do:	do: Thos: Waggoner	notw
Qr: Master Hen: Verrant	do:	do: Robt: Stewart	do:do:
Surgeon Robt: Mckinley	do:	Lieuts: Gustav Splitdorf	k
do: Mate Wm: Congleton	do:	do: Simon Soumain	do:
Capt: Floyer of Hobson's Reg	w	do: Jno: Hambeton	do:
Capt: Robt: Cholmondly	k	do: Jno: Wright	do:
Lieut: Jno: Hansard	k	do: Edmd: Waggoner	do:
do: Wm: Widman	k	do: Robt: Howarth	wounded
do: Walter Crymble	k	do: John Gray	do:
do: Percival Brereton	k	do Walter Stewart	do:
do: John Hart	k	do: Richd: Miller	not wounded
Lt: Coll: Burton	w	do: Wm: Brenaw	do:
Major Wm: Sparke	w	do: Hen: Woodward	do:
Capt: Roger Morris	w		

do: Richd: Bowyer	w		do: Alexr: McNeil	do:	
do: Robt: Ross	w		Surgeon Jas: Craig	do:	
Lts: Theodore Barbat	w		Lieuts: Spendilon	k	
do: Wm: Edmeston	w				
do: John Gladwin	w		Mr: Talbot, Midshipman	k	
Ensigns Richd: Croe	w		Mr. Haines	do:	not w
do: Alexr: McMullen	w				
do: Robt: Stirling	w				
do: John Montresor	w	Total Killed 385	Wounded 328	not wounded 532	

659

(Campbell)

I thought it proper to let you know that I was in the Battle where We were defeated, and we had about Eleven Hundred and Fifty private Men besides Officers and others, And we was attack'd the 9th Day about Twelve o'Clock and held till about Three in the Afternoon and then we were forced to retreat, when I suppose we might bring about 300 whole Men besides a vast many wounded; Most of our Officers were either wounded or killed, General Braddock is wounded but I hope not mortal, and Sr. John St. Claire and many others, but I hope not mortal. All the Train is cut off in a manner. [660]

Thursday July 17th.　　　　　　　　　　　　　　　　　　**(batman)**
We Marched to Fort Cumberlnd, it being 24 miles.[661]

MARYLAND-FORT CUMBERLAND　　　　　　**(Browne)**
Oh! how shall I express my Distraction. This unhappy day at 2 in the after Noon deprived me of my dear Brother in whom I have lost my kind Guardian and Protector and am now left a friendless Exile from all that is dear to me.[662]

PENNSYLVANIA-PHILADELPHIA　　　　**(Pennsylvania Gazette)**
Extract of a letter from an officer at the camp, 35 miles from Fort Du Quesne dated June 30. "We have here about 1300 men, and Colonel Dunbar, with 700 more in about the Great Meadows. The Indian scouts have killed three batmen, a waggoner and one horse belonging to us. Our men are all in high spirits and have plenty of provisions, with which they are regularly served.[663]

July 18 (Friday)
MARYLAND-CAMP 2 MILES WEST OF LITTLE CROSSINGS
Little Bear Camp July ye 18th 1755　　　　　**(Halkett/Disney)**
The Parole is Richmond

At retreat beating the Eldest Capt: to see the Centrys posted And go the Grand Rounds. The Genl to beat at six to morrow Morning. The Surgons to see their sick properly disposed off at Genl Beating And to Attend the Waggons on the march. [664]

Friday July ye 18th.   **(batman)**
We halted and all the wounded Gentlemen was put in the Wards and dressed. [665]

Little Bear Camp 18th July 1755.   **(Ord, Furnis)**
RETURN OF BRASS ORDNANCE howitzers & Cohorn Mortars &ca sent from England, Lost in the Action Near Fort Du Quesne and Distroy'd at the Camp 6 Miles from the Great Meadows by order of General Braddock with the Remain in North America.

SPECIES OF STORES:	SENT FR.ENGLAND	LOST IN ACTION	DISTROY'D AT CAMP	
Light Brass Ordn.Mounted on Traveling Carriages with Limbers, Ammunition Boxes & Elevatg Screws				
12 pounders	4	4		
6 pounders	6	2	4	
Brass Howitzers with Mounted Carriages and Limbers compleat				
8 Inch	4	4		
Brass Cohorn Mortars Mounted on their Beds with Lashing Ropes Compleat:				
4 2/5 Inch	15	3	8	4
Round Shott with Wooden				

391

Bottoms:					
12 pounders			100	100	
6 pounders			450	102	348
Tin Cases fill'd with Iron shott and fix'd with Wooden Bottoms					
12 pounders		400	24	176	200
6 pounders	1200		148	148	904
Spare Round Shott:					
12 pounders	1200		150	1050	
6 pounders	1200		100	1100	
Empty Shells for Howitzers:					
7 2/5 Inch	400		200	200	
Ditto for Cohorns:					
4 2/5 Inch	1500		200	1300	
Corn'd powder Copper hoop'd for the Guns, Howitzers & Small Arms:					
Expended	75				
Whole Barrells	571		34	162	300 [666]

MARYLAND-FORT CUMBERLAND

Fort Cumberland July 18th 1755 (Orme)

Sir (Robert Napier)

As I am perswaded the General would have taken the most early opportunity of informing you of every remarkable event, I take the liberty of transmitting to you by the first express an account of the unhappy affair which happen'd on the 9th of this Month near the Banks of the Monongahela within seven miles of Fort Du Quesne.

After Marching about twenty Miles from this place to a Camp calld the little Meadows, the General finding the delay so great from the extreme line of Baggage and also that it was impossible from the small number of Troops he had to make his line of March secure, he determined to proceed himself with twelve hundred Men, ten pieces of

Ordinance, Ammn and Provisions proportion'd to the undertaking, and left eight hundred Men with the body of the Convoy under the Command of Col⁰ Dunbar with orders to move forward as fast as the Nature of the Service would admit; with this command His Excellency march'd with great expedition and safety, and Encamp'd on the 8ᵗʰ of this instant within ten miles of the French Fort. Here the Guides were all summons'd and question'd as to the first part of the next days March His Excellency having been informd of a very bad and dangerous Defilee called the narrows; upon their report it was judg'd most expedient to pass the Monongahela twice at two different Fords which were neither of them knee deep, by which measure the narrows were to be avoided and a very bad passage of the Turtle Creek. To secure the two passages of the River the General order'd the two Grenadier's Companys as a part of a Detachment which was to be compleated to 300: Men with two Six pounders under the Command of Lieut. Col⁰ Gage with proper Guides to March before break of Day making the two crossings of the Monongahela, of which the first was a mile distance, and to make an advantageous Post at the last, Sir John St. Clair with a working party of 200: Men was to follows at Day break, and the whole was to March at Six. This plan was exactly and punctually executed, and the Artillery, Ammunition, Provisions, Baggage and all the Troops had pass'd the river the second time at one o'clock; as soon as the whole was over the General order'd the two Detachments to advance, and Sir John St. Clair to proceed in making the Road as usual; about half a mile after the Junction of the two Roads Vizᵗ the narrows and the River, a heavy and quick firing was heard in the Front; The General believing a party of French and Indians had taken post, ordered Col⁰ Burton with his Van Guard to reinforce them, and at the same time dispos'd the Column in such a manner as to defend it from any attack and to disengage more men for action. The French and Indians as we found after had possessed the sides and Brow of a Hill In a kind of Semicircular form, from the extremes of which, some of them fired upon one of our advanced Flank Parties, this immediately brought on a general Pannick, the Men could never be perswaded to form regulary, and in great confusion fell back upon the Party which Sir John St. Clair commanded, as did Sir John St. Clair's upon Col⁰ Burton's every exhortion entreaty and perswation was used by the General and Officers to make them advance or fall back into the line of March, examples of all kinds were likewise given by the Genl.

and the Officers, but the Pannock was so univeral and the Firing so executive and uncommon that no order coud ever be restor'd, after three hours or irregularity, and the waste of all the ammunition, during which time allmost all the Officer's were killed or Wounded by advancing sometimes in bodys and sometimes separately in order to encourage the Men, they felt the Field and crossd the River with great precepitation, abandoning the Artillery, Ammunition, Provision, and Baggage, to the Enemy, and their Terror was so great that many of them threw away their Arms and accoutrements, nor could they be stopt till they had run forty Miles notwithstanding the Enemy pursued no further than the River; The General had five Horses shot under him and receiv'd a mortal wound in his Lungs, and in this unhappy state was very near being left in the Enemys power being deserted by the Men and brought off by the assistance of a few Officers who were determined not to forsake him; he died of his wound the 13th Instant. An Express was immediately sent off to Colᵒ Dunbar with orders to send to us Ammunition, Provisions, and Waggons for the wounded, we were then sensible of the good effects of this disposition, for an additional number of Men cou'd have been of no advantage the Pannick being so prevalent, and the want of Provision must have thrown us into the hands of the Enemy.

The Men have by no means recover'd their fright & are so little to be confided in, that Colᵒ Dunbar is movᵍ to this place were I and some other wounded Officer's arrivd from the 17th Inst. under an Escort. I have Inclosed you Sir the most perfect List that could be got and I know it may be much depended upon.

I am Sir, Yʳ most Hᵇˡᵉ & most Obedᵗ Servt

Robt. Orme.

I would have wrote in my own hand but am render'd incapable by the wound in my Thigh. [667]

Sir, (Henry Fox)   (Orme)

The General the day before his Death order'd Me as soon as I was able to transmitt to You, Sir, An Account of the Unhappy Action near the Monongahela about Seven Miles Distant from Fort Duquesne in the Ninth of this Month.

Our Encampment on the Eighth was about ten Miles from the Fort and upon Calling all the Guides the General from the Intelligence he Could Collect determine(d) to pass the Monongahela twice in Order to

Advanced party found Some French and Indians posted on a very advantageous Height some of whom fired upon one of their flank parties which immediately Alarm'd the whole and brought On a very Severe fireing without any Order or Execution. The General immediately sent forward his Van Guard Under the Command of Lieut. Coll. Burton to Sustain the two Detachments and instantlly formed the Column in Such a Manner as to Secure it and to be Able to Bring more Men to Act in Case of Necessity.

The two Advanced parties gave way and fell back Upon Our Van which very much disconcerted the Men and that Added to the Manner of fighting they were quite Unacquainted with struck them with such a pannick that all the Intreaties perswasions and Example of the General and Officers could Avail nothing nor could Order ever be regain'd after fireing away all their Ammunition they gave Ground and left the Artillery Baggage &c in the Hands of the Enemy.

The General was with great Difficulty brought out off the field he had five Horses shott under him and was at last Mortally wounded of which he died the thirteenth.

I had the General Orders to Inform You, Sir, that the behavior of the Officers deserved the very Highest Commendation.

Mr. Morris the Other Aid De Camp and Myself being very dangerously wounded and the Secretary Kill'd all the papers are lost.
₆₆₈

Fort Cumberland   (Orme)
My Dear Governor (Dinwidde)

I am so extremely ill in bed with the wound I have received that I am under the Necessity of employing my friend Capt. Dobson as my scribe. I am informed that Governor Innes has sent you some account of the Action near the Banks of the Monongahela about seven miles from the French Fort. As his Intelligence must be very Imperfect, the Dispatch he sent to you must consequently be so too; you should have had more early Account of it, but every Officer whose business it was to have informed you was either killed or wounded and our distressful Situation put it out of our power to attend to it so much as we would otherwise have done. The 9th instant we passed and repassed the Monongahela by advancing first a part of 300 men which immediatelly followed by another of 200, the general with the Column of Artillery, Baggage and the main body of the Army passed the river the last time, about one o'clock, as soon as the whole had got on the Fort side of

Monongahela we heard a very heavy and quick fire on our front, we immediately advanced in order to sustain them but the Detachment of the 200 and 300 gave way and fell back upon us, which caused such confusion and struck so great a panic into our men that afterwares no military Expedient could be made use of that had any effect upon them, the men were so extremely deaf to the exhortations of the General and the Officers that they fired away in the most irregular manner too their ammunition and then ran off leaving to the Enemy the Artillery, Ammunition, Provisions and Baggage, nor could they be persuaded to stop till they got as far as Gists plantation nor there only in part, many of them proceeding even as far as Col. Dunbar's Party who lay six miles on this side.

The officers were absolutely sacrificed by the unparalleled good behaviour; Advancing before their men sometimes in bodies and sometimes separately, hoping by such an example to engage the soldiers to follow them, but to no purpose. The General had five horses shot under him and at last received a wound through his lungs, of which he died the 13 instant at night. Captain Monies and myself very much wounded. Mr. Washington had two horse shot under him and his clothes shot through in several places, behaving the whole time with the greatest courage and resolution.

Sir P. Halket was killed upon the spot, and according to the best calculation we can as yet make about 28 Officers were killed.

Col. Burton and Sir John St. Clair with 35 Officers wounded and out of our whole number of Officers not above 16 came off the Field unhurt. We imagine there are killed and wounded about 600 men. I have the pleasure to acquaint you that Captain Polson (who was killed) and his company behaved extremely well, as did Captain Stuart and his light horse, who I must beg leave to recommend to you protection and to desire you will be so kind to use your best endeavours to serve him as he has lost by the death of the general the rewards he really deserved by his gallant and faithful attendance on him.

Upon our proceeding with the whole convoy to the Little Meadow we found it impractable to advance in that manner. A Detachment was therefore made of 1200 men with the Artillery, necessary ammunition, Provision and Baggage leaving the remainder with Col. Dunbar, with Orders to join us as soon as possible; with this Detachment we proceeded with saftey and expedition, till the fatal day I have just related and happy it was that this Disposition was made, otherwise the whole must have starved or fallen into the Hands of the enemy as numbers would have been no service to us and our Provision was all lost.

Mr. Shaw put into my Hands a letter from you directed to the General now as then incapaple of any business, it contained Notes of £2000 from South Carolina. I am at a loss to know what to do with them, forgetting the particular appropriation of the Vote of Assembly, though I think I recollect its being voted at the Service of the Expedition in general and at the disposal of General Braddock; these Bills are made payable to him or Order, for which reason they are not negotiable. I desire your advice on this subject, and as it may save time, beg the favor of you to write to Governor Glen about it.

As our number of horses were so much reduced, and those so extremely weak, and many carriages being wanted for the wounded men occasioned our destroying the Ammunition and superfluous part of the Provision left in Col. Dunbar's Convoy, to prevent its falling into the Hands of the Enemy.

As the whole of the Artillery is lost and the Terror of the Indian remaining so strongly in the mens minds, as also the Troops being extemely weakened by Deaths, Wounds and Sickness, it was judged impossible to make any further attempts; therefore Col. Dunbar is returning to Fort Cumberland, with everything he is able to bring along with him. I propose remaining here till my wound will suffer me to remove to Philadelphia, from thence I shall make all possible Dispatch to England.

I am Sir &c [669]

MARYLAND-FORT CUMBERLAND
Sir: Commodore Keppel   (St. Clair)

The personal situation that I am in puts it out of my power to transmit to you in order to be fowarded to England the previous steps to our unlucky defeat, I hope by the time Col. Dunbar who now commands comes here which will be in three days hence that may have strength and spirits enough to dictate the Majesty letters on this Maloncholly subject.

I cannot help requesting of you not to send any ship of war to England until you receive our commandng officer letters for the better information of his Majesty. I have escaped much better, than many of my brother officers, though I was shot through the body amongst the first that were wounded are shot dead upon the spot. [670]

FORT CUMBERLAND, 18 JULY 1755
To: Governor Dinwiddie: (Washington)
   Honbl. Sir - As I am favored with an opportunity, I should think myself inexcusable was I to omit giving you some account of our late Engagement with the French on the Monongahela, the 9th instant.

   We continued our march from Fort Cumberland to Frazier's (which is 7 miles from Duquesne) without meetng any extrodinary event, having only a straggler or two picked up by the French Indians. When we came to this place, we were attacked (very unexpectedly I must own) by abt. three hundred French and Ind'ns; Our numbers consisted of about 1300 well arm'd Men, chiefly Regular's, who were immediately struck with such an inconceivable (deadly) Panick, that nothing but confusion and disobedience of order's prevail'd amongst them: The Officer's in gen'l, behavd with incomparable bravery, for which they greatly suffer'd, there being near 60 kill'd and wound'd. A large proportion, out of the number we had! The Virginia Companies behav'd like Men and died like Soldiers; for I believe out of 3 Companys that were on the ground that day, scarce 30 were left alive: Capt. Peyrouny and all his Officer's, down to a Corporal, were kill'd, Captn Polson had (shar'd) almost as hard a Fate, for only one of his Escap'd: In short, the dastardly behavior of the Regualr troops (so called) (English soldier) expos'd all those who were inclin'd to do their duty to almost certain Death; and at length, in spite of every effort to the contrary, broke and ran as Sheep before the Hounds, leav'g the Artillery, Ammunition, Provisions, baggage, and, in short every individual thing we had with us a prey to the Enemy; and when we endeavor'd to rally them in hopes of regaining (our invaluable) loss, it was with as much the (success) as if we had attempted to have stop'd the wild Bears of the Mountains or rivulets with our feet, for they would break by, in despite of every effort that could be made to prevent it.

   The Genl. was wounded in the shoulder and into the Breast, of which he died three days after, his two Aids de Camp were both wounded, but are in a fair way of Recovery; Col⁰ Burton and Sr J^no St. Clair are also wounded, and I hope will get over it, Sir Peter Halket, with many other brave Officers, were kill'd in the field. I luckily escap'd with't a wound tho I had four Bullets through my Coat and two Horses shot under me. It is supposed that we left 300 or more dead in the Field; about that number we brought off wounded, and it is imagin'd (I believe with great Justice too) that two thirds received their shott from our own cowardly English Soldier's who gather'd themselves into a body contrary to orders, 10 or 12 deep, wou'd then level, Fire and shoot down the Men before them.

I tremble at the consequence that this defeat may have upon our back settlers, who I suppose will all leave their habitations unless there are proper measures taken for their security.

Col⁰. Dunbar, who commands at present, intends as soon as his men are recruited at this place, to continue his march to Phila. into Winter Quarters, so that there will be no Men left here, unless it is the poor remains of the Virginia troops, who survive and will be too small to guard our Frontiers. As Captn. Orme is writg. to your honour I doubt not but he will give you a circumstantial acct. of all things, which will make it needless for me to add more. [671]

Review of the Military Operations in North America. Dinwiddie wished Dunbar to remain and make a new attempt on Dusquesne; but a council of officers unanimously decided the scheme was impracticable, and on the next day (August 2d) began his (Dunbar's) march toward Philadelphia.

The regulars laid the responsibility of defeat on the provincials, alleging "that they were harassed by duties unequal to their numbers, and dispirited through want of provisions; that time was not allowed them to dress their food; that their water (the only liquor, too, they had) was both scarce and of a bad quality; in fine, that the provincials had disheartened them by repeated suggestions of their fears of a defeat should; they be attacked by Indians, in which case the Europeans method of fighting would be entirely unavailing."- Review of the Military Operations in North America from 1753 to 1756. The Gentleman's Magazine asserted these same forces - Irish, Scotch, and English - ran away "shamefully" at Shirley's and Pepperell's regiments, and many deserted. "I must leave a proper number in each county to protect it from the combinations of the Negro slaves, who have been very audacious on the defeat on the Ohio. These poor creatures imagine the French will give them their freedom". - Dinwiddie to Earl of Halifax, 23 July, 1755.

July 18, Tuesday.
Fort Cumberland.   **(Washington)**
Dear Brother: John Augustine Washington

As I have heard, since my arriv'l at this place, a circumstantial acct. of my death and dying speech, I take this early opportunity of contradicting the first and of assuring you that I have not as yet composed the latter. By all the powerful dispensations of Providence, I have been protected beyond human probability and expectation; for I had four bullets through my coat, and two horses shot under me, yet escaped unhurt, altho' death was levelling my companions on every side of me....A weak and feeble state of health obliges me to halt here for two or three days, to recover a little strengh...You may expect to see me there (Mount Vernon) on Saturday or Sunday se'night which is as soon as I can, as I shall take in my Bullskin Plantations on my way.
[672]

Christopher Gist's map of the route **(Gist)**
traveled by Braddock from Cumberland to the vicinity of Fort Duquesne:
Miles From Ft. Cumberland to No.

1 Grove Camp	5
2 George's Creek	5
3 Savage river	5
4 Little Meddowes	5
5 Lawrel rum camp	4
6 Bare Camp	7
7 Lick neer viz. ( ) miles	8
8 Camp 6 East	
Great Meddowes	7
9 Camp 1 West great Meddowes	7
hear is Genl Brad	
10 Rock camp or rock Fort	3
The union camp where the Forces Joyn'd	
11 Gist's house or Plantation	8
12 Camp by Stewarts	5
13 over the river	4
14 Tarripen creek	7
15 Jacob Cabbins	5
16 Lick Camp miles	4
17 camp 3 miles from the Lick	3
18 Monacatootha camp	6
hear Monacatootha's Son Buried	
the 13th of June 1755	

19 Bladen's (?) camp	2
20 head Suger creek	8
21 Mouth Turtle creek	5
To Fort DuQuesne	6
From Fort Cumberland to Fort DuQuesne is	122

The red line for N. 10: is Capt. Dobson's Route to the mouth of Red Stone creek to Destroy the French Barks and Provisions and then Joyn'd the Army at Gist's house N. 11.

The red lines from N. 17: is Gist's Route to the French Fort and back to the Army the crosses on the Black line is the Gen. camp

The Route of the Army under the command of Gen: Braddock to the place of their Defeat.   Laid Down by Christopher Gist   [673]

No specific date is indicated on Gist's map however, it was after the defeat and after the General's interment and at a location where he could confer with others and draw his description of the route, Gist was the expedition's scout.

July 19 (Saturday)

MARYLAND-LITTLE MEADOWS

Camp at the little Meddows July ye 19th: 1755

The Parole is Bristol   **(Halkett/Disney)**

The Genl: to beat to morrow morning at 5 oClock. The whole to be Ready to march half An hour After at Troop beating. [674]

MARYLAND-WILLS CREEK   **(Stewart)**

As I did not till this Moment know of this Opportunity, have scarce Time to inform you, of my having escaped safe from the dreadful Havock we had on the 9th Instant, within Six Miles of the French Fort,-where General Braddock, with 1300 chosen Men and Officers, were attacked by the French and Indians, and after a sharp and bloody Engagement of 3 Hours and 35 Minutes, our Troops yielded Ground; chiefly owing to the Consternation the Indian Method of fighting threw the British into, and for the Want of Officers, most of them being killed or wounded by that Time: Very soon after our giving Way, the Pannic became so general and great, that they shamefully turned their Backs, and in a great Measure, abandoned their General and the Colours-notwithstanding the utmost Efforts of the few remaning Officers to rally and return to the Charge, and tho' they had to retreat upwards of 60 Miles thro' a Wilderness, before they could join the other Division of the Army. As to Particulars, it's impossible yet to give them with any Certainty. We lost all our Artillery, Stores, Provisions, and Baggage of every Kind, by much the greater Number of our Officers, and most People think, at least Half of the Whole Number of Men we carried into the Field that Fatal Day. To give the finishing Stroke to our Misfortune, our great and brave (tho' unfortunate) General, died the 13th Instant. He was wounded in the Arm and Body, and I believe his Misfortune wounded his very Soul. I had the Honour of being close by his Side during the Action, and lost every Thing I had but my Blood, of which not a Drop was spilt, tho' I had two Horses shot under me, one Ball grazed my right Brow, another my Forehead, and a third shot away Sword and Scabard from my Side. I had only a Detachment of my Troops with me of 29 Horses of which 25 were killed. [675]

Saturday July ye 18th.   **(batman)**
   We had several Wounded Officers and Soldiers Ariv'd at the Fort.[676]

July 20 (Sunday)
MARYLAND-MARTINS PLANTATION
Martins Camp July ye 20th: 1755   **(Halkett/Disney)**
The Parole is Monkton
   The Genl to beat to morrow morning at six oClock. All the Surgons here present are to attend the Hospital Waggons. [677]

                                                               (seaman)
   Col. Dunbar with the remains of the Army continued their retreat, and returned to Will's Creek, or Fort Cumberland, the 20th of July. [678]

Sunday July ye 20th.   **(batman)**
   Severall more of the Wounded officers and Soldiers ariv'd here.[679]

Fort Duquesne, July 20, 1755   **(Contrecoeur)**
Captain Contrecoeur to Count La Galisonniere
   The favor with which you have honored me and the role which you play in the Colony leads me to inform you of the complete victory which we have just won from the English three leagues from this fort. 250 French and 650 Indians have defeated 2000 English regular troops

and taken all their cannon and baggage. M. de Beaujeu, who had been named to succeed me in this command, led the party, having as his lieutenant M. Dumas and M. de Ligneris. He was killed on the third discharge from the enemy; these men took his place every well and they were well seconded by all the other officers and cadets. The enemy left 500 men on the filed of battle and have lost their commander and almost all their officers.

I ask you, please, Monsieur, to be helpful at the colony at this time when nothing would please me more than to have to have the officers who served so well under me rewarded for the zeal. Messiuers Dumas and de Ligneris had a great part in our recent success, since victory was very much in the balance when M. de Beaujeu was killed, but these 2 men encouraged our troop so well that all came out for the best and - or, perhaps, I should sav. God put himself on our side...[680]

July 21 (Monday)
MARYLAND-FORT CUMBERLAND   **(batman)**
Colonel Dunbar and his party Ariv'd here, he leaving a Command with the Wounded that was in the Wagons. [681]

July 22 (Tuesday)
MARYLAND-FORT CUMBERLAND
Fort Cumberland July ye 22d: 1755   **(Halkett/Disney)**
The Parole is Boscowen

Each Corps to give into the Director a Return of the No of Sick & Wounded. All Those that have Anything belong: to the Late Capt Tatton or any of the Officers Killd in the Late ingagement of the 44th Regt Are desird to Carry 'em to the Court Martial which is to sitt to morrow morning at 8 oClock. [682]

                                                         (batman)
All the Wagons ariv'd and all the Wounded men was put in the Hospital and Dresed.[683]

Berkebile writes: "The number of Pennsylvania wagons that arrived back at Wills Creek has not been definitely established. For the service of their wagons, 30 owners received payment for a period greater than the 51 days, but of these, only 10 were paid for services beyond what appears to be July 20. Only the wagon of William Douglas, out of 146 wagons involved, seems to have survived the campaign intact. Inasmuch as the other owners were reimbursed for the loss of their wagons, it is likely that those few that arrived back at Fort Cumberland were so badly damaged as to render them unserviceable, and there not worth driving back to eastern Pennsylvania."

MARYLAND-FORT AT WILLS'S CREEK   (St. Clair)
Sir: Robert Napier

I wrote to you a letter of the 12th of June, which I hope you have received by this time, that letter gave you an Account of the obstructions we was like to meet with on our march on account of Carridges; a few days after writing that letter, General Braddock with the Army arrived at the little meadows; about the 17th of June General Braddock sent for me and told me, he laid down a Scheme of his own for marching on, which before that time, had been given to the Brigade Major in orders. The Scheme was, that a detachment should be form'd of those of the British Battalions, which Came from Ireland and that those should march with the artillery togeather with three Companys of the Virginia forces, under the Command of General Braddock, the remaining part of the Army under the Command of Colonel Dunbar, was to follow with the Great Convoy, this step I look'd upon to be a prelude to marching in divisions, which was the only way we Could have brought up our Convoy.

This strong detachment march'd on and arrived at the Strong Camp of the Great-Lick which is Twenty one miles on the other side of Yanehagane and Eighty mile from this fort. The Great advantages of this strong Ground made me propose to the General, to halt with his detachment and bring up Colonel Dunbar with his Convoy; this proposal, was rejected with great indignation; we march'd on 'till the seventh of July Twenty three miles further, I then objected to our marching any longer in that order of march with a Convoy, and proposed, since this small body must march to the french fort, that we should march part of our small numbers and take post before the Fort leaving our Convoy to Come up I urged strongly that no General had hitherto march'd up at midday to the Gates of the Town he was to besiege leading his Convoy and if Genl. Braddock attempted it, he must look to the Consequences.

Tewsday the 8th we march'd to a riseing ground within three quarters of a mile of the Monanganhela and Encamp'd there.

Wednesday the 9th Colonel Gage with about 300 men march'd at daylight, past and repast the Monaganhela where he took post, the Workmen and Cover'ers immediately follow'd and then the rest of the detachment-so that the whole had past by half an hour after Twelve o'Clock, being three miles; The reason of passing the Monaganhela twice was to avoid the Narrows, which is a road on the bank of the River, Commanded by a high hill, which would have taken a days work to have made passable. After Colonel Gage and I had pass'd the river, we received orders from Cap: Morris Aid du Camp to March on; the underwood Continued very thick for about one quarter of a mile beyond the Monaganhela then we Came into an open wood free from underwood with some gradual riseings, this wood was so open the Carridges Could have been drove in any part of it; about a mile on the other side of the last Crossing, we began to feel the Enemys fire and to hear their Shouts; those who were under my Command immediately form'd. On those in my front falling back upon me, I ran to the front to see what the matter was, when I received a Shot through the body. I then return'd to my own people, posted Cap: Polsons Company of Artificers and Cap: Periwees Company of Rangers to Cover my two Cannon. I then went up to General Braddock who was then at the head of his own Guns and beg'd of him for God Sake to gain the riseing ground on our Right to prevent our being Totally surrounded. I know no further of this unlucky affair to my knowledge being afterwards insensible. It will be needless for me to give you any account by hear-say. Our affairs are as bad here as bad Can make them, with regard to my self in particular, I was fully resolved, if we had met with Success to desire leave to have been recalld, finding I could be of little use being never listen'd to: but as our affairs stand at present it is a thing I shall not think of and should be glad of haveing another opportunity of making use of the knowledge I have of the Country and its inhabitants; by the time I shall have your answer, I hope to be in a Condition of doing my duty therefore should be glad you would point it out to me whether its to be here or in New England under General Shirrly. I am with the greatest respect Sir, your most obedient and most obliged humble Servant.   John St Clair. [684]

(St. Clair)
The copies of my letters from the 27th of May to the 9th of July fell into the enemies hands, there were none of them of consequence excepting one to Col. Napier of the 12th of June in which I represented to him the absolute necessity of making a stop near Fort du Quesne by throwing up an entrenchment for our..., and bring up a

second convoy, and opening the communication behind to Pensylvania.

The French also got an original letter of mine which I wrote to the Earl of Hindford, which I had no opportunity of sending back it was to the same purpose as that of Col. Napier. [685]

July 23 (Wednesday)
MARYLAND-FORT CUMBERLAND   **(batman)**

This day their was an Indien sent to the French Fort to the governor (Contrecoeur) to desire him to send the Wrightings (writings) that he had got with the Baggage in the late Ingagement.[686]

WILLS'S CREEK, 23RD OF JULY 1755   **(Gordon)**
Sir, (recipient not stated)

I have not troubl'd you hitherto with any letters, altho' when I took my Leave at London I Receiv'd your Commands to write you the most Remarkable Occurences of our Expedition.

I shall now trouble you with a short Journal of our March & proceedings, from this place to Beyond the Last Crossing of the Monangahela, where we were unfortunatley Defeated.

On the 11th of June we March'd from this fort with much a train of provision & Amunition Waggons, that the first days March Convinc'd us that it was impossible to Get on with so many Carriges so heavily loaded. The General Diminish'd the Carriadges By putting the greatest part of the provisions on Pack horses, & sending Back two of the 6 pounders with their Amunition; in this Reformation we March'd as far as the Little Meadows, which are only Distant 15 miles from our first Camp, yet took us five Days to Get up all our carriages, the Roads Being steep & the horses very weak.

At the Little Meaddows the General order'd another Reform, which Reduc'd us to a Pick'd Body of Eleven hundred men & officers; our Carriadges consisted of two 6 pounders, four 12 pounders, four Howits's, 3 Cowhorns, & 75 Rounds of Amunition, 3 or 4 provision Waggons, which made our whole train of Carriadges three or four & thirty. We Left the Little Meadows the 19th of June with a Resolution of pushing on Directly to fort Du Quesne, & to leave Coll: Dunbar with the rest of our Army & Carriadges to Get up in the Best Manner he cou'd. We Came on Extreamly well, Considering the Difficulty of making the roads, which was so Great, that Altho' Every one us'd

406

their Utmost Endeavor & only halted four Days on the Road, it was the 8th of July Before we Cou'd get within 10 miles of the french fort.

On the 8th we Cross'd the Long Run which was a small Rivulet that runs in to the Monongahela about 12 miles from the F: fort. We were Oblig'd to Cross it many times in the Space of two Miles, in which Distance we came along a Narrow Valley At the widest a Quarter of a Mile, very much Commanded on Both sides By Steep hills. In this March Every proper precaution was taken to secure us, By Detaching all the men that cou'd Be Spar'd from the Advancd party, that day Commanded by C: Burton on our flank the General Likewise orderd 350 men to take possession of the heigths on Each Side; & the Grenadier Company of Sir P: H(alket's) Reg^t, the Advance of the Advanc'd party, to Gain the Rising Ground, which Shut up the Valley in or front. No Enemy appear'd, & we Encamp'd on the last Mention'd Rising Ground, which Brought us within a Small Mile of the River Monongahela.

In our Next Days March we must Either Go along the Narrows, a very Difficult pass, on the Right side Entirely Commanded by high ground & on the Left hemm'd in By the Monongahela; A Small Consultation was held, & it was carryied to Cross the Monongahela at the Nearer end of the Narrows, to keep along the South Side, & to Cross it again Below where turtle Creek runs in, & without the Narrows; As there was Danger Imagin's, the 2 Compys of Grenadiers with 150 men of the two Reg^{ts} Commanded by Col: Gage were Order's to March By 2 o'Clock of the Morning of the 9th to take possession of the Banks of the second Crossing of the River; two of the light 6 pounders were sent along with this party; the rest of our Little Army March'd at four, Cross'd peaceably, & came up with Coll: Gage about Eleven o'Clock in peaceable possession of the furthest Banks of the Last Crossing. Every one who saw these Banks, Being Above 12 feet perpendicularly high Above the Shore, & the Course of the River 300 yards Broad, hugg'd themselves with joy at our Good Luck in having surmounted our greatest Difficultys, & too hastily Concluded the Enemy never wou'd dare to Oppose us.

In an hour which Brought the time about Noon, the Bank was slop'd & passable for Artillery & Carriadges: Coll: Gage with the same Advanc'd party was ordered to (sic) forward; the covering party of the Carpenters & Pioneers followed immediately in his Rear, after them then came two 6 pounders, their Amunition Waggon, & a Guard in their Rear, after them follow'd the Main Body in their Usual Order of March with a strengthen's Rear Guard of 100 men.

The flank partys of the Advance & Main Body were No Stronger than Usual & Coll: Gage's party march'd By files four Deep our front had not Got above half a Mile from the Banks of the River, when the Guides which were all the Scouts we had, & who were Before only about 200 yards Came Back, & told a Considerable Body of the Enemy, Mostly Indians were at hand, I was then just rode up in Search of these Guides, had Got Before the Grenadiers, had an Opportunity of viewing the Enemy, & was Confirm'd By the Report of the Guides & what I saw myself that their whole Numbers did Not exceed 300.

As soon as the Enemys Indians perceiv'd our Grenadiers, they Divided themselves & Run along our right & Left flanks. The Advanc'd party Coll: Gage order'd to form, which Most of them Did with the front Rank upon the Ground & Begun firing, which they continued for several Minutes, Altho' the Indians very soon Dispers'd Before their front & fell upon the flank partys, which only consisted of an officer & 20 men, who were very soon Cut off. The Indians Making their Appearance upon the Rising Ground, on our Right, occasion'd an Order Retiring the Advanc'd Body 50 or 60 paces, there they confusedly form'd again, & a Good many of their Officers were kill'd & wounded By the Indians, who had got possession of the Rising Ground on the Right. There was an Alarum at this time that the Enemy were attacking the baggage in the Rear, which Occasion'd a second Retreat of the Advanc'd party: they had not Retir'd But a few paces when they were join'd By the rest of the troops, Coming up in the greatest Confusion, & Nothing afterwards was to Be Seen Amongst the Men But Confusion & Panick. They form'd Altogeather, the Advanced & Main Body in Most places from 12 to 20 Deep; the Ground on which they then were, was 300 yards Behind where the Grenadiers & Advanc'd party first from'd. The General Order'd the Officers to Endeavor to tell off 150 men, & Advance up the hill to dispossess the Enemy, & another party to Advance on the Left to support the two 12 pounders & artillery people, who were in great Danger of Being Drove away by the Enemy, at that time in possession of the 2 field pieces of the Advanc'd party. This was the Generals Last Order; he had had before this time 4 horses killed under him, & now Reciv'd his Mortal wound. All the Officers us'd their Utmost Endeavors to Get the men to Advance up the hill, & to Advance on the left to support the Cannon. But the Enemy's fire at that time very much Encreasing, & a Number of officers who were Rushing on in the front to Encourage the men Being killed & wounded, there was Nothing to be seen But the utmost panick & Confusion amongst the Men; yet those officers who had been wounded having Return'd, & those that were not Wounded, By Exhorting & threatning had influence to keep a Body about 200 an hour Longer in the field, but cou'd not persuade them Either to Attempt the hill again, or Advance far Enough to support the Cannon, whose officers & men were Mostly kill'd & wounded. The Cannon silenc'd, & the Indian's shouts upon the Right Advancing, the whole Body gave way, & Cross'd the Monnongahela where we had pass's in the Morning, with great Difficulty the General & his Aid de Camps who were Both wounded were taken out of a Waggon, & hurryed along across the River; Coll: Burton tho' very much Wounded attempted to Rally on the Other Side, & made a Speach to the Men to Beg them to get into some Order, But nothing would Do, & we found that Every man wou'd Desert us; therefore we were oblig'd to go along; we march'd all night, & never halted till we Came to Guests's which was near 60 Miles from the place of the Action, we halted that night there, & next Day join'd Coll: Dunbar's party which was 6 miles further.

Thus Sir I have sent you an Account of those transactions Entirely consisting with my own Certain knowledge. I never was a Critick therefore leaves it to you to make what Remarks you see proper, As you are a Much Better Judge in these Matters than I shall Ever pretend to Be. only One thing cannot Escape me, which is, that had our March been Executed in the same manner the 9th as it was the 8th, I shou'd have stood a fair Chance of writing from fort Du Quesne, instead of Being in the hospital at Wills's Creek.

I am a Good Deal hurt in the Right Arm, having Receiv'd a shot which went thro', & shatter'd the Bone, half way Between the Elbow & the wrist; this I had Early, & altho's I felt a Good deal of pain, yet I was too Anxious to allow myself to Quit the field; at the last may horse having Receiv'd three shot, I had hardly time to shift the Sadle on another without the Bridle, when the whole gave way. The passage that was made thro the Bank in the Morning, I found Choack'd up: I was oblig'd to tumble over the high Bank, which Luckily Being of Sand, part of it fell along with me, which kept my horse upon his feet, & I fortunately kept his Back. Before I had got 40 yards in the River, I turn'd about on hearing the Indians Yell, & Saw them Tomohocking some of our women & wounded people, others of them fir'd very Briskly on those that were then Crossing, at which time I Receive'd Another shot thro' the Right Shoulder. But the horse I Rode Escaping, I got across the River, & soon came up with the General, Coll: Burton, & the rest of the officers & men that were along with them, & Continued along with them in the Utmost pain, my wounds not having Been Dress'd untill I came to Guest's.

On the Road I propos'd fortifying a Camp at Licking Creek 10 miles to the Westward of the Crossing of the Yohiogany, a very advantagious Situation, & which Cover'd the Richest part of the Country which Lyes Betwixt Guest's & that, or at least I imagin'd we might have Been join'd By Coll: Dunbar's party at Guest's, where a Good Camp might Easily Been had, which fortifeid with two or three Redoubts in front cou'd have Been defended By our Numbers (above 1000 fitt for Duty) against any force our Enemys cou'd Bring against us.

Instead of all this nothing wou'd Do, But Retiring, & Destroying immense Quantitys of Amunition & Stores, with which Last all our Instruments & Stationary ware shar'd the fate.

Here we are at present, But the talk is of going into Pensilvania, & No talk of putting this fort or the frontiers of this Country in any posture of Defence; as it is at present, 3 pieces of 6 pound Cannon, with the Advantage the Ground wou'd Naturaly give them, cou'd knock the fort to pieces, & nothing after we are gone cou'd hinder 150 french Indians from Ravaging to Alexandria.

I have tir'd My Secretary, & I'm afraid you'll think me too prolix, But I cou'd not help it, & indeed it was my intention, to Lay Before you our Proceedings, & the Situation of Affairs in this Country. Had I had the Use of my Drawing hand, I could have sent you a Sketch of the field of Action, & some other Principal Crossing of the Rivers on our March. I hope soon to Be Able to Lay these things Before you, & will take the opportunity of Describing the Country which we pass'd at the same time; This is all hopes, as Nothing certain is determin'd with Regard to the Lower wound of my Arm, at present I conclude with my best wishes for your health, & always shall Be with the greatest Respect, Sir, your most obligd & obed^t Humble Servt.

Harry Gordon

Wills's Creek   A left hand Subscription

23^d of July 1755

P.S. I shoud Be Extreamly oblig'd to you if you would Be kind Enough to Remind H:R:H of my former petition for a Commission in some Reg^t. I have Reason to Believe that had General Braddock Liv'd I shou'd have Been provided for in some of the Reg^{ts} here. to be Copied for Coll: Napier. [687]

On the 9th Instant the General at the Head of about **(Furnis)** 1200 Men-crossed the Manongahela near Fort DuQuesne. the rear of the Army had scarce forded the River before the advanced Party consisting of 250 Men Commanded by Lieut. Colo. Gage, received a smart fire from behind the Trees which put them into some disorder, upon which the General who was about a quarter of a Mile Distant immediately advanced with the Troops and drew up in an open place, when the Action became general, but the Enemy had greatly the Advantage, by securing themselves behind Trees-in such a manner, as they could not be seen, while our people by keeping togeather in a Body were a Butt for them to fire at, and only threw away their Ammunition the Action began about half an hour past One, and continued until a Quarter past Four, when the Troops gave way, and all methods taken to rally them prov'd ineffectual, so that they were oblig'd to leave all our Artillery and Horses in the Field and to cross the River, in great Confusion, several of the Indians pursued us into the Water, and came up with and scalp'd some of the straglers, but the main body kept'd the field in order to secure the Artillery and Baggage expecting we might rally which was very lucky, for the Soldiers were struck with such a Panick that a small body might have cutt off what remained we are at present uncertain of the number of the french and Indians, but they are computed at about three or four Hundred-and our loss kill'd and wounded about Eight hundred at this time Colo. Dunbar was in the Rear with the rest of the Army, Horses and Provisions about 54 Miles distt. not being able to proceed for want of horses.-On the 11th in the Evening the General with most of the wounded arrived at the Camp, and the next day gave orders to destroy the Stores which were there, and a great Quanitiy of Provisions least they should fall into the hands of the enemy who we then expected would pursue us, the greatest part of the Drivers having gone off with their Horses, on the first Alarm of our defeat.[688]

July 24 (Thursday)

MARYLAND-FORT CUMBERLAND

Fort Cumberland July the 24th 1755　　　　　　　　　　(T. Dunbar)

Sir, (Robert Napier)

The Army under General Braddock proceeding to Fort Duquesne halted at the little Meadows, on the 17th of June there was Orders for a Detachment of About twelve hundred of the best Troops to March, part Under Coll: Gage to march the 18th and the rest the 19th. the Officers for this Detachment were All Named. This was the first Sr Peter Halkett or I knew of this design, the Generall March'd with them leaving Me with the remains of the Army to bring Up About One hundred And fifty Waggons and near three hundred Horse load of bread flower and Bacon, telling Me he never would be more than a days March before Me, so that in Case of Necessity we might joyn in two or three hours, that this was then his Intention is plain for his Orders to Me was to fire A Gun (a Six pounder) if I wanted his Assistance and if he wanted Mine he was to do the Same but if he fired two or more I was to Join him with all the force I had and leave the Convoy.

As soon As he Marched I sent for the Wagon Masters and Commissarys to lett Me know the number of Horses could be furnish'd with Waggons and back loads, and the Quantity of provisions to be taken As Also the Number of Carriages the Artillery would want, when these returns were brought I was told the General had Ordered Six of the Best Horses to be put to each of the Carriages that went with him and many Spare Horses in Case of Accidents As Also the Ablest Horses for back loads, and what remain'd would Only furnish two thirds of the Waggons with four each and for back loads there remained of very bad as many as would take About One half of the provisions.

As soon As I knew this I wrote to the General leting him know the Condition I was in to Execute his Orders, his Answer Express'd anger saying I knew he could not help Me but that Expedients must be Used to bring All Away.

I March'd according to his Orders and took with Me all I could and On My Arrival where I was to halt that night I Ordered All the Horses back to bring Up what was left behind under the Care of a party. The rear division of Waggons did not Arrive untill very late the next Evening the Horses being very bad and Weak, the next day I was

Advised to halt for the Horses were So Work'd they would Not be Able to travile, in this Manner I was Obliged to proceed sometimes 6 or 7 Miles in three days and sometimes four.

I again and Again Sett forth My Scituation to him he Once told Me he sent Me a Waggon and Eleven Horses the first I was and such as could be of little Service, Again he wrote Me he sent me forty Horses tho' unloaded there was but Sixteen could Come they were so wore down, in One Letter I told him it was Impossible I could gett Up with him Unless his Goodness would halt and send Me his Horses to help Me but he did not but proceeded, Some time before the Action He called a Council of Warr when it was proposed taking possession of some strong Camp and halting untill I Joyn'd but it was rejected and He continued Marching untill the Ninth Instant when they fell into the Unhappy Trap at which time I was About fifty Miles from them the next Morning by five o'Clock I had the Account by a follower of the Army that was in the Engagement and in a few hours Another Arrived and About One o'Clock Sr John St. Clair who saw the Whole, the next day in the Evening the General Arrived the Eleventh the 12th We remained in the same Ground which time was Imployed in destroying provisions Ordnance Ammunition &c. by the Generals Orders, by this evening great Numbers of Wounded Officers and Soldiers Arrived and many More that were not. On the 13th We March'd and that day he resign'd the Command to Me After we had got almost a Mile from our Ground, soon After we gott into our ground for that Evening where he died and I proceed to this as was his intention and brought all the Wounded With Me. Here We have fixed a General Hospital and I purpose leaving some of the Independents and provincial Troops to protect them and proceed with the remains of the two Regiments to Philadelphia for Winter Quarters which Capt. Orme tells Me they were all lost, so that I am left to do as I think best, And hope I shall act as Will be agreeable to all I am Accountable to I have wrote to General Shirly and desired his instructions for My future Conduct.

As I was not in the Action I can Only send You such An Account as I could get and believe what I send which I had from Capt. Orme is the same Sent before I could dispatch One.

The Officers by all Account behaved As Well as Men could and the Soldiers don't seem to think they deserve all that is Said. That they fought an invisible Enemy is by All Accounts Certain for I have heard many say both Officers and Soldiers they did not see One of the enemy the whole day tho A warm Constant fire in the front and on both flanks Col⁰ Gage who was in the front and first Attacked declares he does not know he saw One of the Enemy the whole time this Manner of fighting confounded the people; they saw and heard firing and the fatal consequences but few saw an Enemy, that for the Number better could not be found. Many of them had been often tryed and proved themselves so; I am perswaded there is many Accounts of this Affair sent home and that All will not agree.

This Climate by no means agrees with My time of Life and bad Constitution, I was willing to try and hoped I should be Able to go through all that came in my Way, but find it otherwise, therefore beg Your Interest to gett Me leave to go home; was I as able as I am Willing I Assure You I would Gladly Stay.

I have dispatch'd an Indian with a Letter desiring to know what Officers of Ours are prisoners untill I have an Answer to that, Cannot be Certain who is Kill'd, I am Dear Sir, Your most humble and Obedient Servant.   Tho Dunbar [689]

(Gage)

We are arrived here with the remainder of our army, since our unfortunate defeat on the 9th instant, within a few miles of Fort Du Quesne. As I imagine you would be glad to have some particulars of that action. I will give you the best account I can draw for so confused an affair.

General Braddock marched from this place with all his forces, escorting the whole convoy of provisions, ammunition, &c., to a place called the Little Meadows, about twenty-three miles from hence; and finding he had made but very slow progress, chose a detachment of 1200 men, and proceeded towards the French fort as fast as possible, taking with him two six-pounders, four twelve-pounders, and four howitzers: the remainder was left under the command of Colonel Dunbar, to follow with all convenient speed.

The night before the action, I received orders to march the next morning by three o'clock, with two companies of Grenadiers, and 150 men; to pass the Mononghahela,-and to march on the other side, till I would come opposite the place where Frazer's house formerly stood, then repass the river, and post myself on the most convenient spot I should find. These orders were executed without any opposition from the enemy; and I remained on the post we had taken till Sir John Sinclair, who followed me with the working party, came up to me, and the General with the main body was passing the last ford. I then received orders to march on till three o'clock. We had scarcely marched a quarter of a mile from the river, when the guides, who were the only out scouts we had, brought word that the French or Indians were coming. Upon which, the guard in our van came to the right-about, but, by the activity of the officer who commanded them, were stopped from running in, and prevailed on the face again. The detachment was ordered to fix their bayonets, and form in order of battle, with intention of gaining a hill upon our right, which was partly already possess by an officer's party that was scouring our right flank. The first was obeyed in a good deal of hurry, but none of them would stir to the posts assigned them. Though I had all the assistance that could be expected from the officers, not one platoon could be prevailed upon to stir from its line of March, and a visible terror and confusion appeared amongst the men.

By this time, some few shots were fired on the parties who were on the right and left flanks, on which the whole detachment made ready, and notwithstanding all the opposition made by the officers, they threw away their fire, when, I am certain, scarcely two of the men could be seen by them. This fire killed several of our men on the flanking parties, who came running in on the detachment, as did also the vanguard, which completed our confusion. The enemy took advantage of it by coming round us covered by trees, behind which the fire with such success, that most of the officers were in a short time killed or wounded, as also many of the men, and the rest gave way. We found Sir John Sinclair's working party in the same confusion, as also the main body under General Braddock. The same infatuation attended the whole; none would form a line of battle, and the whole army was very soon mixed togeather, twelve or fourteen deep, firing away at nothing but trees, and killing many of our own men and officers. The cannon was soon deserted by those that covered them. The artillery did their duty perfectly well, but, from the nature of the country, could do little execution.

General Braddock tried all methods to draw the men out of this confusion, made several efforts to recover the cannon, and also the drive the enemy from our flanks, as likewise to gain possession of the hill already mentioned. Some few men were at times prevailed on to draw out for this purpose, but before they had marched twenty yards, would fall back to a line of march by files, and proceed to attack in this manner, till an officer, or perhaps a man or two, would be struck down, and then the rest immediately gave way; The men would never make one bold attack, though encouraged to it by the enemy always giving way, whenever they advanced even on the most faint attack.

In this manner the affair continued about two hours and a half, when many of the men began to go off, and the General was wounded; what remained was to endeavour to cover the retreat of the ammnition and provisions, but those that drove the horses went with them. The men that covered the wagons went off by tens and twenties, till reduced to a very small body, which receiving a fire from the enemy, went to the right-about, and the whole were put to flight.

The General was saved by the dexterity of his servants, but all other marks of our disgrace were left upon the field; all our artillery, ammunition, and provisions fell to the enemy's share. It was impossible to rally any body of men for a considerable time, and the General was defended by very few but officers in his repassing of the river. Some bodies of men were with difficulty rallied at different distances, who waited till the general came up, and then marched on with him all that night and all the next day, when we were joined by two companies of Grenadiers, and some provisions from Colonel Dunbar's detachment, and the whole joined the next day.

I have given your Lordship the best account I am able of this shameful affair, and refer you to the public account for a list of the killed and wounded. General Braddock died the fourth night after the action. Sir Peter Halket was killed in the field. I hope that his royal Highness (Cumberland) will think me worth of succeeding Sir Peter in his regiment, as I was the eldest lieutenant-colonel in the action, and should have been appointed colonel to it by General Braddock, had he lived a few day longer. I likewise flatter myself of his protection for the officers of the regiment succeeding to the commissions vacant by this action, as I can with truth assure you, no officers ever behaved better, or men worse. I can't ascribe their behavior to any other cause than the talk of the country people, ever since our arrival in America-the woodsman and Indian traders, who were continualy telling the soldiers, that if they attempted to fight Indians in a regular manner, they would certainly be defeated. These discourses were prevented as much as possible, and the men, in appearance, seemed to shew a through contempt for such an enemy; but I fear they gained too much upon them. I have since talked to the soldiers about their scandalous behavior, and the only excuse I can get from them is, that they were quite dispirited, from the great fatigue they had undergone, and not receiving a sufficient quantity of food; and further, that they did not expect the enemy would come down so suddenly....Most of the wounded are in a fair way of recovery. I received a slight wound in my belly, which is almost well. Poor Nartlo was killed. [690]

Thursday July ye 24th. (batman)

To day the Colonel sent a packet to England. This day all the Wagoners Came to Receive Provisions for to Morrow. They are to be discharged and to Return to their Respective homes. [691]

VIRGINIA-WILLIAMSBURG (Maryland Gazette)
July 4.

Tuesday Evening an Express arrived in Town from the right Honorable the Lord Fairfax, with Letters for his Honour the Governor, acquainting him, that several Parties of French and Indians had lately appeared in the County of Hampshire, on Pattison's Creek, with 8 or 10 miles of Fort Cumberland, that they had kill'd several persons and wounded others, besides committing other Outrages; that the Inhabitants In that Neighborhood were in the greatest Consternation: His Lordship had ordered the Militia under Arms, in Order, if possible, to disperse them; but the Fears of the People, their being in Want of Arms and Ammunitions, give us reason to fear they'll not be able to make Head against them.

Last Night an Express arrive in Town, from our back Settlements, on the Head of Patowmack, confirming the above Account, and further informing us, That five more Families are entirely cut of on Pattison's Creek, by the French and Indians; That most of the Inhabitants were quitting their Plantations and retiring inwards for Safety. [692]

PENNSYLVANIA-PHILADELPHIA (Maryland Gazette)
July 17.

By Several Letters from Cumberland County we are informed, that the Presents made by the Government of the Lower Counties to the Army, consisting of fat Oxen, Sheep, and several Wagons filled with Necessaries, were got safe to the Camp; but that the new Road now cutting, for a communication between the General and this Province, was way-laid by French Indians, in order to cut off any supply: That on the Fourth Instant, at Night, the Commissioners and Road Cutters, tho' they had an escort of Seventy Men, were greatly alarmed, and the next day thirty of the People left them, and the remainder were very uneasy for want of Arms: That Adam Hoops; and Company, who were guarding a convoy of Provisions, were attacked by a Party of Indians upon the road, at a place near Ray's Town, who had killed none, but Hoops, three of his Men, and three Waggoners, made their escape, as did also thirteen soldiers, who were sent by Capt. Hog to meet and guard the provisions that a Parcel of flour, consisting of seven Horse Load, was left at a store beyond Rays town, the Men who convoyed it thither being afraid to proceed any further for fear of the Indians: That after the Return of Mr. hoops, the inhabitants had held a Meeting at M'Dowell's Mill, and on Saturday last thirty Oxen, with Flour and Bread answerable, went off under the Guard for Sixty-four Men, well armed, who it was hoped would meet and take back with them, the thirty Men that had left the Work on the Road, and likewise collect the Waggons and provisions that had been abandoned.[693]

PENNSYLVANIA-PHILADELPHIA   **(Pennsylvania Gazette)**

Extract of a Letter from the Camp, at the Little Meadows, dated June 18, 1755.

"I have nothing material since my last; There is a Party gone this Day of near 500 Men, and To-morrow the General marches with 1000 of the choicest Men; They take but four Howitzers, four Twelve-pounders, twelve Cohorns, and thirty Waggons, with the best Horses, and Spare ones, and the Remainder of their Provisions to be carried on Horses Backs; and they expect to be at the French Fort in less than ten days; and Colonel Dunbar, with the Remainder of the Forces, Carriages, &c. are to march next Monday, so that I hope my next will give you an Account of our being in Fort Du Quesne. The General has sent a Captain and 150 Men to cover your Workmen at the Roads, so that we hope the so much wished for Communication with Philadelphia will soon be opened. We are already greatly distressed for fresh provisions, all our Hopes are on you."

Extract of a Letter from the Camp, at the Great Meadows, dated the First Instant.

"On the 9th of last Month, the whole Army (except 600 Men, with Sir John St. Clair, who marched two Days before) went from Wills's

Creek, and with infinite Difficulty, through the worst Roads in the World, arrived ten Days afterwards at the Little Meadows, where an Abbatis was made by Sir John and two Engineers, encircling the whole camp. Here the Whole halted three Days, then the Baronet with his Party moved forwards, and the second day after the General with four Howitzers, four 12 pounders, 13 Artillery Waggons, besides Ammunition Carts, followed him, and have kept marching ever since, and this Evening it is expected his Excellency will be within 25 miles of the Fort. Colonel Dunbar, with the Remainder of the Army, four Artillery Officers,...Carriages, with Ordinance Stores, and all the Provisions Wagons, from the Rear, among whom I am.

"The Night before last we were alarmed four different Times by the skulking Indians, on whom our out Guards and Centries fired. Tis said this morning the General has had Advice, that 500 Regulars are in full March to the Fort, which is the Reason he is determined to be there before them. As we have had but very little fresh Provisions since we left the Fort at Will's Creek, the Officers as well as private Men have been, and still are, extremely ill of the Flux, many have died. To-morrow Morning we marched again, and are to encamp on the western side of the Great Meadows; from whence we are to proceed after the General, but am fearful it will not be before we have built some Fortification there, and leave a strong party of Men, with a great Deal of Provisions and Artillery Stores, our horses being so weak, for want of Food and Rest, that it is impossible for the whole Rear to join the Front in Five and Twenty Days".

We are sorry to acquaint our Readers, that by Variety of Accounts from the Frontiers it appears, that General Braddock, with 1500 Men, being on the Ninth Instant within a few Miles of Forth Du Quesne, was attacked by the French and their Indians, who fought in the Indians Manner from behind trees, taking Aim, firing in the European manner from behind trees, taking aim, Firing and retreating; but the English kept together in a body, firing in the European Manner and after an Engagement of near three hours, they were obliged to retreat, with the Loss of part of the Artillery and the Baggage; a great Number of Officers and soldiers being killed and wounded. The Remainder had joined Colonel Dunbar, who with his Regiment was bringing up the Rear with the heavy baggage, from Artillery stores, Provisions, &c. and the whole marched back on the Twelfth for Forth Cumberland, where it was expected they might arrive about the Twentieth. "Tis said the General had three horses shot under him, and himself and Sir John St. Clair, are both wounded, but it was hoped not mortally. That the Officers behaved extremely well, but the soldiers could not be kept in Order. In these circumstances most of the Accounts agreed; but there is a great variety in other respects, and therefore, at more...Accounts are hourly expected, we chose to defer other Particulars till we have better Authority for inserting them.

It is hoped that these Southern Colonies, by a vigorous Exertion of their Strength, will soon have a Body of Men upon the Frontiers, capable of repairing our late loss, and effecting their Right to the Country the French have taken possession of.

Extract of a Letter from Annapolis, dated July 20.

" Am told that our Governor intends a visit to either Frederick or Fort Cumberland in a Day or two, with about 250 or 300 Men, 150 of which have already offered to go voluntarily with him, at their own Expense, any where that he shall think fit to send them. A Subscription for raising Money to defend our Friends on the Frontiers, has been...about to which People have subscribed liberally. We keep a military Watch in Force every Night; and in some Parts of the Country...every Day". [694]

MARYLAND-ANNAPOLIS   (Maryland Gazette)
July 24.

By a Letter from an Officer in the Army, and from the Information of Messieurs Joseph Hopkins and James Calder, two young Gentlemen Volunteers, who went from this Province, and who were in the late Action at Monongahela, and are this day come to Town, we have collected the following Particulars, relating to that melancholy Affair.

On the 9th Instant, his Excellency General Braddock, with 1200 Men, selected out of both the Regiments under his command, (Col Dunbar, with part of his Regiment being behind) crossed twice over the River Monongahela, and at one o'clock about 3 Quarters of a mile beyond the River, and 6 miles on this side Fort du Quesne, as they were about to ascend a Hill, they were fired upon, from the Top of the Hill, by a great Number of French and Indians, with a very heavy and quick Fire, which made great Slaughter among our Men, and put them in great confusion, so that the General and his Officers could not keep them in Order, notwithstanding they try'd every military Expedient, and many Entreaties. The Officers, with some of the Men

420

fought gallantly for about 3 hours, when they were forced to retreat. leaving the Artillery, Waggons, Provisions, and Baggage, to the enemy, and many Dead and Wounded. His Excellency General Braddock, after having 5 horses killed under him, was at length shot into the Body, and died on the 13th, and was buried a little beyond the Great Meadows, Sir Peter Halkett, and Mr. Secretary Shrilly, eldest Son to General Shirley, were both kill'd. Many other officers fell with them; ;the Captains Stone (of Lesly's Regiment at Halifax) Tatton, Getbans, Chomley. Polson, Peyronee, Spindiloe, and Hamilton, were all Kill'd; Lieutenants Halkett, Allen, Soumain, Widman, Handfort, Brierton, Hart, and Talbot all kill'd; Ensigns Townsend, Nartloe, Crimble, Splitdorf, Smith and Waggoner, all kill'd; and a great many wounded, among whom are sir John St. Clair, and Mr. Orme Aid de Camp. About 600 of our men are said to be kill'd in the Action; but what Number of the Enemy we have not yet learn'd. Monocatucha, our Friend the Half-King, behaved well, but had his Son Kill'd. Some of the Remainder of the Army join'd Col. Dunbar next Day, and retreated towards fort Cumberland, where we suppose they now are. Tuesday Morning last his Excellency our Governor set out from hence for Frederick County, and lodged that Night at Col. Tasker's (the late Governor Ogle's) Seat, at Bellair. We hear his Excellency intends for Fort Cumberland. [695]

July 24, 1755   **(Dumas)**
To Machault, Minister of the Marine
     When we learned that the enemy was marching toward us with a force very much superior to ours, and with a train of artillery that was quite formidable for a place like this, it was my remonstrance alone that urged M. de Contrecouer to send us to fight them on the road. M. de Contrecouer, who was present with many others, supported my plea...
     M. de Breujeu consequently marched, and under his orders M. Desligneris and I. He attacked the enemy with much daring, but with his troops in total disorder. We fired our first folly while they were out of range. The enemy waited until they were nearer before firing. And in the first moment of combat, one hundred militiaman--one-half of our French forces-shamefully turned tail, shouting "Every man for himself"...

This retreat encouraged the enemy to resound with cries of "Long live the King," and they advanced quickly toward us. Their artillery, having been prepared during this time, commenced firing. This terrified the Indians, who fled. On the enemy's third discharge of musketry, M. de Beaujeu was killed...

It was then, Monseigneur, that by work and gesture I sought to rally the few soldiers who remained. I advanced, with an assurance born of despair. My platoon gave forth with a withering fire that astonished the enemy. It grew imperceptibly, and the Indians, seeing that my attack had caused the enemy to stop shouting, returned to me. Now I sent M. lle chevalier le Borgne and M. de Rocheblave to tell the officers in charge of the Indinas to seize the enemy's flanks. The cannon being in front, encouraged this order. The enemy was attacked on all sides, but fought with an unyielding stubbornness. Entire ranks fell; all the officers perished. And eventually disorder spreading from within put the whole to flight.

The pillage was horrible, on the part of both the French and the Indians. The wounded officers, all of whom had received their wounds at the outset, remained without aid. I sent MM. de Normanville and Saint-Simon to gather the soldiers; all returned. MM. de Carqueville, Leperade, le Borgne, Mommidy, and Hertel were carried off, the first two dying on their arrival at the fort. It meant a great deal to me to find the body of M. de Beaujeu. I found it hidden in a gully near the road.[696]

July 25 (Friday)
MARYLAND-FORT CUMBERLAND
Wills's Creek 25 July 1755.   **(Br. Officer 2)**
Sir, (no indication of addressee)

When every body's expectation was rased to the highest pitch, Concerning the expedition under the Command of General Braddock in America, those who were under his Command, and gave attention to his proceeding, forsaw, what must happen (if any opposition should be made by the Enemy) from the measures taken, and was sorry, so good natured a man should be so much misled by a favourite, or two, who, really had not much experience and were very ignorant of the detail of an Army, how much depend on the Oeconemy (Economy) and Just regulation of every Branch; therefore I presume to lay before you the following remarks, as well as facts, which Can be attested by many, in doing which, I have endeavour'd to advance nothing but what Consists with my own knowledge, or that of the best Authority; neither have I attemped to give any reason for our bad Success to any other person in Europe, as it would not only be great presumtion, but likewise improper; notwithstanding, I shall always think it my Duty to lay before you every Truth, Consisting with my own knowledge, especially things of so much importance to his Majesty and to the Publick, therefore shall make no other Apology for this long narration which I beg your patience to read as something may be mention,d which is overlook'd in other accounts; I know pains have been taken by some (who were deeply Concern'd) to dress up an Account to excuse their own folly, presumtion and manifest ill Conduct: but in Spite of every Gloss Truth will remain and the more the operation if this Expedition is inquired into and the Conduct from the time of dividing the Army to the fatal 9th of July and for three days after things will appear the worse and most deserveing of the severest Censure.

About the 18th of June General Braddock march'd from the Little Meadows with a detachmen(t) of above 1200 men besides Officers as will appear by the inclosed return exclusive of Bat-men Waggoners and other followers of an Army-he took with him the best men of the Artillery tho' the Amunition was not more than make one days firing if there had been occasion again(st) a fort. Also fifty Waggons loaded with different things, to each of which he had six of the best horses-and 400 more horses with back loads of flower &c. and about 100 spare horses-after which he had a supply sent him of one hundred loads of flow'r-upwards of 100 fine fat Oxen and a number of sheep which all joind the day before the action, Consequently fell into the hands of the french.

After all this was fix'd he left Colonel Dunbar with the remainder of the Army to bring 357 Waggons after him, besides 200 back loads and horses only for 100; the Weakest and worst of the horses were left with C. Dunbar and the proportion run to be Just Three Waggons to one sett of bad horses-partly owning to the number of spare ones the General had taken as before mention'd-so you may Judge of the slowness of Col. Dunbar motions marching a little way one day with one sett, then sending Back for another sett &c. therefore every days march (as to distance) took up three days during which time neither man nor beast had any rest and the latter no meat but the leaves of Trees-this way of going on togeather with the Gen's hurry from the little Meadows brought Colonel Dunbar to be near fifty miles in the Gen^{ls}, rear on the day of action. To give you an acco^t of which that will intirely agree with every other, is almost impossible, as most officers, as well as men, differ, in Triffleing Circumstances and even in a few material ones-however the Conducting of the Whole from the beginning might have been retrieved had not a final Issue been put to all by what happed'd last.

On the 9th of July Lt Col. Gage Commanded two Companys of Grs (Grenadiers) which was by way of an advance Guard to the main body under the General as well as for Covering a working party then Cuting the Road under S^r Jo: St. Clair's direction about two o'Clock that day, after Crossing the River Call'd Monanganhely where a Plantation of one fraser had been and within six or seven mile of the french fort Call'd du Queesny (or Kane) and within 3 quarters of mile of the Crossing at frasers house-on the Fort side of Turtle-Creek-The advance Party was attack'd rather from a rising ground by a party of Indians and french in Indian dress. The Number of the Enemy by those who makes the largest allowance did not appear to be above Three hundred and others dont scruple to say did not numbered one hundred. The first fire of the Enemy was on the left of the advance Guard which gradualy Came to the front and extended to their Right something like a half moon, which kill'd about 10 or Twelve Grenadeers-this alarm'd them a little and they return'd the fire, notwithstanding they did not seen the Enemy-which was return'd tho not in a regular manner, but like Poping shots, with little explosion, only a kind of Whiszing noise; (which is a proof the enemys Arms were rifle Barrels) this kind of fire was attended with Considerable execution, which soon put the Grenadiers in some disorder and on the Continuance of the Enemys fire the advance guard was repuls'd but were supported by the working party in their Rear, which afterwards Joind in the disorder; during which time, General Braddock was with the main body about a Quarter of a mile in their Rear-upon the alarm of the advance fire, the General immediately rode to the front and his aid-du-camps after him, some officers after them, and more men without any form or order but that of a parcell of school boys Coming out of s(c)hool-and in an instant, Blue, buff and yellow were inter- mix'd. Soon after an order was given to the main body to move on (that is those who keep'd at their post) without any form or order, but that of the line of march which is four deep faced to the Right or left as occasion might be, with an intention to separate on each side of the road to march Two deep according to his original plan of march a Copey of which I send you inclosed, before I proceed I have only one obvious observation to make on the line of march-which as I before said is 4 deep, instead of three the Usual way-which marches by files-only divides on each side of the line of Waggons, baggage &c. in the Center. Consequently their is a file of two deep on each side of the Waggons on the march but what I'm going to observe, is, that when the Battalion is Compleated (always four deep) the officers are all posted to the front half files (if I may be allow'd the expression) at their respective posts where they were order'd to remain-therefore when the Battalion is faced to the right by files 4 deep-the officers are all on the left flank-it to the left the Contrary-Consequently they're always upon one side-therefore when ever you Come to devide on the center on each side of the waggons and have occasion to form the line-the officers are every one to one Wing-without a single officer to the other. This was a Constant practise with us notwithstanding of the most evident absurdity) but to proceed-one officer, indeed says, he had orders from an aid du camp to double his front, instead of four, to march eight in front, as if one was going to attack a breach-however I believe it was meant only to keep the line of march, in which order the main body moved, without the least direction to officer or man but "March on my lads and keep up your fire" when he Came up with the repuls'd party after passing with difficulty the line of Waggons Baggage Cattle &c. in their front togeather with the Artillery, all which occupy'd the space between the main body And the advance or van Guard or Party whos(e) Confusion had some effect on them and occasion'd their throwing away their fire without seeing the Enemy, which was return'd by them in the manner before describ'd with some execution: but our own fire did much more, however both togeather Contributed not a little to a general disorder; after which, The General would have Changed his disposition (or more properly made one) but the Men were then turn'd stupid and insensible and would not obey their officers in making the intented movements which were unhappily too late attempted. The officers behaved extremely well as possibly Could be, which fact is strengthen'd by the number of kill'd and Wounded-tho' I'm sorry to way the men are accused of misbehaviour, notwithstanding of the number of kill'd and wounded among them, which is Great, Considering the number of Effectives in the field: but I Can't help thinking their misbehaviour is exaggerated, in order to palliate the Blunders made by those in the direction, as they make no allowance for regular Troops being surprised, as was manifestly the Case here, and no manner of disposition made-but one of Certain destruction-in these Circumstances it has generaly I believe been the Case-misbehaviour. Its the general opinion more were kill'd by our own Troops than by the Enemy particularly C. Tatton-by the Grenadiers. The Rear Guard (tho' only a Caps. Command) did more execution than the whole, among the Enemy, as the officer had come to recollect himself Consequently made a dispossition and extended his Guard in advantageous posts behind trees by which he both repuls'd and kill'd a great number. The Ground was extraordinary good when Compared to the rest of the Country. The Trees were high very open and little or no underwood-nor Can any reason be given why they allow'd us to Cross the Monanganhela ¾ of a mile from the Attack-where the banks were vastly high and the most advantageous post for them they possibly Could have, except it was, to lull us in Security, that we had no Enemy, which was too generally believed, on the whole march, and that the Fort would be found abandond'd; there was nothing of Entrenchments-Swivvel-Guns &c. &c. as some officers and several men affirm-which from the best information has no foundation but in their own Brain. Scarce an officer or soldier Can say they ever saw at one time six of the Enemy and the greatest part never saw a Single man of the Enemy.-Col. Gage who Commanded the advance party and distinguish'd himself by Encouraging the men as much as he Could and after they were broke, in rallying them, says, were he put to his oath he Could not say he was above one french or Indian during the action-he had several narrow escapes by shots through both hat & Coat and one which Grased on his belly but did not break the skin, there were a few french and some Indians the french mostly in the Indian dress notwithstand(ing) several were seen in the french uniform-particularly by some who were left in the field of Battle and Crawl'd off afterwards, saw the french take possession of our Guns and over sett some from the Carridges, likewise over turn some of the Waggons, which they scarce would have done had they expected to keep the field; another Circumstance to prove they were not strong of Indians and that they doubted likewise of Success, is, that they never begin scalping, if sure of victory 'till all is over; on the other hand, if the affair is doubtful or if they're sure of being beat they begin scalping when ever opportunity offers, as soon as the've kill'd their man-in this late affair, they scalp'd some very early. I dont apprehend they knew the General was there with the main body, at first-besides they knew very well Col. Dunbar with a strong body was behind him, but they never believed so much as fifty miles-which even few or none of our own officers knew or imagin'd except the General himself and his people, as he had made several remonstrances to the former of his situation to no manner of purpose-the above reasons I give for the Enemys hurry and why they did not pursue, Cross the River, which only a few Indians attempted, but retired agen; it was very natural to imagine, there was a reserve there and that Regular Troops would rally again and return to the field and retake what they lost which I believe might easily have been done; I dont pretend to be a Judge, but submit my Opinion, if it was not a great error in the General to march his whole body without a disposition to support an advance party and without leaving himself a Reserve? whereas, when he found the Advance Guard attack'd had he halted and spoke to the Officers and Men-told them what they might expect and what they were to do, at the same time detach'd some men to support those attack'd but what was more material to (sic) made a disposition and form'd his own line likewise detach'd 100 men on each flank where the attack was to have march'd round the Enemy, which he had time enought to have done, but none of these Steps nor any other but those before mention'd were taken, which occasion'd a Total defeat. The Genl and the rest with him, retreated about 43 miles before ever they thought of sending any acco^t to C. Dunbar at last they did from Guests Settlement within severn miles where Col. Dunbars Camp was at that time-for him to send up some fresh Troops, for a rear Guard, likewise some flower-Amunition &c. and some Empty Waggons for the Sick and wounded which was accordingly done the 11th the same day all Join'd Col. Dunbar. The General in the Action received a shot in the Arm which went through & penetrated his body and tho' I am, and every other person perswaided he was in no Condition to be spoke to or to give orders-notwithstanding, in the General's name, was orders given to destroy every thing in Colonel Dunbar's Camp Provisions of all kinds-upwards of 150 Waggons all the Artillery Stores of every kind and even some officers Baggage &c. &c. &c. The Confusion, hurry and Conflagration attending all this, Cannot be describ'd, but I Can assure you it affected every body who had the least sense of the Honour of His Majesty or the Glory of England at heart, in the deepest manner.

Scandlous as the action was, more Scandlous was the base and hurried Retreat, with the immense destruction and expense to the Nation-what was lost in the Action with what was destroy'd afterwards by our selves, amounted upon a moderate Calculation to near Three hundred Thousand pounds value besides the loss of Blood &c. We Carried with the sweat of our Brows, a pritty Train of Artillery up to the french, which they never Could have obtain'd otherwise. The other part, and the Greatest, which we destroy'd our selves might have been saved perhaps, if things had been left to the management of Col. Dunbar, who for private animosity's &c. never was Consulted-but the most absurd orders given in his camp under the Gen[ls] sanction tho' as I before said from good reasons was thought could not be consulted-how far the adviser's or directors Can answer to God their Country or their own Conscience I shall not determine. I shall conclude this account by telling you the grossest mismanagement has been in this expedition from our landing to our Defeat as every officer except (perhaps) a few, must own on inquiry-happy for our Troops they were not pursued or not a single soul Could have been Saved.

In the time of the Action, The General behaved with a great deal of Personal Courage, which every body must allow-but thats all what Can be said-he was a Man of Sense and good natur'd too tho' Warm and a little uncooth in his manner-and Peevish-with all very indolent and seem'd glad for any body to take business off his hands, which may be one reason why he was so grossly imposed upon, by his favourite-who realy Directed every thing and may Justly be said to've Commanded the Expedition and the Army.

On the 13th after the before mention'd destruction we all March'd-I mean Join'd the Genl in his Retreat-before we had moved far (with Waggons only for the Sick and Wounded) it was discover'd The Train had reserved a Waggon with Powder and Seven Cohorns on which a halt was order'd and Cap: Dobson of Col. Dunbars Regt. who was an acting under aid du camp from the time C. Orme was Wounded-order'd the pioneers to be got togeather-and a hole to be Dug-a little off the road-in sight of the Army-Waggoners-Indian Traders &c &c-where the Cohorns were buried-Who gave him such orders I Cant say but they were accordingly Comply'd with, without any order in

Writeing, at this time the Genl was within a few hours of his Death. This Gentlemans activity in the intrest of C. Orme recommended him so strongley that he was to have been Lt. Colonel to a Regt. from'd from the Independent Companys of which its said Lt. Col. Burton was to be the Colonel-but since the General Death Dobson ask leave of Col. Dunbar to sell his Commission of £1500 to a Lieut.-how far he'll succeed at home is another question. On Sunday the 13 we Came to an encampment within a few miles of the Great Crossing of the Yauchnaganey at which place Genl. Braddock still Continued to give orders 'till he expired at nine oClock same night, and was buried next morning on the high road, that the Army might march over, to deface any marks of a Grave, after which Col. Dunbar took upon him the Command and try'd every method to stop a Licentious Spirit in the Troops-and nothing but the want of powers prevents him makeing examples of some-no person Could Come to a Command under more disadvantages-as he knows nothing of His Majestys intentions nor of Genl. Braddocks instruction-as every paper was lost at the Action, neither Can he obtain any particular information from C. Orme.

When Genl. Braddock landed in America, affairs were by no means in readiness for him, as he expected; Virginia was a bad place, to be supplied in-Pensilvania was infinately better, but we never had recourse there, 'till repeated dissapointments obliged us-a vast deal of time, was spent to little purpose, waiting for Carridges, horses &c. &c. in laying up a Magazine at Wills's Creek of salt provsions flower &c. more than possibly we Could have occasion for-between 7 and Ten Thousand bushells of Oats were laid in, tho' none Issued out, to Enable the horses to go on, in their march (which Oats since the Generals Death, C. Orme gave orders to Sell agen as they were the Generals property-but Col. Dunbar has interposed and will not permit it, as he says they are the Publicks). There were about 300 Waggons hyred at 13[sh] (?) Currency or 10[sh] English money a day, with 4 horses to each Waggon with the value of horses and Waggons ascertain'd if not return'd to the owners-600 back load horses at two shilling a day each-Waggons and horses immensly loaded and little food on the Ground but leaves of Trees-more followers and attendants on this little Army than would have serv'd an Army of 20,000 Men in flanders; a Licentiousness which prevail'd among the Troops, in Consequences of being told, Genl. Braddock was sure of there good behaviour in the day of action, therefore would dispense with the Ceremonial part of

Duty-it's impossible to express the bad effects of this hint-those who were inclin'd to be more exact were not more in favour on that acc[t] never one Deserter punish'd-The Army never seen by the Genl. but once Comeing along the line as Com[r] in Chief; add to all this, The pride, Insolence and overbearing Spirit of the first aid du camp C. Orme-despersing all former military orders ordinances and Customs of an Army in flanders or any where else either in old, or latter times, Commanding and dictateing to every Branch from the lowest to the highest and no bounds of Resentment Again(st) those who would not Bow to Dagon and who had resolution enough to tell him the bad Consequences attending such measures which (to our misfortune) he had always influence enough, to obtain The Generals sanction to.

The heads of both military and Civil Branches with us were despised as ignorant &c and if ever their opinions were ask'd (which was rarely) after a Sneer at them-the Contrary was sure to be follow'd. Poor S[r] Peter Halket who behaved in the late action with the greatest bravery and Coolness-divided his men and fired some platoons by his own Direction, before he was kill'd; at the very time he was approveing of the fire his Men had made before, and biding them to the same again-he was shot through the body. This Gentlemen who had before, given proofs of his abilitys as a Soldier and Confirm'd it by his Death, yet was publickly told-"he was a fool, he wanted leading strings" of which facts there are many Evidences-for some time before he died, he was in Disgrace-and the reasons he gave himself for it was, for his advising to train some people to the Great Guns as we had so few who understood that branch, likewise disapproving of the Line of March and proposeing to build block houses or stockades at proper passes for Magazines both for places of security as well as to encumber our March the less with Carridges-for giving this advice he as took it was foolish and too much presumption-this fact I had from S[r] Peters own mouth-and the same he mention'd to several others-after which he neither was Consulted nor did he ever go near the Genl. but once when he was sent for about some story that had been Carried to the Genl. that he and some others were liveing well when their officers wanted, at which time S[r] Peter only had the King's salt provisions and Could get no other-notwithstanding he was threaten'd with his Regt. and advised to take Care of himself-to which he answer'd he did not depend on it for a livelyhood-and had not his honour been Concern'd he never would have Come on the Expedition.

Col. Dunbar one day, giveing his opinion (when ask'd) with a good deal of reason and instanceing the practise of Great Genls. he had served under &c. was told in presence of Genl. Braddock, by Cap: Orme that it was Stuff, and that he might as well talk of his Grand-Mother to which C. Dunbar reply'd with some Warmth S^r "if she was alive, she would have more sense, more good manners, and know as much of military matters as you do-on which the General interposed and said, Gentlemen you are both Warm-to which Dunbar answer'd- "General, you See the Provocation I got-so it ended then-but his opinion was never ask'd for the future. I forgot to mention, at Will's Creek, The Genl. desired Orme to be admited into the Council of War-which was accordingly done, but Sr Peter finding how every thing went, as he directed he desired every body might afterwards sign their opinion-this gave great offence, so they had no more Councils-Sr Peter declared if ever he Came to ye Command he would dismiss C. Orme next day from the Army and regreted much that the General had such a man about him who's advice would both be the ruin of the General & the expedition.

As to what is before mention'd about C. Dunbar he repeated it when it happen'd and has often mention'd it since. Soon after this the making of the Detachment and divideing the Army was plan'd and believed by everybody-it was done with a Design to vex C. Dunbar, who realy was very much embarrass'd with such such a number of Carridges &c and may other Difficultys-but having no orders how to act he sent for instructions but Could obtain no other-but that he must do the best, and to be on his Guard, as he might expect to be made answerable for his Conduct &c. with several other threating expressions and ordering him not to tease the General with Complaints which sometimes Came at unseasonable hours, during the Seperation, every method was taken to embarrass (to appearance) Col. Dunbar-by sending orders to forward to the Genl. every thing that Could be thought of. C. Dunbars Complaints at last became so well grounded that the General order'd 40 horses to be sent back to him but such methods were taken that only the useless and those near the end were sent-so that only 16, of the 40 was able to Join Dunbar. The General at parting told Col. Dunbar, he would always keep with in three hours march of him-at last when he advanced a Considerable distance, he was heard to say he believed he would be obliged to bring to-till C. Dunbar Join'd him-but that was opposed by C. Orme and orders were then sent to Col. Dunbar to Join the General, the best way he Could with the Convoy at Fort du Quesny (or Kane). Which at the rate he was obliged to go on at Could not have been before Septem^r. They say the principle Councellor with Orme was Lt Col. Burton who was privy to every thing, but this, I Can't affirm, from authority sufficient for you to depend on. When the General separated with his detachment both Reg^{ts} were pick'd and Cull'd without the knowledge either of Sr Peter Halket or Col. Dunbar and the officers names mention'd in publick orders without regard either to tour of Duty-health-fitness or anything else but Just as the projectors pleased (which C. Orme Call'd a new Scheme proper for the Army to follow) after the separation, it then-I mean the part of Col. Dunbar's Regt.-lost its name, and was Call'd Col. Burtons detachment, which in short began to do wonders, and all in a few days, which it seems was intirely oweing to Col Burton-but unluckily in praiseing one so much they depress'd the other and took every opportunity to find fault with Sr Peters detachment in order to set off the other-matters run high, from a dryness among the officers to an indifference and Jelous'y which at last reach'd the men and where it would have ended, if it had more time to Operate in, is hard to tell, but the general Calamity put an end to that; and the remaining part of the Two Regiments heartily agree, in the neglect of Duty, dissobedience of orders, mutinous dispossitions, worst than any Militia I ever saw, Cowardly principles, frighten'd now almost at their own shaddows, or the name of an Indian, partly perhaps from the hurry we were in by a general destruction of every thing, as well as from their own inclinations; Plunder was the word at the Battle, as well as afterwards, but it was plundering ourselves-this is a bad picture of Soldiers and such I'm tyred of, which nothing but the stricktest discipline and greatest severity Can possibly reclaim and I believe they're now in very good hands, I mean in Col. Dunbars if he knew his power which Cap. Orme has taken Care to keep him in the Dark about, and took every method from the beginning to ruin him and make him uneassy, and even since the Generals Death seems equally determin'd to frustrate C. Dunbars designs at least as far as is in his power to do.

In Nine days from the time we Retreated after the Junction of the Genl. we arrived at Wills' Creek where we now are-but Col.Dunbar soon proposes to move to Philadelphia with the Kings Troops 'till he receives orders from England, Pity it was that the Genl. (even after his

Retreat) when he Join'd C. Dunbar-instead of destroying the valueable stores & provisions & making a shameful flight-notwithstanding their was not one Indian or french man in pursute-did not determine on building a stockade at Guests or the Great Crossing where their was fine Ground-in which Case it would have Secured the Fronteers-and been a Cheque on the Enemy our being so far advanced in the Country; we destroy'd provisions enough, which, without any supply would have lasted us all, these six months.

Which way all the Acco^{ts} and Contracts will be settled here is hard to tell but their is an immense sum due for Contracts of one kind and other. I dare say not far short of £100000. The General in some of his Trunks the day of action had Two thousand five hundred pounds all which, with much more money and private effects fell into the Enemys hands-a supply they much Wanted and an ample one it was-from Guests their was a bag of flower left here and thereon the road, least any Soldiers should have been in need of it. Several stragglers have Join'd us since who says they should have starv'd but for Provisions they found on the road-but report, the road was full of Dead and people dieing who with fatigue or Wounds Could move on no further; but lay down to die-this melancholy Acco^t Convinces, what use our Staying, would have been of, to save the life of many a poor fellow.

What we have seen, Convinces us that such an immense number of Waggons and horses will never do to be under the Care of so small a body of Troops. Col. Dunbar affirms that to avoid the Carridges he Could have had live Cattle drove-and flow'r Carried on their backs with out the least trouble to the Army, except to give a Guard to the Conductors-in which Case they would have found one pound of flower and one pound of fresh meat to each man; for within Eight pence Currency a day, where, as the Case stood, each Soldier stands for his Salt provisions and flow'r Three shillings a day & upwards upon the nearest Calculation-this is oweing to the expense of Carridge &c. The Ground was so mountainous from Wills's Creek upwards, that we were all Work'd and sweated for man and beast to get the Waggons up the hills which the horses never Could have done without the men, and be assured notwithstanding it has turn'd out to so little purpose, yet it has been a most fatigueing Campaign, in a Wilderness where nothing is to be seen but wood. We have yet a pretty little march to take to Philadelphia of about 250 miles-we have brought few horses of all we had, here, with us, they being either kill'd or Dead-and vast numbers stole off by the Waggoners and Drivers. This is the Conclusion of the American expedition under General Braddock which was more amply provided for by the Government than any expedition of so small a number ever had been before. The truth of this is very well known to you. I'm heartily sorry I have it not in my power to give a more favourable account which might have been shorten'd if I had avoided some Circumstances-but I thought it best to be particular as they might not Come to your hand so soon-but I'm sure you'll hear all I have advanced and much more-as soon as you have opportunity of seeing any imparital person on this expedition, which will be Ninety-nine out of a hundred. [697]

Nichols writes: "The location of this food dump was near 'main crossing camp', seven miles from Gist's in the direction of Fort Duquesne. Braddock's thoughtfulness saved the lives of some of his men, 'Several stragglers have joined us since who says they should have starved but for provisions they found on the road" (Anonymous Letter, July 25, 1755).

Friday July ye 25th.   **(batman)**
    The men dying so fast daily that they (the survivors) digg holes and throw them in without Reading any service Over them, Altho we haveing two Ministers with us.[698]

July 26 (Saturday)
MARYLAND-FORT CUMBERLAND   **(batman)**
    This day there was a Wounded Soldier Came up who says there was seven more Came from the place of Ingagement together but they all dyed on the Roade and he says there was several dead as he marched along, he not being Able when Ariv'd here hardly to speeke for want of Nurishment, he living on Raw flower (flour) and water when he Came to it, which was left for them (the abandoned wounded) and directions in wrighting to follow and they should find more at such and such places till they Join'd us.[699]

July 27 (Sunday)
MARYLAND-FORT CUMBERLAND   **(batman)**
    This day there beeing divine service, the first we had for 6weeks.[700]

July 28 (Monday)

MARYLAND-FORT CUMBERLAND (batman)

This day the Provost having 56 prisoners, a great many of them this day Recev'd their several punishments due to them by the sentence of a general Cort Martiel.[701]

VIRGINIA-MOUNT VERNON (Washington)

To: Robert Orme

I arrived at home the day before yesterday...I called at Belhaven on purpose to acquaint Maj. Carlyle with your desire, who will use all possible means to procure a Vessel [702.]

July 29 (Tuesday)

MARYLAND-FORT CUMBERLAND (batman)

This day we Rec'd provisions and tryed (tried) several men. Nothing Else Extraordan(ar)y.[703]

July 30 (Wednesday)

MARYLAND-FORT CUMBERLAND (Leslie)

You have heard the disastress termination of our expedition, with the loss of our General and most of the army. What could bravery accomplish against such an attack, as sudden as it was unexpected? the yell of the Indians is fresh on my ear, and the terrific sound will haunt me until the hour of my dissollution. I cannot describe the horrors of that scene; no pen could do it, or no painter delineate it so as to convey to you with any accuracy our unhappy situation. Our friend, Captain John Connyngham is severly wounded, his horse fell on the first fire, and before he could be disengaged from the animal, which had fallen on him, received a wound on his arm; and his life was saved by the enthusiasm of his men, who seeing his danger rushed between the savages and him and carried him in triumph from the spot. I need not tell you that the Captain is indebted for his life to the love his men and for them. Many had sacrificed their lives before he could be extricated from the horse. If you have an opportunity please to communicate the sad intelligence to our friends in Ireland. Tell them I live, but that my feelings have been dreadfully wounded. To tell you what I did, I cannot; suffice it that I acted as all brave men placed like me in a similar position, would act.-We have lost gallant officers and generout friends, not in battle, for that we could bear, but by murder, by savage butchery. The French dared not openly meet us; our's is the loss, theirs the disgrace. When we meet I will give you particulars. Captain Conyngham is doing well. I hope we shall soon be under your hospitable roof in Philadelphia.[704]

Wedensday July 30th.   (batman)

To day we Receved Orders for our Marching on Satterday following. This day their was a Cortmartial held to take an Invantry (inventory) of all the diseased Officers Effects.[705]

July 31 (Thursday)
MARYLAND-FORT CUMBERLAND   (batman)

This day their was a vandue of all the Officers Effects that died in the late Ingagement. This day the governor of Maryland Came hear to Consult with the Colonel what was Best to be done. This day we drumed a man out of Camp upon Suspicion of Robing a Wounded Officer and useing him very ill. He was drum'd thro the line with a Halter about his Kneck.[706]

PENNSYLVANIA-PHILADELPHIA   (Pennsylvania Gazette)

Extract of a Letter from an Officer; dated at Fort Cumberland, July 18, 1755.

"The 9th Inst. we passed and repassed the Monongahela, by advancing first a party of 300 Men, which was Immediately followed by another of 200. The General, with the Column of Artillery, Baggage, and the Main Body of the Army, passed the River the last Time about One o Clock. As soon as the whole had got on the Fort Side of the Monongahela, we heard a very heavy and quick Fire in our front; we Immediately advanced in order to contain them; but the Detachment of the 200 and 300 men gave way, and fell back upon us, which caused such confusion, and struck so great a Panick among our Men, that afterwards no military Expedient could be made use of that had any Effect upon them. The men were so extremely deaf to the Exhortations of the General, and the Officers, that they fired away, in the most irregular Manner, all their Ammunition, and then run off, leaving to the Enemy the Artillery, Ammunition, Provision and Baggage; nor could they be persuaded to stop till they got as far as Gift's Plantation, nor there only in part, many of them proceeding as far as Colonel Dunbar's Party, who lay six miles on this Side.

The Officers were absolutely sacrificed by their unparalleled good Behavior, advancing sometimes in bodies, and sometime separately, hoping by such Example to engage the soldiers to follow them, but to no purpose.

The General had five Horses killed under him, and at last received a wound thro' his right arm into his Lungs, of which he died the 13th instant. Secretary Shirley was shot thro' the head; Capt. Morris wounded; Mr. Washington had two Horses shot under him, and his Clothes shot thro' in several Places, behaving the whole Time with the greatest Courage and Resolution. Sir Peter Halket was killed upon the Spot. Col. Burton, and Sir John St. Clair wounded; and enclosed I have sent you a List of the Killed and Wounded, according to an exact Account as we are yet able to get.

Upon our proceeding with the whole Convoy to the Little Meadows, it was found impracticable to advance in that Manner; the General therefore advanced with Twelve Hundred Men, with the necessary Artillery, Ammunition and Provisions, leaving the main Body of the Convoy under the Command of Col. Dunbar, with orders to join him as soon as possible.

In this manner we proceeded with Safety and Expedition, till the Fatal Day I have just related; and happy it was, that this Disposition was made, otherwise the whole must either have starved, or fallen into the Hands of the Enemy, as Numbers would have been of no Service to us, and our Provision was all lost.

As our Number of Horses was so much reduced, and those extremely weak, and many Carriages being wanted for the wounded Men, occasioned our destroying the Ammunition and superfluous Part of the Provision left in Col. Dunbar's Convoy to prevent its Falling into the Hands of the enemy.

As the whole of the Artillery is lost, and the Troops are so extremely weakened by Deaths, Wounds and Sickness, it was judged impossible to make any farther Attempt; therefore Col. Dunbar is returning to Fort Cumberland, with every thing he is able to bring up with him.

By the particular Disposition of the French and Indians, it was impossible to judge of the numbers they had that Day in the Field. A List of the Officers who were present, and of those killed and wounded in the action on the Banks of Monongahela, the ninth Day of July, 1755.[707]

The casualty list mentioned above could not be included as it was illegible in the compilers copy of this number of the Pennsylvania Gazette.

MARYLAND-ANNAPOLIS   **(Maryland Gazette)**
July 31.

The following is a lost of all the Officers present at the Engagement on the Mononggahela, on the 9th if this instant July, Viz.

Kill'd	Wounded
Major-General Braddock,	Sir John St, Clair, Qr.Mr.Gen.
Sir Peter Halkett	Mat. Lesby, Dep. Quar. Master
William Shirley, Esq; Sec.	Robt. Orme, Esq; Aid de Camp
Capt. Hatton,	Roger Morris, Esq; Aid de Camp
Beckworth,	Lt. Col. Gage, slighty
Gethans,	Col. Burton,
Halkett,	Major Sparkes,
Allen,	Lettler,
Townsend,	Dunbar,
Nartloe,	Treby,
Cholmley,	Simpson,
Crimble,	Locke,
Widman,	Disne,
Handfort,	Kennedy,
Brierton,	Pennington,
Hart,	Power,
Smith,	Ross,
Spendilloe,	Barbutt,
Talbot,	Gladwin,
Stone, of Lascelles,	Edmonton,
Soumaien,	Monthresure,
Polson,	M'Mullen,
Payronee,	Craw,
Hamilton,	Sterling,
Wright,	Buchanan,
Splitdorff,	M'Lead,
Waggoner,	M'Lullen,
Dr. Swenton;,	M'Keller,
	Gordon,
	Williamson,

Floyer, of Hobson's,
Gates,
Howard,
Gray,
Stevens,
Stewart,

The Officers present, who came off unhurt, were,

Geo. Washington, Esq;   Walsham,
Fr. Halkett, Esq; Maj. Brig.   Hawthorn,
Capt. Hobson,   Cope,
Falconer,   Dunbar
Bailey,   Harrison,
Pottinger,   Cowart,
Preston,   Ord,
Dobson,   Harmes,
Morris,   Miller,
        Waggoner,
         Stewart,
        Woodward,
        M'Neil

By Letter in Town we understand, that Col. Dunbar, with the
Remainder of the Two Regiments, and three Independent Companies,
under his Command, were to march from Fort-Cumberland on
Tuesday last for Ray's Town in Pennsylvania. The same Letters
mention the Arrival of one Staut at Fort-Cumberland, who gave them
the following Accounts: That about the Middle of June last, he and his
Family were carried off form the Back Parts of this Province, by a
Party of Indians, to Fort Du Quesne; that when he came thither the
French had not above 400 Men in the Fort; that on the 2d of July,
about 1100 French, and 1300 Indians, came down the Ohio, and in a
few Days afterwards several other large Parties of both French and
Indians arrived also from other parts: That a small party of French,
with about 2000 Indians, were soon after sent out to harass our Army
on their March, who understanding the rout the General had taken,
determined to have disputed his passage over the Monongahela, but
coming too late for that purpose, found him entered into the Valley
where the Action happened: That after the Engagement, the Indians
pursued our People to the Mononghhela, Scalp'd and plundered all
that were left upon the field, except five or six, who not being able to

439

keep pace with the Victors in their Return to the Fort, were all treated in the same Manner, one Virginian only surviving it. (Oh! horrid Barbarity! to kill in cool Blood! But, Protestant Reader, such is the Treatment we may expect to receive from his MOST CHRISTIAN Majesty's American Allies, if ever we should be so unhappy as to fall into their hands, except we give up our Religion, Liberty, and every Thing that is dear and valuable, and submit to be his vassals, and dupes to the Romish Clergy, whose most tender mercies are but hellish cruelties, wherever they have Power to exercise them.)

He further says, that the same day of the Attack, all the Artillery, &c. was carried into the Fort, and the Plunder distributed amongst the Indians; a great number of whom, the second day afterwards, took their Leaves and set out for Canada, carrying this Staut with them a Prisoner, who the first Night afterward made his escape form them, and with much Difficulty, arrived at Fort-Cumberland. almost famished. He says the French have now about 3000 men at the Fort. [708]

August 1 (Friday)
MARYLAND-FORT CUMBERLAND   **(seaman)**

Colonel Dunbar received a letter from Commodore Kepple, desiring the Remains of the Detachment of Seamen might be sent to Hampton in Virginia. Colonel Dunbar gave us our orders, and on the 3rd we left the Army, marched down through Virginia, and on the 18th we arrived on board His Majesty's ship <u>Garland</u> at Hampton. [709]

Friday Augst ye 1st.   **(batman)**

This day the governor left us and we Rec'd four days provisions and orders to march to morrow morning. [710]

August 2 (Saturday)
MARYLAND-CRISOPS   **(seaman)**

On the 2nd, they (Seaman) marched with the Army, and on the 3rd left them. [711]

This day we marched to Colonel Crisops, it beeing   **(batman)**
15 miles. We left in the Fort the Virginia Companyes to garison it. [712]

Nichols indicates the route of Dunbar's retreat was: Winchester, Shippensburg, Carlyle, Lancaster, Philadelphia on August 28th (camp on Society

Hill). After a stay in Philadelphia the troops marched (October 1) to Perth Amboy and then by boat up the Hudson to Albany.

August 3 (Sunday)
VIRGINIA-COXES POTOMAC RIVER   **(batman)**

This day we marched Cross the River Portwomack to Coxes Camp, it being 9 Miles. There was some Indien Corn growing where we incamped in going up the Cuntry, which Oblig'd us to Incamp Close to the River but on the Virginia side.[713]

August 4 (Monday)
VIRGINIA-ENOCKS CAMP

                                                  (batman)

This day we marched to Enocks Camp, it being 16 miles. Very Rainy, but a Pleasant Cuntry.[714]

August 5 (Tuesday)
VIRGINIA-WINCHESTER   **(seaman)**

Arrived at Winchester.[715]

Tuesday Augst 5th.   **(batman)**

This day we marched to Potses Camp, it beeing very Scarce of Water, there beeing no Running Water within a mile of it. This day('s) march is Nigh 16 Miles. As Soon as we Came to our ground we Received fresh Provisions.[716]

August 6 (Wednesday)
VIRGINIA-BILLINGERS   **(batman)**

This day we marched to Widow Billingers, it beeing 9 Miles and we Came to our ground very Early. The People of the House is two old Maids Quakors. Here I went aforigeing (foraging) and it being thin of Plantations that I lost my self in the Night (so) that I was Oblig'd to hire a guide to b ring me to the Camp, it beeing Nigh Eleven O Clock before I ariv'd. [717]

    Hough writes: "On August 6 & 7 most of the survivors of the defeated army encamped here on their way back from the disaster in western Pensylvania." (Winchester-Frederick County Historical Society)

August 7 (Thursday)

VIRGINIA-WINCHESTER   (batman)

This day we halt'd here and I went to Winchester to see that City, it being four miles from our Camp. The City is very Smalle and have only been in Building 15 years. It Consists of 4 Cross Streets and for its defence it have 4 Pieces of Cannon of twelve Poundars Placed in the Center of the town, it beeing a bove a hundred miles from any town. In going to this Town I saw the most Turky Bustards I ever saw in any one place in all my travels, there beeing so many one might have Shot six or Eight at one Shot.[718]

PENNSYLVANIA-PHILADELPHIA   (Pennsylvania Gazette)
Extract of a Letter from Carlisle, dated July 28, 1755.

"Since the late Defeat of our Army, we in these Parts lie much exposed to the Incursions of the Enemy. Most of our Superiors would take Advantage of the Spirit that is at this time among the people, all might be soon relieved. O am confident that were matters well plann'd, and headed by Men of Importance in the different Colonies, there would be no Want of Volunteers sufficient to do the Work, and willing to bear great part of their own expense, or at least would be very willing to pay such a tax as would be sufficient, if it even amounted to Half their Estates. The Single Question now with most People here seems to be, Whether they shall go West, and take a Chance of saving their effects, or East, and loose all."

July 31. By Letters in Town we understand, that Colonel Dunbar, with the Remainder of the Two Regiments, and three Independent Companies, under his Command, were to march from Fort Cumberland on Tuesday last for Ray's Town in Pennsylvania. The same Letters mention the Arrival of one Staub at Fort Cumberland, who gave them the following Accounts: That about the Middle of June last, he and his Family were carried off from the Back Parts of this Province, by a Party of Indians, to Fort Duquesne; that when he came thither the French had not above 400 Men in the Fort; that on the 2d of July, about 1100 French and 1300 Indians, came down the Ohio, and in a few days afterward several other large Parties of both French and Indians arrived also from those Parts: That a small Party of French, with about 2000 Indians, were soon after sent out to harass our Army on their March, who understanding the Rout the General had taken, determined to have defeated his Passage over the

Monongahela, but coming too late for that Purpose, found him entered into the Valley where the Action happened: That after the Engagement the Indians pursued our People to the Monongahela, scalped and plundered all that were left upon the Field, except five or six, who not being able to keep pace with the Victors in their Return to the Fort were all treated in the same manner, one Virginian only surviving it.

He further says, that the same day of the attack, all the Artillery, &c. was carried into the Fort, and the Plunder distributed among the Indians; a great Number of whom, the second Day afterwards, took their leaves, and set out for Canada, carrying this Staub with them a Prisoner, who the first Night afterwards made his escape from them and with much Difficulty arrived at Fort Cumberland, almost famished. He says the French have now about 3000 Men at the Fort. [719]

MARYLAND-ANNAPOLIS   (Maryland Gazette)
August 7.

This day his Excellency our Governor returned home in good Health, from Fort Cumberland, at Wills's Creek.

Col. Dunbar, with the Remains of the European Regiments, marched from Fort Cumberland last Saturday, with all that is ledt of the Train of Artillery; left is expected next Saturday Evening at the Mouth of Concochedgue, in his way to Philadelphia where, we hear, the Regiment will take up their Residence till next Spring. Capt Gates, Rutherford's and Demeres Independent Companies, have also left Fort Cumberland, and are proceeding to New York, where the will General Shirley's Orders. All the Provincial Troops remain at fort Cumberland, under the Command of Governor Innes. If the Companies be immediately completed (as it is said they will) to 50 Men each, we shall not have less than 500 Men left for the Protection of the Frontiers of Virginian this Province, which properly disposed, will it is hoped, be found sufficient to prevent any incursion of Indian parties, who may otherwise have been encouraged by the late unhappy action to invest our borders and destroy the distant inhabitants. [720]

August 8 (Friday)

VIRGINIA-EVENSES   (batman)

This day we marched to John Evenses, it beeing 19 Miles and a fine level Cuntry. Plenty of fruit, both Peaches and Apples. [721]

August 11 (Monday)
MARYLAND-FORT CUMBERLAND

Sir: Col. Dunbar   (St. Clair)

Upon my seeing your letter of the 7th instant to Governour Innes and finding that this place is not to expect any reinforcement from you not withstanding its threatening distress, I think its my busisness to represent a few particulars to you upon that head.

I am persuaded I need not use any arguement to prove the uniqueness and consequences of this place, as you know that it defends the principle intell. of the country, and is at present a considerable deposite of military stores and provisions and tho the enemy...at this time have enough upon their hands to prevent their making any immediate attempt this way, yet I think it is not to be doubted, but they will pay us visit as soon as they possibly can and it is certainly our duty to be prepared for them.

The remedy you propose of having the companys compleated is certainly right, but it is a work of time and probably cannot be done for some months, and as to getting some of the 400 men which Governour Dinwiddie mentioned to you, I doubt they cannot be got either for compleat the company or garrisoning the place because I understand they were meant for a militia that would only serve in case of an expedition and not be tyed down to said service. Besides these difficulties sir I am sorry to tell you that the misfortune of desertion still continuing for every night carry it less or more and there has such a spirit got amongst them that I hear all the remedies that can be applied will prove ineffectural there have been 5 deserters since you went away and with deaths and...our number of men at present fit for duty is reduced to 178 and I am fully persuaded that many of these would have been gone by this time had they been in daily expectation of receiving about six weeks subsistance which could not be paid 'em, this is a disappointment which their paymaster had met with and as soon as they receive the money this misfortune will encrease and I fear will rise to such a height that the few left will probably desert thro fear.

There are two of the Artillery people dead and one discharged from the hospital, gone after you, these are two or three more likely to die, and the rest in such a condition that they cannot help themselves with either victual or drink consequently can be of little use upon a battery and I question if they can stand upon it for half an hour togeather.

These sir are the present circumstances of this place and I leave you to judge whether they ought not to be seriously considered for my part I know no remedy to be depended or untried to be expedited but from your self, therefore hope you will loose no time in resolving upon the subject it is more than probable that all the men under your command and indeed a greater number might be of considerable service in other places and may possibly be wanted, but as they are at too great a distance from the place of action to be of any service for this season, I think it is a pity that as many of them as are necessary should not contribute to the defence of...where there is likely to be...all of their assistance, and sent to it while they are with reach of it.

There Sir are my sentiments upon the subject, I thought it my duty to lay 'm before you and I submit them entirely to your better judgement.[722]

MARYLAND-CONOGOGEE
August 11th 1755
Sir: John St. Clair   **(T. Dunbar)**

I have just now the favor of your letter and as I thought your representation should be properly considered, I called in Lt. Col. Gage, Major Chapman and Major Sparks, and laid your letter before them who after mature deliberation, they first say the scheme formally proposes to send an express to Governour Dinwiddie desiring him to compleat the Virginia Companys...of the 400 men he was raising and said should be ready by the first of September and let their engagement be what they will they may be sent to compleat the company for the present service. In the...place we think as all my proceedings since I came to the command as well as my intentions are sent to General Shirley that I ought not to make any material alterations until I have his instructions which I suspect will meet me at Shippensburg, should we not meet with the General's instructions an expected we design sending proper carriages to bring away such military stores as are not necessary for the defence of the fort in case it should be attacked, and I am your most obed. & hum serv. [723]

VIRGINIA-WILLIAMSBURG
August 11th
Sir: John St. Clair   **(Dinwiddie)**

The service the regulars had done is they have open's the road from F't Cumb'l'd to the Ohio, w'ch will facilitate the invasion of the enemy on our frontiers, w'ch are left to be defended by 400 sick and wounded and the remains of our provincial troops. [724]

VIRGINIA-FREDERICKSBURGH

August 11th.   **(seaman)**

Marched into Fredericksburgh and hired a Vessel to carry the Seamen to Hampton.

August 12 (Tuesday) [725]

This was an independent vessel under Captain Goss.

MARYLAND-ANNAPOLIS

August 1755   **(A. Hamilton)**

Dear Brother: (Gavin Hamilton)

As it may be matter of Entertainment to you to have a circumstantial Account of the late Defeat of our Army under General Braddock, I shall give you a Narrative of the whole Affair, which comes much nearer the truth than many others you may meet with, As it is taken from the mouths of the Principal officers, who were present at that bloody & Tragical Action.

But before I proceed to particulars it will be proper to say Somewhat concerning General Braddock, his behaviour at his first coming to America, and during the time he remained among us, and the Share of Esteem he possessed, not only with the officers and private men of the soldiery in that ill-fated Expedition, but also among peoples of all Ranks and Conditions here, even the Indian Natives.

This Gentleman's behaviour was austere and Supercilious, rough spoken and in Short nothing Engaging appeared in his Conversation. He showed a distant behavior and Reserve, even towards the governors of our Colonys, as if they had been infinitely his Inferiors; shutting himself up like a Bashaw from the Conversation of his own officers, Suffering none of them to hold discourse with him, more than what was just absolutely necessary, At open variance with some and not in Speaking terms with others. For which behavior I never could learn any other reason but his o(wn) haughty and Imperious Temper - Three favorites indeed he had. Some of whom were raw and unexperienced. These were Leut. Col. Burton of Dunbars Regiment,

Capt Orm & Capt Morris his Aids de Camps. Of these was made a Secrete Cabal or Junto, who kept their Schemes entirely to themselves, not permitting the older and more experienced officers to have the least insights into their Measures & Consultations. While he was here at Anapolis (where he staid three days for the coming of the Northern Governors) he would not permit any of our Gentlemen to be introduced to him, and, when on his March to the Ohio, he treated our Country Planters with great harshness & Severity, Taking from them in a Rapacious manner their bought white servants to Recruit his Army, Upon whose labour alone their whole Cropt & years maintenance depended, and gave them for recompense and Satisfaction, good store of Insolent and Abusive Language. In his progress, he threatened the Indian Tribes in a Thrasonick manner to put them all to the Sword, if they did not immediatley join him, and absolutley forbid them to Scalp the prisoners or Slain. The effect of this was Not only the Falling off of a great number of those Indians from our Party, But the Savages laugh'd at his threats, as knowing them to be vain & impracticable upon them, Who are a People of no certain abode or Habitation, being here to day & gone tomorrow. As to the Scalping it was ridiculous to think that they would ever comply with his orders in that respect, That having always Been their constant practice in their Wars against one another, Their Enemys Scalps being not only their Trophies of victory and Badges of honour; but also a Lucrative Article to them and what they Reckoned their pay, As they receive a reward of £5, more or less for each Scalp. By this Sketch of the General I shall leave it to you to Judge how he was belov'd & Esteem'd by his own officers and Men and by people of all Conditions and Ranks here.

Thus gifted and accomplished, After having had a Grand Council of War at Alexandria with the Governors of New England, New York, Pennsylvania and Maryland, he sett out towards the Army in the latter end of Aprile, which was Rendezvou's at Fort Cumberland on Will's Creek, Halkets Regiment having joined Dunbar's there from Winchester, a Town in Virginia, on the other Side Potowmack. They marched from Will's Creek Some time about the middle of June, and mett abundance of difficulty in procuring Waggons & Horses for their Baggage and Amunition, which were now to look for, after the forces had been two Months in the country. This they might well expect in a country Such as this, where the Breed of Horses is small and degenerate, and Few can afford to keep any better, than such as will barely answer for the Drudgery of the Plough. This with the trouble of Clearing away the woods And the difficulty they Found in carrying their Baggage and Artillery over the rugged passes of the Catactan and Allegana Mountains, retarded their March so, That the Month of July was well begun before they got nigh the Monongahela where Fort DuQuesne stands. During this difficult and tedious March they lost but few men by the Incursions of the Indian Enemy, There being only two of their Straglers scalped and kill'd up to this side of the Allegana Mountains and two more amissing. The Indian Sachem or half King Monocatucha, Joined the General with his small Tribe of Indians. Many other Indians of different Tribes also came, but soon afterward left him, upon his publishing orders not to Scalp. The difficultys in this March would not have been complain'd of, as they were unavoidable from the Nature of the Country; But the Principle officers had reason to complain of the Generals insolent and distant behaviour to them. Coll. Dunbar he had an open difference with and on Sundry occasions used him very ill; and with Sir Peter Halket, a Gentleman remarkable for his Civilty and good nature, he was Scarce in Speaking terms and often spoke to him in a huffing manner. Sir John St. Clair, the Quarter Master General, he show'd no more respect to, than if he had been his Lacquai, and he was only barely civil from the teeth outwards to Major George Washington one of his Aids de Camps, a Youth of an undaunted and brave Spirit, whose deserts are beyond my expression, and to whose care alone it was owing that this General was carried alive out of the Field of Battle. In short the aforesaid Triumvirate Orm, Burton and Morris were his only favorites, and the Cabal kept everything in petto, not admitting the others into their Sage and Secrete Consultations, Seeming entirely to despise their Advice. It was said (with what truth I cannot say) That as the General made himself absolutely sure of taking the Fort, There was a Scheme laid by the Junto, that a new Regiment should be formed there, of which Regiment Burton was to have been appointed Colonel, Orm Leut. Col. & Morris Major in prejudice of the older Officers, particulary Sir John St. Clair, who had as yet no particular Command. Such was their Security and opinion of their own ability, that the General and his sage Council took little or no pains to send out Scouts to get Intelligence of the Disposition and face of the Enemy, and the March was managed in a careless and confused manner, and if any person presumed to advise more circumspection and Caution, it was customary with one of the Triumvirate, like those sorts of Fools mentioned in Hudibras, to clap his hand to his pocket and offer to bet a hundred guineas to five shillings that they were in possession of Fort DuQuesne without the least difficulty.

Before the General departed with the Main Body of the Army, and left Coll. Dunbar behind to bring up the heavy Artillery and Baggage, Dunbar at these orders showed some kind of uneasiness and happened to say that he had been 40 years in the Army and had never seen any such Disposition or March, Especially in going into an Enemy's Country. Orm on this said "That his Grandmothers was 75 years of Age when she died and was indeed a very old Woman." This was spoke looking Sneeringly at Dunbar. That old officer made answer "That Were his Grandmother now alive, she would (old as she was) understand more of military affairs and the ordering of a March than such a youngster as he". The General upon this said with some vehemence "Gentlemen you are hot". Dunbar told his Excellency That he left it to him to Judge who had most reason, That it was true he was old, But he thought his age should rather protect him than expose him to the ridicule and insolence of that young Man in his Excellency's hearing.

After this Scuffle and Several other of less consequence too tedious and triffling to relate, The General marched before with 12 pieces of Artillery, 55 Waggons, with a great part of his Ammunition and baggage, 1200 men of the choice of the Army and the Military Chest, and Left Dunbar behind with about 800 men and 72 Waggons to bring up the heavy Artillery and the rest of the Baggage and Ammunition.

Before he reached the Monongahela, our Indian Friend, the half King with some of his Tribe, had once or twice reconnoitred the French Fort and brought the General Intelligence that the Enemy were very strong there, being as he could Judge, about 2200 French Regulars & Irregulars, with a white Flagg and about 3000 of their Indian Friends and Allies. After this advice which Several of the Scouts agreed in, not withstanding the repeated Solicitations of the old officers to regulate the March and be more circumspect. The General let them go on in the same confused manner as before and the Triumvirate still kept laying their Wagers of 100 guineas to 5 shillings and did not stick to charge those with cowardice who talked of watching the Enemy or guarding against their designs.

When they approached the Monongahela, Dunbar with his Party were by this time 50 miles behind (you may probably see this call'd 6 Miles in some of the Triumvirate's Letters published in our News papers) and Monocatucha, the half King, profer'd his Advice that they should proceed no further but Incamp and Fortify the Army on this side of the Monongahela Alleging that if they proceeded towards the Forts, they must of necessity be all Surrounded and cutt off by Superior numbers, having no safe place to Retreat, But this good Advice was disregarded.

Upon the 9th day of July the Army passed the Monongahela twice about eleven o'clock in the morning. That River, which is a branch of the Ohio making a great bend or circumflexure in this place (which is) about seven miles on this Side Fort du Quesne. As Sir John St.Clair and Sir Peter Halket were apprehensive that the Enemy would attack them at this passing of this River (Which they actually intended but came a little too late) they with some difficulty persuaded the General to Form the Army into Battle order. In this order they marched for about a quarter of an hour after they had passed the River, but soon were ordered again to resume the Line of March, and got into their wonted confusion. Sir John at this appeared uneasy and Solicited the General again to form the Army into Line of Battle but to no purpose. Sir John alledged to the General pointing to a Valley with a small rising Hill upon each side scarce half a mile distant from their Front, that the Enemy would attack him there - The General asked him by what intelligence he knew that. He replyed, by the same Intelligence as his Excellency had had of the Indian Sachem, which when the General made slight of Sir John assured him that were he his Enemy and knew his strength and disposition as well as he was assured the French knew it, he would himself undoubtely attack him in the very place, and he judged that the French officer or officers would in common prudence pursue the same Scheme. The General still slighted this advice and Sir John begged that he would only Suffer him with an advance party of 2 or 300 Men, to go and reconnoitere the Fort and bring him proper Intelligence, which request was refused and on they Marched in the same confused manner with Artillery and baggage, and in effect as Sir John had conjectured and they were surprised in that very place with a very hot and heavy Fire on Front and Flank, from a party of French conceal'd in a parcel of high weeds and Brush on the left hand, and a great number of Indians from the rising of the Hill on every hand. This threw them into a terible confusion and the men dropt very fast. Leut. Coll. Gage Led a party in the Front to cover Sir John St. Clair's party, who followed with his Pioneers to clear the woods. The remainder of the Army were behind with the General in a confused Disposition; In the front were 100 Grenadiers, call'd Halkets Grenadiers, as choice men as could any where be seen. These Men bore the first Brunt of the Fire in the Front. Till at last both Sir John St. Clairs & Coll. Gages partys were thrown into the utmost confusion by the tumultuous pressing in and Crowding of the men behind them, who as they were hurried and pushed irregularly forward and ordered to march, earnestly requested to be put into some kind of order and instructed how to proceed. You'll perhaps see in some of our News papers a foolish account from some of the Triumvirate, that the foremost Ranks Falling back on the rest of the Army, as yet not formed. threw them into a pannick and confusion, which neither the entreaties nor threats of the officrs could recover them from, or persuade them to stand their ground But this is as foolish and false a gloss as ever was invented. The Affair was quite the Reverse, and therefore you'll do well not to believe a word of it.

While affairs were in this disorder, Sir John St. Clair again accosted the General and told him, that he was certainly defeated if he did not make a Regular and Speedy retreat, and endeavor to Save the rest of the Army. This was not regarded and Sir John was ordered again to this post. Sir Peter Halket and Leut Col. Gage came also to the Genl. Sir Peter proposed that he should be allowed 200 Men to take possession of an advantagious post which he perceived the Enemy had just left - The General calld him fool and old Woman, telling him that he was fitter to be led than to lead, ordered him to go to his Station and give his advice when it was asked - Sir Peter (that good and worth Man) modestly replyed That he valued not his own life, if the giving up of that would benefit the Cause, but he was grieved, much grieved, to have the said prospect before his eyes of the certain destruction of so many brave men, who deserved a better fate and returning to his station, was in a few minutes after shot dead - Coll. Gage asked his Excellency what he was to do, The Reply was to go and mind his business. The Coll went off, Saying that he could but die at the head of his small remnant of men, For it was now absolutley out of his power to do any Service. Soon after, the confusion and distraction was so dreadful, That the Men fired irregularly one behind another, and by

451

this way of proceeding many more of our Men were killed by their own party than by the Enemy as appeared afterwards by the Bullets which the Surgeons Extracted from the wounded, They being distinguishable from those of the French & Indians by their Size, As they were considerably larger, For the bore of the Enemys Muskets, of which many were picked up, was very small. Among the wounded men there were two for one of these larger bullets extracted by the Surgeons, and the wounds were chiefly on the back parts of the Body, so we may reasonably conclude it must have also been among the killed - Capt Mercer marching with his Company to take possession of an advantagious post, was fired upon by our Men from behind and ten of his men dropt at once - Capt Polson lost many of his men by irregular platooning behind him, on which he faced about and entreated the soldiers not to Fire & Destroy his Men. They replyed they could not help it, They must obey orders, And upon one or two more fires of this Sort Capt Polson himself lost his life being shot directly thro the heart. He jumped at one spring a great distance from the ground and then fell. In Fine between the two Fires of Friends & Enemies that whole Company was destroyed but five. The hundred Grenadiers were also by this time all killd save eleven, three of whom were mortally wounded. A party of these fellows had got behind a large tree which had fell down and making use of it as a brest work, made considerable havock among the Indians. These Fellows the General ordered to be call'd off by his Aid de Camp Washington, who obeyed the order with reluctance. Sir John St.Clair had now received a desperate wound from a Musket Ball that went thro his Shoulder and was followed with a large effusion of Blood. He immediately rode up to the General and speaking to him in Italian told him that he was defeated and all was ruined, to whom, when the General made some scornful Reply Sir John told him That by the fresh bleeding of his wound, he did not expect to Survive many minutes, and therefore could have no Interest in dessembling or saying what he really did not think. Sir John was immediately carried off by his Servant, he having bound him on the Horses back, as he was thro loss of blood unable to keep the Saddle. The General by this time has had five horses kill'd under him and his Aid de Camp Washington two, whose upper coat was almost shot to tatters with musket balls and yet himself unhurt. Soon after this, the General was wounded with a Musket ball which went thro his right arm, his side and lodg'd in the Lungs, and

452

Washington applying to the Soldiers to carry him off the Field, they absolutely refused. At last some good natur'd Waggoners and other people carried him off in a Sort of Bier or Litter upon their Shoulders, he being a gross heavy man and not able to bear the Jolting of a Waggon or Jogging of a Horse.

500 private Soldiers and upwards now lay dead or disabled on the Field, besides officers. The men had now fired away all their Stock of Ammunition and many of them took the Cartridges of powder and shot from the dead and wounded and used that also. There was no other Shift now, but a speedy flight. Great numbers of the officers were killed, all those of the Artillery killd and wounded except one. The Artillery, (which by the bye might easily have been Destroyed or rendered useless) the baggage, ammunition, military Chest, with all the General's plate, of which he had a compleat service, money, letters form the several Governors, papers of Instructions and Accounts fell into the hands of the Enemy Amounting as is thought to £100,000 sterling. The flight was precipitate & confused, many were killed and scalped by the Indians in repassing the Monongahela. Almost all the poor women belonging to the Camp were slaughtered by these Savages. Multitudes of the wounded lay dead upon the road and many died that had no wounds thro faintness, weariness and hungar, the Men having eat little or nothing for 48 hours before the day of Battle and drank only water under an excessive hot sun. In short the poor remainder of them that reached Coll Dunbars Camp appeared like Spirits than men and their wounds alive with Maggots. The Genl died on the road on the 13 of the month, more out of vexation & grief, as is said, than of his wounds, which his surgeon declared were not mortal. He held one Council of War before his death, neigh it was determined & orders given accordingly to Coll Dunbar to destroy all the remainder of the Artillery, Baggage and Ammunition, And this ridiculous Order (tho the Enemy did not make the least feint to pursue) was soon put in execution. The General was buried in a Coffin made of Bark, with little or no Ceremony, a little on the other Side of the Great Meadows. About one hour before his death, he resigned his Command to Coll Dunbar who marched immediatley with the broken remains of the Forces back to Fort Cumberland on Wills Creek, where Leaving the wounded Officers and men, in a few days he took his Rout towards Pensylvania, where he is now arrived. Soon after this defeat, the Indians began to perpetrate their Butcheries on the back part of

Virginia and Maryland and still continue to do so, cutting off many Familys. The French are now Fortifying at the Great Meadows, and our Country here are in a most deplorable situation.

Before I make any remarks upon this unaccountable Transaction, I shall give you the particulars of Sir Peter Halkets death. Just after he had left the General as I have above related, he rode to the head of his Men, and Coursing about to give the necessary orders, he was observed by an Indian Fellow, who sat disabled in the Field, thro'a shot he had received to his knee. This Savage level'd his piece at Sir Peter, as he rode about. which one Capt Ghest a Capt of Militia and a noted Huntsman observing, who had just discarged his musket, he made all possible haste to reload, in order to prevent the danger which threatened Sir Peter, but could not make such dispatch but that the Indian had shot Sir Peter down before he was in readiness to avert the blow.

Ghest however immediatley after step'd up and blew out the Miscreants brains. This is the account I had of that excellent Man's death (tho' from the nature of my Information I cannot vouch the truth of it). Sir Peter's Servant went up to his master body to see it the wound was mortall or in case he was dead to have it decently bestowed or disposed of But the poor fellow at that instant was shot dead, and fell upon his Masters body, a worthy example of duty and fidelity. Thus fell that good and truely heroic Gentleman Sir Peter Halket in the Service of His King and country, a Gentleman much lamented by all who had the honour and pleasure of his acquaintance, of a sweet and affable conversation, and every way accopmlished and qualified as a Gentleman and a Soldier, both in his life and death a lasting honor to his Family. At the same time with Sir Peter fell Mr Secretary Shirly, oldest Son of Major General Shirly, Governor of New England, a youth of promising parts. He was shot thro' the head, as also Leut James Halket, a Gentleman very well esteem'd.

By the whole conduct of this affair, to a man that has but a moderate Share of reflection, it would appear, that the bad Success was chiefly owing to the rash and headstrong conduct of the General, and that he was a person whose Courage and resolution qualified him to execute any orders, if under the Command and direction of another, but by no means capable to Command others himself. For puff'd up with pride and intoxicated with power, extremely self sufficient and confident of his own abilitys, he paid not the least regard to the opinion or advice of others, but rushing headlong on his purpose, and sure of Success, Striving to grasp all the honor and glory of the exploit to himself, impatient of the participation of others, like the Dog in the Fable, he lost the Substance while he snap'd at the Shadow.

By this unfortunate affair, the whole Scheme in America for this Campaign is broke and disconcerted, For at the Grand Council held at Alexandria, before the March of the Army, it was agreed between General Braddock, Major General Shirly and Major General Johnson, That while the First attacked the French fort at Du Quesne, Shirly should invest their fort At Niagara and Johnson that at Crown Point. Had General Braddock, after having been informed that the French were to strong for him at Du Quesne followed advice and fortified his Camp a little on the other side of the Allegeana Mountain, The French not daring to attack him there, would have been obligated to keep their main force at du Quesne, to collect which they had been obliged to evacuate their Forts to the Northward and thus both Niagara and Crown Point would probably have become easy acquitions to Shirly and Johnson. But the General having given the French this fair opportunity of finishing their business at Du Quesne so quickly, the main body of them would have full time to march back to reinforce Niagara, Since Shirley did not depart from Albany till the 25th of July or `16 days after the Battle of Monongahela, And these French Forces would very probably be at Niagara before him. So that we may reasonably Suppose he would not be obliged to be his course of Oswego and Fortify that Garrison, which if he is able to keep from the French will be as great an exploit as can reasonable be expected of him this Campaign. Would the French this Summer make themselves Masters of Oswego, which is but very sorrily Fortified, we shall then be in a miserable condition, For the whole Country will lye open to them, down to Albany, which City they can easily take and extend their Arms & Conquests to the martime part of New York Government without the least difficulty.

It is said that the French themselves, were astonished at this victory it being what they did not at all expect to gain in that place, where they attacked the English; they having only an advanced party of 300 Regulars with four or 500 Indians, that had no other view that to molest Braddock in his March and Scalp some of his men. But after the General Firing began another party of Six or 700 Regulars, who lay a mile behind the advanced party, came up and joined them. The rest of the French were at the Fort entrenched up to their eyes.

The Virginian Forces and officers particularly Major Washington behaved the undaunted bravery in this Engagement, and even the American common Soldier fought and fell like heros. I cannot sufficiently speak the merit of Washington. He is a person well deserving and ought to be distinguished and taken notice of - Major Francis Halket, Sir Peter's son. behaved with remarkable bravery and Courage and showed himself worthy of such a Father. The Courage of our Americans demonstrates that they would make excellent Soldiers, And as we can raise men enough here, we want only money to enable us to oblige the Monsieurs to behave with better Manners - Our Friend the half King by his Gallant behaviour claims his share in the Laurels. He lost his son in the Battle - one thing I must observe with regard to the method of Fighting here among our Savages Indians, who maintain a kind of Running Fight, skulking behind Trees and Bushes, That it is a Folly to Set Regular Troops to Engage them. The only Fit for them are such Forragers as are your Hussars, Hayducks, Wild Tartars or Arabs, or even our own Scots Highlanders for Foot Fighting could manage them very well. Our Backwoods-men here and Huntsmen and many of our American Militia understand better how to Smash these Fellows in their own way than any of his Majesty's Regular Troops. Besides their horrid way of Painting their Bodys all over in time of war and their terrible Screams and barbarous howlings at a general onset. is enough to Strike a pannick into any man, unacquainted with their ways and Customs.

Before I conclude, I would advise you not to credit any Accounts you may meet with in the News papers or elsewhere of this Defeat's being occasioned by the Cowardice of the men. Take my word for it, it is not true. True it is indeed, that after two hours and twenty minutes continual Slaughter, rather than Battle, the men took to their Heels, but at the same time you are to know That these Men did not show their Heels till they had fired away, not only their own, but like wise all the Stock of Cartridges and Shot they could Find about the dead and Wounded, and having no more they threw down their Arms & Fled, In which I think they acted like discreet and prudent men. Many officers were left dead on the field, According to the following List, and 600 private men. The whole Detachment of Sailors, intended to man the Vessels built on Lake Ontario were killed and wounded but five; about

100 were killed and Butchered by the Indians in the repassing of the Monomgahela. Such as lay disabled in the Field of Battle were knocked in the head by the same Barbarians, and but one Virginian prisoner and a Mulatto man, who were able to Travel with them they carried to the Fort. Numbers of the men dropped on the road as they travelled, So that very few got back to Dunbars Camp. And thus ended this dismal and affecting Tragedy-

Account of the officers and Men killed and wounded at the Engagement on the Monongahela.

His Excellency General Braddock died of his Wounds.

Sir Peter Halkets Regiment:

> Sir Peter Halket the Coll., Capt. Charles Tatton, Capt Richard Gethens, Lieut. James Halket, Lieut. James Allan, Lieut. Robert Townsend, Kill'd.
> Lieut Coll. Thos. Gage, Lieut. Will Little (Litteler), Lieut Wm. Dunbar, Lieut. John Trebby (Treeby), Lieut. Andrew Simpson. Lieut Robert Locke, Lieut. Daniel Disney, Lieut Quinlin Kennedy (Quintan Kenedy), Wounded.

Coll. Dunbars Regiment:

> Capt. Robert Chomondly, Lieutenants John Hansand, William Wideman, Walter Crimble, Perregrine B. Regelon (Percival Brereton), John Hart, Kill'd. The last among the wounded as as he could not walk, they knocked him on the head on their way back to Fort Du Quesne and Scalped him.
> Lieut Coll. Ralph Burton, Major Will Sparks, Capt Roger Morris Aid de Camp. Richard Bower (Bowyer), Robert Ross, Lieuts Theodore Barbette (Barbut), William Edmonston, John Gladwin, Ensign Alexander Mcmillan (Macmullan), Richard Croo, Robert Stirling, John Montresure, Wounded.

Artillery:

> Capt Robert Smith, Kill'd, Lieutenants James Buchanan, John MacCulloch, Wounded.

Independent Compy:

> Capt Horatio Gates, Robert Horvath, John Grey, Wounded, Lieut Simeon Foumaign (Sumain), killd.

Light Horse:

> Capt Robert Stewart, Wounded, Lieut Carolus Gresham Splittdorff, kill'd.

Virginian Companys:

Capt William Polson, Chev. Peirinnie, Lieut. John Hamilton, John Wright, Edmund Waggoner, kill'd. Capt Adam Stevens (Stephens), Lieut Walter Stewart, Wounded.

Capt Stone of Coll Laxelle's killd.

Capt Hayler (Hayer), of Coll Hobsons, Wounded.

Sailors:

One midshipman & one Boatswans Mate, killed.

One Ditto-and one Ditto, Wounded.

Of Sailors 9 men killed and Seven Wounded.

386 private men killed and 328 wounded, Many of whom were afterwards kill'd by the Indians and Scalped.

Capt Robert Orme Aid de Camp Wounded.

Mr. Secretary Shirly-kill'd.

Sir John St. Clair, Quarter Master Genl Wounded.

Mr. Lesly Deputy Quarter Master Wounded.

Engineers, Wm. Mckellar, Gordon, Williamson, Wounded,

Sea Officers, Lieutenant Spindelow, Wm. Talbot kill's.

In all 24 officers killed, besides the General and 34 ditto wounded.

Waggons burnt and Lost 200

Horses, kill'd and Lost 130. Alexander Hamilton [726]

August 15 (Friday)

Sir: Col. Napier (St. Clair)

My letter of the 22nd of July gave you an account of the unhappy action of the 9th of that month with the French and Indians, the severity of my wounds at that time prevents my writing to you in as full a manner as I intended, and as I am now a little recovered, I shall be more particular, we have learnt nothing from the French Fort since the action that can be depended upon with any certainty but in general that their numbers were much greater than we imagined, and indeed we had no certain intelligence of their number or of any thing they did for some considerable time before the action, we have likewise heard that the reason of their not pursuing us was their being apprehensive of Col. Dunbars party being at hand and expected that we should return and reengage them next morning. The second day and the next day were taken up in destroying some of our provisions and almost all our military stores, which I think gave the finishing shake to all other attempts for this year, this I believe was one of Mr. Braddocks last orders, and if he had been left to himself, I think he would not have given it, the intention of it was to make waggon room for the wounded and to facilitate our retreat, but I think all this might have been effected with great severity and the stores saved likewise with only taking a little more time.

Colonel Dunbar marched from hence the 2d Instant with the remains of the two British Battalions and the three independent companys of New York, and South Carolina to go to winter quarters in Philadelphia, and left this place garrisoned with the country troops only that number with all the sick and wounded who were not able to march with him. A larger stay would have been very auspitable to the country for they are under daily apprehension of some incursions from the Indians and the country troops desert continually and seem to be no less intimidated than the country people themselves, so that there is a very little dependence upon them. These misfortunes have been represented to Col. Dunbar since his march he is now at Shippenburg, but seems to decline making any movement back this way so that General Shirleys orders and whether they may come time enough to prevent the impending danger is a matter of uncertainty. I am now tolerable recovered of my wound and hope I shall be able to go soon to Williamgsburg to confer with Mr. Dinwiddie about the security of the frontier, and settle some of the perticulars with regard to the establishment of the provinicial troops.

Experience convinces us now that the country was not well chosen for carrying on our expedition, the representations that have been made at home with regard to the advantages of water carriage...so much waggon road have been very partial extremely injudicious; the water carriage at the best of times is very tedious and susceptable to abundance of accidents through the small holes of their bottoms and the scarcity in skillfullness and villany of the watermen in days weather it is quite impassable. That land carriage is long, the country is very mountainous, many of the mountains high steep rocky and stony, the plains between are swampy generally full of...thick woods and troublesome rivers of water. In the best of years there is a scarcity of forrage for cattle and carriages and the country people are the least adapted for military service of any those that I have seen, they are both...and timid we should have avoided most of these disadvantages to the northward, where the country is plentiful and marching is much better and the people of a bold warlike...besides that road would lead us thro a country where people with Indians that would be ready to join us if we made an shew amongst them.

Notwithstanding these opposite circumstances I am still of the opinion that a expedition might be carryed out to the Ohio even from this country and with a moral certainty of success but we must follow different methods from what are observed in our last particularily building small forts in well chosen places and at proper distances These I proposed frequently before but was as often laughed at on account of the time and expense they must take up, but we went then upon an unhappy supposition of certain success and that depended upon our presence only, without the formality of observing military precautions and the dictates of common sence. If actions of this kind was to be carried on again there is one place which I would particularily recommend I mean the complete, the great Luke Creek (mentioned in my last) the ground is naturally strong, the woods very open, the soil rich and abounding with good pasture and the distance from the french fort commodious being only about thirty miles. After saying so much about public business, I must now be leave to speak a word with regard to my own affairs. You know I came here Deputy Quarter Master General with major rank only. I have spared no pain to foward this majority service, I have no chance or prospect of making money nor should I mind that if I was any liklyhood of acquiring a little military skills but the risk to my bones, I have lost all my baggage and about a hundred and thirty pounds worth of horses and to sum all I have lost my commission and so the last loss is the only regretable one, I must beg your favor if you get a copy of it out of the war office, If you can send it a step I shall think it a good recompence for my other loses and shall use any endeavours not to let his Majestys service suffer by it. I am your most hum. & obed. serv. [727]

August 17 (Sunday)
MARYLAND-FORT CUMBERLAND   (Browne)

I went out of my Room supported by 2. The Day is fix'd we are to march the 20 and I am resolved not to stay behind, if I am able to set on a Horse, which I have not been on this 16 Years. [728]

August 18 (Monday)
MARYLAND-FORT CUMBERLAND   (Browne)

460

Very busy packing up for my March which increas'd my Disorder very much. Mr. Cherrington is gone so that I shall not be so happy as to go in his Party. He is the only one I can call my Friend. I can get no Horse so fear I must be left behind.[729]

(seaman)

The seaman in Hampton embarked on board His Majesty's ship Guarland the 18th August, 1755.[730]

August 20 (Wednesday)

MARYLAND-FROM FORT CUMBERLAND   **(Browne)**

I happily met with a Horse. I bought it and set out with my Nurse walking by my Side, all the Gentlemen were gone before.[731]

August 21 (Thursday)

PENNSYLVANIA-PHILADELPHIA   **(Pennsylvania, Virginia Gazette)**

Return of the Troops under General Braddock at Frazer's Plantation, near Monongahela River, July 9, 1755.

Rank	Killed	Wounded	Safe
General	1		
Secretary	1		
Cols. and Lieut. Col.	1	2	
Major		1	
Captains	7	7	7
Lieutenants	11	15	12
2d Lieut. or Ensigns	3	5	6
Midshipmen	1		1
Chaplain		1	
Quarter-Master		1	
Surgeons and mates	1	5	
Sergeants	17	20	21
Corporals and Bombardiers	18	22	21
Gunners	6	8	
Boatswains Mate	1		1
Drummers	2	6	24
Matrosses and private men	383(386)	328	486
Total 1460	456	421	583

Batmen, Officers Servants, and Women, not known. What seems most remarkable is, that all the waggoners from Lancaster and York Counties in this Province (Pennsylvania), who engaged in the service of the Army, have returned safe but two; one of which died by sickness.

We (Pennsylvania Gazette) hear from Virginia, that the Assembly of that Province met on the 5th Instant, and that 40,000 £ is voted for the Defense of their Country. It is said in the Account of the late unfortunate Battle published there, that the Virginia Officers and Troops behaved like Men, and dy'd like Soldiers; for out of three Companies that were there that Day, scarce 30 came safe out of the Field; Capt. Peyroney, and all his Officers down to a Corporal were killed. Captain Polson's Company (who was himself killed) shared almost as hard a Fate, for only one of his escaped. Capt. Stewart, and his Light Horse, behaved gallantly, having 25 killed out of 29, which he bought into the Field But the Regulars were seized with such a Pannick, that their Officers left all Command of them, and they would gather in a Body 10 or 12 deep, contrary to Orders, and them in their Confusion would level, fire and shot down the Men before them, so that many of those killed and wounded received their shots form our own Soldiers. [732]

The causality table above did not appear in the Virginia Gazette until September 5, 1755. The number of Matrosses and Private Men was different as follows: killed 386.

August 28 (Thursday)

PENNSYLVANIA-PHILADELPHIA   **(Pennsylvania Gazette)**
Extract of a Letter from a Gentleman in the Army, dated at Shippensburgh, August 17.

"It gave many here great Concern to see C-----l D-----r reflected on in a Letter from Philadelphia, for Things he was not even acquainted with before executed; nor was there one Field Officer consulted in the Destroying the Artillery, Ammunition, Provisions, &c. at the Camp, where General Braddock joined the Rear Division; This, and our March this Way, was by the General's particular Order. The unhappy Action was on Wednesday, the Ninth of July, and on Thursday Morning, by Five o Clock, the Account of a total Defeat was brought to the Rear Division; may; it was said there was not one escaped; notwithstanding we remained resolved to hear further. This Day many that were wounded came up, and some who were not; their Accounts being more favorable, we resoled to keep our Ground till we heard further. In the Afternoon there came an Order from the General, to send some Waggons to Gift's Plantation, where the General was coming, to bring away the wounded Officers and Soldiers, and to send some refreshments for them; this was immediately done under a strong Guard. The next Morning another Order came, to send the only two Companies of the old Troops, with more Waggons, to Gift's, for the Purpose before mentioned; this was complied with. All this Day Numbers of Wounded and others joined the Rear, and in the Evening the General, with some wounded Officers and Soldiers, joined us. Preparations were immediatelly ordered for setting out next Morning by Order of the General; but the Time required to prepare the Ordnance, &c. to be demolished detailed us; and the next day. the Thirteenth, we marched, leaving People behind to see the Destruction made as ordered; all this was done by the General's own Order, as we were told; and certain it is, that not one of the Field Officers were consulted in it. Nor, on the Division of the Army at the Little Meadows, was either of the Colonels consulted, even in the Picking their Regiments, nor did they know the Design, until in publik Orders. And had the Gentlemen reflected on been in a Hurry, I think it is very plain he might have found Means to have got faster from the Enemy than he did. He has heard what had been said of him, and only observed, that it was severe to reflect on a man from common Report That he desired no favor; he was satisfied what World should say of him all they knew to be Facts; and that a little Time would shew (if any Faults were) where the Faults are to laid. The Soldiers were charged with running away. The Number killed and wounded, it is thought would plainly shew that was not the case; since out of about 1270, 900 were killed and wounded, and all on the Field of Battle. If I were to give my Opinion, I would advise the Publick to be cautious how the reflect, as Reflections cannot be agreeable to wither the innocent or Guilty (if any of the latter.) Such Things may be productive of ill Blood. By the Care taking on either side, it seems to be resolved to cultivate and preserve a good understanding between the Troops and Inhabitants where ever we go.

Tis thought by some we might keep the Field some Months longer, they don't know the Condition we are in. All those that were in the Action did not save any of their Baggage, and the whole now remaining are naked; there is not one who has a second Shirt, scarcely a shoe or hose among them; nay, some without Breeches, and not half the number of Tents to cover them in case of bad Weather.

We hear from Fort Cumberland, that Lieutenant Savage having been out with a scouting Party towards the Great Meadows, returned about the 10th instant, and reported, that having met with some Friend Indians, he learnt from them, that the French were no sooner in Possession of General Braddock's Artillery, than the fell to work upon it, and built and destroyed the Howitzers and Twelve-pounders, not attempting to carry off any thing but the two small six-pounders; as they imagined the Rear under Colonel Dunbar was but a small distance, and that our People would return and attack them inside, not imagining they had obtained so compleat a Victory.

We hear that Colonel Dunbar, with the Army under his Command, will be in this city on Saturday next. [733]

August 30 (Saturday)
MARYLAND-FREDERICK (Browne)

I was very ill and not able to march with the rest. Mr. Anderson was so kind as to leave his Servant to attend me. We march'd at 10 and at 6 we arriv'd at Frederick's Town in Maryland. Mr. Bass came to meet me, he had taken a Lodging for me at the Widow DeButts. I was very much fatigued having marched since I left the Fort 150 Miles, very ill with a fever and Flux.[734]

NEW YORK-NEW YORK (Gates)

As to a history of our Campaign I shou'd be very glad to repeat it to you but am very cautious of writing one as there is so much hazard in letters, they make no scruple of opening both publik and private and here is so much curiosity in this town, (N York) thus far I will inform you Sr that there has not been one true account publish'd as yet a great deal of pro & con in the news papers and yesterday Col. Gage and the Officers of the Van Guard contradicted Captn: Orme's publick letter by an advertisement which you will see in the Phildelphia (sic) Gazette. a few who were the Generals favourites gratefully strive to save his fame by throwing the misfortune of the day on the bad behaviour of the troops, but that was not the case, the main body of the army instead of being form'd in a line of battle, on the Van Guards being attacked moved up in a line of march were flank'd on both sides by the enemy which caused an immediate confusion and so great was the disorder that there was no setting it to rights and from that instant all was lost. the vanguard was near ten minutes engaged before the main body came up of which time the enemy made so good use that fifteen out of eighteen Officers were kill'd and wounded and half of the 300 men that composed it. in this fell poor Stone I cannot say how as I was unluckily shot through the left breast some time before he got his wound, I am not quite recover'd, the ball having cut some string that has deprived me of the use of my left arm. Floyer was shot through the hand which join'd to an extream shatter'd constitution was the death of him he was buried at Wills creek.[735]

September 3 (Wednesday)
MARYLAND-CAMP AT FORT CUMBERLAND
Sir: John St. Clair   **(Stephen)**

I cannot easily believe that Sir John St. Clair would have represented me to Governor Dinwiddie as a person guilty of mal practice, however upon hearing this continualy reported I followed you to Winchester in hopes of having an opportunity of informing myself better but was disappointed and found you gone three days before I got to that place. I would have now come to Williamsburg had not Governor Innes left this place and our Captains ordered me to recruit I having nothing left to do at present but to acquaint you of this report. I expect you will be so good as to let me into this whole affair in order that I may see matters in their proper light depend on it. I will leave no stone unturned to do my self justice and nothing but what is worthy of a gentleman and a soldier to be expected from.[736]

PENNSYLVANIA-PHILADELPHIA   **(Pennsylvania Gazette)**
Extract of a letter from Winchester dated August 28 "Four Indians are killed in Augusta. Eight of them attacked a house and cut a hole in the door, to fire in upon the inhabitants, who were before hand with them, and killed one of the savages through its; upon which they left the door and broke open a piece between the log through which one of them introduced his firelock. The people within rendered it useless by a blow and killed the fellow upon which the rest fled. The other two were killed in a different part of the country. Last Friday two young women were carried off the South Branch of Potowmack by the Indians; there are 100 men in pursuit of them."

From Virginia we hear, that the Governor has passed an Act for giving 40,000 pounds more for maintaining twelve hundred men to defend the frontier, and paying for scalps, at 10 pounds each.[737]

September 5 (Friday)
VIRGINIA-WILLIAMSBURG   (Virginia Gazette)

We hear from Carlisle, that Colonel Dunbar, with the British Forces under his command, was expected to be there last Tuesday.

Annapolis August 14, We hear that his Excellency our Governor, when he was last at the Westward, ordered several small Forts to be erected, for the Defence of the Western Frontier.

Williamsburg September 5, The Troops in the Pay of this Colony, are ordered to be augmented to 1000 Men under the Command of Col. George Washington. The Officers have received their beating Instructions this Week, and immediately set out to raise their several companies. Two great Warriors of the Cherokee Nation, with their Attendants are come to Town, in Order to give a Proof of their Love and Friendship for their Brethern the English and we hear are much pleased with their Enternatinment at the Governor's and the Cloaths and Presents he has made them.[738]

September 10 (Wednesday)
MARYLAND-FREDERICK   (Browne)

Better every day and begin to walk out to see the Town, which is a very Pleasant Place. Most of the People are Dutch.[739]

September 15 (Monday)
MARYLAND-FREDERICK   (Browne)

Rec'd the Comp. of all the English Ladies in the Town, who came to see (me) all at once and gave me an Invitation to their Houses, which I excepted, and was receiv'd with great politeness.[740]

September 20 (Saturday)
MARYLAND-FREDERICK   (Browne)

I had an Invitation to go to a Ball, which was compos'd of Romans, Jews, and Hereticks who in this Town flock togeather. The

Ladys danced without Stays or Hoops, and it ended with a jig from each Lady.[741]

September 25 (Thursday)

MARYLAND-FREDERICK   (Browne)

I receiv'd an Invitation to go out of Town. I went to a farm House & was receiv'd with a friendly wellcome. I had for Breakfast a fine Dish of Fish and a Pig. I stay'd 2 days, and the Good Man and his Wife waited on me home.[742]

September 30 (Tuesday)

MARYLAND-FREDERICK   (Browne)

Parson Miller and his Lady came to see and invited me to his House 6 Miles out of Town. [743]

(Fr. Officer B)

The enemy had three army corps, one of which was destined for the Three Rivers where it was defeated. This corps was three thousand strong and was commanded by General Braudolk. It intended to besiege Fort Duquesne. The troops were equipped with a great deal of artillery-much more than is necessary to besiege forts in this region. Most of it was not needed, although it had cost the King (of England) a great deal. M de Beaujeu, who was in command of the fort, had been informed of the march, and although he had very few men, he had become anxious to prevent the siege; and had therefore determined to attack the enemy. This he proposed to the Indians who were with him, but they at first rejected his opinion and said to him: "Father, you want to die and sacrifice us. The English are more than four thousand, and we are only eight hundred, yet you wish to attack them. Certainly you must see that you are making no sense. We ask of you until tomorrow to make up our minds." They then consulted among themselves, as they always do before marching. The next morning M. de Beaujeu left for the result of their deliberations. They answered that they could not march. M. de Beaujeu, who was kind, affable, and sensible, said to them: "I am determined to confront the enemy. What-would you let your father go alone? I am certain to defeat them!" with this, the decided to follow him. The detachment then was composed of 72 regulars, 146 Canadians, and 637 Indians. The engagement took place four leagues from the fort, the 9th of July, at 1:00 P.M. M. de Beaujeu was killed during the first volley. The Indians, who loved him greatly, avenged his death with all the bravery imaginable. They forced the enemy to take flight after a considerable defeat. This is not extraordinary. Their mode of fighting is quite different from that of the Europeans, which is worthless in this region. The enemy formed a line of battle, and made a front, which allowed those behind the trees to knock over one or two with each shot....One can number the enemy casualties at 1,500 men. M. de Braudolk, their general, was killed, as were many officers....We have lost three officers, among them M. de Beaujeu, and twenty-five soldiers, Canadians, and Indians, with about as many wounded ('Relation dpuis le depart des trouppes de Quebec, jusqu'au 30 du mois de Septembre, 1755").[744]

October 1 (Wednesday)
MARYLAND-FREDERICK (Browne)

The Director is arrived from Philadelphia, but no Letters from England. We are to march as soon as the sick come from Fort Cumberland. [745]

October 5 (Sunday)
MARYLAND-FREDERICK (Browne)

All the Sick are come from Fort Cumberland, but they were obliged to leave some of the Baggage behind, being alarm'd by the Indians.[746]

October 7 (Tuesday)
MARYLAND-FREDERICK (Browne)

An Express is arriv'd from near Fort Cumberland with an Account that the Indians have scalp'd 5 Families, and that they are in the greatest Distress having Bread but for 3 Days and cannot go out for more. [747]

October 8 (Wednesday)
MARYLAND-FREDERICK (Browne)

An Express is arriv'd from Fort Cumberland with an Account that the Indians are near them, and beg some Assistance.[748]

October 9 (Thursday)
MARYLAND-FREDERICK (Browne)

Very busy packing up to go to Philadelphia having but 2 days notice. [749]

October 10 (Friday)
VIRGINIA-FREDERICKSBURG   (Lewis)
Left Fredericksburg under the command of Major Andrew Lewis with eighty men; crossed Rappahannock at the Falls, the men being, most of them, drunk. We marched but seven miles to Picketts; very bad entertainment, no water to had for the soldiers; this night two of my company deserted. The expense, 4s. 51/2d.-7 miles. [750]

Captain Charles Lewis' Journal begins on October 10th, 94 days after the battle. Captain Lewis served with a Virginia militia company on the Braddock Expedition. The entries in the Lewis Journal describe events on the frontier after Braddock's defeat where Colonel George Washington is active in the frontier defense.

Nichols writes: "In August of 1755 Colonel Burton had abandoned the frontier to the hordes of French Indians based upon powerful, self sufficient Fort Duquesne. By the middle of August provincial reconnaissance revealed that there were between 4 and 500 French and Indians at Great Meadows. Fort Cumberland prepared for a siege and the hospital with its sick wounded was transfered to Frederick, Maryland. The House of Burgesses voted £40,000 to augment the Virginia troops to 1,200, and Washington was commissioned colonel of the re-activated Virginia Regiment. Several weeks before Braddock's defeat there had been sporadic French and Indian raids in the vicinity of Fort Cumberland but in the three months following the battle the entire frontier was virtually depopulated by the massacre of settlers and the flight of terrified survivors to safety nearer the seacoast. The Indian raids followed a definite pattern. One large raid on the Pennsylvania frontier was composed of 1400 Indians and French. A week before these 1500 set out from Fort Duquesne they sent out numerous small scouting parties. The main body then moved swiftly over the trails to the frontier and there split into scalping parties of 40 each. One party went against Shamokin, another went down the Juniata, a third covered Harris's Ferry and so on until the whole Pennsylvania frontier was blanketed. Each party thoroughly scouted its objective for several days, and then all attacks were launched at approximately the same time and achieved complete surprise."

Nichols suggests ramifications of the defeat were: anti-Catholic riots in Philadelphia; Virginia colony fears of slave revolt (Lancaster county); great numbers of desertions among provincial troops; and discredited regular troops begin to change in tactics and techniques.

October 11 (Saturday)

VIRGINIA-MARTIN HARDIN'S   (Lewis)

This day I was ordered to march before the company to one Martin Hardin's to provide provisions. I shot a bullock and provided a plenty of bread. In the evening the company came up in high spirits; here we had good entertainment, a merry landlady and daughter; expense, 6s. 2d.-18 miles.[751]

VIRGINIA-WINCHESTER
To: Governor Dinwiddie   (Washington)

No orders are obay'd but what a parley of soldiers of soldiers, or my own drawn sword, enforces; without this, a single horse, for most urgent occasion, cannot be had: to such a pitch has the insolence of these people arrived, by having every point hitherto submitted to them...however, (I have given up none), where his majesty's service requires the contrary...nor will I unless they execute what they threaten, i.e. "to blow out my brains".[752]

Nichols suggests that Washington's implication in the above letter is that Braddock had "spoiled" the people of the back country by excessive leniency.

October 12 (Sunday)
VIRGINIA-NEVILS   (Lewis)

This day Major Lewis and Captain H. Woodward went before to provide for the company and left me the command of the men; took on the march a deserter and drunken schoolmaster. Arrived in the evening at Nevils; bread very scarce. Lieutneant Lowry sent to purchase meal and potatoes. We made a good shift-18 miles. [753]

October 13 (Monday)
VIRGINIA-ASHBY'S GAP   (Lewis)

Marched from Nevils and crossed the ridge at Ashby's Gap. I was this day sent forward to provide for the men-provisions plenty. This day's march was tedious, being cold and rainy and the men very ill-clothed. They came up with me about eight o'clock at night very much fatigued, having marched, this day, 25 miles.[754]

October 14 (Tuesday)
VIRGINIA-WINCHESTER   (Lewis)

This day we marched cheerfully, having but eighteen miles to Winchester. We arrived about three o'clock, and joined the Hon. George Washington, Commander of Virginia Regiment, and Captain George Mercer, A.D.C., with other officers and about forty men-18 miles.

From Fredericksburg seven miles to Picketts; Picketts eighteen miles to Hardens; Hardens eighteen miles to Nevils; Nevils twenty-five miles to Woods; Woods eighteen miles to Winchester-86 miles from Fredericksburg to Winchester.[755]

October 15 (Wednesday)
VIRGINIA-WINCHESTER   (Lewis)
Viewed the town.[756]

October 16 (Thursday)
VIRGINIA-WINCHESTER   (Lewis)
Rested [757]

October 17 (Friday)
VIRGINIA-WINCHESTER   (Lewis)
Rainy and very unpleasant weather.[758]

October 18 (Saturday)
VIRGINIA-WINCHESTER   (Lewis)
Orders to make ready for marching to Fort Cumberland.[759]

October 19 (Sunday)
VIRGINIA-WINCHESTER   (Lewis)
Made ready. This day we had a remarkable battle between two of our servants.[760]

October 20 (Monday)
VIRGINIA-CAPTAIN SMITH'S   (Lewis)
We left Winchester under the command of Major Andrew Lewis, and marched ten miles to Captain Smith's, a very remarkable man. I was this day appointed captain over forty-one men of different

companies; a remarkable dispute between Lieutenant Stanbergen and an Irish woman-10 miles.[761]

October 21 (Tuesday)
VIRGINIA-SANDY TOP MOUNTAIN   (Lewis)

Marched from Captain Smith's and crossed Great Cape Capon, a beautiful prospect and the best land I ever saw. We encamped this night on the top of a mountain. The roads, by far, were the worst this day, and our march was for that reason but thirteen miles. Our men, nevertheless, were in high spirits. About eight o'clock this night a soldier's musket went off in the middle of our encampment without any damage. I think I saw this day some of the most delightful prospects I ever did-13 miles.[762]

October 22 (Wednesday)
VIRGINIA-LITTLE CAPE CAPON   (Lewis)

This day we marched from Sandy Top Mountain to Little Cape Capon. the land very good. We encamped this night at a poor man's house entirely forsaken and the people drove off by the Indians. We found here plenty of corn, oats and stock of all kinds; even the goods and furniture of the house were left behind. This night about nine o'clock, we were joined by the Hon. Colonel George Washington and Captain George Mercer, A.D.C.-15 miles.[763]

October 23 (Thursday)
VIRGINIA-SOUTH BRANCH OF POTOMAC RIVER   (Lewis)

Very bad weather, snow and rain. We marched very slow today, and arrived at the South Branch, where we encamped at a house on the Branch, having come up with Colonel Washington and Captain George Mercer, A.D.C.-9 miles. Very ill-natured people here.[764]

October 24 (Friday)
VIRGINIA-PATTERSON'S CREEK   (Lewis)

A very wet day. We marched to Patterson's Creek, on which we encamped in a deserted house. We found here good corn, wheat and pasturage. Before we marched we discharged our pieces, being wet, and charged them in expectation of seeing the enemy. Colonel

Washington marched before with Captain Ashby's company of
Rangers-14 miles.[765]

October 24 (Friday)
NEW YORK-ALBANY
Sir: Adam Stephen   (St. Clair)

I a few days ago received a letter from you of the 3rd of September
upon the subject of my having represented you to Governour
Dinwiddie as a person guilty of mal practice. I am sorry you had not
received this intelligence before I left Fort Cumberland or that your
note did not overtake me at Winchester and I should in compliance
with your request readily have told you what I know on the subject but
I had not an opportunity of doing it then I shall now.

At my first arrival in this country I had heard of several things you
had done which might very properly be called mal practice. I had
complaints of some myself and I know Sir Peter Halkett had
complaints of some more. Every body that had been at Fort
Cumberland in May last have heard of the Memorial that was drawn
up by some of the Virginia Captains against one another; you were one
of the number, It is like wise known that these memorials was hushed
up for reasons that may not be mentioned.

From these circumstances, Sir I think it must come that your
character was not only in question but very publickly so consequently
what I could not be singular in answering you. I acknowledge to have
mentioned one complaint I had of you to two or three people that was
your (making a case) of a mans disadvantage whom I had ordered
before to be discharged for being a Roman Catholic but I do not know
that I mentioned this to Govenour Dinwiddie nor to any body else with
an intension to hurt you. If I intended that I am certain it was in my
power and the reason why I did not mention this affair to yourself was
least I should be able to hurt you...as I was able some time in hopes
that our future intercourse with his Majestys troops would rectify your
motions in matters of this nature, I over looked, may I stifled that as
well as the other complaints I had of you. This sir is a candid account
of what you desire, and I know of no method left you for...own
language. I know no stone you can turn to convince the world that you
acted like an officer and a gentleman in these affairs, than by applying
to General Shirley for a General Court martial for your vindication,

when there is an opportunity of doing it where the people who made the complaints can be called upon.[766]

NEW FRANCE-AU CAMP DE CARILLON (Lotbiniere)
To: Count d'Argenson, Minister of War

Last autumn, as I had the honor of informing you, the English began to construct a fort at the foot of the Aliganai mountains, and named it Fort Cumberland. The fort is 110 miles form ours on the Belle Riviere, according to their estimation. Last winter, two regiments of regular troops, numbering five hundred men apiece, departed from Europe under the command of General Braddock, and they arrived at Alexandria in Virginia on February 24. The King had given him the commission of general of all the forces in North America, and it was he who was to carry out operations planned at the court in London, invading this country even as it diverted the attention of the French court with a thousand propositions of peace. As soon as he arrived in Virginia, General Braddock began to prepare his campaign, with the intention of marching in early April. He reserved for himself the reduction of the fort on the Ohio, and took all precautions to assure success. However, since he had not been provided for according to his wishes by the provinces of New England (that is the colonies in general) and since he had to wait a long time for the wagons and other things he lacked to be supplied by them, he was not able to leave Fort Cumberland until the first days of June. Our Indians had reported to us during the winter that the English were making great preparations, but M. Duquesne, to whom the news was brought, treated it as a boast and said that it was a flash in the pan. Consequently, he did not take any of the precautions necessary against such a general movement. M. de Vaudreuil arrived in the month of June, and was told that the government was in a marvelous state. M. Duquesne, who had known that his fort was menaced, and sent help there, neglecting totally the other areas. Aid arrived at the place named, and Contrecoeur, knowing that the enemy was only three leagues from Fort Duquesne, sent 891 men, including 250 Frenchmen, the rest Indians, under the command of M. de Beaujeu, the captain of our troops. At 11:00 A.M., Beaujeu found himself face to face with the enemy. He attacked with great vigor, and after five hours of fighting our detachement succeeded in putting totally to rout a vangard of 1,300-odd men, not including wagoners. General Braddock

474

was among them. His rear guard was about eight leagues distant and was not attacked.[767]

Camp du Carillon is at the southern end of Lake Champaign and was taken by the British to become Fort Ticonderoga

October 25 (Saturday)
MARYLAND-FT.CUMBERLAND   **(Lewis)**

Marched from Patterson's Creek and passed many deserted houses. I was this day very curious in the examination of the mischief done in the houses, and was shocked at the havoc made by the barbarous and cruel Indians. At one, Mecraggin's, I found the master of the family, who had been buried but slightly by his friends, after his assassination, half out of the grave and eaten by the wolves; the house burnt, the cornfield laid waste and an entire ruin made. At half-after six we arrived at Fort Cumberland, cold and hungary. We had this day, by Major Lewis' order, two women ducked for robbing the deserted houses-20 miles. Eighty-one miles to Fort Cumberland and one hundred and sixty-seven miles from Fredericksburg.[768]

October 26 (Sunday)
MARYLAND-FT. CUMBERLAND   **(Lewis)**

This day Lieutenant Walter Stuart showed me the Fort. It is a quadrangular fort with four bastions, about one hundred feet in the square; has eleven four-pounders and two smaller mounted. It is situated on the north side of Potomac, in Maryland, on a hill very pleasant, more so, I think, than advantageous; has a romantic prospect from the mountain and is very healthy. I was this day ordered to return to Fredericksburg, but my horse being tired, I was excused. [769]

October 27-30 (Sunday to Thursday)
MARYLAND-FT. CUMBERLAND   **(Lewis)**

Nothing remarkable.[770]

October 31 (Friday)
MARYLAND-FT.CUMBERLAND   **(Hughes)**

I believe I am the first Chaplain who ever saved a Pair of Colours, which I took within fifty Yards of the Cannon, when the Enemy were Masters of them. The French and Indians crept about in small Parties so that the Fire was quite round us, and in all the Time I never saw one, nor could I on Enquiry find any one who saw ten togeather. The Loss killed and wounded 864. The French had 2000 Men, besides Indians, we had six Indians, and they at least as many hundreds, We marched near 400 Miles in three Months, cut 350 thro' Woods, and for the last 200 saw no house but this dirty Fort. Rum 20's a Gallon, the worst brown sugar 4s 6d a Pound, a year old Calf sold to Sir Peter Halket and our Mess a 3£ after the 25th of June a Dollar for a Pint of Rum, so you may judge of our Distress. The whole Country is a Wood.[771]

(Lewis)

An Irishman arrived at the fort with two scalps. It seems he was, the Sunday before, taken prisoner by a party of fifty-two Indians, and being left in the custody of two, while the party proceeded toward the inhabitants; he, with his guard, arrived at the Shanoe camp, and encamped in a deserted house.

About eleven o'clock he was ordered to make up the fire, but refusing to do so, was threatened the tomahawk, but accidently casting his eye on an axe in the house, very convenient to him, he, with it, beat out the brains of the Indian next to him, and with his gun shot the other through the body. Having scalped them he made the best of his way to Fort Cumberland with their scalps, guns, horses, etc. I bought one of the guns for fifty shillings, Maryland currency, being a French piece, very handsome and equally good. This same day a party of volunteers was detached, consisting of one hundred men, rank and file, and eight officers. The Indians having disclosed their designs to McSwain, their prisoner, it is not doubted the party will cut them off.[772]

November 1-3 (Saturday to Monday)

MARYLAND-FT. CUMBERLAND   **(Lewis)**

Nothing remarkable.[773]

November 4 (Tuesday)   **(Lewis)**

The volunteers returned without success; the Indians being supposed to have returned.[774]

November 13 (Thursday)
MARYLAND-FT. CUMBERLAND   (Lewis)

Colonel Stevens arrived this evening with about one hundred recruits with their proper officers; Captain Robert Spotswood, Captain William Peachy; Lieutenants John Hall and King; two volunteers.[775]

November 14-19 (Friday-Wednesday)
MARYLAND-FT. CUMBERLAND   (Lewis)

Nothing material.[776]

November 20 (Thursday)
MARYLAND-FT. CUMBERLAND   (Lewis)

Ensign Bacon arrived at the fort from Patterson's Creek, where he had been to erect a fort. On his way he heard the Indian halloo and saw many tracks of Indians in the woods. This alarmed the fort, but being late it was not possible to send out a party, but orders were given for one hundred men to parade in the morning under Captain Waggoner.[777]

November 21 (Friday)
MARYLAND-FT. CUMBERLAND   (Lewis)

A very bad morning, wet, and still continuing to rain. A party of one hundred men paraded under Captain Waggoner to search for the Indians on Patterson's Creek, according to Ensign Bacon's information of the day before. Mayor Andrew Lewis and myself went volunteers on the command. We returned the same day with the party; no Indians or track of Indians to be seen.[778]

November 22 (Saturday)
MARYLAND-FT. CUMBERLAND   (Lewis)

A very cold day and windy.[779]

November 23-25 (Sunday-Tuesday)   (Lewis)
Nothing remarkable.[780]

November 26 (Wednesday)
MARYLAND-FT. CUMBERLAND   (Lewis)

I went out on this day in company with Major James Livingston, Lieutenant Starke, one sergeant, a corporal, and three privates to Nicholas' Fort on a party of pleasure. It is about five miles from Fort Cumberland, well built, with four bastions. About one o'clock we left this fort and marched one mile below, where we crossed the Potomac River in a canoe. I went on the south side of the river into a house where there was a weaver's loom and a small quantity of the shavings of a wood that people in these parts dye with. Some distance from this house we found in the Indian path about two pounds of swan-shot, supposed by our guide to be dropped there by the Indians in some hurry when they massacred the inhabitants about these plantations. We crossed a small mountain not far from this on whose top you might drop a stone four hundred feet into the Potomac River. We passed another mountain something higher-had much the same propsect. A fine landscape from the top of this mountain; you might drop a stone above five hundred feet perpendicular into the Potomac River. We found here an Indian cap made of bear skin, and then we proceeded on our march to the new store built by the Ohio Company, from whence we crossed the Potomac River, and before night got into Fort Cumberland. This march fatigued me very much, being above fifteen miles, and a great part of it over the mountains.[781]

November 27 (Thursday)
MARYLAND-FT. CUMBERLAND   (Lewis)

A very fine, warm day.[782]

November 30 (Sunday)
MARYLAND-FT. CUMBERLAND   (Lewis)

This day a man unfortunately falling down the bank of the Potomac River opposite the fort, his gun fired and shot a soldier through the leg, who was crossing the river in a canoe.[783]

December 2 (Tuesday)
MARYLAND-CRISSEPS   (Lewis)

Captain Spotswood and self went out as volunteers with a party commanded by Ensign Winter Targie to gather corn from the deserted fields. We arrived about two o'clock at the plantation of one Crisseps, most delightfully situated on land that gave me great pleasure. It was a piece of low ground entirely surrounded by the mountains, the prospect very romantic, high rocks on the sides of the mountains some hundreds of feet perpendicular to the Potomac River. Here we lodged this night in a comfortable house.[784]

December 3 (Wednesday)
MARYLAND-CRISSEPS   (Lewis)

This morning we took our guns, and after directing our men (thirty in number) to gather the corn, we took different courses to hunt for deer and such game as the place afforded. This evening Captain Spotswood went, with a soldier, to the plantation of one Williams, where the houses were burned by savages. The body of a woman layed near one of the houses, her head being scalped and, also, a small boy and a young man. This horrid scene gave us a terrible shock, but I hope with the leave of God we shall still overcome the cruel, barbarous and inhuman enemy.[785]

December 4 (Thursday)
MARYLAND-CRISSEPS   (Lewis)

This morning we intended to hunt again, but soon after day we heard three distinct guns under the Alleghany mountains, wherefore, we were particularly cautious not to venture too far to hunt, lest we should be outwitted by our ever cautious enemy.[786]

December 5 (Friday)
MARYLAND-FT. CUMBERLAND   (Lewis)

This morning we marched to Fort Cumberland, and met, about five miles from Crissep's, a relief commanded by Lieutenant Lynn, of twelve men. We accepted of this relief and gave our command to Mr. Lynn, according to order.[787]

December 6 (Saturday)
MARYLAND-FT. CUMBERLAND   (Lewis)

Five deserters were this day punished, each received one thousand lashes. In this last command I may with the greatest truth aver that I saw the most horrid, shocking sight I ever yet beheld. At a house adjoining the cornfield in which our soldier were employed in gathering corn, we saw the bodies of three different people, who were first massacred, then scalped, and afterwards thrown into a fire. These bodies were not yet quite consumed, but the flesh was on many parts of them. We saw the clothes of these people yet bloody, and the stakes, the instruments of their death, still bloody and their brains sticking to them. The orchards were cut down, the mills destroyed and a waste of all manner of household goods. These people in my opinion were very industrious, having the best corn I ever saw, and their plantation well calculated for produce, and every other conveniency suitable to the station of a farmer.[788]

December 24 (Wednesday)
MARYLAND-FT. CUMBERLAND   (Lewis)

Being Christmas, we were invited to spend the evening with Colonel Stevens, where we spent the time in drinking loyal healths and dancing till eleven o'clock, and them parted in the most amiciable manner.[789]

December 25 (Thursday)
MARYLAND-FT. CUMBERLAND   (Lewis)

Were invited to dine with Colonel Stevens, where we had the most sumptous entertainment. After dinner, drank the royal health and sang some entertaining songs, with three huzzas and roll of drum to every health and song; then took partners and spent the evening in dancing, and about twelve o'clock broke up, well pleased with our generous entertainment. [790]

December 26 (Friday)
MARYLAND-FT. CUMBERLAND   (Lewis)

Sociably spent.[791]

December 27 (Saturday)
VIRGINIA-ASHBY'S FORT   (Lewis)

I was ordered to march with one subordinate, one sergeant, one corporal, and twenty men to take the command of Ashby's Fort; arrived about five o'clock. Met Captain Ashby near the barracks, inquired his number of men and desired to see his list. He informed me he did not know the number and that his lieutenant had the list and was absent. I ordered the drum to beat to arms, when, with much difficulty we got togeather twenty-one men. I appointed Lieutenant John Bacon adjutant, had the article of war read to the men and let them know I was to command them. Mr. Bacon made a most affectional speech to them and then discharged them for the night. They seemed to be mutinous, but were soon convinced after reading orders from Colonel Adam Stevens, that I was their Commander.I gave orders to parade.[792]

END OF CHRONICLES

The compilers original intent was to retrace the road but doing so is problematical not only due to the activities of man through the 243 intervening years, but more importantly due landscape changes caused by nature (water and vegetation). As we have seen many have tried to do this with varying degrees of success. In 1903 Archer B. Hulbert tells us what to look for.

Hulbert writes: "The rough track of this first highway westward may be followed today (1903) almost at any point in all its course between the Potomac and the Monongahela, and the great caverns and gullies which mark so plainly its tortuous course speak as no words can of the sufferings and dangers of those who traveled it during the dark half century when it offered one of the few passages ways to the West. It was a clear, sweet October day when I first came into Great Meadows to make there my home until those historic hills and plains became thoroughly familiar to me. From the Cumberland Road, as one looks southward from Mount Washington across Great Meadows and the site of Fort Necessity, the hillside beyond is well-timbered on the right and on the left; but between the forest lies a large tract of cultivated ground across which runs, in a straight line, the dark outline of a heavy unhealed wound. A hundred and fifty years of rain and snow and frost have been unable to remove, even from a sloping surface this heavy finger mark. Many ears of cultivation have not destroyed, and for many years yet the plow will jolt and swing heavily when it crosses the track of Braddock's Road. I was astonished to find that at many points in Fayette and neighboring counties the old course of the road can be distinctly traced in fields which have for half a century and more been under constant cultivation. If, at certain points, cultivation and the elements have pounded the old track level with the surrounding ground, a few steps in either direction will bring the explorer instantly to plain evidence of its course - except where the road bed is, today, a traveled lane of road. On the open hillsides the track takes often the appearance of a terrace, where, where in the old days the road tore a great hole along the slope, and formed a catchwater which rendered it a veritable bog in many places. Now and then on level ground the course is marked by a slight rounding hollow which remains damp when the surrounding ground is wet, or is baked very hard when the usual supply of water is exhausted. In some places this strange groove may be seen extending as far as any can reach, as though it were the pathway of a gigantic serpent across the world. At time the track, passing the level, meets a slight ridge which, it if runs parallel to its course, it mounts; if the rising ground is encountered at right angles the road ploughs a gully straight through, in which the water runs after each rain, preserving the depression once made by the road. And as I journeyed to and fro in that valley visiting the classic spots which appear in such tender grace in the glad sunshine of a mountain autumn, I never passed a spot of open where this old roadway was to be seen without a thrill; it is impossible to come upon this road without pausing, or to write of it without a tribute. This is particularly true of Braddock's Road when you find it in the forests; everything that savage mark tells in the open country is reechoed in mightier tone within the shadows of the woods. There the wide strange track is like nothing of which you ever or read. it looks nothing like a roadway. it is plainly not the track of a tornado, though its width and straight course in certain places would suggest this. Yet it is never the same in two places; here, it is a side straight aisle covered with rank weeds in the center of the low wet course; there, the forests impinge upon it were the ground is drier; it appears like the abandoned bed of a brook, the large stones removed from its track laying on each side as through strewn there by a river's torrent; there, it swings quickly at right angles near the open where the whole width is covered with velvet grass radiant in the sunshine which can reach it here. In the forests more than elsewhere the deep furrow of the roadway has remained wet, and for this reason threes have not come up. At many points the road ran into marshy round and here a large number of roundabout courses speak of the desperate struggles the old teamsters had on this early track a century ago.

In the forest it is easy to conjure up the scene when this old track was opened - for it was cut through a "wooden country," to use an expression common among the pioneers. Here you can see the long line of sorry wagons standing in the road when the army is encamped; and through many of them were unable to carry their load one foot further-yet there is ever the ringing chorus of the axes of six hundred choppers sounding through the twilight of the hot May evening. It is almost suffocating in the forests when the wind does not blow and the army is unused to the scorching American summer which as come early this year. The wagon train is very long, and though the van may have may have halted on level ground, the line behind stretches down and up the shadowy ravines. The wagons are blocked in all conceivable positions on the hillsides. The condition of the horses is pitiful beyond description. If some are near to the brook or spring others are far away. Some horses will never find water tonight. To the right and left the sentinels are lost in the surrounding gloom" .

Endnotes

1. William Darlington, *Christopher Gist's Journal*, (Ann Arbor: Univeristy Microfilms, 1966, 148-266.
2. Maryland Gazette, 1755.
3. Charles Hamilton, *Braddock's Defeat* (Norman: Univ. of Oklahoma Press, 1959), 7-8.
4. Letterbook of Sir John St. Clair, Jan. 12, 1755 to Dec. 28, 1756 (Microfilm at Univ. of Virginia Library), 1.
5. St. Clair, 2.
6. St. Clair, 3 .
7. Maryland Gazette.
8. Pennsylvania Gazette
9. St. Clair, 10.
10. J. Thomas Scharf, *History of Maryland* (Baltimore: John B. Piet, 1879), 442.
11. Virginia Gazette
12. St. Clair, 15.
13. St. Clair, 12.
14. St. Clair, 13.
15. St. Clair, 15.
16. St. Clair, 46.
17. Stanley Pargellis, *Military Affairs in North America 1748-1765*, (Washington: American Historical Association), 58.
18. Pargellis, 58.
19. Pargellis, 61.
20. Pargellis, 64.
21. St. Clair, 22.
22. St. Clair, 22.
23. Pennsylvania Gazette.
24. St. Clair, 26.
25. St. Clair, 27.
26. St. Clair, 29.
27. St. Clair, 28.
28. St. Clair, 51.
29. Pennsylvania Gazette.
30. Winthrop Sargent, *History of an Expedition against Fort Du Quesne, in 1755*, (Phila: Lippincott, Grambo & Co., 1855), 283.
31. St. Clair, 35.
32. St. Clair, 34.
33. St. Clair, 33.
34. St. Clair, 32.
35. St. Clair, 36.
36. Penn., Maryland,Virginia Gazette.
37. Will H. Lowdermilk, *History of Cumberland, Maryland...* (Baltimore:Regional Publishing Company, 1971), III.
38. Lowdermilk, IV.
39. St. Clair, 37.
40. St. Clair, 38.
41. St. Clair, 40.
42. St. Clair, 39.
43. Lowdermilk, IV.
44. St. Clair, 41.
45. St. Clair, 42.
46. Sargent, 284.
47. Maryland, Virginia Gazette
48. St. Clair, 61.
49. St. Clair, 57.
50. Douglas Southall Freeman, *George Washington: A Biography*, (New York: Scribner's, 1948), 13
51. St. Clair, 66.
52. St. Clair, 76.
53. St. Clair, 67.
54. St. Clair, 70.
55. Virginia Gazette.
56. Sargent, 289.
57. Fairfax Harrison, *With Braddock's Army - Mrs. Browne's Diary*, Virginia Magazine of History and Biography, October 1924, 306.
58. Hamilton, 9.
59. Harrison, 306.
60. Pennsylvania Gazette.
61. St. Clair, 77.
62. St. Clair, 78.
63. Hamilton, 9.
64. Maryland Gazette.
65. Virginia Gazette.
66. St. Clair, 86.
67. Hamilton, 9.
68. John C. Fitzpatrick, *George Washington Colonial Traveler 1732-1775* (Indianapolis: The Bobbs Merrill Co. 1927), 70.
69. St. Clair, 85.

70. Hamilton, 9.
71. Pargellis, 77.
72. St. Clair, 81.
73. St. Clair, 80.
74. Hamilton, 10.
75. Pargellis, 80.
76. Maryland Gazette.
77. St. Clair, 83.
78. St. Clair, 84.
79. Freeman, 18.
80. Virginia Gazette.
81. Sargent, 290.
82. Freeman, 19.
83. Harrison, 306.
84. Hamilton, 10.
85. Harrison, 306.
86. Sargent, 291.
87. Harrison, 307.
88. Lowdermilk, V.
89. Maryland Gazette.
90. Sargent, 291.
91. Lowdermilk, X
92. St. Clair, 87.
93. Lowdermilk, XI
94. Sargent, 358.
95. Lowdermilk, XII.
96. Hamilton, 71.
97. Hamilton, 72.
98. Lowdermilk, XIV.
99. St. Clair, 88.
100. Hamilton, 73.
101. Lowdermilk, XIV.
102. Hamillton, 74.
103. Lowdermilk, XV.
104. Hamilton, 75.
105. Sargent, 297.
106. Lowdermilk, XV.
107. Lowdermilk, XVI
108. Hamilton, 76.
109. St. Clair, 90.
110. Lowdermilk, XVI.
111. St. Clair, 93.
112. Hamilton, 76.
113. Lowdermilk, XVII
114. Sargent, 297.
115. Lowdermilk, XIX.
116. Hamilton, 77.
117. Sargent, 297.
118. *Extracts of Letters from a (British) Officer in one of those Regiments to his friend in London*, Letter I.
119. Lowdermilk, XXI.
120. Sargent, 298.
121. Lowdermilk, XXI.
122. Hamilton, 79.
123. St. Clair, 94.
124. St. Clair, 89.
125. St. Clair, 94.
126. Sargent, 366.
127. Maryland Gazette.
128. Lowdermilk, XXII.
129. Hamilton, 80.
130. Sargent, 367.
131. Lowdermilk, XXIV.
132. Sargent, 229.
133. Sargent, 367.
134. Hamilton, 10
135. Lowdermilk, XXIV.
136. Sargent, 300.
137. St. Clair, 96 .
138. St. Clair, 97.
139. St. Clair, 99.
140. St. Clair, 100.
141. St. Clair, 115.
142. Sargent, 367.
143. Hamilton, 10.
144. Lowdermilk, XXIV.
145. Hamiltin, 81.
146. St. Clair, 99.
147. Sargent, 300.
148. Sargent. 367.
149. Hamilton, 10.
150. Lowdermilk. XXIV.
151. Hamilton, 81
152. Sargent, 367.
153. Hamilton, 10.
154. Lowdermilk, XXIV.
155. Hamilton, 82.
156. St. Clair, 101.
157. St. Clair, 102.
158. Lee McCardell, *Ill-Starred General: Braddock of the Coldstream Guards.* (Pittsburgh: Univ. of Pittsburgh Press, 1958), 169-170
159. Sargent, 368.
160. Lowdermilk, XXIV.
161. Hamilton, 82.
162. St. Clair, 105.
163. Sargent, 368.
164. Hamilton, 10.
165. Pennsylvania Gazette.
166. Lowdermilk, XXV.

167. Hamilton, 82.
168. Sargent, 299.
169. Sargent, 368.
170. Hamilton, 10 .
171. Lowdermilk, XXV.
172. Pargellis, 81-84.
173. McCardell, 168.
174. Hamilton, 82.
175. Sargent, 368.
176. Hamilton, 11.
177. Hamilton, 82.
178. Sargent, 369.
179. Hamilton, 11.
180. Lowdermilk, XXV.
181. Hamilton, 83.
182. Sargent, 307.
183. St. Clair, 107.
184. St. Clair, 110.
185. St. Clair, 111.
186. St. Clair, 112.
187. St. Clair, 113.
188. Sargent, 369.
189. Hamilton, 11.
190. John Bigelow, *Autobiography of
        Benjamin Franklin*, New York:
        G.P. Putman's Sons, 1927), 13.
191. Lowdermilk, XXV.
192. Hamilton, 12.
193. Hamilton, 83.
194. Harrison, 307.
195. Hamilton, 83.
196. Fitzpatrick, 70.
197. Lowdermilk, XXV.
198. Hamilton, 12.
199. Bigelow, 17.
200. Bigelow, 20.
201. Bigelow, 19.
202. Hamilton, 84.
203. Lowdermilk, XXVI.
204. Sargent, 370.
205. Hamilton, 12.
206. Hamilton, 84.
207. Lowdermilk, XXVI.
208. Sargent, 370.
209. Hamilton, 12.
210. Hamilton, 84.
211. Lowdermilk, XXVI.
212. Hamilton, 12.
213. Hamilton, 85.
214. Lowdermilk, XXVI.
215. Sargent, 370.

216. Hamilton, 12.
217. Hamilton, 85.
218. Lowdermilk, XXXXVII.
219. Sargent, 308.
220. Hamilton, 12.
221. Hamilton, 85.
222. Sergent, 370.
223. Hamilton, 12.
224. Harrison, 307.
225. Hamilton, 85.
226. British Officer Letter II.
227. Freeman, 28.
228. Sargent, 370.
229. Hamilton, 12.
230. Sargent, 309.
231. Hamilton, 86.
232. Sargent, 370.
233. Hamilton, 12.
234. Pennsylvania Gazette.
235. Hamilton, 85.
236. St. Clair, 118.
237. Sargent, 371.
238. Hamilton, 13.
239. Hamilton, 86.
240. Sargent, 371.
241. Hamilton, 13.
242. Harrison, 307.
243. Hamilton, 86.
244. Sargent, 371.
245. Hamilton, 13.
246. Fitzpatrick, 72.
247. Harrison, 307.
248. Hamilton, 87.
249. Netherton, 12.
250. Sargent, 371.
251. Hamilton, 13.
252. Harrison, 307.
253. Fitzpatrick, 72.
254. Hamilton, 87.
255. Sargent, 371.
256. Hamilton, 13.
257. Harrison, 308.
258. Bigelow, 26.
259. Elaine G. Breslaw, Drs. Alexander
        and John Hamilton Comments
        on Braddock's Defeat, *Maryland
        Historical Magazine*, Vol. 25,
        No. 2, June 1980, 131-140.
260. Hamilton, 87.
261. Sargent, 372.
262. Hamilton, 13.

485

263. Hamilton, 87.
264. British Officer Letter III.
265. Sargent, 372.
266. Hamilton, 14.
267. Maryland Gazette.
268. Hamilton, 88.
269. Hamilton, 14.
270. Virginia Gazette.
271. Hamilton, 88.
272. Lowdermilk, XXX.
273. Sargent, 373.
274. Hamilton, 14.
275. Lowdermilk, XXXI.
276. Hamilton, 88.
277. Sergent, 309.
278. Sergent, 374.
279. Hamilton, 14.
280. Lowdermilk, XXXII.
281. Lowdermilk, 311.
282. Sargent, 375.
283. Hamilton, 14.
284. Sergent, XXXIII.
285. Sergent. 376.
286. Hamilton, 14.
287. Sargent, XXXIV.
288. Fitzpatrick, 73.
289. Freeman, 32.
290. Hugh Cleland, *Washington in the Ohio Valley*, (Pittsburgh: Univ. of Pittsburgh Press, 1955), 126.
291. Sargent, 376.
292. Hamilton, 14-15.
293. Lowdermilk, XXXV.
294. Sargent, 377.
295. Hamilton, 15.
296. Fitzpatrick, 73.
297. Nichols, 213.
298. Pennsylvania Gazette.
299. Lowdermilk, XXXV.
300. Fitzpatrick, 73.
301. Sargemt, 377.
302. Hamilton, 15.
304. Sargent, 377.
305. Hamilton, 15.
306. Lowdermilk, XXXVI.
307. Sargent, 377.
308. Hamilton, 15.
309. Lowdermilk, XXXVII.
310. Hamilton, 90.
311. Sargent, 310.
312. Sargent, 379.
313. Hamilton, 15.
314. Lowdermilk, XXXVIII.
315. Sargent, 312.
316. British Officer Letter IV.
317. Croghan, 521.
318. Sargent, 379.
319. Hamilton, 15.
320. Lowdermilk, XXXVIII.
321. Sargent, 379.
322. Hamilton, 15.
323. Harrison, 308 .
324. Lowdermilk, XXXVIII.
325. Sargent, 379.
326. Hamilton, 15.
327. Fitzpatick, 73.
328. Harrison, 308.
329. Pennsylvania Gazette.
330. Lowdermilk, XXXIX.
331. British Officer Letter V.
332. Sargent, 380.
333. Hamilton, 16.
334. Fitzpatrick, 74.
335. Maryland, Virginia Gazette.
336. Lowdermilk, XXXIX.
337. Freeman, 44.
338. Hamilton, 92.
339. Lowdermilk, 358.
340. Sargent, 380.
341. Hamilton, 16.
342. Harrison, 308.
343. Lowdermilk, XL.
344. Hamilton, 92.
345. Sargent, 312.
346. Hamilton, 16.
347. Sargent, 407.
348. Harrison, 308.
349. Lowdermilk, XL.
350. Hamillton, 93.
351. Sargent, 358.
352. Hamilton, 16.
353. Harrison, 308.
354. Lowdermilk, XLI.
355. Hamilton, 94.
356. Sargent, 380.
357. Hamilton, 17.
358. Fitzpatrick, 74.
359. Harrison, 309.
360. Lowdermilk, XLII.
361. St. Clair, 133.
362. Hamilton, 95.
363. Sargent, 380.
364. Hamilton, 17.

365. Freeman, 42.
366. Harrison, 309.
367. Lowdermilk, XLIII
368. Hamilton, 96.
369. Sargent, 380
370. Hamilton, 17.
371. Harrison, 309.
372. Pennsylvania Gazette.
373. Lowdermilk, XLIII.
374. Hamilton, 96.
375. Sargent, 323.
376. Fitzpatrick, 75.
377. Sargent, 381.
378. Hamilton, 17.
379. Harrison, 309.
380. Lowdermilk, XLIV.
381. St. Clair, 132.
382. Hamilton, 96.
383. Hamilton, 17.
384. Harrison, 310.
385. Lowdermilk, XLIV.
386. Hamilton, 96.
387. St. Clair, 134.
388. Sargent, 381.
389. Hamilton, 17.
390. Harrison, 310.
391. Lowdermilk, XLIV.
392. Hamilton, 96.
393. St. Clair, 137.
394. St. Clair, 136.
395. Sargent, 381.
396. Hamilton, 18.
397. Harrison, 311.
398. Pennsylvania Gazette.
399. Lowdermilk, XLV.
400. Hamilton, 97.
401. Sargent, 358.
402. Sargent, 381.
403. Harry Grodon, *A Sketch of General Braddock's March - Abstract of a Journal*. This is an annotated map of the route featuring construction detail.
404. Hamilton, 18.
405. Harrison, 311.
406. Lowdermilk, XLV.
407. Hamilton, 97.
408. Sargent, 381.
409. Hamilton, 18.
410. Harrison, 312.
411. Lowdermilk, XLV.
412. Lowdermilk, 135.
413. Hamilton, 97 .
414. Sargent, 381.
415. Hamilton, 19.
416. Harrison, 313.
417. Pennsylvania Gazette.
418. Sargent, XLVI.
419. Sargent, 382.
420. Hamilton, 19.
421. Harrison, 313.
422. Lowdermilk, XLVII.
423. Sargent, 382.
424. Hamilton, 99.
425. Hamilton, 19.
426. Harrison, 314.
427. Lowdermilk, XLVIII.
428. Pargellis, 84.
429. Pargellis, 92.
430. Hamilton, 100.
431. Hamilton, 19.
432. Harrison, 314.
433. Lowdermilk, XLVIII.
434. Lowdermilk, 135.
435. Sargent, 382.
436. Hamilton, 100.
437. Hamilton, 20.
438. Harrison, 315.
439. Lowdermilk, XLIX.
440. Lowdermilk, XLIX.
441. St. Clair, 138.
442. Sargent, 382.
443. Hamilton, 100.
444. Hamilton, 20.
445. Hamilton, 40.
446. Paul E. Kopperman, *Braddock at the Monongahela*, (Pittsburgh: University of Pittsburgh, 1977) , 177.
447. Harrison, 315.
448. Lowdermilk, XLIX.
449. St. Clair, 140.
450. Sargent, 331.
451. Hamilton, 20.
452. Harrison, 315.
453. Lowdermilk, LII.
454. St. Clair, 139.
455. Hamilton, 20.
456. Harrison, 316.
457. Pennsylvania, Gazette.
458. Maryland Gazette.
459. Lowdermilk, LIV.

460. Hamilton, 104.
461. Pargellis, 93.
462. Sargent, 333.
463. Hamilton, 21.
464. Hamilton, 42.
465. Harrison, 316.
466. Lowdermilk, LIV
467. Fitzpatrick, 76.
468. Gordon Abstract of a Journal.
469. Hamilton, 105.
470. Hamilton, 21.
471. Hamilton, 42.
472. Harrison, 317.
473. Hamilton, 108.
474. Gordon Abstract of a Journal.
475. Sargent, 334.
476. Hamilton, 42.
477. Gordon Abstract of a Journal.
478. Sargent, 383.
479. Hamilton, 21.
480. Hamilton, 108.
481. Hamilton, 42.
482. British Officer Letter V.
483. Sargent, 335.
484. Kopperman, 177.
485. Hamilton, 21.
486. Pennsylvania Gazette.
487. Hamilton, 108.
488. Hamilton, 22.
489. Hamilton, 110.
490. Sargent, 336.
491. Hamilton, 22 .
492. Hamilton, 111.
493. Sargent, 336.
494. Hamilton, 43.
495. Hamilton, 22.
496. Freeman, 54.
497. Maryland Gazette.
498. Hamilton, 111.
499. Sargent, 338.
500. Gordon Abstract of a Journal.
501. Hamilton, 44.
502. British Officer Letter V.
503. Hamilton, 22.
504. Pennsylvania Gazette..
505. Hamilton, 111.
506. Hamilton, 22.
507. Hamilton, 111.
508. Hamilton, 22.
509. Hamilton, 112.
510. Sargent, 340.
511. Gordon Abstract of a Journal.
512. Hamilton, 44.
513. Hamilton, 22.
514. Hamilton, 112.
515. Sargent, 340.
516. Hamilton, 44.
517. Sargent, 383.
518. Gordon Abstract of a Journal.
519. Hamilton, 22.
520. Hamilton, 112.
521. Sargent, 341.
522. Hamilton, 45.
523. Hamilton, 23.
524. Hamilton, 113.
525. Gordon Abstract of a Journal.
526. Sargent, 343.
527. Gordon Abstract of a Journal.
528. Sargent, 383.
529. Hamilton, 45.
530. Hamilton, 23.
531. Hamilton, 114.
532. Gordon Abstract of a Journal.
534. Hamilton, 46.
535. Hamilton, 24.
536. Hamilton, 115.
537. Fitzpatrick, 76.
538. Gordon Abstract of a Journal.
539. Sargent, 344.
540. Hamilton, 46.
541. Hamilton, 24.
542. Hamilton, 115.
543. Gordon Abstract of a Journal.
544. Sargent, 344.
545. Hamilton, 46.
546. Hamilton, 24.
547. Hamilton, 116.
548. Sargent, 345.
549. Fitzpatrick, 77.
550. Hasmilton, 46.
551. Hamilton, 24.
552. Hamilton, 117.
553. Gordon Abstract of a Journal.
554. Sargent, 346.
555. Hamilton, 46.
556. Hamilton, 24.
557. Harrison, 317
558. Hamilton, 117.
559. Sargent, 346.
560. Hamilton, 47.
561. Gordon Abstract of a Journal.
562. Fitzpatrick,
563. Hamilton, 24.
564. Hamilton, 118.

565. Sargent, 346.
566. Gordon Abstract of a Journal.
567. Hamilton, 47.
568. Hamilton, 25.
569. Pennsylvania Gazette.
570. Maryland Gazette.
571. Maryland Gazette.
572. Maryland Gazette.
573. Hamilton, 118.
574. Gordon Abstract of a Journal.
575. Sargent, 394.
577. Harrison, 317.
578. Hamilton, 119.
579. Nichols, 327.
580. Hamilton, 47.
581. Hamilton, 25.
582. Hamilton, 119.
583. Sargent, 349.
584. Kenneth P. Bailey, Christopher Gist,
     (Hartford: Archon Books, 1976), 92.
585. Gordon Abstract of a Journal.
586. Hamilton, 47.
587. Hamilton, 25.
588. Kopperman, 266.
589. Kopperman, 259.
590. Hamilton, 119.
591. Sargent, 351.
592. Hamilton, 48.
593. British Officer Letter V.
594. Gordon Abstract of a Journal.
595. Hamilton, 595.
596. Harrison, 317.
597. Kopperman, 259.
598. Kopperman, 253.
599. Hamilton, 120.
600. Sargent, 352.
601. Fitzpatrick,
602. Gordon, Abstract of a Journal.
603. Kopperman, 198.
604. Hamilton, 48.
605. Sargent, 384.
606. Hamilton, 26.
607. Harrison, 317.
608. SCOOUTA: James Smith's Indian
     Captivity Narrative (Columbus:
     Ohio Historical Society, 1978).
609. Kopperman, 267.
610. Kopperman, 259.
611. Sargent, 353.
612. Fitzpatrick, 77.
613. Cleland, 143.
614. Gordon Abstract of a Journal.

615. Kopperman, 186.
616. Hamilton, 49.
617. British Officer Letter V.
618. Kopperman, 174.
619. Kopperman, 178.
620. Sargent, 384.
621. Kopperman, 226.
622. Hamilton, 27.
623. Ohio Hist. Soc., SCOOUTA.
624. Kopperman, 267.
625. Kopperman, 262.
626. Kopperman, 259.
627. Kopperman, 253.
628. Kopperman, 257.
629. Sargent, 357.
630. Hamilton, 53.
631. Kopperman, 253.
632. Maryland Gazette.
633. Maryland, Pennsylvania Gazette.
634. Kopperman, 269.
635. Sargent, 357.
636. Freeman, 84.
637. Harrison, 317 .
638. Kopperman, 271.
639. Hamilton, 121.
640. Kopperman, 184.
641. Sargent, 388.
642. Hamilton, 32 .
643. Harrison, 318.
644. Hamilton, 121.
645. Sargent, 357.
646. British Officer Letter V.
647. Hamilton, 32.
648. Harrison, 318.
649. Hamilton, 123.
650. Hamilton, 32.
651. Pargellis, 129.
652. Hamilton, 124.
653. Fitzpatrick, 78.
654. Hamilton, 33.
655. Bigelow, 109.
656. Hamilton, 125.
657. Hamilton, 33.
658. Hamilton, 125.
659. Hamilton, 54.
660. Kopperman, 180.
661. Hamilton, 33.
662. Harrison, 318.
663. Pennsylvania Gazette.
664. Hamilton, 125.
665. Hamilton, 33.
666. Pargellis, 96.

667. Pargellis, 98.
668. Pargellis, 100.
669. Pargellis, 100.
670. St. Clair, 122.
671. Kopperman, 231.
672. Fitzpatrick, 78.
673. Bailey, front end paper.
674. Hamilton, 126.
675. Kopperman, 229.
676. Hamilton, 33.
677. Hamilton, 126.
678. Sargent;, 389.
679. Hamilton, 33.
680. Cleland, 144.
681. Hamilton, 33.
682. Hamilton, 126.
683. Hamilton, 34.
684. Pargellis, 102.
685. St. Clair, 121.
686. Hamilton, 34.
687. Pargellis, 104-109.
688. Kopperman, 189.
689. Pargellis, 109.
690. Kopperman, 191.
691. Hamilton, 34.
692. Maryland Gazette.
693. Maryland Gazette.
694. Pennsylvania Gazette.
695. Maryland Gazette.
696. Kopperman, 251.
697. Pargellis, 112.
698. Hamilton, 34.
699. Hamilton, 34.
700. Hamilton, 34.
701. Hamilton, 34.
702. Fitzpatrick, 79.
703. Hamilton, 35.
704. Kopperman, 204.
705. Hamilton, 35.
706. Hamilton, 35.
707. Pennsylvania Gazette.
708. Maryland Gazette.
709. Sargemt, 389.
710. Hamilton, 35.
711. Sargent, 389.
712. Hamilton, 35.
713. Hamilton, 35.
714. Hamilton, 35.
715. Sargent, 389.
716. Hamilton, 35.
717. Hamilton, 35.
718. Hamilton, 36.

719. Pennsylvania Gazette.
720. Maryland Gazette.
721. Hamilton, 36.
722. St. Clair, 151.
723. St. Clair, 153.
724. Nichols, 440.
725. Sargent, 106.
726. Breslaw, 131.
727. St. Clair, 155.
728. Harrison, 318.
729. Harrison, 318.
730. Sargent, 106.
731. Harrison, 318.
732. Pennsylvania, Virginia Gazette.
733. Pennsylvania Gazette.
734. Harrison, 319.
735. Kopperman, 195.
736. St. Clair, 182.
737. Pennsylvania Gazette.
738. Virginia Gazette.
739. Harrison, 319.
740. Harrison, 319.
741. Harrison, 319.
742. Harrison, 319.
743. Harrison, 320.
744. Kopperman, 255.
745. Harrison, 320
746. Harrison, 320.
747. Harrison, 320.
748. Harrison, 320.
749. Harrison, 320.
750. *Journal of Capt. Charles Lewis,*
     Fredericksburg, Virginia,
     1755, 11.
751. Lewis, 11.
752. Nichols, 191.
753. Lewis, 11.
754. Lewis, 11.
755. Lewis, 12.
756. Lewis, 12.
757. Lewis, 12.
758. Lewis, 12.
759. Lewis, 12.
760 Lewis, 12.
761. Lewis, 12.
762. Lewis, 12.
763. Lewis, 13.
764. Lewis, 13.
765. Lewis, 13.
766. St. Clair, 183.
767. Kopperman, 260.

768. Lewis, 14.
769. Lewis, 14.
770. Lewis, 15.
771. Kopperman, 203.
772. Lewis, 15.
773. Lewis, 15.
774. Lewis, 15.
775. Lewis, 15.
776. Lewis, 16.
777. Lewis, 16.
778. Lewis, 16.
779. Lewis, 16.
780. Lewis, 16.
781. Lewis, 16.
782. Lewis, 17.
783. Lewis, 19.
784. Lewis, 19.
785. Lewis, 19.
786. Lewis, 20.
787. Lewis, 20.
788. Lewis, 20.
789. Lewis, 21.
790. Lewis, 21.
791. Lewis, 21.
792. Lewis, 21.

SOURCES:

Drake, Samuel. Tragedies of the Wilderness. Boston: Antiquarian Bookstore and Institute, 56 Cornhill. 1844

McCardell, Lee. Ill-Starred General: Braddock of the Coldstream Guards. Pittsburgh: U of Pittsburgh, 1958.

Sargent, Winthrop (Editor). The History of an Expedition against Fort Du Quesne, in 1755. Phila: Lippincott, Grambo & co., For the Historical Society of Pennsylvania. 1855.

Lowdermilk, Will H. History of Cumberland (Maryland) from the time of the Indian Town, Caiuctucuc, in 1728, up to the present day, including Major General Braddock's Orderly Book from February 26 to June 17, 1755 - From Original, in the Congressionsl Library, (Baltimore: Regional Publishing Company, 1971).

Cunningham, Arthur S. "March to Destiny: This being an Attempt to Reconstruct the Muster Rolls of the Braddock Expedition to Fort Duquesne." Typescript, 1992.

Hamilton, Charles, ed. Braddock's Defeat: The Journal of Captain Robert Cholmley's Batman, The Journal of a British Officer and Halkett's Orderly Book. Norman, U. of Oklahoma, 1959.

Hulbert, Archer B. Braddock's Road and Three Relative Papers. Cleveland: Clark, 1903.

Kopperman, Paul E. Braddock at the Monongahela. Pittsburgh: U of Pittsburgh, 1977.

Hazard, Samuel. "Copy of a letter from Major Leslie to a respectable merchant of Philadelphia", Register of Pennsylvania, 5. 1820.

Pargellis, Stanley M. Military Affairs in North America, 1748-1765: Selected Documents from the Cumberland Papers in Windsor Castle. n.p.: Archon, 1969.

Netherton, Ross. Braddock's Campaign and the Potomac Route West Volume 1: Winchester-Frederick County Historical Society. Falls Church, Va. Higher Education Publishing, Inc. 1989.

Hough, Walter S. Braddock's Road Through the Virginia Colony Volume VII: Winchester-Frederick County Historical Society. Strasburg, VA: Shenandoah Publishing Co. 1970.

Darington, William. Christopher Gist's Journal
Ann Arbor: University Microfilms 1966

Ward, Harry M. Major General Adam Stephen and the cause of American Liberty. Charlottesville: University Press of Virginia, 1989.

Fort Ligonier Association. "War of Empire in Western Pennsylvania", Fort Ligonier, PA., 1993.

Bigelow, John, ed., Benjamin Franklin *Autobiography*, New York: G.P. Putnam's Sons, 1927.

Lewis, Charles. Journal of Captain Charles Lewis of Fredericksburg, Virginia, when in the service of the colony of Virginia in the year 1755.

Cameron, Duncan. The life, adventures, and surprizing deliverances, of Duncan Cameron, private soldier in the regiment of foot, late Sir Peter Halkett's.

Bailey, Kenneth P. Christopher Gist: colonial frontiersman, explorer, and Indian agent. Hampton, Conn.: Archon Books, 1976.

Letterbook of Sir John St. Clair, Deputy Quartermaster General-North America Jan. 12 1755 to Dec. 28, 1756 (microfilm at University of Virginia).

Breslaw, Elaine G. "Drs. Alexander and John Hamilton Comment on Braddock's Defeat" Maryland Historical Magazine Vol. 75, No.2, June 1980.

Scharf, John Thomas. History of Maryland from earliest Period to Present Day. Baltimore: John B. Piet, 1879.

Ohio Historical Society. SCOOUTA: James Smith's Indian Captivity Narrative. Columbus, Ohio: 1978

Bailey, Kenneth P. Thomas Cresap Maryland Frontiersman. Boston, Mass.: The Christopher Publishing House, 1944

Lacock, John Kennedy. "Braddock Road" The Pennsylvania Magazine of History and Biography Vol. XXXVII, No.1, 1914.

Gordon, Harry, *A Sketch of General Braddock's March from Fort Cumberland on the 10th of June to ther Field of Battle of the 9th of July*...ABSTRACT OF A JOURNAL.

Wallace, Paul A.W. "Blunder Camp: A Note on the Braddock Road" The Pennsylvania Magazine of History and Biography, 1963.

Older, Curtis L. The Braddock Expedition and Fox's Gap in Maryland. Westminster, Md.: Family Line Publications, 1995.

Nichols, Franklin T. The Braddock Expedition. Ph.D. diss., Harvard University, 1946.

Walzer, John Flexer. Transportation in the Philadelphia Trading Area, 1740 -1775. Ph.D. diss., University of Wisconsin, 1968.

Nichols, Franklin T. "The Organization of Braddock's Army" William and Mary Quarterly, 3rd ser., 4 (1947), pp. 125-47 (this is a excerpt of his 1946 Ph.D. diss.).

Moore, Gay Montague. "Seaport in Virginia - George Washington's Alexandria.", Richmond, VA.: Garrett and Massie, 1949.

Cleland, Hugh. "Washington in the Ohio Valley", Univ. of Pittsburgh Press, Pittsburgh, 1955.

Pennsylvania Gazette. 1755

Virginia Gazette. 1755

Maryland Gazette. 1755

Craig, Neville B. "Jared Sparks Letter and T.C. Atkinson Article" The Olden Time, vol ii., pp. 465-468, 539-544, 1846.

Berkebile, Don H. "Conestoga Wagons in Braddock's Campaign" Bulletin 281: Contributions From the Museum of History and Technology, Papers 1 to 11. 1959. pp.142-153.

Shumway, George, Edward Durell, and Howard C. Frey, "Conestoga Wagon, 1750 - 1850 Freight Carrier for One Hundred Years of American's Westward Expansion", York, PA., 1964.

History of the George Washington Bicentennial Celebration, United States George Washington Bicentennial Commission, Washington, D.C., 1932 (The George Washington Atlas).

The Expedition of Major General Braddock to Virginia with The Two Regiments of Hacket and Dunbar being Extracts of Letters from an Officer in one of those regiments to his friend in London, 1755.

Fitzpatrick, John C. "George Washington - Colonial Traveler 1732-1775", The Bobbs Merrill Company, Indianapolis, 1927

Fitzpatrick, John C. "The Writings of George Washington", Washington, 1931.

Russell, Francis and Editors of American Heritage. "The French and Indian Wars", American Heritage Publishing Co.., Inc., New York.

Bray, George A. "Scalping During the French and Indian War", The Early American Review, Vol II No 3, Spring 1998 (http://earlyamerica.com/review/1998/index.html).

Copeland, David A. "Fighting for a Continent: Newspaper Coverage of the English and French War for Control of North America, 1754-

1760", The Early American Review, Vol. I No. 4, Spring 1997
(http://earlyamerica.com/review/spring97/nrespapers.html).

May, Robin and Embleton, G.A. "Wolfe's Army- Men at-Arms
Series", Osprey-Reed International Books, London, 1994.

Stepp, John W. "Braddock Rock to be Spared", Washington Star
Newspaper, June 12, 1959.

Stephenson, Richard W. "The Cartography of Northern Virginia
Facsimile Reproduction of Maps Dating from 1608 To 1915", Office
of Comprehensive Planning, Fairfax County, Virginia. 1982.

Friis, Herman R. "Guidebook Geographical Reconnaissance of the
Potomac River Tidewater Fringe of Virginia From Arlington Memorial
Bridge to Mount Vernon", Association of American Geographers,
Washington, D.C., 1968.

Smith, Carter (ed.). "Battles in a New Land - A sourcebook on
Colonial America", The Millbrook Press, Brookfield, Conn. 1991

Withington, Charles. 'Building Stones of our Nation's Capital"
U.S.G.S., Washington, D.C. 1975.

Temple, Harry. "Braddocks Road", Ohio Archaeology Quarterly,
XVIII, 438-442, 1909. (Temple was in a group of scholars of the
road that explored the right-of -way that included: Lacock, Larzelere,
Abbot, Weller, E. Murdoch, J.Murdoch, and J. Temple).

Freeman, Douglas Southall. "George Washington: A Biography". New
York: Scribner's, 1948.

Old Peters/Addison Historical Society. "Youghiogheny River Towns",
Addison, PA, 1995.

The Point: Indian Trails to Fort Duquesne
From: The Pittsburg Bulletin, 31 December 1910 by George P.
Donehoo
(http://www.clpgh.org/exhibit/neighborhoods/point/point_n715.html)

The Point: "Diondega" From: A history of the Indian Villages and Place Names in Pennsylvania with Numerous Historical Notes and References, by George P. Donehoo, 1928. (http://www.clpgh.org/exhibit/neighborhoods/point/point_n715. html)

Rotenstein, David S. Historical Archaeology Executive Summary: U.S. Route 9 Improvement Project. Jefferson County, West Virginia, 1996, Pa.: Skelly and Loy, Inc. (re: Vestal's Bloomery, Jefferson County, W. Va.).

Harrison, Fairfax. "With Braddock's Army Mrs. Browne's Diary in Virginia and Maryland", The Virginia Magazine of History and Biography, Vol. XXXII, October, 1924, No.4.

Cappon, Lester J. et al, "Atlas of Early American History - The Revolutionary Era 1760-1790", Institute of Early American History and Culture, Princeton University Press, 1976.

Kopperman, Paul E. and Freiling, Michael J. "A British Officers Journal of the Braddock Expedition - Et Cetera", Western Pennsylvania Historical Magazine, July 1981, pp. 273-287.

Kopperman, Paul E. "An assessment of the Cholmey's Batman and British A Journals of Braddock's Campaign", Western Pennsylvania Historical Magazine 62 (July 1979): 217, n. 36.

Vineyard, Ron. "Virginia Freight Waggons 1750-1850", Colonial Williamsburg Foundation, Williamsburg, Virginia November 15, 1993.

The EXPEDITION of Major General BRADDOCK TO VIRGINIA with the Two Regiments of Hacket and Dunbar Being Extracts of Letters from an Officer in one of those Regiments to his friend in London, describing the March and Engagement in the Woods. Together with many little Incidents Giving a Lively Idea of the Nature of the Country, climate, and Manner in which the Officers and soldiers lived; also the Difficulties they went through in that Wilderness, (London: H. Carpenter, in Fleet-street, MDCCLV).

Volwiler, Albert, T. "George Croghan and the Western Movement 1741-1782", (Cleveland: Arthur H. Clark Co., 1926).

Croghan's Journal, Pennsylvania Archives, Series 2, VI, 521.